T0189794

Communications in Computer and Information Science   **892**

Commenced Publication in 2007
Founding and Former Series Editors:
Phoebe Chen, Alfredo Cuzzocrea, Xiaoyong Du, Orhun Kara, Ting Liu,
Dominik Ślęzak, and Xiaokang Yang

More information about this series at http://www.springer.com/series/7899

S. Rajaram · N. B. Balamurugan ·
D. Gracia Nirmala Rani ·
Virendra Singh (Eds.)

VLSI Design and Test

22nd International Symposium, VDAT 2018
Madurai, India, June 28–30, 2018
Revised Selected Papers

 Springer

Editors
S. Rajaram
Thiagarajar College of Engineering
Madurai, India

N. B. Balamurugan
Thiagarajar College of Engineering
Madurai, India

D. Gracia Nirmala Rani
Thiagarajar College of Engineering
Madurai, India

Virendra Singh
Indian Institute of Technology Bombay
Mumbai, India

ISSN 1865-0929   ISSN 1865-0937 (electronic)
Communications in Computer and Information Science
ISBN 978-981-13-5949-1   ISBN 978-981-13-5950-7 (eBook)
https://doi.org/10.1007/978-981-13-5950-7

Library of Congress Control Number: 2018967043

This Springer imprint is published by the registered company Springer Nature Singapore Pte Ltd.
The registered company address is: 152 Beach Road, #21-01/04 Gateway East, Singapore 189721, Singapore

Preface

VLSI Design and Test (VDAT) is a leading event of the VLSI Society of India. The 22nd symposium in this series, the VLSI Design and Test Symposium (VDAT 2018), was held during June 28–30, 2018, at the Thiagarajar College of Engineering, Madurai, India. The objective of the symposium is to bring together the professional engineers, academics, and researchers from India and abroad to discuss emerging topics of VLSI and related fields on a common platform and to share new ideas, experiences, and knowledge. The chief guest at the event was Dr. Vishwani D. Agrawal, Professor Emeritus, Auburn University, USA.

The scientific program consisted of peer-reviewed paper presentations in two parallel technical sessions. In addition, keynote lectures, presentations by industry professionals, tutorials, a PhD forum, a design contest, and a poster presentation were held during the conference. Research contributions in the following areas were invited for VDAT 2018:

- Digital Design
- Analog and Mixed Signal Design
- Hardware Security
- Micro Bio-fluidics
- VLSI Testing
- Analog Circuits and Devices
- Network-on-Chip
- Memory
- Quantum Computing and NoC
- Sensors and Interfaces

This year we received 231 papers from around the world. After a rigorous review process, the Program Committee selected 39 regular papers and 19 poster papers for the proceedings (the acceptance rate was 25.12%). In all, 150 expert reviewers were involved in rating the papers and on an average each paper received at least three independent reviews. The program of the symposium spanned over three days; the main conference program was preceded by a day of tutorial presentations that had four tutorials delivered by eminent researchers and practitioners in the field. The symposium hosted the following tutorials:

1. Nishit Gupta and Deepak Jharodia, "Taking Reuse to Next Level: Exploiting Transaction Level Modeling (TLM) for Universal Verification Methodology (UVM)"
2. Vijay Kumar Sankaran and Nadeem Husain Tehsildar, "Recent Trends in Modeling and Simulation of Defects in Analog Circuits and Their Applications"
3. Sudeeb Dasgupta, "Tunnel Field Effect Transistors and Reconfigurable Device: A New Paradigm in Emerging Device Technology"
4. Preet Yadav, "IoT Security: The Darker Side of the Cloud"

Several invited talks and keynote speeches were delivered by experts from India and abroad enlightening the participants on various aspects of emerging issues in VLSI research. These talks were delivered by Prof. Vishwani D. Agrawal (Auburn University, USA), Prof. Michiko Inoue (NAIST, Japan), Dr. Neel Gala (RISE Lab., IIT Madras), Mr. Preet Yadhav (NXP Semiconductors, Noida, India), and Dr. Nagi Naganathan (Broadcom, USA). VDAT 2018 was a focused research event encompassing themes related to various disciplines of VLSI.

We sincerely thank all the officials and sponsors for their support in recognizing the value of this conference. We would like to express our thanks to the keynote speakers and the tutorial speakers for kindly agreeing to deliver their lectures. Thanks to the authors and reviewers of all the papers for their quality research work. We heartily thank every member of the Conference Committee for their unyielding support in making this event a success.

July 2018

S. Rajaram
N. B. Balamurugan
D. Gracia Nirmala Rani
Virendra Singh

Organization

VDAT 2018 was organized by the Department of Electronics and Communication Engineering, Thiagarajar College of Engineering, Madurai, Tamilnadu India.

Chief Patron

Karumuttu T. Kannan   TCE, Madurai, India

Patrons

V. Abhai Kumar	TCE, Madurai, India
S. Raju	TCE, Madurai, India
R. Sukanesh	TCE, Madurai, India

Advisory Committee

V. Agrawal	Auburn University, USA
Jaswinder Ahuja	Cadence, India
Virendra Singh	IIT Bombay, India
Susmita Sur-Kolay	ISI, India
Nagi Naganathan	Broadcom, USA
Madhavan Swaminathan	Georgia Institute of Technology, USA
Manoj S. Gaur	IIT Jammu, India
Niranjan Pol	Seagate, India
V. Kamakoti	IIT Madras, India
Chitra Hariharan	Senzopt, Bengaluru, India

General Chairs

Madhavan Swaminathan	GT, USA
S. Rajaram	TCE, Madurai, India
N. B. Balamurugan	TCE, Madurai, India

Program Chairs

Virendra Singh	IIT Bombay, India
V. Kamakoti	IIT Madras, India
D. Gracia Nirmala Rani	TCE, Madurai, India

Tutorial Chairs

P. Vanathi   PSG Tech, Coimbatore
K. Kalyani   TCE, Madurai

Sponsorship Chairs

Chitra Hariharan   Senzopt, Bengaluru, India
J. Ramesh   P.S.G Tech, Coimbatore, India
V. Vinoth Thyagarajan   TCE, Madurai, India

Publicity Chairs

Nagi Naganathan   Broadcom, USA
Niranjan Pol   Seagate, India

Technical Programme Committee

Abu Khari Bin Ain	University of Technology Malaysia, Malaysia
Durgamadhab Misra	New Jersey Institute of Technology, USA
Edward Yi Chang	National Chiao Tung University, Taiwan
Hailong Yao	Tsinghua University, China
H. Hiroshi Iwai	Tokyo institute of Technology, Japan
Ibrahiem El Emary	King Abdulaziz University, Saudi Arabia
Kaustav Banerjee	University of California, Santa Barbara, California
Kewal K. Saluja	University of Wisconsin, Madison
Manoj Sachdev	University of Waterloo, Canada
Shigeru Yamashita	Ritsumeikan University, Japan
Vishwani D. Agarwal	Auburn University, USA
Yuh-Renn Wu	National Taiwan University, Taiwan
Bhadra Pokharel	Tribhuvan University, Nepal
Sanju Shrestha	Tribhuvan University, Nepal
Md. Shohel Sayeed	Multimedia University, Malaysia
Robert Wille	Johannes Kepler University, Austria
Xiao-Zhi Gao	Aalto University, Finland
Thamer M. Jamel	University of Technology, Iraq
Rosula Reyes	Ateneo de Manila University, Philippines
Antonio Rubio	Technical University of Catalonia, Spain
Paulraj M. P.	School of Mechatronic Engineering, Malaysia
Ghulam Muhammad	King Saud University, Kingdom of Saudi Arabia
Rami Joseph Oweis	Jordan University of Science and Technology, Jordan
Aditi Majumder	University of California, Irvine
Claire F. Komives	St. Jose State University, USA
Kin Lu Wong	National Sun Yat-Sen, Taiwan
Yunhe Guan	Xi'an Jiaotong University, China
Zunchao Li	Xi'an Jiaotong University, China

Wenhao Zhang	Xi'an Jiaotong University, China
Al-Sakib Khan Pathan	International Islamic University, Malaysia
Anna W. Babiszewska	Opole University of Technology, Poland
Sattar J. Aboud	Information Technology Advisor, Iraq
Sharifah Hafizah Ariffin	University Teknologi Malaysia, Malaysia
N. Z. Mohammad Hanif	Al Ain University of Science and Technology, UAE
Madhavan Swaminathan	Georgia Institute of Technology, USA
Tulika Mitra	National University of Singapore
Jacob Abraham	University of Texas, Austin, USA
Guru Subramanyam	Dayton University, USA
V. Rajaravivarma	Farmingdale State College, NY, USA
Changkun Park	Soongsil University, Korea
Taehwan Joo	Advanced Institute of Science and Technology, Korea
Tae Wook Kim	Yonsei University, South Korea
Chun-Yu Lin	National Taiwan Normal University, Taiwan
Y.-S. Lin	National Chi Nan University, Taiwan
Yen-Chun Wang	Chung-Yuan Christian University, Taiwan
Chen Feng	Nanyang Technological University, Singapore
Ghazal A. Fahmy	National Telecommunication Institute, Cairo
XueGang Zhang	Institute of RF-&OE-ICs, Southeast University, China
Zhiqun Li	Southeast University, China
Jian Xu	Southeast University, China
Abhijit Karmakar	CEERI, India
Ajit Panda	NIST, India
Amit Prakash Singh	GGS-IPU, India
Anand Bulusu	IIT Roorkee, India
Anjan Chakravorty	IIT Madras, India
Ansuman Banerjee	Indian Statistical Institute, Kolkata, India
Arijit Mondal	IIT Patna, India
Aritra Hazra	IIT Madras, India
Ashutosh Nandi	NIT Kurukshetra, India
Ashwani Rana	NIT Hamirpur, India
BalwinderRaj	NIT Jalandhar, India
Bhadra Pokharel	Tribhuvan University, Nepal
Bijoy Krishna Das	IIT Madras, India
Chandan Kumar Sarkar	Jadavpur University, Kolkata, India
Debashish Dutta	Ministry of Electronics & IT, Govt. of India
Debesh K. Das	Jadavpur University Kolkata, India
Enakshi Bhattacharya	IIT Madras, India
Gaurav Trivedi	IIT Guwahati, India
K. Giridhar	IIT Madras, India
K. Gunavathi	P.S.G Tech, Coimbatore, India
Hafizur Rahaman	IIEST, Shibpur, India
Hemangee Kapoor	IIT Guwahati, India
Jaswinder Ahuja	VLSI Society of India
Jegadhesh	Delhi University, India

John Jose	IIT Guwahati, India
P. Kalpana	P.S.G Tech, Coimbatore, India
J. Klutto Milleth	CEWIT, India
Kunal Banerjee	Intel Labs
Kusum Lata	LNMIIT Jaipur, India
Lava Bhargava	MNIT Jaipur, India
Mahesh Patil	IIT Bombay, India
Manan Suri	IIT Delhi, India
Manoj Saxena	Delhi University, India
Manoj Singh Gaur	MNIT Jaipur, India
N. Mohan Kumar	SKP Engineering Colleges, Thiruvannamalai
N. S. Moorthy	Amrita School of Engineering, Bengaluru
Mridula Gupta	Delhi University, India
Nagendra Krishnapura	IIT Madras, India
Naushad Alam	AMU, Aligarh, India
Neeraj Goel	IIT Ropar, India
Nihar Mohapatra	IIT Gandhinagar, India
Pankaj Pal	NIT Uttarakhand, India
Rajib Kar	NIT Durgapur, West Bengal, India
Raj Sarin	NIT Jalandhar, India
J. Ramesh	P.S.G Tech, Coimbatore, India
Ramesh Vaddi	IIIT Naya Raipur, India
V. Ramgopal Rao	Indian Institute of Technology Delhi
C. P. Ravikumar	Texas Instruments, Bangalore, India
S. R. Ahamed	IIT Guwahati, India
Santosh Biswas	IIT Guwahati, India
Santosh Vishwakarma	IIT Indore, India
P. Saravanan	P.S.G Tech, Coimbatore, India
Shanthi Pavan	IIT Madras, India
Sk Subidh Ali	IIT Tirupati, India
Solaikutty Dhanabal	National Instruments, India
Sougata Kar	NIT Rourkela, India
Soumya Pandit	IRPE, University of Calcutta, Kolkata, India
D. Sriram Kumar	NIT Trichy, India
Subir Roy	IIIT Bangalore, India
Sudeb Dasgupta	IIT, Roorkee, India
Sudip Roy	IIT Roorkee, India
Sujay Deb	IIIT Delhi, India
Surendra Rathod	SPIT, Mumbai, India
Susanta Chakraborti	IIEST, India
Sushanta Mandal	Centurion University, Odisha, India
Usha Mehta	Nirma University, Ahmedabad, India
P. T. Vanathi	P.S.G Tech, Coimbatore, India
Veezhinathan Kamakoti	IIT Madras, India
B.Venkataramani	NIT Trichy, India
Vineet Sahula	MNIT Jaipur, India

Sponsors

- Ministry of Electronics and Information Technology, Government of India
- VLSI Society of India
- Springer
- NEC Technologies

Contents

Hardware Security

Micro Bio-fluidics

VLSI Testing

Analog Circuits and Devices

Memory

Quantum Computing and NoC

Sensors and Interfaces

Digital Design

Efficient Hardware-Software Codesigns of AES Encryptor and RS-BCH Encoder

M. Mohamed Asan Basiri$^{(\boxtimes)}$ and Sandeep K. Shukla

Department of Computer Science and Engineering,
Indian Institute of Technology, Kanpur 208016, India
{asan,sandeeps}@cse.iitk.ac.in

Abstract. The modern real time embedded applications are implemented as a mixture software-hardware designs. In the most of the hardware-software codesigns, the main processor is used to perform the part of the operation in software and to send/retrieve data to/from the hardware or co-processor. This paper proposes efficient hardware-software codesigns for AES encryptor and RS-BCH concatenated encoder, where the latency and hardware cost lie in between the fully hardware and software based designs. The synthesis results show that our proposed hardware-software codesigns of 128-bit AES and RS(255,239)-BCH(2184,2040) serial concatenated error correction encoder achieve 85% and 40% of reduction in switching power dissipation over the conventional folded AES design and [8] using Artix-7 FPGA implementation respectively.

Keywords: AES · BCH · Cryptography · Error correction codes · Hardware-software codesign · Reed-Solomon

1 Introduction

Latency and hardware cost (number of slices and power dissipation) are the two important metrics in any hardware-software codesign. Here, the performance and flexibility are achieved via hardware and software respectively. The fully software based design requires more latency than fully hardware based and hardware-software partition based designs. Similarly, the hardware cost of fully software based design is less than the fully hardware based and hardware-software partition based designs. In the hardware-software partition based designs, a part of the operations are done with software and the other parts will be done with hardware. Usually, the operations take more cycles in the software will be preferred to do with hardware. Figure 1 shows the comparison of various metrics in the hardware-software codesigns.

The co-processors are used as hardware accelerators to improve the performance of certain operations. The co-processors will be controlled by the main processor that will be used for general tasks and the co-processor will be used for special tasks. Figure 2 shows the digital signal co-processor designs with and

© Springer Nature Singapore Pte Ltd. 2019
S. Rajaram et al. (Eds.): VDAT 2018, CCIS 892, pp. 3–15, 2019.
https://doi.org/10.1007/978-981-13-5950-7_1

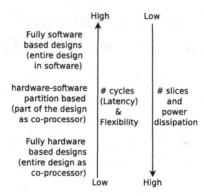

Fig. 1. Comparison of various metrics in the hardware-software codesigns

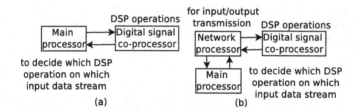

Fig. 2. Digital signal co-processor design flavours (a) without network processor and (b) with network processor.

without network processor. Figure 3 shows the complete block diagram of 32-bit Microblaze, custom IP (AES/RS-BCH co-processor), and other peripherals with 32-bit AXI_LITE bus interconnect using Xilinx Vivado. Here, the peripheral AXI timer is used to measure the number of cycles required for the operations involved in the software (32-bit Microblaze). DLMB and ILMB represent data and instruction side local memory buses respectively.

1.1   Related Works

Advance Encryption Standard (AES) is the most popular block cipher used in the cryptography [1]. The general AES VLSI architectures are classified into two categories, they are parallel and folded. In parallel design, the separate hardware components compute each round. In folded designs, the hardware is present for one round and the remaining rounds will be done with reuse of the hardware that exists. Therefore, hardware cost for parallel AES design is greater than folded. Latency for folded AES design is greater than parallel design. Figure 4(a) and (b) show the 128-bit AES parallel and folded designs respectively. Here, the output cipher text will be produced after 10 rounds. Each round includes byte sub, shift row, mix column, and add key.

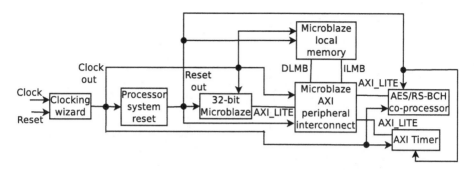

Fig. 3. Block diagram of 32-bit Microblaze, AES/RS-BCH co-processor, and other peripherals with AXI_LITE using Xilinx Vivado

The following literature are found in the hardware-software codesign implementations of AES. The parameterized parallel AES design is proposed in [2], where the hardware for two rounds are combined and the remaining rounds are done with hardware reuse strategy. Four T-boxes based folded AES co-processor is proposed in [3], where the conventional S-box is combined with four multiplication constants used in the mix column to produce four T-boxes. Hardware-software partitioning based AES is described in [4]. In [5], Euclidean algorithm based S-box and mix column are done with co-processor. The remaining operations are done with software. In [6], four co-processors are used for AES operation and each one corresponds to one particular round function. In [7], mix column is designed as a co-processor and the remaining operations are done with software.

The demand for high data rate reliable communication needs the high performance hardware-software codesigns of forward error correction codes, where the redundant parity bits are added to the message bits to allow the receiver to detect and correct the errors that have been occurring during the transmission. In general, error correction codes are classified into block codes, convolution codes, concatenated codes, Turbo product codes and so on. The most widely used block codes in the digital communication and digital storage systems are BCH and Reed Solomon (RS) codes. Given a finite field $GF(2^m)$ (with $m \geq 3$), a t-error correcting BCH code, denoted as $\text{BCH}[n, k, t]$ encodes k-bit message to a n-bit code word by adding $(n - k)$ parity bits, where $n \leq 2^m - 1$ and $(n - k) \leq mt$. The generator polynomial $G(x)$ of the t-error correcting BCH is found to be the least common multiple of the minimal polynomials that is shown in (1). The parity polynomial $R(x)$ is shown in (2), where $D(x)$ is the k-bit message.

$$G(x) = m_1(x).m_3(x).m_5(x)....m_{2t-1}(x) \tag{1}$$

$$R(x) = (x^{n-k}.D(x))\%G(x) \tag{2}$$

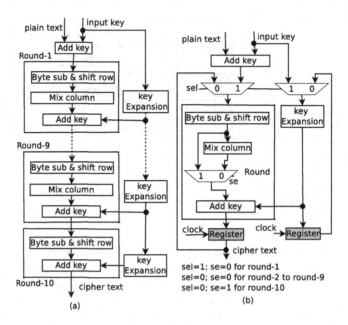

Fig. 4. 128-bit AES (a) parallel and (b) folded designs

Similarly, given a finite field $GF(2^m)$, a t-error correcting RS code, denoted as $\mathrm{RS}[n, k, t]$ encodes k-symbol message to a n-symbol code word by adding $(n-k)$ parity symbols, where $n \leq 2^m - 1$, and $t = floor(n - k/2)$, m is the number of bits per symbol. The generator polynomial $G(x)$ of the t-error correcting RS is expressed in (3), where α is a primitive element in $GF(2^m)$ and i is an arbitrary number. The code word polynomial $C(x)$ is shown in (4), where $D(x)$ is the k-symbol message.

$$G(x) = (x + \alpha^i).(x + \alpha^{i+1}).(x + \alpha^{i+2})...(x + \alpha^{i+2t-1}) \qquad (3)$$

$$C(x) = x^{n-k}.D(x) + R(x) \qquad (4)$$

The RS-BCH concatenated error correction codes are shown in [8,9], where the inner and outer encoders are used. The output from the inner encoder will be encoded again with outer encoder. Figure 5 shows the RS(255,239)-BCH(2184,2040) serial concatenated error correction encoder design.

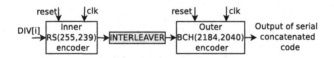

Fig. 5. RS-BCH based serial concatenated error correction encoder

1.2   Contribution of This Paper

In all the fully hardware based designs, hardware cost is compromised. Similarly, latency is compromised in fully software based designs. Our objective is to design efficient hardware-software codesigns for AES encryptor and RS-BCH concatenated encoder in such that both latency and hardware cost are not much be compromised. The synthesis results show that the latency and hardware cost of proposed designs lie in between the fully hardware and software based designs.

The rest of the paper is organized as follows: Sect. 2 describes the proposed hardware-software codesign of AES encryptor. Section 3 explains the proposed hardware-software codesign of RS-BCH concatenated encoder. Design modelling, implementation, and results are shown in Sect. 4, followed by a conclusion in Sect. 5.

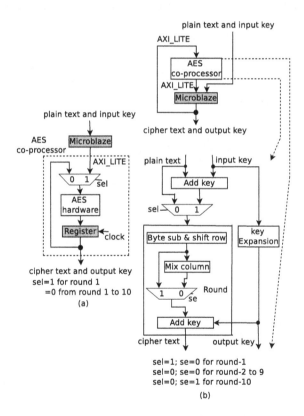

Fig. 6. AES (a) conventional folded design with synchronous registers as a co-processor (b) proposed hardware-software codesign

2   Proposed Hardware-Software Codesign of AES

In the fully hardware based approach, the entire AES is implemented as a co-processor. The inputs for this co-processor are sent from the main processor of the system. The hardware cost of this approach is much higher while the latency is low. Also, the outputs from the co-processor are sent to the main processor at the end of the operation. In this design, the hardware synchronous registers act as pipeline registers, which are used to send the cipher text and key from previous round of AES to the present round. Due to the involvement of these registers dynamic power dissipation is high. Also, the hardware registers consume a significant portion of hardware utilization. Figure 6(a) shows the conventional AES folded design with synchronous registers as a co-processor, where the hardware for a round is repeatedly used for all the 10 rounds. In the fully hardware based design, the architecture as shown in Fig. 4(b) will act as a co-processor, where the input plain text and key are arrived from main processor. In the hardware-software partitioning based approach, a part of the AES (Ex: Mix column) is implemented as a co-processor and rests of the AES are implemented as software in the main processor. Therefore, this approach requires the interaction between main processor and co-processor for each round. Here, the latency is much higher while the hardware cost is kept minimum.

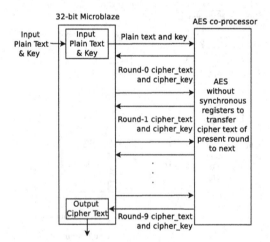

Fig. 7. Communication between Microblaze and AES co-processor at each round using the proposed hardware-software codesign as shown in Fig. 6(b)

In the proposed design, the co-processor includes the entire hardware for single round of AES without hardware registers. Now, each round operation will be performed at co-processor. At the end of each round, the cipher text and output key will be sent to the main processor. Then these values will be sent back to co-processor from the main processor to perform next round of operation. Due to the absence of hardware synchronous registers, dynamic power dissipation and the number of slices of the proposed design are much less than fully hardware based approach. Since the entire AES round operation is done with co-processor, the latency of the proposed design is less than fully software based and existing hardware-software partition based designs. Figure 6(b) shows the proposed hardware-software codesign of AES, where the main processor is Microblaze. Here, AXI_LITE is the bus connection between custom-IP (AES co-processor) and 32-bit Microblaze. Figure 7 shows the communication between Microblaze and AES co-processor at each round. In both the cases as shown in Fig. 6(a) and (b), the Microblaze main processor cannot be avoided. The number of communications between the Microblaze and AES co-processor in the proposed design is greater than existing design as shown in Fig. 6(a) and this will cause some extra latency. This will be the trade-off in this proposed design.

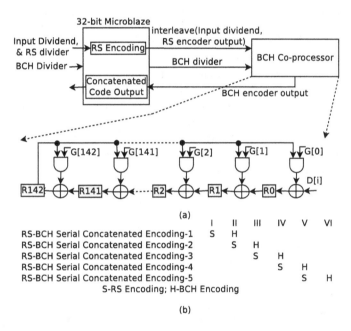

Fig. 8. (a) Proposed hardware-software codesign based RS(255,239)-BCH(2184,2040) serial concatenated error correction encoder and (b) the proposed compact scheduling used in (a).

3   Proposed Hardware-Software Codesign of RS-BCH Serial Concatenated Error Correction Encoder

In the proposed hardware-software codesign based RS(255,239)-BCH(2184,2040) serial concatenated error correction encoder, the RS encoding is done with software in 32-bit Microblaze and the BCH encoding is done with hardware in the co-processor. Figure 8(a) shows the aforementioned approach. The RS encoding output from the 32-bit Microblaze is sent along with the dividend inputs to the BCH co-processor. Now, the BCH encoding is done with hardware co-processor. According to the Eqs. 2 and 4, the RS/BCH encoding is nothing but the concatenated result of the remainder $R(x)$ and the input $D(x)$, where $R(x) = (x^{n-k}.D(x))\%G(x)$. Figure 8(a) shows the LFSR based bit serial divider architecture for BCH encoder with the length of generator polynomial as 144. Since the most significant bit (msb) of generator polynomial is 1, 143 numbers of AND gates and XOR gates are used. The first 143 bits of the generator polynomial $G[0]$ to $G[142]$ act as a divisor, while $G[143] = 1$. Initially, the registers $R0$ to $R142$ are in the reset condition. From the first cycle onwards, each bit of the dividend $DIV[i]$ is sent to the circuit from msb to least significant bit (lsb) during each cycle, where i is varied from 2039 to 0. The required remainder will be produced after passing the lsb of the dividend. Finally, the BCH encoded output is the required serial concatenated error correction encoding output that is sent back to the 32-bit Microblaze. Here, the hardware part (BCH encoding) will be started after completing the software execution (RS encoding), because the outer encoding (BCH encoding) requires the output from the inner encoder (RS encoder). Therefore, there is a dependency between the software portion and the hardware portion. So, the software portion is idle during the execution of the hardware portion. Our proposed design utilizes this dependency to achieve multiple concatenated encoding in parallel, that is named as the compact scheduling. In compact scheduling, the software portion will be busy with second concatenated encoding while the hardware portion is busy with the first concatenated encoding. This phenomenon is similar to the conventional synchronous pipelined implementation. Figure 8(b) shows the proposed compact scheduling based five numbers of RS(255,239)-BCH(2184,2040) serial concatenated error correction encodings.

4   Design Modelling, Implementation, and Results

All the existing and proposed hardware-software codesigns are modelled/verified using Verilog HDL and synthesised using Xilinx vivado with 28 nm Artix-7 Nexys-4 FPGA (XC7A100T-CSG324) device. The actual FPGA devices used in the reference papers for all the existing techniques are different. All the existing techniques are implemented as per the reference papers using one particular aforementioned FPGA device. Therefore, the comparisons with proposed technique are valid. In all the hardware-software co-designs mentioned in this paper, the software and hardware portions are implemented with c and $verilog\ HDL$ respectively. In all the cases, the co-processor will get the inputs from the main processor and results from the co-processor will be sent to the main processor (32-bit Microblaze). Tables 1 and 2 show the performance analysis and hardware cost of various hardware-software codesigns of 128-bit AES respectively. The synthesis results clearly show that the latency and hardware cost of proposed AES design lie in between the fully hardware based and hardware-software partition

Table 1. Performance analysis of various hardware-software codesigns of 128-bit AES using Artix-7 Nexys-4 FPGA (XC7A100T-CSG324) with Xilinx Vivado (100 MHz)

	AES functions				# cycles in S		# cycles in H		# cycles
	BS&SR	MC	AK	KE	1 task	40 tasks	1 task	40 tasks	Inter commu -nication (for 1 task)
Compiler based	S	S	S	S	530736	21368593	0	0	0
Conventional folded with LUT based SBOX	H	H	H	H	523	18660	10	400	$3(\frac{128}{32})$
Parallel with LUT based S BOX (without pipeline)	H	H	H	H	354	11900	1	40	$3(\frac{128}{32})$
Parameterized parallel with LUT based SBOX [2]	H	H	H	H	438	15260	5	200	$3(\frac{128}{32})$
T-boxes based folded [3]	H	H	H	H	591	21380	10	400	$3(\frac{128}{32})$
Partition based [4]	S	H	H	H	18951	755780	10	400	$4 \times 10(\frac{128}{32})+3$
Partition based [4]	S	H	H	S	37422	1494620	10	400	$3 \times 10(\frac{128}{32})+3$
Partition with Euclidean algorithm based SBOX [5]	H	H	S	S	39716	1502374	10	400	$2 \times 10(\frac{128}{32})+2$
Four co-processors based [6]	H	H	H	H	6786	269180	39	1560	$9 \times 10(\frac{128}{32})$
Partition based [7]	S	H	S	S	40677	1624820	9	360	$2 \times 9(\frac{128}{32})$
Proposed design with one co-processor (Fig. 6(b))	**H**	**H**	**H**	**H**	**3810**	**150140**	**10**	**400**	$4 \times 10(\frac{128}{32})+3$

Here, BS, SR, MC, AK, KE , H, and S are byte sub, shift row, mix column, add key, key expansion, hardware, and software respectively. In parameterized parallel design [2], hardware for two AES rounds is considered as co-processor. Also, the number of cycles required for the communication between the 32-bit Microblaze and co-processors for 40 tasks is the multiplication between the 40 and the cycles required for 1 task. The irreducible polynomial used in $GF(2^8)$ 128-bit AES is $x^8 + x^4 + x^3 + x + 1$.

based existing designs. In the fully hardware based designs, all the AES functions (BS&SR, MC, AK, and KE) are designed with hardware (H). The latency of our proposed AES hardware-software codesign is greater than fully hardware based parallel and folded designs, because of inter communication overhead between the co-processor and Microblaze. Since the fully hardware based designs (conventional folded, parallel, [2], and [3]) require synchronous hardware registers, the dynamic power is much greater than the hardware-software partition based ([4-7]) and proposed designs. Here, the co-processor in the proposed AES design is called for each round. Therefore, 10 intercommunications are required in the proposed AES design for each task. During each round, four 128-bit data (plain text, input key, cipher text, and output key) are transferred between the 32-bit Microblaze and the co-processor as a number of 32-bit chunks. The plain text and input key are transferred from the 32-bit Microblaze to the co-processor. Similarly, the cipher text and output key are transferred from the co-processor to 32-bit Microblaze. Three extra 32-bit chunks are used to transfer the control signals such as *sel* and *se* (as shown in Fig. 6(b)) from the 32-bit Microblaze to the co-processor. Each 32-bit data transfer between the 32-bit Microblaze and the co-processor requires one cycle. Therefore, the total number of cycles required to transfer the data between the 32-bit Microblaze and the co-processor for one AES encryption in the proposed design is equal to $4 \times 10(\frac{128}{32}) + 3 = 163$.

Table 2. Hardware cost of various hardware-software codesigns of 128-bit AES using Artix-7 Nexys-4 FPGA (XC7A100T-CSG324) with Xilinx Vivado (100 MHz)

	Utilization		Power (w)	
	# Slices	# LUTs as logic	Switching power	Leakage power
Compiler based	832	2043	0.029	0.098
Conventional folded with LUT based SBOX	2922	5987	0.181	0.098
Parallel with LUT based S BOX (without pipeline)	3402	11971	0.419	0.099
Parameterized parallel with LUT based SBOX [2]	4522	6569	0.213	0.098
T-boxes based folded [3]	3060	7613	0.241	0.098
Partition based [4]	1056	2795	0.046	0.099
Partition based [4]	981	2791	0.032	0.098
Partition with Euclidean algorithm based SBOX [5]	1957	5893	0.032	0.098
Four co-processors based [6]	1481	4243	0.035	0.098
Partition based [7]	978	2444	0.027	0.098
Proposed design with one co-processor (Fig. 6(b))	**1277**	**3683**	**0.028**	**0.098**

The plain text and input key are transferred from the 32-bit Microblaze to the co-processor while the cipher text is transferred from the co-processor to 32-bit Microblaze in the fully hardware based designs such as conventional folded, parallel, [2], and [3]. Therefore, the total number of cycles required to transfer the data between the 32-bit Microblaze and the co-processor for one AES encryption in the fully hardware based design is equal to $3\left(\frac{128}{32}\right) = 13$. The synthesis results show that our proposed hardware-software codesign of 128-bit AES achieves 85% of reduction in switching power dissipation over conventional folded design using Artix-7 FPGA implementation.

Table 3. Performance analysis and hardware cost of various hardware-software codesigns of RS(255,239)-BCH(2184,2040) serial concatenated error correction encoder using Artix-7 Nexys-4 FPGA (XC7A100T-CSG324) with Xilinx Vivado (100 MHz)

	Functions		# cycles in S		# cycles in H		# cycles
	RS	BCH	1 task	5 tasks	1 task	5 tasks	inter communi-cation (for 1 task)
Compiler based	S	S	26988612	135152245	0	0	0
Fully hardware based [8]	H	H	2358	7539	(2040+239)	5(2040+239)	$(2\lceil\frac{143}{32}\rceil + \lceil\frac{15\times8}{32}\rceil + \lceil\frac{239\times8}{32}\rceil)$
Proposed design (Fig. 8(a))	**S**	**H**	**221467**	**894340**	**2040**	**2040**	$(\lceil\frac{15\times8}{32}\rceil + 2\lceil\frac{143}{32}\rceil + \lceil\frac{239\times8}{32}\rceil)$

	Utilization		Power (w)	
Compiler based	832	2043	0.029	0.098
Fully hardware based [8]	2497	7944	0.098	0.098
Proposed design (Fig. 8(a))	**2011**	**6358**	**0.059**	**0.098**

Here, S and H represent software and hardware respectively. Also, the number of cycles required for the communication between the 32-bit Microblaze and co-processors for 5 tasks is the multiplication between the 5 and the cycles required for 1 task. For RS(255,239) encoding, $GF(2^8)$ arithmetic [10] is used.

Table 3 shows the performance analysis and hardware cost of various hardware-software codesigns of RS(255,239)-BCH(2184,2040) serial concatenated error correction encoder. The cycles used in the hardware from the first task will never be considered, because both the hardware and software work in parallel from the first task onwards due to the compact scheduling as shown in Fig. 8(b). During the last task, the hardware works alone while the software is idle. Therefore, the number of cycles for the co-processor using the proposed design as shown in Fig. 8(a) for 5 tasks is equal to the 1 task. Also, the 15 numbers of 8-bit chunks as a output from RS encoder, the 239 numbers of 8-bit chunks as a input of the RS encoder, and the 143-bit data as divider for BCH encoder need to be transferred from the 32-bit Microblaze to the co-processor in the proposed concatenated error correction encoder design. Similarly, the 143-bit data as output from the BCH encoder needs to be transferred from the co-processor to the 32-bit Microblaze. Therefore, the total number of cycles required to transfer the data between the 32-bit Microblaze and the co-processor for one RS-BCH concatenated error correction encoding in the proposed design is equal to $\lceil\frac{15\times8}{32}\rceil + 2\lceil\frac{143}{32}\rceil + \lceil\frac{239\times8}{32}\rceil = 74$. Here, the 16th digit of the divisor used in the RS encoder is 1 due to the generator polynomial with length 16. Similarly, the 144th bit of the divisor used in the BCH encoder is 1 due to the generator polynomial with length 144. Therefore, the lengths of the outputs (remainders) of RS and BCH encodings are 15 digits each with 8-bits and 143-bits respectively. The synthesis results show that our proposed hardware-software codesign of RS(255,239)-BCH(2184,2040) serial concatenated error correction encoder achieves 40% of reduction in switching power dissipation over [8] using Artix-7 FPGA implementation.

5   Conclusion

This paper proposes low power AES folded encryptor and RS-BCH concatenated error correction encoder using FPGA based hardware-software codesign. In the first implementation, synchronous registers are avoided in the co-processor, where the results after each round will be passed from the co-processor to Microblaze and again back from Microblaze to co-processor for the next round of operations. In the second case, the compact scheduling based hardware-software partitioning is used, where both the software in Microblaze and hardware in co-processor work in parallel to improve the performance. The synthesis results show that our proposed hardware-software codesigns of 128-bit AES and RS(255,239)-BCH(2184,2040) serial concatenated error correction encoder achieve 85% and 40% of reduction in switching power dissipation over the conventional folded AES design and [8] using Artix-7 FPGA implementation respectively.

References

1. Mohamed Asan Basiri, M., Shukla, S.K.: Hardware optimizations for crypto implementations. In: IEEE International Symposium on VLSI Design and Test, pp. 1–6 (2016)
2. Anwar, H., et al.: Parameterized AES-based crypto processor for FPGAs. In: IEEE Euromicro Conference on Digital System Design (DSD), pp. 465–472 (2014)
3. Chaves, R., Kuzmanov, G., Vassiliadis, S., Sousa, L.: Reconfigurable memory based AES co-processor. In: IEEE International Parallel and Distributed Processing Symposium, pp. 1–8 (2006)
4. Otero, C.T.O., Tse, J., Manohar, R.: AES hardware-software codesign in WSN. In: IEEE International Symposium on Asynchronous Circuits and Systems (ASYNC), pp. 85–92 (2015)
5. Baskaran, S., Rajalakshmi, P.: Hardware-software codesign of AES on FPGA. In: ACM International Conference on Advances in Computing, Communications and Informatics, pp. 1118–1122 (2012)
6. Heinrich, E., Staamann, S., Joost, R., Salomon, R.: Comparison of FPGA-based implementation alternatives for complex algorithms in networked embedded systems - the encryption example. In: IEEE International Conference on Emerging Technologies and Factory Automation, pp. 1449–1456 (2008)
7. Hasamnis, M.A., Limaye, S.S.: Design and implementation of Rijindael's encryption algorithm with hardware/Software codesign using NIOS II processor. In: IEEE Conference on Industrial Electronics and Applications (ICIEA), pp. 1386–1389 (2012)

8. Zhang, L., Wang, Z., Hu, Q., Zhang, J.: High speed concatenated code codec for optical communication systems. In: IEEE International Symposium on Photonics and Optoelectronics, pp. 1–4 (2009)
9. Yuan, J., Ye, W., Jiang, Z., Mao, Y., Wang, W.: A novel super-FEC code based on concatenated code for high-speed long-haul optical communication systems. Opt. Commun. **273**, 421–427 (2007)
10. Mohamed Asan Basiri, M., Shukla, S.K.: Flexible VLSI architectures for Galois field multipliers. Integration VLSI Journal **59**, 109–124 (2017)

High Level Synthesis and Implementation of Cryptographic Algorithm in AHIR Platform

Abhimanniu Raveendran$^{(\boxtimes)}$, Sanjay Dhok, and Rajendra Patrikar

Center for VLSI and Nanotechnology,
Visvesvaraya National Institute of Technology, Nagpur 440010, India
abhimanyu.raveendran@gmail.com, sanjaydhok@gmail.com, rajendra@computer.org

Abstract. This paper proposes a High Level Synthesis (HLS) design methodology that translates complex algorithms modeled in high level language to hardware description. The existing HLS strategies fails to provide adequate abstraction to the underlying hardware details and thus limits software programmers from designing complex and advanced cipher algorithms. In this paper the method of generating synthesizable Register Transfer Level (RTL) design from algorithm is accomplished through an open framework called AHIR, an acronym for *a hardware intermediate representation*. The integrated design flow intends to generate layout from algorithm with minimal human intervention and thus offers software programmers with ample opportunities to design application specific digital hardware. The paper discusses several highlights of the design flow including savings in verification, rapid prototyping and shorter time to market together with various performance overheads. The cipher algorithms implemented in this paper includes the widely accepted Advanced Encryption Standard (AES) along with other established lightweight algorithms namely PRESENT, Light Encryption Device (LED) which are effective for resource constrained applications. A comparative performance analysis was carried out between the high level design approach and the traditional RTL style based on their FPGA and ASIC implementation.

Keywords: High level synthesis · AHIR · AES · LED · PRESENT

1 Introduction

Digital design flow has undergone drastic changes over the past decade. Among the various attempts much efforts were focused on abridging the gap between digital designers and software programmers. A great deal of attention was laid on abstraction at a higher level and automating the digital design flow with minimal human intervention. Every design goes through either an application specific design flow which mainly concentrates on performance or a Field Programmable Gate Array (FPGA)/embedded processor based design that focuses more on

S. Rajaram et al. (Eds.): VDAT 2018, CCIS 892, pp. 16–27, 2019.
https://doi.org/10.1007/978-981-13-5950-7_2

other aspects like rapid deployment on a generic platform. This paper gives more significance on performance as we look to implement algorithms in hardware for resource constrained devices like Internet of Things (IoT) and hence more focus was given to Application Specific Integrated Circuit (ASIC) even though we look to bring about their comparisons with the other as and when required. The performance metrics in highlight are die area, power consumption and speed of operation of the chip.

The HLS followed in this work employs AHIR intermediate representation. AHIR is an open platform developed by IIT Bombay. It acts as a transition layer between high level compilation and hardware synthesis. It takes advantages from software level optimization and also the decoupled approach followed in AHIR helps for reuse or sharing of computational resources. One of the major challenges designers often confront is market pressure to produce a digital system with better performance in shorter time. The bottle neck to the above issue is the time, cost and resources utilized for the verification process. Almost 70% of cost incurred for design of digital hardware accounts to verification. Hence any novel design flow that minimizes verification effort would be considered appropriate. The HLS approach presented here replaces traditional RTL verification with a software level verification which accounts for savings and also makes digital hardware design accessible to large set of people.

Cryptography has become integral part of any device as data safety and security has become targets for attacks and are of prime concern. Over the years both the software and hardware implementation of cipher algorithms has been studied in detail to alleviate data security attacks along with their respective performance aspects. Our design approach incorporates merits from both domains, the ease of building algorithm in high level language at software level and the performance when security algorithms are implemented in hardware.

Among many available block ciphers we chose The Advanced Encryption Standard or **AES**, the symmetric block cipher algorithm because it is widely accepted and standardized. It offers ease of implementation and favorable defense against various attack techniques. With regard to challenges and security solutions for resource constrained devices like IoT's and Smart Cards, various tailored versions of existing ciphers were developed commonly termed as *Lightweight Cryptography*. In this work we have included two most commonly preferred lightweight cryptography algorithms viz. **PRESENT** and **LED** as part of the work. A graphical user interface which gives a front end for the user was also developed. It wraps the entire design flow but enables the user to disassemble individual steps and thus have an effective debugging facility at each step throughout the entire process.

The rest of the contents in this paper is organized as follows: Sect. 2 gives an overview of various cipher algorithms implemented in this paper. Section 3 describes in detail the HLS flow using AHIR. The automated C to GDS tool is presented in Sect. 4. Sections 5 and 6 describes the FPGA and ASIC implementation and analysis of various designs respectively. The results of the work carried out and discussions are covered in Sects. 7 and 8 presents Conclusion.

2   Cryptographic Algorithms: An Overview

Security has been an area of major concern in modern digital systems. Encryption of data using cryptographic algorithms offers confidentiality, authentication and integrity of data. This section gives an overview of one of the most commonly used standards for encryption, The Advanced Encryption Standard (AES) along with other light weight cryptographic algorithms that can be implemented in resource constrained devices.

2.1   Advanced Encryption Standard (AES)

AES is a symmetric block cipher which operates on plain text of length 128 bits. The key length for AES can be 128, 192 or 256 bits. The proposed work assume key length of 128 bits. The encryption process consists of 10 rounds for 128 bit key length. This step is implemented using *for* loops in C. The last round is little different from the others in that it does not include one operation. Each round performs a series of operations in sequence namely a single byte substitution using substitution box, shifting of rows, mixing of columns (skipped for last round) and an Exclusive-OR with specific round key [8]. The most critical operation in this encryption process is the mixing of column step, in which the block is multiplied by a fixed matrix. We have implemented this step in an optimized manner to reduce area with the help of macros and without using LUT method. The detailed algorithm is shown in Fig. 1. The operations carried out in each of the rounds are implemented as individual C *functions* which acts on the globally available plain text.

2.2   PRESENT Cipher Algorithm

PRESENT is a lightweight block cipher based on substitution permutation (SP) network. Encryption process includes 31 rounds and block length is 64 bits. The key length chosen in this paper is 80 bits. Each of the 31 rounds consists of the following three steps viz. *AddRoundKey, SboxLayer, pLayer*. The algorithm is explained in Fig. 2. The above steps are implemented as C functions. *AddRoundKey* involves an Exclusive-OR operation with key. The Substitution box is implemented as a look up table (LUT). This LUT is utilized in *SboxLayer* step to provide nibble by nibble in each cycle. The step *pLayer* does a bit permutation based on fixed locations [9]. The prefixed locations of each of the 64 bits of plain text is provided as a LUT to the function. The above algorithm is considered useful for extremely resource constrained environments because of its efficient hardware implementation, moderate security features and above all simplicity. This paper implements PRESENT starting from C level and analyses its merits.

2.3   Light Encryption Device (LED) Block Cipher

LED is another lightweight block cipher that has many similarities with AES. It was primarily developed for hardware implementation. LED works on 64

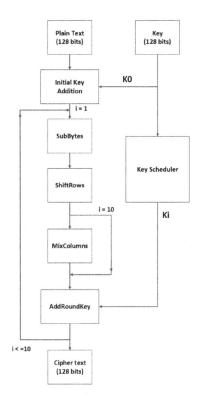

Fig. 1. AES algorithm

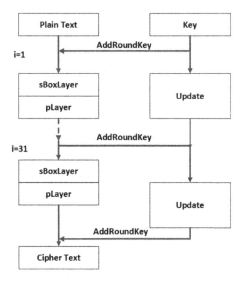

Fig. 2. PRESENT algorithm

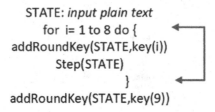

STATE: *input plain text*
for i= 1 to 8 do {
addRoundKey(STATE,key(i))
Step(STATE)
}
addRoundKey(STATE,key(9))

Fig. 3. Light Encryption Device (LED) algorithm

bit plain text and key size employed in this paper is 64 bit. The various processes involved are *addRoundKey* which does Exclusive-OR operation with key and then the method *step(STATE)* which comprises of four rounds of encryption. Each of these four rounds uses the following operations in sequence viz. *AddConstants, SubCells, ShiftRows* and *MixColumnSerial* implemented as C *funtions*. The function *AddConstants* performs EXOR operation with a round constant matrix (provided as LUT). *SubCells* function does substitution by nibbles method using PRESENT substitution box. *ShiftRows* function in C shifts the elements arranged of block array. The critical *MixColumnSerial* step multiplies the block array with a fixed array [10]. Figure 3 describes LED algorithm.

3   High Level Synthesis Flow

The HLS flow described in this paper is organized as a 3 tier model. Modeling a complex algorithm at C level, HLS using AHIR framework tools and HDL verification using software testbench respectively forms the entire model. The ease of modeling in high level language, reliable verification method and shorter turn around time are major highlights of this flow.

3.1   Software Level Modeling and Verification

The algorithmic description of a digital system is modeled in a software language like C. A test infrastructure is also written at this stage to verify the C model using standard C compilers like gnu compiler collection (gcc). This test infrastructure is further utilized for hardware verification at a later stage.

3.2   C to VHDL Conversion Using AHIR

A Hardware Intermediate Representation (AHIR) is a set of tools that converts an algorithm written in C to synthesizable vhdl which can be used for hardware generation [1–3]. AHIR flow is illustrated in Fig. 4.

C Language to LLVM Byte Code. The algorithm written in C language is first converted into Low Level Virtual Machine (LLVM) byte code using clang compiler which supports LLVM framework.

LLVM Byte Code to AHIR Assembly (Aa) Code. The LLVM byte code is then compiled into an intermediate assembly representation known as AHIR assembly (Aa) code. This Aa code consists of modules (just like C functions) which can communicate through (first in first out) FIFO pipes.

AHIR Assembly (Aa) Code to Virtual Circuit (vC) Code. The AHIR assembly (Aa) code is then converted into a virtual circuit which consists of modules disassembled as control path, data path and storage.

Virtual Circuit (vC) Code to VHDL. A VHDL description consisting of modules, memory spaces and FIFO buffers is generated from the virtual circuit code.

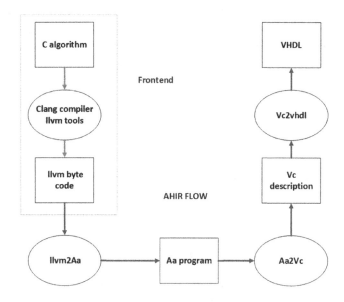

Fig. 4. High level synthesis flow

3.3   HDL Verification Using C - VHDL Co Simulation

The simulator used for the flow is open source GHDL simulator which allows for peripheral language interface. GHDL is an open source VHDL compiler or simulator assembled on gcc. GHDL offers reasonable support and hence a preferred choice as a VHDL simulator.

The peripheral language in this context is C language and is made to interface with design under test (DUT) written in vhdl. Once the vhdl models gets elaborated and simulated in simulator, VHPI (VHDL Procedural Interface) mechanism enables to access the data from these vhdl models. The VHPI standard by

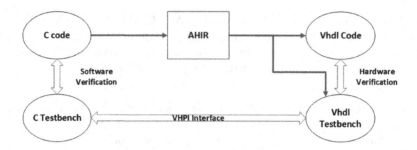

Fig. 5. C-VHDL cosimulation

IEEE is implemented as C functions forming a library in C. All the peripheral interface applications are compiled in C and linked to a shared library.

The algorithm and the testbench is specified in C. AHIR converts the C model into vhdl. The initial C testbench itself is employed in verifying the generated vhdl instead of writing a separate testbench. The process builds a vhdl testbench that instantiates the DUT. It has a foreign architecture through which C testbench interacts with DUT as illustrated in Fig. 5. The traditional methodology does this through rigorous verification through writing vhdl test benches which requires huge effort. The above methodology of writing testbenches at a higher abstraction level saves the time and cost for stringent verification and also helps in rapid prototype deployment.

4   Automated C to GDS Flow

The automated C to GDS tool generates digital Integrated Circuits (IC) from algorithm as shown by its GUI in Fig. 6. The tool employs a flow that takes C specifications as input. AHIR converts it into VHDL and also generates various executable files to verify the design at software level and at hardware level. Hardware level verification or simulation was done using GHDL Simulator. Synopsys *Design Compiler* was employed to Synthesis RTL to gate level netlist. This step was followed by equivalence checking performed by Synopsys *Formality* and the synthesized netlist is then mapped to SCL 180 nm technology library. Placing of standard cells, Clock Tree Synthesis and Routing is done using Cadence *Innovus* and finally the design was exported in GDSII foundry format. A front end graphical user interface was also developed that ensures ease of usage.

5   FPGA Implementation

The AES encryption and decryption modules was written in verilog using a round based architecture [8]. Simulation of encryption module is done using Xilinx ISE 14.7 as shown in Fig. 7.

The AES algorithm which is also described in C, was translated to VHDL using the design methodology presented in this paper. The resulting VHDL

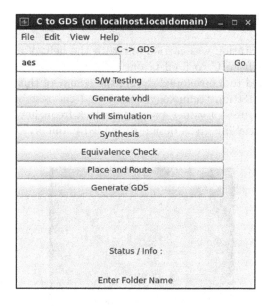

Fig. 6. Front end GUI

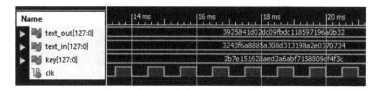

Fig. 7. Xilinx simulation of AES

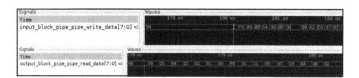

Fig. 8. GHDL simulation of AES

was verified and simulated using standard AES test vectors using C-vhdl Co-simulation flow. The simulation is performed with the help of open source GHDL simulator as shown in Fig. 8.

The FPGA implementation of both the design styles was done on Xilinx Kintex-7 XC7K325T FFG900C FPGA. The resulting device utilization are enlisted in Table 1.

6   ASIC Implementation

The ASIC implementation was carried out with the help of a completely automated flow staring from C to final layout. The entire design flow was carried
out by the integrated tool developed during the course of this work. The design
is mapped to SCL 180 nm technology library and the rest back end processes
assumes standard figures of values except the clock frequency to which the tool
must try to synthesize any given design (provided manually).

Fig. 9. ASIC Layout of AES

The final layout generated from the C description of AES through the automated tool is shown in Fig. 9.

7   Results and Discussions

Table 1 compares FPGA implementation of the design starting with C specification against the traditional RTL style. The RTL design and the C level
design both were synthesized on to Xilinx Kintex-7 FPGA board. The resulting implementation indicates that C level design utilizes more of the available
device resources compared to the other. The high utilization results in FPGA
implementation does not hamper the higher abstraction flow as long as the flow
helps in rapid deployment of the exact design and reducing the effort and the
cost incurred for the same.

The results of ASIC implementation of AES following the two design styles
are tabulated in Table 2. From the results it can be inferred that handwritten
RTL is still a way ahead of C level abstraction. The die area required is more for
C level style even though power dissipation results are of same order. Various
experiments carried out during the course of this work suggests that lack of
expressing parallelism in C, inefficient cell libraries and restricted usage of C
constructs are accountable for the above obscure results.

Table 1. Resource utilization for FPGA Implementation.

AES algorithm	No. of Slice Registers (407600)	No. of Slice LUT's (203800)	No. of bonded IOB's (500)	BUFGCTRL (32)
RTL	1408	9417	385	1
C Level	53807	45493	66	1

Table 2. Performance characteristics for ASIC Implementation

AES algorithm	Area (mm^2)	Power (mW) @ 10 MHz	Max Freq. (MHz)
RTL	2.0	12	28
C Level	3.2	16	77

Table 3. ASIC synthesis results of cipher algorithms

Algorithm	Area (mm^2)	Power (mW) @ 50 MHz	Max Freq. (MHz)
AES	3.2	80	77
LED	1.2	30	55
PRESENT	1.4	26	50

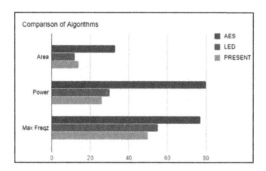

Fig. 10. Analysis of cipher algorithms

Table 3 shows the ASIC implementation results of lightweight algorithms viz. LED and PRESENT along with standard AES. These light weight algorithms were modeled in C true to AHIR specification. The automated design flow was made use of in achieving the final layout once these designs were synthesized and mapped to the technology library. The amount of effort incurred during this process was minimal compared to traditional style. The table data shows the die area and power obtained for each of the algorithm which when laid out as an ASIC.

Figure 10 (relatively scaled) clearly depicts that light weight algorithms are more efficient in terms of chip area and power dissipation compared to standard

AES. This adds to the advantage of the above mentioned abstract level design flow that it encourages designers to develop efficient cryptographic algorithms for the modern day resource constrained applications.

8   Conclusion

In this paper a design flow was presented that converts an algorithmic description in C into digital hardware. The abstract design procedure was completely automated that offers programmers with limited understanding of Hardware Description Language (HDL) to design digital hardware. The paper explored HLS implementation details of standard AES along with lightweight cipher algorithms viz. LED and PRESENT that can potentially replace traditional heavy weight algorithms for emerging technological applications like IoT's. The results obtained through this work reflects the fact that the hardware generated may not compete with hand-coded implementation in terms of performance but when the overall design cycle is considered the savings attained outruns the performance overheads. The design flow can be made more competent by exploring optimization techniques at various levels. Future ventures aim to develop end to end mapping along with software based on-board logic analysis and debugging.

References

1. Sahasrabuddhe, S.D., Raja, H., Arya, K., Desai, M.P.: AHIR: a hardware intermediate representation for hardware generation from high-level languages. In: 20th International Conference on VLSI Design, January 2007
2. Arvind, Nikhil, R., Rosenband, D., Dave, N.: High-level synthesis: an essential ingredient for designing complex ASICs. In: International Conference on Computer Aided Design (ICCAD 2004), November 2004
3. Sahasrabuddhe, S.D.: A competitive pathway from high-level programs to hardware. Ph.D. dissertation, IIT Bombay (2009)
4. AhirV2: from algorithms to hardware-An overview Madhav Desai Department of Electrical Engineering Indian Institute of Technology, Mumbai, 400076, India, 22 February 2015
5. Budiu, M., Goldstein, S.C.: Pegasus: an efficient intermediate representation. School of Computer Science, Carnegie Mellon University, Technical report, April 2002
6. Gupta, S., Dutt, N., Gupta, R., Nicolau, A.: SPARK: a high-level synthesis framework for applying parallelizing compiler transformations. In: International Conference on VLSI Design, January 2003
7. ModelSim Foreign Language Interface for c VHDL Co-Simulation- by Andre Pool
8. Daemen, J., Rijmen, V.: AES Proposal: Rijndael, NIST AES Proposal. www.esat. kuleuven.ac.be/rijmen/rijndael/
9. Bogdanov, A., et al.: PRESENT: an ultra-lightweight block cipher. In: Paillier, P., Verbauwhede, I. (eds.) CHES 2007. LNCS, vol. 4727, pp. 450–466. Springer, Heidelberg (2007). https://doi.org/10.1007/978-3-540-74735-2_31

10. Light Encryption Device, Jian Guo Institute for Infocomm Research, Singapore, Thomas Peyrin Axel Poschmann Nanyang Technological University, Singapore, Matt Robshaw Applied Cryptography Group, Orange Labs, France, CHES 2011 Proceedings of the 13th International Conference on Cryptographic Hardware and Embedded Systems
11. A recent review on lightweight cryptography. in IoT In: 2017 International Conference on I-SMAC (IoT in Social, Mobile, Analytics and Cloud) (I-SMAC), Palladam, India, February 2017
12. Analysis of lightweight cryptographic solutions for Internet of Things. Indian J. Sci. Technol. **9**(28) (2016). https://doi.org/10.17485/ijst/2016/v9i28/98382

A Hardware Accelerator
for Convolutional Neural Network
Using Fast Fourier Transform

S. Kala[1($\boxtimes$)], Babita R. Jose[1], Debdeep Paul[2], and Jimson Mathew[3]

[1] Cochin University of Science and Technology, Kerala, India
{kalas,babitajose}@cusat.ac.in
[2] Department of Electrical Engineering, Indian Institute of Technology Patna,
Patna, India
debdeep.ee15@iitp.ac.in
[3] Department of Computer Science and Engineering,
Indian Institute of Technology Patna, Patna, India
jimson@iitp.ac.in

Abstract. Convolutional Neural Networks (CNN) are biologically inspired architectures which can be trained to perform various classification tasks. CNNs typically consists of convolutional layers, max pooling layers, followed by dense fully connected layers. Convolutional layer is the compute intensive layer in CNNs. In this paper we present FFT (Fast Fourier Transform) based convolution technique for accelerating CNN architecture. Computational complexity of direct convolution and FFT convolution are evaluated and compared. Also we present an efficient FFT architecture based on radix-4 butterfly for convolution. For validating our analysis we have implemented a convolutional layer in Virtex-7 FPGA.

Keywords: Convolutional neural networks · Hardware complexity · FFT · FPGA · VLSI

1 Introduction

Deep Convolutional Neural Networks (DCNN) algorithms for machine learning, based on feed forward networks have become very attractive for the researchers recently. Convolutional Neural Network is considered as a variant of Deep Neural Network (DNN). In recent years CNN has become the solution for various computer vision applications. CNNs find applications in face recognition, image classification, video surveillance etc. and are recently used in several machine learning challenges such as Natural Language Processing (NLP) and speech recognition. CNNs are widely used in Big Data analysis which requires high performance. In CNNs feature extraction and classification are done in a single model.

© Springer Nature Singapore Pte Ltd. 2019
S. Rajaram et al. (Eds.): VDAT 2018, CCIS 892, pp. 28–36, 2019.
https://doi.org/10.1007/978-981-13-5950-7_3

Accelerating CNN architecture on various platforms were presented by various research groups. In [1] design space algorithm for a high performance DCNN implementation in FPGA platform is presented. CNNs implemented in Graphics Processing Unit (GPU) is presented in [2]. In [20] convolutions are computed in Fourier domain and are then reused in the whole network. The architecture has been implemented in GPU. But GPU based architectures are not suited for mobile applications due to energy dissipation. General Purpose Processors (GPP) are also not efficient for CNN implementation [7]. Machine learning algorithms are highly parallel in nature. However this parallelism cannot be exploited in GPPs. FPGA based CNN accelerators are proposed in [3,4,6–10]. In [5], a face detection system is implemented in CNN which can be used for low power applications. CNNs for document image classification is proposed in [13]. A framework for CNN approximation called Ristretto, has been proposed in [14] which reduces the bit width of arithmetic used in the architecture along with multiplierless computation. Various techniques for parallelism can be utilized in different layers of CNN so as to improve the performance of the network. In [7] a high performance CNN accelerator in which all the layers work in parallel is proposed. They have used different computing methods to optimize computation and memory in convolution and fully connected layers. CNN architecture in [16] proposes techniques for utilization of all the resources by dynamic configuration of data. But they have limitations of off-chip memory bandwidth. Performance of various convolution techniques are evaluated in [21]. They have implemented ResNet-20 model in ARM Cortex A53. Google has proposed Google LeNet, where the issues of computation when using large size filters are addressed [18]. They have introduced parallel pipelining technique and used 1×1 convolutions. Most of the researchers have done their techniques and optimizations taking the state-of-art CNN, AlexNet [2] as the base architecture. ASIC based accelerator proposed by [11], gives high performance but with limitations in flexibility. FPGA is suitable accelerator for CNN due to its efficiency and flexibility.

Motivation

CNN has a special network architecture using convolution layers and fully connected layers. Convolution layer is computationally intensive and accounts for more than 90% of the overall computation. Convolution layers are compute bound and fully connected layers are memory bound. So a flexible hardware is required for accelerating CNN. CPU and GPU are not efficient enough for mobile applications. Convolution algorithms are parallel and by using FPGA platform, parallelism can be exploited. Computation overhead can be minimized by utilizing fixed point arithmetic instead of floating point. Accelerating CNNs using FFT can reduce the number of multiplications involved in computation of convolution when compared with conventional techniques [20]. This paper discuss about acceleration of CNNs based on FFT in FPGA and the hardware complexity analysis of convolution layer. We have taken AlexNet CNN as the basic architecture.

Rest of the paper is organized as follows. Section 2 gives a brief overview of CNN architecture. Section 3 describes various schemes for convolution in CNN. Proposed FFT architecture is discussed in Sect. 3.1. Section 3.2 deals with the hardware complexity analysis of various convolutional schemes. Implementation and results are discussed in Sect. 4. Section 5 concludes the paper.

2   Overview of CNN

Input data are organized and fed to the first layer of CNN which produces feature maps. Proceeding layers take this as the input and give new feature maps as the outputs. Figure 1 shows a simple CNN model. Convolutional layers, pooling layers and fully connected layers are the main components in a CNN. Convolutional layers takes the input image and convolves it with kernal to produce feature maps. Pooling layer gives the maximum or average value the features over a sub area in the image. Fully connected layer can be treated as a multi-layer perceptron where each neuron in the previous layer is connected to every other neuron in the next layer. So the weights will be higher and thus fully connected layers are memory intensive. In [11] and [12] these weights are stored in on-chip memory. But when the size of the network becomes large, external memory will be required which calls for bandwidth bottleneck.

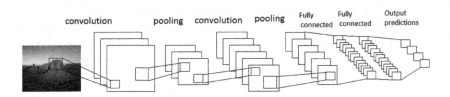

Fig. 1. Simple CNN model

First CNN which was developed for handling real world problem was LeNet [17]. Later a scaled version of LeNet with modifications like maxpooling and ReLU was proposed by researchers from University of Toronto [2]. The implementation, called AlexNet was run on GPU and won the ImageNet competition in 2012. State-of-art CNN model for object recognition, AlexNet classifies 224×224 image into 1000 categories [2]. It has five CONV (convolution) layers and three FC (Fully Connected) layers. Convolution layers extract features from the input image. After first, second and fifth CONV layers, three maxpooling layers for subsampling along with ReLU (Rectified Linear Units) nonlinearity function is applied. Alexnet CNN model is shown in Fig. 2. Number of operations in convolution layer and the number of weights in fully connected layer are discussed in [7]. Numbers show the resource requirement of CONV layer and memory requirement of FC layers. Recent works in CNN, like, GoogleNet and ResNet consists of large number of convolutional layers [18,19].

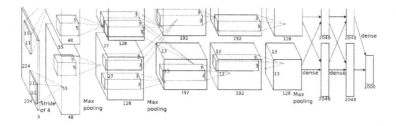

Fig. 2. AlexNet architecture

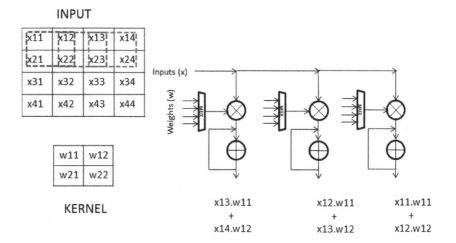

Fig. 3. Direct convolution

3   Convolution Schemes

One of the crucial operation in CNN is convolution. Efficiency of CNN architecture depends on the efficiency of convolution layer. Convolution can be performed using conventional method, also called Direct convolution as shown in Fig. 3. This is a slow process since each pixel in the image is multiplied with each of the weight in the kernel. Here, a single stride is taken for performing convolution. As the image size increases, number of MAC (multiply and accumulate) operations also increases. Real time CNN architecture comprises of several channels of input features and many convolutional layers.

Another method of performing convolution is using FFT, which is a faster technique. Convolution can be efficiently performed in frequency domain. Equation (1) gives mathematical representation of FFT based convolution.

$$x(n) * h(n) = IFFT\{FFT(x(n)) \times FFT(h(n))\} \tag{1}$$

Here, Fourier transform of the input image and kernel are taken thereby transforming them to frequency domain. Both FFTs should be of same length for element-wise multiplication. Perform inverse FFT to get the results in time domain. Figure 4 shows FFT based convolution scheme. FFTs of the input feature and the kernel are taken and are multiplied together. To perform matrix multiplication, augmentation is done. Inverse FFT is computed for the result.

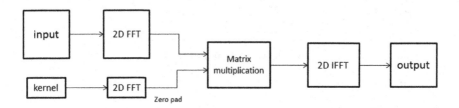

Fig. 4. FFT convolution scheme

3.1 Proposed FFT Architecture

FFT architecture based on radix-2 and radix-4 are used in our implementation. Radix-2 decimation in frequency (DIF) FFT architecture using single-path delay feedback (SDF) for 16 point FFT is shown in Fig. 5. Here, log_2N stages are required for computing a one dimensional (1D) FFT of size N. A complex multiplier is used after each stage for twiddle factor multiplication. Radix-4 FFT based on parallel architecture using *mode select* signal is used for developing higher order FFTs as shown in Fig. 6 [15]. All the four inputs are fed in parallel to the engine. That is, the butterfly unit receives all four inputs in a single clock cycle. Since the architecture is parallel and there is a control signal to decide which output has to be generated from four outputs, latency can be reduced and reordering is not required.

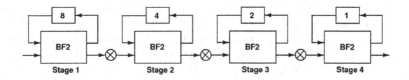

Fig. 5. Radix-2 SDF FFT architecture for N = 16

Control Signals

Mode select signal is a two bit control signal based on which we can select the output to be generated, unlike in conventional radix-4 butterfly unit. In conventional radix-4 butterfly unit, outputs are generated in a particular order. This requires the output to be reordered before giving it to the next stage. Since

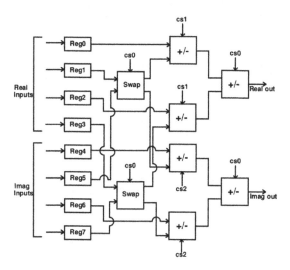

Fig. 6. Radix-4 FFT architecture

our output is already in required order, we can reduce significant amount of intermediate memory, which is used in output reordering. Also, as buffers are reduced, latency is reduced significantly. Signal cs0 decides whether to swap the real and imaginary data. Adder or subtractor is selected according to cs1 and cs2. Mode selection signal is a two bit signal which can be used to generate other control signals. *Mode* can be varied using an up-counter. LSB of *mode* can be taken as cs0 signal and MSB is taken as cs1 signal. An XOR operation of the two bits in *mode* will generate cs2 signal. Table 1 shows the control signals cs0, cs1, cs2 and *mode*. Proposed two dimensional (2D) FFT architecture is developed using cascade of one dimensional FFTs based on radix-4 butterfly units. Latency can be significantly reduced using the control signal *mode select* [15]. Since output from first one dimensional FFT is already in reordered form using *mode select*, there is no need of intermediate memory within a 1D FFT. FFT of the input features and kernels can be computed using cascade of radix-2 or radix-4 engines based on the size. Figure 7 shows the block diagram of two dimensional FFT architecture. Within a 1D FFT, intermediate memory is avoided and within two 1D FFTs, buffer size is reduced in this architecture, when compared to conventional cascade of 1D FFTs. Input memory takes the streaming input and provides it in parallel to the first 1D FFT. Inter-processing block requires buffers to store the output to be fed to second FFT block. Both 1D FFTs are identical in this architecture. For larger size FFTs, number of stages within a 1D FFT should be increased, which will not consume intermediate buffer in our implementation. Inverse FFT can be computed using FFT and its conjugates as given in Eq. (2).

$$IFFT = conj(FFT(conj(x)))/length(x) \qquad (2)$$

Table 1. Mode selection in radix-4 butterfly

cs0	cs1	cs2	Mode	Output
0	0	0	0 0	X(0)
1	0	1	0 1	X(1)
0	1	1	1 0	X(2)
1	1	0	1 1	X(3)

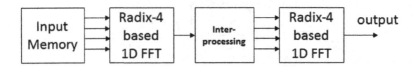

Fig. 7. 2D FFT architecture

3.2 Complexity Analysis

Consider an image of size $n \times n$ and kernel $k \times k$. In case of direct convolution, each pixel requires $O(k \times k)$ computations. i.e., each element in the input image feature map is individually computed using multiplication and accumulation operation with the kernel. Thus the 2D convolution will have complexity of $O(n^2 \times k^2)$. Total number of operations required in direct convolution is $(n - k + 1)^2 \times k^2$. FFT based convolution has a complexity of $O(n^2 log(n))$.

Convolution parameters in AlexNet model are given in Table 2. Table 2 gives input size and kernel size in various convolution layers. Three channels of input image, each with size 224×224 are fed to CONV 1 layer. CONV 1 has kernel of size 11×11 with stride 4. It produces 96 features of size 55×55 which are fed as input to next layer. Considering the direct convolution in CONV 1 layer, there are 105 million MAC operations and 34k parameters. CONV 2 layer has 224 million MAC operations and 307k parameters. This shows the computational complexity of convolutional layers in CNN architecture.

Table 2. CONV layer parameters in AlexNet CNN

Layer	Features (channels)	Size	Kernel	Stride
Input image	3	224×224		
CONV 1	96	55×55	11×11	4
CONV 2	256	27×27	5×5	1
CONV 3	384	13×13	3×3	1
CONV 4	384	13×13	3×3	1
CONV 5	256	13×13	3×3	1

Table 3. Comparison of convolution schemes

Parameters		FFT convolution	Direct convolution
Slice LUTs	Used	1176	2481
	Available	41000	41000
	Util %	2.87	6.05
Flip Flops	Used	1974	4795
	Available	82000	82000
	Util %	2.41	5.85
DSP48 and BRAM	Not used in this implementation		

4 Implementation and Results

For validating the analysis, we have implemented convolution layer in Virtex-7 FPGA platform. Both direct convolution scheme and FFT based convolution for 4×4 feature size and 2×2 kernel size were implemented. For FFT based convolution, two dimensional Fourier Transform of 4×4 feature and 2×2 kernel were taken. Kernel size 2×2 has to be augmented to 4×4 for matrix multiplication and IFFT is computed on the result. For hardware implementation, we have used fixed point arithmetic with 16 bits as the word length. For complex multiplication, we have used four real multipliers which are pipelined signed booth multipliers, and two adders. Comparison of resource utilization in terms of slice LUTs of direct convolution and FFT based convolution layer is given in Table 3. Table 3 shows that resources are utilized more in case of direct convolution. Since our implementation was based on a small matrix, DSP blocks and Block RAMs were not used. FFT based convolution is more advantageous when kernel size is large.

5 Conclusion

Convolutional Neural Network is a widely used learning algorithm which is used in Computer Vision and non-Vision applications. CNNs consists of massive number of neurons and are computationally intensive. CNN contains a stack of convolutional layers and fully connected layers where, convolutional layers are computationally complex and fully connected layers are memory intensive. In this paper we present various convolution schemes in CNNs. Complexity analysis of direct convolution and FFT based convolution are performed. For experimental results, we have implemented both the schemes in Virtex-7 FPGA. We have taken an input size of 4×4 and kernel size of 2×2. Resource utilization of both convolution techniques are evaluated. Comparison shows that FFT based convolution reduces the utilization of slice LUTs when compared to direct convolution. FFT based convolution reduces the complexity of computation and give better performance when the kernel size is large.

References

1. Motamedi, M., Gysel, P., Akella, V., Ghiasi, S.: Design space exploration of FPGA-based deep convolutional neural networks. In: Proceedings of the ASP DAC, pp. 575–580 (2016)
2. Krizhevsky, A., Sutskever, I., Hinton, G.E.: ImageNet classification with deep convolutional neural networks. In: Advances in Neural Information Processing Systems, pp. 1097–1105 (2012)
3. Solazzo, A., Del Sozzo, E., De Rose, I., De Silvestri, M.: Hardware design automation of convolutional neural networks. In: IEEE ISVLSI (2016)
4. Peemen, M., Setio, A.A.A., Mesman, B., Corporaal, H.: Memory-centric accelerator design for convolutional neural networks. In: ICCD (2013)
5. Farabet, C., Poulet, C., Han, J.Y., LeCun, Y.: CNP: an FPGA based processor for convolutional networks. In: FPL (2009)
6. Ma, Y., Suda, N., Cao, Y., Seo, J.-S., Vrudhula, S.: Scalable and modularized RTL compilation of convolutional neural networks onto FPGA. In: FPL (2016)
7. Li, H., et al.: A high performance FPGA-based accelerator for large-scale convolutional neural networks. In: FPL (2016)
8. Qiu, J., et al.: Going deeper with embedded FPGA platform for convolutional neural network. In: FPGA (2016)
9. Zhang, C., et al.: Optimizing FPGA-based accelerator design for deep convolutional neural networks (2015)
10. Farabet, C., et al.: Hardware accelerated convolutional neural networks for synthetic vision systems. In: ISCAS (2010)
11. Chen, Y., et al.: DaDianNao: a machine-learning supercomputer. In: IEEE/ACM International Symposium on Microarchitecture, pp. 602–622 (2014)
12. Du, Z., Fasthuber, R.: ShiDianNao: shifting vision processing closer to the sensor. In: ACM International Symposium Computer Architecture (ISCA) (2015)
13. Kang, L., Kumar, J., Ye, P., Li, Y., Doermann, D.: Convolutional neural networks for document image classification. In: 22nd International Conference on Pattern Recognition (2014)
14. Matthias, G.P.: Ristretto: hardware-oriented approximation of convolutional neural networks. MSc thesis, UC Davis (2016)
15. Kala, S., Nalesh, S., Maity, A., Nandy, S.K., Narayan, R.: High throughput, low latency, memory optimized 64K point FFT architecture using novel radix-4 butterfly unit. In: IEEE International Symposium on Circuits and Systems, ISCAS, pp. 3034–3037 (2013)
16. Chakradhar, S., Sankaradas, M., Jakkula, V., Cadambi, S.: A dynamically configurable coprocessor for convolutional neural networks: In: ACM SIGARCH Computer Architecture News, vol. 38, pp. 247–257. ACM (2010)
17. LeCun, Y., Bottou, L., Bengio, Y., Haffner, P.: Gradient-based learning applied to document recognition. Proc. IEEE 86(11), 2278–2323 (1998)
18. Szegedy, C., Reed, S., Sermanet, P., Vanhoucke, V., Rabinovich, A.: Going deeper with convolutions, pp. 1–12 (2014)
19. He, K., Zhang, X., Ren, S., Sun, J.: Deep residual learning for image recognition. In: CVPR (2016)
20. Mathieu, M., Henaff, M.: Fast training of convolutional networks through FFTs. In: ICLR (2014)
21. Abtahi, T., Kulkarni, A., Mohsenin, T.: Accelerating convolutional neural network with FFT on tiny cores. In: ISCAS (2017)

Reconfigurable VLSI-Architecture of Multi-radix Maximum-A-Posteriori Decoder for New Generation of Wireless Devices

Rahul Shrestha[1(✉)] and Ashutosh Sharma[2]

[1] School of Computing and Electrical Engineering, Indian Institute of Technology
(IIT) Mandi, Mandi 175005, Himachal Pradesh, India
rahul_shrestha@iitmandi.ac.in
[2] Center for VLSI and Embedded System Technologies, International Institute
of Information Technology (IIIT) Hyderabad, Hyderabad 500032, Telangana, India
ashutosh.sharma@research.iiit.ac.in
https://faculty.iitmandi.ac.in/~rahul_shrestha/

Abstract. This work presents new flexible-architecture for maximum-
a-posteriori (MAP) decoder with multi-radix modes to support various
throughputs at different levels of power consumption. We have designed
major internal blocks of MAP decoder using extensive steering logic to
support radix-2/4/8 operating modes. These designs enable efficient clock-
gating of our decoder for low-power consumption in different operating modes. This decoder-architecture is post-layout simulated in 65 nm-
CMOS process and its performance analysis showed that the bit-error-
rate (BER) of 10^{-4} could be achieved at 5 dB. Implementation result
shows that the suggested MAP decoder could achieve throughput in the
range $270-810$ Mbps with the corresponding power consumption range
of $12.24-37.67$ mW. In comparison to the state-of-the-art, our design
achieved 38% higher throughput and 61% lower power consumption.

Keywords: Wireless communication · Channel codes ·
MAP decoding · VLSI architectures · VLSI design

1 Introduction

For the last two decades, turbo code has become dominant choice of various
wireless-communication systems, like IEEE 802.16 (Fixed & Mobile WiMAX),
WCDMA, HSDPA, 3GPP-LTE, 4G-LTE-A, as a forward error correction (FEC)
code due to its near-optimal error-correction performance to Shannon's limit [1].
Achievable throughput of turbo decoder is one of the key factors in its evolution
and the state-of-the-art value compliant to 4G wireless communication systems
is more than 1 Gbps [2,3]. However, the new generation of radio must support
various other features like IoTs, cloud computing and vehicular communications along with the mobile communication and broadband data. Hence, the

© Springer Nature Singapore Pte Ltd. 2019
S. Rajaram et al. (Eds.): VDAT 2018, CCIS 892, pp. 37–48, 2019.
https://doi.org/10.1007/978-981-13-5950-7_4

flexibility is a key feature that needs to be incorporated in such radios. As we know, MAP decoder based on Bahl-Cocke-Jelinek-Raviv (BCJR) algorithm is the major block responsible for the design of high-throughput turbo decoder [5] and thereby, it is high-time to propose new and flexible MAP-architecture. In literature, Chen-Hun Lin et al. reported scalable MAP-decoder (which performs single & double binary turbo-decoding) to support various 3G wireless standards and it supports only dual-mode throughputs up to 500 Mbps [6]. However, it is necessary to enhance this throughput range as well as maximize the achievable throughput.

In this work, we present new solution for this problem by proposing reconfigurable very-large scale-integration (VLSI)-architecture for the MAP decoder in order to support different throughputs for various features of new radio. This design can be configured to perform decoding in either of radix-2/4/8 operating modes delivering various data rates. Internal architectures of MAP decoder like state-metric and logarithmic-likelihood-ratio (LLR) computation units are redesigned for supporting these modes. We have additionally used clock-gating technique to lower the power consumption. Rest of this paper is organized as follows: Sect. 2 presents specification and theoretical background of MAP decoding. The proposed VLSI architectures along with qualitative analysis for MAP decoding are included in Sect. 3. Section 4 incorporates performance analysis, implementation results and comparison. Finally, this paper concludes in Sect. 5.

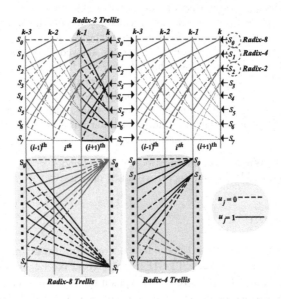

Fig. 1. Radix-2, 4 & 8 trellis stages for the computation of one, two and three LLRs, respectively, in each computation cycle of MAP decoding.

2   Preliminaries

We incorporated channel-coding specifications of 4G-LTE-A wireless communication standard [7] for our decoder architecture and its eight-states radix-2 trellis-graph, shown in Fig. 1, is generated using the convolutional-encoder (CE) transfer function $G(D) = [1, (1+D+D^3)/(1+D^2+D^3)]$ with the constraint length (K_r) of four. Each CE used in the construction of turbo code for 4G-LTE-A standard (in order to support a code-rate of 1/3) must have a code-rate of $r = 1/2$ and thereby, we considered the same in this work [8]. The proposed decoder-architecture is design for the sliding-window based MAP decoding [9] for which the block-size (N) and sliding-window-size (M) are 6144 and 24 respectively. Since $r = 1/2$ for the systematic CE, there is a transmission of information bits u_j and encoded parity bits $x_j \forall j = \{1, 2, 3, \ldots N\}$. At the receiver end, the soft demodulator provides $2 \times N$ a-priori LLR values to the MAP decoder input-side and are represented as λu_j and $\lambda x_j \forall j = \{1, 2, 3, \ldots N\}$. For every state transition in i^{th} stage of the trellis graph with N stages, there are 16 state transitions and each of them is associated with a branch metric which is denoted by $\gamma_i(s_m, s_n) \forall \{m, n\} \in \{0, 1, 2, \ldots 7\}$ where s_m and s_n are previous and present states respectively. Thereby, the branch metric for each state transition in j^{th} trellis stage can be computed as $\gamma_j(s_m, s_n) = \{u_j \times L(u_j)/2\} + l_c/2 \times \{u_j \times \lambda u_j + x_j \times \lambda x_j\}$ where l_c and $L(u_j)$ are channel reliability and logarithmic a-priori probability respectively [9]. Rather than computing all $2 \times S_N$ branch metrics where S_N is total number of states in the trellis graph ($S_N = 8$ in this work), we need to compute only $\log_2(2 \times S_N)$ parent branch metrics and use them in repetitive fashion to cover all state transitions [10]. In this work, state metric computation is performed in three different ways: radix-2, 4 & 8 which process single, double and triple trellis stages, respectively, in each clock cycle. Figure 1 represents three stages of radix-2 trellis graph where s_0, s_1 and s_2 represent different states for radix-2, 4 & 8 forward state-metric computations respectively (as backward state-metric computations also follows the same method, we considered only forward state-metric computation for clarity). Thereby for radix-8, one of the forward state metric of state s_0 is computed as [11]

$$\alpha_k(0) = max\{\alpha_{k-1}(0) + \gamma_{i+1}(0,0), \alpha_{k-1}(1) + \gamma_{i+1}(1,0)\} \qquad (1)$$

where

$$\alpha_{k-1}(0) = max\{\alpha_{k-2}(0) + \gamma_i(0,0), \alpha_{k-2}(1) + \gamma_i(1,0)\} \quad \& \qquad (2)$$

$$\alpha_{k-1}(1) = max\{\alpha_{k-2}(2) + \gamma_i(2,1), \alpha_{k-2}(3) + \gamma_i(3,1)\} \qquad (3)$$

where

$$\alpha_{k-2}(0) = max\{\alpha_{k-3}(0) + \gamma_{i-1}(0,0), \alpha_{k-3}(1) + \gamma_{i-1}(1,0)\}, \qquad (4)$$

$$\alpha_{k-2}(1) = max\{\alpha_{k-3}(2) + \gamma_{i-1}(2,1), \alpha_{k-3}(3) + \gamma_{i-1}(3,1)\}, \qquad (5)$$

$$\alpha_{k-2}(2) = max\{\alpha_{k-3}(4) + \gamma_{i-1}(4,2), \alpha_{k-3}(5) + \gamma_{i-1}(5,2)\} \quad \& \qquad (6)$$

$$\alpha_{k-2}(3) = max\{\alpha_{k-3}(6) + \gamma_{i-1}(6,3), \alpha_{k-3}(7) + \gamma_{i-1}(7,3)\}. \qquad (7)$$

Similarly, radix-4 computation of forward state-metric for state s_1 is performed as

$$\alpha_k(1) = max\{\alpha_{k-1}(2) + \gamma_{i+1}(2,1), \alpha_{k-1}(3) + \gamma_{i+1}(3,1)\} \tag{8}$$

where

$$\alpha_{k-1}(2) = max\{\alpha_{k-2}(4) + \gamma_i(4,2), \alpha_{k-2}(5) + \gamma_i(5,2)\} \quad \& \tag{9}$$

$$\alpha_{k-1}(3) = max\{\alpha_{k-2}(6) + \gamma_i(6,3), \alpha_{k-2}(7) + \gamma_i(7,3)\}. \tag{10}$$

Finally, the radix-2 forward-state metric for s_2 is computed as [11]

$$\alpha_k(2) = max\{\alpha_{k-1}(4) + \gamma_{i+1}(4,2), \alpha_{k-1}(5) + \gamma_{i+1}(5,2)\}. \tag{11}$$

On completing the computation of all branch, forward and backward state metrics, a-posteriori LLRs $\Gamma_i \; \forall \; j = \{1, 2, 3, \ldots N\}$ are determined for radix-2, 4 & 8 depending on the mode of operation. Detail discussion on the qualitative analysis of this process is presented in Sect. 3 along with the proposed VLSI architectures.

3   Proposed VLSI Architectures

This section presents the suggested architecture of state-metric-computation and LLR-computation units. Overall MAP-decoder architecture which integrates these units is also presented here.

3.1   State-Metric Computation-Unit Architecture

Basically, state-metric computation-unit (SMCU) computes a forward/backward state metric for each state and thereby, S_N such units are stacked to compute all the state metrics of each trellis stage in MAP decoder. We have proposed a reconfigurable architecture for such SMCU that computes state metrics for radix-2/4/8 MAP decoding. This architecture has been presented based on Eqs. (1–11), as discussed earlier. The key challenge is to reliably route the branch and state metrics for different operating modes. As the radix value scales up (from radix-2 to radix-8), traversing of trellis becomes deeper for the state-metric computation of present state and the number of branch as well as state metrics of previous states, required for state metric calculation, gradually increases. The proposed SMCU VLSI-architecture has been presented in Fig. 2. Analyzing this architecture bottom-up, Rad2-SMCU computes the state metric for radix-2 operating mode from (11). Subsequently, three such units are aggregated to construct Rad4-SMCU block for the calculation of radix-4 state metric using (8–10). Finally, these units are integrated with the multiplexer/de-multiplexer network to build reconfigurable SMCU which determines radix-8/4/2 state metrics for a given state depending on the values of select lines *sel0* and *sel1*, as shown in Fig. 2. For example, when the value of *sel1* is high then all the state metrics of $(k-3)^{th}$ stage and branch metrics of $(i-1)^{th}$ stage, for radix-8 computation, are passed to Rad4-SMCU blocks through first stage of multiplexers. Subsequently,

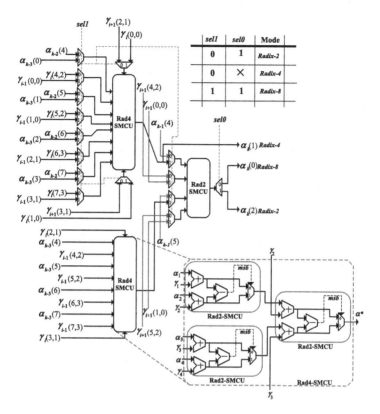

Fig. 2. Proposed VLSI architecture of reconfigurable SMCU for radix-2/4/8 operating modes.

next multiplexer-stage releases two computed radix-4 state-metrics which are then fed to Rad2-SMCU along with respective branch metrics. Eventually, if *sel0* is high then de-multiplexer releases radix-8 state metric $\alpha_k(0)$, as shown in Fig. 2. Similarly, this design can be used for radix-2/4 state-metric computation by changing the values of select lines.

3.2 Reconfigurable VLSI Architectures of LLR Computation Unit and MAP Decoder

Computation of LLR for the multi-radix MAP decoder is a crucial and complex operation where radix-2, 4 and 8 operating modes must produce 1, 2 and 3 LLRs, respectively, in every computation cycle. Each stage of trellis graph for radix-4 and 8 (derived from three and two stages, respectively, of radix-2 trellis) is shown in Fig. 1. Considering radix-2 LLR computation, the transition probability for any arbitrary state transition $s_p \rightarrow s_q$ is computed as [9]

$$\lambda_{p:q} = \alpha_{k-1}(p) + \gamma_{i+1}(s_p, s_q) + \beta_k(q) \ \ \forall \ \ p \in S_N \ \& \ q \in S_N. \tag{12}$$

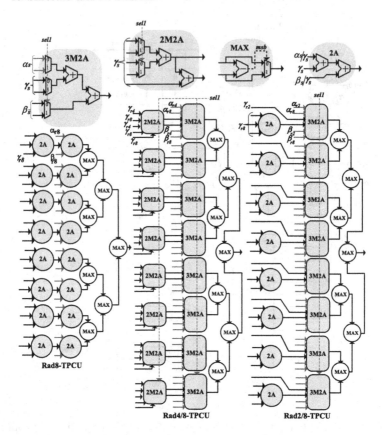

Fig. 3. Proposed reconfigurable VLSI-architectures of submodules used for computing transition probabilities in LCU.

Referring Fig. 1, LLR of $(i+1)^{th}$ stage is computed as

$$\Gamma_{i+1} = max_{\delta:u_j=1}\{\lambda_{p:q}\} - max_{\delta:u_j=0}\{\lambda_{p:q}\} = \lambda_{p:q}^1 - \lambda_{p:q}^0 \qquad (13)$$

where δ: $u_j = 1/0$ represents set of all state transitions for u_j is 0 or 1 [2]. Similarly, LLRs are computed for all the trellis stages to complete radix-2 decoding. In case of radix-4 LLR computation, two of the radix-2 trellis stages are combined as one stage, as shown in Fig. 1. If $s_{q'}$ represents an intermediate state between $s_p{\rightarrow}s_q$ transition then its probability is computed as

$$\lambda_{p:q':q} = \alpha_{k-3}(p) + \gamma_{i-1}(s_p, s_{q'}) + \gamma_i(s_{q'}, s_q) + \beta_{k-1}(q). \qquad (14)$$

Figure 1 shows that there are four state transitions from previous stage towards each of the sink states in radix-4 trellis. Thereby, four transition probabilities for each of such states are represented as $\lambda_{p:q':q}^{00}$, $\lambda_{p:q':q}^{10}$, $\lambda_{p:q':q}^{11}$ and $\lambda_{p:q':q}^{01}$. Thereby, LLRs for $(i-1)^{th}$ and i^{th} trellis stages those are computed in one computation cycle are [12]

$$\Gamma_{i-1} = max_{\delta:u_j=1}\{\lambda^{10}_{p:q':q}, \lambda^{11}_{p:q':q}\} - max_{\delta:u_j=0}\{\lambda^{00}_{p:q':q}, \lambda^{01}_{p:q':q}\}, \tag{15}$$

$$\Gamma_{i} = max_{\delta:u_j=1}\{\lambda^{11}_{p:q':q}, \lambda^{01}_{p:q':q}\} - max_{\delta:u_j=0}\{\lambda^{00}_{p:q':q}, \lambda^{10}_{p:q':q}\}. \tag{16}$$

Similarly, there are eight state-transitions towards each sink state of radix-8 trellis stage, as shown in Fig. 1, where each transition probability is computed as

$$\lambda_{p:r:s:q} = \alpha_{k-3}(p) + \gamma_{i-1}(s_p, s_r) + \gamma_i(s_r, s_s) \\ + \gamma_{i+1}(s_s, s_q) + \beta_k(q) \tag{17}$$

where s_r and s_s are intermediate states at $k-2$ and $k-1$ stages respectively. Therefore, three LLRs in each computation cycle of radix-8 decoding are calculated as [12]

$$\Gamma_{i-1} = \max_{\delta:u_j=1}\{\lambda^{100}_{p:r:s:q}, \lambda^{110}_{p:r:s:q}, \lambda^{111}_{p:r:s:q}, \lambda^{101}_{p:r:s:q}\} \\ - \max_{\delta:u_j=0}\{\lambda^{000}_{p:r:s:q}, \lambda^{010}_{p:r:s:q}, \lambda^{011}_{p:r:s:q}, \lambda^{001}_{p:r:s:q}\}, \tag{18}$$

$$\Gamma_{i} = \max_{\delta:u_j=1}\{\lambda^{110}_{p:r:s:q}, \lambda^{010}_{p:r:s:q}, \lambda^{011}_{p:r:s:q}, \lambda^{111}_{p:r:s:q}\} \\ - \max_{\delta:u_j=0}\{\lambda^{000}_{p:r:s:q}, \lambda^{100}_{p:r:s:q}, \lambda^{101}_{p:r:s:q}, \lambda^{001}_{p:r:s:q}\}, \tag{19}$$

$$\Gamma_{i+1} = \max_{\delta:u_j=1}\{\lambda^{011}_{p:r:s:q}, \lambda^{111}_{p:r:s:q}, \lambda^{101}_{p:r:s:q}, \lambda^{001}_{p:r:s:q}\} \\ - \max_{\delta:u_j=0}\{\lambda^{000}_{p:r:s:q}, \lambda^{100}_{p:r:s:q}, \lambda^{110}_{p:r:s:q}, \lambda^{010}_{p:r:s:q}\}. \tag{20}$$

The transition probability computations from (12), (14) and (17) indicate that the number of branch metrics involved in such computation varies for different operating modes of multi-radix MAP decoding. Prior to the design of LLR computation unit (LCU), we propose architectures for its three integral modules: radix-8 transition-probability computation-unit (Rad8-TPCU), flexible-radix-4/8 transition-probability computation-unit (Rad4/8-TPCU) and flexible-radix-2/8 transition-probability computation-unit (Rad2/8-TPCU). Figure 3 shows these new reconfigurable architectures where γ_{r8}, γ_{r4} and γ_{r2} represent branch metrics for radix-8, 4 and 2 operating modes respectively. Similarly, α_{r8}/β_{r8}, α_{r4}/β_{r4} and α_{r2}/β_{r2} represent forward/backward state metrics for the same. Internal architectures of their sub-modules like 3M2A, 2M2A, 2A and MAX have been presented in Fig. 3. Proposed architectures of Rad4/8-TPCU and Rad2/8-TPCU can be reconfigured using *sel1* signal to compute transition probabilities of radix-4/8 and radix-2/8 operating modes respectively. Unlike, Rad8-TPCU computes transition probability for only radix-8 mode. On integrating these computation units along with the MAX comparator network, we finally present the proposed VLSI architecture of LCU in Fig. 4. It shows that the transition probabilities computed using eight TPCUs are fed to the network of MAX comparators which calculates the LLRs for radix-2, 4 and 8 operating modes based on (13), (15 and 16) and (18–20) respectively.

We adopted sliding-window based MAP decoding where the entire trellis length is segregated into N/M windows and each of which comprises of M trellis stages [9]. Figure 5 shows the suggested decoder architecture which is an aggregation of various sub-modules like: branch metric computation unit (BMCU),

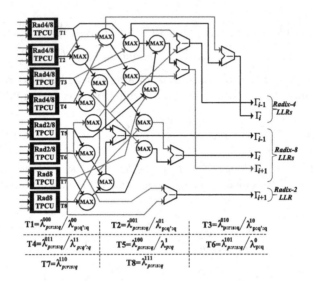

Fig. 4. Proposed VLSI-architecture of LLR computation unit for multi-radix MAP decoding.

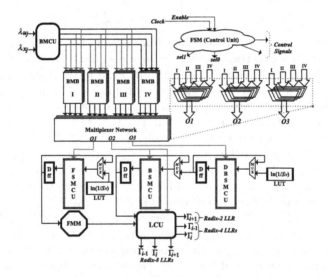

Fig. 5. Overall reconfigurable VLSI-architecture of multi-radix MAP decoder.

branch-metric memory banks (BMBs), multiplexer network (MuN), forward-SMCU (FSMCU), backward-SMCU (BSMCU), dummy-BSMCU (DBSMCU), forward-state metric memory (FMM) and LCU. BMCU computes parent branch metrics based on the equations discussed in Sect. 2 and BMBs are used for storing these values for different sliding windows. FSMCU as well as BSMCU comprises of S_N SMCUs for computing all the forward/backward state metrics of each trellis stage. DBSMCU has been included to perform dummy backward recursion to estimate the values of backward state-metric while starting the actual backward recursion [10]. Subsequently, this unit is initialized using $\ln(1/S_N)$ equi-probable value (stored in LUT) to start the dummy backward recursion, as shown in Fig. 5. MuN has been incorporated to route the branch metrics into FSMCU, BSMCU and DBSMCU for different sliding windows. Additionally, a finite state machine (FSM) based control unit has been designed to generate various control signals (like *sel1* and *sel0*) to operate this data-path of MAP decoder in radix-2/4/8 operating mode. Finally, computed values of forward & backward state-metrics and branch metrics are fed to LCU for computing the LLRs, as discussed earlier.

4   Experimental Results and Comparison

We performed Monte-Carlo simulation of the reconfigurable MAP-decoding algorithm, in the additive-white Gaussian-noise (AWGN) channel environment, based on the specifications of LTE-A wireless standard discussed in Sect. 2.

Figure 6 shows the BER plots at different E_b/N_0 values (in decibel) for radix-2, 4 and 8 MAP decoding. It can be observed that the suggested MAP decoder for different operating modes delivers identical performance. This design has been synthesized and post-layout simulated using UMC 65 nm-CMOS process; thereby, its final chip-layout and implementation results are presented in Fig. 7 and Table 1 respectively. In the proposed MAP-decoder architecture shown in Fig. 5, critical path lies in FSMCU/BSMCU/DBSMCU and all other units are feed-forward architectures which are coarse-grain pipelined in this work. Therefore, maximum clock frequency of MAP decoder operating in radix-8 mode is

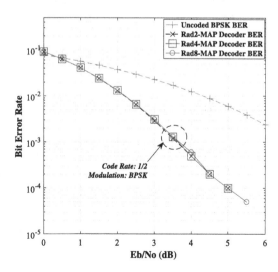

Fig. 6. Performance analysis of the proposed reconfigurable MAP, compliant to LTE-Advanced wireless standard.

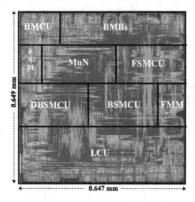

Fig. 7. ASIC chip layout incorporating 397k cell count.

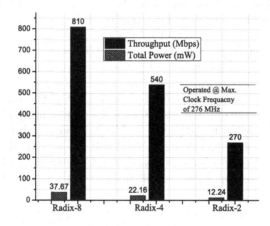

Fig. 8. Power-&-throughput analysis of the proposed reconfigurable MAP when operated at max. clock frequency.

Table 1. Comparison of the proposed MAP decoder with the reported works

	[13]-2005	[14]-2006	[6]-2011	[2]-2014	This work
Technology (nm)	180	130	130	130	**65**
Supply (V)	1.8	1.2	1.2	1.2	**1**
Area (mm^2)	8.7	1.96	1.28	2.12	**0.42**
Scaled Area @ 65 nm (mm^2)	1.13	0.49	0.32	0.53	**0.42**
Max. Clk. Freq. (MHz)	285	238	125	526	**276**
Total Power (mW)	330	528	97.83	NA	**12.24−37.67**
Radix-r	$r = 2$	$r = 16$	$r = 4$	$r = 2$	$r = 2/4/8$
Throughput (Mbps)	285	952	500	526	**270−810**

276 MHz. Suggested architectures from Figs. 2 and 3 indicates that minimum and maximum number of units are activated while operating in radix-2 and 8 modes respectively. Thus, our architecture can deliver throughputs from 270 to 810 Mbps with variable power consumptions, using clock-gating technique, as plotted in Fig. 8. Implementation results of the proposed decoder are compared with the reported works from literature, as listed in Table 1.

5 Conclusion

This paper presented new VLSI-architectures for various internal modules (like FSMCU, BSMCU, DBSMCU and LCU) and overall MAP decoder which supported multi-radix operating modes. Such decoder-core can be suitable integrated to design parallel-turbo decoder to support multi gigabit data-rates at different power levels. This makes turbo decoder to support various contemporary features like IoTs, cloud computing and vehicular communications. Our design consumed moderately lower power, delivered higher throughput and supported largest dynamic range in comparison to the reported works, as listed in Table 1.

Acknowledgement. The authors would like to thank Science and Engineering Research Board (SERB), Department of Science and Technology (DST), Govt. of India, for supporting this research work.

References

1. Berrou, C., Glavieux, A., Thitimajshima, P.: Near Shannon limit error correcting coding and decoding: turbo codes. In: Proceedings of IEEE International Conference on Communications, vol. 40, no. 8, pp. 1064–1070 (1993)
2. Shrestha, R., Paily, R.P.: High-throughput turbo decoder with parallel architecture for LTE wireless communication standards. IEEE Trans. Circ. Syst. I Reg. Papers **61**(9), 2699–2710 (2014)
3. Ilnseher, T., Kienle, F., Weis, C., Wehn, N.: A 2.15 GBit/s turbo code decoder for LTE advanced base station applications. In: Proceedings of International Symposium on Turbo Codes and Iterative Information Processing (ISTC), pp. 21–25 (2012)
4. Boccardi, F., Heath, R.W., Lozano, A., Marzetta, T.L., Popovski, P.: Five disruptive technology directions for 5G. IEEE Commun. Mag. **52**(2), 74–80 (2014)
5. Bahl, L.R., Cocke, J., Jelinek, F., Raviv, J.: Optimal decoding of linear codes for minimizing symbol error rate. IEEE Trans. Inf. Theory **20**(2), 284–287 (1974)
6. Lin, C.-H., Chen, C.-Y., Wu, A.-Y.: Area-efficient scalable MAP processor design for high-throughput multistandard convolutional turbo decoding. IEEE Trans. Very Large Scale Integr. (VLSI) **19**(2), 305–318 (2017)
7. 3GPP; Technical Specification Group Radio Access Network, "E-UTRA; Multiplexing and Channel Coding (Release 10) 3GPP," 3GPP, TS 36.212, Rev. 10.0.0 (2011) Std
8. Bhat, P., et al.: LTE-advanced: an operator perspective. IEEE Commun. Mag. **50**(2), 104–114 (2012)

9. Woodard, J.P., Hanzo, L.: Comparative study of turbo decoding techniques: an overview. IEEE Trans. Veh. Technol. **49**(6), 2208–2233 (2000)
10. Benkeser, C., Burg, A., Cupaiuolo, T., Huang, Q.: Design and optimization of an HSDPA turbo decoder ASIC. IEEE J. Solid-State Circ. **44**(1), 98–106 (2009)
11. Studer, C., Benkeser, C., Belfanti, S., Huang, Q.: Design and implementation of a parallel turbo-decoder ASIC for 3GPP-LTE. IEEE J. Solid-State Circ. **46**(1), 8–17 (2011)
12. Sun, Y., Zhu, Y., Goel, M., Cavallaro, J.R.: Configurable and scalable high throughput turbo decoder architecture for multiple 4G wireless standards. In: Proceedings of International Conference on Application-Specific Systems, Architectures and Processors, pp. 209–214 (2008)
13. Lee, S.-J., Shanbhag, N.R., Singer, A.C.: A 285-MHz pipelined MAP decoder in 0.18 um CMOS. IEEE J. Solid-State Circ. **40**(8), 1718–1725 (2005)
14. Tang, C.-H., Wong, C.-C., Chen, C.-L., Lin, C.-C., Chang, H.-C.: A 952MS/s max-log MAP decoder chip using radix-4.4 ACS architecture. In: Proceedings of IEEE Asian Solid-State Circuits Conference (A-SSCC), pp. 79–82 (2006)

Design of High Speed 5:2 and 7:2 Compressor Using Nanomagnetic Logic

Shantanu Agarwal, G. Harish, S. Balamurugan[iD], and R. Marimuthu[(✉)][iD]

Vellore Institute of Technology, Vellore, Tamilnadu, India
{shantanu.agrawal2015,g.harish2015,sbalamurugan,rmarimuthu}@vit.ac.in

Abstract. There are many attempts being made to design circuits in the post-CMOS scenario. One such attempt includes the Nanomagnetic logic. In this logic, a top-down methodology is followed. This paper presents the design of high speed 5:2 and 7:2 compressors using Nanomagnetic logic.

Keywords: Post-CMOS · High speed · Compressor · PNML

1 Introduction

The development of complementary metal-oxide-semiconductor was very successful. A lot of work has been done in CMOS since then which has helped to reduce the area, power consumption and various factors in-order to improve the working and the efficiency [1,2]. This has not prevented the researchers to discover and implement new technologies to achieve the same functionality as the CMOS circuit would achieve but with increased efficiency.

There are a lot of problems and challenges being faced in the post - CMOS scenario. Constant efforts are being made to improve the working of the digital circuits in terms of power consumption, area. In [3], a standard methodology has been followed for benchmarking the various beyond - CMOS devices and a comparison of those devices is done. Nanomagnetic logic is one such technology in which the circuits are designed using magnets. In this logic, there are two methods for designing - Perpendicular Nanomagnetic Logic (pnml) and In- plane Nanomagnetic logic (inml).

Nanomagnetic logic offers non-volatile means to perform various Boolean and non-Boolean functions. In Nanomagnetic logic, it is possible to perform a significant scaling of the area and is also one of the lowest power consuming technology [3]. There is a certain set of Boolean operations that can be performed on Nanomagnetic logic. The initial stage for a majority of them include the Inversion (INV), Conjunction (AND), Disjunction (OR) [3–6] and if-then-else (MUX) [7,8]. With the aid of these primitives, other Boolean operations can be performed to simplify the circuitry.

In [9], the concept of Majority Inverter Graphs has been presented along with their manipulation using the Magnetic Boolean algebra technique. In this paper,

S. Rajaram et al. (Eds.): VDAT 2018, CCIS 892, pp. 49–60, 2019.
https://doi.org/10.1007/978-981-13-5950-7_5

the concepts of Majority Inverter Graphs are utilized to optimize the logic for 5:2 and 7:2 compressor using the MagCAD tool which is a part of the ToPoliNano design suite [10].

This paper is divided into 4 parts. The first part deals with the 5:2 and 7:2 compressors and their basic design. The second part deals with the design of 5:2 and 7:2 compressors on the MagCAD tool. The third part deals with the 5:2 and 7:2 compressor design using the Magnetic Boolean simplifications. The fourth part deals with the Results and Discussions where the latency and area of the circuits are specified.

2   Exact Compressors

Compressors are meant for accumulating the partial products during multiplication process. It reduces the partial products in the reduction stage. Several compressors were proposed and utilized in various sizes of multipliers [11–14]. For example, a 5:2 compressor means that there are 5 operands which can be reduced to 2 in the addition process and keeping the carries and the sums separate. In this paper, we have used the full adder as the most primitive compressor which is also known as the 3:2 compressor. Each 3:2 compressor has a delay of 2 XOR gates. As in [15], we have used three 3:2 compressors to design the 5:2 compressor and subsequently 5 full adders to design the 7:2 compressor on the MagCAD tool.

The block diagram of a 5:2 compressor is shown in Fig. 1. There are seven inputs out of which, five are direct inputs and two are carry-in bits of the previous stage. There are four outputs, out of which, two are carry-out bits to the next stage and two are sum and carry. The equations for sum and carry are shown below:

$$Sum = X_1 \oplus X_2 \oplus X_3 \oplus X_4 \oplus X_5 \oplus C_{in1} \oplus C_{in2} \tag{1}$$

$$Carry = ((X_1 \oplus X_2 \oplus X_3) \oplus (X_4 \oplus X_5 \oplus C_{in1}) \bullet C_{in2}) \\ + \overline{((X_1 \oplus X_2 \oplus X_3) \oplus (X_4 \oplus X_5 \oplus C_{in1}))} \bullet ((X_1 \oplus X_2 \oplus X_3)) \tag{2}$$

A 7:2 compressor is similar in structure to a 5:2 compressor except for the fact that it consists of two 3:2 compressors in the first stage followed by three 3:2 compressors in the subsequent stages. This paper utilizes the conventional 7:2 Compressor model for the analysis. There are seven inputs and four carry inputs from the previous stages. The block diagram is shown in Fig. 2. The expression for the sum and carry of a 7:2 compressor is shown in Eqs. 3 and 4

$$Sum = X_1 \oplus X_2 \oplus X_3 \oplus X_4 \oplus X_5 \oplus X_6 \oplus X_7 \oplus C_{in1} \oplus C_{in2} \oplus C_{in3} \oplus C_{in4} \tag{3}$$

$$Carry = (b \bullet C_{in3}) + (b \bullet C_{in4}) + (C_{in3} \bullet C_{in4}) \tag{4}$$

where,
$$b = a \oplus C_{in1} \oplus C_{in2}; a = (X_1 \oplus X_2 \oplus X_3) \oplus (X_4 \oplus X_5 \oplus X_6) \oplus X_7$$

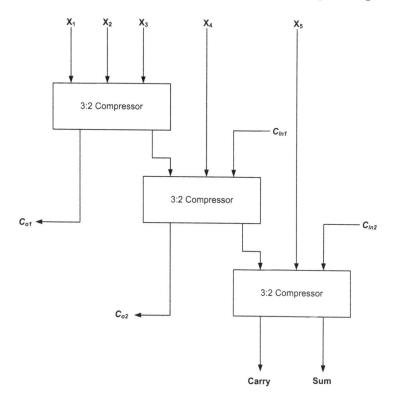

Fig. 1. 5:2 Compressor.

3   Compressor Using Nanomagnetic Logic

In this section, the 5:2 and 7:2 compressor as mentioned above are designed using Nanomagnetic logic on the MagCAD tool. We have utilized the pnml (perpendicular nanomagnetic logic) technology in which building blocks are nanomagnets interacting with an anti-ferromagnetic material.

The circuit for a 3:2 compressor using the Nanomagnetic logic is shown in Fig. 3. It is evident in the figure that a 3:2 Compressor has three inputs and two outputs, namely the sum and carry. Using this circuit, we design the 5:2 compressor by cascading three 3:2 compressors as shown in Fig. 4.

3.1   Design of an Adder Using Simplification Rules

As described in [9], there are various rules for simplifying the nanomagnetic circuits like the substitution rule, relevance rule, complementary associativity rule. The simplified version of the Full adder is obtained using the above-mentioned properties. This Full Adder obtained has a small bounding area and also the latency is reduced as we will observe in this paper.

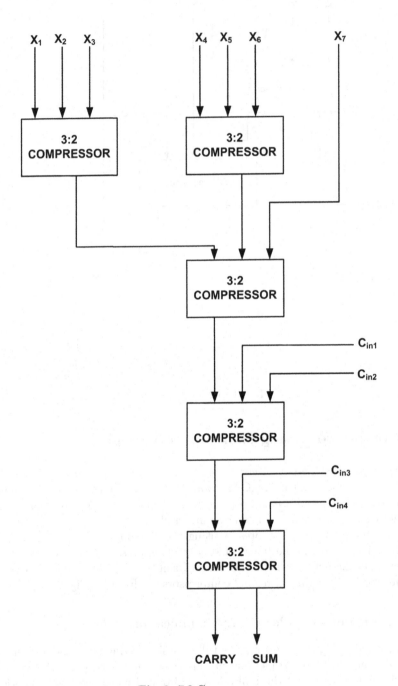

Fig. 2. 7:2 Compressor.

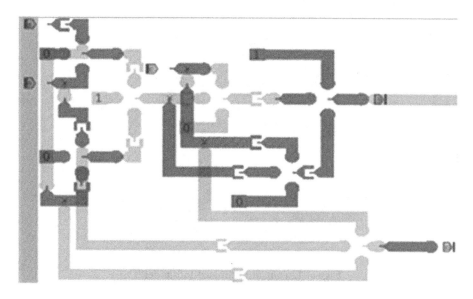

Fig. 3. 3:2 Compressor using MagCAD tool.

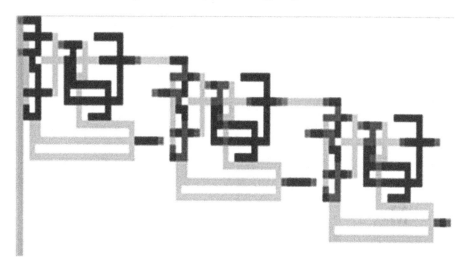

Fig. 4. 5:2 Compressor using MagCAD tool.

We have utilized the full adder circuit obtained in [9] to design the 5:2 and 7:2 circuits in this section. The simplified 5:2 Compressor is shown in Fig. 7.

The optimized full adder is obtained by using the substitution and the relevance theorems which are explained in [9]. The resultant figure relating the simplified expression is shown in Fig. 6.

This optimized Full Adder is obtained using the substitution and the relevance rules. As shown in Figs. 3 and 5, the differences between the Full adders

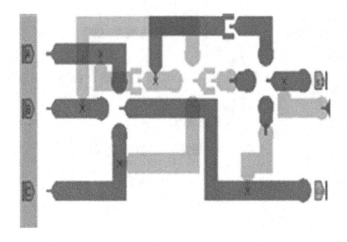

Fig. 5. Layout of optimized full adder.

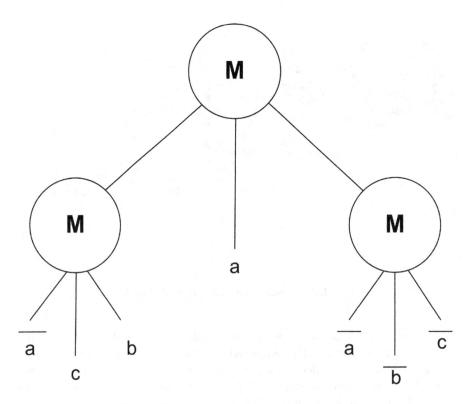

Fig. 6. Optimized full adder - relevance rule.

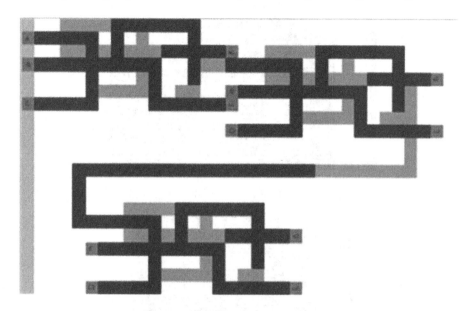

Fig. 7. Optimized 5:2 Compressor.

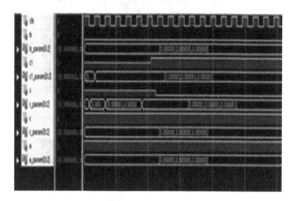

Fig. 8. Timing diagram of full adder.

designed using Magnetic Algebra and without Magnetic Algebra is evident in terms of the area of the structure.

4   Results and Discussions

In this section, we have calculated the latency and the area of the various circuits which were mentioned in the previous sections. The Timing diagram for the Full adder is shown in Fig. 8 and the timing diagram for the simplified Full adder is shown in Fig. 9. As we can observe, the latency of the full adder obtained using Boolean simplifications is lesser when compared to the conventional full adder.

56   S. Agarwal et al.

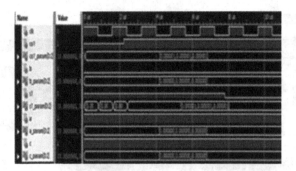

Fig. 9. Timing diagram of simplified full adder.

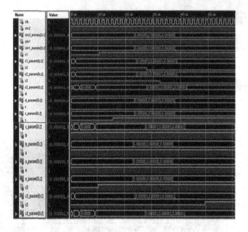

Fig. 10. Timing diagram of 5:2 Compressor.

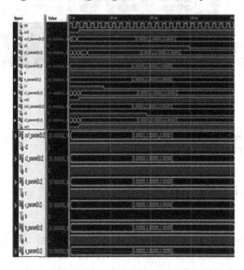

Fig. 11. Timing diagram of simplified 5:2 Compressor.

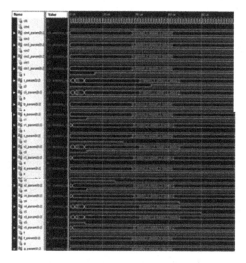

Fig. 12. Timing diagram of 7:2 Compressor.

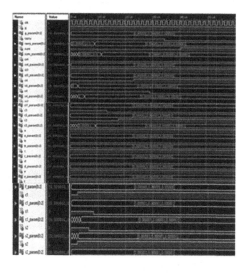

Fig. 13. Timing diagram of simplified 7:2 Compressor.

The timing diagram for the conventional un-simplified 5:2 compressor is shown in Fig. 10.

The timing diagram of simplified 5:2 compressor using magnetic Boolean algebra is shown in Fig. 11.

As evident from the timing diagrams, the latency for the simplified 5:2 Compressor is smaller than the un-simplified 5:2 Compressor and there is a reduction in area for the simplified 5:2 Compressor when compared to the un-simplified

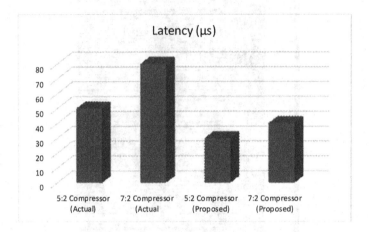

Fig. 14. Latency of different compressors.

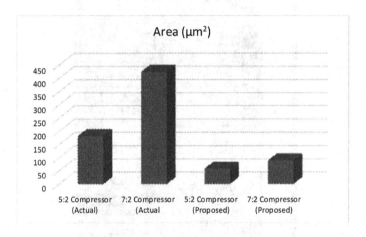

Fig. 15. Bounding box area of different compressors.

Table 1. Result analysis of compressors.

Compressor	Area (μm^2)	Latency (μs)
5:2 Compressor (Actual)	181.44	50
7:2 Compressor (Actual)	424.08	80
5:2 Compressor (Proposed)	58.59	30
7:2 Compressor (Proposed)	88.97	40

compressor. Similarly, the timing diagrams of 7:2 Compressors without and with Magnetic Boolean Algebra are shown in Figs. 12 and 13 respectively.

The Bounding box area is the area of the smallest rectangle that contains an object (Table 1). Figures 14 and 15 show the simulation results of various compressors.

5   Conclusion

This paper has presented an implication of a post-CMOS technology on Digital Circuits. As mentioned in the paper, the post-CMOS pose many different challenges and problems. In the Nanomagnetic logic, circuits are designed using magnets. Different Boolean Algebra reduction rules have been derived to simplify these circuits in -order to reduce the power, latency and the bounding area. The substitution rule, the relevance rule has reduced the circuit area and latency.

The Compressor circuits have been designed using the MagCAD tool. The latency of the circuits, bounding box area was calculated for the circuits. Using the Magnetic Boolean Algebra rules, the Boolean expressions representing the circuit were reduced and this implication results in a decrease in the bounding box area and the latency of the circuit. Nanomagnetic logic offers an opportunity to design circuits in the post-CMOS technology and thereby resulting in improved performance of the circuit.

References

1. Balamurugan, S., Ghosh, S., Atul, Marimuthu, R., Mallick, P.S.: Design of low power fixed-width multiplier with row bypassing. IEICE Electron. Express **9**(20), 1568–1575 (2012)
2. Balamurugan, S., Srirangaswamy, B., Marimuthu, R., Mallick, P.S.: FPGA design and implementation of truncated multipliers using bypassing technique. In: Proceedings of the International Conference on Advances in Computing, Communications and Informatics, pp. 1111–1117. ACM, Chennai (2012)
3. Nikonov, D.E., Young, I.A.: Overview of beyond-CMOS devices and a uniform methodology for their benchmarking. In: Proceedings of IEEE, 2498–2533. IEEE (2013)
4. Stamps, R.L., et al.: The 2014 magnetism roadmap. J. Phys. D: Appl. Phys. **47**(33), 333001 (2014)
5. Rudell, R.L., Sangiovanni-Vincentelli, A.: Multiple-valued minimization for PLA optimization. IEEE Trans. Comput. Aided Des. Integr. Circuits Syst. **6**(5), 727–750 (1987)
6. Brayton, R.K., Rudell, R., Sangiovanni-Vincentelli, A., Wang, A.R.: MIS: a multiple-level logic optimization system. IEEE Trans. Comput. Aided Des. Integr. Circuits Syst. **6**(6), 1062–1081 (1987)
7. Brayton, R., Mishchenko, A.: ABC: an academic industrial-strength verification tool. In: Touili, T., Cook, B., Jackson, P. (eds.) CAV 2010. LNCS, vol. 6174, pp. 24–40. Springer, Heidelberg (2010). https://doi.org/10.1007/978-3-642-14295-6_5
8. Bryant, R.E.: Graph-based algorithms for boolean function manipulation. IEEE Trans. Comput. **100**(8), 677–691 (1986)

9. Amarú, L., Gaillardon, P.-E., De Micheli, G.: Majority-inverter graph: a novel data-structure and algorithms for efficient logic optimization. In: Proceedings of the 51st Annual Design Automation Conference, pp. 1–6. ACM, San Francisco, CA, USA (2014)

10. Riente, F., et al.: MagCAD: tool for the design of 3-D magnetic circuits. IEEE J. Explor. Solid-State Comput. Devices Circuits **3**, 65–73 (2017)

11. Marimuthu, R., Mallick, P.S.: Design of efficient signed multiplier using compressors for FFT architecture. J. Eng. Sci. Technol. Rev. **10**(2), 108–113 (2017)

12. Marimuthu, R., Elsie Rezinold, Y., Mallick, P.S.: Design and analysis of multiplier using approximate 15-4 compressor. IEEE Access **5**, 1027–1036 (2017)

13. Marimuthu, R., Pradeepkumar, M., Bansal, D., Balamurugan, S., Mallick, P.S.: Design of high speed and low power 15-4 compressor. In: International Conference on Communication and Signal Processing, pp. 533–536. IEEE, Melmaruvathur (2013)

14. Marimuthu, R., Bansal, D., Balamurugan, S., Mallick, P.S.: Design of 8-4 and 9-4 compressors for high speed multiplication. Am. J. Appl. Sci. **10**(8), 893–900 (2013)

15. Menon, R., Radhakrishnan, D.: Majority-inverter graph: high performance 5: 2 compressor architectures. In: IEE Proceedings-Circuits, Devices and System, pp. 447–452. IET (2006)

A Comparative Exploration About Approximate Full Adders for Error Tolerant Applications

M. Priyadharshni and S. Kumaravel[(✉)]

VIT, Vellore, Tamil Nadu, India
{priyadharshni.m,kumaravel.s}@vit.ac.in

Abstract. Arithmetic units such as adders and multipliers play an essential role in the performance of Digital signal processor (DSP) systems. The efficiency of the Processors are influenced by the speed and power consumption of arithmetic units. It is improved by adopting approximate computing in arithmetic units with acceptable degradation in the output. Approximate computing is an emerging topic in the past decades, it aims to achieve promising design approach with the sacrifices in computational quality for error resilient applications. Approximate computing can be adopted both in hardware level and software level of research. This paper provides an elaborative investigation about approximate computing on full adders which is explored at the hardware level. The approximation is applied to full adders either at gate level or transistor level. Further, ripple carry adder is designed for varying bit width with different degrees of approximation using these approximate Full adders. Ripple carry adder is estimated based on the structural analysis such as Area, Delay Product (ADP) and Power, Delay Product (PDP) and error matrix such as pass rate, error rate, Normalized Error Distance (NED) and Mean Error Distance (MED). The ripple carry adders are designed in Verilog HDL and stimulated in Synopsys Design Compiler (DC) using tsmc 65 nm standard cell library typical corner whereas, the error characteristics is done in MATLAB.

Keywords: Approximate computing · Approximate full adder · Error matrix · Ripple carry adder · Structural analysis

1 Introduction

DSP Processors are widely used in digital image/signal processing applications which are highly error tolerant. Error-tolerant applications will accept the output with some degrees of degradation since these applications are limited to human perception. The arithmetic and logical operations are mostly performed in DSP by using arithmetic units (ALU). The complexity of arithmetic and numerical

Supported by organization VIT.

S. Rajaram et al. (Eds.): VDAT 2018, CCIS 892, pp. 61–74, 2019.
https://doi.org/10.1007/978-981-13-5950-7_6

operations are also determined by the ALU such as adders and multipliers. So the adders and multipliers play major in designing DSP processors where we can adopt the approximate computing. The main motivation of approximate computing [5] is to achieve best design approach with a reduction in the complexity but with the trade-off accuracy in the results for error resilient applications.

The approximation is done in two levels, both in the hardware level and software level of abstraction [5]. In the software level of approximation, some levels in the algorithms are eliminated and at the hardware level, the design of circuits is modified. By adopting the approximation at the hardware level, Approximate adders/multipliers are designed which are used in the processors to overcome the major drawback of DSP such as system complexity and power dissipation. Adders have attracted researcher's attention in designing approximation since adders are the most fundamental data operator. The key motivation in designing the approximate adders is to reduce the lifetime of carry propagation and the circuit complexity. The lifetime of carry propagation is depended on the length of the critical path. The longest lifetime of carry propagation is approximately equal to log2(n) [7] and less than log2(n)+12 [9]. In the worst case, lifetime of carry propagation is equal to N (rarely happens).

In this paper, approximate adders are evaluated based on their structural analysis and error metrics. Structural analysis are related to hardware related figures of merit like gate count [8], area, power and delay including the compound metrics such as area-delay product (ADP) and power-delay product (PDP). The error characteristics [4] of approximate adders are determined based on their Pass rate, error rate, error distance, mean error distance (MED) and normalized error distance (NED).

This paper makes the following contributions.

1. A collection of approximate adders which include recent designs are considered.
2. Approximate adders are evaluated based on their gate count, pass rate and error rate.
3. Further, the evaluation includes designing the ripple carry adder using approximate adders in the given set. Ripple carry adder is designed for varying bit width with different degrees of approximation.
4. Ripple carry adders are evaluated based on their design metrics and error metrics by using random 1 lakh test stimulus vectors.

2   Approximate Adder

Two methodologies are used in redesigning the full adder.

1. Approximation in the gate level of full adder.
2. Approximation in the transistor level of full adder.

2.1 Approximation in the Gate Level of Full Adder

Inexact Full Adders (INXA). Three inexact full adders [1] are implemented by applying the approximation in the gate level and they are implemented with less number of transistors. In these inexact adders one of the full adder output is approximated and the other output has the accurate result.

INXA1. This adder is designed by maintaining the accurate sum signal and the carry signal is approximated. The gate level implementation of INXA1 is shown in the Fig. 1 and the truth table is given in the Table 1 (col 14 and 15). In the truth table a tick mark represents the accurate output is equal to the exact output and the cross mark represents the unequal i.e erroneous outputs. The INXA1 produces the accurate sum and 2 error out of 8 cases in carry signal.

Gate Count Calculation: The implementation of 1-bit INAX1 requires 2 XOR gate and 1 NOT gate. For the sake of comparison, assume that 1 basic gate [8] is equal to 1 gate count and the number of gate count is used to determine the area of the adders. Then XOR gate is limited to 2-input basic gates (AND,OR and NOT), it requires 2 AND gate, 1 OR gate and 1 NOT gate [6]. Then INXA1 is implemented by using 4 AND gate, 2 OR gate and 2 NOT gate.

Total number of basic gates used in INXA1 = 9 basic gates.

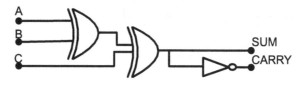

Fig. 1. INXA1

INXA2. INXA2 is formulated by maintaining the accurate results in the carry signal and approximate result in the sum signal. In INXA2, the second XOR gate in the exact full adder is replaced with OR gate. The gate level implementation of INXA2 is shown in Fig. 2. The truth table of INXA2 in Table 1 (col 16 and 17), which shows that the sum signal has 2 errors out of 8 cases whereas carry signal is remained with accurate output.

Gate Count Calculation: 1-bit INXA2 requires 1 XOR gate, 2 OR gate and 2 AND gate. When the XOR is limited to 2-input basic gates then INXA2 is implemented by using 4 AND gate, 1 NOT gate and 3 OR gate.

Total number of basic gates used in INXA2 = 8 basic gates.

INXA3. INXA3 is demonstrated by applying approximation in the sum signal and carry signal remains as exact. The gate level diagram of INXA3 is shown in Fig. 3 and the truth table is shown in Table 1 (col 18 and 19). INAX3 produces 2 errors out of 8 cases in the sum signal.

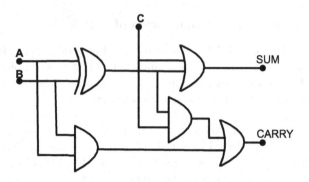

Fig. 2. INXA2

Gate Count Calculation: INXA3 utilizes 1 XOR gate, 2 AND gate, 1 OR gate and 1 NOT gate. After the limitation on XOR gate then INXA3 is redesigned by using 4 AND gate, 2 NOT gate and 2 OR gate.

Total number of basic gates used in INXA3 = 8 basic gates.

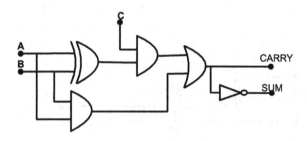

Fig. 3. INXA3

Approximate Full Adders (AFA). AFAs [2] are constructed by modifying the conventional Full adder in the gate level and they also designed as the output of carry signal is independent of carry input. The common approach used in these AFAs are to reduce the length of carry lifetime when it is implemented in the multibit adders. AFAs are implemented by applying approximation only in the carry signal.

AFA_1 *and* AFA_2. In AFA_1, the output of carry signal is considered as the input of A. In AFA_2, the input of B is considered as the output of carry signal. AFA_1 and AFA_2 produces 2 error out of 8 cases in the carry signal. The gate level logic implementation of AFA_1 and AFA_2 is shown in the Figs. 4 and 5 and the truth table of AFA_1 and AFA_2 is shown in the Table 1 (column 6 and 7) and (column 8 and 9) respectively.

Gate Count Calculation: Both AFA_1 and AFA_2 are realized by using 2 XOR gate. Due to the limitation, they bring about by using 4 AND gate, 2 OR gate and 2 NOT gate.

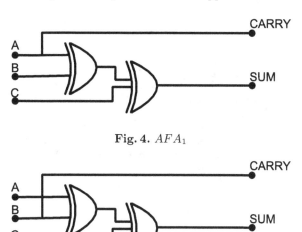

Fig. 4. AFA_1

Fig. 5. AFA_2

The total number of basic gates used in AFA_1 and $AFA_2 = 8$ basic gates.
AFA_3. In AFA_3, the output of carry signal is viewed as A.B. The truth table of AFA_3 is shown in the Table 1 (Column 10 and 11) and gate level implementation is shown in the Fig. 6.

Gate Count Calculation: AFA_3 is performed by using 2 XOR gate and 1 AND gate. After the limitation applied to the XOR gate, AFA_3 is realized by using 5 AND gate, 2 OR gate and 2 NOT gate.

The total number of basic gates used in $AFA_3 = 9$ basic gates.
AFA_4. In AFA_4, the output of carry signal is executed as A+B. The gate level circuit diagram is shown in Fig. 7 and the truth table is shown in Table 1 (column 12 and 13).

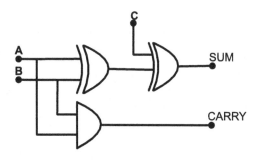

Fig. 6. AFA_3

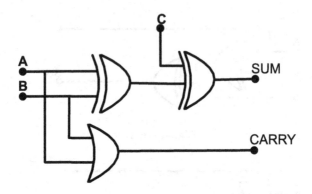

Fig. 7. AFA_4

Gate Count Calculation: 2 XOR gate and 1 OR gate are used to construct AFA_4. 4 AND gate, 3 OR gate and 2 NOT gate are utilized to construct AFA_4 after the limitation applied over the XOR gate.

The total number of basic gates used in $AFA_4 = 9$ basic gates.

Table 1. Truth table of approximate full adders.

Inputs			Exact outputs		AFA_1		AFA_2		AFA_3		AFA_4		INXA1		INXA2		INXA3	
x1	x2	x3	Carry	Sum	Carry	Sum	Carry	Sum	Carry	Sum	Carry	Sum	Carry	Sum	Carry	Sum	Carry	Sum
0	0	0	0	0	0✓	0✓	0✓	0✓	0✓	0✓	0✓	0✓	0✓	0✓	0✓	0✓	0✓	1✗
0	0	1	0	1	0✓	1✓	0✓	1✓	0✓	1✓	0✓	1✓	1✗	1✓	0✓	1✓	0✓	1✓
0	1	0	0	1	0✓	1✓	1✗	1✓	0✓	1✓	1✗	1✓	0✓	1✓	0✓	1✓	0✓	1✓
0	1	1	1	0	0✗	0✓	1✓	0✓	0✗	0✗	0✓	1✓	0✓	1✓	0✓	1✓	1✗	1✓
1	0	0	0	1	1✗	1✓	0✓	1✓	0✓	1✓	1✗	1✓	0✓	1✓	0✓	1✓	0✓	1✓
1	0	1	1	0	1✓	0✓	0✗	0✓	0✗	0✓	1✓	0✓	1✓	0✓	1✓	1✗	1✓	0✓
1	1	0	1	0	1✓	0✓	1✓	0✓	1✓	0✓	1✓	0✓	0✗	0✓	1✓	0✓	1✓	0✓
1	1	1	1	1	1✓	1✓	1✓	1✓	1✓	1✓	1✓	1✓	1✓	1✓	1✓	1✓	1✓	0✗

2.2 Approximation in the Transistor Level of Fulladder

The reduction in circuit complexity, node capacitance, and dynamic power dissipation are achieved by removing some of the transistors from the transistor level representation of the accurate full adder. For the sake of comparison, all the approximate full adders are represented in gate level and approximate adders with minimum error are considered for the exploration.

Approximate Mirror Adder. Different Approximate adders are acquired by extracting some of the transistors from the economical representation of a full adder called mirror adder (MA) [3]. When removing some transistors from MA it results shorter delay (i.e) faster charging and discharging of node capacitance is achieved.

AMA1. AMA1 is implemented by using eight transistors which are accomplished by removing some of the transistors from conventional MA. It is done by verifying that extraction process does not result in the short or open circuit in AMA1. AMA1 produces 2 errors out of 8 cases in the sum signal and one error out of 8 cases in the carry signal.

Gate Count Calculation: The AMA1 is achieved by using 3 AND gate, 2 OR gate and 1 NOT gate.

The total number of basic gates used in AMA1 = 6 basic gates (Fig. 8).

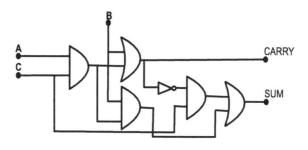

Fig. 8. *AMA*1

AMA2. AMA2 is implemented as carry signal is computed first then a buffer is added to get the sum signal. The output of sum signal is equal to complimentary of carry signal for 6 cases out of 8 cases with an error in 2 cases. The output carry signal remains as accurate. The truth table of AMA2 is shown in table and gate level representation is shown in the figure.

Gate Count Calculation: The gate level characterization of AMA2 is based on its Transistor representation and it is achieved by using 2 AND gate, 2 OR gate and 1 NOT gate.

The total number of basic gates used in AMA2 = 5 basic gates (Fig. 9).

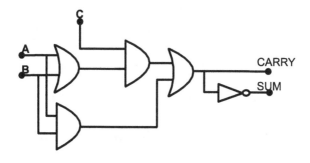

Fig. 9. *AMA*2

Approximate XNOR/XOR Based Adder (AXA). AXA [10] is proposed by approximating XOR/XNOR based exact full adder. AXA achieves less transistor count and reduction in power dissipation with the trade-off accuracy when compared to the exact full adder.

AXA1. AXA1 is implemented with 6 transistors, 4 transistor for XNOR and 2 for pass transistor logic. In AXA1 the output of XNOR gate is equal to the output of the sum signal which leads to 4 errors out of 8 cases in sum signal whereas carry signal is remained accurate by cascading the output of XNOR gate with pass transistor logic.

Gate Count Calculation: The gates utilized for implementing AXA1 is 1 XOR gate, 1 NOT gate, 1 OR gate, and 2 AND gate. When the XOR is limited to the 2-input basic gate, the total gates utilized for AXA1 is 2 NOT gate, 2 OR gate, and 4 AND gate.

The total number of basic gates utilized for AXA1 = 8 basic gates (Fig. 10).

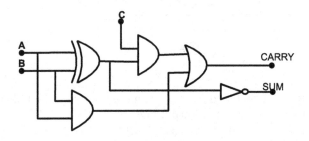

Fig. 10. *AXA*1

AXA2. The design of AXA2 is the extension of AXA1. In order to reduce the error in the sum signal, a pass transistor configuration (2 transistors) is used, which leads to 2 errors out of 8 cases in sum signal. The carry signal remained same.

Gate Count Calculation: AXA2 requires 1 XOR gate, 1 NOT gate, 1 OR gate, and 3 AND gate for the gate level characterization of AXA2. Due to the limitation, 2 NOT gate, 2 OR gate and 5 AND gate are utilized for the demonstration of AXA2.

The total basic gates used in AXA2 = 9 basic gates (Fig. 11 and Table 2).

3   Structural Analysis of Approximate Adder

Ripple Carry adders for n = 20 are designed using approximate adders with different degrees of full adder approximation (DFA) for example: 12:8 the first 8 LSB adders are approximate adders and the remaining adders are accurate

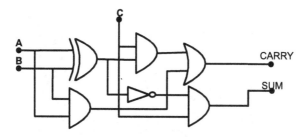

Fig. 11. $AXA2$

Table 2. Truth table of approximate full adders.

Inputs			Exact outputs		AMA1		AMA2		AXA1		AXA2	
x1	x2	x3	Carry	Sum	Carry	Sum	Carry	Sum	Carry	Sum	Carry	Sum
0	0	0	0	0	0✓	0✓	0✓	1✗	0✓	1✗	0✓	0✓
0	0	1	0	1	0✓	1✓	0✓	1✓	0✓	1✓	0✓	1✓
0	1	0	0	1	1✗	0✗	0✓	1✓	0✓	0✗	0✓	0✗
0	1	1	1	0	1✓	0✓	1✓	0✓	1✓	0✓	1✓	0✓
1	0	0	0	1	0✓	0✗	0✓	1✓	0✓	0✗	0✓	0✗
1	0	1	1	0	1✓	0✓	1✓	0✓	1✓	0✓	1✓	0✓
1	1	0	1	0	1✓	0✓	1✓	0✓	1✓	1✗	1✓	0✓
1	1	1	1	1	1✓	1✓	1✓	0✗	1✓	1✓	1✓	1✓

adders. The designed adders are coded in Verilog HDL and simulated using Verilog compiler simulator (VCS). These different adders are synthesized in Synopsys Design compiler (DC) using TSMC 65nm standard cell library typical corner. The switching activity of ripple carry adder for 1 lakh random test stimulus vectors are recorded in the .saif file and used in DC for detailed power analysis. Area, Power, and delay obtained from the DC compiler, which promotes the comparative study of the approximate adders. The structural analysis of approximate adders is based on their gate count, Area and Delay Product (ADP), Power and Delay Product (PDP) and Area and Power Product (APP). Table 3 gives the detailed analysis of ripple carry adder with different of approximation (DAR). ADP, PDP, APP values are represented in Figs. 12, 13 and 14 respectively. AFA shows attains lowest values in the compound metrics by maintaining the equal gate count when compared to other approximate adders in the set.

4   Error Analysis of Approximate Adder

Pass rate, error rate, mean error distance (MED) and normalized error distance (NED) are the error metrics considered for the evaluation of error characteristics of the approximate adder. Error distance is given as difference between the exact results and accurate results. MED is the mean value of error distance.

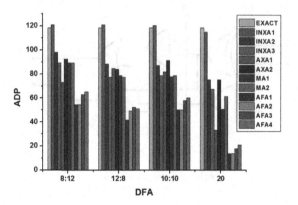

Fig. 12. ADP

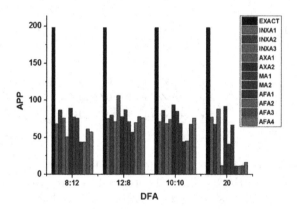

Fig. 13. APP

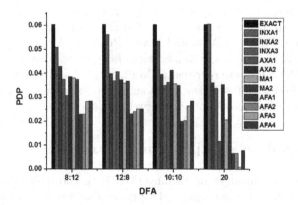

Fig. 14. PDP

Table 3. Structural comparison of ripple carry adder using approximate adders for different degrees of approximation

Designs	Degrees of approximation for N = 20	Area	Delay	Power
Exact	20	623.2	0.19	0.3179
	10:10	623.2	0.19	0.3179
	8:12	623.2	0.19	0.3179
	12:8	623.2	0.19	0.3179
INXA1	20	383.2	0.3	0.202
	10:10	400.8	0.3	0.1782
	8:12	402.8	0.3	0.1696
	12:8	402.8	0.3	0.1874
INXA2	20	375.2	0.2	0.1804
	10:10	436	0.2	0.1976
	8:12	445.2	0.22	0.1947
	12:8	420.4	0.21	0.1901
INXA3	20	420.4	0.16	0.2106
	10:10	392.8	0.2	0.0.1752
	8:12	425.2	0.21	0.1787
	12:8	386.8	0.2	0.1842
AFA1	20	151.2	0.09	0.0732
	10:10	334.4	0.15	0.1324
	8:12	321.2	0.17	0.1351
	12:8	383.2	0.13	0.1769
AFA2	20	151.2	0.09	0.0736
	10:10	334.4	0.15	0.135
	8:12	321.2	0.17	0.1352
	12:8	378	0.13	0.1851
AFA3	20	199.2	0.09	0.00962
	10:10	385.2	0.15	0.17534
	8:12	370	0.17	0.1658
	12:8	402.8	0.13	0.1931
AFA4	20	210.8	0.1	0.0785
	10:10	400.8	0.15	0.1895
	8:12	361.6	0.18	0.1583
	12:8	393.6	0.13	0.1937
AMA1	20	317.6	0.16	0.1285
	10:10	430.8	0.18	0.1979
	8:12	425.6	0.21	0.1817
	12:8	436	0.18	0.1996
AMA2	20	361.6	0.17	0.1847
	10:10	392.8	0.2	0.1752
	8:12	425.2	0.21	0.1787
	12:8	386.8	0.2	0.1841
AXA1	20	183.6	0.18	0.0645
	10:10	409.2	0.2	0.1813
	8:12	348	0.21	0.1464
	12:8	469.6	0.18	0.2264
AXA2	20	442	0.17	0.2079
	10:10	455.6	0.2	0.2062
	8:12	462.4	0.2	0.1932
	12:8	418.8	0.2	0.1869

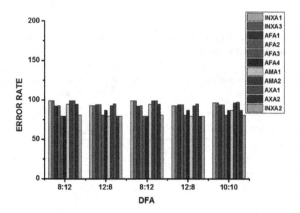

Fig. 15. Error rate.

$$NED = \frac{Mean\ value\ of\ Error\ Distance}{Magnitude\ of\ maximum\ possible\ error} \tag{1}$$

$$Pass\ Rate = \frac{Number\ of\ correct\ outputs}{Total\ number\ of\ outputs} \tag{2}$$

$$Error\ Rate = \frac{Number\ of\ incorrect\ outputs}{Total\ number\ of\ outputs} \tag{3}$$

1 lakh random test stimulus vector are generated and recorded for detailed error analysis, which is done in MATLAB. Pass rate and error rate of all the adders are represented in Figs. 15 and 16 respectively. Table 4 provides the NED values of ripple carry adder.

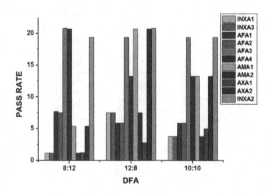

Fig. 16. Pass rate.

Table 4. Ned values of ripple carry adder for different degrees of approximation.

Designs	N = 20	N = 10:10	N = 8:12	N = 12:8
INXA1	4.685×10^{-1}	6.17×10^{-2}	1.8×10^{-3}	4.24×10^{-4}
INXA2	1.22×10^{-1}	8.336×10^{-1}	5.68×10^{-2}	4.104×10^{-2}
INXA3	4.678×10^{-1}	4.5×10^{-2}	1.6×10^{-3}	3.44×10^{-4}
AFA1	2.209×10^{-2}	2.209×10^{-2}	2.209×10^{-2}	4.21×10^{-3}
AFA2	3.15×10^{-2}	2.209×10^{-2}	2.209×10^{-2}	4.21×10^{-3}
AFA3	2.235×10^{-2}	2.209×10^{-2}	4.128×10^{-2}	2.23×10^{-3}
AFA4	3.15×10^{-2}	6.689×10^{-2}	4.128×10^{-2}	6.689×10^{-2}
AMA1	1.57×10^{-2}	2.97×10^{-2}	1.633×10^{-1}	4.2×10^{-4}
AMA2	4.678×10^{-1}	4.497×10^{-2}	1.6×10^{-3}	3.45×10^{-4}
AXA1	4.371×10^{-1}	7.05×10^{-3}	1.34×10^{-3}	2.27×10^{-4}
AXA2	3.07×10^{-2}	5.56×10^{-2}	1.6×10^{-3}	4.104×10^{-2}

5 Conclusion

Approximate adders are used in the DSP processor and in the error resilient application to reduce the circuit complexity with some acceptable degradation in the output. The approximation is applied to full adders either at gate level or at the transistor level. The probability of erroneous outputs in the approximate full adder at the gate level is less when compared to the probability of erroneous output in the approximate full adder at the transistor level. Further, the analysis is extended to the multi-bit adder, which is designed by using the approximate full adders in different degrees of approximation. The designed ripple carry adder is evaluated based on their Structural and error characteristics. Among all the approximate adders taken for the exploration, AFA1 and AFA2 shows a reasonable balance between the area and accuracy.

References

1. Almurib, H.A., Kumar, T.N., Lombardi, F.: Inexact designs for approximate low power addition by cell replacement. In: 2016 Design, Automation and Test in Europe Conference and Exhibition (DATE), pp. 660–665. IEEE (2016)
2. Dutt, S., Nandi, S., Trivedi, G.: Analysis and design of adders for approximate computing. ACM Trans. Embed. Comput. Syst. (TECS) **17**(2), 40 (2018)
3. Gupta, V., Mohapatra, D., Raghunathan, A., Roy, K.: Low-power digital signal processing using approximate adders. IEEE Trans. Comput.-Aided Des. Integr. Circ. Syst. **32**(1), 124–137 (2013)
4. Liang, J., Han, J., Lombardi, F.: New metrics for the reliability of approximate and probabilistic adders. IEEE Trans. Comput. **62**(9), 1760–1771 (2013)
5. Mittal, S.: A survey of techniques for approximate computing. ACM Comput. Surv. (CSUR) **48**(4), 62 (2016)

6. Oklobdzija, V.: The Computer Engineering Handbook. Computer Engineering Series. CRC Press, Boca Raton (2001)
7. Parhami, B.: Computer Arithmetic: Algorithms and Hardware Designs. Oxford University Press, Inc., New York (2009)
8. Townsend, W.J., Swartzlander, E.E., Abraham, J.A.: A comparison of Dadda and Wallace multiplier delays. In: Advanced Signal Processing Algorithms, Architectures, and Implementations XIII, vol. 5205, pp. 552–561. International Society for Optics and Photonics (2003)
9. Verma, A.K., Brisk, P., Ienne, P.: Variable latency speculative addition: a new paradigm for arithmetic circuit design. In: Proceedings of the Conference on Design, Automation and Test in Europe, pp. 1250–1255. ACM (2008)
10. Yang, Z., Jain, A., Liang, J., Han, J., Lombardi, F.: Approximate XOR/XNOR-based adders for inexact computing. In: 2013 13th IEEE Conference on Nanotechnology (IEEE-NANO), pp. 690–693. IEEE (2013)

Analog and Mixed Signal Design

A PVT Insensitive Low-Power
Differential Ring Oscillator

Nishtha Wadhwa$^{(\boxtimes)}$ ⓘ, Pydi Ganga Bahubalindruni ⓘ, and Sujay Deb ⓘ

IIIT-Delhi, Okhla Industrial Estate, Phase III, New Delhi 110020, India
{nishthaw,bpganga}@iiitd.ac.in

Abstract. This paper presents novel low-power seven stage differential ring oscillators, which are robust against PVT variations. This work consider two different circuits, namely, current starved and negative skewed PMOS ring oscillators. Power consumption is minimized in these circuits by employing DTMOS (below 0.6 V) technique that adjusts the threshold voltage of the PMOS transistor in a dynamic way. In addition, circuit performance is made robust against PVT variations by using a self biased compensation technique. The biasing circuit changes the control voltage of the differential ring oscillator to maintain a constant frequency. Circuits simulations are carried out in standard 65 nm technology with a supply voltage of 0.5 V. The worst case variation in frequency of oscillation is <4% over a temperature range of −75 °C to 150 °C. Process corners have resulted in 2% variation compared to the nominal, on the other hand 1% relative variation is observed when power supply is within the range of ±5% of nominal value. Proposed current starved and skewed PMOS ring oscillators show a power consumption of 186 nW at 41 MHz and 4.2 μW at 1.5 GHz, respectively, from the simulations. Both these circuits maintains the power delay product of 0.2 fJ. Given the robust performance against PVT, these circuits can find the potential applications in IoT devices.

Keywords: Differential ring oscillator · PVT insensitive circuits ·
Current starved · Negative skewed delay · DTMOS

1 Introduction

In modern processors and system-on-chip applications, power consumption is increasing as chips are getting larger and operating frequency increases [1]. On the other hand, high speed data communication systems demand high frequency clocks and low power dissipation for reliable operations [2]. On-chip timing signal generators (oscillators) are one of the main building blocks in the afore mentioned applications, which demand a frequency of operation ranging betweens tens of MHz to few GHz [3].

Among different architectures of oscillators, LC resonators uses inductors that are very bulky, difficult for on-chip realization and provides limited frequency tuning. The other architecture is the quartz crystal oscillators, which

© Springer Nature Singapore Pte Ltd. 2019
S. Rajaram et al. (Eds.): VDAT 2018, CCIS 892, pp. 77–87, 2019.
https://doi.org/10.1007/978-981-13-5950-7_7

provide excellent stability against PVT (Process, Voltage and Temperature) variations. However, they impose limitations for on-chip integration. On contrary, conventional CMOS ring oscillators (RO) are preferred because of their simplicity and ability to generate multiphase clocks that are used as various control signals for data path [2,4,5]. Typically ROs are sensitive to PVT variations and low-power consumption is a stringent requirement in many applications [6]. Design of on-chip oscillators that can ensure robust frequency of oscillation against PVT variations together with low-power consumption is quite challenging. Some designs employ external references to tune the frequency of oscillation, whereas, others employ on-chip stable voltage reference generation [7]. Another well known PVT insensitive technique is constant g_m biasing [8]. In this topology the transistors are biased such that their transconductance is independent of PVT variations. However, the drawback of this topology is that the on-resistance of the switches in the switch capacitor implementation are not linear unless complex topologies like bootstarpping is used. This work introduces simple self compensated biasing circuit that provides a stable control voltage to maintain a constant frequency with temperature, voltage and process variations.

Significant work has been done in addressing low power requirements of RO. Dynamic Threshold MOSFETS (DTMOS) is one of the well known approach to achieve low power consumption. This technique utilizes dynamic body bias as the substrate (or body) and gate of PMOSFET are tied together. Therefore, input gate voltage forward biases the source-substrate junction owing to the body effect, which decreases the threshold voltage V_t in ON state. When the PMOSFET is turned off, V_t returns to its original high value [9].

Another common architecture is the current starved (CS) ring oscillator. In this circuit, current supplied to each inverter is restricted to promise low power consumption, however, it imposes a limitation on the frequency of oscillation [10,11]. On the other hand, by using negative skewed delay approach the frequency of the RO can be improved by increasing number of high-to-low and low-to-high transitions, but it imposes limitation on the power consumption [2]. By employing DTPMOS in the negative skewed topology, power delay product (PDP) can be improved. Further this proposed circuit is made robust against PVT variations by employing the afore mentioned self compensating bias circuit.

The rest of the paper is organized as follows. Section 2 demonstrates the proposed circuit design and its operating principle. Section 3 presents the simulation results and discussions and finally the conclusions are drawn in Sect. 4.

2   Circuit Description

A ring oscillator comprises of an odd number of inverters connected in a series and then back-coupled to provide an unstable state that leads to oscillations [8]. In order to improve the noise performance in ROs, a differential scheme is used. Differential circuits are generally preferred to single-ended circuits in noisy environments because the substrate noise appears as a common mode signal on the differential output and hence, its impact is several orders of magnitude lower as compared to the single-ended output [12].

2.1   Dynamic Threshold MOSFETS

For low-power applications DTPMOS is used as shown in Fig. 1 in which PMOS transistor M_p is connected in the DTPMOS configuration. DTMOS technique can be applied to both NMOS and PMOS in the SOI (Silicon On Insulator) technology. However, the same technique cannot be applied to the NMOS transistors in the conventional Bulk-CMOS technology because all NMOS transistors share the same substrate and it can only be applied to the PMOS transistors since every transistor is isolated in its own n-well. To extend the application of the DTMOS to the NMOS in Bulk-CMOS technology triple well has to be used [13].

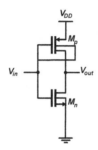

Fig. 1. Circuit schematic of a simple inverter using DTPMOS (M_p)

From (1) it is clear that if threshold voltage increases the substrate current will decrease for PMOS.

$$I_{sub} = I_0 \frac{W}{L} e^{\frac{V_{gs} - V_t}{nV_t}} \tag{1}$$

From (2), the threshold voltage of DTPMOS depends on V_{bs}. Forward bias across the junction reduces the junction width and the depletion region charge density, which inturn reduces V_t that results in higher driving capability. Whereas, reverse bias increases the depletion region width and hence increases body charges due to which V_t also increases resulting in low leakage current there by saving power. Thus the threshold voltage of M_p is changed dynamically according to the input voltage level i.e. operating state of the circuit. Hence, DTPMOS enables the circuit to operate under the low supply voltage and suitable for low-power applications.

$$V_t = V_{t0} - \gamma(\sqrt{|-2\phi_F|} - \sqrt{|-2\phi_F + V_{bs}|}) \tag{2}$$

where,
V_{t0} is the threshold voltage when $V_{sb} = 0$
γ is the body-effect coefficient
$2\phi_F$ is the silicon surface potential at the onset of the strong inversion and it's equal to -0.6 V for typical p-type substrates
V_{sb} is the source to body voltage

The general architecture for the Differential CSRO and Differential Skew RO employing DTPMOS technique is shown in Fig. 2. In this MOSFETS M_{p1}, M_{n1} and $M_{p1'}$, $M_{n1'}$ forms the differential pair. Transistors M_{bp} and M_{bn} provide biasing current to the circuit. For lower biasing current the transistors operate in near-subthreshold region and hence the power consumption can be minimized [14].

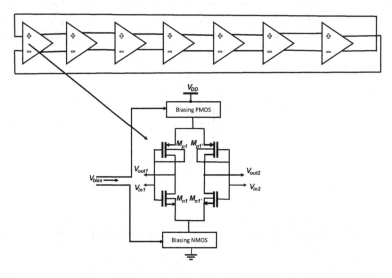

Fig. 2. Proposed differential 7-stage RO circuit

2.2   Current Starved (CS) RO

One of the proposed design consists of seven stage Differential current starved ring oscillator (DESIGN I), which employs DTPMOS along with self-biased technique shown in Fig. 4. For high speed operation and low power consumption, the aspect ratios of PMOS to NMOS are maintained between 1.5–1.7 gives equal rise and fall resistances. For the clear explanation single stage Current starved RO is considered as shown in Fig. 3 [17] but simulations are carried out for the differential stage as per design shown in Fig. 2. In this it can be seen that by varying the bias voltage the time to charge and discharge the gate capacitance of the stage can be varied and consequently the frequency. As power is directly proportional to frequency, so less power means less frequency. This means that CSRO can b used for low power applications.

PVT Insensitive Circuit: PVT insensitive bias voltage for proposed ROs is generated using the circuit shown in Fig. 4.

In the literature all PVT biased circuits are implemented using BJT [5]. In order to be compatible with CMOS only process, the proposed work implements the basing circuits only with MOSFETs. PMOS and NMOS transistors $M_{p'}$,

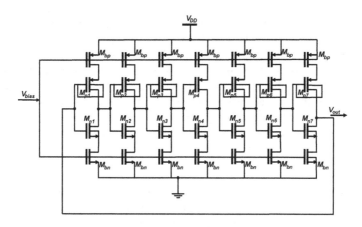

Fig. 3. 7-stage current starved ring oscillator (CSRO) employing DTPMOS technique

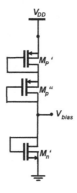

Fig. 4. Circuit schematic of proposed self-compensated biasing circuit only with MOSFETs

$M_{p''}$ and $M_{n'}$ are in the form of diode connected configuration. Through the mathematical analysis, the following Eq. (3) is derived, which shows that the biasing voltage is independent of temperature as it cancels out variation in the threshold voltage of both NMOS and PMOS that are used in the biasing circuit, by choosing the aspects ratios as per (4).

$$V_{cntr} = V_{DD} - 2[\sqrt{\frac{\mu_n C_{ox}(W/L)_n}{\mu_p C_{ox}(W/L)_p}}(V_{gs} - V_{tn}) + |V_{tp}|] \tag{3}$$

$$(\frac{W}{L})_n = \frac{\mu_p}{\mu_n}(\frac{W}{L})_p \tag{4}$$

The NMOS that is used, makes the voltage change inversely proportional to temperature in order to compensate the temperature changes. PMOS is used for compensating the process variations as it helps to cancel out the threshold voltage variations. The biasing voltage that is provided to the ROs are independent of oxide thickness, mobility and threshold voltage by considering Eqs. (3) and (4). So, the variations due to the process are getting cancelled out. The final mathematical Eq. (3) that is derived shows that V_{cntr} is direct function of V_{gs} which minimizes the voltage variations. If supply voltage varies V_{gs} also varies with the same amount so the biasing voltage remains constant irrespective of the supply voltage variations.

2.3 Skewed RO

The second proposed design is Differential negative skewed PMOS RO (DESIGN II) which also incorporates the PVT insensitive biasing voltage together with DTPMOS to reduce the power consumption. The general architechure is presented in Fig. 2. For this design also simulations are carried out for differential topology but for the explanation single stage Skew PMOS RO is considered as shown in Fig. 5. The basic principle of PMOS negative skewed RO is that the input of the PMOS is connected to the negative delay elements, so it prematurely makes the PMOS 'on' when low to high output transitions occur. This helps to compensate the performance of PMOS that is usually less than that of NMOS. Similarly when high to low transition occurs PMOS is prematurely 'off' before NMOS turns 'on' which speeds up the operation and thereby increasing the frequency of operation [2]. In this circuit as the number of transitions are much higher, it ensures high frequency of operation with slight increase in power consumption, which can be lowered by DTPMOS technique. In the same way by connecting negative delay elements to the NMOS, negative skewed NMOS RO can be designed. As the mobility of electrons is greater than that of mobility of holes, NMOS skewed is used to provide high frequency of operation but consumes high power as well. Due to which the power delay product is increased compared to negative skewed PMOS. Therefore, PMOS negative skewed technique is considered as better PDP can be obtained from this.

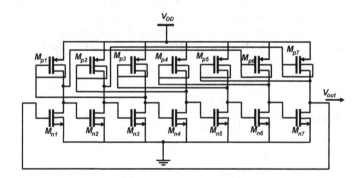

Fig. 5. Circuit schematic of single ended negative skewed PMOS RO.

3   Results and Discussion

The proposed circuits (DESIGN I and DESIGN II) are simulated in standard 65 nm technology. PDP is the measure of the energy and is defines as the product of average power and the gate delay t_p given by,

$$t_p = \frac{1}{2 * n * frequency} \qquad (5)$$

where n is the number of stages. For the comparison purpose, the proposed Design I is compared with the constant g_m biasing circuit (for a faired comparison, this circuit is also simulated under similar conditions). It can be observed from Fig. 6 that it shows >30% variation in frequency of oscillations with variation in temperature.

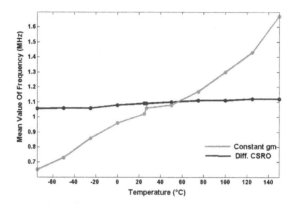

Fig. 6. Comparison of DESIGN I with respect to constant g_m biasing and proposed self biasing technique.

In addition, greater variations in frequency of oscillations have been observed for process and voltage variations. For the proposed circuits the temperature versus frequency and temperature verses PDP is compared in Fig. 7a for DESIGN I and Fig. 7b for DESIGN II, respectively. From these figures it can be observed that Design I has shown a frequency variation <4% but the PDP is constant over a wide range of temperature ranging from −75 °C to 150 °C and it consumes a power of 186 nW at 41 MHz. Whereas, in the Design II the frequency of oscillations is around 1.5 GHz and the PDP is constant for the wide range of temperature from −75 °C to 150 °C with the power consumption of 4.2 μW. The phase noise of Design I is −85 dBc/Hz at 1 MHz frequency and for Design II is −90 dBc/Hz at 1 GHz frequency. As per the results we see that the Design I consumes very low power and Design II operates at much higher frequency with the supply voltage of 0.5 V.

Design I and Design II responses are presented in Fig. 8a and b, respectively. Tables 1 and 2 show the variation in the frequency and PDP with respect to

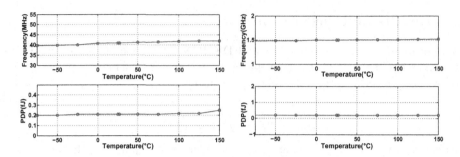

Fig. 7. Proposed Design I and Design II frequency and PDP variation against temperature.

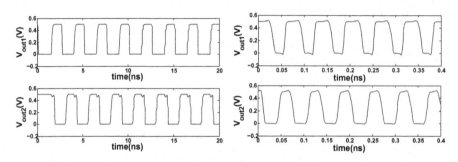

Fig. 8. Proposed Design I and Design II response.

different process corners and supply voltages (typical and ±5%) for the Design I. It can be seen from the table that with the process, the variation is 2% and 1% relative variation is observed when power supply is within the range of ±5% of nominal value. The same amount of variations are observed for Design II with respect to process and voltage in Tables 3 and 4.

Tables 5 and 6 shows the monte carlo analysis at different temperatures. It can be inferred that <5% of mismatch variations in power was observed for Design I and Design II.

Table 7 compares the proposed work with the state of art. As it can be noticed that in the lower technology nodes the ROs are giving the inferior performance interms of PDP. In high speed applications of RO's, the main concern is low power consumption and high frequency of operation. The proposed circuits satisfies both these conditions. They are giving less power without much compensating with the frequency. It can also be seen that the proposed Design II gives the best performance in terms of frequency of operation and the Design I interms of power consumption but both gives the PDP of same range.

Table 1. Process variations for Design I with supply voltage of 0.5 V and temperature of 27 °C

Process	Frequency (MHz)	PDP (fJ)
SS	40	0.21
TT	41	0.21
FF	41.5	0.25
FS	42.8	0.2
SF	40	0.26

Table 2. Voltage variations for Design I with typical conditions and temperature of 27 °C

Voltage (V)	Frequency (MHz)	PDP (fJ)
0.45	40.8	0.2
0.50	41	0.2
0.55	41.5	0.21

Table 3. Process variations for Design II with supply voltage of 0.5 V and temperature of 27 °C

Process	Frequency (GHz)	PDP (fJ)
SS	1.45	0.21
TT	1.5	0.21
FF	1.55	0.24
FS	1.43	0.2
SF	1.5	0.22

Table 4. Voltage variations for Design II with typical conditions and temperature of 27 °C

Voltage (V)	Frequency (GHz)	PDP (fJ)
0.45	1.49	0.21
0.50	1.5	0.21
0.55	1.53	0.22

Table 5. Parameters obtained through monte carlo simulations for Differential CSRO

Temperature (°C)	−75	27	150
Mean(μ) nW		184.27	186.091	188.7
Standard deviation(σ) nW	36.72	38.185	40.17

Table 6. Parameters obtained through monte carlo simulations for Differential Skewed RO

Temperature (°C)	−75	27	150
Mean(μ) μW	3.9	4.1	4.4
Standard deviation(σ) μW	0.71	0.86	0.997

Table 7. Performance Comparison with other works

Work description	Tech. (nm)	V_{DD}(V)	Freq. (MHz)	Power (uW)	PDP (fJ)	Temp. Coeff. (ppm/°C)
Diff. CS RO [1]	45	1	90	25	69	263
Diff. CS RO [15]	60	4	0.68	400	2900	324
Diff. RO [16]	65	5	1200	13200	1100	NA
Diff. CS RO [12]	180	1.8	432	500	1157	NA
Diff. CS RO [5]	250	2.74	7	1500	11000	315
Skew RO [2]	800	1.2	0.15	42.6	142000	40
Proposed Design I	65	0.5	41	0.186	0.20	200
Proposed Design II	65	0.5	1500	4.2	0.207	170

4   Conclusions

This paper proposes seven stage Differential CS and the Negative skewed PMOS RO that are able to compensate the PVT variations and ensures low power consumption and high frequency of operation respectively. The aspects ratios of PMOS to NMOS are chosen in the range of 1.5–1.7. Use of DTPMOS helps to consumes low power by adjusting the threshold voltage. The self biasing circuit that is exploited helps to compensate the variations of 4% for temperature, 2% for process and 1% for voltage respectively. The circuits shows excellent performance interms of power consumption, frequency of oscillations and stability. These two proposed circuits provides potential applications in IoT.

Acknowledgment. The authors would like to thank everyone who helped with this work, including the project by early career research grant ECR/2017/000931.

References

1. Datta, B., Burleson, W.: Low-power and robust on-chip thermal sensing using differential ring oscillators. In: Midwest Symposium on Circuits and Systems, pp. 29–32 (2007)
2. Lee, S.-J., Kim, B., Lee, K.: A novel high-speed ring oscillator for multiphase clock generation using negative skewed delay scheme. IEEE J. Solid-State Circ. **32**(2), 289–291 (1997)
3. Tang, Y., Aktas, A., Ismail, M., Bibyk, S.: A fully integrated dualmode frequency synthesizer for GSM and Wideband CDMA in 0.5/spl mu/m CMOS. In: Midwest Symposium on Circuits and Systems, vol. 2, pp. 866–869 (2001)
4. Hajimiri, A., Limotyrakis, S., Lee, T.H.: Jitter and phase noise in ring oscillators. IEEE J. Solid-state Circ. **34**(6), 790–804 (1999)

5. Sundaresan, K., Allen, P.E., Ayazi, F.: Process and temperature compensation in a 7-MHz CMOS clock oscillator. IEEE J. Solid-State Circ. **41**(2), 433–442 (2006)
6. Mandal, M., Sarkar, B.: Ring oscillators: Characteristics and applications (2010)
7. Linares-Barranco, B., Rodriguez-Vazquez, A., Sanchez-Sinencio, E., Huertas, J.: Frequency tuning loop for VCOs. In: International Symposium on Circuits and Systems, pp. 2617–2620 (1991)
8. Razavi, B.: Design of analog CMOS integrated circuits (2001)
9. Niranjan, V., Gupta, M.: An analytical model of the bulk-DTMOS transistor. J. Electr. Devices **8**(2010), 329–338 (2010)
10. Wang, Y., Chan, P.K., Li, K.H.: A compact CMOS ring oscillator with temperature and supply compensation for sensor applications. In: Computer Society Annual Symposium on VLSI, pp. 267–272 (2014)
11. Zhang, X., Apsel, A.B.: A low-power, process-and-temperature-compensated ring oscillator with addition-based current source. IEEE Trans. Circ. Syst. I Regular Papers **58**(5), 868–878 (2011)
12. Dermentzoglou, L., Tsiatouhas, Y., Arapoyanni, A.: A built-in selftest scheme for differential ring oscillators. In: International Symposium on Circuits and Systems, pp. 448–452 (2005)
13. Elgharbawy, W., Bayoumi, M.: A novel ultra-low-energy bulk dynamic threshold PMOS scheme. In: Midwest Symposium on Circuits and Systems, vol. 3, pp. 1388–1391 (2003)
14. Harrison, R.R., Charles, C.: A low-power low-noise CMOS amplifier for neural recording applications. IEEE J. Solid-State Circ. **38**(6), 958–965 (2003)
15. Shyu, Y.-S., Wu, J.-C.: A process and temperature compensated ring oscillator. In: Asia Pacific Conference on ASICs, pp. 283–286 (1999)
16. Sebastiano, F., Breems, L.J., Makinwa, K.A., Drago, S., Leenaerts, D.M., Nauta, B.: A 65-nm CMOS temperature-compensated mobility-based frequency reference for wireless sensor networks. IEEE J. Solid-State Circ. **46**(7), 1544–1552 (2011)
17. Nayak, R., Kianpoor, I., Bahubalindruni, P.G.: Low power ring oscillator for IoT applications. Analog Integr. Circ. Sig. Process. **93**(2), 257–263 (2017)

Optimal Transistor Sizing of Full-Adder Block to Reduce Standby Leakage Power

Prateek Gupta$^{(\boxtimes)}$, Shubham Kumar, and Zia Abbas

Center for VLSI and Embedded Systems Technologies (CVEST),
International Institute of Information Technology, Hyderabad, Hyderabad, India
{prateek.g,kumar.shubham}@research.iiit.ac.in, zia.abbas@iiit.ac.in

Abstract. In this paper, two one-bit full adder design techniques are explored for reduced power consumption in standby mode. The proposed algorithm based techniques compute optimal transistor sizing for variable operating conditions (temperature, supply voltage) to achieve desirable leakage power and speed for a full-adder circuit. Both techniques use 'SLEEP' signal to drive full adder circuit to lower standby mode leakage state without even degrading the performances in active mode. The investigation has been carried out for 45 nm, 32 nm, 22 nm Metal Gate High-K PTM models and all the simulation characterizations are carried out using HSPICE simulation tool. Performance comparison of both techniques after optimization has been done over a complete range temperature $(-40\,^\circ\mathrm{C}-125\,^\circ\mathrm{C})$ and $\pm 5\%$ variation in supply voltage. The resultant designs are tested on large full-adder based digital circuits to analyze the reduced standby leakage power. The results show that up to 97% of standby leakage reduction can be obtained with $(0.4{-}15)\%$ delay overhead using the proposed methods of full-adder design.

Keywords: CMOS · Leakage power · Propagation delay ·
Minimum Leakage Vector (MLV) · Input Vector Control (IVC) ·
Power Gating (PG)

1 Introduction

The addition is a conspicuous part of arithmetic operations in the processors. Thus power efficient and operating variation-aware full adder cell plays a decisive role in a large portion of the VLSI chips. With the progressive downscaling of VLSI technology for performance improvement in computing systems led to an enormous increase in leakage power. As an example, sub-threshold leakage is increasing with the reduction in the transistor threshold voltage, which is scaled down with the supply voltage for maintaining high speed and supply voltages are scaled to withstand the electric field. This exponential increase in subthreshold leakage current can be observed from Eq. (1).

$$I_{ds} = K(1 - e^{(-V_{ds}/V_T)})e^{(V_{gs}-V_T+\eta V_{ds}/nV_T)} \tag{1}$$

© Springer Nature Singapore Pte Ltd. 2019
S. Rajaram et al. (Eds.): VDAT 2018, CCIS 892, pp. 88–99, 2019.
https://doi.org/10.1007/978-981-13-5950-7_8

where η is drain induced barrier lowering coefficient and K, n are technology functions. Leakage current increases by the factor of 10 with reduction of the threshold voltage by 100 mv [1]. The other leakage components are Reverse Junction Bias Current, Band-to-Band Tunneling (BTBT), Tunneling through and into Gate Oxide, Injection of hot carriers from substrate to gate oxide, Gate induced drain leakage (GIDL), Punch through, etc, all together contribute to total static power dissipation in nanoscale MOS. Sub-threshold leakage is still dominating leakage components [2], Gate oxide leakage currents have been partially limited by the introduction of high-K dielectrics in CMOS technologies [3]. Hence, leakage minimization techniques for modern technology nodes are of great importance. Leakage current also depends on the input vector of the circuit because of transistor stacking effect [4]. Determining Minimum Leakage Vector and applying it to the circuit in an idle state can cause a significant reduction in overall leakage. This popular leakage reduction technique is called Input Vector Control (IVC) [5]. Figure 1 depicts variation in leakage power with input vectors applied on full-adder cell at 45 nm, 32 nm and 22 nm Metal Gate High-K technology under normal operating conditions (NOC, $V_{supply} = 1.0$ V, temperature $= 25\,°C$). It can be observed from Fig. 1 that leakage at input vector (111) which is the MLV of the cell is significantly lesser (about 1.4 times) than leakage at input vector (001) which is the worst leakage state (WLS) of the cell. Also, one can gate both the pull-up and pull-down network using PMOS and NMOS transistors to provide almost two orders of magnitude leakage power savings [6], this technique is called power gating [7]. Motivated by the above observation, we propose a performance-aware design approach to find the optimal transistor sizing of each transistor in full adder cell based on Evolutionary Algorithm. The idea is to switch every FA cell in a complex circuit/Integrated Circuit to its MLV state using IVC during standby mode with as little performance overhead as possible, especially in the circuits where low power is prime concern. The standby leakage is also reduced with determining optimal transistor sizing for power gated full adder cell and compared the performance of both types of designs.

In this paper an optimized sizing of 1-bit full adder cell has been found for minimum standby leakage power at different technology nodes such as 45 nm, 32 nm, 22 nm and the obtained results of the 1-bit full adder cell are applied on various applications for efficient and improved performance. The targeted 1-bit full adder cell consist of 28 transistors in mirror configuration with three input (A, B and C_i) and two output nodes (sum and carry), and is a basic building block for many important complex circuits such as ripple carry adder, carry select adder, carry skip adder, arithmetic and logic unit etc. The sum (S) and carry output (C_{out}) are given by:

$$S = A \oplus B \oplus C_i \tag{2}$$

$$C_{out} = A \cdot B + (A \oplus B) \cdot C_i \tag{3}$$

In the past years, many comparisons are done between different full adder topologies, however, no optimal sizing of each transistor calculated using evolutionary techniques for nanoscale technology nodes has been reported. In the present work

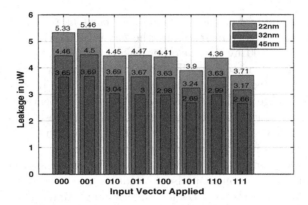

Fig. 1. Variation in leakage with input vector at different technology nodes in full adder circuit.

a brief idea about incorporating verse techniques such as input vector control (IVC) and power gating (PG) with latest evolutionary algorithms to find the robust sizing of each transistor in the circuit for the scaled technology nodes has been reported. The results are calculated using HSPICE PTM model cards for state of the art technology nodes. The rest of the paper is divided as follows: Sect. 2 is the survey of related work; Sect. 3 discusses the proposed design approach; Sect. 4 discusses the experimental results on few applications of full-adder followed by a conclusion and future work in Sect. 5.

2   Background

Many techniques have been discussed in past to overcome the leakage in the VLSI chips. In [1,6], a survey of different leakages reduction techniques have been reported including dual-threshold CMOS, multi-threshold CMOS, variable threshold CMOS, forced transistor stacking, input vector control (IVC), power gating (PG), etc. A comparison of subthreshold and total leakage currents for all the possible input combinations of 4 input NAND cell and it's MLV estimation has been done in [8]. To calculate MLV in combinational circuits, a different method called weighted partial Max-SAT based algorithm has been proposed in [9]. In order to reduce the leakage current in VLSI circuit, a combination of gate replacement and IVC has been proposed in [10]. Different sources of leakage power and their control in standby and active mode in CMOS circuits is given in [11]. A performance comparison between different topologies of full adder cell has been done in [12]. Device sizing and yield calculation has been done in [13,14] for several standard digital cells including full adder circuit at different operating and process conditions.

Many evolutionary algorithms are also available such as genetic algorithm, particle swarm optimization algorithm, artificial bee colony algorithm etc to achieve minimum leakage value while keeping the constraints on other performances in the circuits [15,16].

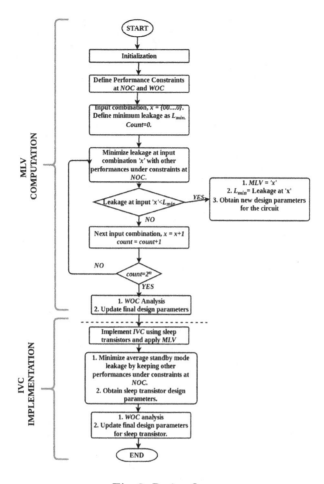

Fig. 2. Design flow.

3 Proposed Approach and Implementation

The evolutionary algorithms such as Ant colony optimization, particle swarm optimization (PSO) are generic population based metaheuristic algorithms. In presented work, in order to calculate the minimum leakage vector and optimal transistor sizing, we have implemented PSO algorithm [17], is basically inspired from nature such as bird flocks or fish schools. We have applied single objective PSO to obtain minimum leakage value and corresponding optimal transistor sizing keeping the propagation delays in bounds. PSO algorithm along with collective local unimodal search (PSO-CLUS) [18] is used in this paper to avoid the premature convergence of the solution in the high dimensional and multimodal problem.

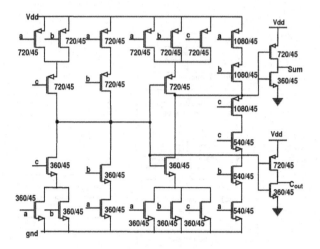

Fig. 3. Nominal full adder cell (45 nm) [13].

The proposed design approaches involve two different ways to reduce the standby mode leakage power and to find optimal transistor sizing; Input Vector Control (IVC) and Power Gating (PG). Both the reported techniques involve PSO-CLUS algorithm [18] to find its associated performance parameters.

Approach I - For IVC approach, the design flow for estimating the optimal sizing of each transistor in circuit under test is displayed in Fig. 2. It involves two steps; MLV computation and MLV implementation.

MLV computation initializes with defining the performance constraints i.e. the leakages and delays constraints for normal operating condition (NOC) [V_{supply} = 1.0 V, temperature = 25 °C] and worst operating conditions (WOC) [V_{supply} = 1.05 V (for leakage computation), V_{supply} = 0.95 V (for delays computation), temperature = (−40 °C to 125 °C). The initial sizing of used 28-T nominal full adder mirror type circuit has been taken from [13] is shown in Fig. 3. Then we minimize the leakage at MLV keeping the delays in the bound of 10–15% overhead of its initial values while evaluating the sizing of each transistor. The MLV is the input vector which gives the minimum leakage value among all possible vectors in full adder cell. This MLV can drive the complete circuit at its minimum leakage power consumption. Thus, finally, this step gives us the MLV with the optimal sizing of each transistor.

Now, we come to second step MLV implementation. This MLV is applied to the circuit by applying Input Vector Control technique implemented using transmission gate technology as a single NMOS or PMOS pass transistor suffers from a threshold drop. While transmission gates fix this problem at the cost of two transistors in parallel [19]. Thus we obtain the sizing of sleep transistors by the algorithm and minimize average standby mode leakage power keeping all delays and area in same bound as we defined for initial sizing for NOC and WOC.

Approach II - The second design approach involves stand-by mode leakage reduction using power gating technique. It entails two additional transistors (sleep transistors) in 28-T full adder cell. One PMOS connected between Vdd and pull up network (PUN) and one NMOS between ground and pull down network (PDN) applied by sleep and its complementary signal at its gate terminal respectively. The initialization approach here is same as mentioned in approach I. It facilitates the reduction of standby mode leakage by turning off the sleep transistors and creates a virtual vdd and gnd. In Active mode, the sleep transistors are turned on thus the circuit functions as usual. Again, the optimal sizing of all transistors in the full adder including sleep transistors calculated using the mentioned algorithm.

With these approaches, we would see in the result section that standby mode leakage reduced from 28% upto 97%.

After applying the proposed approaches using HSPICE tool on 28-T full adder cell, the final transistor sizing obtained are shown in Figs. 4, 5 and 6 for 45 nm, 32 nm, 22 nm technology nodes respectively. From Figs. 4, 5 and 6(a), The MLV for the respective circuit is obtained and applied to it through transmission gate using approach I, so as to drive the circuit in standby mode with minimum power consumption. For sleep signal (Sl) equals to zero, MLV is passed from node 'A', 'B', 'C' to node 'a', 'b', 'c' respectively and circuit functions in standby mode. While when sleep signal (Sl) equals to one it remains in active mode and it works normally and normal input combinations are passed from input to output.

In Figs. 4, 5 and 6(b) the dotted line represents virtual Vdd and virtual ground connection made by the power gated transistors connected in PUN and PDN. Here also, the optimal sizing of all the transistors has been calculated by the mentioned algorithm with HSPICE tool. With approach II, the circuit functions in standby mode as soon as Sl = 0 thus power consumption is minimum and when Sl becomes 1, it works normally. The sizing that is the ratio of width (W) and length (L) of the transistor is in (nanometer/nanometer) units. The corresponding performance's results at these sizings are given in Table 1 that will be discussed in detail in the result section.

3.1   For 45 nm Technology

Figure 4 represents final FA circuit with optimal transistor sizing for 45 nm technology node obtained from proposed approaches. The length has been taken as constant and width have been varied in the applied algorithm to obtain desired performance parameters.

As it can be clearly seen from Fig. 4(a) that MLV for such circuit is obtained as '100' which has been applied to it through the transmission gate using approach I. Figure 4(b) represent the final sizing obtained after applying proposed approach II to the power gated FA cell.

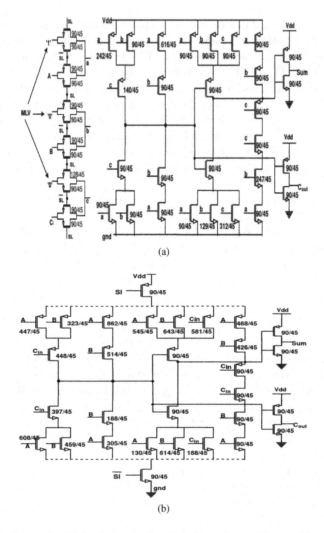

Fig. 4. Full adder cell with final obtained optimal transistor sizing at 45 nm technology (a) Using approach I (with IVC) (b) Using approach II (with PG).

3.2 For 32 nm Technology

The proposed approach is also applied on 28-T full adder for 32 nm technology node and obtained transistor sizing is shown in Fig. 5. Figure 5(a) shows final transistor sizing obtained from approach I, which is written across each transistor and the MLV obtained for such circuit is '100' which has been applied to it using transmission gate. Whereas Fig. 5(b) shows final sizing obtained after applying proposed approach II to power-gated FA cell.

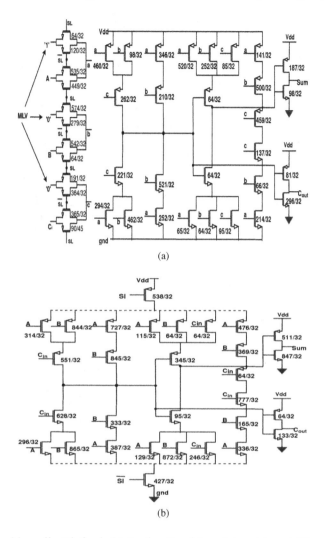

Fig. 5. Full adder cell with final obtained optimal transistor sizing at 32 nm technology (a) Using approach I (with IVC) (b) Using approach II (with PG).

3.3 For 22 nm Technology

Figure 6 represents final transistor sizing obtained after applying proposed approach on 22 nm FA cell. Here MLV obtained is '111' which has been applied to FA using approach I as shown in Fig. 6(a). Whereas Fig. 6(b) shows final transistor sizing obtained after applying proposed approach II on power gated FA cell.

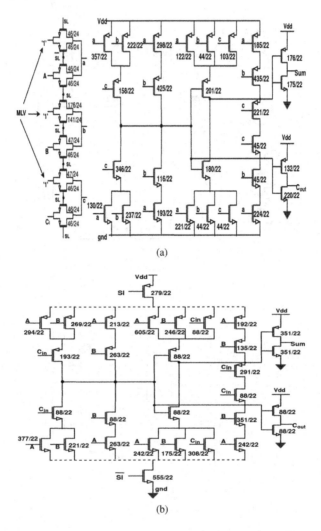

Fig. 6. Full adder cell with final obtained optimal transistor sizing at 22 nm technology (a) Using approach I (with IVC) (b) Using approach II (with PG).

4   Simulation Results

Table 1 shows the leakage, delay and area obtained by applying the proposed approaches at NOC on full adder cell. These performance's results are obtained at corresponding transistor sizings which are as shown in Figs. 4, 5 and 6. The sizing of nominal full adder cell is given in Fig. 3, which has been taken from [13]. From Table 1, The percentage leakage reduction in standby mode for 45 nm,

Table 1. Standby mode leakage, delay and area obtained.

Technology used	Full adder type	Standby leakage (uW)	Delay (ps)	Total area (10e–15 sq.mt.)
45 nm	Nominal	3.08	11.8	753.3
	Approach l (with IVC)	0.71	11.3	215.7
	Approach ll (with PG)	0.06	13.3	415.1
32 nm	Nominal	3.35	10.05	380.9
	Approach l (with IVC)	2.4	11.3	327.9
	Approach ll (with PG)	0.81	11.8	390.6
22 nm	Nominal	4.51	8.68	180.0
	Approach l (with IVC)	3.01	9.2	129.8
	Approach ll (with PG)	0.17	8.72	156.6

32 nm, 22 nm for IVC approach is 77%, 28.3%, 33.2% respectively and that for PG approach is around 97.4%, 75.8%, 96.2% respectively. It is also clear from Table 1 that with some penalty to the delay, the leakage, as well as area used both are reduced significantly. In Table 1, It need to be noted that with proposed approach I both leakage and delay for 45 nm technology has been reduced by 77% and 4.2%. The Proposed method is also tested to prove It's functionality as well as It's efficiency on some large applications of full adder such as 32-bit ripple carry adder, 32-bit arithmetic and logic unit (ALU), 32-bit carry select adder and 32-bit carry skip adder and compared the results for different technology nodes as shown in Fig. 7. Since we have three inputs in FA cell, thus we check for all 8 combinations ie. from 000 to 111 to find input vector with minimum leakage. For a circuit with many inputs such as 32-bit ALU, we take random 1000 or more samples.

The time taken to complete the HSPICE simulation of full adder cell for single technology node is around three hours for 400 iterations of the mentioned algorithm using 12 core, 32 GB RAM Cent-OS machine.

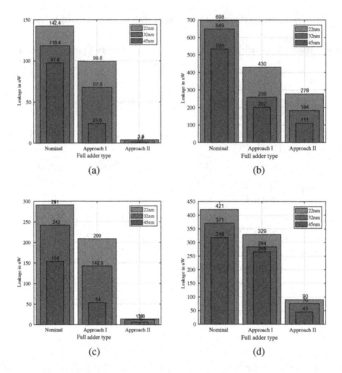

Fig. 7. Leakage comparison of nominal values versus optimal leakage obtained from proposed approaches at 45 nm, 32 nm, 22 nm technology for (a) 32 bit Ripple carry adder. (b) 32 bit ALU. (c) 32 bit Carry select adder. (d) 32 bit Carry skip adder.

5 Conclusion and Future Research

In this paper we have proposed the design approach to find the optimal transistor sizing of the 28-T full adder cell and it's applications for different technology nodes and at different operating conditions. The standby mode leakage has been reduced up to 97% with some penalty on delay in few cases and reduced area up to 71%.

The future work may include considering the process variation also into account so as to make the device more robust and improve circuit's performance. The functioning of the proposed approach including evolutionary and other algorithms which can converges to global minimum for advanced VLSI technologies, like SOI, SOS and FINFETs are inevitable.

References

1. Deepaksubramanyan, B.S., Nunez, A.: Analysis of subthreshold leakage reduction in CMOS digital circuits. In: 2007 50th Midwest Symposium on in Circuits and Systems, MWSCAS 2007, pp. 1400–1404 (2007)
2. Abbas, Z., Olivieri, M.: Impact of technology scaling on leakage power in nano-scale bulk CMOS digital standard cells. Microelectron. J. **45**(2), 179–195 (2014)
3. Lee, B.H., Song, S.C., Choi, R., Kirsch, P.: Metal electrode/high-k dielectric gate-stack technology for power management. IEEE Trans. Electron Devices **55**(1), 8–20 (2008)
4. Mukhopadhyay, S., Neau, C., Cakici, R.T., Agarwal, A., Kim, C.H., Roy, K.: Gate leakage reduction for scaled devices using transistor stacking. IEEE Trans. Very Large Scale Integr. Syst. **11**(4), 716–730 (2003)
5. Abdollahi, A., Fallah, F., Pedram, M.: Leakage current reduction in CMOS VLSI circuits by input vector control. IEEE Trans. Very Large Scale Integr. Syst. **12**(2), 140–154 (2004)
6. Roy, K., Mukhopadhyay, S., Mahmoodi-Meimand, H.: Leakage current mechanisms and leakage reduction techniques in deep-submicrometer CMOS circuits. Proc. IEEE **91**(2), 305–327 (2003)
7. Singh, H., Agarwal, K., Sylvester, D., Nowka, K.J.: Enhanced leakage reduction techniques using intermediate strength power gating. IEEE Trans. Very Large Scale Integr. (VLSI) Syst. **15**(11), 1215–1224 (2007)
8. Chinta, V., Kudithipudi, D.: Minimum leakage vector pattern estimation. In: 2007 50th Midwest Symposium on Circuits and Systems, MWSCAS 2007, pp. 1066–1069. IEEE (2007)
9. Singh, A., Gulati, K., Khatri, S.P.: Minimum leakage vector computation using weighted partial MaxSAT. In: 53rd IEEE International Midwest Symposium on Circuits and Systems (MWSCAS), pp. 201–204. IEEE (2010)
10. Yuan, L., Qu, G.: A combined gate replacement and input vector control approach for leakage current reduction. IEEE Trans. Very Large Scale Integr. (VLSI) Syst. **14**(2), 173–182 (2006)
11. Fallah, F., Pedram, M.: Standby and active leakage current control and minimization in CMOS VLSI circuits. IEICE Trans. Electr. **88**(4), 509–519 (2005)
12. Alioto, M., Palumbo, G.: Analysis and comparison on full adder block in submicron technology. IEEE Trans. Very Large Scale Integr. (VLSI) Syst. **10**(6), 806–823 (2002)
13. Abbas, Z., Olivieri, M.: Optimal transistor sizing for maximum yield invariation-aware standard cell design. Int. J. Circ. Theory Appl. **44**(7), 1400–1424 (2016)
14. Abbas, Z., Mastrandrea, A., Olivieri, M.: A voltage-based leakage current calculation scheme and its application to nanoscale mosfet and finfet standard-cell designs. IEEE Trans. Very Large Scale Integr. (VLSI) Syst. **22**(12), 2549–2560 (2014)
15. Man, K.-F., Tang, K.-S., Kwong, S.: Genetic algorithms: concepts and applications [in engineering design]. IEEE Trans. Ind. Electr. **43**(5), 519–534 (1996)
16. Xue, B., Zhang, M., Browne, W.N., Yao, X.: A survey on evolutionary computation approaches to feature selection. IEEE Trans. Evol. Comput. **20**(4), 606–626 (2016)
17. Eberhart, R., Kennedy, J.: A new optimizer using particle swarm theory. In: 1995 Proceedings of the Sixth International Symposium on Micro Machine and Human Science, MHS 1995, pp. 39–43. IEEE (1995)
18. Arasomwan, M.A., Adewumi, A.O.: Improved particle swarm optimization with a collective local unimodal search for continuous optimization problems. Sci. World J. **2014** (2014)
19. Weste, N.H., Harris, D.: CMOS VLSI Design: A Circuits and Systems Perspective. Pearson Education India, New Delhi (2015)

A 31 ppm/°C Pure CMOS Bandgap Reference by Exploiting Beta-Multiplier

R. Nagulapalli[1], K. Hayatleh[1], S. Barker[1], S. Zourob[1], N. Yassine[1], and B. Naresh Kumar Reddy[2(⊠)]

[1] Oxford Brookes University, Wheatley Campus, Oxford OX33 1HX, UK
khayatleh@brookes.ac.uk, raja.cedt@gmail.com
[2] Department of Electronics and Computer Engineering,
K. L. University, Guntur, India
naresh.nitg@gmail.com

Abstract. Often Bandgap Reference performance limits the SNR of the bio-medical transceiver, hence sensitivity. In this paper, conventional beta multiplier has been explored to design a new low voltage pure CMOS bandgap architecture, which avoids op-amps and resistors, hence very less mismatch and area. Line sensitivity has been improved by adding an extra gain stage in the circuit. The circuit implementation of the proposed technique was done in 65 nm TSMC CMOS technology to generate 460 mV output voltage. The minimum operating voltage of the circuit is 650 mV. Post-layout simulation results are as follows, 31 ppm/°C temperature coefficient against temperature variation of $-40°$ to $125°C$, 0.5% regulation against supply variation of $0.65-1$ V and 0.42% PVT variation. Circuit draws 2.3 A current from 650 mV from power-supply. The proposed band gap reference occupies 0.00144 mm^2 silicon area.

Keywords: Bandgap reference · Regulation ·
Temperature coefficient · Micro watt · Bio-medical opamp ·
Monte Carlo

1 Introduction

Ultra-low power temperature independent bandgap voltage reference circuits are very critical for variety of low power biomedical circuits. They must be integrated with complex system on chip (SOC), hence the performance should independent of power supply noise and work under the presence of large thermal gradients. Unfortunately, CMOS scaling demands reduced power supply voltage (V_{DD}) to limit the internal junction electric fields to maintain long term reliability without reducing the threshold voltage (V_{TH}) of the transistor because reduced V_{TH} creates large leakage problem for the digital circuits. Hence voltage reference should work low V_{DD} demanded by the chosen technology node. Though circuit can work at this voltage meeting stringent performance specifications is challenging, because second order effects like Drain Induced Barrier lower, velocity saturation, reverse short channel effects degrades transistors small signal parameters

© Springer Nature Singapore Pte Ltd. 2019
S. Rajaram et al. (Eds.): VDAT 2018, CCIS 892, pp. 100–108, 2019.
https://doi.org/10.1007/978-981-13-5950-7_9

(g_m, g_{ds}). The first bandgap reference has been proposed in BJT technology [2] by adding scaled version of PTAT and CTAT. V_{BE} of a BJT biased with constant current can be expressed as

$$V_{BE} = V_T \ln(1 + I_c/I_s) \tag{1}$$

Where V_T is thermal voltage (KT/q 26 mV), I_C is bias current and I_S is reverse saturation current, which will increase with temperature. From (1) V BE has negative temperature coefficient (-2 mV/0 °C), hence it is Complimentary to Absolute temperature (CTAT) voltage. If two bipolar devices operating at unequal current densities, then difference between their V_{BE} is having PTAT nature, hence it is proportional to absolute temperature (PTAT) voltage.

$$\Delta V_{BE} = V_T \ln n \tag{2}$$

By adding V_{BE} and with a proposer scaling factor we could get first order bandgap reference with very good temperature stability, results $\sim$1.2 V across PVT (equal to silicon bandgap voltage at 0 K). Unfortunately getting good quality BJT devices in CMOS process is very costly, so researchers have been exploiting parasitic vertical PNP devices formed nwell to design bandgap reference circuits [3]. But vertical pnp devices have very poor current gain ($\sim$4) due to the wider base formed by nwell, this will add some error. Due to the fact that V_{BE} is not very linear with $-$ve slope, there have been few higher order bandgaps called curvature compensation [4]. Since the output voltage is $\sim$1.2 V, this architecture can't be used with latest CMOS technologies, for example in 90 nm CMOS technology supply voltage is 1.2 V, but the worst-case voltage could drop below this and 65 nm CMOS will have 1 V power supply voltage. Use of nonstandard devices like DTMOST instead of BJT could potentially achieve less than 1.2 V, but at the cost of low reproducibility, poor portability and poor yield [5]. By using the resistive potential divider, a reference voltage of 0.7 V has been achieved [6], but this has curvature error. A well working sub 1 V bandgap reference with pnp devices has been proposed in [7], which results in high accuracy out of all existing circuits. All above explained circuits comes under BJT based bandgap, which are not power efficient because BJT devices needs high bias current.

Unfortunately, bio-medical and sensor applications, need to run on micro watt power level with low voltage, hence there has been a separate filed of bandgaps which are designed with pure CMOS devices without having requirement of BJT or special devices [8–11]. To minimize the operating voltage, range every one avoided Cascode opamps and current mirrors and biased in the sub-threshold region to carry less than μA currents. Most of the designs are relaying on the fact that threshold voltage of MOS transistor also decreases with temperature, hence this can be used as CTAT. Based on trans-linear principle PTAT has been realized.

Unfortunately, all the designs using Opamps to self-bias the bandgap reference like all pnp based designs, but the opamp draws significant percentage of power budget allocated for the entire bandgap. [8] utilized the so-called beta-multiplier to release the bandgap, but in this design temperature drift of the opamp offset contribute major temperature coefficient error. In the present paper, a modified beta multiplier has been explored [10], which is area efficient compared to original beta-multiplier and a novel bandgap has been proposed to which avoids opamps to get the best power efficiency suitable for biomedical requirements and it is only used MOS transistors and avoids even resistors to further optimize the area.

2 Modified Beta Multiplier

Conventional Beta multiplier [9] shown in Fig. 1(a). It is a self-bias circuit, which generates a constant g m bias and works as follows. By assuming K is ratio of M 2 and M 1 aspect ratio (W/L), the bias current can be expressed as follows.

$$I_{M2} = \frac{2}{\mu_n C_{ox}(W/L)_2} \frac{1}{R_B^2} \left(1 - \sqrt{\frac{\beta_1}{\beta_2}}\right)^2 \qquad (3)$$

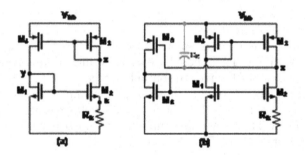

Fig. 1. Beta multiplier (a) Conventional (b) Proposed in [10].

Where μ_n is the electron mobility, Cox is the gate capacitance of the unit square transistor. General choice of transistor ratio is 4 times, hence VGS2 is half of the VGS1. Hence the voltage across resistor is as follows.

$$V_{GS1} - V_{GS2} = IR_B \ and \ \frac{V_{ov}}{2} = IR_B \ hence \ g_m = \frac{1}{R_B} \qquad (4)$$

Fundamentally this is a negative feedback system, where M_2 and M_1 current is monitored and adjusted M1 gate voltage in appropriate way [9]. The transfer function of the loop can be expressed as follows (Fig. 3)

$$\frac{g_{m2}(1 + SR_BC_B)g_{m4}}{(1 + g_{m2}R_B + SR_BC_B)(1 + \frac{SC_X}{g_{m3}})(1 + \frac{SC_Y}{g_{m3}})g_{m3}g_{m1}} \qquad (5)$$

Where gm, C is the trans-conductance of respective transistor, capacitance of respective node. Interesting observation from (2) is the DC gain is lesser than 1, but unfortunately there is zero frequency at $1/R_BC_B$ which will increase the

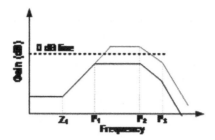

Fig. 2. Loop gain frequency response.

gain with frequency. The danger is if gain increases above unity, this may cause serious oscillations in the step response. The model bode plot has been shown in Fig. 2, as it shows if P1 higher than required value, gain will increase 1 and becomes stable. The next dominate pole g_{m2}/C_B so to prevent the gain increases the above unity, this pole needs to be at as low frequency as possible, hence C_B needs to increase. This circuit contains all low impedance nodes so to compensate the circuit, every node requires much larger compensation capacitor. To solve this problem Fig. 1(b) has been proposed, which basically works on the same principle but it compares M1 current with M2 current (on the contrary in the Fig. 1(a)) and adjusted the gate of M1, but to enable the negative feedback a common source (CS) amplifier has been added to provide the inversion. The main advantage of this method is, there is a clear high impedance at drain of M3 which enables frequency compensation with small capacitor. A capacitor CC been added from node x to supply such that any high frequency noise will be suppressed by keeping V_{gs5} constant. Since it is a self-bias circuit, a start-up circuit will be needed to avoid zero current operating point, which wasn't shown in these figures. The bias current in the circuit behaves like PTAT, because to keep gm constant with respect to temperature, current needs to increase to compensate the mobility (μ_n) degradation. The voltage across the resistor also will be PTAT.

3   Proposed Technique

As explained in the introduction, the principle of bandgap reference is to add the scaled version of PTAT and CTAT voltages. The threshold voltage (VTH) of the Transistor will decrease with the temperature with $-0.3\,\mathrm{mV}/0\,°\mathrm{C}$ coefficient, so this will be used as CTAT voltage. Figure 2 describes the proposed circuit including the startup circuit. $M_1 - M_6$ forms the Beta-Multiplier and MB3 forms the resistor, it's drain voltage can be expressed as follows

$$V_{DSB3} = V_Y = V_{GS1} - V_{GS2} = \eta V_T \ln\left(\frac{\beta_1}{\beta_2}\right) \tag{6}$$

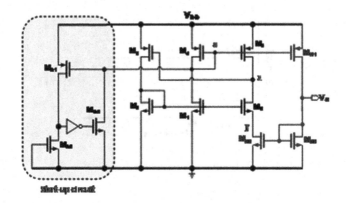

Fig. 3. Proposed differential pair based VGA.

From (3), vds is a having PTAT nature and current also has PTAT nature. By mirroring this current through M_3, M_{B1}, M_{B2}, the resistance of triode region biased MB3 can be control. The transistor currents can be expressed as follows

$$I_{dB2} = \frac{\beta_{B2}}{2}(V_o - V_{th})^2 \tag{7}$$

$$I_{dB3} = \frac{\beta_{B2}}{2}\left(2(V_o - V_{th}) - \frac{V_y^2}{2}\right) \tag{8}$$

By combining (4) and (5) we can express output voltage as follows.

$$V_o = V_{th} + V_y\left(\frac{\beta_{B3}}{\beta_{B2}} + \sqrt{\left(\frac{\beta_{B3}}{\beta_{B2}}\right)^2 - \frac{\beta_{B3}}{\beta_{B2}}}\right) \tag{9}$$

By combining (3) and (6) we can deduce the bandgap reference voltage as follows.

$$V_o = V_{th} + \eta V_T \ln\left(\frac{\beta_2}{\beta_1}\right)\left(\frac{\beta_{B3}}{\beta_{B2}} + \sqrt{\left(\frac{\beta_{B3}}{\beta_{B2}}\right)^2 - \frac{\beta_{B3}}{\beta_{B2}}}\right) \tag{10}$$

First term in the above equation represents CTAT and second term represents PTAT. Interesting observation is PTAT voltage scaling term is function of aspect ratio of transistors, which will have absolute minimum PVT and mismatch sensitive. This is one of the advantage compared to [8,12]. To find relation between the device sizes for the minimum temperature dependence of the output, derivative of (7) should be equal to zero. By doing this, the following condition for the devices aspect ratios can be derived.

$$\ln\left(\frac{\beta_2}{\beta_1}\right)\left(\frac{\beta_{B3}}{\beta_{B2}} + \sqrt{\left(\frac{\beta_{B3}}{\beta_{B2}}\right)^2 - \frac{\beta_{B3}}{\beta_{B2}}}\right) = 2.6627 \tag{11}$$

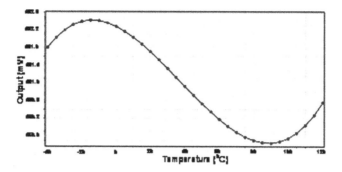

Fig. 4. Temperature stability of the reference voltage.

Device sizes needs to be adjusted per (8) for minimal temperature sensitivity and the output voltage is approximately close to sum of V_{th} and V_{ov} of the M_{B2}. The minimum operating voltage of the circuit limited by the transistor stack MB2, MB1, the required voltage is $V_{th} + V_{ov} + V_{dsat}$, which will be in the order of 400–500 mV, but in the present design we have allocated much higher voltage for the VDS of MB2. This can even be go down if anyone can use low voltage devices, in the present design we are limiting multiple flavour of the devices to save the mask cost. In the previously proposed architectures, opamp is the one which is limiting the minimum operating voltage to the high value ∼0.8 V. The design uses minimum channel length devices in the beta multiplier to easily adopt and scale for other technologies.

4 Simulation Results

To demonstrate the functionality of the bandgap, a prototype has been developed in 65 nm CMOS Technology. The minimum supply voltage at which the circuit could work without breaking its performance is 0.65 V, the nominal designed output reference voltage is 461 mV at 650 °C. The circuit draws 2.3 μA current at room temperature.

Figure 4 shows the temperature sensitivity of the reference voltage, it's peak to peak variation is 2.8 mV while temperature changes from −40° to 120 °C. The temperature sensitivity is 31 ppm/°C which can be calculated as follows.

$$PPM/°C = \frac{V_{0ma} - V_{0min}}{V_{0mean}(T_{max} - T_{min})}10^6 \qquad (12)$$

Figure 5 shows the reference voltage variations across Process, Voltage, temperature (PVT) corners results 11.2 mV variation with a mean of 461 mV, means 2.42% variation.

As explained in the introduction, a low voltage operation and insensitivity to the supply variation is the ultimate goals of the present days reference circuits, Fig. 6 shows the line regulation at room temperature. Circuit works with full performance starting from 1 V to minimum of 650 mV, below this voltage output

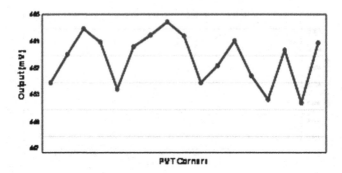

Fig. 5. PVT variation of the reference voltage.

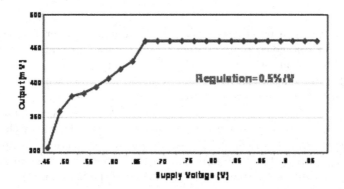

Fig. 6. Line regulation of the reference voltage.

voltage drops significantly. The change in the output voltage is 0.806 mV while supply drops from 1 V to 650 mV hence the line regulation is ~0.5 V. Compared to state of art [8, 12] this is a tremendous improvement, this is due to the extra loop gain contribution by $M_5, M_6(g_{m5}/g_{m6})$ to the beta multiplier. This extra loop gain will also improve frequency response of the power supply rejection as well at low frequency (up to the loop bandwidth frequency) [11]. Batch production quality is the final goal for analog circuits, because there will be lot of mismatch among the wafers and bandgap circuit from each wafer should perform with-in the specification limits. To evaluate this, a 500-point Monte Carlo simulation were performed. Figure 7 shows the histogram of the output voltage, the mean (μ) of Vout is 460.5 mV and its standard deviation (σ) is 1.9 mV, means a coefficient of variation (σ/μ) of 0.42%. The predicted reason for this better performance is lack of opamps and resistors, generally opamp offset be the most dominate contributor and resistors makes the circuit very big, hence by avoiding the both opamp and resistors makes this architecture is insensitive to the process mismatch. Figure 8 shows the layout of the reference proposed reference, it occupies 1440 μm², most of the area occupied by the de-capacitor on node

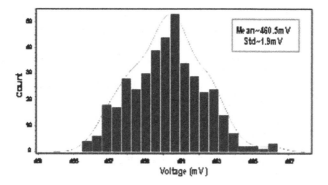

Fig. 7. Mismatch of the reference voltage.

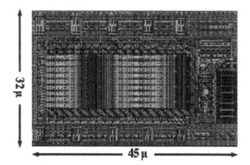

Fig. 8. Layout of the bandgap reference.

a and dummy transistors surrounding the main active devices to minimize the mismatch contribution.

5   Conclusion

In this paper an opamp and resistor less pure CMOS, low voltage micro watt bandgap reference proposed. Circuit has been achieved 31 ppm temperature coefficient and 2.4% PVT sensitivity. 2.3 W is the total power consumption at room temperature and suitable for bio-medical and wearable applications.

References

1. De Vita, G., Iannaccone, G.: A sub-1-V, 10 ppm/°C, nanopower voltage reference generator. IEEE J. Solid-State Circuits **42**(7), 1536–1542 (2007)
2. Brokaw, A.P.: A simple three-terminal IC bandgap reference. IEEE J. Solid-State Circuits **SC–9**, 388–393 (1974)
3. Razavi, B.: Design of Analog CMOS Integrated Circuits. McGraw-Hill, New Work (2001)

4. Malcovati, P., Maloberti, F., Fiocchi, C., Pruzzi, M.: Curvature-compensated BiC-MOS bandgap with 1-V supply voltage. IEEE J. Solid State Circuits **36**, 1076–1081 (2001)
5. Annema, A.-J.: Low-power bandgap references feature DTMOSTs. IEEE J. Solid-State Circuits **34**, 949–955 (1999)
6. Neuteboom, N., Kup, B.M.J., Janssens, J.: A DSP-based hearing instrument IC. IEEE J. Solid-State Circuits **32**, 1790–1806 (1997)
7. Banba, H., et al.: A CMOS bandgap reference circuit with sub-1-V operation. IEEE J. Solid-State Circuits **34**, 670–674 (1999)
8. Nagulapalli, R., Hayatleh, K.: A 0.6 V MOS-only voltage reference for biomedical applications with 40 ppm/°C temperature drift. J. Circuits Syst. Comput. **27**(8), 1850128 (2018)
9. Nagulapalli, R., et al.: J. Circuit Syst. Comp. https://doi.org/10.1142/S0218126618501281
10. Liu, S., Baker, R.J.: Process and temperature performance of a CMOS beta-multiplier voltage reference. In: Proceedings of IEEE MWSCAS 1998, pp. 33–36, August 1998
11. Nicolson, S., Khoman, P.: Improvements in biasing and compensation of CMOS opamps. In: Proceedings of ISCAS, vol. 1, pp. 23–26, May 2004
12. Sansen, W.M.: Analog Design Essentials. Springer, Boston (2006). https://doi.org/10.1007/b135984. ISBN 978-0-387-25746-4
13. Nagulapalli, R., Hayatleh, K., Barker, S., Zourob, S., Yassine, N., Sridevi, S.: A microwatt low voltage bandgap reference for bio-medical applications. In: 2017 International Conference on Recent Advances in Electronics and Communication Technology (ICRAECT), pp. 61–65 (2017)

Supply and Temperature Independent Voltage Reference Circuit in Subthreshold Region

Vineysarathi Kokkula$^{(\boxtimes)}$, Akash Joshi, and Raghvendra Deshmukh

Center for VLSI and Nanotechnology, Visvesvaraya National Institute of Technology, Nagpur 440010, Maharashtra, India
viney.sarathi6@gmail.com, akash.joshi@students.vnit.ac.in, rbdeshmukh@ece.vnit.ac.in

Abstract. This paper presents a voltage reference circuit, operating in sub-threshold region. The circuit is made tolerant to temperature and supply variations. The temperature tolerant behaviour of reference circuit is achieved by incorporating the difference of gate to source voltages of high Vth and standard Vth transistors. The bias voltage for the reference circuit is generated using a bias circuit and made temperature insensitive using a variable load with digital trimming technique. The circuit is simulated with 0.18 μm CMOS models. Reference voltage variation with supply is 6.25 mV/V, variation with temperature is 9.37 uV/C in 0 °C to 100 °C temperature sweep. The power consumption is 50 nW at room temperature with 0.8 V as supply voltage. Power Supply Rejection Ratio (PSRR) of the proposed circuit at room temperature with 0.8 V supply is simulated to be −72 dB at 100 Hz and −23 dB at 1 MHz.

Keywords: Reference voltage · Subthreshold · CMOS

1 Introduction

Voltage reference circuit has a wide range of applications like Analog to Digital Converters (ADCs), switched capacitor circuits, DRAM, flash memory and few more. It is one of the important analog blocks in most of the chips. Its power consumption, stability and performance effect the overall performance of the chip. Considering the rapid growth in low power applications and electronics moving towards power-autonomous ICs, there is a need of voltage reference circuit to be designed with ultra low power consumption with better performance. However, the bandgap reference (BGR) circuits need very high value of resistors to allow the circuit to have nano amperes of current. So BGR circuits are not preferable. Analog blocks always stay in on condition once the power of the chip is on. They consume a lot of standby power.

© Springer Nature Singapore Pte Ltd. 2019
S. Rajaram et al. (Eds.): VDAT 2018, CCIS 892, pp. 109–120, 2019.
https://doi.org/10.1007/978-981-13-5950-7_10

Voltage References are mainly classified in to two types. Bandgap references (BGR) and MOSFET-Only references. The use of BGR restrict the minimum supply required to atleast 1 V. This limits usage of BGRs to applications with sub-1 V supply. In some MOSFET-Only references, the difference of gate to source voltages of high Vth and low vth transistors is used to generate a constant voltage [3,7,9]. The other important technique to generate MOSFET-only reference is by averaging CTAT and PTAT voltages to generate a ZTC reference [1,4,6].

There are wide ranges of Voltage References designed in the literature [1–10]. Temperature and Supply insensitive BGR designs are mentioned [2,10]. These BGR designs are settled in terms of performance but these are not preferred because of the reasons mentioned earlier. Threshold voltage usually has negative temperature coefficient (NTC) and thermal voltage (V_T) has positive temperature coefficient (PTC). The former concept is utilised to generate compliment-to-absolute-temperature (CTAT) voltage and the later helps in designing proportional-to-absolute-temperature (PTAT) voltage as mentioned in [1,4,6]. In this situation, to get a zero temperature coefficient voltage reference, either an averaging circuit is implemented as in [4,6] or a method of PTAT imposing on CTAT is used [1]. Native nMOS transistors are used as current sources and then a stack of one or more pMOS transistors are used to generate reference voltage in [3]. The generated reference voltage is scalable depending on the number of pMOS transistors in the stack. But this stack is limiting the minimum supply to be used.

In this work, the concept of superposition of threshold voltage property and thermal voltage property as in [7] is used to get zero temperature coefficient reference voltage. The circuit is made to operate in subthreshold region such that the power consumption is in nano watts and no resistors are used to avoid occupying large area. Our idea in implementing this circuit is to consume low power, occupy small area and have reference voltage insensitive to supply and temperature variations. This proposed design is better in terms of PSRR, temperature coefficient and area compared to other designs mentioned in references.

The next section of this paper goes through working principle and explains different blocks of the design. It explains the expressions involved in the design. It also gives an idea how PTAT and CTAT parameters are handled to make the design temperature tolerant. In Sect. 3, simulation results are presented. In Sect. 4, layout of the biasing circuit and reference circuit are illustrated. Performance comparison is presented in Sect. 5, followed by conclusion in Sect. 6.

2 Circuit Description and Working

In this design, a biasing circuit and a reference circuit are used to get a constant reference voltage with respect to supply variations. A critical load transistor in the biasing circuit is trimmed digitally to get the biasing voltage tolerant to temperature variations. The switching automation is achieved using a combination of ring oscillator, counter and a digital switching circuit. It is explained in the following subsections how this circuit is going to make the reference voltage constant with respect to supply and temperature variations.

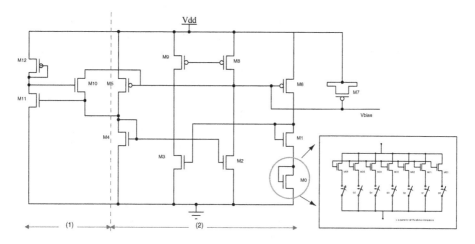

Fig. 1. Biasing circuit

2.1 Biasing Circuit

In Fig. 1 shows the biasing circuit. It basically consists of two parts. Part (1) is the startup circuit. Part (2) is a beta multiplier circuit with negative feedback. This start up circuit switches off once the normal functioning of part (2) is ensured. This will reduce the unnecessary power consumption. At room temperature *Vbias* node provides biasing voltage of 548.5 mV approximately. In the above circuit, if the temperature changes, the current flowing through beta multiplier changes, which in turn changes the biasing voltage *Vbias*. So, we found a critical load in the circuit, whose dimentions can change the current in the circuit accordingly. That critical transistor is found out to be **M0**. The key point here is if load is made variable which can be tuned or trimmed, using that load the current in beta multiplier is varied such that *Vbias* is always constant. So, instead of using a single transistor **M0**, a transistor matrix is used as shown in Fig. 1. Now, switching of this matrix is done automatically when temperature changes, using a ring oscillator and digital switching circuit. The detailed description of automatic switching is explained in next subsections. This temperature variation tolerant bias voltage is needed to bias a current source in the reference voltage circuit, which is also described in the next section. Simulations of the above circuit are performed with temperature varying from 0 °C to 100 °C and Vbias is plotted and is shown in Simulations section.

2.2 Reference Circuit

Figure 2 represents Voltage Reference circuit. In the figure *Vbias* is taken from biasing circuit shown in Fig. 1. In the reference circuit, transistor M0 acts like a current source. M1 is a standard threshold voltage (Vth) transistor and M2, M3 are high vth transistors. The usage of high Vth transistor is because of the reason that threshold voltage of that transistor has more negative temperature coefficient, compared to standard vth transistor. The reason for using high Vth transistor would be more clear after the mathematical analysis. The reference voltage achieved from this design is found out to be 194.6 mV approximately.

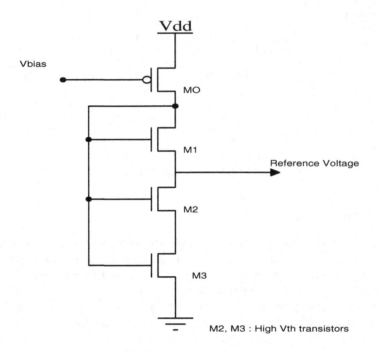

Fig. 2. Reference voltage circuit

The following mathematical analysis proves how the output remains insensitive with respect to temperature.

The equation of drain current flowing in a MOSFET is given by

$$I_d = I_s \left[\exp(V_{gs} - V_{th})/n\phi_t\right] (1 - \exp(-V_{ds}/n\phi_t)) \tag{1}$$

where Is is sub-threshold saturation current, n is sub-threshold slope factor and ϕ_t is thermal voltage.

Now we can write current flowing through transistor M1 as

$$I_{ref} = I_{s1} \left[\exp(V_{gs1} - V_{th1})/n\phi_t\right] \tag{2}$$

We have neglected Vds term because from simulations we observed that it is greater than $4\phi_t$. In that case the term approaches 1 with 2% error. Current flowing through transistor M3 can be written as

$$I_{ref} = I_{s3} \left[\exp(V_{gs3} - V_{th3})/n\phi_t\right] (1 - \exp(-V_{ds3}/n\phi_t)) \tag{3}$$

We can't neglect Vds term here because it is well below $4\phi_t$, hence the current is sensitive to it's variation.

From Fig. 2, the output voltage **Vref** can be written as

$$V_{ref} = V_{gs3} - V_{gs1} \tag{4}$$

On solving Eqs. (2) and (3) to get Vref as mentioned in Eq. (4)

$$V_{ref} = (V_{th3} - V_{th1}) + n\phi_t \ln(I_{s1}/I_{s3}) + n\phi_t \ln(1 - \exp(-Vds3/n\phi_t)) \tag{5}$$

The term $(V_{th3} - V_{th1})$ has -ve slope with increasing temperature because V_{th3} is the threshold voltage of high V_{th} transistor. The remainder of the equation has positive slope with increasing temperature. With proper adjustment of widths of M1, M2 and M3 we can get constant voltage reference with respect to temperature.

The simulation results of reference circuit with supply and temperature variations are discussed in simulations section.

2.3   Ring Oscillator

Frequency of the ring oscillator in Fig. 3 at room temperature is 165.4 KHz. The gate to source voltage of MOS transistors in ring oscillator is high (i.e.0.8 V), then in that case if the temperature increases the current through individual transistor decreases. This causes increase in raise and fall delays. Concluding, as the temperature increases frequency of the ring oscillator decreases. The variation of frequency with temperature is shown in Fig. 4.

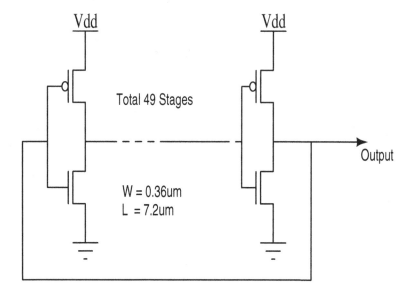

Fig. 3. Ring oscillator

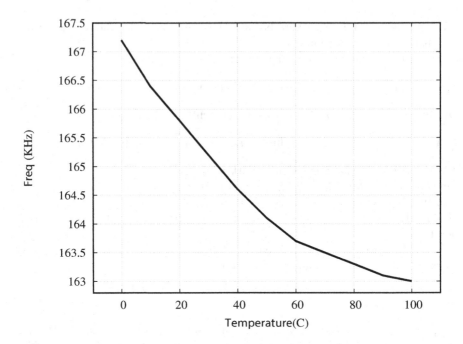

Fig. 4. Frequency of ring oscillator with temperature

This concept of frequency varying with temperature is utilised to detect temperature changes in the ambience of reference circuit. Based on these changes in temperature, width of M0 in biasing circuit will be trimmed automatically by using a counter and a digital switching circuit.

2.4   Counter and Digital Switching Circuit

A counter is designed such that it is clocked from the output of ring oscillator. Then the change in temperature changes clock frequency and hence the count value. The counter designed is of 11-bit. The size of the counter is chosen according to the setup convenience. This count value will be given to a digital switching circuit in the next stage. Based on count value the transistor will be digitally switched to keep the bias voltage Vbias constant.

2.5   Block Diagram

The block diagram is shown in Fig. 5. The block diagram visualizes the mechanism used to achieve constant voltage reference. The arrow marks in the block diagram represents the flow of control. *Reset* and *Enable* signals are provided externally depending upon the frequency of ring oscillator.

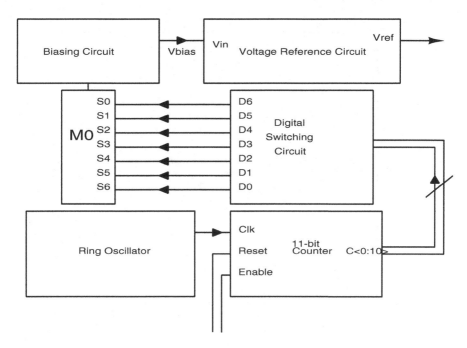

Fig. 5. Block diagram of whole setup

3   Simulations and Results

3.1   Biasing Circuit

Biasing voltage is made insensitive to temperature variations using automatic trimming of transistor M0 in biasing circuit, which provides constant bias to a current source in reference circuit placed next to it. The bias voltage with variation in temperature is plotted and shown in Fig. 6.

3.2   Reference Circuit

From simulation results of reference circuit shown in Fig. 7, we can observe that reference voltage is 194.42 mV and is almost constant for a supply range of 560 mV to 800 mV. The variation is found out to be 6.25 mV/V. From Fig. 8, we can observe that reference voltage is almost constant with respect to temperature variations. The temperature is swept from 0 °C to 100 °C. The variation is found out to be 7.83 uV/°C in 0 °C to 60 °C sweep and it is 11.7 uV/°C in 60 °C to 100 °C sweep.

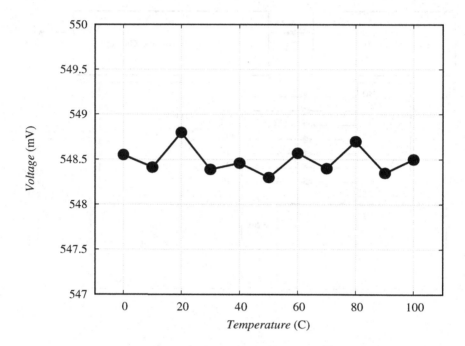

Fig. 6. Vbias with respect to temperature

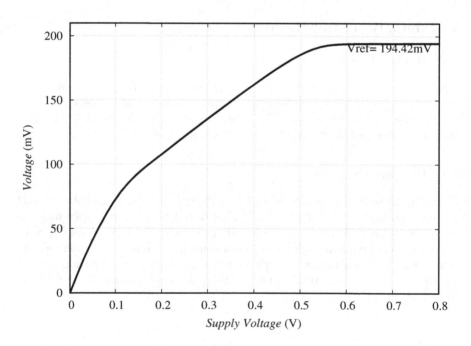

Fig. 7. Reference voltage variation with Supply

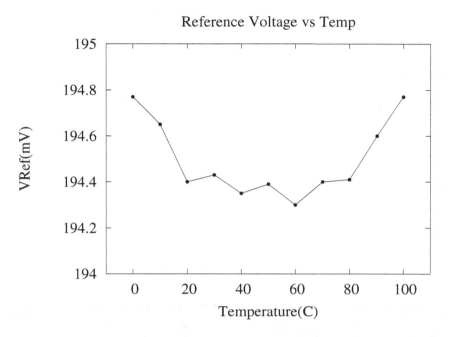

Fig. 8. Reference voltage variation with Temperature

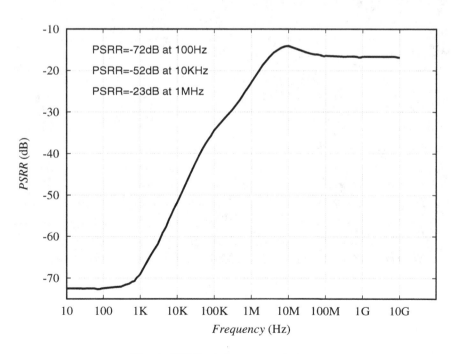

Fig. 9. PSRR of the proposed circuit

PSRR: PSRR of the proposed circuit is calculated and is found out to be −72 dB at 100 Hz and −23 dB at 1 MHz. This is calculated at room temperature with 0.8 V as supply voltage. The figure −72 dB is sufficient to show it is suppressing the fluctuations in supply reaching the output. PSRR variation with frequency is shown in Fig. 9.

Power Consumption: For a supply voltage of 0.8 V and temperature maintained at 27 °C, the total current flowing is found out to be 72 nA. Power consumption is 57 nW. The power consumption in the range of tens of nano watts is achieved due to the fact that circuit is operating in subthreshold region.

4 Layout

Layout of the biasing circuit, reference circuit along with trimming circuit is shown in Fig. 10. These trimming circuit switches have buffers to avoid improper switching. The area of the proposed layout is (47.465 * 36.81) um². Post layout simulations are verified with schematic simulations.

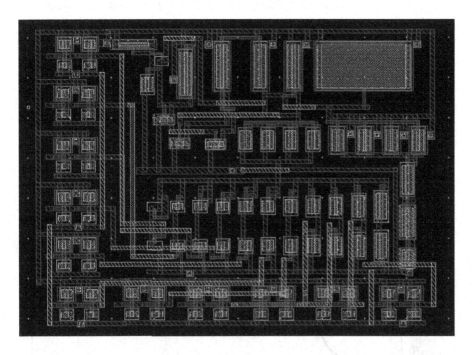

Fig. 10. Layout of the Biasing circuit and Reference circuit along with buffers

Table 1. Comparision with different works

Parameter	This work	Ref. [1]	Ref. [2]	Ref. [3]	Ref. [4]	Ref. [8]	Ref. [9]
$Technology$	180 nm	180 nm	350 nm	180 nm	180 nm	350 nm	180 nm
$Reference Voltage (mV)$	194.4	755	1.17(V)	1.25(V)	350.8	745	118.46
$Temp.Coeff.(PPM/C)$	9.37(avg)	34	12.75	8 to 53	76	15(avg)	63.6
$Supply range (V)$	$0.56 - 1.8$	$1.1 - 1.8$	NA	$1.4 - 3.6$	$0.85 - 1.8$	$1.4 - 3$	$0.45 - 1.8$
$Area(mm^2)$	0.0017	0.0598	0.487	0.0025	0.023	0.055	0.012
$Power(nW)$	57	4.6	29	35e − 3	120 @ 0.8 V	300	14.6
$PSRR(dB)@100\,Hz$	−72	−9 @10 Hz	NA	−41	−65	−45	−44.2
$Temp.range(in C)$	0 to 100	−15 to 140	−10 to 110	0 to 100	0 to 75	−20 to 80	−40 to 125
$Variaton with supply$	6.25 mV/V	NA	2.3 mV/V	4.34 mV/V	0.54 mV/V	NA	1.2 mV/V
$Usage of resistors$	No	No	Yes	No	No	No	No

5   Performance Comparision

This work is compared with works done in [1–4, 8, 9]. A reference voltage of 755 mV is achieved in [1], but the problem with that design is that it needs a minimum supply voltage of 1.1 V. The reference voltage in [2], has a very small TC of 12.75 mV/C and low power consumption 29 nW. But this design is occupying area of 0.487 mm², which is almost 100 times the area used in our design. Moreover, this is a BGR reference circuit which limits minimum supply voltage also. Reference voltage of 1.25 mV and very small area of 0.0025 mm² is achieved through the work [3], but the reference value itself keeping restriction on minimum supply voltage. The work presented in [4] has the least variation with respect to changes in supply voltage, but it needs manual switching and passive capacitors internally and externally to be connected. The external capacitor to be connected is a very high value capacitor. Apart from this it is discrete component and occupies high area. Reference voltage is 740 mV in [8], where the design requires minimum supply voltage of 1.4 V. For [8], there are 5 transistors assumed to have no mismatch. Very low Power consumption and very good line regulation of 14.6 nW and 1.2 mV/V respectively, is achieved through the design [9]. Minimum supply of only 0.45 V is enough for [9]. But design considerations are complex in that work. Maintaining transistor, M5 in their design, in saturation is having a constraint. There is a body bias Vb1 which can't be too large or too small. Each has their own effect on performance (Table 1).

6   Conclusion

In this work, we proposed a Voltage Reference circuit which is tolerant to supply variations and temperature variations. The circuit is designed in CMOS 0.18 μm technology. An automatic digital trimming technique is incorporated to maintain constant reference voltage with respect to temperature variations. The design is verified with schematic and post layout simulations. A power consumption of 50 nW is more encouraging for power autonomous applications. Temperature coefficient of 9.37 ppm/°C and a PSRR of −72 dB ensure good performance of the design.

References

1. Liu, Y., Zhan, C., Wang, L.: An ultralow power subthreshold CMOS voltage reference without requiring resistors or BJTs. IEEE Trans. Very Large Scale Integr. (VLSI) Syst. **26**(1), 201–205 (2018)
2. Lee, J.M., et al.: 5.7 A 29nW bandgap reference circuit. In: IEEE International Solid-State Circuits Conference - (ISSCC) Digest of Technical Papers, San Francisco, CA, pp. 1–3 (2015)
3. Lee, I., Sylvester, D., Blaauw, D.: A subthreshold voltage reference with scalable output voltage for low-power IoT systems. IEEE J. Solid-State Circ. **52**(5), 1443–1449 (2017)
4. Chatterjee, B., Modak, N., Amaravati, A., Mistry, D., Das, D.M., Baghini, M.S.: A sub-1 V, 120 nW, PVT-variation tolerant, tunable, and scalable voltage reference with 60-dB PSNA. IEEE Trans. Nanotechnol. **16**(3), 406–410 (2017)
5. Albano, D., Crupi, F., Cucchi, F., Iannaccone, G.: A sub- kT/q voltage reference operating at 150 mV. IEEE Trans. Very Large Scale Integr. (VLSI) Syst. **23**(8), 1547–1551 (2015)
6. Anvesha, A., Baghini, M.S.: A sub-1V 32nA process, voltage and temperature invariant voltage reference circuit. In: 2013 26th International Conference on VLSI Design and 2013 12th International Conference on Embedded Systems, Pune, pp. 136–141 (2013)
7. Zeng, Y., Huang, Y., Zeng, M., Tan, H.-Z.: A 1.2nW, 2.1ppm/∘C subthreshold CMOS voltage reference without resistors. In: IET International Conference on Information and Communications Technologies (IETICT 2013), Beijing, pp. 112–116 (2013)
8. Ueno, K., Hirose, T., Asai, T., Amemiya, Y.: A 300 nW, 15 ppm/C, 20 ppm/V CMOS voltage reference circuit consisting of subthreshold MOSFETs. IEEE J. Solid-State Circ. **44**(7), 2047–2054 (2009)
9. Wang, Y., Zhu, Z., Yao, J., Yang, Y.: A 0.45-V, 14.6-nW CMOS subthreshold voltage reference with no resistors and no BJTs. IEEE Trans. Circ. Syst. II: Expr. Briefs **62**(7), 621–625 (2015)
10. Klimach, H., Costa, A.L.T., Monteiro, M.F.C., Bampi, S.: Resistorless switched-capacitor bandgap voltage reference with low sensitivity to process variations. Electron. Lett. **49**(23), 1448–1449 (2013)

CMOS Implementations of Rectified Linear Activation Function

P. Priyanka$^{(\boxtimes)}$, G. K. Nisarga, and S. Raghuram

Department of ECE, Ramaiah Institute of Technology, Bengaluru 560054, India
priyankaplnlll@gmail.com,
nishakrishnamurthy426@gmail.com, raghuram@msrit.edu

Abstract. Deep Neural Networks have become an increasingly favourite choice for a variety of machine learning tasks. Two important components are largely responsible for this success, improved neural network functionalities, and availability of suitable hardware for training large complex networks. Using these types of novel networks and functions, Deep Neural Networks have been shown to be very highly efficient for various classification tasks. As the next level of optimization, dedicated ASIC and FPGA ICs are being developed, to realize Deep Neural Networks. This provides an additional level of performance optimization beyond traditional software-based implementations. Towards this direction, in this work, we have developed CMOS circuits for realizing the highly popular Rectified Linear (ReLu) activation function. The ReLu activation function has largely replaced the traditional sigmoid activation function due to better learning rates and reduced computational requirements. With dedicated CMOS implementations of such functions, we get better operating speed with lower power consumption, leading to improved real-time implementations of classification tasks.

Keywords: Deep Neural Networks · CMOS ·
Rectified Linear Activation Function · Neuromorphic circuits

1 Introduction

The publication of the results of the Imagenet challenge using Deep Convolutional Neural Networks has given a boost to the use of Neural Networks in classification tasks. The challenge required the classification of 1.2 million images into 1,000 different classes. While existing methods showed Top-5 error rates were 28.2% and 25.6%, the approach used in [1] reduced the error rate significantly to 17%. There were various novelties in [1], and the eventual empirical proof of their effectiveness has lead to their widespread adoption in different types of classification and recognition tasks. A significant novelty was the use of a new type of Neural Network (NN) layer, called the Convolutional layer. This layer shares the same set of weights across the whole input, thereby extracting a certain feature anywhere in the input. Further, multiple features (i.e., set of weights) are extracted at each input level. Secondly, the network is deep, it has a total of eight layers. The combination of the convolutional layer and the deep network allowed for the hierarchical extraction of features. i.e., features are extracted in a bottom up manner, with the lower layers recognizing simple features

© Springer Nature Singapore Pte Ltd. 2019
S. Rajaram et al. (Eds.): VDAT 2018, CCIS 892, pp. 121–129, 2019.
https://doi.org/10.1007/978-981-13-5950-7_11

such as edges, higher layers recognizing specific combinations of edges and eventually, the top layers recognizing a specific entity in the input. [1] consists of six such convolutional layers in series, with two consecutive fully connected layers in the end, and a 1000-way softmax layer at the output. Such networks are also called as Deep Convolutional Neural Networks (DCNNs). Another significant difference in [1] was that for every convolutional layer and the two fully connected layers, the neuron did not use the traditional sigmoid activation function, but rather chose a Rectified Liner (ReLu) activation function. The activation function is applied to the outputs of a layer, before passing it on as input to the subsequent layer. Starting with [1], all DCNNs have continued to use the ReLu function as the activation function in the neuron. In this section, we have briefly described the state-of-the-art in Neural Networks, the DCNNs. In the next section, we describe attempts at Silicon implementations of the activation function of the Artificial Neuron.

2   Silicon Neuronal Implementations

Hardware implementations are traditionally used for mature algorithms when further optimizations in performance are not possible at the software level. Examples are the popularity of DSP chips, and more recently, digital implementations of the AES algorithm. There have been several works (such as that have built Application Specific Integrated Circuits (ASICs) that have reproduced the functionality of the DCNN and its layers and are referred to as Deep Neural Network accelerators [2]. In this work however, we are more concerned with ASIC implementations of the Silicon Neuron, rather than the full DCNN. In the rest of this section, we discuss some implementations that have realized the later functionality using ASICs.

2.1   Artificial Neuron

The Artificial Neuron (AN) consists of inputs, which model the dendrites in the biological neuron. The inputs are weighted and then summed, before an activation function is applied to produce an output, which represents the activation of the axon. The AN is modeled as follows:

$$op = \sum_{i=1}^{n} f(w_0 + w_i a_i) \tag{1}$$

In the above equation, ai represents the input, and wi represents a weight. An activation function f is then applied on the weighted sum, producing the output of the AN. The activation function is traditionally a tanh squashing function. Since the late 1980s, Silicon implementations of the biological neural networks have been undertaken, forming the domain popularly known as neuromorphic engineering [3]. Complex analog circuits have been devised, which allow also for training of the AN silicon implementation. However, with recent research showing the superior properties of the ReLu activation function [4], there is a need to update the Silicon neuronal circuit before it can be used in Neuronal architecture implementations. In the next section, we briefly discuss the ReLu activation function.

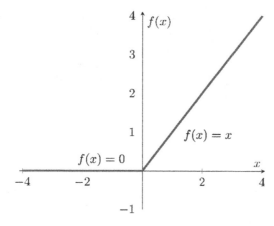

Fig. 1. The Rectified Linear Activation Function

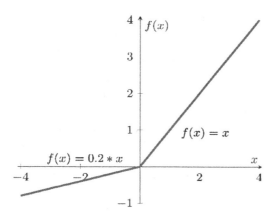

Fig. 2. The Parametric Rectified Linear Activation Function

2.2 ReLu Activation Functions

The ReLu activation function is succinctly represented as f(x) = max (0, x), i.e., if the inputs are positive or zero, the output is equal to the input. If the input is negative, the output is squashed to zero. The function is graphically represented in Fig. 1.

The reason for changing the activation function from the long traditional sigmoid function to the ReLu function are listed in [5]:

1. The increase in the learning rate, i.e., the number of iterations required for convergence is lesser.
2. They reduce the complexity of computations involved with the tanh function.

[5] also mentions some issues such as "dying": if the network has learned a large negative bias, then the output of the ReLu will always be zero. To improve this situation (and thereby the accuracy) [5] has proposed a Parametric ReLu or PReLu unit, where there is a small but nonzero slope in the negative regions. An example of this function is shown in Fig. 2. The function can be represented as in (2), where p is a parameter that can be learned.

$$f(x) = \begin{cases} x : x \geq 0 \\ p.x : x \leq 0 \end{cases} \qquad (2)$$

In this section, we have discussed the commonly used ReLu function, and a recent variant, the PReLu function. Next, we discuss our CMOS Circuit implementations for realizing these functions in hardware. Prior to that, we briefly discuss some existing approaches for these implementations.

2.3   Existing Activation Function Implementations

The primary objective of a hardware implementation is to improve performance and power consumption simultaneously. In this direction, DSP circuits and AES hardware implementations are popular examples. The earlier versions discussed in [3] were producing spikes, like the biological neuron. However, in more modern implementations discussed in [6], the hardware implementations focus on exactly replicating the DCNN, rather than the biological neural network, as done in [7]. Hence, in the rest of this paper, we will also refer only to the DCNN rather than the biological neural network.

An important point to be noted is that the implementations presented in [6] are completely digital - for all the neuronal activities (product, sum, and activation) digital representations and circuits are used. In contrast, we propose analog CMOS circuits, since their footprint in much smaller, and thereby come with additional improvements in speed and power consumption. The activation functions are usually nonlinear. In [6] the sigmoid function is represented as three piecewise linear portions: when the input is large in magnitude (positive and negative), the output saturates to a constant value. When the input is switching from positive to negative, the output is a line with unity slope (i.e., input equals output). Hence, we see that not only is a digital implementation of an activation function more complex, it also is inaccurate.

In the next section, we discuss the CMOS circuits we have developed for the ReLu and PReLu activation functions.

3   CMOS Activation Circuits

From the waveform in Fig. 1, we see that some sort of rectification function is required to be performed. Further, we restrict our self to CMOS only (no BJT or Diode) in order to keep all related penalties low. A Full wave MOS Rectifier is presented in [8]. Here, a circuit is developed that does full wave rectification for RF circuits. To adapt this for our case, we need to modify it to a Half-Wave-Rectifier, with the output staying at 0 V for all negative values of input.

3.1   ReLu CMOS Circuit

The proposed ReLu CMOS circuit is depicted in Fig. 3. For realizing the ReLu functionality as shown in Fig. 1, we modify the circuit in [8] in such a way that only half-wave rectification occurs. When the input is positive, PM1 and NM2 are ON, and the output follows the input. When the input is negative, PM2 and NM1 are ON: in [8] the resistor connection allows the input to be reflected at the output with an opposite polarity. In our case, we have removed this feedback resistor, thereby the output stays at GND through PM2, thereby giving the required ReLu activation function.

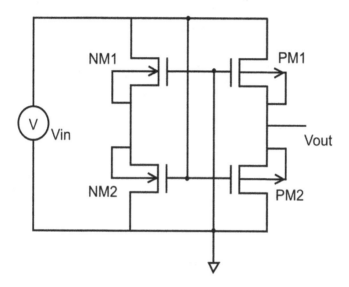

Fig. 3. Rectified Linear CMOS Circuit

3.2   Parametric ReLu

For realizing the PReLu functionality as shown in Fig. 2, the circuit from Fig. 3 is modified and the proposed CMOS circuit is depicted in Fig. 4. The modification required is realized by using an additional NMOS (NM3). NM3 alters the working of the ReLu circuit only for the negative inputs. NM3 acts as a diode-connected MOS-FET, since gate and drain are shorted, producing a small and non-zero linear slope for the negative inputs. The linear slope corresponds to the parameter $p.x$, for the negative inputs as described in Eq. 2.

An alternate circuit for PReLu is shown in Fig. 5 and it depicts a saturated output for the negative inputs. In this circuit, NM3 does not function as a diode connected transistor, hence instead of producing a small linear slope in the negative region, the output saturates at a small negative voltage.

The circuits developed in this section are very compact compared to their digital counterparts. Further, as we shall see from the waveforms in the next section, we will see that there is no compromise in accuracy either.

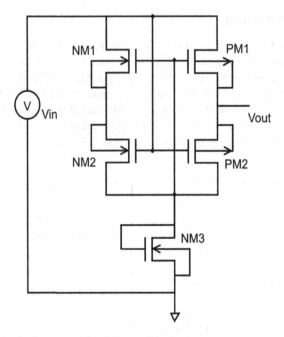

Fig. 4. Parametric Rectified Linear CMOS Circuit (without saturation)

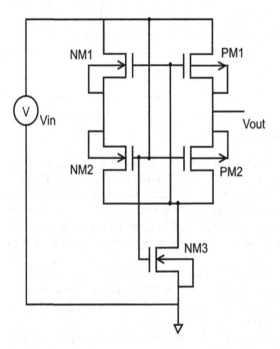

Fig. 5. Parametric Rectified Linear CMOS Circuit (with saturation)

4 Results and Discussion

The proposed CMOS circuits for ReLu and PReLu (with and without saturation) in Figs. 3, 4 and 5, respectively are implemented using standard 0.18 μm technology and are characterized with Spectre simulator under Cadence environment. The voltage input (Vin) fed into the circuits, ranges between −3 V and 2 V, which fits the requirements of digital circuits.

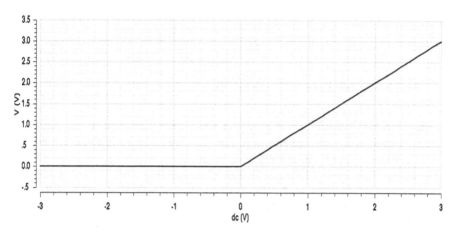

Fig. 6. Simulation result of proposed ReLu circuit

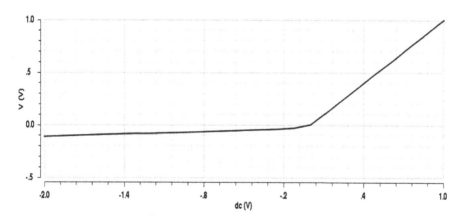

Fig. 7. Simulation result of proposed Parametric ReLu (without saturation) circuit

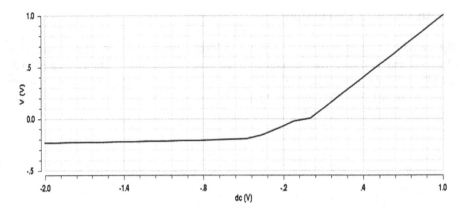

Fig. 8. Simulation result of proposed Parametric ReLu (with saturation) circuit

The simulated waveforms of proposed ReLu and Parametric ReLu (with and without saturation) circuits, are shown in Figs. 6, 7 and 8 respectively. It is observed from Fig. 6 that proposed ReLu circuit has better results with very low error of 0.011 and from Fig. 7, the slope of Parametric ReLu for negative cycles of input is observed to be 0.05. Further, the simulated graph of PReLu with saturation is depicted in Fig. 8. The functionalities of ReLu and PReLu obtained from the proposed CMOS circuits are in consistent with the ideal functions.

5 Conclusion

In this work we have realized most widely used ReLu activation function followed by its variant Parametric ReLu. The structures does not require complex circuit design while simulation results are also of high accuracy. Low power consumption and compact nature has made the circuits more reliable. The proposed circuits find their application in real time realization of classification tasks and are better than their digital counterparts in this regard. Further, the proposed circuits of the activation functions can be used in the implementation of single artificial neuron. It can also be used as a framework for the development of layout design and to create an artificial neural network standard library, integral part being the activation function. Also, the CMOS implementations provide improved real time implementations of the classification tasks of the deep neural networks.

References

1. Krizhevsky, A., Sutskever, I., Hinton, G.E.: Imagenet classification with deep convolutional neural networks. Adv. Neural Inf. Process. Syst. **5**, 1106–1114 (2012)
2. Chen, Y.-H., Emer, J., Sze, V.: Using dataflow to optimize energy efficiency of deep neural network accelerators. IEEE Micro **37**(3), 12–21 (2017)
3. Douglas, R., Mahowald, M., Mead, C.: Neuromorphic analogue VLSI. Annu. Rev. Neurosci. **18**(1), 255–281 (1995)
4. Vinod, N., Hinton, G.E.: Rectified linear units improve restricted boltzmann machines. In: Proceedings of the 27th International Conference on Machine Learning (ICML-10) (2010)
5. He, K., et al.: Delving deep into rectifiers: surpassing human-level performance on imagenet classification. In: Proceedings of the IEEE International Conference on Computer Vision (2015)
6. Chen, Y.-H., Joel, E., Vivienne, S.: Eyeriss: a spatial architecture for energy-efficient dataflow for convolutional neural networks. In: 2016 ACM/IEEE 43rd Annual International Symposium on Computer Architecture (ISCA). IEEE (2016)
7. Merolla, P.A., et al.: A million spiking-neuron integrated circuit with a scalable communication network and interface. Science **345**(6197), 668–673 (2014)
8. Yilmaz, M., Tunkar, B.A., Park, S., Elrayes, K., Mahmoud, M.A.E.: High-efficiency passive full wave rectification for electromagnetic harvesters. J. Appl. Phys. **116**(13), 134902 (2014)

Voltage Level Adapter Design for High Voltage Swing Applications in CMOS Differential Amplifier

Ashfakh Ali[✉], Arpan Jain, and Zia Abbas

Center for VLSI and Embedded Systems Technologies (CVEST), International
Institute of Information and Technology (IIIT) Hyderabad, Hyderabad, India
{huluvallay.md,arpan.jain}@research.iiit.ac.in,
zia.abbas@iiit.ac.in

Abstract. This work focuses on circuit level technique that achieves high
swing in single ended output differential amplifiers like differential amplifier
with active current mirror load, telescopic cascode, folded cascode etc. This
technique is designed in such a manner that it can be visualized as a 2-terminal
black box. Now, these 2-terminals can be connected to the conventional single
ended differential amplifiers enhancing their swing without degrading other
parameters like gain, bandwidth, CMRR etc. This black box achieves its performance consuming less power and minimum circuitry area. All the simulation
characterization and validation has been made through UMC 180 nm technology node in Cadence.

Keywords: CMOS · Differential amplifier · Current mirror load ·
Quiescent point · Voltage swing · Transconductance

1 Introduction

The differential amplifier is probably the most widely used building block in analog
and mixed signal circuits design. The advantage of differential over single ended
amplifier is higher rejection to environmental noise [1]. Differential amplifier with
active current mirror is more commonly used topology for single ended output without
sacrificing the gain. The important performance parameters of differential amplifier are
gain, bandwidth, linearity, noise (CMRR) and output voltage swing. Output swing is
the maximum and minimum limit at the output voltages where output follows input
linearly. Beyond these limits, the relation between the input and output voltages
become nonlinear, therefore avoided. In general for maximum output voltage swing,
DC operating point of output voltage is preferred to be set at middle of supply voltage
i.e. $(V_{dd} - V_{ss})/2$. In practical design, we often end up at different output operating
voltages that reduces the output voltage swing. Therefore, in analog circuits, voltage
shifter is required that should change the output voltage to a desired value in order to
further provide the maximum voltage swing. There are different methods used to shift
the output bias voltage for achieving high swing, for example, in high swing two-stage
amplifiers; first stage is used for high gain while second stage is used for high swing,

alternately resistance divider circuit used in feedback to bias the output dc operating point. However, most of the techniques either affect other performance figures such as gain attenuation or cost heavy additional circuitry (consequently consume more power and area), etc. The proposed analog *level adaptor* can shift the quiescent point of output voltage to achieve the maximum voltage swing without affecting the requisite performances like gain, bandwidth, power, etc. with minimum additional circuitry.

2   Differential Amplifier with Active Current Mirror Load

There are many single ended differential amplifiers reported previously, for example folded cascode, telescopic, active current mirror, etc. The differential amplifier with active current mirror load (depicted in Fig. 1) has been chosen as test case to illustrate the proposed concept. However, it is equally valid for other designs where high voltage swing is required.

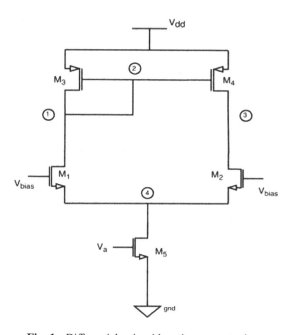

Fig. 1. Differential pair with active current mirror

Considering transistors M_1 & M_2 and M_3 & M_4 are matched i.e. width and length (W/L) are equal and identical threshold voltages. In the reported differential amplifier, current source in a mirror arrangement serves as the load and output is single ended.

From the circuit, upward resistance seen at *node1* is $1/g_{m3}$ while upward resistance seen at *node3* is r_{o4}. In general, $r_{o4} \gg 1/g_{m3}$. Therefore, this is differential amplifier with asymmetric load. However, single ended gain of this amplifier i.e. $g_{m1,2}.(r_{o2} \| r_{o4})$ is same as the differential gain of the conventional differential amplifier with symmetric load [1–5].

$g_{m1} = g_{m2} = g_{m1-2} = $ transconductance of nMOS
$g_{m3} = g_{m4} = g_{m3-4} = $ transconductance of pMOS
$r_{o1} = r_{o2} = r_{o1-2} = $ drain-source resistance of nMOS
$r_{o3} = r_{o4} = r_{o3-4} = $ drain-source resistance of pMOS

Node1 & *node2* are shorted in the circuit so they have the same voltage. Gate voltage (Vbias) and source voltages of M1 and M2 are connected to the same potential, therefore, carrying equal gate to source voltages. Similarly, the sources of M3 and M4 are connected to Vdd and gates of M3 and M4 are at similar potential i.e. *node2*, so providing equal gate voltage of M3 and M4.

Now, if the voltage at *node1* is higher than the voltage at *node3*, then the source to drain voltage of M3 will be lesser than source to drain voltage of M4. Since M3 and M4 are operating at equal source to gate voltages (VsgM3 = VsgM4 = VsgM3-M4), as a result, the current in left branch will be lesser than the current in the right branch. However, the drain to source voltage of M1 is more than drain to source voltage of M2, again the gate to source voltages of M1 and M2 are same, indicating that the current in left branch of differential amplifier is more than current in right branch. Such contradictory analysis take us to an observation that the voltage at *node1* cannot be more than the voltage at *node3*. A similar contradiction arises if we consider the voltage at *node1* is less than the voltage at *node3*. Consequently, such contradictions confirm that voltage at *node1* and *node3* must be same.

$$\text{Operating voltage at } node1 = V_{dd} - V_{sg,M3-M4}$$
$$\text{Operating voltage at } node3 = \text{Operating voltage at } node1$$
$$V_{node-3} = V_{dd} - V_{sg,M3-M4}$$

If an AC signal is applied to the gates of M1 and M2 then voltages at *node1*, *node2*, *node3* and *node4* will change, however, M4 will remain in saturation until voltage at *node3* reaches $V_{dd} - V_{sg} + |V_{tp}|$.

$$V_X = V_{dd} - V_{sg,M3-M4} + |V_{tp}|$$

Where V_X is the output voltage at which M4 enters into triode region.

So maximum upward swing possible $= V_X - V_{node-3} = |V_{tp}|$.

It is obvious, the maximum available upward swing is small (i.e. V_{tp}), accordingly the overall maximum swing (upward and downward) is also small (i.e. $2.V_{tp}$). Therefore, this small voltage swing will be the limiting factor for the efficient use of differential amplifier in various applications.

3 Proposed Voltage Level Adapter (VLA)

The proposed Voltage Level Adapter (VLA) is capable of shifting the quiescent voltage in order to achieve the high voltage swing without degrading the amplifier performance figures (e.g. gain, bandwidth, etc.).

The proposed idea is presented in Fig. 2, ensuring that the voltage at *node2* follows *node1* without having the same potential, and support to maintain a voltage gap. This voltage gap can be utilized to shift the output quiescent voltage. Recalling from Fig. 1; *node1* and *node3* have the same quiescent voltage, therefore, shifting the quiescent voltage at *node1* will shift the quiescent voltage at *node3*. Now, to shift the quiescent voltage at *node1*, direct connection of *node1* & *node2* should be avoided, this can be established by placing a new circuit in between the *node1* and *node2*, and affirming that *node2* follows *node1* i.e. if the voltage at *node1* is incremented/decremented then the node2 must be incremented/decremented in agreement.

Transistor sizing [6–8] can be an alternative solution for shifting down the quiescent point i.e. improving the voltage swing. However, in complex analog circuit's transistor sizing may affect other performances. Moreover, such transistor sizing techniques are circuit design dependent. While the proposed idea is applicable at circuit level and works as a black box i.e. valid for other similar designs without degrading the other performance of the circuit under test (CUT) with minimum extra circuit.

3.1 PMOS Based VLA

Consider the Fig. 2, *node2* is connected to the source terminal of extra circuitry and gate terminal of M3. As no current can flow through the gate, therefore, M6 will not take any current from *node2*. Now, if we look at *node1*, it is connected to gate terminal of extra circuitry and drain terminal of M3, again no current can flow through the gate, M6 is not taking any current from *node1*. This observation take us to a conclusion that pMOS extra circuitry is not disturbing the operating currents in differential amplifier. Moreover, this extra circuitry ensures that *node2* will follow *node1*. This can be justified mathematically from small-signal equivalent circuit in Fig. 3.

Apparently from Fig. 3, input is applied at the gate and output is taken from the source. Since every current source has finite internal resistance, so $r_{o,CS}$ is the output resistance of the current source and $r_{o,PMOS}$ is the source to drain resistance of the pMOS in VLA. From small- signal model (Fig. 3).

$$V_1 = V_{out} - V_{in}$$

$$V_{out} = g_m (V_{out} - V_{in}) \times r_{o,PMOS} \| r_{o,CS} \tag{1}$$

$$r_{o,PMOS} \| r_{o,CS} \approx (r_{o,PMOS}/2) \ (As \ r_{o,CS} \approx r_{o,PMOS}) \tag{2}$$

$$V_{out} = g_m(V_{out} - V_{in}) \times (r_{o,PMOS}/2)$$

$$V_{in}\left[g_m \cdot (r_{o,PMOS}/2)\right] = V_{out}\left[g_m \cdot (r_{o,PMOS}/2) - 1\right]$$

$$\frac{V_{out}}{V_{in}} = \frac{g_m \cdot (r_{o,PMOS}/2)}{g_m \cdot (r_{o,PMOS}/2) - 1} \approx 1\left[\text{As } g_m \cdot (r_{o,PMOS}/2) \gg 1\right]$$

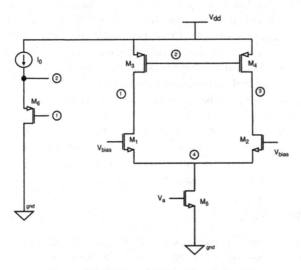

Fig. 2. PMOS based Voltage level adapter

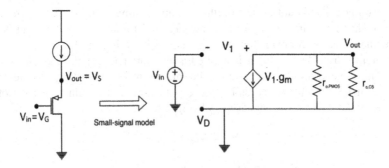

Fig. 3. Small-signal model of pMOS based VLA

The gain of the pMOS based VLA is slightly higher than the differential amplifier with active current mirror load. This can be examined from the mathematical justification discussed above i.e. $V_{out}/V_{in} > 1$. The same has been justified through simulations and reported in Fig. 6 and Table 2.

It is evident from Table 2, with the proposed idea, performance values are slightly improved along with the shift in quiescent voltage leading to proper utilization of output voltage swing (Fig. 5). Table 1 report the device dimensions and other network elements used in VLA based differential amplifier.

However, the power is slightly degraded on the other hand. Furthermore, to reduce the power consumption of VLA, we can drive the pMOS transistor of VLA into the subthreshold region. Note, reducing the power is not in the scope of presented work. Circuits operating in subthreshold will work in nano-Amp current, therefore, power can be reduced from µW to nW.

Since the subthreshold operation can offer limited shift of quiescent voltage, cascading two or more pMOS in VLA can solve the problem, as depicted in Fig. 4. Since subthreshold operation has its own challenges of sensitivity to temperature, process variations, etc. Therefore, it is left as a future scope.

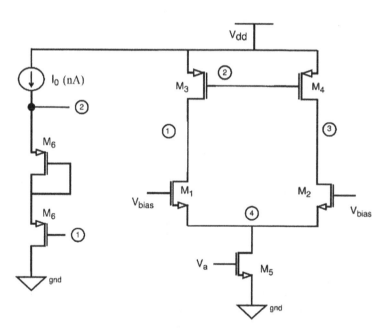

Fig. 4. VLA operating in subthreshold

4 Results

All simulation and validation for the targeted circuit has been carried out in the Virtuoso (Cadence) using UMC 180 nm PDK. It can be observed from Fig. 5(a) output bias point is asymmetric i.e. 1.25 V which led to clipping of the output while in Fig. 5 (b) pMOS based VLA is used to shift the quiescent point to the required level i.e. 0.6 V in the presented case, therefore clipping is avoided and maximum voltage swing can be availed.

As discussed earlier, DC gain of the pMOS based VLA is slightly higher than the differential amplifier with active current mirror load. The 3 dB bandwidth with proposed pMOS based VLA is almost equal to that of the differential amplifier with active current mirror load. The phase margin of pMOS based VLA is more than 60°, therefore, confirming the stable system.

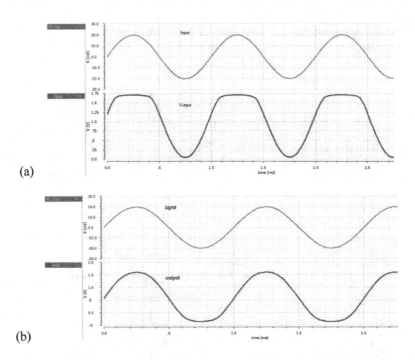

Fig. 5. Input and Output plot displaying swing characteristics of differential amplifier with (a) active current mirror load (b) pMOS based VLA

The proposed pMOS based VLA can be visualized as a 2-terminal black box (shown in Fig. 7) i.e. it can be connected to other single ended differential amplifiers without disturbing the operating currents.

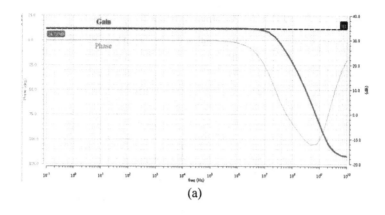

(a)

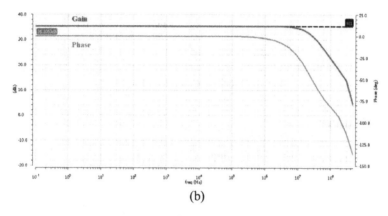

(b)

Fig. 6. Gain and phase plot of Differential amplifier with (a) current mirror load (b) pMOS based VLA

Table 1. MOSFET dimensions and network elements used in VLA and differential amplifier with current mirror load

$M_1 - M_2$	50 μm/500 nm
$M_3 - M_4$	30 μm/180 nm
M_5	40 μm/200 nm
M_6	50 μm/500 nm
$+V_{dd}$	+1.8 V
$-V_{ss}$	−1.8 V
I_d ($M_1 - M_4$)	50 μA
I_d (M_5)	100 μA
I_d (M_6)	90 μA
Operating mode	All $M_1 - M_6$ in saturation

Table 2. Performance figure comparison

Performance figures	CML differential amplifier	Proposed PMOS based VLA
DC gain	34.737 dB	36.335 dB
3 dB Band Width	22.19 MHz	22.8 MHz
Phase margin	75.2°	62°

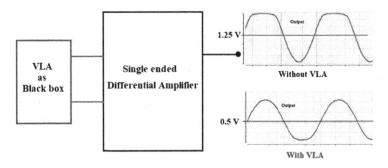

Fig. 7. Block box diagram of VLA

5 Conclusion

In this work, a circuit level idea for improving the voltage swing in the single ended differential amplifier without disturbing the operating current and other requisite performances such as gain, bandwidth, etc. has been presented. To achieve desired output quiescent voltage in complex analog amplifiers can be difficult by transistor sizing i.e. tuning W/L ratio, as adjusting (W/L) ratio may led to degrade the other parameters. The proposed VLA is very useful to shift output quiescent voltage even in complex analog amplifiers without disturbing other performances. The VLA circuit design is simple and applicable to any other single ended differential amplifier. Power dissipation of the circuit under test with proposed VLA can be further improved by operating the pMOS in subthreshold region.

References

1. Razavi, B.: Design of Analog CMOS Integrated Circuits, 22nd edn. Tata McGRAW-HILL, Bangkok (2002)
2. Allen, P.E., Holberg, D.R.: CMOS Analog Circuit Design, 3rd edn. Oxford University Press, Oxford (1987)
3. Butkovic, Z., Szabo, A.: Analysis of the CMOS differential amplifier with active load and single-ended output. In: IEEE MELECON 2004, May 12–15, Dubrovnik, Croatia (2004)
4. Corsi, F., Marzocca, C.: An approach to the analysis of the CMOS differential stage with active load and single-ended output. IEEE Trans. Educ. **46**(3), 325–328 (2003)

5. Paulik, G.F., Mayer, R.P.: Differential amplifier with current-mirror load. IEEE Trans. Educ. **55**(2), 233–237 (2012)
6. Abbas, Z., Olivieri, M., Yakupov, M., Ripp, A.: Design centering/yield optimization of power aware band pass filter based on CMOS current controlled current conveyor (CCCII+). Microelectron. J. **44**(4), 321–331 (2013)
7. Abbas, Z., Yakupov, M., Olivieri, M., Ripp, A., Strobe, G.: Yield optimization for low power current controlled current conveyor. In: Proceedings of 25th Symposium on Integrated Circuits and Systems Design (SBCCI), pp. 1–6 (2012)
8. Abbas, Z., Olivieri, M.: Optimal transistor sizing for maximum yield in variation aware standard cell design. Int. J. Circuit Theory Appl. **44**, 1400–1424 (2016)

Layout Design of X-Band Low Noise Amplifier for Radar Applications

I. Stefigraf$^{(\boxtimes)}$ and S. Rajaram

M.E. Communication Systems, Department of Electronics and Communication
Engineering, Thiagarajar College of Engineering, Madurai, India
stefigraf154@gmail.com

Abstract. This paper presents a x-band low noise amplifier design using different transistor, biasing, technology and matching network. The design of the front end low noise amplifier is one of the challenges in radio frequency receivers, which needs to maintain good impedance match, enough power gain and low noise figure within the required band. The key parameters are such as input return loss (S_{11}), output return loss (S_{22}), gain (S_{21}) and noise figure are simulated by using 'Advanced Design System (ADS)' and results are shown.

Keywords: ADS · Noise factor · Input return loss · Output return loss · LNA (Low Noise Amplifier)

1 Introduction

RADAR stands for Radio detection and ranging which is used for air traffic control, aircraft navigation, ship navigation and safety. Based on functionality and major features the Radar can be classified into general pulse radar, military range resolution radar, pulse compression radar and synthetic aperture radar. The radar functionality can be analyzed by using this equation [1]

$$P_r = \frac{P_t G_t \sigma A_{er}}{(4\pi R^2)^2} \tag{1}$$

The range of RADAR measured in terms of nautical mile. Low Noise Amplifier (LNA) is the first block that comes in the receiver section, after the signal is received at antenna, it is important for an LNA to have high gain and low noise figure [2]. The important parameter to be considered while designing an LNA are input and output matching network, power consumption, noise figure and gain. Matching network is used to increase the gain, gain flatness and VSWR.

2 Literature Survey

Bias inductor is used to improve the input impedance and also increase the gain of an LNA. Noise figure value depends on DC operating point and width of the transistor [2]. Cascode transistor is used to suppresses the miller effect of the input device. To achieve

S. Rajaram et al. (Eds.): VDAT 2018, CCIS 892, pp. 140–156, 2019.
https://doi.org/10.1007/978-981-13-5950-7_13

better performance of an LNA by using cascade topology [3]. Two factors are affecting the noise and linearity performance which completely depends on the Gate to source voltage and width of the transistor. Dual common source transistors are used to reduce the noise figure value and also improve the gain of an LNA [4]. A higher value of unity current gain frequency is used to obtain high gain and low noise figure [5]. Maximum power transfer occurred from a source and load impedances are complex conjugate of each other narrow band matching can be done using RLC circuits and feedback network around active circuits. Current reuse inductors are used to increase the gain of an LNA but in high frequency ranges it suffers from high insertion loss [6]. For low noise applications transistors are biased at low current level. It is used to obtain minimum noise figure [7]. At higher frequency the noise figure value takes normally low when the gate noise is taken into account. Tuned amplifiers are mostly used in communication circuits to provide better amplification of required signal and filter out the unwanted signal. Series gate inductance is used to match the real and imaginary part of the noise impedance. Gain bandwidth product is independent of center frequency [8].

3 Design Parameters

3.1 Transistor Selection

Low Noise Amplifier is designed by using different transistors like BJT, MOSFET, PHEMT and GaAsFET. BJT can be used for some specific frequency ranges. FET (CMOS and PHEMT) is suitable for high frequency ranges. GaAsFET generates very little noise compare with other transistors. It is used in several radio frequency applications like space communication, radio astronomy and armature radio.

3.2 DC Biasing Network

It is used to select the precise operating point of the transistor. Biasing is done by using several ways like fixing V_{GS}, feedback resistor, constant current source, fixing gate voltage V_G and connecting a resistance in a source, resistive divider biasing and current mirror biasing.

3.3 Stability

Stability can be determined with the help S parameter, proper terminations and matching network. The stability is measured by using 'Rollet stability factor (K)' and Δ.

$$\Delta = |S_{11}S_{22} - S_{12}S_{21}| \tag{2}$$

$$K = \frac{1 - |S_{11}|^2 - |S_{22}|^2 + |\Delta|^2}{2|S_{12}S_{21}|} \tag{3}$$

Unconditional stable condition: **K > 1** and $\Delta < 1$.

3.4 Matching Network

Matching network is used to maximize the power transfer and also enhances the signal to noise ratio. Series or parallel combination of inductance and capacitance can be added to provide an impedance transformation. Matching components capacitor also act as dc blocks and inductor provides dc biasing. Different matching networks are available. The available matching networks are

- Matching with lumped components
- Stub matching network
- T and Pi matching network

In L matching network Q value is fixed. Q value normally taken from the square root of transformation ratio. Two L matching network connected in cascaded to form a PI matching network. Dual L matching network forms the T matching. It is suitable for source and load termination parasitics are inductive in nature (Fig. 1).

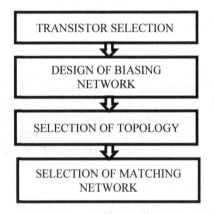

Fig. 1. Low Noise Amplifier design steps

Step 1: Optimum device width

$$Q = |c|\sqrt{\frac{5\gamma}{\delta}}\left[1 + \sqrt{1 + \frac{3}{|c|^2}\left(1 + \frac{\delta}{5\gamma}\right)}\right] \tag{4}$$

Where γ is white noise factor set between 2–3.
δ takes 2–3 times the value of γ.
$\alpha = 0.85$
The equation for device width

$$W = \frac{3}{2C_{OX}QL\omega R_S} \tag{5}$$

Step 2: Find gate source capacitance

$$C_{gs} = \frac{2 \times W \times C_{ox} \times L}{3} \tag{6}$$

Step 3: Find device transconductance

$$g_m = \sqrt{2K'_n I_D \frac{W_{OPT}}{L}} \tag{7}$$

Step 4: Find the transistor unity gain frequency

$$\omega_T = \frac{g_m}{C_{gs}} \tag{8}$$

Step 5: Expected noise figure value

$$F_{min} = 1 + 2.3 \left[\frac{\omega}{\omega_T} \right] \tag{9}$$

4   Different LNA Topologies

To access all the above design goals different LNA topologies like Common Gate (CG), Common Source (CS), CS with resistive terminations with shunt-series feedback, CS with inductive source degeneration, folded cascode, current reuse, common source with cascode inductive source degeneration, dual common source structures are available.

4.1   Common Source Stage with Inductive Load

The real part of impedance value is suppressed by using this inductive load. Inductor consumes a smaller voltage drop compared with resistor. This topology sustains small supply voltages (Fig. 2).

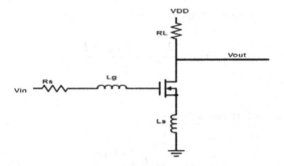

Fig. 2. Inductive source degeneration topology

4.2 Shunt Series Amplifier

Resistive feedback network generates broadband capability. It produces thermal noise continuously due to the feedback resistor R_F. It gives better noise figure value compared with other topology. NF value is obtained by using (Fig. 3)

$$F \geq 2 + 4(\gamma/\alpha)\left(\frac{1}{g_m R}\right) \tag{10}$$

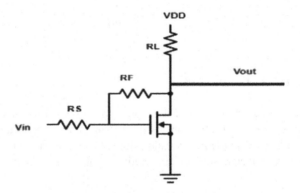

Fig. 3. Shunt series feedback topology

4.3 Common Gate Topology

The input impedance of CG stage is (Fig. 4)

$$Z_{in} = \frac{1}{g_m} \tag{11}$$

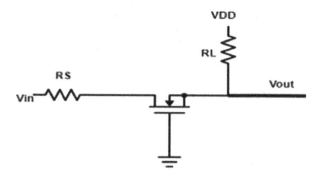

Fig. 4. Common gate topology

Channel length modulation is neglected the input impedance of the CG stage is low. Input return loss value can be diminished with the help of gate to source capacitance and transconductance value. Transistor width is directly proportional to transconductance value. Low gain, high Value and low power consumption are the major detriment of the common gate topology. NF is expressed in terms of

$$NF = 1 + \gamma + 4\frac{R_S}{R_L} \tag{12}$$

4.4 Comparison of Different LNA Topologies

See Table 1

Table 1. Comparison of different LNA topology

Topology	Gain	Power consumption	Noise figure
Common gate	Low	High	Moderate
Common source	High	Low	High
Current reuse	High	High	Low
Cascode	High	Low	High
Resistive feedback	Moderate	Low	High

5 Simulation Results

5.1 Cascaded CS with Inductive Source Degeneration LNA Using PHEMT

The circuit consists of cascaded combination of two PHEMT transistors. Source inductance is used to create a resistive input impedance without the need of noisy resistor. PHEMT is suitable for high frequency applications. It has good noise and low power consumption capability. Output of the first common source stage is given to the input of the next amplifying stage. It is used to boost the gain of an LNA and also increases the stability. Advantage of PHEMT transistors are low voltage operation, no need for negative supply voltage, no thermal run away. The combination L and C forms the tank circuit which is used to convert the load impedance in to the input impedance of the subsequent stages. At resonance frequency inductance and capacitance effect revoke each other gain becomes $g_m R$ (Figs. 5, 6 and 7).

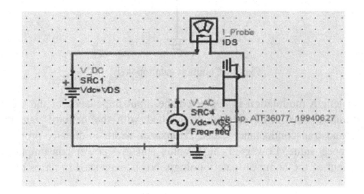

Fig. 5. DC biasing circuit

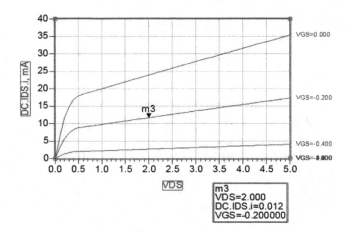

Fig. 6. Device IV characteristics

Figure 8 shows the plot between stability factor vs frequency. The obtained stability factor (K) value is 1.02.

Figure 9 shows the S parameter value of LNA it achieves a S_{11} value is −10.119 dB at 10 GHz. The obtained output return loss value is −15.317 dB at 10 GHz. It achieves a good return loss value. S_{22} is the output voltage reflection coefficient. The gain value for a LNA design using PHEMT is 20.486 dB (Fig. 10).

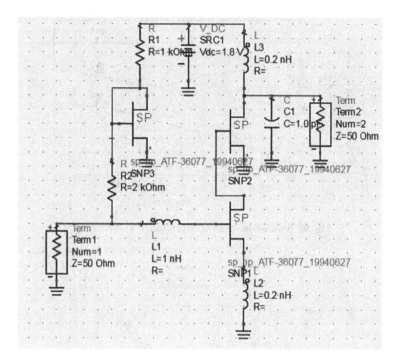

Fig. 7. Cascaded LNA circuit using PHEMT circuit

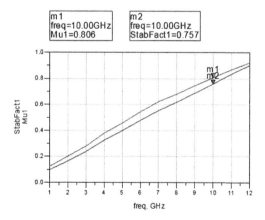

Fig. 8. Simulation result of stability factor

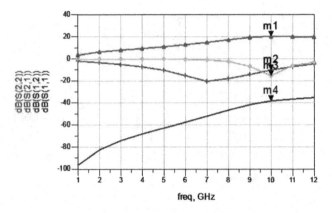

Fig. 9. Simulation result of S parameter Vs frequency

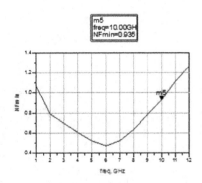

Fig. 10. Simulation result of noise figure

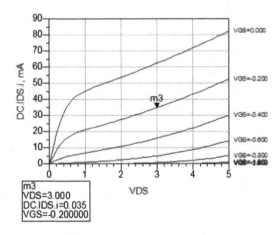

Fig. 11. Device I-V characteristics

5.2 Cascode CS Stage with Inductive Source Degeneration LNA Using GaAs FET

Stability of the transistor scrutinized by using this simulation setup, by connecting two terminal impedances in between the transistor. A simple parameter sweep is accomplished at a frequency range of 1 GHz to 12 GHz with a step size of 1 GHz. From this simulation results we obtain the S parameter value (Figs. 11, 12 and 13).

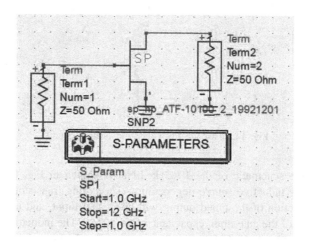

Fig. 12. Simulation setup for S parameter calculation

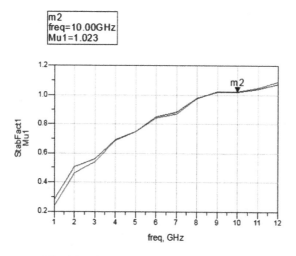

Fig. 13. Simulation result of stability value

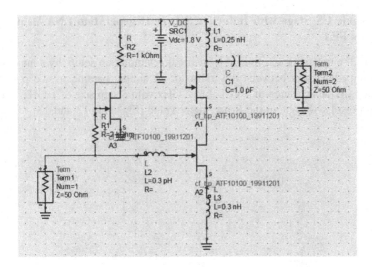

Fig. 14. Cascode LNA with GaAs FET circuit

The complete schematic of the 10 GHz LNA is shown in Fig. 14. The method employed here is inductive source degeneration. Cascoding transistor M2 is used to reduce the interaction of the tuned output with the tuned input, and also it is used to reduce the effect of the gate-drain capacitance Cgd of M1. The inductors L_g and L_s are chosen to provide the desired input impedance matching. Inductor L_d and capacitance C_d of the transistors M2 form a parallel tank circuit to match the LNA at 10 GHz Fig. 14. Schematic of the Proposed LNA transistor (M3), resistor R1 and R2 form a current mirror bias circuit. In order to minimize the power over head problem by choosing the small fraction of the transistor width. Miller effect is defined as the multiplication of the stray capacitance (C_{gs}) by the voltage gain. Current buffer stage at the output of an amplifier reduces the miller effect which leads to increase the performance of an LNA (Figs. 15 and 16).

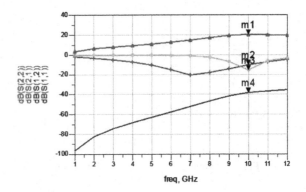

Fig. 15. Simulation result of S parameter Vs frequency

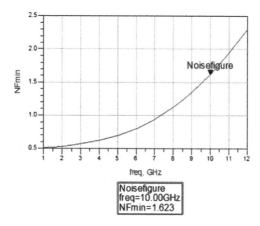

Fig. 16. Simulation result of noise figure

5.3 Cascoded LNA Using Parallel Structure

Parallel combination of MOSFET is sufficient for high power applications. Dual common source transistors are connected in parallel. It is used to enhance the device current handling capability. Drain to source resistance and gate threshold voltage are the major concern of the parallel connection of MOSFET. It produces the thermal run away problem. In order to reduce the thermal run away problem small resistor is connected in series with source (Figs. 17, 18, 19 and 20).

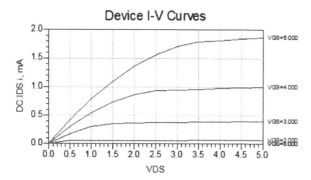

Fig. 17. Device IV characteristics

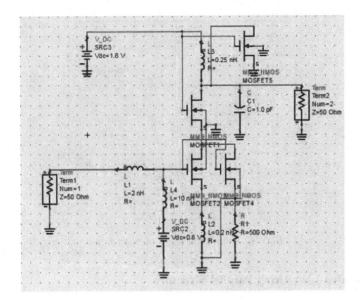

Fig. 18. Cascaded LNA with parallel MOSFET

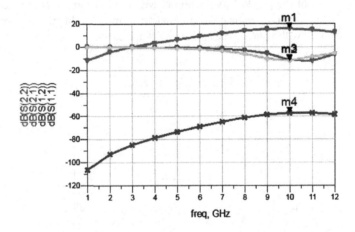

Fig. 19. Simulation result of S parameter value using parallel MOSFET

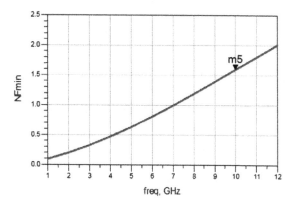

Fig. 20. Simulation result of noise figure

5.4 Cascoded LNA Design Using LC Matching Network

To achieve better matching additional input and output matching network is designed using a lumped LC components. To measure the input impedance by using Z parameter analysis. Match the source impedance Z_S to the input impedance at the input side. The dip occurs at the resonance frequency depends on the input and output loops (Fig. 21).

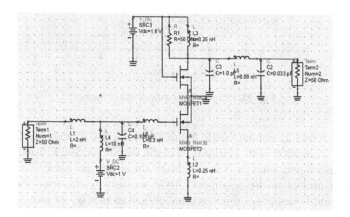

Fig. 21. Cascoded LNA using LC matching network

Figure 22 shows a S parameter value of LNA using LC matching network. S_{11} provides a good input impedance matching at −10.460 dB. It is the measure of input voltage that is reflected at the terminal. The obtained output return loss value is −29.862 dB.

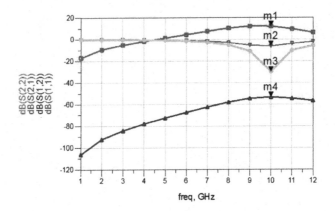

Fig. 22. Simulation result of S parameter value using LC matching network

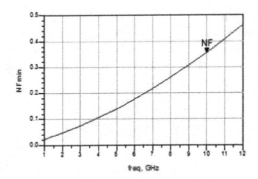

Fig. 23. Simulation result of noise figure

Figure 23 shows a minimum noise figure value of LNA. The obtained noise figure value is low compared with PHEMT, GaAsFET and MOSFET using LNA. The simulated noise figure value is 0.36 dB. MOS transistors are used to rectify all the noise sources present in the amplifier. CMOS transistor suffer from thermal noise, flicker noise and noises arises from parasitic capacitances (Fig. 24 and Table 2).

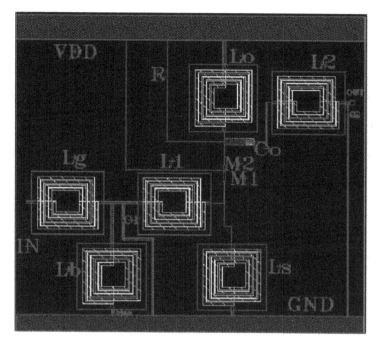

Fig. 24. LNA layout

Table 2. Results

S. no	Parameter	Simulation result of LNA using PHEMT	Simulation result of LNA using GaAsFET	Simulation result of LNA using parallel MOSFET	Simulation result of LNA using LC matching
1	Frequency	10 GHz	10 GHz	10 GHz	10 GHz
2	S_{11}	−10.119 dB	−15.127 dB	−10.177 dB	−10.460 dB
3	S_{12}	−38.173 dB	−17.316 dB	−57.150 dB	−53.293 dB
4	S_{21}	20.489 dB	2.730 dB	10.883 dB	10.606 dB
5	S_{22}	−15.317 dB	−12.003 dB	−29.523 dB	−29.862 dB
6	NFmin	0.935 dB	1.623 dB	1.732 dB	0.36 dB

6 Conclusion

The designed LNA is simulated using cascoded and cascaded topology with different techniques. The results are simulated using Advanced Design System software. The LNA is characterized by obtaining its power gain, input return loss, output return loss and noise figure. Gain value depends on the source inductance (Ls) value and the device properties. Compared with different methodology CS topology with parallel tank circuit using PHEMT gives better results. The layout of the LNA has been designed using CADENCE tool.

References

1. Richards, M.A.: Fundamentals of Radar Signal Processing. McGraw-Hill, New York (2005)
2. Razavi, B.: Design of Analog CMOS Integrated Circuits. McGraw-Hill, New York (2011)
3. Pozar, D.M.: Microwave Engineering, 4th edn. Wiley, New York (2011)
4. Yasami, S., Bayoumi, M.: An ultra-low power current reused CMOS low noise amplifier for x-band space application. In: 19th IEEE International Conference on Electronics, Circuits, and Systems (ICECS 2012), pp. 673–676 (2012). ISBN 978-1-4673-1260-8
5. Senthilkumar, D., Pandit khot, U., Jagtap, S.: Design and comparison of different matching techniques for low noise amplifier circuit. Int. J. Eng. Res. Appl. 3, 403–408 (2013). ISSN 2248-9622
6. Gore, S.S., Phade, G.M.: Design challenges and performance parameters of low noise amplifier. Int. J. Innov. Eng. Technol. (IJIET), 3(1) (2013). ISSN: 2319-1058
7. Lessi, C., Karagagianni, E.: An x-band low noise amplifier design for marine navigation radars. Int. J. Commun. Netw. Syst. Sci. 7, 75–82 (2014)
8. Fallahnejad, M., Najmabadi, Y., Kashaniniya, A.: Design and simulation of low noise amplifier at 10 GHz by using GaAs high electron mobility transistor, 10(5), 29–34 (2015). Ver. II, e-ISSN 2278-1676, p-ISSN 2320-3331
9. Sahin, N., Yelten, M.B.: A 0.18 m CMOS X-BAND low noise amplifier for space applications. In: IEEE First New Generation of CAS (2017)

Hardware Security

A Novel Approach to Detect Hardware Malware Using Hamming Weight Model and One Class Support Vector Machine

P. Saravanan[1(✉)] and B. M. Mehtre[2]

[1] Department of ECE, PSG College of Technology, Coimbatore, India
dpsaravanan@gmail.com
[2] Centre for Cyber Security, Institute for Development and Research in Banking Technology (IDRBT), Hyderabad, India

Abstract. Internet of Things (IoT) is an upcoming research area in cyber security and since common security measures are not implemented in these devices, they are most vulnerable to cyber attacks. Though IoT devices are vulnerable to both hardware and software malware attacks, the impact of hardware vulnerabilities will be significant since the devices once fabricated cannot be modified or updated. Among the major hardware vulnerabilities, hardware malware also known as hardware trojan (HT) is critical as it can control, modify, disable or monitor the key information in the device. While many techniques have been explored in the literature to detect HT at the gate level netlist, their computational complexity is very high and detection accuracy is relatively low. In order to reduce the computational complexity and improve the detection accuracy, a novel approach is proposed in this work to detect HT in the gate level netlist using Hamming weight model and unsupervised anomaly based detection method. The leakage power supply current signatures for both HT-free and HT-infected circuits are derived from Hamming weights of the random input sequence. The current signatures are then normalized and applied to one class support vector machine which acts as an anomaly detector to identify the HT-infected circuits. The process parameter and environmental noise variations are considered while characterizing the gates for different Hamming weights. The proposed method is evaluated on ISCAS85 C17 benchmark circuit using 16 nm process technology node in HSpice. A detection accuracy of 100% is achieved even when there is a single malicious gate in the HT-infected circuit. Experiments with other benchmark circuits show that the proposed methodology performs well.

Keywords: Hardware Trojan · Hardware malware · Hardware security · Hamming weight model · One class support vector machine · Leakage current

1 Introduction

Outsourcing has become a buzz word since the semiconductor industry has shifted gears to improve productivity and strike a balance between abstraction and automation. The key benefits of outsourcing the design and fabrication process in Integrated Circuit (IC)

© Springer Nature Singapore Pte Ltd. 2019
S. Rajaram et al. (Eds.): VDAT 2018, CCIS 892, pp. 159–172, 2019.
https://doi.org/10.1007/978-981-13-5950-7_14

design flow are better time to market, lower cost and increased focus towards differentiating technology. However, the major risks in outsourcing are the reliability issues where an adversary can tamper IC supply chain management with the help of HTs. The HT is a piece of extra logic that is added to the design or modified from the original design for malicious purposes in IC design flow. To make it more stealthy and avoid being detected in chips, HTs are designed in an intelligent manner and are triggered in rare conditions so that traditional testing strategies cannot effectively detect them.

The major challenges in HT detection are the generation of efficient test patterns necessary to activate HT so that their impact can be observed either in the functional or non-functional characteristics of the design beyond process and environmental variations [1]. Side channel analysis plays a key role in HT detection since they are non-destructive and non-invasive. The very first work on HT detection using side channel analysis was proposed in [2] where a set of genuine fingerprints of an IC family was produced utilizing side channel information such as power, temperature and electromagnetic profiles. The ICs in the field are then verified using statistical tests against the fingerprints.

A circuit partitioning based approach to detect and locate embedded HTs was proposed in [3]. Further, a switching activity based analysis was performed to create a difference between the actual and the HT-infected circuit to make them easily observable. The sensitivity of a power supply transient signal to detect HT was investigated under a variety of adverse conditions in [4]. A power gating scheme to facilitate the screening of an IC for HT infection was proposed in [5]. A calibration scheme was suggested in it to reduce the impacts of process variations. By extracting the controllability and observability of signals in the given netlist, low testability signals were identified and their susceptibility to HT were observed in [6]. Gate level characterization in the presence of measurement noise and manufacturing variability was proposed in [7]. Linear equations were formed based on the measurements of side channel parameters and were processed by using linear programming method in order to arrive at the scaling factors which were then statistically analysed to determine the presence of hardware Trojans.

A reverse engineering based HT detection using one class support vector machine (OCSVM) was presented in [8]. The images obtained from the imaging step of reverse engineering are pre-processed and the features extracted from them are then used to characterize and classify IC's physical layout. Most of the earlier work was focussed towards switching activity based power supply transient signals. Though the sensitivity of the power supply transient signal was evaluated in the presence of measurement noise, the impact of leakage current is not considered in their work which is a serious issue in nanometric technologies. This work proposes a novel approach to detect HT in gate level netlists using Hamming weight model and OCSVM. The OCSVM characterizes baseline models of a state of normalcy and identifies attacks based on deviations from the models.

The major contributions in this paper are:

- The proposed approach uses Hamming weight based encoding to map the test patterns to the leakage power signatures in order to reduce the computational complexity during reference model characterization.

- The proposed approach detects HT even in the presence of manufacturing variability and environmental noise.
- Since static power is used, the HT can be detected even when there is no activity in the system i.e. the HT need not be fully activated.
- OCSVM is employed at the gate level netlist to detect HT with minimal false positive and false negative errors.
- The proposed approach is scalable and can be extended to any large circuit using circuit partitioning techniques.
- The proposed approach detects HT in a non-invasive and non-destructive manner.

The paper is organized as follows. Section 2 gives an overview about HT detection methods. Section 3 covers the significance of Hamming weight model to characterize leakage power dissipation. Section 4 explores one class classification concepts and OCSVM along with data normalization techniques. Section 5 describes the proposed approach to detect HT using OCSVM. The performance analysis is done on Sect. 6. Section 7 concludes the paper with noted references.

2 Hardware Trojan Overview

HT is a malicious addition or alteration in the design either by inserting extra redundant logic or by modifying the existing logic in a stealthy manner in order to fulfill the adversary's objectives. HT can change the functionality [affects the availability service], reduce the reliability [affects the integrity service] or leak valuable information [affects the confidentiality service] in the design. The major taxonomies in HT detection methods are Pre-silicon, Post-silicon, Design for Trust and Manufacturing for Trust as shown in Fig. 1 [9].

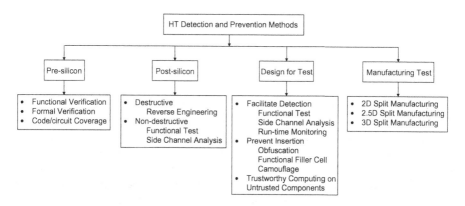

Fig. 1. Various HT detection and prevention methods

In pre-silicon methods, either formal or functional verification techniques are used. In post-silicon methods, either destructive or non-destructive techniques are used. Functional testing algorithms play key role in non-destructive techniques. In addition, side channel analysis (SCA) can also be used since the malicious modification will definitely impact the side channel parameters in the design. A preventive measure can also be taken to avoid HT insertion during the design phase of the system. And finally split manufacturing techniques can also be used to gain the trust against HT insertion. In most of the cases, traditional hardware testing cannot effectively detect HT due to their stealthy nature. Since HT can be inserted at any phase of the IC design flow, it will be very difficult to develop a single countermeasure to detect HT in all the abstraction levels of IC design flow.

3 Hamming Weight Based Power Model

The power model exploits the mathematical approaches to estimate the power consumption of the circuit. Since static power consumption always exists irrespective of the switching activities in the circuit, it can be modeled as a function of the input patterns. It has been proved in literature that the leakage power consumption in a circuit has a strong correlation to the Hamming weight of the input patterns. The Hamming weight model calculates the number of occurrences of the binary value 1 in the input patterns of the circuit. At the gate level, the Hamming weight and leakage current are negatively correlated since the leakage current in NMOS transistor is more when compared to the leakage current in PMOS transistor. The leakage current of the NOT gate is given in Table 1 which shows the inverse relationship between Hamming weight and leakage current [10].

Table 1. Leakage current in NOT gate (16 nm technology).

Input	Hamming weight	I_{leak} (pA)
0	0	104.8360
1	1	3.8210

4 One Class Classification

The basic requirement of any machine learning algorithm is to have a training dataset that represents some parameter/feature space of the system and testing dataset that represents the practical environment. The major challenge is to train the algorithm using many classes in the training dataset and once trained successfully then it can be deployed in the field to identify the correct class in the testing dataset. In reality, the availability of testing dataset is very limited in most of the applications. So the traditional multiclass machine learning algorithms cannot be applied in these applications and the right solution is to go for one class classifiers. The one class classification algorithms are basically unsupervised anomaly based detection algorithms. The primary assumption in one class classification is that information or the dataset is available in abundance for one class, the target class. In HT detection applications, the target class is focused on dataset that belongs to normal or HT-free circuits. The main task in one class classification is to define a boundary around the target class so as to maximize the normal data acceptance while minimizing outlier data acceptance [11]. The outliers in this case belongs to the HT-infected circuits.

4.1 One Class Support Vector Machine

SVMs are traditionally used in binary classification tasks. Given two classes, the objective of SVMs is to find the best hyperplane that has the largest separation margin between the two classes of samples. This objective results in a sparse solution as the hyperplane is only affected by the samples that are close to it, the support vectors. One class SVM proposed by Scholkopf et al. [12] finds the optimal boundary characterizing the training samples in the form of a hypersphere. In this work, radial basis function (RBF) kernel is used in one class support vector machine. This kernel nonlinearly maps training samples and keeps the number of hyper parameters that influences the complexity of model selection very minimum.

4.2 Data Normalization

It is necessary to apply normalization in the training samples before applying them to OCSVM. The main advantage of scaling is to avoid samples in greater numeric ranges dominating those in smaller numeric ranges. Another advantage is to avoid numerical difficulties during the calculation. Because kernel values usually depend on the inner products of feature vectors, large attribute values might cause numerical problems. In this work the training and testing samples are normalized to the range [0, 1].

5 Proposed Methodology

This section covers the proposed methodology to detect HT in the gate level netlist. The leakage current (I_{leak}) is characterized by using 16 nm PTM model cord and the simulation is carried out by using HSpice. The process parameters are varied by running Monte Carlo simulation with Gaussian distribution. The machine learning part using one class support vector machine (OCSVM) is implemented in Python 3.6.

The proposed methodology consists of two phases to detect the HTs in the given netlist. The first phase characterizes each gate in the given netlist for leakage current (I_{leak}) consumed by the gate as a function of Hamming weight based test patterns. Instead of characterizing different gates in the circuit, a common single type of gate can be characterized in this phase. The logic synthesis tool is then forced to map only to the characterized gates so that the whole characterization process can be simplified. In this work, a 2 input NAND gate is characterized and is applied to ISCAS85 C17 benchmark circuit.

The proposed approach makes use of Hamming weight based test patterns instead of exhaustive test patterns which reduces the complexity in characterizing gates. For example, a 2 and 3 input NAND gate requires only 3 and 4 Hamming weight based test patterns whereas it requires 4, 8 exhaustive test patterns as given in Tables 2 and 3. To generalize, an n-input gate requires only n + 1 Hamming weight based test patterns which is far less when compared to 2^n exhaustive patterns. The I_{leak} is measured for each Hamming weight based test pattern in the presence of 2.5%, 5%, 7.5% and 10% variations in process parameters such as threshold voltage (Vth), temperature, effective channel length (Leff) and thickness of the gate oxide (Tox). In addition, Gaussian noise is added in 50 dB, 60 dB, 70 dB, 80 dB and 90 dB signal to noise ratio (SNR) values in order to consider environmental noise.

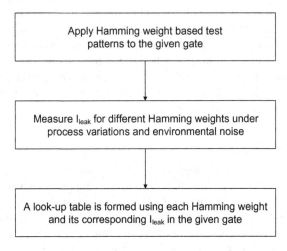

Fig. 2. Proposed methodology (Phase 1)

Table 2. Leakage current in 2-input NAND gate.

Input	Hamming weight	I_{leak} (pA)
00	0	206.7267
01	1	105.0462
10	1	105.0462
11	2	7.6416

In the first phase, as shown in Fig. 2, the complete Hamming weight based test patterns are applied to the gate and the I_{leak} is measured under process parameter variations and environmental noise. Then, a look-up table is formed by using the measured currents for the different Hamming weight based test patterns. The second phase has got two sections such as training phase and detection phase as shown in Fig. 3. In the training phase, the I_{leak} for the circuit under test is estimated through Hamming weight model for a random sequence of inputs. First, the test patterns in the random sequences are applied and are propagated from the primary input to the primary output of the given netlist. Then, the Hamming weight is calculated at the input of each gate in the netlist. The I_{leak} for the corresponding Hamming weight is obtained from the look-up table generated from the first phase. Finally, I_{leak} obtained from each gate through Hamming weight model are summed up to estimate the total I_{leak} of the given netlist. The summed up I_{leak} is pre-processed by using normalization process and then used to train the OCSVM.

Table 3. Leakage current in 3-input NAND gate.

Input	Hamming weight	I_{leak} (pA)
000	0	309.5699
001	1	207.0873
010	1	207.0873
011	2	105.4791
100	1	207.0873
101	2	105.4791
110	2	105.4791
111	3	11.4618

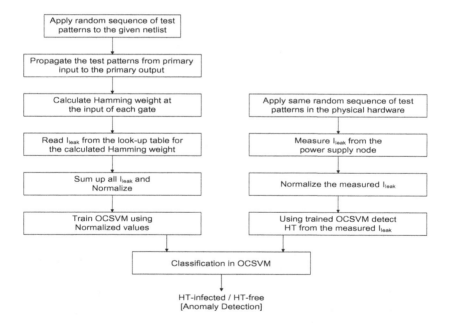

Fig. 3. Proposed methodology (Phase 2)

In the detection phase, the I_{leak} measured from the actual circuit is used to check for outliers in the trained OCSVM. In this phase, the same random sequence of test patterns which was applied earlier during the training phase, is applied to the physical hardware of the actual circuit and I_{leak} is measured. The measured I_{leak} is pre-processed by using normalization process and then tested in the trained OCSVM. Based on the outliers, the decision on whether the actual physical hardware is HT-infected or not can be made.

6 Results and Discussion

In this work, the default OneClassSVM command in Python is used to detect the HT-infected circuits. In OCSVM, RBF kernel is used with 'degree' as 3 and 'nu' is set as 0.2 and gamma is set as 'auto'. The ISCAS85 C17 benchmark circuit is considered as HT-free circuit. In the HT-free circuit, we deliberately included HT with a size of 1 to 6 redundant 2-input NAND gates with dummy outputs. The redundant gates are connected to C17 circuit at different nodes in order to examine the randomness of HT insertion phase.

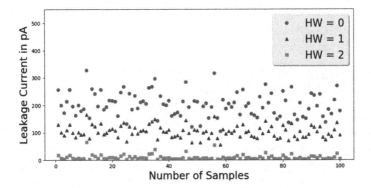

Fig. 4. I_{leak} of 2-input NAND gate for Vth variations

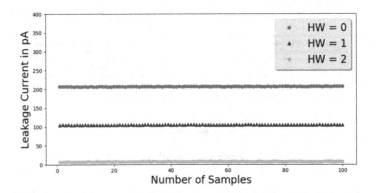

Fig. 5. I_{leak} of 2-input NAND gate for temperature variations

6.1   Gate Level Characterization

All real measurements are affected by environmental noise and hence to represent the effects of electronic noise, a Gaussian noise (AWGN) of 50 dB, 60 dB, 70 dB, 80 dB and 90 dB SNR is added in all simulations in this work. Since HT-free circuit has only 2-input NAND gates, the look-up table is formed between Hamming weight and I_{leak} by characterizing 2-input NAND gate for both process parameter and environmental noise variations. For 70 dB SNR, the variations in I_{leak} for 5% variations individually in threshold voltage (Vth), temperature, effective channel length (Leff) and gate oxide thickness (Tox) are shown in Figs. 4, 5, 6 and 7 respectively. It can be observed from Figs. 4 and 7 that the threshold voltage and gate oxide thickness are the dominant factors in process parameter variations that affect I_{leak} when compared to other parameters. Figure 8 gives the variations in I_{leak} for combined 5% variation in all process parameters.

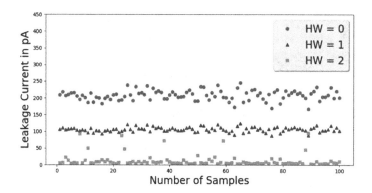

Fig. 6. I_{leak} of 2-input NAND gate for Leff variations

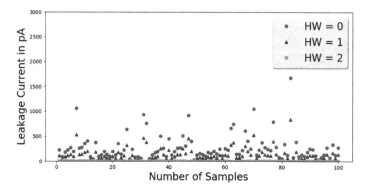

Fig. 7. I_{leak} of 2-input NAND gate for Tox variations

6.2   OCSVM Training Phase

Three random sequence of test patterns are formed in this work termed as S1, S2 and S3 for the HT-free circuit. Each sequence is applied to the HT-free circuit and the test patterns are propagated from primary input to primary output. At the input of each gate in the HT-free circuit, Hamming weights are calculated. The corresponding I_{leak} for each Hamming weight is obtained from the Look-up table and the I_{leak} is summed up for all the gates. The OCSVM is trained with summed up I_{leak} after normalizing the dataset.

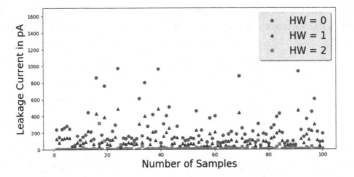

Fig. 8. I_{leak} of 2-input NAND gate for all process parameter variations

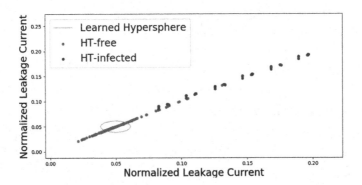

Fig. 9. DA for 2.5% variation in process parameters at 90 dB SNR

6.3   HT Detection Phase

In this phase, HT-infected C17 circuit is excited with the same sequence of test patterns and the I_{leak} for all circuits are measured and normalized. The trained OCSVM is tested with the normalized I_{leak} and the outlier is detected. The contour plots of the proposed detection method are shown in Figs. 9, 10 and 11 for 2.5%, 5% and 10% variations in process parameters and 90 dB, 70 dB and 50 dB SNR values in environmental noise respectively. The OCSVM effectively forms the hypersphere by learning the variations in the normalized leakage current which helps in proper detection of HT-infected circuits. A given netlist is treated as HT-infected if it lies outside the learned hypersphere in the contour plot.

Table 4. Performance analysis of proposed work.

Process parameter variations	Environmental noise [SNR in dB]	Input Sequence 1 (S1)			Input Sequence 2 (S2)			Input Sequence 3 (S3)		
		FPR (%)	FNR (%)	ACC (%)	FPR (%)	FNR (%)	ACC (%)	FPR (%)	FNR (%)	ACC (%)
2.5%	90	0	20	100	0	19.75	100	0	20	100
	80	0	20	100	0	20	100	0	19.75	100
	70	0	19.75	100	0	20	100	0	20	100
	60	0	19.75	100	0	19.75	100	0	20	100
	50	0	19.75	100	0	19.75	100	0	20	100
5%	90	0	20.25	100	0	20.25	100	0	20.25	100
	80	0	20.25	100	0	20.25	100	0	20.25	100
	70	0	20	100	0	20.25	100	0	20	100
	60	0	20.25	100	0	20.25	100	0	20.25	100
	50	0	20.25	100	0	20.25	100	0	20	100
7.5%	90	0	20.25	100	0	20	100	0	20	100
	80	0	20.25	100	0	20	100	0	20	100
	70	0	20.25	100	0	20	100	0	20.25	100
	60	0	20.25	100	0	20.25	100	0	20	100
	50	0	20	100	0	20.25	100	0	20.25	100
10%	90	0	20.25	100	0	20.25	100	0	20.25	100
	80	0	20.25	100	0	20.25	100	0	20	100
	70	0	20.25	100	0	20.25	100	0	19.75	100
	60	0	20	100	0	20.25	100	0	20.25	100
	50	0	20.25	100	0	20	100	0	20	100

6.4   Performance Analysis

To evaluate the performance of the proposed approach, three different metrics known as detection accuracy (DA), false positive rate (FPR) and false negative rate (FNR) are employed in this work. The detection accuracy gives the ratio of number of HT-infected circuits detected to the total number of HT-infected circuits. The false positive rate of classification is the ratio of number of false positive circuits to the total number

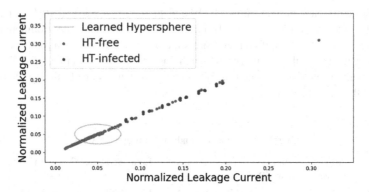

Fig. 10. DA for 5% variation in process parameters at 70 dB SNR

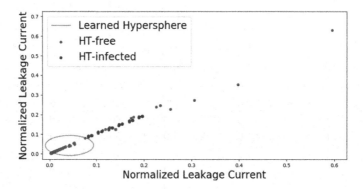

Fig. 11. DA for 10% variation in process parameters at 50 dB SNR

of false positive and true negative circuits. The false negative rate of classification is the ratio of number of false negative circuits to the total number of false negative and true positive circuits.

The total number of HT-free training samples considered in this work is 400 and the total number of HT-infected samples is 48. The detection accuracy of our proposed work for different random sequence of inputs is tabulated in Table 4 where it can be observed that the detection accuracy is maintained at 100% even under the process parameter variations and environmental noise variations. The values of FNR in Table 4 are not support vectors and are just an indication of spread in the training samples. The detection accuracy of our proposed work with various benchmark circuits is given in Table 5.

Table 5. Detection accuracy of proposed work.

Benchmark circuits	No. of gates	Detection accuracy [%]
C17	6	100
C432	160	100
C499	202	100
C880	383	99
C1355	546	99
C1908	880	98

7 Conclusion

A novel approach to detect HT in gate level netlist is proposed in this work by exploiting Hamming weight based leakage model to derive the power supply current signatures. OCSVM is employed as an anomaly detector to identify the HT-infected circuit from the HT-free training samples. The proposed work is evaluated on ISCAS85 C17 benchmark circuit with HT-infected circuit of varying size from 1 to 6 gates. The power supply current traces are extracted from the HT-free circuit by varying both process parameters and environmental noise. The experimental results demonstrate that it is possible to achieve almost 100% detection accuracy even in the presence of a single malicious gate in the HT-infected circuit. The proposed approach is scalable and can be applied to any large sized gate level netlists by using circuit partitioning techniques.

References

1. Chakraborty, R.S., Wolff, F., Paul, S., Papachristou, C., Bhunia, S.: *MERO*: a statistical approach for hardware Trojan detection. In: Clavier, C., Gaj, K. (eds.) CHES 2009. LNCS, vol. 5747, pp. 396–410. Springer, Heidelberg (2009). https://doi.org/10.1007/978-3-642-04138-9_28
2. Agrawal, D., Baktir, S., Karakoyunlu, D., Rohatgi, P., Sunar, B.: Trojan detection using IC fingerprinting. In: Proceedings of IEEE Symposium on Security Privacy, pp. 296–310, Berkeley (2007)
3. Banga, M., Hsiao, M.S.: A region based approach for the identification of hardware Trojans. In: Proceedings of IEEE International Workshop Hardware Oriented Security Trust (HOST), pp. 40–47, Anaheim (2008)
4. Rad, R., Plusquellic, J., Tehranipoor, M.: A sensitivity analysis of power signal methods for detecting hardware Trojans under real process and environmental conditions. IEEE Trans. Very Large Scale Integr. (VLSI) Syst. **18**(12), 1735–1744 (2010)
5. Yuan, C., Chang, C.H., Chen, S.: A cluster-based distributed active current sensing circuit for hardware Trojan detection. IEEE Trans. Inf. Forensics Secur. **9**(12), 2220–2231 (2014)
6. Hassan, S.: COTD: reference-free hardware Trojan detection and recovery based on controllability and observability in gate-Level netlist. IEEE Trans. Inf. Forensics Secur. **12**(2), 338–350 (2017)
7. Sheng, W., Potkonjak, M.: Scalable hardware Trojan diagnosis. IEEE Trans. Very Large Scale Integr. (VLSI) Syst. **20**(6), 1049–1057 (2012)

8. Chongxi, B., Forte, D., Srivastava, A.: On application of one-class SVM to reverse engineering-based hardware Trojan detection. In: Proceedings of 15th IEEE International Symposium on Quality Electronic Design (ISQED), pp. 47–54, Santa Clara (2014)
9. Kan, X., Forte, D., Jin, Y., Karri, R., Bhunia, S., Tehranipoor, M.: Hardware Trojans: lessons learned after one decade of research. ACM Trans. Des. Autom. Electron. Syst. (TODAES) **22**(1), 1–6 (2016)
10. Alioto, M., Giancane, L., Scotti, G., Trifiletti, A.: Leakage power analysis attacks: a novel class of attacks to nanometer cryptographic circuits. IEEE Trans. Circuits Syst. **57**(2), 355–367 (2010)
11. Tax, D.: One-class classification: concept-learning in the absence of counter-examples. Ph.D. dissertation, Delft University of Technology (2001)
12. Scholkopf, B., Williamson, R.C., Smola, A.J., Shawe-Taylor, J., Platt, J.C.: Support vector method for novelty detection. In: Proceedings of Advances in Neural Information Processing Systems (NIPS), pp. 582–588 (1999)

Detecting Hardware Trojans by Reducing Rarity of Transitions in ICs

Tapobrata Dhar$^{(\boxtimes)}$, Surajit Kumar Roy, and Chandan Giri

Indian Institute of Engineering Science and Technology, Shibpur, Howrah 711103,
West Bengal, India
taporata.dhar91@gmail.com, suraroy@gmail.com, chandan@it.iiests.ac.in

Abstract. The fabless nature of the integrated circuits (ICs) manufacturing industry has made it prone to various kinds of attacks that can
compromise the security of the IC. The inclusion of malicious circuitry
in the original IC is one such attacks which has the potential to create
a critical failure in the functioning of the ICs. Such kinds of clandestine
circuitry is known as Hardware Trojan Horses (HTH) and they are often
inserted in the circuit in such a way that they are very difficult to detect
during the testing phase. The secretive nature of HT is attributed to the
fact that they are often inserted in the parts of the IC where there is relatively less transitions. In this paper, a technique is suggested that aids
in raising the number of transitions all over the IC which in turn helps
in stimulating and/or activating the malicious HT circuit. The transition probability is increased in the IC by using 2-to-1 MUXs which are
inserted in specific parts of the circuit. The 2-to-1 MUXs feed signals to
the various parts of the IC with respect to weighted signal probability
during the testing phase. The main goal of this paper is to increase the
overall transition probability throughout the IC with an optimal number
of 2-to-1 MUX insertions.

Keywords: Design for testing · Hardware trojan ·
Transition probability

1 Introduction

In the current IC manufacturing scenario, the manufacturers often have to
depend on various third-party companies that provides them with the necessary
tools in various phases of the process to manufacture their ICs. The dependence
on third-party companies in the manufacturing process exists because carrying
out all the manufacturing stages by one company is extremely expensive. Using
third party IPs (3PIP), depending on computer-aided design (CAD) tools created by other companies to design the IC, outsourcing the fabrication to other
companies are some of the practices which can leave the integrity of the IC at
stake. This is because less trustworthy elements in any of these phases have the
power to jeopardise the functionality of the original intended IC by incorporating

S. Rajaram et al. (Eds.): VDAT 2018, CCIS 892, pp. 173–185, 2019.
https://doi.org/10.1007/978-981-13-5950-7_15

malicious modifications in the circuitry that has the potential to wreak havoc in critical applications.

Modifications in the circuitry through insertion or resizing of gates can occur in the design, fabrication or manufacturing phases of the IC. They can be of hardware modifications where application-specific integrated circuits (ASIC), commercial-off-the-shelf (COTS) parts, micro-controllers, microprocessors, digital signal processors, or network processors are altered physically or even modifications in the firmware like field-programmable gate array (FPGA) bit-streams [17]. Components with hardware trojans can lead to failures in mission critical operations. This is an unacceptable condition especially when they are used in military equipments, nuclear plants or aerospace industries, because for them the slightest malfunction can lead to devastating results [2].

The hardware trojans are deemed stealthy because they are often inserted in nodes with low controllability and observability. This ensures that they are only activated in rare conditions of logical states. Compared to the infected host, the hardware trojans are negligible in size [15]. Standard automatic test pattern generation (ATPG) techniques are insufficient for efficient detection of the malicious circuits since they are designed according to the netlist of the trojan-free version of the original circuit [18].

Test patterns need to be efficient in detecting presence of hardware trojans. Hardware trojan detection can be improved by applying both test patterns and side channel analysis methods. Proper test patterns chosen such that the trojan activity is enhanced all the while reducing the circuit activity helps in their detection using transient power analysis [3]. On the other hand, in the method of delay analysis, any abnormal delay in the path of the signal due to the presence of gates of the trojan circuit can be observed by applying proper test patterns. These are chosen such that the inputs of trojans present in the circuit undergoes transition [10].

The reduction of the condition of rarity that activates the trojan circuit is explored in this paper. Generation of transitions in the trojan circuit leads to their activation. The transition probability of each net has been determined by using geometric distribution, and is used to derive the expected number of clock cycles which would be required for a transition to take place. Nets with low transition probability are identified and are highlighted for reduction of rarity in their transition condition. To increase the transition probability in the nets with low controllability and observability without changing the functionality of the original circuit, scan-in and scan-out registers paired with 2-to-1 MUXs are used.

During the testing phase, these 2-to-1 MUXs provide the signals based on the weighted signal probability in order to raise the transition probability of the target nets. The MUXs are inserted in such a way that all the nets in the circuit achieve the maximum possible transition probability which would ensure the activation, or, at the very least, transition in the rare nets where insertion of hardware trojan are possible. This process is carried out with the objective in mind that overall transition probability throughout the circuit is increased with the optimal number of 2-to-1 MUX insertions, such that significant area overhead is not incurred.

The experiments conducted by us showcases the decrease in rarity of transition in nets with minimal 2-to-1 MUX insertion in polynomial time. In large trojan circuits, such decrease in rarity of transition in nets would promote transitions in the trojans' trigger. This would help them to be detected using side-channel analysis techniques. In case of trojans of small sizes, reducing the rarity of nets also gives rise to the chance of fully activating the hardware trojan circuit and its detection by observing the erroneous result in the output.

The paper has been structured as follows: Sect. 2 of this paper shows the related works where various measures for dealing with hardware trojans is stated, Sect. 3 states the motivation behind the proposed technique, Sect. 4 introduces the proposed method for detection of hardware trojans, Sect. 5 includes the simulation results of the experiments conducted and lastly, Sect. 6 ends the paper with concluding statements.

2   Related Works

There are various methods of facilitating detection of hardware trojans inserted within a circuit. They include approaches like reverse engineering, logic testing, IP trust verification and side-channel analysis, design for security approaches of the circuit under test (CUT) and runtime monitoring of the circuit [4].

Reverse engineering process is used to determine the internal components of an IC. Meticulous separation of the components of an IC is conducted such that the underlying logic is revealed. Such a process is categorised as a destructive process since the original circuit is unobtainable after the reverse engineering is conducted on it. Although this process has a hundred percent success rate detecting trojans, it is deemed as an impractical one because currently it is very expensive and time-consuming which does not yield acceptable throughput [13].

Side-channel analysis on ICs are used to monitor their parametric values, especially transient current analysis that is useful for detecting switching activity within the IC [11], static current analysis which is used in the absence of switching by analysing the cumulative consumption of leakage current of the static CMOS gates by undesired components [1] and path delay analysis where propagation delay of signals is monitored in the circuit to detect the presence of any malicious modification [12]. However, with the ever decreasing size of the IC, the existence of noise in the analysis results due to environmental and process variations makes the side-channel analysis on its own an ineffective source of detecting hardware trojans [5].

Logic testing is a method used to detect hardware trojans by exciting the IC to a phase in which the rare trigger condition of the hardware trojan is achieved during testing phase, thus detecting its presence by confirming the payload output. This is achieved by acquiring a compact set of test patterns which are statistically probable to trigger any malicious circuits [8,9]. Test patterns can also be generated using genetic algorithms and boolean satisfiability algorithms by detecting possible payload nodes using probabilistic analysis [14].

Design for Security approach proposes the inclusion of extra hardware components in the circuit. This can help obfuscating the circuit design such that the attacker finds the process of inserting hard to detect trojans difficult [6,7]. In this approach, the extra hardware can also be used for improving the controllability and observability of the circuit by increasing the transition probability of the signals within it. In this way, during the testing phase, the low probability nets are more inclined to get excited thus revealing the presence of any malicious circuit through parametric analysis or direct triggering of the payload [15,19].

3   Motivation

The hardware trojans are covert in nature primarily because they are introduced in the nets of the host circuit where the controllability and observability values are low. It also implies that the insertion points of hardware trojans in the host have less transition probability compared to the other portions of the circuit.

This observation has prompted the need for introducing methods to identify such points in the circuit and increase their transition probability so that state transitions or activation of inserted malicious circuitry can become more probable during the testing phase. This would lead to detection of any inserted hardware trojans by observing deviations in parametric values through side-channel analysis, or observing erroneous values at the output in case of successful trigger activation. The transition probability of the nets can be improved by applying DFT techniques which can be activated in the testing phase. Previous works involving this concept has been done by a Salmani et al. [15] and Zhou et al. [19] as stated in Sect. 2.

However, Shekarian et al.'s [16] work introduced a technique where a net with transition probability lower than the threshold can be introduced in the circuit using nets closest to the threshold and a single AND/OR gate. This invalidates the previously mentioned techniques since it shows how easily a hardware trojan with low detectability can be inserted even with transition probability improvement mechanisms.

This encourages us to use better techniques to increase the transition probability of the nets such that mere inclusion of a single gate does not easily affect the transition probability by lowering its value to an alarming extent. One of the ways in which this can be achieved is by ensuring that all the nets in a given circuit has the maximum possible transition probability.

Transition probability in a net is maximum only when signal in the net in question is random. This can only be achieved when the signal probability of net i being '1' (say Pr_i^1) and the signal probability of being '0' (say Pr_i^0) are of the same value, which is 0.5. Therefore, the probability of generating a transition in signal from '0' to '1' or '1' to '0' in the ith net can be evaluated as $TP_i = Pr_i^1 \times Pr_i^0 = 0.25$.

In Fig. 1, nets G10, G13 and G15 have initial transition probabilities of 0.049735, 0.109375 and 0.131836 respectively. These are regarded as nets which are susceptible to hardware trojan infection. In [19], this same circuit has been

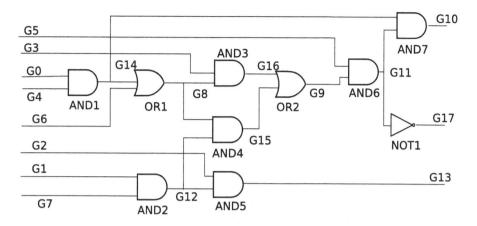

Fig. 1. Sample circuit

used where they declared the threshold transition probability TP_{th} as 0.15. Based on that declaration, using WSP and inserting two 2-to-1 MUXs in nets G12 and G14 they succeeded in raising all the nets' transition probability to more than that of TP_{th}. Compared to their results, using technique in [15] would require three insertions of dSFFs. Therefore technique in [19] would be considered superior among the two.

However, technique in [19] leaves G8, G10, G14 and G12 with transition probability 0.152344, 0.172257, 0.187500 and 0.187500 respectively. Even though all of these transition probabilities are above the previously declared TP_{th}, these nets are susceptible to compromise. This is because an adversary can take any of these two nets and create a net with severely low transition probability using only one AND or OR gate. Therefore, it is a noticeable fact that increasing the transition probability just above a declared threshold is not sufficient to ensure prevention of addition of a difficult-to-detect malicious circuit since this security measure can be circumvented by using technique mentioned in [16].

It should be our objective to increase the transition probability of every single net in the circuit such that they are all close to 0.25. One way of achieving that goal is by progressively adding 2-to-1 MUXs in the circuit according to the current transition probabilities and the logical depth of each net. The insertion point is chosen such that nets with lower transition probabilities and lower logical depth are preferred for their insertions. The logical depth of the nets are selected as a parameter because preferring nets with lower logical depth as insertion point would ensure the increase in overall transition probability since it would have the chance of including a lot of nets in its fan-out region. In doing so, changes in transition probability in a certain net will have the chance to be propagated a lot more, thereby optimising the required number of 2-to-1 MUX insertions.

Using our technique, upon four additions of 2-to-1 MUXs in G11, G0, G1 and G5 with WSPs 0.937500, 0.937500, 0.937500 and 0.875000 respectively, the resulting circuit will have nets with transition probability above 0.179443.

The resulting circuit will exhibit only 3 nets with transition probability less than 0.2 among total 25 nets. To detect the peak of our result, we simulate this technique until we find a stagnant or oscillating values in the overall mean and variance of transition probability in the entire circuit. Once such oscillation is detected, the simulation is halted with the peak value of mean and variance. The results should be judged by noticing the maximum value of mean and lowest value of variance.

4   Proposed Method

In this section, the proposed algorithm for maximising the transition probability of all the nets in a circuit will be discussed.

The transition probability in a particular section of the circuit is improved by using 2-to-1 MUX which is coupled with scan register. This results in a uniform structure helps using an optimal number of pin-outs even when there are a large number of insertions. In order to manipulate the logical value of a certain net, the insertion of a 2-to-1 MUX attached to a scan chain which provides the logical values is used. Such an architecture has proven to be the most efficient manner of increasing transition probability first introduced in [19].

In the test architecture, when the test enable (TE) signal is active, the commencement of test mode takes place. In this mode, the input of the target nets is supplied by the flip-flops in the scan chain through the 2-to-1 MUXs. The circuit retains its normal functionality when the TE signal is switched back to inactive mode.

A concern arises in such a setup, that an adversary can be made aware of such preventive techniques and can design their hardware trojans such that they would only operate when the TE signal is in the inactive state. In such a case, it is highlighted in [15] that repeated toggling of the TE signal excites the trojan into having an increased number of transitions. Such activity would enable the detection of any hardware trojans since it would affect the parametric values significantly.

The main objective of inserting the 2-to-1 MUXs is to reduce the difference in signal probability of being '1' and '0' as much as possible. Improving the transition probability of the input net of a sub-circuit which is the most influential. In case of the output of an AND gate, a low transition probability can insinuate that either the $Pr_i^0 >> Pr_i^1$ or that $Pr_i^0 << Pr_i^1$. With the transition probability of an AND gate evaluated as $Pr_i^1 = \prod_{k=1}^{N} Pr_k^1$, where k is the number of inputs of the AND gate, it is noted that the resultant signal probability has the tendency to be less than 0.5.

In the first case, the input net with the lowest Pr_j^0 contributes most to the lowering of the resultant transition probability. Increasing the transition probability of that net will have the maximum impact on the resultant net's transition probability of the AND gate. Similarly, for the second case, choosing the net with the minimum signal probability and decreasing its value to one around 0.5 contributes to the increase in the resultant transition probability.

Similar logic is applied while improving the transition probability in other gates. In this way, the increase in transition probability is ensured. It is also observed that applying weighted signal pattern, as opposed to random patterns, contributes in significantly better improvement in terms of transition probability in the output net. The process of choosing the optimal weighted signal probability is described in the next subsection.

4.1 Application of Weighted Signal Probability

Using weighted signal pattern can significantly optimise the insertion of 2-to-1 MUXs as opposed to just using random patterns. Using it can ensure elimination of rare nets in a circuit with an optimal number of 2-to-1 MUX insertions.

Algorithm 1. Algorithm to generate WSP

Input : WSP, $TargetNet$ and $Net - List$
Output: $Prob$

1 SP $\leftarrow$ EvalSignalProbability($Net - List$);
2 TP $\leftarrow$ EvalTransitionProbability(SP);
3 maxMean $\leftarrow$ 0;
4 minVar $\leftarrow$ 1;
5 **foreach** $value\ of\ WSP$ **do**
6 $\quad$ EvalTransitionProbability($TargetNet, Net - List, WSP_i$);
7 $\quad$ Mean $\leftarrow$ MeanEval($Net - List$);
8 $\quad$ Variance $\leftarrow$ VarianceEval($Net - List$);
9 $\quad$ **if** Mean $>$ maxMean and Variance $<$ minVar **then**
10 $\quad\quad$ maxMean $\leftarrow$ Mean;
11 $\quad\quad$ minVar $\leftarrow$ Variance;
12 $\quad\quad$ $Prob \leftarrow WSP_i$;
13 $\quad$ **end**
14 **end**

The weighted signal patterns are generated by using a linear feedback shift register (LFSR) having multiple AND and OR gates coupled with their output lines thus yielding signal probabilities of the form $(0.5)^n$. In this work the weighted signal probability list $\{1.0, 0.9375, 0.875, 0.75, 0.5, 0.25, 0.125, 0.0625, 0.0\}$ is used.

Having established the weighted signal probability (WSP) list, the question of choosing the correct signal probability which would provide the best results arises. When an insertion point in the candidate net is established, consulting the WSP list, the effect of using every WSP in the target net is evaluated. The overall mean and variance of transition probability in the circuit is evaluated at each application of WSP value at the candidate net. Algorithm 1 describes the process that has been applied. The WSP value for which the mean of transition probability in the entire circuit is maximum and at the same time the variance in transition probability value is minimum is chosen.

This technique ensures that the choice in WSP which contributes to the maximum overall improvement in transition probability in the entire circuit is the best one.

4.2   Algorithm to Select Insertion Points

The 2-to-1 MUXs are inserted in the circuit with the objective in mind that the overall transition probability of each and every net in the entire circuit is improved. In this section, the procedure of selecting the insertion points of the 2-to-1 MUX is discussed.

Algorithm 2. Proposed Algorithm

Input   : $Net - List$
Output: $Net - List$

1 Logical_Depth $\leftarrow$ EvalLogicalDepth($Net - List$);
2 SP $\leftarrow$ EvalSignalProbability($Net - List$);
3 TP $\leftarrow$ EvalTransitionProbability(SP);
4 I_MINTP $\leftarrow$ GetInputNet($Net - List$, TP);
5 LDOrder $\leftarrow$ OrderNet(I_MINTP, Logical_Depth);
6 NetHealth $\leftarrow$ HealthEval(LDOrder, TP);
7 TargetNet $\leftarrow$ SelectMinimum(NetHealth, $Net - List$);
8 Prob $\leftarrow$ EvalProbability(WSP, TargetNet, $Net - List$);
9 Insert2-to-1MUX($Net - List$, Prob, TargetNet);
10 $Net - List \leftarrow$ UpdateNetList($Net - List$);

Inserting a 2-to-1 MUX in the input of a gate yields to improvement of transition probability in its fan-out. The input of the gate with the lowest transition probability is chosen for this purpose. Improving the transition probability in the input with the lowest transition probability will result in maximum improvement of the transition probability in the output gate. This is because inputs with the lowest transition probability in a gate has the highest impact in the transition probability of its output. The array I_MINTP is constructed to store all such inputs for each gate.

The insertion points are chosen such that improvement of transition probability in one point in the circuit can lead to the propagation of the improvement in its fan out. To make this possible, nets with inputs that have lower logical depth are preferred. With the I_MINTP array, the logical depth of each input with lowest transition probability is noted. The health function described in Algorithm 2 comprises of the parameters of logical depth of inputs with minimum transition probability and the transition probability of the output net. The function is constructed such that it highlights the insertion points which can have the highest impact of overall improvement in the net. The minimum value in this array is chosen which directs to the gate in which the 2-to-1 MUX insertion would take place.

The algorithm is repeated until it detects oscillating or constant values of the overall mean and variance of the transition probability in the circuit in further 2-to-1 MUX additions. When it does so, the point of commencement of oscillation is detected and that is marked as final improvement of transition probability in the circuit. This method ensures that the maximum possible transition probability is achieved in all of the nets in the circuit, all the while inserting an optimal number of 2-to-1 MUXs.

4.3 Example

Applying this algorithm on Fig. 1, the WSP value of 0.937500 shows to be the best choice out of the list of WSP values for overall increase in transition probability of the circuit when a 2-to-1 MUX is added in G11. Using this value shows that the mean value of transition probability increases and the variance value in transition probability decreases in the overall circuit. This implies that he transition probability of all the nets in the circuit improves, tending to converge to the value 0.25. Similarly, to exhibit the best overall increase, the WSP values of 0.937500, 0.937500 and 0.875000 are chosen when the 2-to-1 MUXs are inserted at points G0, G1 and G5 respectively at subsequent iterations of the program.

In Fig. 1, the insertion points G11, G0, G1 and G5 are chosen as the insertion points for 2-to-1 MUXs in subsequent iterations, prioritised by their output transition probability and logical depth of their inputs. The WSP values as stated in the previous section are applied in those insertion points and the resultant circuit will have nets with transition probability above 0.179443. The resulting circuit will exhibit only 3 nets with transition probability less than 0.2 among total 25 nets.

Table 1. Results obtained by applying the proposed algorithm on s27, s298, s386, s1423 and s5378 circuits

Benchmark circuit	No. of nodes	No. of nets	No. of insertions	Nets with TP $\in [0, 0.1]$		Nets with TP $\in (0.1, 0.15]$		Nets with TP $\in (0.15, 0.2]$		Nets with TP $\in (0.2, 0.25]$		Insertion %
				Before	After	Before	After	Before	After	Before	After	
s27	21	30	1	0	0	7	0	6	11	17	19	4.54%
s298	145	261	4	11	8	15	18	45	46	190	189	2.74%
s386	182	358	24	61	22	27	42	48	66	222	228	13.11%
s1423	756	1290	39	98	56	83	90	242	232	867	912	5.15%
s5378	3045	4619	23	1024	936	295	295	400	455	2900	2933	0.755%

5   Experimental Results

The proposed algorithm is verified using simulations on ISCAS'89 benchmark circuits. The algorithm has been constructed using C language. The signal probabilities of all the primary inputs have been initialised to 0.5. The simulations have been run on a computer with Intel(R) Core(TM) i3 560 @ 3.33 GHz processor and 4 GB RAM.

The algorithm has been applied to s27, s298, s386, s1423 and s5378 ISCAS'89 benchmark circuits. The number of required insertion points to achieve a higher mean value in transition probability is seen to be directly proportional to the size of the circuits.

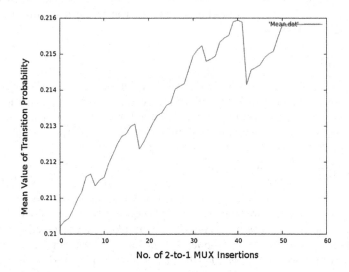

Fig. 2. Mean TP value of overall circuit per insertion of 2-to-1 MUX in s1423.

The results of the simulation is shown in Table 1. This table highlights the impact on transition probability that the insertion of 2-to-1 MUXs have on these benchmark circuits. The percentage of new insertions in order to counteract the state of rarity of the nets are evaluated. Running the algorithm on s5378 has the minimum impact on area overhead since the insertion percentage is shown to be only 0.755%. On the other hand, s386 shows to exhibit maximum area overhead with the insertion percentage of 13.11%. Figure 2 shows the progressive increase in overall mean transition probability value in s1423 circuit per 2-to-1 MUX insertion. Figure 3 showcases the overall variance value of transition probability in the entire circuit and how each insertion of 2-to-1 MUX influences it.

Table 1 denotes the count of nets after final insertion with transition probabilities $TP \leq 0.1$, $0.15 \geq TP > 0.1$, $0.2 \geq TP > 0.15$ and $TP > 0.2$ respectively. The table shows that maximum number of nets in the circuits have their transition probability improved beyond the value 0.15. Such an improvement ensures that lowering of the transition probability in the net is made much more difficult by adding only a negligible number of extra gates in the circuit. It is to be noticed that apart from s27, the rest of the benchmark circuits shows a number of nets with transition probabilities below 0.15. These nets should be considered

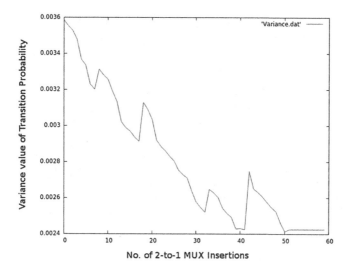

Fig. 3. Variance of TP value of overall circuit per insertion of 2-to-1 MUX in s1423.

as a critical part of the resultant circuit and should be monitored for they have more chance of being compromised by an adversary.

6   Conclusion

In order to detect insertion of malicious hardware trojans in the circuit we have proposed a logical testing algorithm which would increase the overall transition probability of circuits. This strategy is used to excite the nets which has low controllability and/or observability which results in transitions in those nets. Such transitions enables the detection of malicious circuits having the affinity to the inserted in those regions through side-channel analysis or even direct triggering of the trojans yielding the erroneous result at the output.

The transition probabilities of all the nets of the circuit under test are increased to their maximum possible values. This is achieved by inserting 2-to-1 MUXs with weighted signal probability into specific regions of the circuit with low logical depth and low transition probability. The resultant circuit shows a significant improvement in transition probability such that further reduction of their value cannot be achieved through negligible additions in the circuit.

References

1. Aarestad, J., Acharyya, D., Rad, R., Plusquellic, J.: Detecting Trojans through leakage current analysis using multiple supply pad I_{rmDDQ}s. IEEE Trans. Inf. Forensics Secur. **5**(4), 893–904 (2010). https://doi.org/10.1109/TIFS.2010.2061228
2. Adee, S.: The hunt for the kill switch. IEEE Spectrum **45**(5), 34–39 (2008). https://doi.org/10.1109/MSPEC.2008.4505310

3. Banga, M., Hsiao, M.S.: A region based approach for the identification of hardware Trojans. In: 2008 IEEE International Workshop on Hardware-Oriented Security and Trust, pp. 40–47, June 2008. https://doi.org/10.1109/HST.2008.4559047
4. Bhunia, S., Hsiao, M.S., Banga, M., Narasimhan, S.: Hardware Trojan attacks: threat analysis and countermeasures. Proc. IEEE **102**(8), 1229–1247 (2014). https://doi.org/10.1109/JPROC.2014.2334493
5. Bowman, K.A., Tang, X., Eble, J.C., Menldl, J.D.: Impact of extrinsic and intrinsic parameter fluctuations on CMOS circuit performance. IEEE J. Solid-State Circuits **35**(8), 1186–1193 (2000). https://doi.org/10.1109/4.859508
6. Chakraborty, R.S., Bhunia, S.: Security against hardware Trojan through a novel application of design obfuscation. In: 2009 IEEE/ACM International Conference on Computer-Aided Design - Digest of Technical Papers, pp. 113–116, November 2009. https://doi.org/10.1145/1687399.1687424
7. Chakraborty, R.S., Bhunia, S.: Security against hardware Trojan attacks using key-based design obfuscation. J. Electron. Test. **27**(6), 767–785 (2011). https://doi.org/10.1007/s10836-011-5255-2
8. Chakraborty, R.S., Wolff, F., Paul, S., Papachristou, C., Bhunia, S.: *MERO*: a statistical approach for hardware Trojan detection. In: Clavier, C., Gaj, K. (eds.) CHES 2009. LNCS, vol. 5747, pp. 396–410. Springer, Heidelberg (2009). https://doi.org/10.1007/978-3-642-04138-9_28
9. Huang, Y., Bhunia, S., Mishra, P.: MERS: statistical test generation for side-channel analysis based Trojan detection. In: Proceedings of the 2016 ACM SIGSAC Conference on Computer and Communications Security. CCS 2016, pp. 130–141. ACM, New York (2016). https://doi.org/10.1145/2976749.2978396
10. Jin, Y., Makris, Y.: Hardware Trojan detection using path delay fingerprint. In: 2008 IEEE International Workshop on Hardware-Oriented Security and Trust, pp. 51–57, June 2008. https://doi.org/10.1109/HST.2008.4559049
11. Narasimhan, S., et al.: Hardware Trojan detection by multiple-parameter side-channel analysis. IEEE Trans. Comput. **62**(11), 2183–2195 (2013). https://doi.org/10.1109/TC.2012.200
12. Rai, D., Lach, J.: Performance of delay-based Trojan detection techniques under parameter variations. In: 2009 IEEE International Workshop on Hardware-Oriented Security and Trust, pp. 58–65, July 2009. https://doi.org/10.1109/HST.2009.5224966
13. Rostami, M., Koushanfar, F., Karri, R.: A primer on hardware security: models, methods, and metrics. Proc. IEEE **102**(8), 1283–1295 (2014). https://doi.org/10.1109/JPROC.2014.2335155
14. Saha, S., Chakraborty, R.S., Nuthakki, S.S., Anshul, Mukhopadhyay, D.: Improved test pattern generation for hardware Trojan detection using genetic Algorithm and Boolean satisfiability. In: Güneysu, T., Handschuh, H. (eds.) Cryptographic Hardware and Embedded Systems - CHES 2015. LNCS, vol. 9293, pp. 577–596. Springer, Heidelberg (2015). https://doi.org/10.1007/978-3-662-48324-4_29
15. Salmani, H., Tehranipoor, M., Plusquellic, J.: A novel technique for improving hardware Trojan detection and reducing Trojan activation time. IEEE Trans. Very Large Scale Integr. (VLSI) Syst. **20**(1), 112–125 (2012). https://doi.org/10.1109/TVLSI.2010.2093547
16. Shekarian, S.M.H., Zamani, M.S., Alami, S.: Neutralizing a design-for-hardware-trust technique. In: The 17th CSI International Symposium on Computer Architecture Digital Systems (CADS 2013), pp. 73–78, October 2013. https://doi.org/10.1109/CADS.2013.6714240

17. Tehranipoor, M., Koushanfar, F.: A survey of hardware Trojan taxonomy and detection. IEEE Des. Test Comput. **27**(1), 10–25 (2010). https://doi.org/10.1109/MDT.2010.7
18. Wang, X., Tehranipoor, M., Plusquellic, J.: Detecting malicious inclusions in secure hardware: challenges and solutions. In: 2008 IEEE International Workshop on Hardware-Oriented Security and Trust, pp. 15–19, June 2008. https://doi.org/10.1109/HST.2008.4559039
19. Zhou, B., Zhang, W., Thambipillai, S., Jin, J.T.K., Chaturvedi, V., Luo, T.: Cost-efficient acceleration of hardware Trojan detection through fan-out cone analysis and weighted random pattern technique. IEEE Trans. Comput.-Aided Des. Integr. Circuits Syst. **35**(5), 792–805 (2016). https://doi.org/10.1109/TCAD.2015.2460551

Enhanced Logical Locking for a Secured Hardware IP Against Key-Guessing Attacks

R. Sree Ranjani[1(✉)] and M. Nirmala Devi[2]

[1] Department of Electronics and Communication Engineering,
Amrita School of Engineering, Coimbatore, India
r_sreeranjani@cb.amrita.edu
[2] Amrita Vishwa Vidyapeetham, Coimbatore, India
m_nirmala@cb.amrita.edu

Abstract. The vulnerability of hardware Trojans in digital integrated circuits (IC) and their prevention methods are studied in the past decade. The focus of this work is to prevent the hardware Trojan insertion by a built-in locking mechanism known as hardware encryption. The main objective of the techniques proposed is to build a secured logical locking such that (i) an incorrect key will result a functionally locked design and (ii) it is difficult to attain the secret key. In order to build a strong hardware encryption technique, the locking key is to be placed at high observable nodes of the design. Furthermore, the proposed scheme will address the key-guessing attacks like Brute force attack, Hill climbing attack and as well as path sensitization attacks, and provide the corresponding countermeasures. Experimental results present a highly secured locking mechanism with acceptable design overhead, when the proposed technique is employed on ISCAS'85 benchmark circuits.

Keywords: Hardware locking · Key-gates insertion ·
High observability nodes · Output corruption · Design-for-security

1 Introduction

The emerging hardware threat in large number of applications, from consumer electronics all the way to defense systems is considered as a growing concern. These threats occur when the fab-less Integrated Circuit (IC) companies are outsourcing their de- sign to external untrusted foundries for manufacturing process. Intellectual property (IP) piracy, illegal IC overbuilding, reverse engineering and malicious circuit insertion known as hardware Trojans (HT) are the major hardware vulnerabilities [11, 12, 14]. The main goal of adversary in untrusted foundry is: (1) to obtain the design functionality by reverse engineering or (2) to gain design knowledge that enables its manipulation. The adversary in the foundry may have access to the GDS-II file of the design and claim the IP ownership by means of reverse-engineering. Due to these threats, the semiconductor industries lose several billion dollars every year [5]. Thus, an IC design engineer has a major challenge to produce a secured design such that the adversary may fail to obtain the circuit functionality through reverse-engineering. Challenges of IC industries

© Springer Nature Singapore Pte Ltd. 2019
S. Rajaram et al. (Eds.): VDAT 2018, CCIS 892, pp. 186–197, 2019.
https://doi.org/10.1007/978-981-13-5950-7_16

to regain the trust of end-users are discussed in [16]. From which design-for-security (Dfs) techniques are considered to be authentic and hence chosen.

2 IP Piracy Threat Model and Defenses

The main objective of the attacker is to determine the secret key by defeating the purpose of logical locking. This is to functionally unlock the circuit and to add the Trojans in the netlist, or to make pirated copies of IPs, and illegally sell them in the market. The attacker with the knowledge of logical locking can easily insert Trojans by analyzing the structural behavior of the design. The attacker with the help of functional IC from the end-user will try to obtain the key of the encrypted netlist either from the IC design (1), or from the layout (2) or from the mask (3) during fabrication, by means of reverse engineering or from the packaging unit (4), that is manufactured non-functional IC as shown in Fig. 1.

To prevent IP piracy, techniques like IC camouflaging [10], split manufacturing [6], watermarking [13], Trojan activation [9], logic encryption [3, 12, 17], online checking [2] are proposed as countermeasures. Among these techniques, logic encryption also known as logical locking or logic obfuscation is one of the popular countermeasure to IP piracy and Trojan insertion. In logic encryption henceforth known as hardware encryption, additional key-gates are added to the original design to mask/hide the circuits functionality. When the correct key inputs are applied the encrypted/locked design is unlocked or else the functionality of the circuit is locked/incorrect. The manufactured IC is activated by the designer with the correct keys stored in a tamper-proof memory. Illegally overproduced ICs are also cannot be used without unlocking the design with the correct keys. Such a scheme is implemented in this work and has been validated on combinational benchmark circuits.

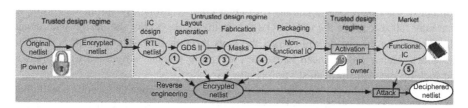

Fig. 1. Ending piracy of integrated circuits (EPIC) design flow [12]

3 Metrics for Logical Locking

To evaluate the proposed logical locking scheme, the following metrics are considered: (i) Hamming distance (HD) between the logically locked netlist and the original netlist, when an incorrect key is applied [9]. (ii) Number of key-gates inserted to produce an optimum HD value of 50% faulty output, when an incorrect key is applied to the encrypted design [8].

4 Background and Objective

The key-gates used for hardware encryption techniques are XOR/XNOR gates [9, 12, 17], multiplexers [9], AND/OR gates [3], in some encryption techniques a combination of all the above gates are also used [7]. In EPIC [12], XOR/XNOR key-gates are inserted randomly into the design, when an invalid key is applied the original logic is inverted by the key-gates to produce a wrong output. When a valid key is applied, these locking keys act as buffer and produce a correct logical output. However, the attacker can easily guess the valid keys to unlock the circuit with the basic encryption knowledge and random insertion of key-gates does not always produce an incorrect output for an invalid keys. Hence, locations of key-gates place an important role in locking the digital circuits for security.

In order to enhance the logical locking technique by producing high output corruption, the key-gates are placed at the high fault impact nodes based on fault analysis approach [8, 9]. The locations of inserting key-gates are selected upon three basic phenomena of IC testing principle such as: fault excitation, fault propagation and fault masking. The basic idea is upon applying an incorrect key, either a stuck-at-0 (s-a-0) or stuck-at-1 (s-a-1) are excited and these faults are propagated towards the output to corrupt a maximum number of output bits. The nodes with maximum fault impact are the potential locations to insert key-gates. For an incorrect key the designer will controllably corrupt the 50% of output bits by the fault excitation and propagation method.

However, by means of path sensitization attack [17] an attacker will extract the keys inserted by both randomly and fault analysis methods. This is done by sensitizing the key-bit to the output for a specific input pattern and upon applying the same input patterns to the encrypted netlist, the key-value can be revealed. Yasin *et al.* [17] had inserted the key-gates at the locations to mitigate the path sensitization attack by increasing the interface between the key-gates. However, it is difficult to find a large number of interfacing key locations for bigger circuits. Moreover, an increased clique size may fail to corrupt the output bits for an invalid keys. For the design with small clique size, the adversary will extract the keys through Brute-force attack is a major drawback. Hence an enhanced hardware encryption scheme is required to strengthen the locking mechanism against various attacks.

The main goal of a designer is to insert a key-gate at the specific locations, such that it should produce a high output corruption for wrong keys and this increases the attackers ambiguity. Moreover, the key extraction should be difficult for an attacker. The proposed work is to satisfy the above mentioned criterias by inserting key-gates at the specific locations. In this scheme, the strengthened key-gates are inserted on the nodes with high testability measure called observability. Thus the proposed encryption approach ensures high output corruption for incorrect keys and increases the attackers ambiguity to postulate the valid key by examining the output. The key-length of the proposed scheme is fixed to *10*, taken from the primary input bits of the circuit. The adversary has to attempt for 2^{10} input combinations to reveal the key-input and this is difficult with a sufficiently large key-bit size. The encryption key-gates are distributed at different locations and this makes a path sensitization attack practically impossible.

The proposed hardware encryption scheme is evaluated against a several security attacks like brute-force attack, hill-climbing attack and shows that the encrypted design is secured from most of the addressed attacks.

5 Proposed Hardware Encryption Scheme

The proposed hardware encryption technique with *10 bits* of valid key from the primary input to unlock the encryption module is discussed here. The technique is divided into two phases: (1) Identification of location to insert key-gates and (2) Insertion of hardware encryption module. Figure 2 presents the proposed work flow. Circuit-under test (CUT) to be encrypted is given as the input, and the testability measure for each gate are analyzed to determine the controllability and observability values [1]. The nodes with high observability values are chosen as a node of interest to insert the encryption module. This is because when an incorrect key is applied, the nodes with high observability values will propagate the faults excited by the proposed encryption module towards the output. Thus the encrypted netlist is obtained and the input patterns are applied to validate it. If a valid primary input key is applied the encrypted netlist is functionally unlocked to produce a correct output, whereas if an invalid key is applied the design is logically locked and produce an incorrect output bits. Thus the proposed hardware locking mechanism will secure the IP from the malicious modification, illegal overproduction, etc.

The design to be encrypted is give as an input to the testability measure Algorithm. 1, which analyses the nets of the design and calculates the controllability values of each nets. By using the controllability values, the observability values of each nets are calculated. Once the computation is done, the average of all observability values is calculated and it represents the *observability threshold value* (θ). Then a range is set to segregate the nodes of the design as *low observable* (LO) nodes between the range of ($0 \leq \theta/2$), *medium observable* (MO) nodes between the range of ($\theta/2 < \theta$ and *high observable* (HO) nodes between the range of ($\theta \leq \theta_{max}$), where θ_{max} is a maximum observability value.

5.1 Identification of Location to Insert Key-Gates

The location of key-gates plays a vital role in encryption technique, as sometimes the randomly placed key-gates are failed to corrupt the output bits due to fault masking. In the proposed scheme, the nodes are selected based on the testability measure called observability. The observability of any node is defined as a difficulty in observing each node. Here, the nodes with high observability (HO) are chosen as a node of interest to insert key-gates. This is because when an invalid key is applied, the encrypted module will excite a fault in these nodes and the excited faults are easily propagated towards the output without masking the excited faults. If the high observability nodes are faulty, then they will corrupt the output bits and the Hamming distance between correct and corrupted output will be high. Algorithm. 1, describes the gate selection based on the testability measures as shown in Fig. 3 [1]. It overcomes the need for having the in-built design-for-test (DfT) features in the circuit and hence dependence on EDA tool is overcome.

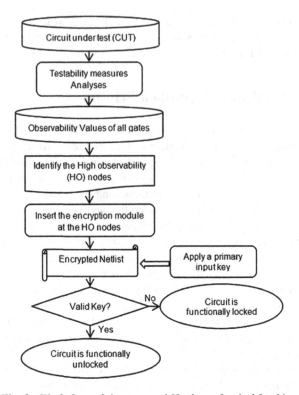

Fig. 2. Work flow of the proposed Hardware Logical Locking

Once the nodes of interest are selected, the encryption module is inserted on these nodes. To produce a *50%* bit flipping in the primary output the selected number of XOR gates are inserted in the chosen HO nodes.

5.2   Insertion of Hardware Encryption Module

Conventionally, the basic gates like XOR/XNOR/MUX or combination of all these gates are used as key-gates for logical encryption techniques. However, the adversary will attain the hidden keys either by brute-force attacks or by the path sensitization attacks. Hence a strengthened hardware locking is required to protect the IP from various threats. The proposed encryption module consists of two parts as: a trigger and a payload as shown in Fig. 4. When a specific set of key input patterns are applied to the trigger part of the encryption module, the trigger circuit will generate an intermediate key to be applied to the payload which will produce output *0* logic. The output of the payload is applied as an input for the distributed XOR gates, where the other input of the XOR gate is the output nodes of high observability gates. Hence for a valid primary input key, the payload produce a *0* output and the XOR gate now acts as a buffer to propagate the logic value of high observability nodes towards the output. This results in a correct functionality of the encrypted design. The trigger circuit is designed with a

Controllability calculation

Combinational 0-controllability, cc0(z)= min (cc0(a), cc0(b))+1;
Combinational 1-controllability, cc1(z)= cc1(a), cc1(b)+1;
Observability calculation

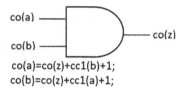

co(a)=co(z)+cc1(b)+1;
co(b)=co(z)+cc1(a)+1;

Fig. 3. Sample Observability calculation of AND gate [1]

logical gates, such that on applying a correct sequence of specific set of input patterns it produces a *0* logic at the input of XOR gate to propagate the correct logical value of the HO node to the next level of the design. Whereas, if the sequence of specific set of input patterns is incorrect, it produces a logic *1* to the input of XOR gate which excites the faults at the HO node and propagated towards the primary outputs.

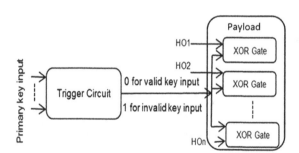

Fig. 4. Block diagram of proposed hardware encryption module

Thus when a wrong input key is applied to the encryption module, the payload will produce output logic *1*, which will excite an XOR gate to reverse the logic of the high observability nodes of the circuit. Then the excited faults at the nodes of interest are propagated towards the output to produce a high output corruption. This results in an incorrect functionality of the encrypted design. Once the encrypted design is unlocked the circuit will perform the normal function for all applied input patterns.

Algorithm 1. Generate the list of nodes to insert encryption module

---

Input: Circuit under test

Output: Identifying HO gates, based on the observability threshold (θ). Whereas, θ is the average of observability and θ_{max} is the maximum observability value of all gates in the design.

1. **Read** Input text File and assign the values of Input, Output nodes and Gates details to corresponding variables
2. Declare a variable level and set to 1
3. Iterate the List of Gates to identify the processable gates (i.e., if both inputs to the gates are available for processing).
4. Calculate Observability values for the current Gate inputs using SCOAP Observability calculation as shown in Fig. 3 [1].
5. List of Gates with the corresponding controllability and observability values and identify the nodes with high observability
6. **for** all gates in circuit do
7. Calculate the node Observability (No)
   find the Observability threshold (θ)
   if ($\theta \leq No \leq \theta_{max}$) then
   select the gate as high observability (HO) gate.
   end if
8. **end** for

---

6 Experimental Results

The proposed encryption scheme is evaluated on ISCAS'85 benchmark suites. The testability measures are analyzed and the encryption module is inserted in the original design with the distributed XOR Key-gates. Then the encrypted design is re-synthesized using Synopsys Design Vision tool [4] with SAED_EDK 90 nm technology. The key-length of the encrypted design is fixed to *10* bit and the area, power and delay overhead of the encrypted netlist with the original netlist are evaluated in Table 1.

If there exists *m* number of HO nodes, the design require one common trigger and payload module with *m* number of XOR gates to encrypt the design. By using Synopsys Design Vision compiler [4], the entire encrypted netlist is synthesized to calculate area, power and timing tools. It is observed that area overhead is within *10%* even for the large circuits like c6288 and c7552. Whereas, the power overhead of ISCAS'85 benchmark circuits are of minimum overhead at an average of *6.419%* and the delay overhead for most of the circuits is *0%*, as its critical path does not contain any key-gate.

The ability of the proposed encrypted scheme is evaluated, by calculating the hamming distance between the original output bits and the encrypted designs outputs. The average percentage of output corruption for a randomly generated input patterns are shown in Table 2. It is observed that *50.652%* of Hamming distance is achieved when a wrong key is applied with less percentage overhead of area, power and delay. Thus the enhanced encryption scheme satisfy all the criteria together, such as a wrong key gives corrupted output when a key-gates are inserted at a specific HO nodes and the adversary will fail to access the key easily, as a set of input sequence is given as a valid key. As the determined sequence of key-bits are extracted from the primary input of the design, it is practically impossible for the attacker to apply brute-force to extract the correct key-combination. Path sensitization attack is also fails to extract the keys, because the key-gates are distributed throughout the design at the HO nodes. Thus the proposed encryption module is highly secured against the key-guessing attacks (Fig 5).

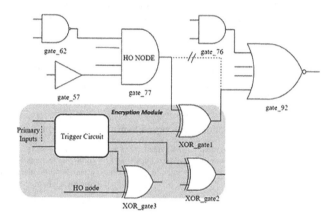

Fig. 5. Insertion of Hardware Encryption module at the HO node of c5315 benchmark circuit

Table 1. Overhead results of the encrypted netlists with the original design

ISCAS'85 circuits	Overhead (%)		
	Area	Power	Delay
c17	45.106	8.04	11.11
c432	24.761	2.26	0
c499	10.175	3.82	0
c1355	29.512	1.42	0
c1908	13.344	9.43	0
c2670	16.214	13.76	0
c3540	11.626	11.65	0
c5315	9.913	7.161	0
c6288	9.536	5.414	0
c7552	5.472	1.24	0
Average	*17.565*	*6.419*	*1.111*

7 Security Analysis Against Key-Guessing Attacks

The proposed encryption module is evaluated against several key-guessing attacks like brute-force attack, Hill-climbing attack and path sensitization attack. The brute-force attack initially apply the random input patterns to check the output of the encrypted netlist with the unlocked netlist. The attacker will try all possible keys to unlock the design. If the key-length of the encryption module is small it is possible to reveal the key, in the proposed method the key-length is fixed to *10* bits of the primary input of the design and a sequential set of input patterns are used to unlock the design functionality. Table 2 describes the evaluation of the enhanced hardware encryption scheme on ISCAS'85 benchmark circuits. It is observed that an average of *50.652%* of Hamming distance obtained for the encrypted circuit and thus the maximum output corruption proves that the proposed technique is a strengthened locking mechanism against a brute-force attack. It is clear from Table 2, that the output corruption is independent of number of input patterns and it depends on the number of XOR gates considered to encrypt the design.

Table 2. Evaluation of proposed hardware encryption

Circuit	No. of Primary Inputs	No. of Primary Outputs	Total No. of Gates	Observability threshold Value (θ)	Maximum observability value (θ_{max})	# of HO nodes	% of Input vectors corrupting Outputs when 10000 Random patterns applied	Corrupted output bits when wrong key is applied (%)
c17	5	2	6	2.333	5	2	100	50
c432	36	7	160	34.693	89	64	98.5	57.14
c499	41	32	202	157.821	299	128	98	46.87
c1355	41	32	546	204.904	351	344	99	50
c1908	33	25	880	75.652	259	505	98.8	52
c2670	233	140	1269	164.912	574	569	99	50
c3540	50	22	1669	108.564	529	594	98.25	50
c5315	178	123	2307	74.882	226	893	97.98	49.59
c6288	32	32	2406	422.716	754	1275	99	50
c7552	207	108	3513	538.281	892	1532	98.78	50.92
Avg	*72.11*	*52.3*	*1049.44*	*138.497*	*342.888*	*590.6*	*98.581*	*50.652*

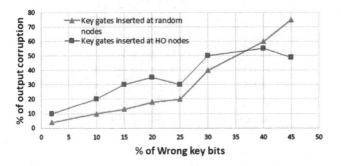

Fig. 6. Evaluation of c5315 against Hill-climbing attack

Moreover, hill-climbing attack is a process of randomly flipping the bits of keys to reduce the Hamming distance between the corrupted output and the original output. The attacker will reveal the key by reducing the Hamming distance to zero. The sustainability of the proposed encryption method against this attack, the design encrypted based on the testability measure is considered with the randomly inserted key gates.

Table 3. Evaluation of the proposed node selection method with fault analysis based logic encryption scheme

Circuits	Fault analysis method [8]			Proposed method		
	No. of XOR/XNOR gates	HD (%)		No. of XOR gates	HD (%)	
		Random nodes	FA nodes		Random nodes	HO nodes
c17	6	42	51	2	40	50
c432	17	29	50	12	27	57.14
c499	40	26	50	37	32	46.87
c1355	28	19	50	34	29	50
c1908	42	26	50	18	33	52
c2670	28	26	50	20	38	50
c3540	22	23	50	18	20	50
c5315	97	15	44	88	82	49.59
c6288	27	32	50	20	32	50
c7552	89	13	46	80	76	50.92

Figure 6 shows the difference in the output bit corruption on *c5315* benchmark circuit. This shows that the Hamming distance between the correct and observed output bits grows linearly with respect to the number of HO nodes. The linearity behavior of the output bits may allow the attacker to reach the correct key by flipping the input patterns. However, in the proposed scheme, output corruption decreases slowly when a number of HO nodes considered decreases. It is observed that more-than *10%* of output bits are corrupted by encrypting *5* HO nodes while for a random insertion of key-gates produces less than *5%* of corruption at the output bits. Thus by flipping one input bit will effect many key-gates, as they are distributed throughout the design and hence a single key flips will produce a high output corruption. Thus the proposed method strengthens the encryption scheme by restricting the extraction of valid primary key using the Hill-climbing attack. By encrypting about *25%* of HO nodes strengthens the design with a maximum output corruption of *50.652%* on average. Thus an optimum HD value of *50%* is obtained from the proposed scheme. This is because, if all bits flips the attacker gets the original circuit by just inverting them. *95%* is as bad as *5%*, *97%* is as bad as *3%* and so forth.

The other common attack used by the attacker to extract the key bits is the path sensitization attack, in which the keys are extracted with the help of functionally working IC available in the market. This is possible by sensitizing the key-bit towards the output and the outputs of both functionally unlocked IC and encrypted IC can be observed. If the output bits are same for a similar input key, the attacker will observe the key-value. However, this process of reveling the key-bit by comparing its functional logical values is not possible in the proposed method. This is because of the other key-gates will interfere in the sensitization path of distributed encryption nodes and this will stop the attacker to sensitize the path towards the output. Moreover, if the primary input key differ for each IC then the attacker will be deceived with the path sensitization attack.

8 Discussion

The proposed enhanced logical locking scheme is evaluated on ISCAS'85 benchmark circuits and their results are compared with the existing fault analysis (FA) based logic encryption method are shown in Table 3. It is observed that the proposed scheme requires less number of key-gates than the FA based scheme. Even for the large circuits like c7552 with total gates of *3513* produces an output corruption of *50.92%* of HD with *80* XOR gates as a key gates. Whereas, FA based encryption scheme [8] requires *86* XOR/XNOR gates, which produces an output corruption of *46%* only with HD as a metric. The above observation justify the superiority of the enhanced logical locking scheme over the state-of-the-art of FA based logic encryption technique.

9 Conclusion and Future Work

The proposed enhanced logic encryption technique is a primary input key based hardware locking mechanism. An average of *50.652%* output corruption is produced when a wrong key is applied and the key size is *10* bits of the primary input, so it is not easy to unlock the circuit with the random attempts. These two characteristics of the proposed scheme strengthen the encryption scheme, so that the adversary has to put more effort to reveal the valid keys. Extra hardware is required to ensure high security of the design, which is practically reasonable for large circuits. The encrypted design is preserved against the brute-force attacks, hill-climbing attacks and path sensitization attacks, since the adversary will fail to extract the unlocking key. Recently, SAT solvers are used to extract the valid input keys to unlock the encrypted design [15]. However, in the proposed scheme key-length is a random *10* bits of the primary input, so applying SAT-based attacks is assumed difficult. The future direction of this work is to establish a formal proof of resistance of the proposed encryption technique against SAT-based attack and to validate the strength of the encryption module against various hardware attacks.

References

1. Bushnell, M., Agrawal, V.: Essentials of electronic testing for digital, memory and mixed-signal VLSI circuits, vol. 17. Springer Science & Business Media, Boston (2004)
2. Chakraborty, R.S., Pagliarini, S., Mathew, J., Sree Ranjani, R., Nirmala Devi, M.: A flexible online checking technique to enhance hardware trojan horse detectability by reliability analysis. IEEE Trans. Emerg. Topics Comput. **5**(2), 260–270 (2017)
3. Dupuis, S., Ba, P.S., Di Natale, G., Flottes, M.L., Rouzeyre, B.: A novel hardware logic encryption technique for thwarting illegal overproduction and hardware trojans. In: 2014 IEEE 20th International On-Line Testing Symposium (IOLTS), pp. 49–54. IEEE (2014)
4. Guide, D.V.U., Version, D.: March 2010. synopsys R (2010)
5. Jose, S.: Innovation is at risk as semiconductor equipment and materials. Semiconductor Equipment and Material Industry(SEMI) (2008)
6. Kahng, A.B., Lach, J., Mangione-Smith, W.H., Mantik, S., Markov, I.L., Potkonjak, M., Tucker, P., Wang, H., Wolfe, G.: Watermarking techniques for intellectual property protection. In: 1998, Proceedings of Design Automation Conference, pp. 776–781. IEEE (1998)
7. Lee, Y.W., Touba, N.A.: Improving logic obfuscation via logic cone analysis. In: 2015 16th Latin-American Test Symposium (LATS), pp. 1–6. IEEE (2015)
8. Rajendran, J., Pino, Y., Sinanoglu, O., Karri, R.: Logic encryption: a fault analysis perspective. In: Proceedings of the Conference on Design, Automation and Test in Europe, pp. 953–958. EDA Consortium (2012)
9. Rajendran, J., Zhang, H., Zhang, C., Rose, G.S., Pino, Y., Sinanoglu, O., Karri, R.: Fault analysis-based logic encryption. IEEE Trans. Comput. **64**(2), 410–424 (2015)
10. Rajendran, J.J., Sinanoglu, O., Karri, R.: Is split manufacturing secure? In: Proceedings of the Conference on Design, Automation and Test in Europe, pp. 1259–1264. EDA Consortium (2013)
11. Rostami, M., Koushanfar, F., Karri, R.: A primer on hardware security: models, methods, and metrics. Proc. IEEE **102**(8), 1283–1295 (2014)
12. Roy, J.A., Koushanfar, F., Markov, I.L.: Ending piracy of integrated circuits. Computer **43**(10), 30–38 (2010)
13. Salmani, H., Tehranipoor, M., Plusquellic, J.: New design strategy for improving hardware trojan detection and reducing trojan activation time. In: 2009 IEEE International Workshop on Hardware-Oriented Security and Trust, HOST 2009, pp. 66–73. IEEE (2009)
14. Sree Ranjani, R., Nirmala Devi, M.: Malicious hardware detection and design for trust: an analysis. Elektrotehniski Vestnik **84**(1/2), 7 (2017)
15. Subramanyan, P., Ray, S., Malik, S.: Evaluating the security of logic encryption algorithms. In: 2015 IEEE International Symposium on Hardware Oriented Security and Trust (HOST), pp. 137–143. IEEE (2015)
16. Tehranipoor, M., Salmani, H., Zhang, X., Wang, M., Karri, R., Rajendran, J., Rosenfeld, K.: Trustworthy hardware: trojan detection and design-for-trust challenges. Computer **44**(7), 66–74 (2011)
17. Yasin, M., Rajendran, J.J., Sinanoglu, O., Karri, R.: On improving the security of logic locking. IEEE Trans. Comput. Aided Des. Integr. Circuits Syst. **35**(9), 1411–1424 (2016)

SARP: Self Aware Runtime Protection Against Integrity Attacks of Hardware Trojans

Krishnendu Guha(✉) ⓘ, Debasri Saha ⓘ, and Amlan Chakrabarti ⓘ

A. K. Choudhury School of Information Technology, University of Calcutta,
Kolkata, India
{kgchem_rs,acakcs}@caluniv.ac.in, debasri_cu@yahoo.in

Abstract. Globalization of the modern semiconductor design industry has evicted the hardware root of trust. Security principles are compromised at runtime due to the implantation of malicious circuitry or Hardware Trojan Horse (HTH) in the vulnerable stages of System on Chip (SoC) design, from less trusted third parties. Runtime security from integrity attacks or erroneous result generation due to HTHs is the focus of this work. The prevailing techniques adopt a redundancy based approach. Several limitations are associated with the redundancy based approach like inability to perform multitasking in a multitasking environment, inability to adapt to aging, use of fault diagnosis even in normal scenario and severe overhead in area and power. Incorporation of observe, decide and act (ODA) paradigm in the design of a SoC makes it self aware. We propose a self aware approach for facilitating runtime security, which overcomes the limitations of the existing redundancy based approach. Low overhead in area and power and better throughput than the redundancy based approaches as observed in experimental results aid its application for practical scenarios.

Keywords: Self awareness · Runtime security ·
Hardware Trojan Horse

1 Introduction

The recent era has witnessed the advent of the embedded domain which has redefined challenges for modern age system on chip (SoC) designers. Some of these include reduction of cost in SoC designing and meeting of stringent marketing deadlines. To achieve such objectives, the semiconductor design industry has adopted the globalization strategy which includes integration of intellectual properties (IPs) from different third party IP (3PIP) vendors and outsourcing the various phases of VLSI design to different parts of the world [2]. However, trust is a serious concern in globalization where malicious circuitry or Hardware Trojan Horse (HTH) may be implanted in the 3PIPs [11] or in less trusted foundries [17].

© Springer Nature Singapore Pte Ltd. 2019
S. Rajaram et al. (Eds.): VDAT 2018, CCIS 892, pp. 198–209, 2019.
https://doi.org/10.1007/978-981-13-5950-7_17

Research in this arena gained significant attention after HTH was recognized by the US government in 2005 as a significant threat to mission critical applications [1]. A HTH comprises of a trigger and a payload. The trigger enables it to remain dormant during testing and evade detection. The payload comprises of a malicious functionality which threatens the security principles of the SoC, after getting activated at runtime. Due to this, normal SoC testing methodologies is ineffective to tackle HTH threats. Logic testing and side channel analysis is commonly used to detect a HTH [2]. Logic testing involves creation of test vectors to generate the trigger state of a HTH, but such a technique renders ineffective in a complex architecture where the HTH is large and spreads over a set of IP cores. In side channel analysis, aid of external parameters like delay, critical path, power or a combination of all are sought to detect a HTH, with respect to a reference or golden architecture [16]. However, such a technique is ineffective where the size of a HTH is negligible compared to the size of SoC. Moreover, obtaining a golden model is difficult. This led to the development of statistical models [18]. Alternative design for trust methodologies were also proposed like the obfuscation technique for key based circuit structures [15] and layout filler technique to prevent insertion of a HTH in the empty spaces of a layout [17]. Several other techniques were proposed but none could provide a full proof protection. This led to the development of runtime security methodologies which are termed as the last line of defense by eminent researchers of this arena [2].

Our work focuses on tackling integrity attacks at runtime caused due to the vulnerability of hardware in an IP core, which generally performs a complex function or operation. Integrity attacks are basically active attacks which generate erroneous results and possess the capability to jeopardize a perfectly operating system.

The prevailing runtime security techniques utilizes a redundancy based approach to facilitate security from such vulnerability [8–10]. In this approach, several IP cores are procured from different 3PIP vendors, which perform the same functionality. Redundancy is introduced by executing the same task in all the IP cores simultaneously. As different IPs is procured from different vendors, possibility of existence of the same HTH in all cores is negligible. Moreover, time of HTH trigger will be different in different cores. Thus, possibility of same and simultaneous error generation in all cores is eliminated by satisfaction of these constraints, termed as distribution due to diversity constraints [11]. After task completion in all IP cores, fault diagnosis is applied to select the correct result. Several fault diagnosis strategies are proposed to generate trust at runtime. Comparison of results was proposed in [8], while [9] uses a polling methodology. Better results using weighted polling was demonstrated in [10].

Several limitations persist in such an approach. Though several IP cores are utilized, yet no multitasking is facilitated as the same task is executed in parallel in all of them. Fault diagnosis is performed naively, irrespective of fault occurrence. No mechanism is present which can adapt to aging. At least three cores are required for its successful execution. Increase in the number of IP cores enhances trust. However, overhead in area and power for a single task execution increases proportionally with the increase in number of cores.

Another runtime security methodology is the self aware approach. Self awareness can be incorporated on a chip by designing it based on the observe-decide-act (ODA) paradigm [19]. Such a technique involves consistent monitoring of runtime operations, i.e. observe. Based on this, it learns the natural scenario. On encountering an unnatural scenario, it triggers its deciphering unit or the fault diagnosis phase. The self aware module must act to bypass the unnatural scenario or adapt to it, if it is harmless. Self aware security strategy tackling confidentiality attacks of HTH was proposed by us in [12,13]. The proposed methodology facilitated intelligent fault diagnosis, i.e. performing fault diagnosis only when a vulnerability is detected and had the capability to adapt to aging. Self aware security strategy to mitigate availability attacks at runtime due to delay inducing HTHs was also proposed by us in [14].

In this work, we propose a self aware approach ensuring protection against integrity attacks of a HTH. Such a mechanism removes the limitations of the redundancy based approaches discussed earlier. In this technique, a self aware module is associated with each core of a multitasking environment. Thus, performance of each core is consistently monitored. Only if vulnerability is detected, the task is redundantly executed on some other core for fault diagnosis. Based on fault diagnosis, it either adapts to the new scenario if aging takes place or inhibits the operation of its host on detection of fault.

The paper is organized as follows. Section 2 discusses the threat model which jeopardizes the integrity of a system at runtime. The proposed security methodology is presented in Sect. 3. Comparison of the proposed methodology with the existing redundancy based approaches is also discussed in the same section. Section 4 deals with implementation and results and the paper concludes in Sect. 5.

2   Threat Model

2.1   Overview of SoC Design

Several phases are associated in the design of SoC architecture. It starts with the design phase where identification of a list of IPs is carried out by the SoC designer or integrator to fulfill the requirements of a given specification. The SoC designer then procures such IPs from one or more 3PIP vendors and integrates them to generate the register transfer level (RTL) description of the SoC design. After performing high level synthesis, netlists are generated. Layouts are generated after performing logic and physical synthesis on these netlists. The layouts are then sent for fabrication and after testing, the manufactured SoC's are deployed.

2.2   Attack Scenario

Scope lies in the implantation of Hardware Trojans in any phase of SoC design [2]. However, in this work, we only focus on the RTL design phase, which features

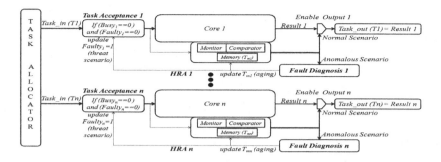

Fig. 1. Incorporation of security elements in an n core SoC architecture

procuring IPs from different 3PIP vendors. Trustworthiness of the 3PIP vendors is a significant concern in recent times [11]. We consider that the SoC designer is trusted and the environment in which the 3PIPs are integrated to generate the SoC is also secure. Hence, the CAD tools used for this purpose are also considered trusted, along with activities performed in the foundry.

2.3 Possible Trojan Structure

A basic HTH architecture essentially comprises a trigger module and a payload module [2]. The trigger mechanism might be external or internal. Reception of signals via sensors or antenna generally describes an external trigger. A combinational or a sequential circuit like a counter or a comparator facilitating activation via a rare combination of internal node values may be an internal trigger. Via the trigger, an HTH is able to remain dormant during testing and prevent detection.

For this work, the HTH trigger comprises of a counter and a comparator. The counter is initially set to 0, which increments its value with each operation. On reaching a pre-decided desired value, set by the adversary, it enables the effect of the malicious operation encapsulated in the payload.

The malicious functionality encapsulated in the payload module may vary according to the need of the adversary and is responsible for the threats posed by the HTH.

In this work, as only integrity issues are focused, the HTH payload comprises of additional undesired logic instructions, which leads to the generation of erroneous results.

3 Proposed Security Methodology

3.1 Self Aware Runtime Protection (SARP)

An n core homogeneous multitasking environment is considered. Similar to the redundancy based approaches, each IP core is assumed to be procured from different 3PIP vendors. To facilitate security, we associate with each core, i, where $i = \{1, 2, ...n\}$, two one bit status registers ($Faulty_i$ and $Busy_i$), a hardware

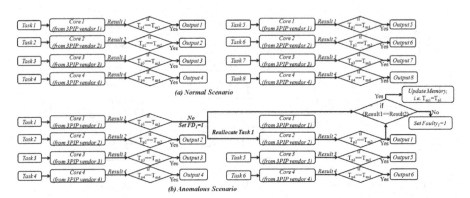

Fig. 2. Diagrammatic representation of security activity for (a) Normal Scenario (b) Anomalous Scenario

runtime agent (HRA_i) and a fault diagnosis module (FD_i). The two registers indicates the dynamic status of core i based on its runtime activities. HRA_i comprises of a monitor and a comparator, in addition to a register, which serves as its memory. It is associated with monitoring the runtime performance of core i and on detecting any anomaly, triggers the fault diagnosis module. The fault diagnosis module classifies the anomalous scenario either as aging or HTH threat. It adapts to aging by updating memory of HRA, else inhibits operations of the core by updating $Faulty_i$ to 1.

For detection of a HTH, we adhere to the clock sweeping methodology demonstrated in [4]. This works on the fact that the payload of a digital HTH introduces some additional logic or instructions. Hence, the number of clock cycles elapsed for task completion after HTH trigger must be greater than the normal scenario. However, an IP core may comprise of several paths from its input to output. Being an offline detection strategy, [4] classified and compared the timing of all the paths. However, for runtime security, this would incur a severe overhead in area and time. Time padding is a convention used for such scenarios [5]. Additional delay inducing structures are added in the design which aligns the timing of the paths. Such technique is also effective for mitigating confidentiality attacks via timing analysis. Even techniques like algorithmic balancing and masking are also prevalent which ensures alignment of the various paths during design to mitigate difference in the values of side channel parameters and ensure confidentiality of a system [6,7]. For this work, we also assume such IP cores where the total time incurred in generating the result is independent of the path traversed, and equivalent to the timing of longest path.

Incorporation of the security elements in an n core SoC architecture is shown in Fig. 1. The diagrammatic representation of security methodology is shown in Fig. 2. The security mechanism is also illustrated in Algorithm 1 and enumerated below.

Algorithm 1. Self Aware Runtime Protection (SARP)

Input: $Task\_in$
Output: $Task\_out$
begin

    for *input task, $Task\_in$, allocated to*
    $IP\_core\_i[f_i(Faulty_i, Busy_i, Input_i, Result_i)]$ **do**

        Task Acceptance **begin**
            if $Faulty_i == 0$ **and** $Busy_i == 0$ **then**
                Set $Input_i = Task\_in$;
                Set $Busy_i = 1$;

        Evaluation of Runtime Performance (Monitor of HRA_i) **begin**
            always @ (posedge clk)
            if *Task execution in progress* **then**
                $T_{pi} = T_{pi} + 1$

        Detection of Anomaly (Comparator of HRA_i) **begin**
            if $T_{pi} == T_{mi}$ **then**
                Set $Task\_out = Result_i$;
                Set $Busy_i = 0$;
                Reset T_{pi};

        else
            Trigger Fault Diagnosis, i.e. $FD_i = 1$

        Fault Diagnosis **begin**
            if $FD_i == 1$ **then**
                task reallocated to another core j, i.e.
                $IP\_core\_j[f_j(Faulty_j, Busy_j,\ Task\_in, Task\_out)]$
            if $Result_i == Task\_out$ $(i.e.Result_j)$ **then**
                Set $Busy_i = 0$;
                Set $T_{mi} = T_{pi}$ //Adapt to Aging;
                Reset T_{pi} and FD_i

            else
               Set $Faulty_i = 1$ //Status update for Fault

Task Acceptance: A task, $T(Task\_in, Task\_out)$ is accepted for execution by a core, i only if the core is neither faulty nor busy. The decision is based on the two status registers. $Faulty_i = 0$ indicates core i is active, while $Faulty_i = 1$ indicates operations of core i has been inhibited. $Busy_i = 0$ indicates core i is free for executing a task, while $Busy_i = 1$ indicates core i is performing a task.

Evaluation of Runtime Performance: Dynamic evaluation of runtime performance is the demand of the current scenario. Cycles per instruction is a dynamic measure of runtime performance for general processors [20]. However, as the set of instructions are fixed for hardware IP cores, it reduces to number of clock cycles elapsed for task completion by the core. This is termed as Embedded Timing Analysis (ETA) [3].

The monitor of HRA determines the ETA or the runtime performance of its host core for the present iteration, i.e. T_{pi}. It is basically a counter with an internal clock. This counter is reset before performing a new task.

Detection of Anomaly: The comparator of the HRA is responsible for detection of anomaly. T_{mi} represents the value of the memory register of HRA_i, which stores the worst case value of ETA encountered for task completion. This is initially set during testing, for a particular operational environment, and needs to be performed each time whenever a different operational environment is selected. As we adhere to a differential analysis of T_{pi} and T_{mi} for ensuring security, effects of process variation is also nullified. If $T_{pi} = T_{mi}$, then the core is considered fault free and the result of task completion is generated as output, i.e. $Task\_out = Result_i$. Else, some anomalous scenario have been encountered. It may either be due to aging or due to some Trojan activity. In such a case, the Fault Diagnosis mode is triggered.

Fault Diagnosis: In fault diagnosis, the same task is made to execute on a fault free core, j where $i \neq j$. The result of the host core, i.e. $Result_i$ is compared with the result of the fault free core, which is basically the task output, i.e. $Task\_out$. If both are same, then the additional ETA encountered is considered as a cause of aging. However, if the results differ, then an attack to integrity by HTH is confirmed.

Status Update: If aging is the scenario, then adapting to the new scenario is necessary for task performance in future. This is done by updating the value of T_{mi} to T_{pi}. However, if malicious scenario is detected, the status register $Faulty_i$ is set to 1, inhibiting task allocation to the core in future.

3.2 Comparison with Existing Redundancy Based Approaches [8, 10]

Multitasking: Though redundancy based approaches uses a multi-core environment, yet do not facilitate multitasking as the same task is executed in parallel. Our proposed approach (SARP) facilitates multitasking and only executes a task redundantly on some other core, when an anomalous scenario is encountered. This enhances throughput of the system.

Adaptation to Aging: Degradation of performance due to aging is inherent [18]. However, no provision for adaptation to aging is present in the redundancy based recovery techniques. SARP considers this factor and updates its action with time.

Intelligent Fault Diagnosis: Fault diagnosis, i.e. comparison or polling of results to select the correct one among all is used every time in redundancy based approaches, even when no malicious action takes place. SARP utilizes fault diagnosis intelligently, i.e. only when an anomalous scenario is detected.

Resource Utilization for Correct Result Generation during Attack. During attack, for correct result generation, at least three cores are needed by the redundancy based approaches, while only two cores are needed by our proposed approach to ensure generation of correct result. Hence, reduction of resource overhead is facilitated.

4 Implementation and Results

Design of the IP cores, attack scenarios and security modules is performed using Verilog in Xilinx Vivado Platform, targeted for ZynQ xc7z020-1clg484 evaluation board. Their behavioral correctness is validated in Xilinx ISim Simulator. Leonardo Spectrum of Mentor Graphics is used to generate the netlist files for 180 nm technology node. The netlists are imported in Pyxis ASIC platform of Mentor Graphics to analyze overhead incurred in area and power for 180 nm technology node. We choose some standard ISCAS 89 benchmark IPs and a 128 bit Advanced Encryption Standard (AES) cryptocore for experimentation.

4.1 Experimental Validation

For experimental validation, we consider a homogeneous two core SoC architecture. Sensitivity of clock in the monitor is of utmost importance to detect an unnatural scenario (which may be HTH action or aging). Lower is the periodicity of the clock, better is its sensitivity. We use a clock of periodicity 1 ns. We generate two scenarios as described below for experimentation.

Scenario 1 (S1) (Generation of Attack): HTH can be implanted in any stage of VLSI design. Vulnerability in the RTL design phase due to the untrustworthiness of 3PIP vendors is very common and has aroused considerable research interest in recent times [11]. For experimental analysis, we instantiate verilog code for a HTH and introduce it in the RTL of one of the IP cores of the two core SoC, just before final output is generated. The trigger of the HTH comprises of a 6 bit counter and activates the payload when the counter reaches $(111111)_2$. The payload comprises of an additional AND operation with logic 0, and utilizes one additional clock unit for its operation, such that the result generated is erroneous.

Scenario 2 (S2) (Aging): The second scenario represents aging, where we have modeled one of the IP cores in such a fashion that it takes an additional two clock cycles to generate its results after a certain time interval.

Table 1 provides the actual timing and the associated ETA values. As evident from experimental results of Table 1, for scenario S1, status of affected core after fault diagnosis due to HTH action renders inactive. However, after fault diagnosis for scenario S2, status of core due to aging remains active.

Table 1. Detection and fault diagnosis using SARP

IP Core	s5378		s9234		s15850		AES	
Scenario	S1 (Threat)	S2 (Aging)	S1 (Threat)	S2 (Aging)	S1 (Threat)	S2 (Aging)	S1 (Threat)	S2 (Aging)
Timing (ns) (normal IP)	14.21	14.21	20.56	20.56	29.79	29.79	40.68	40.68
ETA (normal IP)	15	15	21	21	30	30	41	41
Timing (ns) (affected IP)	15.31	16.65	21.66	22.96	30.87	31.93	41.79	42.91
ETA (affected IP)	16	17	22	23	31	32	42	43
Status after FD	Inactive	Active	Inactive	Active	Inactive	Active	Inactive	Active

4.2 Overhead and Throughput Analysis

Overhead Analysis: We analyze the overhead incurred in area and power, due to our security elements over the experimental cores in this section. To facilitate a secure environment, at least two cores are needed. Hence, we start with two cores and increment the number of cores (k) accordingly. Table 2 shows the overhead incurred in area and power for the various experimental IP cores. During fault diagnosis in an architecture with more than two cores, finding the core on which task reallocation has taken place incurs an additional overhead. Hence, a slight increment in overhead is associated with the increase in number of cores.

Throughput Analysis: Redundancy based approaches is silent on multitasking, though utilizes a multitasking environment. Our proposed approach facilitates multitasking and only executes a task redundantly on some other core, when an anomalous scenario is encountered. This enhances throughput of the system. A comparison of throughput showing the efficiency of our proposed approach to that of the approaches utilizing redundancy is demonstrated in this sub section.

Table 2. Overhead analysis of area and power

IP core	Number of cores (k)									
	$k = 2$ % increase in		$k = 3$ % increase in		$k = 4$ % increase in		$k = 5$ % increase in		$k = 6$ % increase in	
	Area	Power	Area	Power	Area	Power	Area	Power	Area	Power
s5378	6.33	3.01	6.87	3.29	7.42	3.56	8.31	3.92	9.51	4.38
s9234	4.02	1.72	4.36	1.87	4.71	2.04	5.27	2.24	6.03	2.51
s15850	2.81	1.01	3.06	1.09	3.29	1.19	3.68	1.31	4.22	1.46
AES	1.28	0.72	1.60	0.78	1.89	0.85	2.35	0.94	2.71	1.05

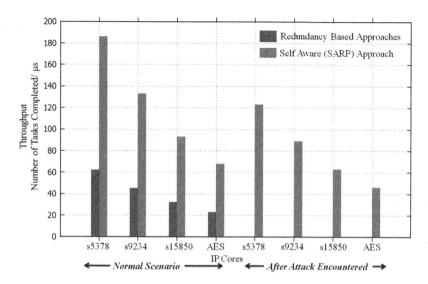

Fig. 3. Throughput analysis

A multitasking environment is selected with three cores for analysis of this scenario. This is due to the fact that at least three cores are required by any of the redundant techniques to function properly. As our proposed approach facilitates multitasking, throughput incurred is three times than the throughput obtained when the redundant technique is utilized for normal scenario, i.e. when no fault is incurred. This is evident from the graphical representation illustrated in Fig. 3 for the environment entitled *"Normal Scenario"*.

When a fault occurs in any one of the cores due to an attack or threat encountered, the techniques which utilizes redundancy ceases to function. Hence, throughput is nil. This is because the redundant techniques will need at least three cores to select the correct result via comparison or majority polling. However, our proposed approach can still function, detect anomaly and ensure recovery with at least two cores. Hence, two times throughput is still obtained when a fault in any one of the three cores is incurred. This is evident from the graphical presentation provided in Fig. 3 for the scenario entitled *"After Attack Encountered"*.

5   Conclusion

Hardware security has became an arena of concern in recent times due to globalization of semiconductor design industry. The present work focuses on integrity threats of HTHs. Existing runtime security techniques follow a redundant approach and suffer from a lot of limitations. We propose a self aware approach which overcomes these limitations by facilitating multitasking, providing consistent core monitoring, using intelligent fault diagnosis and having capability to adapt to aging. Experimentation is performed using ISCAS 89 benchmarks and

AES cryptocore. Low overhead and better throughput than existing methodologies as evident from Table 2 and Fig. 3 respectively, depicts the efficiency of our proposed technique.

Acknowledgement. This work is sponsored by the Department of Science and Technology, Government of India, INSPIRE Fellowship Number: 150916.

This research is supported by TEQIP Phase III, University of Calcutta (UCT-CU).

This work has also been supported partially through resources and financially by SMDP-C2SD project of the University of Calcutta, funded by MeitY, Government of India.

References

1. Defense Science Board: Task Force on High Performance Microchip Supply, February 2005. http://www.acq.osd.mil/dsb/reports/ADA435563.pdf
2. Bhunia, S., Hsiao, M.S., Banga, M., Narasimhan, S.: Hardware Trojan attacks: threat analysis and countermeasures. Proc. IEEE **102**(8), 1229–1247 (2014)
3. Taabatabaei, S., Ivanov, A.: Embedded timing analysis: a SoC infrastructure. IEEE Des. Test **19**(3), 22–34 (2002)
4. Xiao, K., Zhang, X., Tehranipoor, M.: A clock sweeping technique for detecting hardware Trojans impacting circuits delay. IEEE Des. Test **30**(2), 26–34 (2013)
5. Askarov, A., Zhang, D., Myers, A.C.: Predictive black box mitigation of timing channels. In: Proceedings of the 17th ACM Conference on Computer and Communications Security (CCS 2010), pp. 297–307. ACM, New York (2010)
6. Coron, J.-S., Goubin, L.: On boolean and arithmetic masking against differential power analysis. In: Koç, Ç.K., Paar, C. (eds.) CHES 2000. LNCS, vol. 1965, pp. 231–237. Springer, Heidelberg (2000). https://doi.org/10.1007/3-540-44499-8_18
7. Jayasinghe, D., Ignjatovic, A., Parameswaran, S.: NORA: algorithmic balancing without pre-charge to thwart power analysis attacks. In: 30th International Conference on VLSI Design, pp. 167–172 (2017)
8. McIntyre, D., Wolf, F., Papachristou, C., Bhunia, S., Weyer, D.: Dynamic evaluation of hardware trust. In: IEEE International Workshop on Hardware Oriented Security and Trust 2009 (HOST 2009), pp. 108–111 (2009)
9. Beaumont, M., Hopkins, B., Newby, T.: SAFER PATH: security architecture using fragmented execution and replication for protection against Trojaned hardware. In: Proceedings of Design, Automation and Test in Europe Conference and Exhibition (DATE), pp. 1000–1005 (2012)
10. Amin, H.A.M., Alkabani, Y.: Selim: system-level protection and hardware Trojan detection using weighted voting. J. Adv. Res. **5**, 499–505 (2014)
11. Liu, C., Rajendran, J., Yang, C., Karri, R.: Shielding heterogeneous MPSoCs from untrustworthy 3PIPs through security driven task scheduling. IEEE Trans. Emerg. Top. Comput. **2**(4), 461–472 (2015)
12. Guha, K., Saha, D., Chakrabarti, A.: RTNA: securing SOC architectures from confidentiality attacks at runtime using ART1 neural networks. In: 19th International Symposium on VLSI Design and Test, pp. 1–6 (2015)
13. Guha, K., Saha, D., Chakrabarti, A.: Real-time SoC security against passive threats using crypsis behavior of geckos. J. Emerg. Technol. Comput. Syst. **13**(3), 1–26 (2017). Article 41

14. Guha, K., Saha, D., Chakrabarti, A.: Self aware SoC security to counteract delay inducing hardware trojans at runtime. In: 30th International Conference on VLSI Design, pp. 417–422 (2017)
15. Chakraborty, R.S., Bhunia, S.: Security against hardware Trojan attacks using key-based design obfuscation. J. Electron. Test. **27**(6), 767–785 (2011)
16. Narasimhan, S., et al.: Hardware Trojan detection by multiple-parameter side-channel analysis. IEEE Trans. Comput. **62**(11), 2183–2195 (2013)
17. Xiao, K., Forte, D., Tehranipoor, M.: A novel built-in self-authentication technique to prevent inserting hardware Trojans. IEEE Trans. Comput. Aided Des. Integr. Circuits Syst. **33**(12), 1778–1791 (2014)
18. Huang, K., Liu, Y., Korolija, N., Carulli, J.M., Makris, Y.: Recycled IC detection based on statistical methods. IEEE Trans. Comput. Aided Des. Integr. Circuits Syst. **34**(6), 947–960 (2015)
19. Sarma, S., Dutt, N., Gupta, P., Venkatasubramanian, N., Nicolau, A.: Cyber physical system on chip: a self aware MPSoC paradigm with cross-layer virtual sensing and actuation. In: Proceedings of Design, Automation and Test in Europe Conference and Exhibition (DATE), pp. 625–628 (2015)
20. Zhai, X., Appiah, K., Ehsan, S.: A method for detecting abnormal program behavior on embedded devices. IEEE Trans. Inf. Forensics Secur. **10**(8), 1692–1704 (2015)

A VLSI Architecture for the PRESENT Block Cipher with FPGA and ASIC Implementations

Jai Gopal Pandey[1,2(✉)], Tarun Goel[2], Mausam Nayak[1,3],
Chhavi Mitharwal[1,3], Sajid Khan[4], Santosh Kumar Vishvakarma[4],
Abhijit Karmakar[1,2], and Raj Singh[1,2]

[1] CSIR- Central Electronics Engineering Research Institute, Pilani 333031, India
{jai,abhijit,raj}@ceeri.res.in,
nayak.mausam@gmail.com, chhavimitharwal@gmail.com
[2] Academy of Scientific and Innovative Research (AcSIR), CSIR-CEERI,
Pilani 333031, India
tarungoel.com@gmail.com
[3] Banasthali Vidyapith, Vanasthali, Rajasthan 304022, India
[4] Indian Institute of Technology Indore, Simrol, Indore 453552, India
{phd1601102015,skvishvakarma}@iiti.ac.in

Abstract. The infrastructure of internet-of-things (IoT) and cyber-physical systems (CPS) is based on the security of communicated data. Here, lightweight cryptography plays a vital role in IoT/CPS resource-constrained environments. In this paper, we propose an architecture for the PRESENT lightweight block cipher and its VLSI implementations in an FPGA and ASIC. The input-output ports of the architecture are registered and datapath is based on 8-bit. It requires 49 clock cycles for processing of 64-bit *plaintext* with 80-bit user key. The FPGA implementation of the proposed architecture is done in Xilinx Virtex-5 device in comparison to an existing design improved performance has been obtained. Further, an ASIC implementation of the architecture is done in SCL 180 nm technology where gate equivalent (GE) of the design is 1608 GEs and area of chip is 1.55 mm². At 100 MHz operating frequency, total power consumption of the chip is 0.228 mW. A throughput of 130.612 Mbps, energy 112.15 nJ, energy/bit 14.018 nJ/bit, and 0.813 efficiency is obtained.

Keywords: PRESENT block cipher · Lightweight cryptography ·
VLSI architecture · FPGA · ASIC

1 Introduction

The foundation of internet-of-things (IoT) [1], cyber-physical systems (CPS) [2, 3] and edge computing [2] technologies heavily rely on communicated data. As shown in Fig. 1, data can be between human-to-machines and their any combination [4]. In this fast-growing computing infrastructure, small computing devices are deployed for sensing, control, communication and computation needs. Subsequently, deployment trend of devices for IoT/CPS applications, bring a drastic change in designing of electronic circuits and associated systems. Here, the design metrics are being optimized for resource, latency, power and bandwidth [1].

© Springer Nature Singapore Pte Ltd. 2019
S. Rajaram et al. (Eds.): VDAT 2018, CCIS 892, pp. 210–220, 2019.
https://doi.org/10.1007/978-981-13-5950-7_18

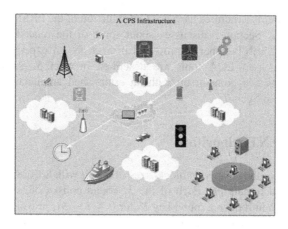

Fig. 1. A modern infrastructure of IoT, CPS and edge computing technologies.

Secure communication is very essential for restricting access of information to unauthorized persons or machines [3, 5, 6]. In this concern, cryptography plays a vital role. In cryptography, the encryption operation is used to convert data into a secure form that is known as ciphertext. Hardware-based security solutions with symmetric key cryptography algorithms are ideally suited to meet the IoT/CPS security challenges [5]. In a survey of lightweight-cryptography ciphers [7], it has been mentioned that, efficient implementation of the ciphers are closely dependent on the selection of appropriate architectures for achieving low implementation complexity and high performance. In the context of lightweight cryptography, ISO/IEC 29192-2 has standardized symmetric block cipher algorithm PRESENT in the year 2012 [8]. The algorithm provides adequate security goals along with hardware-oriented performance attributes which makes it a prominent choice for developing lightweight cryptographic applications [9].

In this paper we propose a hardware architecture for the PRESENT block cipher and its VLSI implementations for a field-programmable gate array (FPGA) device and an application-specific integrated circuit (ASIC). The architecture is based on 8-bit datapath, works on the 64-bit input and of 80-bit user key and provides 64-bit ciphertext in 49 clock cycles. The FPGA implementation of the architecture is done in Xilinx Virtex xc5vlx50 device and the architecture is proposed with an existing 8-bit datapath based architecture. In comparison, the proposed architecture outperforms in performance. The ASIC implementation of the proposed architecture is done in SCL 180 nm technology. Here, the chip operates on 3.3 V and the core works at 1.8 V. Total power consumption of the chip is 2.45 mW; where, the dynamic component is 0.211 mW and the static one is 0.016 mW. With 100 MHz operating frequency obtained a throughput of 130.162 Mbps, energy 112.15 nJ, energy/bit 14.018 nJ/bit are obtained. The efficiency of the design is 0.813. Total area of the chip is 1.55 mm^2 with 1608 two input NAND gate equivalent (GE).

Rest of this paper is structured as: a brief introduction of the PRESENT algorithm is provided in Sect. 2. Section 3 discusses about some of the related work. An architecture for the PRESENT cipher is proposed in Sect. 4. An experimental setup and detailed about the used EDA tools are described in Sect. 5. Section 6 provides experimental results and comparison with an established architecture. Finally, conclusions are given in Sect. 7.

2 The PRESENT Algorithm

The PRESENT algorithm works on block sizes of 64-bit with 80/128-bit user keys and requires 31 internal rounds [9]. Each of the 31 round consist of an XOR operation, which is required to introduce a round key K_i for $0 \leq i \leq 31$, in which K_{31} is used for post-whitening operation. Further, there is a linear bit-wise permutation layer and a non-linear substitution layer that uses a 4-bit S-box. The algorithmic steps is depicted in Fig. 2. It requires mainly four functions, which are explained in the following subsections.

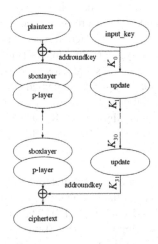

Fig. 2. A top-level algorithmic description of PRESENT cipher.

2.1 The Key Schedule

The cipher requires a unique round key (K_i) in each round, where the input key is $K(k_{79}k_{78}\ldots k_0)$ for 80-bit key or $K(k_{127}k_{126}\ldots k_0)$ for 128-bit key length.

2.2 Add Roundkey Operation (AddRoundKey)

With current state $b_{63}\ldots b_0$ and for the given leftmost 64-bit of the round key $K_i = k_{63}^i\ldots k_0^i$ (or $K_i = k_{127}^i\ldots k_{64}^i$); $0 \leq i \leq 31$. The *AddRoundKey* operation is defined as $b_j = b_j \oplus k_j^i$ for $0 \leq j \leq 63$ [9].

2.3   Substitution Box Layer

The cipher requires a 4-bit S-box (S) as $\mathbb{F}_2^4 \rightarrow \mathbb{F}_2^4$ [9]. 64-bit current state $b_{63}\ldots b_0$ is taken as 16, 4-bit words $w_{15}\ldots w_0$. Where, $w_i = w_4 \times i + 3 \parallel w_4 \times i + 2 \parallel w_4 \times i + 1 \parallel w_4 \times i$ for $0 \leq i \leq 15$. The updated state value is provided by $S[w_i]$ [9]. Here, the S-box is used in each rounds and key scheduling operation.

2.4   Bit Permutation (p-Layer)

Bit permutation layer is used to move bit i of the *State* to bit position $P(i)$ [9].

3   Some of the Existing VLSI Architectures for the PRESENT Block Cipher

Architectural space exploration with iterative, parallel and serial variants are discussed in [10, 11]. The serial architecture provided by [12], requires 303 clock cycles for complete encryption. A rough estimate of the gate count is around 1100, 2-input *NAND* gates, known as gate equivalents (GEs). Iterative type of architectures are reported in [10, 11, 13]. The architectures of [10, 11] take 250 clock cycles for complete processing with 1100 GEs. The architecture of [13] is based on 64-bit datapath, 33 clock cycle latency and requires 57 slices for 64-bit key and 69 slices for 128-bit on Xilinx xc5vfx70t FPGA device.

Architectures provided in [10, 12] are based on 8-bit datapath. To bring external 80-bit plaintext and 128-bit key, 16 clock cycles are needed. To process the intermediate State for the encryption operation, 31 clock cycles are required. As the output of the architecture is of 8-bit, it also needed an 8 clock cycles for producing the output. Thus, the total latency of the architecture is 55 clock cycles with 1800 GEs. The architecture of [12] when implemented in Xilinx Virtex-5 xc5vlx50 FPGA device takes 87 slices [12] with 47 clocks latency. Maximum clock frequency 221.64 MHz and throughput is 341.64 Mbps.

4   A VLSI Architecture for the PRESENT Lightweight Block Cipher

A proposed architecture for the PRESENT block cipher is shown in Fig. 3. Here, 8-bit datapath is selected, it provides an optimal trade-off in terms of power and performance. The three main components of the architecture are: encryption engine, key scheduling and a controller. The key scheduling block takes 80-bit input key and generates thirty one intermediate round keys for the 31 individual rounds of the cipher. The permutation is a simple bit-transposition, which needs connecting wires only. The main building blocks of the proposed architecture are arranged in different subsections and described below.

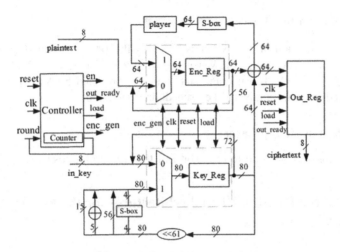

Fig. 3. Proposed architecture for the PRESENT cipher.

4.1   Datapath of the Proposed Architecture for the Encryption Operation in the PRESENT Cipher

The proposed architecture is based on 8-bit datapath consisting a 64-bit *Enc_Reg* and an 80-bit *Key_Reg* register. These registers are used for storing internal states of the encryption operation and intermediate round keys respectively. Two 64-bit and an 80-bit (or a 128 bit) multiplexers are used to switch the data between load and round computation phases. The datapath contains *sboxlayer* (16 S-boxes) and one S-box for 80-bit (two S-boxes for 128-bit key) for the key scheduling operation. Along with this, one 64-bit XOR gate, 5-bit XOR gate and a 3-bit and one 5-bit up-counters are also used. The *plaintext* is loaded in first clock cycle and in next clock cycle multiplexer is used to switch the data. Subsequently, for next 31 cycles all intermediate states are computed.

Data is available at the *Enc_Reg* and XORed intermediate round key. Further, the mixed State is passed to the *sboxlayer*, which provides 64-bit data concurrently to the P-layer. After that, data is passed to the *Enc_Reg* through a multiplexer shown in Fig. 3. In last clock cycle, ciphertext is available at the *Out_Reg* register. Thus, a total of 10 + 31 + 8 = 49 clock cycles are required to encrypt a single block of 64-bit plaintext. The key processing unit works in on-the-fly mode with each round. A 64-bit register is used to store the round key, the first leftmost 64-bit of key register is XORed with the intermediate state. The *sboxlayer* is implemented by area-optimized combinational logic circuit.

4.2   A Controller for the Proposed Architecture

A controller shown in Fig. 4 is designed to generate various required signals for the key generation and encryption engine. There are six states in the FSM, it generates four control signals which are: *en*, *io_load*, *en_gen* and *out_ready*.

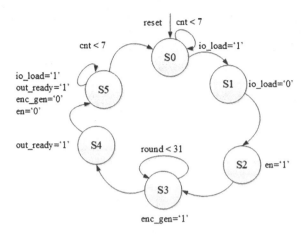

Fig. 4. A FSM for the PRESENT cipher architecture.

In state S0 the signals *io_load* = '1', enables the *Enc_Reg* register for storing first byte of *plaintext* and the user key is also stored in the same clock cycle. The state remains in S0 for 8 clock cycles, by this complete 64-bit of *plaintext* and 64-bit of the 80-bit user key are stored in the respective registers. The remaining 2 bytes of data is stored in subsequent two clock cycles of states S1 and S2. In state S2, the signal *en* = '1', enables a 5-bit up-counter for counting 31 rounds of the cipher. In state S3, multiplexers are switched and the *enc_gen* signal is used to start the intermediate operations by enabling the encryption and key registers. The state remains in S3 until counter value reaches 31. Then, the state is switched to state S4, where counter is disabled by *en* = '0' and *out_ready* signal is switched to logic '1'. First byte of ciphertext is available after 42 clock cycles; further in state S5, the state remains in the same state for next eight clock cycles and ciphertext is available through the output register (*Out_Reg*). Thus, the architecture requires a total of 49 clock cycles to produce 64-bit registered ciphertext for the 80-bit user key. Similarly, for 128-bit user key the controller needs six more clock cycles to produce a registered output.

5   Experimental Setup and Used EDA Tools

The proposed architecture is implemented in VHDL language and simulated in *Modelsim* simulator. This simulator is also utilized to generate switching activity interchange format (SAIF) file. One hundred random vectors are used to compute dynamic power dissipation with Xilinx *XPower Analyzer* [14] tool. The tool requires two additional files that are FPGA device-specific. The first file is a physical representation of the design mapped to the components in native circuit description (NCD) format. The second file is a physical constraints file (PCF). These files are generated by synthesizing the design for Xilinx Virtex-5 xc5vlx50 FPGAs device using Xilinx *ISE Design Suite* [15]. After validating the proposed architecture in FPGA device, an ASIC implementation of the architecture in SCL 180 nm technology [16] is done. Here, Synopsys *Design Compiler* is used for synthesis. To perform physical design and power analysis, Synopsys *IC Compiler* and *Power Compiler* tools are utilized [17]. Performance of the architecture is evaluated in terms of throughput, maximum frequency, power, energy, energy/bit and efficiency, which are computed as:

$$Throughput = \frac{(\max imum\,frequency \times total\,no.\,of\,bits)}{latency} \tag{1}$$

$$Energy = \frac{(power \times latency)}{operating\,frequency} \tag{2}$$

$$Efficiency = \frac{throughput}{gate\,equivalent} \tag{3}$$

The gate equivalent (GE) is replaced by total number of consumed slices for the FPGA implementation.

6 Experimental Results and Discussion

Experimental results for simulation, synthesis and an ASIC implementation are provided. These results are arranged in different subsections and described below.

6.1 Simulation Result of the Proposed Architecture

A snapshot of the simulation result from *Modelsim simulator* is shown in Fig. 5. Here 64-bit data X"000...0" as a *plaintext* and 80-bit data X"FF...F" as user key are provided to the implemented architecture. Each data of the *plaintext* and key is sent in byte-wise fashion. In the simulation, first byte of the registered output is obtained after 42 clock cycles that is shown at the first cursor in Fig. 5. In subsequent 7 clock cycles, all the output bytes as X"E72C46C0F5945049" are available which is pointed-out by the second cursor in Fig. 5.

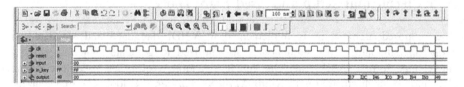

Fig. 5. A simulation result for the proposed architecture with 64-bit plaintext and 80-bit key in *Modelsim* simulator.

6.2 Results for the FPGA Implementation and Comparison with an Existing Architecture

An FPGA synthesis result for the proposed architecture is performed and the design is compared with an existing architecture. In comparison, the selected design metrics are: LUTs, registers and total number of consumed slices for resource comparison. Performance of the design is compared for latency, maximum operating frequency, throughput (1), energy (2) and efficiency (3). The FPGA device synthesis and comparison result is shown in Fig. 6. As shown in the figure, in comparison to architecture of [12] in the proposed architecture, with 5.7% lesser FPGA slices, there is 50.4% gain in frequency, 28.4% higher throughput, 35.6% increased efficiency.

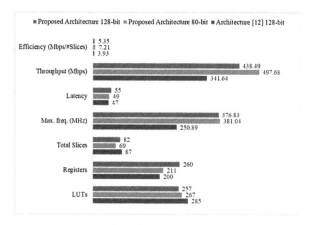

Fig. 6. An architectural comparison between the proposed architecture and the architecture [12] in Xilinx Virtex-5 xc5vlx50-1ff324 FPGA device.

Xilinx *XPower Analyzer* tool [14] with its default settings is used for performing power analysis with Virtex-5 xc5vlx50-1ff324 FPGA device. Power consumption of the proposed architecture at the maximum operating frequency is given in Table 1.

Here, power distribution in terms of dynamic power and static power is provided. Here, a set of one hundred random vectors are used. The associated components of the dynamic power are also provided. Total dynamic power dissipation is 49.63 mW for 64-bit key and 27.73 mW for the 128-bit key. Apart from computing power dissipation at the maximum operating frequencies, power is also computed at a constant frequency of 13.56 MHz. This particular operating frequency is most commonly used in RFID applications and in IoT transmitters [11]. Table 2 shows the computed power, energy and energy/bit for both 80 and 128-bit user keys.

Table 1. Power consumption at maximum operating frequency for Xilinx Virtex-5 xc5vlx50-1ff324 FPGA device

Elements		Value	
		80-bit	128-bit
Dynamic power (P_D) (mW)	Clock	14.86	19.60
	Logic	14.86	3.21
	Signals	19.26	4.34
	IOs	0.85	0.59
	Total	49.63	27.73
Static power (P_S) (mW)		422.06	421.81
Total power ($P_D + P_S$) (mW)		471.69	449.54
Energy (nJ)		60.66	65.61
Energy/bit (nJ/bit)		0.95	1.03

Table 2. Power consumption at 13.56 MHz operating frequency for Xilinx Virtex-5 xc5vlx50-1ff324 FPGA device

Elements		Value	
		80-bit	128-bit
Dynamic power (PD) (mW)	Clock	1.68	2.87
	Logic	4.65	4.77
	Signals	9.41	9.37
	IOs	0.33	0.33
	Total	16.07	17.33
Static power (PS) (mW)		421.68	421.69
Total power (PD + PS) (mW)		437.45	439.03
Energy (nJ)		1.58	1.78
Energy/bit (nJ/bit)		0.025	0.028

6.3   Results for the ASIC Implementation in SCL 180 nm Technology

The ASIC implementation of the proposed architecture is done in SCL 180 nm technology. Here, all the data is obtained after completing *placement and routing (PnR)* of the design. The core requires, clock (*clk*), reset, 8-bit input data, 8-bit user key and 8-bit output. Where, *pc3d01* is used as an input pad; *pc3o01* for output pad and *pc3c01* for the clock pad, and *pfrelr* is used as corner pads. For supplying 3.3 V power, *pvda* pad is used with *pv0a* as ground. Similarly, for 1.8 V power, *pvdi* pad is used with *pv0i* as ground. Area of the complete chip is 1.55 mm^2 and it takes 1608 two input *NAND* gate equivalent of standard cells. The standard cell area is 0.029594 mm^2, where, pad cell area of 0.770 mm^2, core size area 0.296283 mm^2 and pad core size area is 0.555293 mm^2.

Performance of the proposed architecture in terms of power dissipation, throughput, energy, energy/bit and efficiency in SCL 180 nm technology is given in Table 3. Here, Synopsys *Design Compiler, IC Compiler, Power Compiler* and *Prime Time* tools are used for physical design and power analysis. *Power Compiler* tool requires *SAIF* and standard parasitic exchange format (*SPEF*) files. The *SPEF* file is generated by *IC compiler* tool after completing place and route (*PnR*) and the *SAIF* file is obtained by *ModelSim* tool. At 100 MHz clock frequency, total power dissipation is 0.2288 mW for the 80-bit key and 0.27267 mW for the 128-bit key. *Design Compiler* and *IC compiler* tools provide netlist in Verilog format at multiple stages of the design. The netlists generated by the tools are used to perform functional simulations using *ModelSim* simulator. The simulations results match with the simulation result of Fig. 5. Finally, conclusion of the paper is drawn in next section.

Table 3. Performance of the architecture in SCL 180 nm technology.

Elements		Utilization
Dynamic power (PD) (mW)	IO Pads	0.087
	Switching	0.051
	Cell Internal	0.073
	Total	0.211
Static power (PS) (mW)		0.0163
Total power (PD + PS) (mW)		0.228
Throughput (Mbps)		130.612
Energy (nJ)		112.15
Energy/bit (nJ/bit)		14.018
Efficiency		0.813

7   Conclusion

We presented a VLSI architecture for the PRESENT block cipher algorithm. Datapath of the architecture is based on 8-bit and it requires 49 clock cycles for processing of 64-bit *plaintext*, 80-bit user key. An FPGA implementation of the architecture is done in Xilinx Virtex-5 xc5vlx50 device. In comparison to an existing architecture, the proposed architecture shows improvement in performance. Also, an ASIC implementation of the proposed architecture is done in SCL 180 nm technology. Area of the chip layout is 1.55 mm^2, with 1608 gate equivalent (GE). At 100 MHz operating frequency, total power consumption of the chip is 0.228 mW. A throughput of 130.612 Mbps, energy 112.15 nJ, energy/bit 14.018 nJ/bit, and 0.813 efficiency is obtained. The proposed design can be utilized in IoT/CPS applications for data security.

Acknowledgement. The authors would like to thank Director, CSIR-CEERI, Pilani, Rajasthan, India and Ministry of Electronics and Information Technology (MeitY), Govt. of India for providing necessary resources to carry out this research. This work has been carried out under the SMDP-C2SD project, sponsored by MeitY.

References

1. Alioto, M. (ed.): Enabling the Internet of Things. From Integrated Circuits to Integrated Systems. Springer, Cham (2017). https://doi.org/10.1007/978-3-319-51482-6
2. Shi, W., Dustdar, S.: The promise of edge computing. Computer **49**(5), 78–81 (2016)
3. Lee, E.A., Seshia, S.A.: Introduction to Embedded Systems: A Cyber-Physical Systems Approach. MIT Press, Cambridge (2016)
4. Russell, S.J., Norvig, P.: Artificial Intelligence: A Modern Approach. Pearson Education Limited, Malaysia (2016)
5. Xu, T., Wendt, J.B., Potkonjak, M.: Security of IoT systems: design challenges and opportunities. In: Proceedings of the 2014 IEEE/ACM International Conference on Computer-Aided Design, pp. 417–423. IEEE Press (2014)
6. Pathan, A.-S.K.: Securing Cyber-Physical Systems. CRC Press, Boca Raton (2015)
7. Eisenbarth, T., Kumar, S.: A survey of lightweight-cryptography implementations. IEEE Des. Test Comput. **24**(6), 522–533 (2007)
8. ISO/IEC 29192-2:2012. Information technology–security techniques–lightweight cryptography – part 2: Block ciphers
9. Bogdanov, A., et al.: PRESENT: an ultra-lightweight block cipher. In: Paillier, P., Verbauwhede, I. (eds.) CHES 2007. LNCS, vol. 4727, pp. 450–466. Springer, Heidelberg (2007). https://doi.org/10.1007/978-3-540-74735-2_31
10. Rolfes, C., Poschmann, A., Leander, G., Paar, C.: Ultra-lightweight implementations for smart devices – security for 1000 gate equivalents. In: Grimaud, G., Standaert, F.-X. (eds.) CARDIS 2008. LNCS, vol. 5189, pp. 89–103. Springer, Heidelberg (2008). https://doi.org/10.1007/978-3-540-85893-5_7
11. Lara-Nino, C.A., Diaz-Perez, A., Morales-Sandoval, M.: Lightweight hardware architectures for the PRESENT cipher in FPGA. IEEE Trans. Circ. Syst. I Reg. Papers **64**, 2544–2555 (2017)
12. Hanley, N., ONeill, M.: Hardware comparison of the ISO/IEC 29192-2 block ciphers. In: IEEE Computer Society Annual Symposium on VLSI (ISVLSI) 2012, pp. 57–62. IEEE (2012)
13. Pandey, J.G., Goel, T., Karmakar, A.: An efficient VLSI architecture for PRESENT block cipher and its FPGA implementation. In: Kaushik, B.K., Dasgupta, S., Singh, V. (eds.) VDAT 2017. CCIS, vol. 711, pp. 270–278. Springer, Singapore (2017). https://doi.org/10.1007/978-981-10-7470-7_27
14. Xilinx: Xilinx power estimator user guide
15. Xilinx: ISE design suite
16. Semi-conductor Laboratory (SCL), Gov. of India (2018)
17. Synopsys: Synopsys products (2018)

Efficient Data Compression
Scheme for Secured Application Needs

Ravi Kashyap[1] ⓘ, Twinkle Verma[1] ⓘ, Priyanka Kwatra[1] ⓘ,
and Sidhartha Sankar Rout[2(✉)] ⓘ

[1] Jaypee Institute of Information Technology, Noida, India
ravi.kashyapl996@gmail.com, twinkil724@gmail.com,
kwatrapriyanka@gmail.com
[2] Indraprastha Institute of Information Technology Delhi, New Delhi, India
sidharthas@iiitd.ac.in

Abstract. The widespread availability of 3G/4G network could make Intelligent Traffic Systems (ITS) capable of wirelessly connecting to the data networks. The near future possibility of 5G communication would make this service more promising. The applications like traffic management and military where ITS plays an important role, demands a huge amount of secure data transmission. Massive data transfer is always a costly affair in terms of power, performance and reliability. A suitable data compression technique equipped with robust encryption methodology can leverage the burden of extensive data transportation. The shrunken data transmitted can be decrypted and decompressed at the receiver end, and there by the original information can be recovered. This paper demonstrates an efficient way of lossless data compression using a blend of Static and Instantaneous encoding named as SIN Compression. The proposed scheme encodes the data based upon a suitable threshold point that eliminates the large number of iterations used in traditional compression methods. For an experiment performed over a 16×16 pixel image; the SIN compression shows 60% of performance, 64% of area, and 69% of power improvement over the original lossless Huffman compression.

Keywords: Compression · Encryption · Secured applications

1 Introduction

Continuous edge detection of object image can help in defining the segmentation of image and thereby finding the discontinuities in the image files. These image processing techniques help military people identifying a suspicious object inside the range [1]. These can also assist the doctors to identify the location of foreign objects in the body [2]. These techniques need continuous image of the object area to be clicked, processed and transmitted for further analysis. So, highly sensitive applications such as medical and military, where human life and border security are under risk, cannot afford unsecured and inefficient information transmission. Whereas data security is of utmost importance for these applications; at the same time quick data transmission with low power consumption are highly desirable. Efficient compression of data with a high compression ratio can shrink the data even more than 50%. This reduces the

© Springer Nature Singapore Pte Ltd. 2019
S. Rajaram et al. (Eds.): VDAT 2018, CCIS 892, pp. 221–230, 2019.
https://doi.org/10.1007/978-981-13-5950-7_19

transmission time and power consumption drastically. The data storage requirement also decreases significantly. Being an encoding technique, compression also strengthens the encryption effort. Along with multiple fault tolerant techniques to maintain the data integrity, encryption of data is a required post-compression mechanism to keep the data secured during transmission. Using a known key to sender and receiver, a unique encrypted cipher can be generated which is secure enough to be transmitted. On the reception of the data, it is required to retrieve the original information. A decryption technique can extract the original compressed information from the received cipher by using the known key. The decompression process now can reconstruct the initial information. The extracted information can be approximate or exact to the original, depending on whether the compression technique is lossy or lossless. Secured application area like military, demands exact information back after decompression, so this paper deals with only lossless compression techniques. In traditional approach, Huffman technique is widely accepted for compression. Though this technique has various advantages, it has several disadvantages as well. Thus, in order to overcome those disadvantages, we have proposed a novel compression technique named as SIN compression. The introduced method can be effectively used for the applications that demand a low power and high speed data processing. The processing benefits in the proposed method are achieved by reducing the number of iterations while assigning codes to the corresponding symbols.

The major contributions of this work are summarized as follows:

1. Development of SIN technique for efficient compression and decompression
2. FPGA implementation to validate our proposed compression technique

Rest of the paper is organized as follows. Section 2 discusses previous work done for efficient data processing for communication. A demonstration of complete methodology used in this work, and the data processing techniques required are explained in Sect. 3. Comparison of Huffman and the proposed SIN technique is discussed in Sect. 4. Supporting results are produced in Sect. 5, and Sect. 6 concludes the work.

2 Related Work

Both compression and encryption are two major steps required for efficient as well as secure data transmission. Numerous works have been done on data compression for several past decades. The basic concept behind data compression is to eliminate the redundancy in the original information. Popular compression technique like Huffman, encodes the highly repeated symbols with less bits and thereby reduces the size of the information [3]. Other popular methods like Arithmetic coding, LZW method etc. also performs compression of data efficiently [4–7]. Maintaining data security during transmission is very much essential to protect the information from malicious attack. Data encryption is the widely used technique to safeguard the transmitted data. Multiple researchers have come up with several such encryption standards like Advanced Encryption Standard (AES), Data Encryption Standard (DES), Triple DES, Blowfish etc. [8–10]. Among all these, AES is popularly adopted for data encryption.

In this work we have proposed an efficient compression mechanism SIN, which can improve the data processing speed by reducing the number of iterations during the symbol encoding phase. This can also eliminate the performance bottlenecks of techniques like Huffman encoding, where a translation table needs to be sent along with the coded message.

3 Methodology and Data Processing

This section gives an overview of multiple data processing stages which are required for secured and efficient data transmission. Figure 1 clearly demonstrates all these processing steps. At sender side continuous images are clicked which need to be transferred to the receiver end for immediate object detection. Rather than transmitting the original image, edge detected images with considerably reduced size can be sent which carry required features for the object detection.

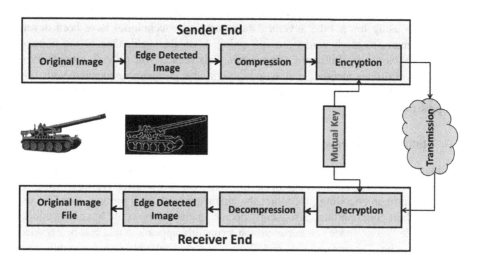

Fig. 1. Data processing and communication flow of edge detected image.

An edge detected image size can further be reduced by a suitable compression mechanism. In this paper we have proposed a novel compression technique named as SIN, which takes considerably less cycles to compress the data. Our method has been validated by comparing it with widely popular Huffman compression technique which is highly iterative in nature to assign code to each symbol. The next section explains the compression algorithm, the shortcomings of Huffman technique, and shows how the proposed technique can overcome those limitations.

After data compression, we have used 128 bit AES encryption to maintain the security and integrity of the data. The data encryption is achieved by a unique keyword which is known to both the sender and the receiver. The encrypted data stream is transmitted through the channel to the receiver side.

The reverse engineering is required to be performed at the receiver end to get back the original information. A decryption phase with the help of the same key-word can retrieve back the original compressed information. The output of the decryption stage is provided to the decompression module to regenerate the original information.

4 Compression Techniques and Comparisons

Most of the applications nowadays are data centric. So, huge amount of data are expected to be exchanged continuously. Massive data processing and transmission always drive the attention towards the total power consumption and the performance needed. Realistically these data contains significant redundancy. The techniques which can effectively remove all the redundancies or at-least lessen it to a great extent are known as compression techniques. These methods can enhance the meaningful data density in both storage device and communication process. Compressing data will allow more information to be transmitted through the channel without disturbing the performance and power budget. Data Compression is the process of encoding digital information using fewer bits. Several data compression techniques have been developed and many research works are still going on in this field. One of the popular existing techniques is Huffman Compression. This section will provide a brief introduction to Huffman method, and will highlight the problems associated with this method. The later part of this section gives a detailed description of proposed SIN compression technique.

4.1 Huffman Compression

Huffman encoding is a variable length character encoding scheme which can provide tighter packing of data in comparison to fixed length character representation. In standard Huffman encoding procedure, the characters with high probability of occurrence get short codes and the infrequently occurring characters would have long codes. For example "white space" character which frequently appears in text can be encoded with a single bit. The approximate code length of a particular character or symbol can be represented as given by [5].

$$\text{code length} = \log_2(\text{symbol probability}) \tag{1}$$

Here symbol probability represents the probability of occurrence of a symbol in terms of relative frequency. Now we would consider a case of text with ASCII characters where each symbol takes eight bits. The above expression would reduce the length of a symbol to a two bit code if the same appears once in every four symbols. This reduces the total size occupied by the same symbol to one fourth of its initial size. Multiple researches have reported that Huffman encoding can compress a text up to 40 to 55% [6].

The 3 major disadvantages of Huffman compression can be summarized as below:

1. Large number of iterations required to perform the repetitive sorting of symbol frequencies
2. Size of the translation table, that is required for compression
3. Complexity of decompression process

Huffman technique starts with figuring out the frequency distribution of each input symbol. Then for the encoding process, it creates binary tree with sorted frequency values where the process iteratively adds up the two lowest frequencies present in the list and sorts the remaining frequencies along with the generated resultant again. This process repeats itself till the time all the symbol frequencies are considered. The complete process of code generation is shown in Fig. 2. Huffman encoding strategy introduces the time complexity of the operation to as large as O(nlogn) in case of 'n' different symbols [11]. This gets synthesized to be a complicated hardware resulting huge power and performance overhead.

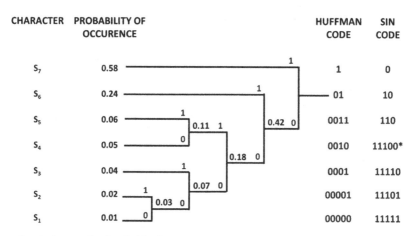

* at S_4 denotes the threshold point

Fig. 2. Code assignment for Huffman and SIN technique.

A translation table is required in Huffman process which holds all the symbols and the corresponding codes for them. The size of the translation table increases drastically if the input symbol size increases. For example the table size jumps from 256 entries to 64K entries when the size of each input symbol would change from 8-bit representation to 16-bit representation. Implementation of such a large size translation table is impractical in most of the cases. And also transferring this large table to the receiver side would add up high overheads in terms of power and communication bandwidth.

The complexity of Huffman decompression process is equally exhaustive like its compression process. With the arrival of compressed data stream, each input bit is compared with the corresponding bit of the codes present in the received translation table. This process repeats itself until a complete match would happen. This decoding exercise continues till the last bit of the received data stream and proves to be a highly iterative method.

4.2   SIN Compression

This paper proposes an efficient compression scheme named as SIN compression, which adopts a unique coding technique that reduces the iterations to a large extent. This method provides much better power and performance figures w.r.t. Huffman compression with a comparable compression ratio as shown in next section. SIN technique sorts the frequencies of all the symbols in decreasing order and smartly decides a threshold point. Instantaneous and static coding methods are used intelligently across the threshold point to get the final SIN codes for each symbol. Figure 3 shows the algorithm for the proposed scheme.

```
1.  input (m symbols) // m <= 2ⁿ
2.  determine frequencies of m symbols
3.  sort frequencies in descending order from fₘ, fₘ₋₁ ... f₁
4.  [m:2ⁿ⁻¹] total_bits = 0 // size of total_bits is 'm'
5.  for (i=m; i>=2ⁿ⁻¹; i--)
6.    consider i as threshold point
7.    for (j=m; j>i; j--)
8.      code[j] = {(m-j){1},0}
9.      total_bits[i] = total_bits[i] + fⱼ * bits(code[j])
10.   for (k=j; k>=1; k--)
11.     code[k] = {len(code[j+1]){1}, binary(k)}
12.     total_bits[i] = total_bits[i] + fₖ * bits(code[k])
13.  find(smallest(total_bits[p] ∀ p>=2ⁿ⁻¹))
14.  SIN code : code related to smallest(total_bits[p])
```

Fig. 3. Pseudo code for the proposed SIN compression.

Threshold point is the heart of the proposed method. Symbols having frequencies more than the frequency at the threshold point would be assigned instantaneous code. This has been shown in Fig. 2 and coded at line number 8 in Fig. 3. Beyond threshold point, this method assigns static code to rest of the symbols which can be realized at line number 11 of Fig. 3. Following example from Fig. 2 will clarify the assignment of static code.

As can be seen in Fig. 2, S_4 is the threshold point. So, all the symbols below this point including S_4 will be given static code. Since there are 4 such symbols, two binary bits are sufficient to encode them. But to distinguish these codes from the instantaneous codes we append 1's in front of these 2 bit codes. The number of 1's to be appended is decided from the bit length of the code just before the threshold point. This method gives pretty similar compression ratio in comparison to the Huffman method as shown in the result section.

Line number 6 in the above algorithm would decide the threshold point value from the value of variable 'i' after all the iterations. These iterations would go from 'm' till '2^{n-1}' where 'm' is total number of symbol present and 'n−1' is equal to "$\lfloor \log_2 m \rfloor$". We have taken a fair assumption that the threshold point would be present somewhere between the maximum frequency symbol and the symbol present at the 2^{n-1} location. This reduces the time and operation complexities to at-least half or even more. To prove our assumption we have run total of 100 simulations. For this, we have experimented with 10 different symbol sets and each set is considered for 10 different frequency distribution generated by random frequency generator. The simulation gives us a better compression ratio in 98% of cases when the threshold point is between 'm' and 2^{n-1} location, proving our assumption is an acceptable one. The results of these simulations are summarized in Fig. 4.

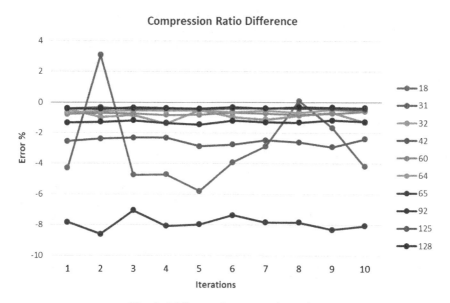

Fig. 4. Difference in compression ratio.

In the above simulation, we have calculated the percentage errors for differences in the compression ratios between two cases. One case is the compression ratio when the threshold point is considered at 2^{n-1} location. Second case is the minimum of all compression ratios when the threshold point is individually considered for all the symbols after 2^{n-1} location. A negative percentage error indicates that 2^{n-1} location being considered as the threshold point generates better compression ratio. This case can be observed for 98% of instances from Fig. 4.

The excessive sorting iterations in Huffman technique are completely absent in case of SIN, only except the first instance. This enormously reduces the area and power overhead. The time complexity reduces to the order of O(n) in case of 'n' different symbols. Although the data path becomes little complex because of multiple addition and multiplication operations, but the measure is not so high, since the iteration stops at 2^{n-1} point in the proposed method.

In case of SIN method, translation table is not required for compression. This can be considered as the second major benefit over Huffman method. This gives relief in terms of storage space. We only need to send the threshold point information to the receiver for decompression process unlike the huge translation table in case of Huffman.

The third benefit can be observed in the decompression stage. In the proposed method unlike the Huffman technique, we need not compare the incoming data bits with the corresponding bits of all the symbol codes. We will take the example of Fig. 2 to explain the decompression process. If in the incoming data stream a continuous "111" pattern comes, then we can conclude that the current code is one among the static codes. So, for next two input data bits four comparisons are required to detect the exact matching. The process of input data decode is pretty straightforward till the threshold point which is an instantaneous code. Whenever there is a "0" after less than three 1's pattern, it indicates the end of one symbol and the corresponding symbol can be easily decoded using its instantaneous nature. This process considerably reduces the number of iterations in the decompression phase.

5 Experimental Setup and Results

The proposed SIN algorithm is a fast compression method suitable for applications like military which demands continuous and high speed information transmission. Here for experimental purpose we have considered processing of edge detected image. The image to be processed is first converted to a binary text file using MATLAB. The complete data processing flow as shown in Fig. 1 is performed for both Huffman and SIN compression and the comparisons are shown for compression ratio, area, power and performance. Area and power consumption is measured for 90 nm technology and synthesized with the Synopsys design compiler tool. Same design is also synthesized on Xilinx Vivado for Artix 7 FPGA to get an estimation of resource utilization in terms of configurable LUTs and flip-flops. A 16 × 16 pixel image is considered for initial prove of concept. This 256 bit image file is broken into 32 symbols of 8-bit width each. Total 9 different symbols are present with frequency distribution ranging from 9 to 1.

Table 1. Comparison of Huffman vs. SIN for 16 × 16 image size.

Design parameters	Huffman	SIN	Improvement (%)
Compression ratio	1.273	1.326	4.2
Power (uW)	779.756	238.489	69.41
Area (um^2)	107747.139	36254.323	66.35
LUTs	61526	16169	74.04
Flip-flops	1100	675	38.63
Compression time (us)	2.325	0.88	62.26
Decompression time (us)	0.95	0.35	63.15

Table 1 compares different parameters for Huffman and SIN compression on the above described image.

We can observe a significant improvement in area and power in case of SIN compression over the Huffman with similar compression ratio. This is because; the number of iterations are reducing considerably both during compression and decompression phase. Simulations are run for a 100 MHz clock, and results show remarkable improvements in compression and decompression time. The only overhead associated with SIN method is the requirement of threshold calculation circuit. From the experiment we found this overhead is between 2% to 5% in terms of area, power and performance.

To realize the performance improvement for larger data sets, we have considered few more cases with large image sizes. Table 2 summarizes the implementation results for different image sizes.

Table 2. Comparison for different image sizes.

Image size	Compression ratio		Data processing time (us)	
	Huffman	SIN	Huffman	SIN
128 × 128	1.684	1.595	364.75	56.765
128 × 64	1.409	1.21	196.01	32.275
64 × 64	1.171	1.305	117.92	17.355
64 × 32	1.044	1.133	61.14	10.235

This can be observed from the above table that both the compression techniques provide more or less similar compression ratios for different image sizes. The table also shows total time consumed by the complete data processing stages including compression, encryption, decryption and decompression. The encryption standard used is common for both the data processing flows having Huffman as well as SIN technique. This justifies the difference in processing time is only due to the difference in total time taken by both compression and decompression phases. The results show significant improvements in simulation time in case of SIN technique for all the image sizes we have considered.

Table 3. Comparison with existing compression techniques.

Images	Huffman		Shannon Fano		LZ77		SIN	
	CR	DPT	CR	DPT	CR	DPT	CR	DPT
Cameraman (512 × 512)	1.192	.546	1.093	2.641	1.424	128.3	2.092	.073
Female (256 × 128)	1.704	.069	1.099	2.439	1.427	113.7	1.934	.012
House (128 × 64)	1.543	.023	1.120	1.978	1.813	97.18	1.623	.005
Tank (64 × 64)	1.136	.016	1.217	2.273	1.324	103.2	1.972	.003
Tree (64 × 32)	1.249	.009	.915	1.480	1.667	63.54	2.556	.003

CR: Compression Ratio, DPT: Data Processing Time

All the above results are generated from the hardware synthesis of the designs. We have generated few more results by software simulation in Python to compare the SIN technique with 3 other existing compression methods. Table 3 demonstrates the comparison and proves the proposed method to be an efficient one.

6 Conclusion

In this work we have proposed a novel compression technique named as SIN compression which can efficiently serve the application areas like military and ITS where high speed continuous data communication is the foremost requirement. This technique can reduce the number of sorting iterations significantly in comparison to the traditional techniques like Huffman. The improvements in SIN method are achieved in retaliation to the small overhead associated with the threshold circuit. Thereby the proposed technique gives considerably good compression of data with remarkable processing speed improvement of around 60% over the existing Huffman technique. Since the design complexity reduces for SIN algorithm, we have achieved around 66% area improvement and 69% reduction in power consumption.

References

1. Khashman, A.: Automatic detection of military targets utilising neural networks and scale space analysis. In: RTO IST Symposium on New Information Processing Techniques for Military Systems (2000)
2. Zhao, Y.-Q., Gui, W.-H., Chen, Z.-C., Tang, J.-T., Li, L.-Y.: Medical images edge detection based on mathematical morphology. In: 27th Annual International Conference of the Engineering in Medicine and Biology Society, pp. 6492–6495. IEEE (2005)
3. Huffman, D.: A method for the construction of minimum redundancy codes. Proc. IRE **40**, 1098–1101 (1952)
4. Witten, I.H., Neal, R.M., Cleary, J.G.: Arithmetic coding for data compression. Commun. ACM **30**(6), 520–540 (1987)
5. Welch, T.A.: A technique for high-performance data compression. Computer **17**(6), 8–19 (1984)
6. Heghbati, H.K.: An overview of data compaction techniques. Computer **14**(4), 71–75 (1981)
7. Carreto-Castro, M.F., Ramirez, J.M., Ballesteros, J.L., Baez-Lopez, D.: Comparison of lossless compression techniques. In: IEEE Proceedings of the 36th Midwest Symposium on Circuits and System, vol. 2, pp. 1268–1270 (1993)
8. Daemen, J., Rijmen, V.: AES proposal: Rijndael. In: Banksys/Katholieke Universiteit Leuven, Belgium, AES submission (1998)
9. National Bureau of Standards - Data Encryption Standard, FIPS Publication 46 (1977)
10. Schneier, B.: Description of a new variable-length key, 64-bit block cipher (Blowfish). In: Anderson, R. (ed.) FSE 1993. LNCS, vol. 809, pp. 191–204. Springer, Heidelberg (1993). https://doi.org/10.1007/3-540-58108-1_24
11. Pi, C.W., Yuan-Rung, Y., Chun-Liang, L., Hung-Yi, C.: A memory efficient Huffman decoding algorithm. In: 19th International Conference on Advanced Information and Applications, Taipei, Taiwan, vol. 2, pp. 475–479 (2005)

Micro Bio-fluidics

Effective Method for Temperature Compensation in Dual Band Metal MEMS Resonator

Amol Morankar[1]([⊠]) and Rajendra Patrikar[2]([⊠])

[1] Riva Labs (P) Limited, Nagpur, India
morankaramol@gmail.com
[2] Center for VLSI and Nanotechnology,
Visvesvaraya National Institute of Technology, Nagpur, India

Abstract. Metal MEMS resonator fabricated using CMOS compatible process suffers from poor temperature compensation and low quality factor. The design, simulation and fabrication of complicated composite structures using SiO2 & metals, to achieve low temperature coefficient of frequency may be difficult, expensive and time consuming. A real time temperature compensation technique using stress induced frequency compensation through mixed mechanical and electrical coupling scheme in dual band metal MEMS resonator for future dual frequency filters and oscillators is proposed. Mechanical coupler forces all the clamped-clamped beams to vibrate at uniform resonant frequencies. Whereas placement of mechanical couplers at low and high velocity points ensures minimum variations in mode shapes irrespective of the variations in temperature of clamped-clamped beams. Electrical coupling lessen the parasitic capacitance that appears across the input-output ports therefore provides better out of band rejection. The technique achieved a temperature coefficient of frequency of -4.4 ppm/°C at ambient temperature.

Keywords: MEMS resonator · Dual band · Temperature compensation · Temperature coefficient of frequency

1 Introduction

Several homogeneous and heterogeneous wireless communication networks and systems are capable of multiband operations. Design of miniaturized multiband transceiver plays an important role in creating multiband operations a commercially viable solution. Currently the research in MEMS resonators is focused on its deployment in multiband transceivers and replacement of SAW and BAW devices. Aluminum Nitride (AlN) thin FBAR and SAW resonators are limited in the capability of multiband frequency responses on the same chip [1–3]. Metal MEMS resonator fabricated using CMOS compatible process suffers from poor temperature compensation and low quality factor (Q) [4–6].

To address thermal stability of MEMS resonators based on capacitive transduction mechanism passive temperature compensation techniques, such as the stress induced frequency compensation [7], composite structures consisting of silicon dioxide [8], and degenerate doping [9], without consuming excessive power [10] or requiring

© Springer Nature Singapore Pte Ltd. 2019
S. Rajaram et al. (Eds.): VDAT 2018, CCIS 892, pp. 233–241, 2019.
https://doi.org/10.1007/978-981-13-5950-7_20

complicated active compensation parabolic-type control circuits [11] are demonstrated. Composite structures consisting of silicon dioxide have been recently used for temperature compensation; since it is easy to process and has temperature coefficient of expansion (TCE) of opposite sign as compared to most other materials commonly used in MEMS. However, the design, simulation and fabrication of complicated composite structures, to achieve low temperature coefficient of frequency (TCF) may be difficult, expensive and time-consuming. Suppression of spurious responses due to change in temperature of the beam is desirable, to achieve single chip dual band frequency response solutions.

In this paper, an attempt has been made to improve the TCF of dual band metal MEMS resonator using stress induced frequency compensation in real time. Temperature compensation in dual band metal MEMS resonator was explored using mixed mechanical and electrical coupling scheme. Mechanical coupler forces all the beams to vibrate at uniform resonant frequencies. Whereas placement of mechanical couplers at low and high velocity points ensures minimum variations in mode shapes irrespective of the variations in temperature of clamped-clamped (CC) beams. Better stop band rejection can be achieved through electrical coupling. It achieves non-addition of unwanted and spurious responses and also reduces parasitic capacitance across the input-output ports [12]. Dual band metal MEMS resonator design using Euler Bernoulli's beam theory, fabrication, simulation using COMSOL multiphysics software and experimental results are discussed.

2 Device Design

Practically CC beams in an array experiences temperature variation. That results in changes in vibration shapes and natural frequencies due to compressive thermal loads and expansion for each CC beam. Therefore it is necessary to provide temperature compensation with the help of stiff mechanical couplers. Theses coupler forces all the beams to vibrate at uniform resonant frequencies irrespective of the variations in temperature of CC beams. Placement of mechanical couplers at low and high velocity points ensures minimum variations in mode shapes.

Dual band metal MEMS resonator consists of four mechanically coupled CC beams, input-output electrodes and mechanical couplers. The centre frequency of the CC beam resonator can be exactly decided by selection of material and geometrical parameters of CC beam. Placement of mechanical couplers at precise node points achieves high mechanical coupling, controllable bandwidth and thermal stability. Euler Bernoulli equation for the resonance frequency f is given using Eq. (1)

$$f = \frac{1}{2\pi\sqrt{12}} \beta_n^2 \sqrt{\frac{Y}{\rho}} \frac{t}{L^2} \tag{1}$$

where L is length, w is width and t is thickness of the beam, ρ is density and Y is Young's modulus of the structural material respectively and βn is mode coefficient. The bandwidth of the filter is given using Eq. (2)

$$BW = \frac{f}{k_r(x)} \frac{k_c}{k_{12}}$$ (2)

where BW is the required bandwidth, kc is the stiffness of the coupler, kr(x) is the stiffness of the resonator at point x from the anchor and k12 is the normalized coupling coefficient for the given filter type. Stiffness of coupling beam can be obtained using Eq. (3)

$$k_c = \omega w_c t \sqrt{E\rho}$$ (3)

where wc is width of the couplers that can be chosen to satisfy desired stiffness of the coupler. Desired bandwidth and Q can be obtained by determining the location of mechanical coupling between two CC beams through couplers. It can be precisely obtained using location of point x from the anchor as mention in Eq. (2). Desired bandwidth can be obtained independently for resonant mode 1 and 3 through node points. In this design, node points were obtained through Eq. 2 when operated in mode 1 and 3. It was designated to achieve Q around 125 in air. Therefore mechanical couplers were connected at node points (1/3rd of the beam length) when operated in resonant mode 1 as shown in Fig. 1. Whereas in case of resonant mode 3, node points were identified at the 1/3rd of the X. X is equal to 1/3rd of the length of the CC beam as shown in Fig. 2. Thus desired bandwidth can be set by controlling the location of node points separately for each band at the design stage. Additionally these mechanical couplers assist in maintaining the vibration shapes & resonant frequencies of the CC beam due to change in temperature. Secondly it facilitates use of multi-beam resonators for high power applications. Finally it generates sharp and narrow frequency response that would have been difficult due to use of many beams in resonators. Large number of beams in resonators without mechanical couplers generates flat frequency response due to minor variations in dimensions during the fabrication of the beams. Feed through cancellation was obtained through precise placement of input-output electrodes beneath the CC beam as shown in Fig. 3. Thus electrical coupling using placement of input-output electrodes was explored. When the resonator observes variation in the mode shapes due to change in temperature, constituent resonators tends to move towards and away from the output electrode 1 and 2 respectively or vice-versa. Thus the output current I_{o1} and I_{o2} obtained from output electrodes 1 and 2 respectively, flows in opposite directions. Finally the total output current I_o can be obtained by summing the I_{o1} & I_{o2} together representing the entire output. Thus better stop band rejection and attenuation of undesired modes due to variation in temperature was achieved due to cancellation of feed through current.

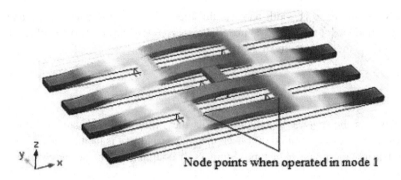

Fig. 1. CC beam with node points when operated in mode 1

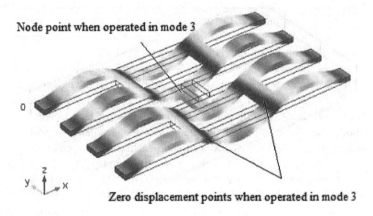

Fig. 2. CC beam with node and zero displacement points when operated in mode 3

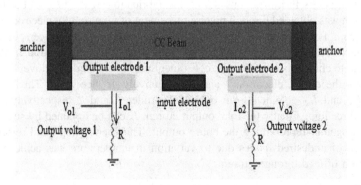

Fig. 3. Placement of input-output electrodes

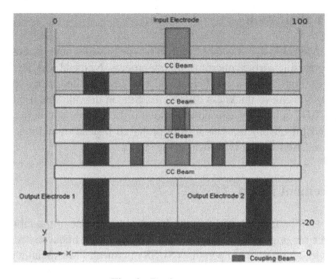

Fig. 4. Device structure

3 Device Structure

In this study, CC beam resonator array composed of four identical mechanically coupled CC beams were selected to serve as basic resonant tank shown in Fig. 4. These CC beams were mechanically coupled at designated node points. Input-output electrodes were provided for interfacing with external circuitry. Slim mechanical couplers are connected to each CC beam at node points. The four identical micromechanical CC beams are anchored to the substrate by stiff contact anchors. Two output electrodes increases transduction area and transduction gap was kept in the submicron range. The length of the mechanical couplers was selected to be less than quarter wavelength of the operating frequencies.

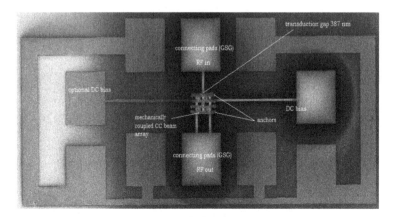

Fig. 5. FESEM image of the fabricated device

4 Device Fabrication

The metal MEMS resonator was fabricated on n-type Si wafer having resistivity greater than 1000 Ω-cm using surface micromachining process. Ni metal was used as structural material due its high stiffness coefficient and can be deposited using simple electroplating process to achieve thickness of 500 nm. Silicon dioxide was used as sacrificial layer and 5:1 BHF solution was used to remove it. Entire fabrication process required four masks and lift off process was mostly preferred instead of etching. The FESEM image of the released device is shown in Fig. 5.

5 Measurement Setup

Experiments were performed to obtain the frequency response of the fabricated device at temperatures ranging from 10 °C to 60 °C. To determine frequency response of the fabricated device at different temperatures SUSS microtech PM8 vacuum probe station, Agilent E8267D vector signal generator, Keithley 4200 SCS and Agilent E4407B series spectrum analyzer were employed. The input DC voltage Vdc = 5v and AC input power at 0 dBm was applied to the resonator, and then the resonator was allowed to resonate at all resonant modes. Initially the temperature was set at 10 °C and then incremented with steps of 5 °C till 60 °C. During the course of experiment, measurements were taken after every 30 min so as to allow the temperature to settle.

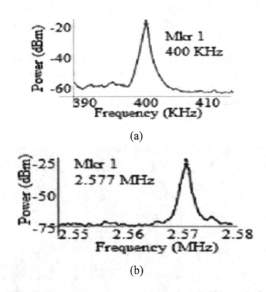

(a)

(b)

Fig. 6. Frequency response (a) mode 1 & (b) mode 3

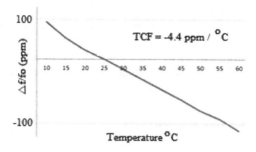

Fig. 7. Frequency stability measurement for temperature from 10 °C to 60 °C

6 Results and Discussion

In this design, temperature compensation was explored using mixed electrical and mechanical coupling scheme. Mechanical coupling at low and high velocity points when operated in mode 3 and 1 respectively was explored. Also coupling beam length was chosen to be shorter to reduce spurious modes and avoid reduction in resonant frequency due to complex structure. Selection of more than two mechanical couplers per CC beam ensures minimum variations in mode shapes and frequencies due to change in temperature. Experimental results clearly indicates stiff mechanical couplers of smaller size and precise placement of couplers at node points ensured thermal stability in the range of ± 100 ppm when operated in mode 1 (400 kHz) and mode 3 (2.557 MHz) from 10 °C to 60 °C as shown in Fig. 6. The TCF of −4.4 ppm/°C was achieved due to electrodeposited nanocrystalline nickel on chromium at room temperature bearing dense and

Table 1. MEMS resonator physical & electrical parameters summary

Parameter	Value	Unit
Beam length, L	76	μm
Beam width, w	8	μm
Structure thickness, t	0.513	μm
Electrode to resonator gap	0.387	μm
Coupling beam length, L_c	10	μm
Coupling beam width, w_c	8	μm
DC voltage (Vdc)	5	V
DC current (Idc)	0.5	pA
Mode 1		
Resonant Frequency	400	KHz
Bandwidth	3	KHz
Q	133	–
Mode 3		
Resonant Frequency	2.577	MHz
Bandwidth	20	KHz
Q	129	–

simple structure. Table 1 summarizes the measured physical and electrical parameters for the proposed mechanically coupled CC beams resonator. Figure 7 shows the plot of frequency stability measurement for temperature from 10 °C to 60 °C. Also it is possible to set desired bandwidth and Q by controlling the positioning of node points and dimensions of the mechanical coupler. Additionally the proposed resonator achieves better performance at moderate (+5 V) MEMS bias DC voltage and consumes 2.5 pW of power.

7 Conclusion

Dual band metal MEMS resonator with a method to achieve better temperature compensation and controllable bandwidth through mixed mechanical and electrical coupling scheme is proposed. The technique achieved a temperature coefficient of frequency (TCF) of -4.4 ppm/°C at temperature from 10 °C to 60 °C. It was achieved due to electrodeposited nanocrystalline nickel on chromium at room temperature that bears dense and simple structure. Selection of more than two mechanical couplers per CC beam ensures minimum variations in mode shapes and frequencies due to change in temperature. The device is CMOS process compatible, operates at nominal +5 V and consumes 2.5 pW of power. Further thermal stability can be elevated at higher temperatures by addition of Fe & P in the solute and annealing at temperature below 150 °C. The technique may be verified using CMOS-MEMS integration.

Acknowledgment. A part of the reported work (fabrication) was carried out at the IITBNF, IITB under INUP which is sponsored by DeitY, MCIT, Government of India.

References

1. Basu, J.D., Bhattacharyya, T.K.: Microelectromechanical resonators for radio frequency communication applications. Microsyst. Technol. **17**, 1557–1580 (2011)
2. Wang, Y., Feng, C., Lamers, T., Feld, D., Bradley, P., Ruby, R.: FBAR resonator figure of merit improvements. In: Proceedings IEEE Ultrasonic Symposium, pp. 861–863 (2010)
3. Gong, S., Piazza, G.: Monolithic multi-frequency wideband RF filters using two-port laterally vibrating lithium niobate MEMS resonators. IEEE J. Microelectromech. Syst. **23**(5), 1188–1197 (2005)
4. Zhang, H., Liang, J., Zhou, X., Zhang, H., Zhang, D., Pang, W.: Transverse mode spurious resonance suppression in lamb wave MEMS resonators: theory, modeling, and experiment. IEEE Trans. Electron Devices **62**(9), 3034–3041 (2015)
5. Patel, M., Bhattacharjee, K., Reed, J., Zhgoon, S.: Temperature compensation of longitudinal leaky SAW with silicon dioxide overlay. In: Proceedings IEEE Ultrasonic Symposium, pp. 1006–1010 (2008)
6. Gao, A., Gong, S.: Harnessing mode conversion for spurious mode suppression in AlN laterally vibrating resonators. IEEE J. Microelectromech. Syst. **25**(3), 450–458 (2016)
7. Hsu, W.-T., Nguyen, C.C.: Stiffness-compensated temperature insensitive micromechanical resonators. In: 15th IEEE International Conference on Micro Electro Mechanical Systems, pp. 731–734 (2002)

8. Tabrizian, R., Casinovi, G., Ayazi, F.: Temperature-stable silicon oxide (SilOx) microme-chanical resonators. IEEE Trans. Electron Devices **60**(8), 2656–2663 (2013)

9. Ng, E., et al.: Localized, degenerately doped epitaxial silicon for temperature compensation of resonant MEMS systems. In: 17th International Conference on Solid-State Sensors, Actuators and Microsystems (Transducers Eurosensors XXVII), pp. 2419–2422 (2013)

10. Hopcroft, M., et al.: Active temperature compensation for micromachined resonators. In: Technical Digest Solid-State Sensor, Actuator and Microsystems Workshop, pp. 364–367 (2004)

11. Ho, G., Sundaresan, K., Pourkamali, S., Ayazi, F.: Micromechanical IBARs: Tunable high-q resonators for temperature-compensated reference oscillators. J. Microelectromech. Syst. **19**(3), 503–515 (2010)

12. Chen, Chao-Yu., Li, M.-H., Chin, C.-H., Li, S.-S.: Implementation of a CMOS-MEMS Filter Through a Mixed Electrical and Mechanical Coupling Scheme. J. Microelectromech. Syst. **25**(2), 262–274 (2016)

Deadlock Detection in Digital Microfluidics Biochip Droplet Routing

Jyotiranjan Swain[✉] and Sumanta Pyne

Department of Computer Science and Engineering,
National Institute of Technology, Rourkela 769008, Odisha, India
jrswain85@gmail.com, pynes@nitrkl.ac.in

Abstract. Digital Microfluidics Biochip (DMFB) is one of the trending research areas. It is used extensively in genetic research and medical diagnostics. Droplet routing is one of the essential tasks in DMFB. The goal is to transport all the droplets to their respective destination cells to perform the desired operation without colliding with each other. To avoid unwanted interference between two droplets, fluidics constraints are defined. Deadlock occurs when two droplets stop advancing to next cell due to the violation of fluidics constraints. This leads to higher routing time. In this paper, we defined the conditions for deadlock and detect the deadlock before its occurrence. The proof is presented also. The simulation result shows improvement in routing time.

Keywords: DMFB · Droplet routing · Deadlock · Routing time

1 Introduction

Digital microfluidics Biochip (DMFB) or Bio-MEMS or cyber-physical MEMS is a handheld device, that is capable of automating biochemical reactions or assays. DMFBs are extensively used in DNA research works, medical diagnostics, studying particulate matters in the environment etc. These devices have following advantages over the traditional biochemical laboratory.

- Portability: Traditional laboratory equipments are huge and immobile. DMFBs are small and hand-held devices offering high portability [1].
- Precision analysis: Manual sample preparation in the range of nano/picoliter is error-prone as it involves human intervention. DMFB can automate sample preparation by eliminating or minimizing human role, Hence giving a very small margin of error in the result [10].
- On spot or Point of Care analysis: Traditional experimentation takes longer time as it involves the overhead of sample transportation to the lab. DMFBs can collect the sample, perform the biochemical reaction and generate result instantaneously on the spot [8].
- Flexibility: A single DMFB can be reused for multiple assays just by reprogramming the chip. This is called dynamic reconfiguration [13].

© Springer Nature Singapore Pte Ltd. 2019
S. Rajaram et al. (Eds.): VDAT 2018, CCIS 892, pp. 242–253, 2019.
https://doi.org/10.1007/978-981-13-5950-7_21

Due to above features Biochips are used extensively in clinical or medical diagnostics e.g. measuring sugar or glucose level in blood [1], genetic research like DNA sequencing, PCR analysis [1], Law enforcement application like preventing drunk driving by checking blood alcohol level, explosive detection and drug discovery [3].

The first generation of digital microfluidics devices are called analog devices. These devices have micro-channels integrated into the chip. These devices are designed for a specific chemical reaction. To perform an assay continuous fluids are pumped along the channels to specific points of the chip where multiple liquids are mixed. These devices suffers from contamination, inflexibility and absence of fault tolerance capability [1,2,5]. The second generation of Biochips are capable of generating discreet droplets in volume of nano/pico liters. These devices are based on electro-wetting principle. The individual droplets are manipulated by switching on or off the electrodes beneath the cell on which they reside. This behavior of electrodes mirrors with values of a bit i.e. 0 or 1. Hences these devices are also called digital microfluidics biochip (DMFB). One of the important task in DMFB is droplet routing i.e. moving all the droplets from their source cell to their destination cell without violating fluidic constraints. The aim is to minimize total number of cells used by the all droplets or latest arrival time (the time at which the last droplet reaches its destination) or both [3].

The remaining portion of the paper is organized as follows, Sect. 2 gives a brief description of the digital microfluidics system. Section 3 present droplet routing and related works. The proposed method and proof is elaborated in Sect. 4. The experimental result and analysis are given in Sect. 5. Finally the papers end with the conclusion and future work.

2   Digital Microfluidics System

Digital microfluidics system consists of three components i.e. PC controller, micro-controller and digital microfluidic biochip. The PC controller maps various assay operations like mixing, splitting etc. to the chip and generates an activation sequence of electrodes. The activation sequence specifies which electrodes to be switched on at the various instant. The microcontroller takes the activation sequence as input and generates corresponding signals and sends it to the biochip to power on/off the electrodes [23].

The biochip consists of two parallel glass plates each one painted with a hydrophobic material. The upper plate contains a single continuous ground electrode, while the bottom plate contains a series of uniform sized evenly spaced electrodes. The fluidic droplet is squeezed in between the plates as shown in Fig. 1.

The bottom plate is viewed as a two-dimensional array of cells or electrodes. The droplets reside on the cells and manipulated using electro-wetting principle. When the voltage is applied to a static aqueous droplet, its contact angle and the pressure decreases. This induces an electromagnetic force that stretches the droplet's contour towards the higher voltage potential. This phenomenon is called electro-wetting. Each cell in the biochip is capable of performing basic operations like transport (moving a droplet from one cell to another), mixing

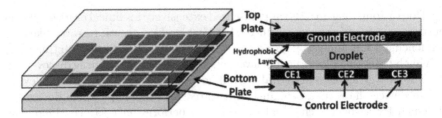

Fig. 1. Digital microfluidic biochip [21]

(merging two droplets), splitting (dividing a droplet into two smaller droplets) and store (keeping the droplet at a cell for a specific time period). The additional capability like heating and detection can also be added to the biochip [1]. The biochemical reactions or assays are represented as a directed acyclic graph (DAG). Each node in DAG is an assay operation and the edges represent the interoperational dependencies. Chemical synthesis on a digital microfluidics contains three stages i.e. scheduling (when the operations are to occur), placing (where the operations are to be performed) and routing (how the operations are to be executed) [22].

3 Droplet Routing

In scheduling, the start and end times of individual operations are assigned. In placing various operations are mapped to modules to increase cell utilization. Once scheduling and placement are finished, droplet routing is performed. Each droplet has source and destination cells. The goal of the droplet routing is to transport all the droplets from their source to the destination cell, simultaneously without colliding or interfering with any other droplets. To prevent unwanted mixing of droplets, fluidic constraints are defined [1,2]. Two type of constraints is defined i.e. static and dynamic. The static constraint defines the rules for static droplets while dynamic constraint specifies rules for mobile droplets. The target is to maintain a gap of at least one cell between two droplets.

Let D_i and D_j are two non adjacent droplets. $(X_i(t), Y_i(t))$ denote the position of D_i at time t [1–3].

Static Constraint:
R1: $| X_i(t) - X_j(t) |$ > 1
R2: $| Y_i(t) - Y_j(t) |$ > 1
R3: R1 OR R2 = True
Dynamic Constraint:
R4: $| X_i(t+1) - X_j(t) |$ > 1
R5: $| Y_i(t+1) - Y_j(t) |$ > 1
R6: $| X_i(t) - X_j(t+1) |$ > 1
R7: $| Y_i(t) - Y_j(t+1) |$ > 1
R8: (R4 OR R5) AND (R6 OR R7) = True
The experimental proof of the fluidics constraint is illustrated by Su et al. [1].

3.1 Related Work

Droplet routing is a vital component in the chemical synthesis using DMFB. Several authors have proposed many routing techniques. Su et al. [1] presented a divide and conquer method. It assumes solving a series of subproblem optimally will lead to the optimal final solution. The route of a droplet is considered a summation of a series of subproblems. A subproblem constitutes the portion of the route to travel by the droplet in a specific time period. Hence solving a series of subproblem leads to suboptimal solutions. If routes of any droplets are not found then the replacement of modules are done and route discovery process is restarted. Xu et al. [8] used a clique partition method for suboptimal solution. A clique formed by grouping droplets having cells sharing same row or column in the next move. Griffith et al. [5] considered the DMFB as a network of components. Various components like street, interconnect, bridge, source, sink and work area are defined. Virtual architecture is defined to avoid interference among droplets while traveling. To avoid deadlock, the rate of injection of droplets are controlled. Akella et al. [6] proposed a vertex coloring approach on the virtual architecture to eliminate deadlock. A transition graph is generated and nodes are colored in such a way that no two adjacent nodes have the same color. The total time for routing is equal to the chromatic number of the graph. Yuh et al. [7] introduced a two-stage routing method. In global routing, a rough route for droplet is estimated and in detail routing phase the exact path is determined by applying wait cycles. Grissom et al. [21] used the same architecture as in [5]. They have avoided deadlock by defining clockwise and anticlockwise movement in intra and inter rotaries. They also limited the number of droplet in a module to 3. They also further improved the solution by introducing pre-stalling i.e. When the number of stalls added to a route reaches a threshold, The route is modified by adding all the stalls at the beginning of the route and rerouted [22]. Cho et al. [10] introduced bypassability and concession zone. The bypassability refers to the number of routes available to bypass a droplet without violating fluidic constraints, while concession zone consists of a set of cells with dimensions greater than or equal to 3×1. Droplets are processed in descending order of bypassability. In case of deadlock, droplets having minimum route length are moved to concession zone to provide path for longer route droplets. Zhao et al. [12] find disjoint paths (both vertex and edge) for droplets. Initially, they find vertex disjoint path, if any portion of the route can't be routed then edge-disjoint paths are found from that point. Singha et al. [26] applied CSMA/DA for droplet routing. Roy et al. [2] present a total parallel method of droplet routing. Here the cells are numbers as the time cycle at which they reside on it. Two consecutive cells should have a timestamp difference of at least 2. The deadlock is solved by using stall, detour or backtracking. Roy et al. [13] presented a best selection path based on Hightower line search method. The routes are selected based on the number of crossovers. Roy et al. [14] presented a clustering-based approach for droplet routing. Here clusters are formed by grouping 2-net operations and 3-nets operations separately. Bhattacharya et al. [24] presented a total parallel routing method. They solve the deadlock by finding the both stalling and detour. The best among these two is selected to break the deadlock. Bohringer et al. [4] mapped the droplet routing to motion path planning for multiple robots. He introduced prioritized A* algorithm for droplet routing. If there exist a path then it returns optimal path. Huang et al. [11] used vector analysis to construct global routing tracks for the droplets. To avoid collision there is a gap of at least one row or column of cells between tracks. Pan et al. [15] and Juarez [3] used ant colony optimization for droplet routing. Pan et al. represent the pheromone value as the time traveled by the droplet and the target. While Juarez define crossover and mutation functions to generated optimal solutions.

3.2   Problem Formulation

All the method discussed above allows the droplets to be in deadlock. To beak deadlock stalling, detouring and backtracking is used. Other methods include controlling the rate of injection of droplets or defining the way droplet moves across various modules on the biochip. The performance of a deadlock is measured by the two parameters i.e. the number of cells along a route and latest arrival time. optimizing both these parameters is an NP-hard problem [4]. Here we try to optimize the latest arrival time by detecting deadlock before it can happen. The goal is so that necessary solutions can be applied to prevent deadlock to happen.

Let two non adjacent droplets D_i and D_j are at (X_i, Y_i) and (X_j, Y_j) at time t. Move the droplets to their destination modules such that no two droplets become adjacent to each other i.e. fluidic constraints should hold always. Reduce the latest arrival time by detecting deadlock and resolve it by applying stalling and detouring.

4   Proposed Method

All the work discussed earlier allows the droplets to enter into deadlock and then take necessary action to recover from the deadlock. Our aim is to detect deadlock before its occurrence and take necessary steps to avoid the deadlock. For this we need to detect the deadlock by identifying the cases which leads to deadlock. We assume that, Each movement of the droplet abide by the fluidic constraints. Deadlock happens when two droplets halts at current cell they are in as they can't move to their next cell as they will become adjacent after next move. To prevent unwanted mixing, a conflict zone is defined around a droplet. A conflict zone contains all the cells surrounding a droplet. Deadlock happens when a droplet enter into conflict zone of other. So detection of deadlock can be seen as overlapping of rectangles. Where a rectangle is the conflict zones of a droplet.

Claim: Deadlock occurs if a droplet enters into conflict zone of another droplet.

Proof: The conflict zone of a droplet consists of all the cells that are adjacent to cell currently occupied by the droplet. If any droplet enters into any one of the cell of the conflict zone in next move, then it is guaranteed to be adjacent to another droplet. This results a violation of fluidic constraints. As fluidic constraints don't allow any movement that results in adjacency between droplets. So the droplets are engaged in deadlock.

It has been observed that, The number of cells between two droplets in deadlock is 1 or 2. There is no guarantee that deadlock will happen if the number of cells between droplet is 1 or 2. It depends on the direction of movement of the droplet. Based on these observations deadlock can occur in three cases.

Case 1: When both droplets moves to the same cell.
Let D_1 and D_2 are two droplets in cells (X_1, Y_1) and (X_2, Y_2) respectively at time t. If both of them moves to same cell in next move, Then
$$| X_1(t+1) - X_2(t+1) | = 0$$
$$| Y_1(t+1) - Y_2(t+1) | = 0$$

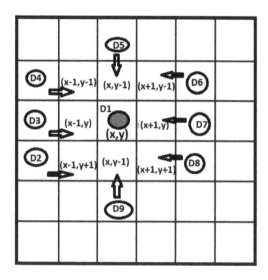

Fig. 2. One of the droplet is static

In next two cases, the next move of the droplet results in adjacency between cells. There are two cases i.e. when one of the droplet is static and the other one is both of the droplets are mobile.

Case 2: When one of the droplet is static.
Let D_i is a static droplet residing in cell (x, y) at time t. It will be part of a deadlock if any droplet tries to enter into its conflict zone. The conflict zone of D_i contains 8 cells surrounding it. Let D_j for j = 2 to 9 be the droplets tries to enter one of the cells in the conflict zone. It has been observed that deadlock can happen in two configuration when the next move of the droplet becomes diagonally adjacent or non diagonally adjacent.

Non-diagonal Cells: D_3, D_5, D_7 and D_9

D3
$| X_1(t+1) - X_3(t+1) | = 1$
$| Y_1(t+1) - Y_3(t+1) | = 0$

D7
$| X_1(t+1) - X_7(t+1) | = 1$
$| Y_1(t+1) - Y_7(t+1) | = 0$

D5
$| X_1(t+1) - X_5(t+1) | = 0$
$| Y_1(t+1) - Y_5(t+1) | = 1$

D9
$| X_1(t+1) - X_9(t+1) | = 0$
$| Y_1(t+1) - Y_9(t+1) | = 1$

Diagonal Cells: D_2, D_4, D_6 and D_8

D2
$| X_1(t+1) - X_3(t+1) | = 1$
$| Y_1(t+1) - Y_3(t+1) | = 1$

D6
$| X_1(t+1) - X_7(t+1) | = 1$
$| Y_1(t+1) - Y_7(t+1) | = 1$

D4
$| X_1(t+1) - X_5(t+1) | = 1$
$| Y_1(t+1) - Y_5(t+1) | = 1$

D8
$| X_1(t+1) - X_9(t+1) | = 1$
$| Y_1(t+1) - Y_9(t+1) | = 1$

Case 3: When both of the droplet are mobile. Let D_i moved to cell (x, y) at time t+1 from (x−1, y). then its conflict zone also moved t as shown in the Fig. 3. Then deadlock to happen the droplet has to enter into the new conflict zone of the droplet.

Non-diagonal Cells: D_3, D_5 and D_7

D3
$| X_1(t+1) - X_3(t+1) | = 0$
$| Y_1(t+1) - Y_3(t+1) | = 1$

D7
$| X_1(t+1) - X_7(t+1) | = 0$
$| Y_1(t+1) - Y_7(t+1) | = 1$

D5
$| X_1(t+1) - X_5(t+1) | = 1$
$| Y_1(t+1) - Y_5(t+1) | = 0$

Non-diagonal Cells: D_2, D_4, D_6 and D_8

D2
$| X_1(t+1) - X_3(t+1) | = 1$
$| Y_1(t+1) - Y_3(t+1) | = 1$

D6
$| X_1(t+1) - X_7(t+1) | = 1$
$| Y_1(t+1) - Y_7(t+1) | = 1$

D4
$| X_1(t+1) - X_5(t+1) | = 1$
$| Y_1(t+1) - Y_5(t+1) | = 1$

D8
$| X_1(t+1) - X_9(t+1) | = 1$
$| Y_1(t+1) - Y_9(t+1) | = 1$

From above observations we can detect deadlock in following way. Let two non adjacent droplets D_i and D_j are at (X_i, Y_i) and (X_j, Y_j) at time t. Then both droplets are said to be in droplet if any one of the following condition satisfies

C1: $| X_i(t+2) - X_j(t+2) | = 0$ AND $| Y_i(t+2) - Y_j(t+2) | = 0$
C2: $| X_i(t+2) - X_j(t+2) | = 1$ AND $| Y_i(t+2) - Y_j(t+2) | = 0$
C3: $| X_i(t+2) - X_j(t+2) | = 0$ AND $| Y_i(t+2) - Y_j(t+2) | = 1$
C4: $| X_i(t+2) - X_j(t+2) | = 1$ AND $| Y_i(t+2) - Y_j(t+2) | = 1$

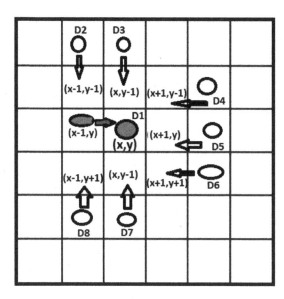

Fig. 3. One of the droplet is static

5   Simulation Results and Analysis

We have used UCR microfluidics static simulator [28] for our experimentation. It is an open source simulator and licensed for academic research purpose only. It is written in C++ and Java. It offers visual display of droplet movement which helps in easy debugging. We have executed our experimentation on a 32-bit Window 7 machine having 2 GB RAM and Intel core i7 processor operating at 3.4 GHz. For each experiment, Path scheduler [22] used for scheduling phase. We have performed our experimentation, for two type of architectures i.e. virtual topology and free topology. Virtual topology has fixed motion path for droplets [5,6,21] and for placing of modules Path placer [23] used. In free topology, there is no restriction of movement path for droplets and Krammer placer is used for placing. The operating frequency is set at 100 Hz. The performance analysis is done by comparing routing time measured in millisecond.

We have taken three routers i.e. Cho Router [10], Roy Router [2] and Grissom router [22] for their efficiency and implemented the proposed deadlock detection condition in each protocol. Most literature use following three type of benchmark i.e. PCR, In vitro and protein based. Polymerase Chain Reaction(PCR) benchmark is commonly used for used in molecular biology for exponential DNA amplification. In-vitro diagnostics is used for identifying metabolic disorders. These benchmarks use four human physiological fluids (plasma, serum, urine, and saliva) to measure levels of glucose, lactate, and glutamate. Calorimetric protein assay based on the Bradford reaction are used in protein crystallization. It is a commonly used technique for protein analysis and subsequent drug design.

Table 1. Virtual topology

Benchmark	Nodes		Cho [10]		Roy [2]		Grissom [22]	
	Total	Non I/O	Original	Proposed	Original	Proposed	Original	Proposed
PCR	16	7	52	48	49	43	56	52
In Vitro 1	20	8	74	65	67	65	83	81
In Vitro 2	30	12	124	116	113	108	134	126
In Vitro 3	45	18	Failed	237	Failed	312	185	174
In Vitro 4	60	24	216	214	198	195	242	245
In Vitro 5	80	33	282	281	262	260	316	310
Protein 1	118	62	Failed	700	680	640	941	902
Protein Split 1	28	14	124	121	122	118	195	187
Protein Split 2	58	30	325	312	318	289	4521	4429
Protein Split 3	118	62	Failed	800	680	665	941	920
Protein Split 4	238	126	Failed	Failed	1401	1380	1914	1845
Protein Split 5	478	254	Failed	Failed	2900	2854	3910	3791

It predicts the three-dimensional arrangement of the constituent amino acids, which in turn indicates the specific biological function of a protein.

The simulation result for virtual topology is listed in Table 1. The Roy router [2] outperform other routers, the reason is the shortest route generation due to the use of Sokoup's algorithm for route discovery. But it fails to work for few benchmarks like in-vitro 3. The possible reason is to inability to resolve the deadlock in compaction phase. Our proposed method, able to successfully route the droplet in in-vitro 3 case and marginally improve the routing time. Cho router [10] gives good performance compared to Grissom router [22] but failed for benchmarks like in vitro 3, Protein 1, Protein split 3, 4 and 5 The reason for failure is, these benchmarks are dense and the frequent attempt to move the droplet to the concession zone and break the deadlock. Our proposed method able run in vitro 3 and Protein 1, but failed in other three cases. We also observed small improvement in routing time. Grissom router [22] able to execute all the benchmarks successfully as it guarantees deadlock free. But the number of cycles needed to execute is worst among the three routers. The modified version of performs better than the original one. The improvement in routing time increases as the assay becomes denser.

The simulation result for free topology is given in Table 2. Here also Roy router [2] outperform other routers. But it fails to work for few benchmarks like protein 1 and protein split 3. Our proposed method, able to successfully route the droplets in case of in-vitro 3. The modified Roy router able to run on all the benchmarks with better routing time. Cho router [10] gives good performance over Grissom router [22] but less than Roy router. It is not able to run for benchmarks like Protein 1, Protein split 3, 4 and 5. The modified version able to run for Protein 1 and routing time is significantly improved for all benchmarks. Grissom router [22] is designed for virtual topology, hence it failed in most cases due to the absence of detouring, backtracking mechanisms.

Table 2. Free topology

Benchmark	Nodes		Cho [10]		Roy [2]		Grissom [22]	
	Total	Non I/O	Original	Proposed	Original	Proposed	Original	Proposed
PCR	16	7	75	61	73	62	Failed	81
In Vitro 1	20	8	122	106	115	97	188	168
In Vitro 2	30	12	201	176	189	160	273	259
In Vitro 3	45	18	238	201	235	191	Failed	402
In Vitro 4	60	24	329	292	314	285	Failed	Failed
In Vitro 5	80	33	452	411	431	392	Failed	Failed
Protein 1	118	62	Failed	586	Failed	498	Failed	501
Protein Split 1	28	14	248	219	245	206	326	287
Protein Split 2	58	30	492	450	498	391	Failed	Failed
Protein Split 3	118	62	Failed	721	Failed	689	Failed	Failed
Protein Split 4	238	126	Failed	Failed	1904	1542	Failed	Failed
Protein Split 5	478	254	3656	Failed	3679	3206	Failed	Failed

The modified version able to run few more benchmarks like In vitro 3 and protein 1 but failed in other cases with a slight improvement in routing time. From the simulation result, we can conclude that detecting deadlock before its occurrence improves the performance of the protocols.

6   Conclusion and Future Work

DMFB is one of the trending research area. Microfluidics is the study of devices that manipulate nanoliter droplets through a network of micro-channels. The first generation of microfluidics devices consist of microchannels pasted inside the chip and fluids are flown along these channels to perform various chemical reactions. To remove its inflexibility and fault tolerance, the second generation biochips are designed. These devices able to generate tiny size droplets having volumes in nanoliter range. It consists of 2D - array of electrodes called cells. The droplets reside on these cells and manipulated by switching on or off the electrodes beneath the cells. Droplet routing is one the important task in it. The goal of the droplet routing is to transport all the droplets to their destination without colliding with each other. All the proposed methods allow the droplets to enter into deadlock and then take necessary action to resolve the deadlock. The action includes stalling, detouring and backtracking. Deadlock can happen between two droplets when both of them becomes adjacent in next move. In other words, deadlock can occur only when the droplets becomes diagonally or non-diagonally adjacent. Hence to reduce to latest arrival time, we need to detect deadlock before it happen and take necessary action to prevent it. In this paper we defined the conditions for deadlock occurrence and presented a proof for it. We perform our experiment using UCR microfluidics static simulator and taken three router i.e. Cho router, Roy router and Grissom router. The experimental result show, Roy router performs best and able to run most of the benchmarks, while Grissom router able to execute all the benchmarks in virtual topology, but failed to execute most benchmarks in free topology. The modified version of all these three protocols includes the deadlock detection and performance is slightly better than the original In future we plan to implement these three routers with stalling, detouring and backtracking and study the performance.

References

1. Su, F., Hwang, W., Chakrabarty, K.: Droplet routing in the synthesis of digital microfluidic biochips. In: Proceedings of the Conference on Design, Automation and Test in Europe, DATE 2006, Munich, Germany, 6–10 March 2006, pp. 323–328 (2006)
2. Roy, P., Rahaman, H., Dasgupta, P.: A novel droplet routing algorithm for digital microfluidic biochips. In: Proceedings of the 20th Symposium on Great Lakes Symposium on VLSI, GLSVLSI 2010, Rhode Island, USA, 16–18 May 2010, pp. 441–446 (2010)
3. Juarez, J., Brizuela, C., Martínez, I., Velázquez, K., Lozano, E.: A genetic algorithm for the routing of droplets in DMFB: preliminary results. In: Proceeding of 2014 IEEE International Conference on Systems, Man and Cybernetics (SMC), San Diego, CA, USA, pp. 3808–3815 (2014)
4. Bohringer, K.F.: Towards optimal strategies for moving droplets in digital microfluidic systems. In: Proceeding of IEEE International Conference on Robotics and Automation, pp. 1468–1474 (2004)
5. Griffith, E., Akella, S.: Coordinating multiple droplets in planar array digital microfluidics systems. Int. J. Robot. Res. **24**(11), 933–949 (2005)
6. Akella, S., Griffith, E.J., Goldberg, M.K.: Performance characterization of a reconfigurable planar-array digital microfluidic system. IEEE Trans. Comput. Aided Des. Integr. Circuits Syst. **25**, 340–352 (2006)
7. Yuh, P.H., Yang, C.-L., Chang, Y.-W.: BioRoute: a network-flow based routing algorithm for digital microfluidic biochips. In: Proceeding of IEEE/ACM Computer-Aided Design, ICCAD 2007, San Jose, CA, USA, 4–8 November 2007
8. Xu, T., Chakrabarty, K.: A cross-referencing-based droplet manipulation method for high-throughput and pin-constrained digital microfluidic arrays. In: Proceedings of Design Automation and Test in Europe, April 2007, pp. 552–557 (2007)
9. Yuh, P.-H., Sapatnekar, S., Yang, C.-L., Chang, Y.-W.: A progressive-ILP based routing algorithm for Cross referencing biochips. In: Proceedings of Design Automation Conference, June 2008, pp. 284–289 (2008)
10. Cho, M., Pan, D.Z.: A high-performance droplet routing algorithm for digital microfluidic biochips. IEEE Trans. Comput. Aided Des. Integr. Circuits Syst. **27**(10), 406–419 (2008)
11. Huang, T., Ho, T.: A fast routability - and performance-driven droplet routing algorithm for digital microfluidic biochips. In: Proceedings of IEEE ICCD, Lake Tahoe, CA, pp. 445–450 (2009)
12. Zhao, Y., Chakrabarty, K.: Cross-contamination avoidance for droplet routing in digital microfluidic biochips. In: Proceeding of Conference on Design, Automation and Test in Europe, DATE 2009, Nice, France, 20–24 April 2009, pp. 1290–1295 (2009)
13. Roy, P., Bhattacharya, R., Rahaman, H., Dasgupta, P.: A best path selection based parallel router for DMFBs. In: IEEE International Symposium on Electronic Design, ISED 2011, Kochi, India, pp. 176–181 (2011)

14. Roy, P., Rahaman, H., Dasgupta, P.: Two-level clustering-based techniques for intelligent droplet routing in digital microfluidic biochips. Integr. **45**(3), 316–330 (2012)
15. Pan, I., Dasgupta, P., Rahaman, H., Samanta, T.: Ant colony optimization based droplet routing technique in digital microfluidic biochip. In: International Symposium on Electronic System Design, pp. 223–229 (2011)
16. Roy, P., Howladar, P., Bhattacharjee, R., Rahaman, H., Dasgupta, P.: A new cross contamination aware routing method with intelligent path exploration in digital microfluidic biochips. In: Proceedings of 8th International Conference on Design & Technology of Integrated Systems in Nanoscale Era, (DTIS), Abu Dhabi, United Arab Emirates, 26–28 March 2013
17. Pan, I., Samanta, T.: Weighted optimization of various parameters for droplet routing in digital microfluidic biochips. In: Thampi, S., Abraham, A., Pal, S., Rodriguez, J. (eds.) Recent Advances in Intelligent Informatics. AISC, vol. 235, pp. 131–139. Springer, Cham (2004). https://doi.org/10.1007/978-3-319-01778-5_14
18. Wang, Q., Shen, Y., Yao, H., Ho, T.-Y., Cai, Y.: Contamination-aware routing flow for both functional and washing droplets in digital microfluidic biochips. In: Proceeding of 19th Workshop on Synthesis And System Integration of Mixed Information technologies, (SASIMI 2015), Yilan, Taiwan (2015)
19. Bhattacharya, R., Rahaman, H., Roy, P.: A new heterogeneous droplet routing technique and its simulator to improve route performance in digital microfluidic biochips. In: Proceedings of 2016 International Conference on Microelectronics, Computing and Communications, MicroCom, Durgapur, India, 23–25 January 2016
20. Maftei, E., Pop, P., Madsen, J.: Routing-based synthesis of digital microfluidic biochips. In: Proceedings of International Conference on Compilers, Architectures and Synthesis for Embedded Systems (CASES 2010), Scottsdale, Arizona, USA, 24–29 October 2010, pp. 41–50 (2010)
21. Grissom, D., Brisk, P.: A high-performance online assay interpreter for digital microfluidic biochips. In: Proceedings of the 22nd Great Lake Symposium on VLSI, (GLS-VLSI), Salt Lake City, UT, USA, 3–4 May 2012, pp. 103–106 (2012)
22. Grissom, D., Brisk, P.: Fast online synthesis of digital microfluidic biochips. IEEE Trans. Comput. Aided Des. Integr. Circuits Syst. (TCAD) **33**(3), 356–369 (2014)
23. Grissom, D., Brisk, P.: Path scheduling on digital microfluidic biochips. In: Proceedings of 49th Design Automation Conference, (DAC), San Francisco, CA, USA, 3–7 June 2012, pp. 26–35 (2012)
24. Bhattacharya, R., Roy, P., Rahaman, H.: Homogeneous droplet routing in DMFB: an enhanced technique for high performance bioassay implementation. Integr. VLSI J. **60**, 74–91 (2018)
25. Sait, S., Youssef, H.: VLSI Physical Design Automation: Theory and Practice. IEEE Press, New York (1995)
26. Singha, K., Samanta, T., Rahaman, H., Dasguptay, P.: Method of droplet routing in digital microfluidic biochip. In: Proceeedings of the 2010 IEEE/ASME International Conference on Mechatronics and Embedded Systems and Applications (MESA), QingDao, China, 15–17 July 2010
27. Bazargan, K., Kastner, R., Sarrafzadeh, M.: Fast template placement for reconfigurable computing systems. IEEE Des. Test Comput. **17**(1), 68–83 (2000)
28. Grissom, D., et al.: An open-source compiler and PCB synthesis tool for digital microfluidic biochips. Integr. VLSI J. **51**, 169–193 (2015)

Fabrication of Molybdenum MEMs Structures Using Dry and Wet Etching

Sandeep Singh Chauhan[1], Niharika J[1(✉)], M. M. Joglekar[2], and S. K. Manhas[1]

[1] Microelectronics Laboratory, Department of Electronics and Communication Engineering, Indian Institute of Technology Roorkee, Roorkee 247667, India
sandy.dec2014@iitr.ac.in, nijgup@gmail.com
[2] Department of Mechanical and Industrial Engineering, Indian Institute of Technology, Roorkee 247667, India

Abstract. This paper presents a novel method to make molybdenum (Mo) MEMS structures by using both wet and dry etching methods complementing each other to do fabrication in less time by using bulk micromachining process. These planar structures can find a wide range of applications which includes pressure sensors, micro-hotplates owing to the property of Mo to be thermally stable at high temperature, and RF switches due to the mechanical stability of Mo. In the present work, the n-type Si substrate is used on which an oxide layer is grown by thermal oxidation and then high-quality Mo thin film of thickness 900 nm is deposited by DC magnetron sputtering. This paper also describes a very effective method to address the problem of stiction during the releasing process of MEMs structures. The Mo film is characterized by atomic force microscopy (AFM) and X-ray diffraction (XRD) and MEMs structures are characterized by field emission scanning electron microscopy (FE-SEM).

Keywords: DC sputtering · Dry etching · Molybdenum film ·
MEMs structures · Wet etching

1 Introduction

Integration and application of MEMs structures have been increasing along with CMOS technology. Different MEMs structures such as cantilever beam for micro switch [1], Silicon on Insulator (SOI) diaphragm for capacitive sensing devices, patch antenna and filters [2], interdigitated micro cantilever array for sensitive sensor and parallel detection of multiple analytes [3]. Straight beam, T shaped beams for energy harvester [4, 5] bulk micro machined cantilever structures also used for micro resonators and accelerometers [6]. The MEMs structures fabricated in present work are Mo-based. Mo has very good adhesion to SiO_2 as compared to Pt and Au, whereas, Al and Ti have the tendency to get oxidized easily in the environment [7]. Mo is a refractory metal which is highly resistant to wear and heat. It has a melting point of 2610 °C. It has high thermal shock resistance due to its low coefficient of thermal expansion [8].

© Springer Nature Singapore Pte Ltd. 2019
S. Rajaram et al. (Eds.): VDAT 2018, CCIS 892, pp. 254–263, 2019.
https://doi.org/10.1007/978-981-13-5950-7_22

Crystalline Mo films having body-centered cubic structure and {110} planes have least surface energy and high planar density. This high planar density improves the quality factor of Mo MEMs structures [9]. Mo being a refractory material shows much less change in expansion coefficient with temperature. Sputtered Mo film has the resistivity of 10–11 $\mu\Omega$-cm [10]. Mo is a CMOS process compatible material has a high Young's modulus of elasticity of 3.4 $\times$ 10^{12} dynes/cm^2 which is beneficial from the switching point of view [11]. Mo is an ideal mechanical material for RF MEMS capacitive switches as it shows very less rate of change of actuation voltage with rising in temperature and hence provides temperature robust process which is low cost and gives good yields. Mo provides the good balance between thermal expansion coefficient and resistivity required for these switches. The Mo switches are said to operate up to 150 °C and have pull in voltage change of 0.03 V/°C. Mo switches can operate 20 billion cycles without failure [10]. Mo can also be used as a bottom electrode for AlN based devices for applications like FBAR filters, sensors, actuators and energy harvester [5, 12].

The silicon dioxide layer between the Mo and silicon can act as a dielectric and this whole assembly can function as a capacitive switch. Doped silicon being a semiconductor can act as a bottom electrode. The dielectric film in between helps to prevent stiction between two conducting layers but provides a low impedance path between the two contacts. This minimizes insertion loss. When the switch is actuated, the metal-dielectric-metal sandwich provides low impedance path to surrounding waveguide this prevents the RF signal from traveling beyond switch [13]. Since oxide films are very fragile, so deposition of Mo over it and releasing a cantilever can ease the handling of cantilever [14]. The sensitivity of cantilever is proportional to the square of the length of the cantilever beam and fabricating long cantilever can be a problem due to stiction problem [3]. The voltage required to turn on the MEMS switch decreases as we increase the length of the cantilever beam so it is an advantage to get a higher length cantilever beam. The use of the dielectric material in between the two metal contacts in the switch is to avoid stiction problem [15].

So, releasing of long MEMs structure with ease is a potential research problem to be solved. By using RIE we get large grains because RIE has plasma which anneals the structure. And this reduces the interfacial area between the contact solids and hence helps in avoiding stiction [16]. Dry etching is said to produce lesser defects in fabricated cantilever than wet etching. The defects can be indicated from the shift in natural frequency of oscillation of cantilever from the theoretically calculated value [12]. It is very important that no residue is left behind after releasing of the cantilever as this residue may result in undesired capacitance ratio i.e. on and off position of the switch which is one of the potential application [13]. The higher gap between the MEMs structure and the substrate is beneficial for sensing application as high depth means the pull-in voltage when the cantilever has deflected 1/3rd of the gap increases. Pull-in voltage is the maximum dc voltage that the cantilever can sustain. Hence, as the distance between the cantilever and substrate increases the maximum deflection that cantilever can sustain without breaking increases and hence the limit of detection also increases [17].

The Sect. 2 of the paper gives detail on the fabrication process for deposition of Mo thin film, fabrication and releasing of Mo MEMs structures. In Sect. 3, the results are discussed where the characterization of Mo film has been explained in details and then the SEM results of MEMs structures are discussed. The next subsection in Sect. 3 discusses the etching behavior.

2 Experimental Details and Fabrication Process Flow

The n-type silicon wafer was taken and 300 nm oxide layer was grown after RCA cleaning. After that, 900 nm thick Mo thin film was deposited at 200 W plasma power and 5 mbar pressure. The target to substrate spacing was kept at 55 mm. The positive photoresist AZ1512HS was used to pattern the structures on Mo thin film and the corresponding developer AZ351B was used to develop the pattern. This positive photoresist also acts as a mask for the wet etching of both Mo and SiO_2 layers. The etchant used for Mo was H_3PO_4:HNO_3:CH_3COOH: DI water mixed in the ratio of 15 ml: 9 ml: 5 ml: 33 ml. The optimized etch rate of Mo was 200 nm/min. Further, the SiO_2 layer was etched in buffered HF at an etch rate of 90 nm/min. This was followed by dry and wet etching of Si substrate. KOH is an anisotropic wet etchant for Si. IPA was added to KOH to reduce the frequency of occurrence of hillocks and to obtain smooth silicon surface. Moreover, added IPA in KOH solution also reduce etchant surface tension which helps in releasing hydrogen bubbles and in dissolving organic contaminants. Addition of IPA avoids micro masking effect and produces smooth etching. The etchant for Si was 20 g of KOH pellets dissolved in 50 ml of DI water and 12 ml of IPA heated at 75 °C temperature. All the experimental parameters are listed in Table 1.

Table 1. Thin film deposition parameters and etching recipe.

Process	Parameters	Etchants
Oxidation	Oxide thickness of 300 nm at 1050 °C with O_2 flow rate of 0.5 l/min	BOE with the etch rate of 90 nm/min
Molybdenum sputtering	900 nm thick Mo film, deposited at 350 °C, 200 W, 30 sccm Ar flow, 5 mbar pressure, with 55 mm target to substrate spacing	H_3PO_4:HNO_3:CH_3COOH: DI water. obtained etch rate 200 nm/min
Dry etching	70 W RIE plasma power, 20 Pa pressure	SF_6 (35 sccm), Ar (20 sccm), O_2 (10 sccm), etch rate of 1 μm/min
Si bulk etching	At 75 °C	KOH solution, etch rate 0.85/1.38 μm/min

The complete fabrication process flow is shown in Fig. 1. The etch rate of Si in KOH is 1.38 μm/min with the dry etching process. During this process of releasing cantilever SiO_2 and Mo acts as a mask for silicon wet etching. This was the main etching step to take advantage of high etch rate in wet etching. This was preceded by dry etching i.e. RIE was done for 15 min at 70 W plasma power and 20 Pa pressure to obtain high aspect ratio and low roughness of side walls. The process took total 1 h, 25 min as compared to 2 h and 30 min which is a very short time to obtain the MEMs structures. The fabricated MEMs structures are rectangular bridges, simple, and array cantilevers. Length of the cantilever is 50 μm to 250 μm and width varying from 10 μm to 40 μm. To avoid stiction of the MEMs releasing structures the sample after wet etching process was placed in acetone carefully and the acetone was allowed to evaporate naturally.

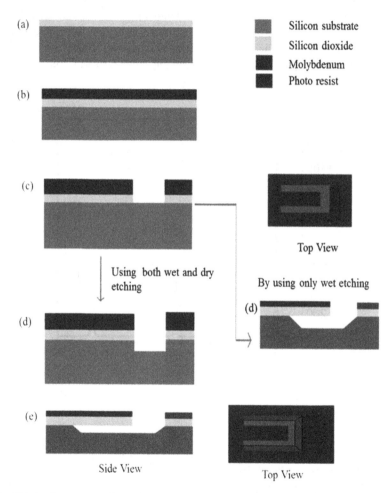

Fig. 1. Fabrication process flow of microcantilever structure (a) Silicon substrate with grown silicon dioxide, (b) Mo layer sputtered on top of oxide layer, (c) Spin coating of photoresist, lithography, patterning, and etching of Mo & silicon dioxide, (d) dry etching of bulk silicon, (e) after wet etching and final released microcantilever structure.

3 Results and Discussion

XRD is used to analyze the crystallographic properties of the Mo thin film deposited on SiO₂/Si substrate. It uses Cu-Kα radiation with the wavelength of $\lambda = 0.1540$ nm. The peak intensity obtained along (110) orientation at 40.5 confirms the deposited Mo film with body centred cubic structure. This shows there is some compressive stress. As seen in the Fig. 2 third peak of Mo corresponds to (200) plane [18]. The additional peaks correspondingly are seen due to the high-temperature deposition which was done to smoothen the surface and to obtain highly crystalline structures. The increase in peak intensity and the decrease in the full width at half maximum (FWHM) are indicative of high crystallinity [6]. Figure 3 shows a high quality deposited Mo thin film with the average surface roughness of 2 nm.

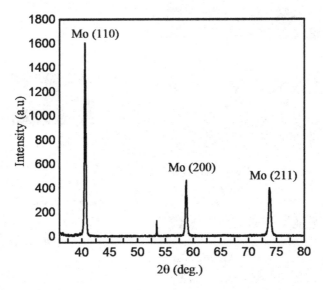

Fig. 2. XRD pattern of sputtered Mo thin film on SiO₂/Si substrate at the plasma power of 200 W, and Ar flow rate of 30 sccm.

As seen from Fig. 4 the SEM images of wet etched MEMs structures are not released with good demarcation even though the etched depth is 158 μm and this is one of the reason dry etching has been done before wet etching. The other reasons being that the MEMs structures release time also reduces. In the wet etching process due to more directional etching of KOH in (100) directions, we can see convex corner etching profile. The reason for the etch time reduction with the first dry etching followed by the wet etching process is that the Si is vertically exposed. It means remaining convex corners after dry etching are comparatively less. So, the isotropic wet etching proceeds easily to release highly demarcated Mo MEMs structures. Hence, dry followed by wet etching

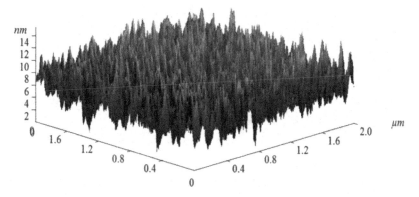

Fig. 3. AFM images of deposited Mo film on SiO_2/Si substrate at Ar flow rate of 30 sccm with the measured average surface roughness of 2 nm.

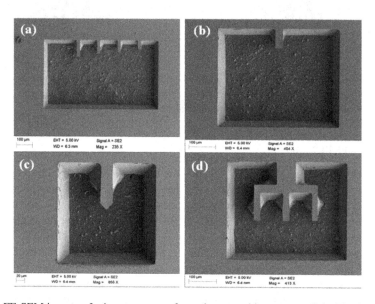

Fig. 4. FE-SEM images of microstructures after only wet etching process (2 h, 25 min). (a) The array of the cantilever beam, (b) single cantilever beam, (c) Microcantilever with the pointed tip, (d) Branched cantilevers.

process promotes faster and completely released MEMs structures (Fig. 5). The etch depth is 118 μm in this method. The sidewalls of the cantilever are defined by (111) plane which is a self-limiting plane so does not etch easily. The surface of Si when etched hillocks form as seen in Fig. 4 and faces of these are composed of <111> planes.

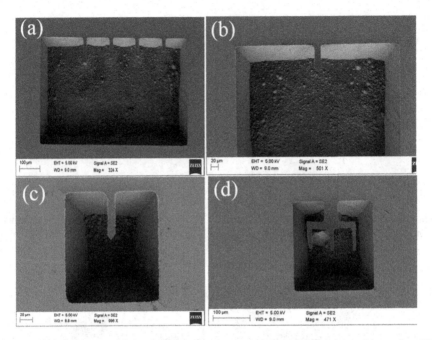

Fig. 5. FE-SEM images of completely released microcantilevers after dry etching using RIE system followed by the wet etching process (1 h, 25 min). (a) Cantilever beam array, (b) Single cantilever beam, (c) Micro cantilever with pointed tip, (d) Branched cantilevers.

3.1   Etching Behavior

The etching of Si along <110> and <100> plane is 10 to 100 times faster than along <111> plane. The anisotropic etching of Si stops by itself when all slow etching planes <111> meet. As in Fig. 6 depicting the etching behavior of Si the V-shaped grooves are formed by anisotropic etching of Si by KOH solution. As reported in literature the angle between (111) plane and (100) plane is 54.74°, thus V grooves are formed [19]. The benefit of using dry etching before wet etching is that the V grooves form late and hence etching stops slow since <111> planes take time to be exposed. The Fig. 7 shows dry etched vertically exposed Si above which we have SiO_2 and Mo. Since Si layer is vertically exposed it can be etched laterally fast when exposed to the KOH solution and the MEMs structure easily released. The advantage of using dry etching by RIE is that SF_6 can be made isotropic. The planar selectivity of KOH for planes <110>, <100>, and <111> is 600:400:1. This means that the (111) gets etched least followed by (100) plane and (110) plane is the one that is etched most. The main advantage of bulk micromachining is that it can be used quickly and uniformly over large Si area at low cost. The cavity will have four concave corners with <111> plane. The undercutting at convex corners <110> plane in wet anisotropic etching is used in fabricating suspended microstructures like cantilever beams in silicon bulk micromachining process. Undercutting at convex corner occur due to the emergence of high indices crystallographic planes. These crystallographic planes have the high etch rate in comparison to <100> plane and hence cantilevers get released. By using dry etching we expose the convex corner planes which can then be easily etched by KOH solution [20].

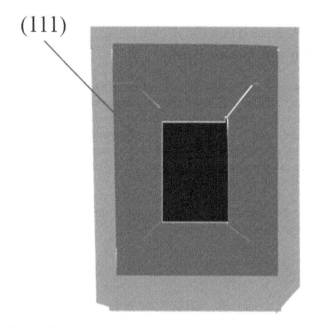

Fig. 6. Etching profile of bulk silicon substrate after both wet and dry etching process.

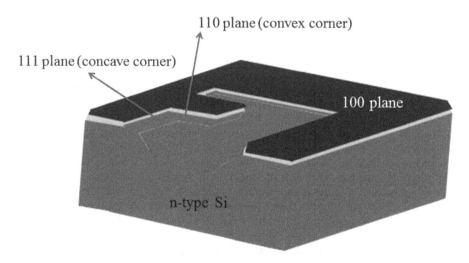

Fig. 7. The orientation of different planes and the formation of the convex and concave corners during the releasing process of the cantilever.

Whenever the requirement is to get undercutting the sides are slightly misaligned from (110) planes and thus large cavity is obtained this property is exploited to release the MEMs structures fast by first aligning the sides by dry etching. Undercutting is only obtained along the convex corner and not along the concave corner [21]. So, we conclude that the MEMs structures are easily released with first dry etching followed by the wet etching process.

4 Conclusion and Future Work

This paper presents the use of both dry and wet etching together to complement each other to release the cantilever in lesser time. Compared to the convex corner it's very difficult to get rid of the concave corner by corner compensation method and it is said to be difficult to get rid of (111) planes during anisotropic wet etching so the proposed method can be very helpful to release MEMs structures easily. This work can be extended by depositing needy and active material layer on Mo MEMs structures and can be used for various applications.

Acknowledgment. The authors thank to Institute Information Centre (IIC), IIT Roorkee for their support in characterization of deposited thin films.

References

1. Chandra, S., Bhatt, V., Singh, R., Sharma, P., Pal, P.: MEMS prototyping using RF sputtered films. Indian J. Pure Appl. Phys. **45**, 326–331 (2007)
2. Luo, W.-J., Pan, Y.-J., Yang, R.-J.: Transient analysis of electro - osmotic secondary flow induced by dc or ac electric field in a curved rectangular microchannel. J. Micromech. Microeng. **15**, 1–11 (2005)
3. Pires, N.M.M., Dong, T., Hanke, U., Hoivik, N.: Recent developments in optical detection technologies in lab-on-a-chip devices for biosensing applications. Sensors (Switzerland) **14** (8), 15458–15479 (2014)
4. Iqbal, A., Mohd-Yasin, F.: Comparison of seven cantilever designs for piezoelectric energy harvester based on Mo/AlN/3C-SiC. In: RSM 2015 Proceedings, pp. 1–4 (2015)
5. Chauhan, S.S., Manhas, S.K., Joglekar, M.M.: Fabrication of cantilever MEMs structure of C-axis grown AlN film for energy harvester application. In: 18th ICIT Conference, Lyon, France, pp. 984–988. IEEE (2018)
6. Singh, R., Kumar, M., Chandra, S.: Growth and characterization of high resistivity C-axis oriented ZnO films on different substrates by RF magnetron sputtering for MEMS applications. J. Mater. Sci. **42**(12), 4675–4683 (2007)
7. Mele, L., Santagata, F., Lervolino, E., Sarro, P.M.: A molybdenum MEMS microhotplate for high-temperature operation. Sens. Actuators A Phys. **88**, 173–180 (2012)
8. Sharma, J., Fernando, S., Tan, W.M.: Integration of AlN with molybdenum electrodes and sacrificial amorphous silicon release using XeF 2. J. Micromech. Microeng. **24**(3), 35019 (2014)
9. Rao, L.L.R., Singha, M.K., Subramaniam, K.M., Jampana, N., Asokan, S.: Molybdenum microheaters for MEMS-based gas sensor applications: fabrication, electro-thermo-mechanical and response characterization. IEEE Sens. J. **17**(1), 22–29 (2017)

10. Goldsmith, C., et al.: Performance of molybdenum as a mechanical membrane for RF MEMS switches. In: MTT-S International Microwave Symposium, Boston, USA, pp. 1229–1232. IEEE (2009)
11. Brown, R.B., Ger, M.L., Nguyen, T.: Characterization of molybdenum thin films for micromechanical structures. Micro Electromech. Proc., 77–81 (1990). 3764178
12. Yao, Z.J., Chen, S., Eshelman, S., Denniston, D., Goldsmith, C.: Micromachined low-loss microwave switches. J. Microelectromech. Syst. 8(2), 129–134 (1999)
13. Park, J.Y., Kim, H., Chung, K.W., Bu, B.U.: Monolithically integrated micromachined RF MEMS capacitive switches. Sens. Actuators A 89, 88–94 (2001)
14. Patil, G.D., Kolhare, N.R., Bhosale, P., Rokade, A.I.: Cantilever type switch design. Int. J. Res. Eng. Technol. 4(1), 402–406 (2015)
15. Lee, C., Hsu, W.: Modification on surface roughness by combining dry and wet etching. In: Proceedings of SPIE, vol. 5116, pp. 627–635 (2003)
16. Hwang, D.-H., Lo, Y.-C., Chin, K.: Development of a systematic recipe set for processing SU8-5 photoresist. In: Proceedings of SPIE Device and Process Technologies for MEMS and Microelectronics, vol. 4592, pp. 131–139 (2001)
17. Haluzan, D.T., Klymyshyn, D.M., Achenbach, S., Börner, M., Jaber, N.R.: Reducing pull-in voltage by adjusting gap shape in electrostatically actuated cantilever and fixed-fixed beams. Micromachines 1, 68–81 (2010)
18. Dementyeva, M.G., Meisner, L.L., Lotkov, A.I., Mironov, Y.P.: X-ray diffraction studies of the molybdenum thin films magnetron-sputtered on the TiNi alloy surface. Fundam. Modif. Process., 182–185 (2014)
19. Håkan, E.G.A., Rosengren, L., Bäcklund, Y.: Fabrication of 45° mirrors together with well-defined v-grooves using wet anisotropic etching of silicon. J. Microelectromech. Syst. 4(4), 213–219 (1995)
20. Pal, P., Sato, K., Chandra, S.: Fabrication techniques of convex corners in a (1 0 0)-silicon wafer using bulk micromachining: a review. J. Micromech. Microeng. 17(10), R111–R133 (2007)
21. Pal, P., Singh, S.S.: A simple and robust model to explain convex corner undercutting in wet bulk micromachining. Micro Nano Syst. Lett. 1, 1 (2013)

Continuous Flow Microfluidic Channel Design for Blood Plasma Separation

Jagriti Srivastava[✉] and Rajendra Patrikar

Centre for VLSI and Nano-Technology,
Visvesvaraya National Institute of Technology, Nagpur 440010, India
jagriti19ss@gmail.com, rajendra@computer.org

Abstract. Various clinical blood diagnostics tests are performed on plasma, necessitating an efficient microfluidic device for blood plasma separation. Microfluidics devices are being explored for such applications and many of them are successfully deployed. This work demonstrates a passive microchannel design for continuous flow blood-plasma separation. The design uses the multistage bifurcations and constrictions to separate blood plasma. Simulation results show that the more plasma yield is obtained by reducing the angle of bifurcation, decreasing the constriction width and by increasing the bifurcating stages. The simulation shows that yield obtained after optimizing the geometry is 97.03%.

Keywords: Blood · Plasma · Microfluidic · Microchannels ·
Continuous flow · Passive separation

1 Introduction

Blood carries with it the information regarding the functioning of the body that is vital for clinical diagnosis. Blood is comprised of four basic components: plasma, red blood cells, white blood cells, and platelets where the plasma constitutes of 55% of the blood. Blood test discovers substances such as tumor marker, an electrolyte that indicates various infections, diseases, and cancers [1]. More than 90% of the tests [2] which are indicative of Bone marrow disorders, Kidney disease, Edema, Hepatitis, Human Immunodeficiency Virus, inflammatory bowel disease, Leukemia, Liver disease, Malnutrition are performed on the plasma. So the more efficient separating techniques are required to obtain pure plasma.

Centrifugation is one of the two conventional methods for blood plasma separation. Centrifugation method requires longer time and a large amount of sample moreover they do not contribute to integration for the development of point-of-care clinical diagnostic devices [3]. Another one is membrane-based filtration where there occurs a clogging of pore due to a large number of cells in the sample which reduces the efficiency of separated plasma [4]. Microfluidic deals with the smaller sample volume resulting in the reduction of fabrication cost, lower cost per measurement, shorter analysis time and is minimally invasive to the patient. Microfluidic simplifies and parallelizes the analysis steps and benefits

© Springer Nature Singapore Pte Ltd. 2019
S. Rajaram et al. (Eds.): VDAT 2018, CCIS 892, pp. 264–277, 2019.
https://doi.org/10.1007/978-981-13-5950-7_23

in automation and integration. The elimination of the need for portability and storage increases the quality, efficiency, and reproducibility of the component in microfluidic devices [5].

The microfluidic systems for blood plasma separation can be categorized into Active and Passive systems. The Active separation method requires the application of external force fields such as gravity [6], magnetic force [7], electric force [8] and acoustic force [9]. Hence requires external power to induce the force. Moreover, high conductivity suspension of blood causes heating inside the device [10] and prolonged exposure to the magnetic field can change the native immuno-phenotype of the cell [11]. Whereas the passive systems require lesser sample volume, zero power consumption, and allows better system integration for point-of-care devices. Another advantage of the passive system is that they do not require extra systems for external force field hence they are cost-effective and easy to handle. A detailed study of passive approaches for blood plasma separation has been assembled in a review by Tripathi et al. [12]. The passive separation can either be cell sized or bio-mimetic. The various approaches for cell sized separation are: capillarity [13], cross-flow filtration [14,15], hydrodynamics and lateral displacement around obstacles [16,17]. But for these approaches there is a need for high level skills for controlling the pillars and gaps as mentioned by Tachi et al. [18] and hence fabrication is difficult as mentioned by Chandra et al. [19] and Xiang et al. [20].

The bio-mimetic separation deigns are simple, least challenging to fabricate and can be easily integrated into LOC. The bio-mimetic plasma separation are classified by Zweifach Fung bifurcation effect which can be achieved either by constrictions as stated by Hou et al. [21] or curved cross sections or by both. Over the years many designs have been developed for passive bio-mimetic separation with the curved cross sections which are mostly spirals or the serpentine structures [22]. But Zhang et al. [2] showed that curved channels are not good choice for micro-channel in case of both high flow-rate and low flow-rate [20]. At high flow-rate contributes to coupling of centrifugal migration and Dean Vortex. While at a lower flow-rate there is very minor contribution of cell in migration. So in this work the passive design which is geometrical equivalent of spiral structure have been modified and used for continuous flow separation as shown in Fig. 1. The continuous flow systems can potentially examine and adjust the parameters for separation continuously [21]. This increases the throughput of the device.

2   Theory and Measurement

2.1   Zweifach-Fung Effect/Bifurcation Law

Svanes and Zweifach [24] observed the decrease in hematocrit which is the ratio of RBC to the total volume of blood, when the capillaries were compressed using micro-occlusion techniques. They also observed that the branch with higher velocity tends to have more hematocrit leading side branches with negligible hematocrit when the marginal blood flow passes down by the branch. The cell then enters into the region of bifurcation follows the channel which has higher flow-rate compared to the channel with lower flow-rate. Further Pries *et al.* [23] also observed that the branches with lower flow rates had the reduced hematocrit. This can be observed from the Fig. 1. For this, the velocity of main(RBC) channel should be higher than that of side (plasma) channel. The velocity depends upon the diameter of the particle and hence the diameter of a channel is of great importance. Tripathi *et al.* has a provided a detailed study of the structures employing Zweifach Fung effect.

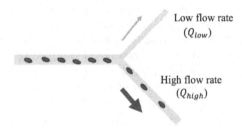

Fig. 1. Representation of the Zweifach-Fung bifurcation law [12]

2.2 Inertial Migration

For the microfluidic devices with lower Reynolds number($\Re << 1$), fluidic properties and dynamics are governed by Stokes equations. In this case, the drag force comes into the picture. The microfluidic devices with $1 < \Re < 500$ are the inertial devices. Size dependency of hydrodynamic forces in microfluidic channel leads to the inertial migration of particles/cells within the cross-section of the channel. This creates a drift that allows the focusing of the particles between the stream of fluids. This lift force results into a cell-free layer along the wall of the channel. The expression for induced lift force is given by:

$$F_L = \frac{\wp_p \pi d^3 U^2}{6 D_h} \tag{1}$$

where, $\wp_p$ is the density of particle, d is the diameter of particle, U is the average velocity of fluid and D_h is the hydraulic diameter of the channel. The lateral migration of particle is the result of the shear lift forces (F_{LS}) and the wall lift force (F_{LW}). The former force is due to parabolic nature of fluid velocity and lateral is due to the interaction between particles and walls deviating away from the particles from the wall. Constriction increases the flow-rate increasing the shear stress focusing the particles towards the center. The expression for the drift induced by the constriction of the particles is given by:

$$F_{dr} \approx 2.7 \frac{L_c R^3}{w_c h^2_c} \tag{2}$$

where L_c, w_c, h_c are the length, width and height of constriction respectively and R is the radius of a sphere having same radius as a cell (Fig. 2).

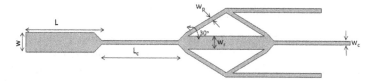

Fig. 2. Geometry of microchannel with constriction and 1st stage bifurcation with angle 30°

The working of the structure presented in this paper employs the theory of hydrodynamic forces. It uses symmetrical bifurcation of the flow across the channel. Alternately the constrictions have been provided by making the channel width first from 250 μm(w) to 100 μm(w_c) and then to 50 μm(w_c). After bifurcation the main channel width(w_r) reduces to 200 μm and the width of plasma(w_p) channel is 100 μm for 100 μm constriction width and 50 μm for 50 μm constriction channel width. The angle of the bifurcating channel is varied as 60°, 45° & 30°. Figure 2 shows the structure with single stage with 50 μm constriction width as well as plasma channel width considering bifurcation angle to be 30°. The cascaded structure has been developed and stages are varied as 1, 3 and 5 each for different structures with the different angle of the side channel. The outlet flow-rate of plasma is evaluated from both forwardly as well as backwardly leaned side channel. The length of the constricted channel(L_c) and main channel(L) is 1 mm while that of side channel varies with the angle.

3   Design Calculations

The design comprises a main channel(RBC) and the side channels(plasma) with alternate bifurcating loops and constriction. Various structures having the different angle, the number of loops and constrictions have been employed and summarized in Tables 1 and 2. The depth for each of the structure is considered to be 70 μm. The experiments have been performed keeping flow-rate at the inlet of 0.1 ml/h and constriction width of 50 μm. The effect of various parameters on flow-rate has been calculated to analyze the device for plasma efficiency as below:

3.1   Channel Resistance(R_{ch})

The resistance offered to the fluid depends upon the viscosity, length, width, and height of the microchannel. The channel with lower flow-rate offers higher resistance and higher flow-rate offers lower resistance. Hence the flow-rate ratio between the main channel and side(plasma) channel can be obtained by calculating the resistance ratio at the bifurcation. For rectangular channel the resistance is given as:

$$R_{ch} = 12 \frac{\vartheta L_{ch}}{1 - 0.63 \frac{h_{ch}}{w_{ch}}} \times \frac{1}{w_{ch} h^3_{ch}} \tag{3}$$

where, ϑ is the viscosity of the blood, L_{ch} is the length, h_{ch} is the height and w_{ch} is the width of the channel respectively.

3.2   Pressure and Pressure Gradient

The channel with high flow-rate has more pressure gradient than the channel with low flow-rate. This is due to the differential pressure and the shear lift force acting on the particles. The shear lift force is more in the channel where flow-rate is higher generating torque on the particle, due to which it focuses towards the higher flow rate channel after reaching the bifurcation. Constriction also escalates the flow influencing the pressure gradient. Pressure depends upon the channel resistance and the channel's flow-rate and is given as:

$$\Delta P = Q_p.R_p = Q_r.R_r \tag{4}$$

where Q_p, Q_r, R_p and R_r are the flow-rates and resistances of side(plasma) channel and main(RBC) channel respectively.

3.3   Reynolds Number($\Re$)

At higher flow-rate with higher $\Re$, the focusing of the particle at the center improves. And at lower flow-rate, the focusing of this concentrated particle gets destroyed. The expression for Reynolds Number at the inlet is given by:

$$\Re = \frac{\rho.\nu.D_h}{\vartheta} \tag{5}$$

where ρ is the density of the blood, D_h is the hydraulic diameter of the microchannel, ν is the average velocity and ϑ is the viscosity of the blood.

3.4   Flow Rate Ratio (F_Q)

Flow rate ratio is the ratio of flow-rates at the outlet of the RBC channel to that of Plasma channel. Zhang et al. [2] works present that the purity of plasma decreases with increase in flow-rate ratio while for some the efficiency of plasma was higher for the higher ratio.

$$F_Q = \frac{Q_r}{Q_p} \tag{6}$$

where, Q_p and Q_r are the flow-rates of the side(plasma) channel and main(RBC) channel respectively.

3.5   Yield

The plasma yield can be obtained by measuring volume fraction of RBCs in plasma channel to the total volume fraction of the RBCs. In our case we have considered volume fraction (phid) of RBCs to be 0.01.

Table 1. Variations in flow-rate for Plasma channel and RBC channel

Design no.	Angle	Stage(s)	W_p μm	W_r μm	L_{ch} mm	Q_p ml/h	Q_r ml/h
1	30°	1	50	200	4.5	0.0093	0.0359
2		3	50	200	9.5	0.0086	0.057
3		5	50	200	14.5	0.0084	0.055
4	45°	1	50	100	4.5	0.00735	0.058
5		3	50	200	9.5	0.0064	0.057
6		5	50	200	14.5	0.0073	0.0575
7	60°	1	50	100	4.5	0.0093	0.053
8		3	50	200	9.5	0.0082	0.058
9		5	50	200	14.5	0.0125	0.061

Inlet flow-rate was taken to be 0.1 ml/h

Table 2. Variations in values of Velocity and Reynolds number for the Plasma channel and RBC channel.

Design no.	Angle	Stage(s)	Velocity(m/s)		$\Re$	
			v_p	v_r	$\Re_p$	$\Re_r$
1	30°	1	0.742	2.856	43.25	101.34
2		3	0.683	4.53	39.8	160.7
3		5	0.671	4.45	39.1	157
4	45°	1	0.583	4.56	33.98	161
5		3	0.527	4.53	30.7	160
6		5	0.585	4.57	34.1	162
7	60°	1	0.741	4.22	43.2	149.7
8		3	0.654	4.59	38.1	162
9		5	0.996	4.84	58.06	171

The values are calculated using Eqs. 4, 5 and 6

4   Computational Analysis

The microfluidic Blood Plasma separator model was designed and simulated using COMSOL Multiphysics software. COMSOL solves the Navier-Stokes equation for almost all fluid flow models. There is an incompressible liquid Newtonian flow for constant density. The stationary analysis of incompressible liquid is modeled by Navier-Stokes equations using partial differential equations(PDE) is given by

$$\varrho(u * \triangledown)u = \triangledown[-pI + \kappa\{\triangledown u + (\triangledown u)^T\} + F] \tag{7}$$

$$\varrho \triangledown *u = 0 \tag{8}$$

where, u, ϱ, p, κ are fluid velocity, fluid density, fluid pressure, kinematic viscosity respectively. The Eq. (7) describes the conservation of momentum from Newton's second law. Equation (8) is the continuity equation where zero indicates that the fluid is incompressible.

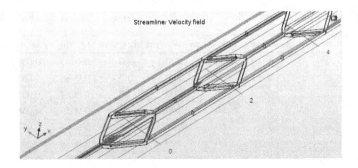

Fig. 3. 3D view of the streamlines for the velocity profile for multistage bifurcating microchannel.

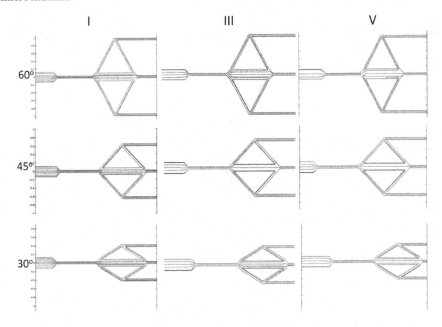

Fig. 4. Streamlines for the continuous phase velocity for different stages with different bifurcation angle for 50 μm channel width.

The simulation for our structure has been carried out in two steps. The first steps involves the use of Laminar flow model in COMSOL. And in the next step Mixture model, laminar flow has been used. The Laminar flow model is used to obtain the velocity profile, streamline and pressure gradient profile of the structure. While mixture model is used to calculate the volume fraction of the continuous phase and dispersed phase materials.

For Laminar flow model simulation, firstly the 3D geometry has been selected and the stationary study method was used. For the material basic property that are density $(1000 \, \text{kg/m}^3)$ and dynamic viscosity $(0.001 Pa.s)$ was selected and PDMS as a boundary layer was given. Average velocity was used which was calculated by dividing flow-rate by area. At the outlet the zero pressure as suppress backflow was used. After the computation, in the results the average over surface for the velocity was used and plotted in 1D plot graph. The total 3 structures were simulated. The stages were varied from 1 to 5. Figure 3 is the result for this simulation.

In the next step, Mixture model was used. The mixture model uses one set of Naiver-Stokes, one set of continuity and one set of the transport equation. This model assumes the density of each phase to be constant. For mixture model, the continuous phase should be liquid while the dispersed phase could be the particles, bubbles or droplets. We can provide the mixture of the two phases as input using this model. For the mixture properties, plasma was considered to be continuous phase material and RBC to be dispersed phase material. The dynamic viscosity for plasma was taken to be $0.001 Pa.s$ and density for plasma was taken as $1000 \, \text{kg/m}^3$ and for RBC it was $1095 \, \text{kg/m}^3$. Since RBCs contains almost 99% of the cellular components the dispersion phase volume fraction(phid) was taken to be 0.01 with an average velocity of 0.01 m/s. Figures 4, 5 and 6 shows the result out of this simulation.

5 Results and Discussions

5.1 Simulation Results

The change in volume fraction of dispersed phase RBC in the main channel and plasma channel has been listed in Tables 3 and 4. It can be seen as the phid decreases there is an increase in yield and hence the plasma purity is increased. From the laminar model, it can be observed that when the mixture flows by the constriction, the velocity is lower near the side channels and so the RBC moves to the central region of the microchannel. Also, the velocity is higher in the central region. Hence the RBCs flows at a higher velocity in the microchannel. As the mixture progresses in the channel it faces bifurcation after constriction so there are lesser chances for already localized RBCs to enter into the bifur-cating side channels. So only the purified plasma enters through the bifurcation. It can be observed from Fig. 4 (with respect to the streamlines) that purified plasma(continuous phase) enters side channel rendering lesser plasma entry into the main channel after each bifurcating stage.

For the larger angle, there are chances that the after constriction the RBCs to enter into plasma channel because of the gradual expansion as shown in the Figs. 5 and 6 for the structures at 1st stage. It can be seen that for lesser constriction width there is a lesser chance for RBCs to enter the plasma channel. Increasing the bifurcating stages reduces the level of RBCs from plasma channel as it can return back from the backwardly leaned side channel. But from Tables 3 and 4 we can see that the phid is decreasing in plasma channel till stage 3 but after the 5th stage it is again increasing. Hence the optimized structure must not contain more than three stages of bifurcation for the present structure. It can also be observed that yield obtained is more for the structure with lesser

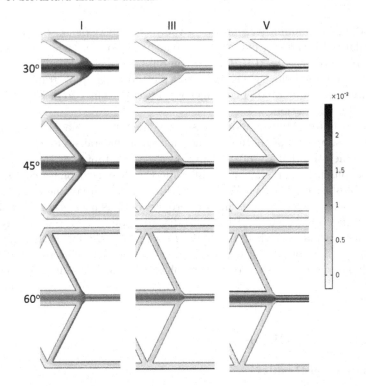

Fig. 5. Volume Fraction of RBCs near the bifurcating stage 1,3 & 5 for angle 30° 45° 60° with constriction width of 100 μm.

constriction width i.e. for 50 μm channel. Hence the calculations and results shown in Tables 1 and 2 are derived only for the structure with constriction width as 50 μm.

Increasing the angle in both the cases we can see that the yield gets reduced. However, from the Table 3, we can observe that for 3 stage design at angle 60° we get the highest yield of 89.33%. But then after reducing constriction width, the yield is highest for angle 30° as seen in Table 4. It can also be seen that as the phid for RBC decreases we get higher yield at the higher flow-rate ratio. As the phid decreases the yield increases and hence increase in the plasma purity. So by varying number of stages and angle of side channel an optimized model has obtained i.e. 3 stage 30° angle of bifurcation with 50 μm constriction width.

5.2 Comparitive Analysis

Comparing the structures and narrowing width from 100 μm to 50 μm, we found that the better yield is gotten by utilizing 50 μm channel. From the Fig. 6 and Table 4, the highest yield of plasma obtained, therefore, the pure plasma can be gotten by utilizing the Design number 2, which is the structure with three stages, 30° bifurcating point, and constriction width 50 μm. In this way contrasting

Table 3. Differences in phid and yield for the plasma and RBCs.

Design no.	Angle	Stage(s)	$(phid)_p(1)$	$(phid)_r(1)$	Yield %
1	30°	1	2.8E−3	15.4E−3	84.6
2		3	2.2E−4	15.2E−3	87.35
3		5	2.21E−4	14.9E−3	87.13
4	45°	1	3.44E−3	15.01E−3	81.42
5		3	2.8E−3	16.0E−3	85.11
6		5	2.86E−3	15.2E−3	84.16
7	60°	1	4.5E−3	14.5E−3	76.31
8		3	1.76E−3	15.0E−3	89.33
9		5	4.02E−3	15.7E−3	79.89

Constriction width=100 μm

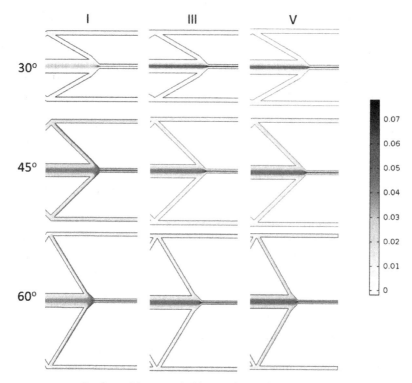

Surface: Dispersed phase volume fraction(1)

Fig. 6. Volume fraction of RBCs near the bifurcating stage 1,3 & 5 for angle 30° 45° 60° with constriction width of 50 μm.

Table 4. Differences in phid, yield and flow-rate ratio for the plasma and RBCs.

Design no.	Angle	Stage(s)	$(phid)_p(1)$	$(phid)_r(1)$	Yield %	F_Q
1	30°	1	$1.16E{-}3$	$16.8E{-}3$	93.5	3.86
2		3	$5.9E{-}4$	$19.3E{-}3$	97.03	6.62
3		5	$6.18E{-}4$	$18E{-}3$	96.67	6.54
4	45°	1	$2.77E{-}3$	$15.9E{-}3$	85.16	7.82
5		3	$1.97E{-}3$	$16.4E{-}3$	90.16	8.91
6		5	$1.79E{-}3$	$14.8E{-}3$	89.21	7.9
7	60°	1	$5.3E{-}3$	$14E{-}3$	72.5	5.69
8		3	$4.56E{-}3$	$20.3E{-}3$	81.7	7.07
9		5	$5.02E{-}3$	$17.9E{-}3$	78.1	9.18

Constriction width=50 μm

the present work and diverse structures keeping the channel width same i.e. 50 μm. Figure 7 demonstrates the comparison of the present work with mostly used Spiral microchannel, T-shaped structure and with the structure like Zhang et al. with slight alteration by changing constriction width and the number of the bifurcating stages. The volume fraction of the dispersed phase in RBC channel as well as in the plasma channel for different structures is stated in Table 5 for the Fig. 7.

Figure 7(a) is the simulation of the basic spiral structure keeping the parameters same as that we have kept for the present work. Same parameters are kept for simulation of the other structures as well as explain in the Computational Analysis section. Another method for separation includes T-shaped structure [12] and has been compared using same constriction channel width as shown in Fig. 7(b). Figure 7(c) is the modified structure presented in the work [2] where we have modified the width of constriction. Similarly, for the structure in Fig. 7(e) which is presented in work [3] is another biomimetic design using serpentine structure. For this structure the channel width is modified as per our design. Instead of the constriction channel width of 150 μm we have designed it using 50 μm and similarly the width of inlet is changed from 450 μm to 350 μm, respectively the channel width and height has been scaled and modified comparative to our design.

The yield is obtained through simulation by evaluating phid across the plasma as well as the RBC channel and are enlisted in Table 5. We can see that for same plasma channel width(constriction width), the same velocity at the inlet and same parameters for different designs we have different yield. Also, we can see that the yield for our structure is highest. The lowest yield we get is out of the spiral structure, although the spiral structures are improved and varied to obtain the higher yield but then there arise difficulties in fabrication, whereas the structure presented in this paper can be easily fabricated. Thus the highest yield is obtained using the structure from Fig. 7(e).

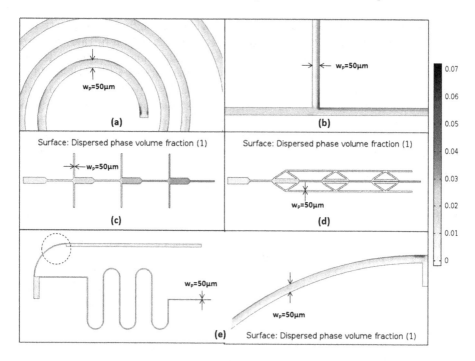

Fig. 7. Comparison of the volume fraction of RBCs for (a) Spiral microchannel structure, (b) T-shape microchannel structure, (c) 3-Stage microchannel for [2], (d) This work, and (e) Mirochannel design with Serpentine structure, with plasma channel width of 50 μm and velocity v = 0.01 m/s.

Table 5. Differences in phid for the plasma and RBCs with Yield of the Plasma.

Design	$(phid)_p(1)$	$(phid)_r(1)$	Yield %
(a)	9.2E−3	11.4E−3	55.34
(b)	9.1E−3	18.8E−3	67.38
(c)	6.4E−3	33.9E−3	84.11
(d)	5.9E−4	19.3E−3	**97.03**
(e)	9.95E−3	14.63E−3	59.52

6   Conclusion

A passive structure of the microchannel for the continuous flow blood plasma separation has been investigated using COMSOL Multiphysics. The simulation results show that due to constriction there is an increase in velocity in the main channel leaving the plasma channels with lower flow rate. Results show that the plasma purity increases with increase in flow rate ratio. From the result, it can be concluded that constriction helps in increasing the flow-rate of the RBC channel and it focuses the particle into centre after which the bifurcation directs the plasma to the side channels. Hence reducing constriction width further will give more pure plasma. Results obtained shows that bifurcation at angle 45° is not a good choice for microchannel structure as the flow-rate as well as the yield is much lower compared to others. After simulating and comparing the design with different structures we concluded that the highest plasma yield obtained from the volume fraction is 97.03% for the 3 stage bifurcation at angle 30°. Hence the optimized structure obtained after varying constriction width, bifurcating angles and number of the bifurcation stages is 3-stage 30° microchannel which is the Design Number 2 from Table 1.

References

1. Vaidyanathan, K., Vasudevan, D.M.: Organ specific tumor markers: what's new? Indian J. Clin. Biochem. **27**(2), 110–120 (2012)
2. Zhang, J., Wei, X., Xue, X., Jiang, Z.: Structural design of microfluidic channels for blood plasma separation. J. Nanosci. Nanotechnol. **14**(10), 7419–7426 (2014)
3. Jang, H., Haq, M.R., Ju, J., Kim, Y., Kim, S.M., Lim, J.: Fabrication of all glass bifurcation microfluidic chip for blood plasma separation. Micromachines **8**(3), 67 (2017)
4. Liu, C., et al.: Membrane-based, sedimentation-assisted plasma separator for point-of-care applications. Anal. Chem. **85**(21), 10463–10470 (2013)
5. Kovarik, M.L., et al.: Micro total analysis systems: fundamental advances and applications in the laboratory, clinic, and field. Anal. Chem. **85**(2), 451–472 (2012)
6. Huh, D., et al.: Gravity-driven microfluidic particle sorting device with hydrodynamic separation amplification. Anal. Chem. **79**(4), 1369–1376 (2007)
7. Jung, Y., Choi, Y., Han, K.H., Frazier, A.B.: Six-stage cascade paramagnetic mode magnetophoretic separation system for human blood samples. Biomed. Microdevices **12**(4), 637–645 (2010)
8. Pommer, M.S., et al.: Dielectrophoretic separation of platelets from diluted whole blood in microfluidic channels. Electrophoresis **29**(6), 1213–1218 (2008)
9. Petersson, F., Åberg, L., Swärd-Nilsson, A.M., Laurell, T.: Free flow acoustophoresis: microfluidic-based mode of particle and cell separation. Anal. Chem. **79**(14), 5117–5123 (2007)
10. Nakashima, Y., Hata, S., Yasuda, T.: Blood plasma separation and extraction from a minute amount of blood using dielectrophoretic and capillary forces. Sens. Actuators B Chem. **145**(1), 561–569 (2010)
11. Fukuda, S., Schmid-Schönbein, G.W.: Centrifugation attenuates the fluid shear response of circulating leukocytes. J. Leukoc. Biol. **72**(1), 133–139 (2002)
12. Tripathi, S., Kumar, Y.B., Prabhakar, A., Joshi, S.S., Agrawal, A.: Passive blood plasma separation at the microscale: a review of design principles and microdevices. J. Micromech. Microeng. **25**(8), 083001 (2015)
13. Maria, M.S., Chandra, T.S., Sen, A.K.: Capillary flow-driven blood plasma separation and on-chip analyte detection in microfluidic devices. Microfluid. Nanofluidics **21**(4), 72 (2017)
14. Lee, K.J., Wu, R.M.: Simulation of resistance of cross-flow microfiltration and force analysis on membrane surface. Desalination **233**(1–3), 239–246 (2008)

15. Yeh, C.H., Hung, C.W., Wu, C.H., Lin, Y.C.: Using the developed cross-flow filtration chip for collecting blood plasma under high flow rate condition and applying the immunoglobulin E detection. J. Micromech. Microeng. **24**(9), 095013 (2014)
16. Wu, Z., Hjort, K.: Microfluidic hydrodynamic cell separation: a review. Micro Nanosyst. **1**(3), 181–192 (2009)
17. Sun, J., et al.: Size-based hydrodynamic rare tumor cell separation in curved microfluidic channels. Biomicrofluidics **7**(1), 011802 (2013)
18. Tachi, T., Kaji, N., Tokeshi, M., Baba, Y.: Simultaneous separation, metering, and dilution of plasma from human whole blood in a microfluidic system. Anal. Chem. **81**(8), 3194–3198 (2009)
19. Maria, M.S., Rakesh, P.E., Chandra, T.S., Sen, A.K.: Capillary flow-driven microfluidic device with wettability gradient and sedimentation effects for blood plasma separation. Sci. Rep. **7**, 43457 (2017)
20. Li, X., Chen, W., Liu, G., Lu, W., Fu, J.: Continuous-flow microfluidic blood cell sorting for unprocessed whole blood using surface-micromachined microfiltration membranes. Lab Chip **14**(14), 2565–2575 (2014)
21. Wei Hou, H., Gan, H.Y., Bhagat, A.A., Li, L.D., Lim, C.T., Han, J.: A microfluidics approach towards high-throughput pathogen removal from blood using margination. Biomicrofluidics **6**(2), 024115 (2012)
22. Rafeie, M., Zhang, J., Asadnia, M., Li, W., Warkiani, M.E.: Multiplexing slanted spiral microchannels for ultra-fast blood plasma separation. Lab Chip **16**(15), 2791–2802 (2016)
23. Pries, A.R., Secomb, T.W.: Microvascular blood viscosity in vivo and the endothelial surface layer. Am. J. Physiol. Heart Circ. Physiol. **289**(6), H2657–H2664 (2005)
24. Svanes, K., Zweifach, B.W.: Variations in small blood vessel hematocrits produced in hypothermic rats by micro-occlusion. Microvasc. Res. **1**(2), 210–220 (1968)

Real Time Mixing Index Measurement of Microchannels Using OpenCV

Khuushi[✉], Vanadana Jain, Rajendra Patrikar,
and Raghavendra Deshmukh

Visvesvaraya National Institute of Technology, Nagpur, India
Khuushi.105022@gmail.com

Abstract. One of the main figures of merit for quantification of microchannels is mixing index (MI). The main challenge is to calculate the MI in real time, which is needed for improvising the performance of microfluidic system. In this contrast, present work is demonstrated the real time MI calculation using open source computer vision (OpenV) image processing tool. The MI application (MI-App) is developed by using Qt software which provide simple and easy platform to the end user. All open source software is handled through the Raspberry Pi which makes our system low cost and portable. The approach present in this work will helpful in various bio-medical applications.

Keywords: Mixing index · Real-Time · OpenCV · Micro-channels · Image processing

1 Introduction

Microfluidics have found their importance in biotechnology and chemical analyses due to miniaturization of devices. Microchannels play an important role in such devices. Microchannels are used for various applications like mixing, dielectrophoresis, separation, on paper microfluids, etc. A microchannel can be either active or passive [2, 3]. Irrespective of the mechanism used, every channel is quantified through its velocity at the outlet and inlets, pressure drop along the path and mixing index/mixing efficiency. Out of these, mixing index is the most common figure of merit used for quantification of microchannels.

In the past, various methods that use mathematical methods have been employed to determine the mixing of coloured liquids. Images captured while mixing takes place are used to perform calculations. A high resolution expensive camera is used. In this paper we focus on analysing the mixing efficiency in real time and in utmost cost effective method. A new application has been developed using open source software OpenCV and a cost effective camera have been used. The software is developed in C++ language on QT which is also an open source software. Absolute mixing index (AMI) [4] and Relative mixing index (RMI) are some of the most common methods used for mixing index calculations. In AMI the grayscale image is scaled from 0–255 to 0–1 and the deviation of intensity of each pixel from the mean of all the pixels intensities in the region of interest is measured [4]. The standard deviation is thus calculated. The value 0 indicates maximum mixing and 1 indicates no mixing. RMI is also a similar process

S. Rajaram et al. (Eds.): VDAT 2018, CCIS 892, pp. 278–284, 2019.
https://doi.org/10.1007/978-981-13-5950-7_24

but it takes under consideration the ambient light intensities [1]. This is done by dividing the standard deviation value at the point of care by the standard deviation at the inlet. Hence, the change in values due to ambient light is cancelled. The ratio is then subtracted from 1 which gives a more intuitive result, implying 1 as complete mixing and 0 as no mixing. In both the above methods the deviation of the pixel intensities is compared with the average of intensities of all the pixel in the region of interest. The average intensity here is assumed to be the intensity value of the mixed solution, which may or may not be true. For example, a mixer having low efficiency will have an average intensity value different than that of the intensity of a 100% mixed solution. In the presented paper, the intensity of a 100% mixed solution is fed before the experiment is started. This gives an estimate of a value the software needs to reach for a 100% mixing.

In the previously mentioned methods i.e., Absolute Mixing Index and Relative Mixing Index, both the reagents have been assumed to have same intensities which is a very specific case. However practically the color of both the reagents may or may not be same and there is a requirement of selection of the reference reagent intensity value. Hence, in the presented work different cases are considered and then calculation is performed. The GUI is designed in a user friendly manner and does not need any expertise to understand it.

The given paper is divided into 5 sections, Sect. 2 describes the different cases for the selection of the reference reagent. In Sect. 3, the GUI of the application (MIApp) is explained. Section 4 deals with the experiments undertaken and its results, a low cost technique for fabrication of microchannel with paper as a substrate has also been discussed and Sect. 5 is the conclusion.

2 Mixing Index Derivation

Mixing index is generally calculated by converting the image captured into 8-bit grayscale image. The intensities are in the range of 0–256. For mixing index calculation the intensities are normalized to be 0 for minimum value and 1 for maximum value. The basic formula is to normalize the intensities and then standard deviation is calculated which gives a value of 0 for complete mixing and 0 for no mixing as shown in Eqs. 1 and 2. In order to make the mixing index more intuitive the standard deviation is subtracted from. Now, 1 and 0 represent maximum and minimum mixing respectively (as in Eq. 3) [6].

$$I_{norm} = \frac{Ii - Iref}{Imix - Iref} \tag{1}$$

$$I_{std} = \sqrt{\frac{(1 - Inorm)^2}{N}} \tag{2}$$

$$MI = 1 - I_{std} \tag{3}$$

Here, Inorm is the normalized pixel intensity value, Ii is the grayscale intensity value of the pixel, Imix is the intensity of completely mixed region and Iref is the intensity of completely unmixed region. The above mention mechanism holds true only when the grayscale intensity of the solution at both the inlets is same, i.e., the color, brightness and contrast of both the reagents to be mixed is same. For different colors of reagents to be mixed the formulas show ambiguity hence it needs to be modified, for proper selection of Iref. There can be three different practical cases (1) when Imix is between Ir1 and Ir2 where, Ir1 and Ir2 is the intensity of reagent 1 and reagent 2 respectively. Here Ir1 is assumed smaller than Ir2. For example, mixing ink with water, (2) when Imix is greater than Ir1 and Ir2, example, mixing NaOH solution with a solution of phenolphthalien in ethyl alchohol. (3) when Imix is lesser than Ir1 and Ir2, the example of this situation is when a solution of sodium hypochloride and sodium hydroxide bleaches a food coloring solution. It has been observed that in all the three cases considering the minimum of the two intensities gives incorrect mixing index, which is obvious, since the mixing index should be 0 at both Ir1 and Ir2. Hence, selection of Iref is critical.

Case I: when I_{mix} is between I_{r1} and I_{r2}. When the minimum value, i.e., I_{r1} is considered to be I_{ref} all the pixel intensity values larger than I_{mix} and smaller than or equal to I_{r2} will return a value of I_{norm} which is greater than 1. Now, if in the selected region of interest the density of such pixel intensities is more, the mixing index is negative. Also, if the I_{r2} is considered as I_{ref} all the pixels, in the region of interest, having intensities less than that of I_{mix} will contribute to wrong value of mixing index. Therefore, in this case

$I_{ref} = I_{r1}$ for $I_i <= I_{mix}$ and $I_{ref} = I_{r2}$ for $I_{ref} > I_{mix}$.

Case II: when I_{mix} is greater than I_{r1} and I_{r2}. In this case, since both values are less than I_{mix}x, care has been takes that mixing index is 0 at both I_{r1} and I_{r2}. Assuming I_{ref} as I_{r2} is justified for pixels inside the region of interest, having intensity values which are greater than I_{r2}. For values less than I_{r2}, considering value of I_{ref} as I_{r1} may return wrong values, as practically pixels having intensity values very close to I_{r2} should return a mixing index value to approximately 0. Hence, a value I_{med} has been calculated which lies between I_{r1} and I_{r2} such that all pixel intensities larger than I_{med} should take I_{ref} value as I_{r2} and pixel intensities smaller than I_{med} should take I_{ref} value as I_{r1}.

Case III: when I_{mix} is lesser than I_{r1} and I_{r2}. This case is quite similar to case 2. In this case for all intensity values less than I_{med}, I_{ref} is I_{r1} and for values greater I_{med}, I_{ref} is I_{r2}. This may look same as that of case 2 but the formula for calculation of I_{med} is different.

3   Application (MI-APP)

A system has been setup which comprises of a cost-effective camera having a resolution of (1280×1800) which suffices the requirement in this particular application. The processor used is Broadcom BCM2837 which is the in-built in Rasp-berry pi 3 as shown in Fig. 1. The compact size and cost-effective elements in this setup makes it easily available to everybody. A user-friendly GUI has been developed using open source platform. The calculation of mixing index in this paper has been done through image processing using Open source Computer Vision (OpenCV) libraries. Another open source software QT has been used which provides IDE environment. Libraries of OpenCV have been linked with QT and an application is built using C++ language. The coloured image is converted to grayscale and the intensities of this converted image are then used for mixing index calculations. The algorithm used for converting RGB to grayscale is such that it preserves the salient feature of the coloured image such as contrast, sharpness, shadow and image structure [7].

Fig. 1. Experimental setup and GUI of the application for real time measurement of mixing efficiency

The Fig. 1 shows the GUI developed in QT environment. The webcam option helps the user to analyze mixing index in real time. Video feature in the application can be selected to load a pre-captured video and measure the mixing index. Once the start button is clicked a new window gets opened which shows the video capture or the captured date from web-cam. Three new windows pop up which asks the user to select the reagent 1, reagent 2 and the completely mixed value, respectively. It must be kept in mind that before performing the experiment for analyzing the mixing efficiency of a micromixer we must know the resultant colour change when there is a 100% mixing efficiency. The application then prompts to select a region where the mixing needs to be measure in the mixer. The mixing index is then displayed for each frame.

4 Results and Discussion

In order to check the credibility of the application few experiments have been performed using different reagents. A t-mixer has been fabricated on paper using low-cost wax curing mechanism. A t-mixer was printed on filter paper using laser-jet printer. The thickness of the channel is 3 mm. Wax was then rubbed along the printed pattern very precisely. In order to avoid seepage of wax into the channel, it was ensured that the layer of wax was not too thick. The wax patterned filter paper was kept on hot plate for 5 s at 1200c. The wax seeped in vertically through the filter paper making hydrophobic walls. Any liquid now dropped inside the channel would follow the micro channel path as shown in the Fig. 2.

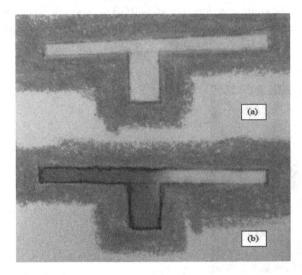

Fig. 2. (a) the red ink flowing only through channel and there is no leakage (b) introducing inks of two different colors does not cause any leakage. (Color figure online)

After fabrication of the channel two different solution were introduced in the inlets with the help of syringes and the whole mixing process was recorded though a camera. The video was then played using the developed application and the mixing efficiency was analyzed.

In this experiment a red and a blue ink solution has been used as reagents and it turns purple on mixing. Snapshots at different time frames have been captured and are shown. Figures 3, 4 and 5 show the mixing indexes at the outlet at 56 s, 72 s and 90 s which is 0.672, 0.847 and 0.917 respectively. It can be observed from these figures that as the time increases, the liquids get more time to interact in turn increasing the mixing index.

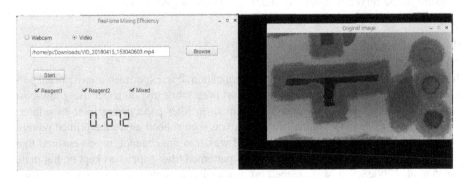

Fig. 3. Mixing index measured at 56 s using Mi-App (Color figure online)

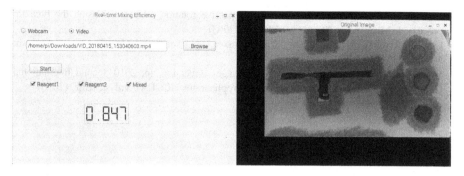

Fig. 4. Mixing index measured at 72 s using Mi-App (Color figure online)

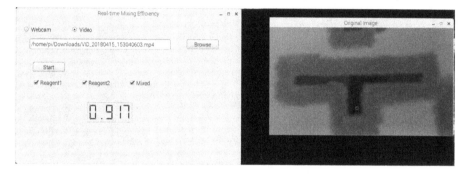

Fig. 5. Mixing index measured at 90 s using Mi-App (Color figure online)

5 Conclusion

Various experiments are successfully performed by using MI-app. The use of all open source libraries and IDE, camera and Raspberry Pi ensures that the device is reasonably priced. The application developed is user friendly and intuitive. This makes the device suitable for many researchers which are having limited resource. The application is still in development form and a lot of improvement is possible to enhance the microfluidic system efficacy.

References

1. Hashmi, A., Xu, J.: On the quantification of mixing in microfluidics. J. Lab. Autom. **19**(5), 488–491 (2014)
2. Lee, C.-Y., et al.: Microfluidic mixing: a review. Int. J. Mol. Sci. **12**(5), 3263–3287 (2011)
3. Nguyen, N.-T., Wu, Z.: Micromixersa review. J. Micromech. Microeng. **15**(2), R1 (2004)
4. Liu, R.H., et al.: Passive mixing in a three-dimensional serpentine microchannel. J. Microelectromech. Syst. **9**(2), 190–197 (2000)
5. Stroock, A.D., et al.: Chaotic mixer for microchannels. Science **295**(5555), 647–651 (2002)

6. Park, S.-J., et al.: Rapid three-dimensional passive rotation micromixer using the breakup process. J. Micromech. Microeng. **14**(1), 6 (2003)
7. Cha, J., et al.: A highly efficient 3D micromixer using soft PDMS bonding. J. Micromech. Microeng. **16**(9), 1778 (2006)
8. Saravanan, C.: Color image to grayscale image conversion. In: 2010 Second International Conference on Computer Engineering and Applications (ICCEA), vol. 2. IEEE (2010)

Novel RF MEMS Capacitive Switch for Lower Actuation Voltage

Sagar B. Dhule[✉] and Vasu Pulijala

Center for VLSI and Nanotechnology, Visvesvaraya National Institute of Technology, Nagpur 440010, India
sbdhule810@gmail.com, p.vasu@ece.vnit.ac.in

Abstract. In this work, we propose a novel RF MEMS Capacitive Switch for lower Actuation voltage. The comparative studies of MEMS Switches have been performed based on (a) geometrical changes in structure model shape (Clamped-Clamped beam, flexure support beam, meander beam, meander flexure beam) and (b) material used (Copper, Aluminium and Gold). A Novel structure is proposed by optimizing the air gap between the bridge and electrode, incorporating holes in cantilever structure and by changing length and width of anchor which also lead to better RF performance of Switch. The beams are designed based on the Coplanar Waveguide with RO4003-FR4 as the substrate. The values thus obtained for the novel switch design gives very less Actuation Voltage of 7.5 V, very less Insertion Loss i.e. -0.065 dB and Isolation as -46.8 dB over the range of 30 GHz–40 GHz. The static and dynamic analysis of these MEMS switches is done using COMSOL Multiphysics and the RF simulations using Ansoft HFSS electromagnetic simulator based on finite element method (FEM).

Keywords: MEMS capacitive shunt switch · RO4003-FR4 substrate · Actuation voltage · Insertion loss · Isolation

1 Introduction

Microelectromechanical Systems (MEMS) is the integration of mechanical elements, sensors, actuators, and electronics on silicon substrate through micro fabrication technology. Wherein Radio Frequency (RF) MEMS is the technology which is emerging over the years for its potential of implementing systems for the next generation of Communication Applications [1]. It has many advantages considering minimum power, good RF performance and its integration capability with low cost, smaller size and increase in functionality [2].

MEMS switch offers very less DC power consumption, low insertion loss, low intermodulation and relatively high isolation over the conventional solid state switches [3–5]. MEMS switches are classified as (*i*) Series Capacitive MEMS Switches and (*ii*) Shunt Capacitive MEMS Switches. The series switches are suitable over the low frequency ranges and hence shunt switches are preferred for

© Springer Nature Singapore Pte Ltd. 2019
S. Rajaram et al. (Eds.): VDAT 2018, CCIS 892, pp. 285–294, 2019.
https://doi.org/10.1007/978-981-13-5950-7_25

high frequency applications [6]. The physical connection of capacitive switches is either resistive (metal-metal contact) or capacitive (metal-insulator-metal contact). In resistive contact there is a chance of membrane getting short with the electrode which does not happen in the case of capacitive contact because of insulator layer in between the metal-metal contact. So for better isolation, capacitive connection is preferred over the resistive contact [1,7]. The electrostatic discharge, high switching time and low power handling are some of the limitations in the working of the switch [5].

Electrostatic force, thermally induced force and magnetic force are the actuation mechanisms employed for the switch. Electrostatic actuation is used because of the compatibility with other electrical devices and systems, low power consumption and low switching time. It is essential to lower the actuation voltage in order to use the switch in wireless communication [8]. The wire-bonding in the package leads to introduction of undesirable impedance mismatch in the RF device and the complete package which may cause signal losses. Thus to eliminate the losses and to ease the Fabrication of RF MEMS switches, Printed Circuit Boards are preferred over other substrates as both the RF devices can be directly fabricated over single PCB without any wire-bonding [2,9].

In this work a comparative study of different membrane structures (Fig. 1(a)–(c)) of electrostatically actuated shunt capacitive switches is done. Combining the advantages of the structures, a novel device structure as shown in Fig. 1(d) is designed which gives the optimized results of all the structures.

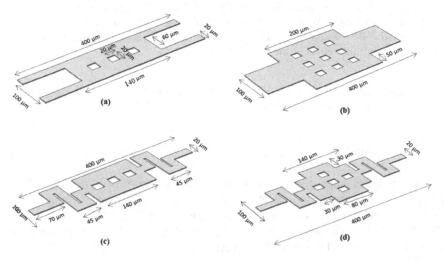

Fig. 1. Different bridge structure of membrane, (a) Design I, (b) Design II, (c) Design III, (d) Design IV.

1.1   Electrostatic and Electromechanical Modeling of Switches

The study of MEMS also constitutes the study of Electrostatics and Electrome-chanical physics of the MEMS devices. On the application of the voltage to the electrode, charges get accumulated across the membrane of the switch resulting in an electrostatic force acting on it which results in the actuation of the membrane. The switch remains in the ON condition until the electrostatic force is acting on it. When the voltage is OFF the membrane comes back to its original place within a specified time which is called the switching time. The Electrostatic Force acting on the membrane is given as [7,10]

$$F_e = \frac{\epsilon_0 A V^2}{2\,g_0{}^2} \tag{1}$$

The actuation voltage needed to deflect the membrane to overcome the airgap is derived from the electrostatic force as [7]

$$V_a = \sqrt{\frac{8\,k\,g_0^3}{27\epsilon_0 A}} \tag{2}$$

Where, k is the stiffness (spring) constant, A is the overlapping area of the membrane over the electrode, g_0 is the air gap between the electrode and membrane.

The displacement of the membrane on the application of the actuation voltage is given to be [7]

$$d = g_0 = \frac{F_e a^3 (3-a)}{6\quad E\quad I_z}) \tag{3}$$

Where, Iz is the Moment of Inertia and is given as [7]

$$I_z = (\frac{t^3 w}{12}) \tag{4}$$

Here, E is the Young's Modulus; d is the deflection of cantilever which is equivalent to the air gap between electrode and the membrane; l is the length of cantilever; a is the distance from anchor to middle of electrode; w and t is the width and thickness of cantilever.

1.2   Structural Design and Geometry

The working of MEMS switches basically depends on the geometry of the bridge structure. In this work four bridge structures with same length but different shapes are proposed. Meander shapes with few holes incorporated in it are employed so as to reduce the stiction, stiffness of beam and the switching time. The substrate used in the work is RO4003FR4 with thickness of 0.5 μm and the thickness of copper over it is 35 μm. The Coplanar Waveguide is the base for the bridge structure where the dimensions of the Ground line is 150 μm × 1000 μm and the dimensions of signal line is 120 μm × 1000 μm. Gap between the Ground to Signal plane & Signal to Ground plane is 90 μm. The thickness of the bridge is $2\,\mu m$. Also the membrane should be thick enough to create restoring force to regain its original position [4]. A thin layer of $0.2\,\mu m$ of Si_3N_4(used as the dielectric material) is deposited over the signal line. A capacitive path is formed using dielectric to avoid any short circuit of transmission line to ground [5]. The different bridge structures designed in this work are as given in Fig. 1. The Design IV as shown in Fig. 1(d) is the combination of Design II and Design III as shown in Fig. 1(b) and (c) respectively. The stiffness constant varies with the change in geometry of the Bridge structure is as follows from [3, 4, 7]:

For Design I:

$$k = 32Ew\left(\frac{t}{l}\right)^3 \tag{5}$$

For Design II:

$$k = 2Ew\left(\frac{t}{l}\right)^3 \tag{6}$$

For Design III & Design IV:

$$k = 4Ew\left(\frac{t}{nl}\right)^3 \tag{7}$$

Where, n is the meanders in the structure.

For RF MEMS switches there is always trade off in actuation voltage and the insertion loss. So the main focus of this paper is to minimize the actuation voltage without affecting insertion loss. This can be achieved by (a) minimizing the air gap between cantilever and signal line (b) increasing in the common area which is overlapping between the signal line and bridge structure (c) reducing the stiffness (spring constant) of the beam by varying the length, thickness of the beam and by using different shape bridge structures [6]. More actuation area leads to more upstate capacitance which further increases the insertion loss. So, relative variation is done to achieve both low actuation voltage and less insertion loss.

Holes are incorporated in the structure to make the mechanical movement smoother and to minimize the spring constant. With the increase in meanders, the stiffness constant can be decreased and thus less Pull in Voltage will be required for the cantilever structure to actuate to overcome the airgap. A novel design as shown in Fig. 1(d) is made out of combining two structures which gives improved results for all parameters.

1.3 Simulations and RF Analysis

The static analysis of the MEMS Switches are carried out on the COMSOL Multiphysics Version 5.3. The devices are simulated for the mentioned bridge structures shown in Fig. 1. The simulations are performed for the same membrane but with different materials like copper (Young's Modulus $= 130 \times 10^{9\prime}P_a'$), Aluminium (Young's Modulus $= 70 \times 10^{9\prime}P_a'$), Gold (Young's Modulus $= 78 \times 10^{9\prime}P_a'$) so as to compare the change in Actuation Voltage with change in membrane material. Young's Modulus is less for Aluminium thus gives lower actuation voltage when used as membrane material. Also with the increase in width of signal line, actuation voltage decreases as it is inversely proportional to overlapping area, but it also affect the RF parameters at the same time.

The displacement observed for the different structures shown in Fig. 1 i.e. for Design I, Design II, Design III, Design IV are shown in the Figs. 2, 3, 4, and 5 respectively. The displacement should be equal to the air gap between bridge and electrode and the obtained displacement for all the structures is $0.8\,\mu$m as the airgap is of $0.8\,\mu$m. After fabrication of devices, actuation voltage may increase due to: (i) Buckling of switch membrane because of internal stress, (ii) Variation in airgap due to buckling & (iii) Contamination of metal during the process (changes Young's Modulus) [9].

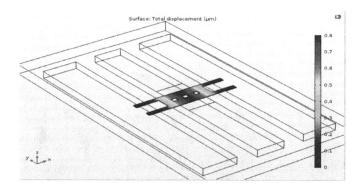

Fig. 2. Displacement of membrane for Design I.

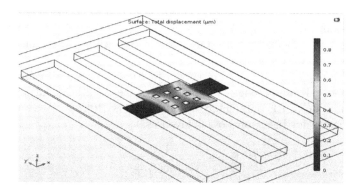

Fig. 3. Displacement of membrane for Design II.

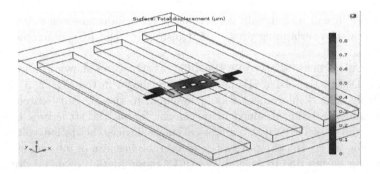

Fig. 4. Displacement of membrane for Design III.

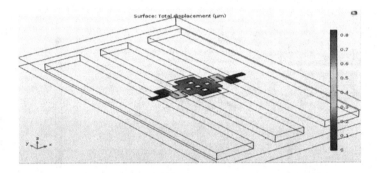

Fig. 5. Displacement of membrane for Design IV.

For the switch to work over RF & Microwave frequencies, it should have low Insertion Loss and high Isolation [5]. The RF analysis is done using Ansys HFSS. The simulations are carried out for the switches in both 'UP' state (OFF state of the switch) and 'DOWN' state (ON state of the switch) to get insertion loss and isolation results respectively.

The RF Simulations results are shown in Figs. 6, 7, 8 and 9 for Design I, Design II, Design III and Design IV respectively. The essential equations required for the calculation of RF parameters are given below [10]:

The Equation for Insertion Loss is given as,

$$S_{21} = \frac{1}{1 + jwC_d\frac{Z_0}{2}} \tag{8}$$

The UP_State & DOWN_State Capacitance is calculated as,

$$C_u = \frac{\epsilon_0\,A}{g_0 + \frac{t_d}{\epsilon_r}} \tag{9}$$

$$C_d = \frac{\epsilon_0\epsilon_r A}{t_d} \tag{10}$$

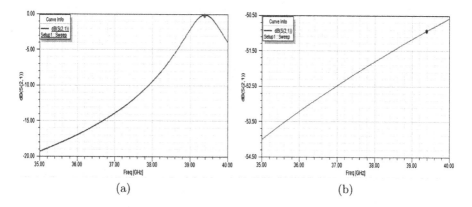

Fig. 6. (a) Insertion loss of Design I (b) Isolation of Design I

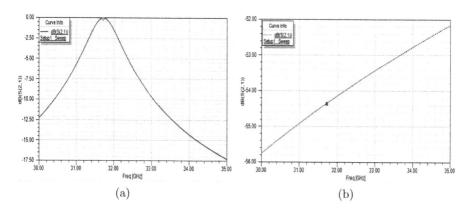

Fig. 7. (a) Insertion loss of Design II (b) Isolation of Design II

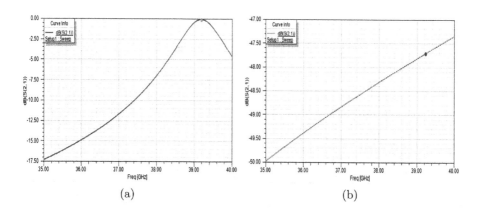

Fig. 8. (a) Insertion loss of Design III (b) Isolation of Design III

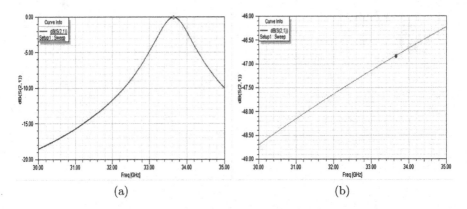

Fig. 9. (a) Insertion loss of Design IV (b) Isolation of Design IV

The Capacitance ratio should be high so as to get high isolation and can be measured as,

$$\frac{C_d}{C_u} = \frac{\frac{\epsilon_0 \epsilon_r A}{t_d}}{\frac{\epsilon_0}{g_0 + \frac{t_d}{\epsilon_r}} A} \qquad (11)$$

The structures are designed in HFSS 3D Design Model in HFSS. The frequency at which the switch is working can be changed by varying the signal width of the coplanar waveguide. The change in the membrane material doesn't affect the RF parameters significantly. For Aluminium material, the change in RF parameters for respective design structures is as given in Table 1.

Table 1. Comparison of RF parameters (30 GHz–40 GHz)

Structure	Insertion loss (dB)	Isolation (dB)
Design I	−0.09	−51
Design II	−0.06	−54.5
Design III	−0.075	−47.75
Design IV	−0.065	−46.8

The Insertion Loss and Isolation for all four designs are observed for frequencies in the range of 30 GHz–40 GHz. The UP state capacitance calculated is 129.41 fF and the DOWN state capacitance is 5.15 pF. The calculated Capacitance ratio is 39.80.

2   Results and Comparison

The actuation voltage (applied over the electrode for the simulated displacement), shown in Table 2, are compared for different membrane materials: Copper, Aluminium and Gold for all the designs.

Table 2. Comparison of actuation voltage variation

Material	Design 1	Design 2	Design 3	Design 4
Copper	27.35 V	26 V	15 V	10 V
Aluminium	16.5 V	16 V	9.5 V	7.5 V
Gold	21.5 V	20 V	11.5 V	8.5 V

As can be observed from Table 2, Aluminium gives better actuation voltages for all the designs. Hence, Aluminium is used as the membrane material for Design IV while comparing with other works as shown below in Table 3.

Table 3. Comparison of different capacitive RF shunt switches

References	[3]	[14]	[4]	[10]	This work
Substrate	Silicon	GaAs	Pyrex glass	PCB	RO4003-FR4(PCB)
Actuation voltage	18.3 V	25 V–40 V	4.8 V–6.3 V	15 (30) V	7.5 V
Capacitance ratio	16.5	-	-	-	39.80
Insertion loss (dB)	0.29	0.8	0.25–0.7	0.3	0.06–0.09
Isolation (dB)	20.5	20	30–40, 30	20	46–54
Frequency (GHz)	35	40	20–50	20	30–40

3 Conclusion

The main objective of this paper is to design a novel structure by comparing the various parameters of different MEMS Switches for Lower Actuation Voltage without affecting RF parameters like Insertion Loss and Isolation. Thus in the analysis of design of different structures and the material, a novel structure is designed and simulated. Lower Actuation Voltage and improved RF characteristics are achieved for Aluminium material over Copper and Gold. Thus the material used to build the membrane structure of the RF MEMS Switch is Aluminium. The Design IV as shown in Fig. 1(d) is the novel design giving lower Actuation Voltage i.e. 7.5 V, low Insertion Loss i.e. -0.065 dB and Higher Isolation i.e. -46.8 dB with Aluminium as the membrane material. The improved performance in this work could be attributed to the geometry, thickness, number of holes and its size in the membrane structure of the Switch.

References

1. Ananthasuresh, G.K.: Micro and Smart Systems. Wiley, Hoboken (2012)
2. Chang, H.P., Qian, J., Cetiner, B.A., De Flaviis, F., Bachman, M., Li, G.P.: RF MEMS switches fabricated on microwave-laminate printed circuit boards. IEEE Electron Device Lett. **24**(4), 227–9 (2003)

3. Jmai, B., Rajhi, A., Gharsallah, A.: Controllable bridge of the RF-MEMS: static analysis. In: 2017 International Conference on Green Energy Conversion Systems (GECS), 23 March 2017, pp. 1–4. IEEE (2017)
4. Shekhar, S., Vinoy, K.J., Ananthasuresh, G.K.: Surface-micromachined capacitive RF switches with low actuation voltage and steady contact. J. Microelectromech. Syst. 26(3), 643–52 (2017)
5. Molaei, S., Ganji, B.A.: Design and simulation of a novel RF MEMS shunt capacitive switch with low actuation voltage and high isolation. Microsyst. Technol. 23(6), 1907–1912 (2017)
6. Li, M., Zhao, J., You, Z., Zhao, G.: Design and fabrication of a low insertion loss capacitive RF MEMS switch with novel micro-structures for actuation. Solid-State Electron. 1(127), 32–37 (2017)
7. Rebeiz, G.: RF MEMS Theory, Design, and Technology. Wiley, New Jersey (2003)
8. Raman, R., Shanmuganantham, T.: Design and modeling of RF MEMS metal contact switch for wireless applications. In: 2016 International Conference on Control, Instrumentation, Communication and Computational Technologies (ICCICCT), 16 December 2016, pp. 268–271. IEEE (2016)
9. Chang, H.P., Qian, J., Cetiner, B.A., De Flaviis, F., Bachman, M., Li, G.P.: Design and process considerations for fabricating RF MEMS switches on printed circuit boards. J. Microelectromech. Syst. 14(6), 1311–1322 (2005)
10. Shah, D.R.: Study of RF-MEMS capacitive shunt switch for microwave backhaul applications. IOSR J. Electron. Commun. Eng. (IOSR-JECE) 12(1), 57–65 (2017). e-ISSN: 2278-2834, p-ISSN: 2278-8735. Ver.III
11. Persano, A., Cola, A., De Angelis, G., Taurino, A., Siciliano, P., Quaranta, F.: Capacitive RF MEMS switches with tantalum-based materials. J. Microelectromech. Syst. 20(2), 365–370 (2011)
12. Silva, M.W., Barbin, S.E., Kretly, L.C.: Fabrication and testing of RF-MEMS switches using PCB techniques. In: 2009 SBMO/IEEE MTT-S International Microwave and Optoelectronics Conference (IMOC), 3 November 2009, pp. 96–100. IEEE (2009)
13. Ketterl, T., Weller, T.: X-Band MEMS capacitive shunt switches with metal-insulator-metal contacts for improved isolation. In: 2006 IEEE Annual Wireless and Microwave Technology Conference. WAMICON 2006, 4 December 2006, pp. 1–5. IEEE (2006)
14. Shekhar, S., Vinoy, K.J., Ananthasuresh, G.K.: Design, fabrication and characterization of capacitive RF MEMS switches with low pull-in voltage. In: 2014 IEEE International Microwave and RF Conference (IMaRC), 15 December 2014, pp. 182–185. IEEE (2014)

VLSI Testing

A Novel Countermeasure Against Differential Scan Attack in AES Algorithm

Jayesh Popat$^{(\boxtimes)}$ and Usha Mehta

Institute of Technology, Nirma University, Ahmedabad, Gujrat, India
popat_jayesh@yahoo.co.in, usha.mehta@nirmauni.ac.in
http://www.nirmauni.ac.in

Abstract. The Design for Testability (specifically scan designs) is standard testing techniques for Digital cores for achieving high fault coverage and to provide better controllability and observability. However, such test architectures in the chip containing secret data mostly becomes the instrumental for secret information leakage. The attacker may use different implementation attacks to leak the secret data. In this paper, we first analyse the existing scan designs from security perspective. We demonstrated that how the secret key is retrieved by differential scan attack (DSA) in case of symmetric encryption standards (AES). Furthermore, it is also shown that AES along with time compactor also fails to provide sufficient security. We then propose novel prevention mechanism, Modular Exponentiation Secure Scheme (ME-SS), which clears the insecure states of all the existing techniques. Our experimental results show that the proposed countermeasures can effectively insulate all the information related to cipher key from DSA.

Keywords: DFT · AES · Differential Scan Attack (DSA) · MISR · Modular Exponentiation Secure Scheme · Cipher key

1 Introduction

In today's era, the advancement in fabrication technology along with huge design complexity make it feasible to produce small, high speed and in-expensive computing devices. In recent years, portable devices and smart cards come with in-built cryptographic hardware which is generally considered as highly complex computing device. These devices also hold the private confidential information. The ultimate motive of cryptography is to make the communication secure and hence the algorithm must be as mathematical complex as possible. The crypto-algorithm can be possible to implement in software as well as hardware. But, hardware implementation is fast and giving high throughput [1]. Since the hardware implementation holds the confidential information, the security of the crypt-chips becomes crucial. Therefore, the attacks carried out on such crypto-hardware were drawing attention in researcher community in past two decades. Several countermeasures against such attacks are also reported in publication.

There are basically two processes involved in any Cryptography algorithm. Encryption and Decryption. Encryption is the way toward encoding data with the goal that the unapproved people can't recognize the data. All the encryption algorithms

© Springer Nature Singapore Pte Ltd. 2019
S. Rajaram et al. (Eds.): VDAT 2018, CCIS 892, pp. 297–309, 2019.
https://doi.org/10.1007/978-981-13-5950-7_26

change input data, known as plain text, into jumbled format, known as cipher text. The approved individual has the capacity to translate the data back into original form utilizing decryption algorithms. Two kinds of cryptographic algorithms available for information security are asymmetric public key and symmetric secret key cryptography. In Asymmetric key cryptography algorithm, keys used for encrypting and decrypting messages are not the same, often called public key and private key. On the other hand, symmetric key cryptography algorithm uses the same key while performing encrypting and decrypting process, which is viable while taking care of a lot of information [2].

The crypto-hardware holds the sensitive confidential information. When attacked, the result will be personal information loss, compromised valid user access and financial theft. Once internal architecture along with hardware implementation details are examined and studied by the attacker, the attack can easily be performed without even decoding complex mathematics of algorithm. Although the private key isn't recovered by attacker in some cases, there are still chances of disturbing crypto-hardware functionality or denial of service attack which brings about failures in stable system. Several implementation attacks are reported in publications and analyzed in next section. The attacks on public key crypto-algorithms like RSA [3], stream cipher [4] and Elliptic Curve Cryptosystems (ECC) [5] as well as private key crypto-algorithms like Data Encryption Standard (DES) [6] and Advanced Encryption Standard [7] are reported in literature.

The paper discusses about the crypto-algorithm (particular AES) hardware implementation and mainly focuses on the test-infrastructure (especially scanchain) based attack. Also, existing countermeasures against scan attacks are reviewed and a novel countermeasure to make the AES full secure is presented in detail. This paper is organized in following sections. Different implementation attacks on crypto hardware and existing countermeasures are described in Sect. 2. Section 3 describes fundamental highlights of AES algorithm and Sect. 4 shows the basic differential scan-based attack for AES and AES with time compactor. The proposed countermeasure based on Modular Exponentiation scheme to avoid attacks is proposed in Sect. 5. Section 6 includes the result analysis in terms of performance. At last, conclusion and future work are presented in Sect. 7.

2 Implementation Attacks and Countermeasures

Several attacks on crypto-hardware are reported in [8–19]. According to implementation technique, the hardware attacks on crypto-hardware system are classified in the three basic categories: 1. Side-channel Attack 2. Fault injection attack 3. Test-infrastructure attack. The main goal of the attacker is to retrieve confidential data stored in crypto-hardware although having many goals in mind. All of these attacks are practically implementable and hence called Implementation attacks.

2.1 Side Channel Attacks

Side channel attacks are generally carried out on the non-primary interface of the crypto systems like timing [8], power [9] and EM analysis [10] to retrieve confidential data.

2.2 Fault Attacks

The faults are injected in the crypto-chips and then manifestation of fault is captured and can be exploited for the benefit of attacker. Under-powering and power spikes [11, 12], clock glitches [13], Temperature attacks [14], optical attacks [15], EM fault injection [16] are reported fault injection methods. All fault injection techniques work on same principle: by changing physical property of chip, they make transistor to switch improperly. But, these methods differ in fault injecting property.

2.3 Test-Infrastructure Attack

Test infrastructure (Design for Testability-DfT) now-a-days are introduced in the chip early during the IC design cycle to easily detect manufacturing defect. However, the attacker takes advantage of such existing test infrastructure to reveal secret data from crypto-chips. Most widely used test infrastructure nowadays are Scan-chins, the attacker exploits the same to retrieving the confidential data stored on the chip. The detailed explanation about AES and scan attack on AES hardware implementation are presented in Sects. 3 and 4. The attack is also applicable on other symmetric ciphers like RSA, DES, and ECC. It can simply be applied using 1-bit different plaintext without knowledge of physical implementation of algorithm. Thus, it is also called differential attack [17–19].

The side-channel attacks require costly source and measuring equipment to leak secret from crypto-hardware. Furthermore, the fault injection may need expensive setup to execute fault injection. But, the fault injection methods mainly focus on tamper data stored in memory, make semiconductor device to conduct incorrectly and malfunctioning of the device. On the other hand, the test-infrastructure based attacks don't require costly instruments and aiming only to retrieve confidential data from crypto-hardware rather to focus on malfunctioning it. In this paper, we mainly focus on the test-infrastructure based attack and countermeasures against it. The next sub-section deals with countermeasures against this attack in detail.

2.4 Countermeasures Against Scan-Based Attack on Crypto-Hardware

As the key contribution in this paper is to analyze test-infrastructure(scan) based attack and propose novel countermeasure against such attacks, the state-of-art countermeasures against scan-based attack on crypto-hardware are Built-in self-test, on-chip test comparison, inserting inverters in scan-path, masking (round register or compactor output), Noise Injection in Scan Output, Secure Test Access Mechanism.

Built-in Self-test. The iteration of encryption process is used to implement self-test procedure [20]. For instance, the output is fed back to encryption chip input for certain round and then final signature is generated. This signature is then compared with golden signature stored on-chip. BIST works as a natural countermeasure against scan-based attack at the cost of extra hardware.

On-Chip Test Comparison. The expected response which generally stored on external tester to compare against the actual captured response for individual test pattern. This method instead is used to transfer the same expected response on-chip using scan-out pin. The extra hardware required on-chip for the comparison of actual and expected responses. Only one-bit pass/fail per pattern is coming out and hence scan-based attack is not feasible in this case [21].

Inserting Inverters in Scan-path. The crypto-chip full scan architecture is divided into arbitrary number of sub-chains and also inverters are place in random order at the output of certain scan-cells. The inverter placement and number of scan-chain is only known to test engineer and designer. Due to this, the attacker can get flipped intermediate state of cipher and hence it is hard for him/her to process further and leak the secret data. However, the differential attack is still possible as the inversion effect is cancelled out when taking output differences [22].

Masking Round Register or Compactor Output. The author describes two different masking methods. In first method, it is suggested to mask the round register output of AES and then unmask it for subsequent operation. Due to this method, the scanned-out data which represent the intermediate state of the cipher, is always masked during test-mode. To unmask the intermediate state, an extra EX-OR operation is performed after round register. In second method, the compacted response of the cipher is getting EX-ORed with 128-bit pseudo random bits. This is called Extended LFSR(eLFSR). The seed value of LFSR can never be retrieved. In both cases, the attacker cannot observe the actual intermediate state of cipher and hence the scan-based attack is not possible. Crypto-chip performance may be compromised due to area overhead and longer critical path [17].

Noise Injection in Scan Output. In this method, the author suggested to use LFSR along with TRNG (True Random Number Generator). TRNG hides actual value of some of the LFSR output bits and hence 50% scan cell output bit becoming noisy while other 50% remains unchanged. This kind of masking has to be applied at every clock cycle to make scan-based attack unsuccessful. Similar to previous attack, crypto-chips may suffer in performance due to area overhead during testing [23].

Secure Test Access Mechanism. This technique is also known as secure-scan DFT technique [7]. The crypto-chip is allowed to work in two different modes in this method: Secure mode and Insecure mode. In the insecure mode, the chip can make transition from test mode to normal mode same as traditional DFT. But in secure mode, the chip is only allowed to function in normal mode. Any transition from secure mode to insecure mode is only possible through power-off reset. This will erase all intermediate information of cipher stored in round register. Hence, the differential attack is not possible. Nevertheless, the technique requires extra set of register to hold secret key related information and also modification in test controller is also required to alter the initialization of test session.

3   Advanced Encryption Standard (AES)

In this section, we examined symmetric key AES cipher and its implementation detail. The study mainly focuses on this algorithm because it is developed most recently and provides high security. Recent cryptographic application specific integrated circuits (ASICs) and coprocessors are created using AES algorithm [24] known as Rijndael cipher, can be implemented efficiently in both hardware and programming [25]. Advanced Encryption Standard is symmetric key block cipher. This implies that the key used for encrypting the message will be same during decryption as well. The block size in AES is 128-bit, which means plaint text and cipher text are of 128-bit. However, secret key bits may vary from 128 to 192 to 256 bits with respect to 10, 12 or 14 rounds of cipher. AES implementation requires the basic four steps to be performed. (1.) Add Round Key, (2.) Substitution Bytes (S-BOX), (3.) Shift Rows (4.) Mix Columns Operation. Key generation unit, is utilized for producing ten distinct keys for ten different rounds of operation. Input to each round will be in the form of state matrix. In the paper, we only consider 10 rounds of operation with 128-bit of key size [26]. The basic architecture of AES is illustrated below in Fig. 1.

4 Differential Scan Attack (DSA)

The attack known as Differential Scan Attack (DSA) based on observing scanchain states is described in the state-of-art research. The following sections give details of the DSA on simple as well as time-based response compactor (MISR) based AES.

4.1 Application of DSA on AES

The differential attack is usually conducted on the fact that particular plain text input pair is capable of producing output pairs having unique hamming distance after first round of ciphering. For example, the plain text with one-bit difference (p2 = p1 ⊕ 1) in 0th bit of a byte, are encrypted using first round of AES, the hamming distance between two outputs (o1, o2) corresponding to (p1, p2) can have 4 unique S-Box input values as shown in Table 1 [7, 17]. The procedure of scan-based attack on round register of AES cipher has following two steps.

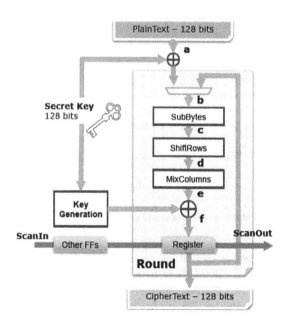

Fig. 1. AES structure [18].

Algorithm 1 . Determining Round Register Flops

1: Apply plaintext from primary input in Functional mode.

2: Run the AES cipher for only one round.

3: Switch to test mode.

4: Shift out the content of scan chain. This is output response f_1.

5: Repeat the above steps for another plaintext with one-bit difference.

6: Scan-out the output response f_2. .

7: Compute output difference of previous two plaintexts ($f_1 \oplus f_2$).

8: Flip-flops with a value of one correspond to the flops in the round register.

9: Repeat all above steps until all the flip flops of round register are identified.

(1.) Determining exact position of round register flip-flops in entire scan-chain of chip. This procedure is summarized in Algorithm 1 [7].

(2.) Retrieve specific key byte corresponding to onebit different plain text input byte. This procedure is summarized in Algorithm 2 [7].

It should be noted that a single bit change in a particular byte of plain text will cause the four-byte change in first round output due to Mix-Column operation. As it can be seen from Algorithm 2 that two different key bytes (k1 & k2), corresponding to two values of S-Box input for a single unique hamming distance, are retrieved when each individual plain text input pair is processed using the Algorithm 2.

Algorithm 2 . Secret key recovery using Differential Scan Attack

1: Apply plaintext input to cipher in functional mode.

2: Run the AES cipher for only one round.

3: Switch to test mode.

4: Shift out the round register data. This is output response f_1.

5: Repeat the above steps for another plaintext input with one-bit difference in a byte, keeping remaining bytes unchanged.

6: Shift out the output response f_2. .

7: Compute hamming distance of previous two output response ($f_1 \oplus f_2$).

8: If hamming distance is 9, 12, 23 or 24 then determine corresponding unique S-Box input pair (b_1, b_2)

9: Compute key byte by EX-Oring corresponding S-Box input pair with plain text ($k_1 = a \oplus b_1$) and ($k_2 = a \oplus b_2$)

10: Repeat the previous steps for each pair of plaintext that differ in the least significant bit of a byte ($a_1 = a_2 \oplus 1$).

11: Repeat all previous steps for all bytes of plaintext to retrieve all remaining key bytes.

The similar procedure is carried out on remaining 15 bytes of plain text and for every plain text byte two different key bytes (k1 & k2) are retrieved. To determine correct key byte out of two, the procedure of checking correct encryption output after first round from 216 possibilities. So, the key byte search complexity comes down from 2^{128} to 2^{16}.

Table 1. Hamming distances with unique S-BOX input corresponding to input bit-difference positions [7, 17]

Bit position	Hamming distance	S-BOX unique inputs
0th bit	9	(226,227)
	12	(242,243)
	23	(122,123)
	24	(130,131)
1st bit	12	(72,74)
	23	(152,154)
	24	(17,19)

4.2   Application of DSA on AES with Time Compactor (MISR)

The standard structure of Scan chain based Multiple Input Signature Register is shown in Fig. 2. It contains flip-flops and EX-OR gates to produce compacted test response, generally referred as Signature [18]. We have considered 16- chains (M0 to M15) with 16-bit MISR along with the seed value 0000H. Each chain is 8-bit long (totally 16 * 8 = 128 bits). Although entire round register content is not observable directly by attacker in case of response compactor, the attack is still possible to retrieve confidential information of AES cipher by observing the signature register. The basic steps of DSA mentioned in previous section are also performed. In addition, the extra effort to recover the exact key bytes in the presence of response compactor (MISR) are described below in Algorithm 3 [17, 19].

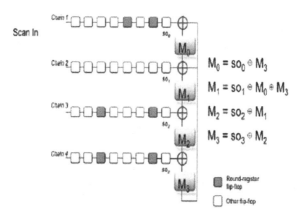

Fig. 2. MISR scheme [18]

Algorithm 3. Secret key recovery in the presence of MISR compactor

---

1: Compute the output difference of the compacted responses (R_1 and R_2) of the two plaintexts a_1 and a_2 that differ in the least significant bit ($a_1 = a_2 \oplus 1$)

2: If $R_1 \oplus R_2 = 1$ (odd), consider the hamming distance 9 and 23, Otherwise, consider the hamming distance 12 and 24.

3: Switch to test mode.

4: Compute the possible key byte with the help of S-Box inputs and the plaintexts. (same as existing attack).

5: Discard all the keys except the ones with maximum occurrence K_1 (11 keys).

6: Repeat the previous steps for each pair of plaintext that differ in the second least significant bit ($a_1 = a_2 \oplus 2$) and compute K_2 (13 keys).

7: Take the intersection of two key sets to retrieve the correct key ($K_1 \cap K_2$).

---

5 Proposed Modular Exponentiation Security Scheme for Countermeasure Against DSA

In the proposed work, a novel countermeasure is developed to secure the key from the attacker and is shown the Fig. 3. A novel Modular Exponentiation security scheme (ME-SS) is applied as a countermeasure to prevent attacker from retrieving the key using one-way function. The below sub-section describes the ME-SS in detail.

5.1 Modular Exponentiation Security Scheme (ME-SS)

This scheme is basically implemented using HDL by performing below mentioned three steps. (1.) Pre-calculation Module (2.) Modulo exponentiation (3.) Control Module.

Pre-calculation Module. This module is used to pre-calculate the 128-bit secret key value and 16-bit prime modulus value and store them in memory. These values are going to be utilized by subsequent steps. In crypto-hardware implementation, it is suggested that these values are kept as secret as AES encryption round key.

Modulo Exponentiation. The modular exponentiation is calculated using Square & Multiply operation. It will make the algorithm calculation speedy and hence cycles required will be less. The multiplication is carried out if the key bit is equal to 1, else square operation is executed. This is the most important step of this scheme.

Control Module. This module connects different modules with each other and hence data flow is stream lined. To achieve expected outcome, top module implements a hardware which regulates flow with several conditions.

The main goal of this strategy is to prevent key bytes from being retrieved by attacker using DSA at the same time test quality for normal operations should not be compromised. It is noted that by using this method the MISR output is one more time encrypted by Modular Exponentiation scheme and signature bits are randomized. Initially, plaintext is encrypted using AES cipher after first round operation. The cipher text present in the round register is compacted using time compactor scheme i.e. MISR. In the proposed work, the modular exponentiation (X^Y mod N) based security scheme is applied after the time compactor. The X is message to be encrypted (MISR output in our case), Y is exponent or secret key, and N is the prime modulus is the prime number of 16-bit. The modular exponentiation scheme should not be considered as RSA public key algorithm due to the following differences.

- Unlike RSA, where public components (Y and N) to be known to everyone. We propose to keep Y and N as secret as the AES key. So, the secret key Y and prime modulus N have to be kept as conceal as private key of AES.

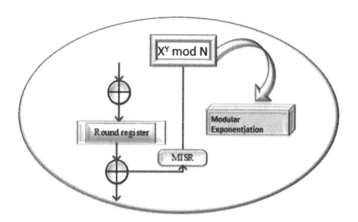

Fig. 3. Modular Exponentiation Secure Scheme

- The RSA required procedure initially to generate public key component public key, prime modulus and private key component private key, prime modulus using two prime numbers. We have not considered the same as the proposed procedure involved only encrypting the MISR output in every case with private key only. As shown in Fig. 4, the MISR output signature is compared against ATE golden signature traditionally. Furthermore, the proposed scheme is shown in Fig. 5. The MISR output is encrypted using ME-SS scheme and compared with encrypted golden signature on ATE without extra hardware overhead. The ATE/tester must be loaded with encrypted test patterns response so that this procedure will not disturb the basic ATE testing operation.

– Differential attack on RSA [3] will not be applicable here as those are applied during decryption of the cipher data using private key component. In our case, we don't propose any decryption of output message after any round of AES cipher. At the same time, decryption process of modular exponentiation will not be same as traditional RSA deciphering.

Subsequently, the overall attack procedures are carried out as discussed in Sub-sect. 4.2. But, there is no maximum repeating key bytes are found and thus no secret key bytes are retrieved using the same procedure.

6 Results and Discussion

The proposed design of AES with Security Scheme is described in Verilog HDL, simulated in Xilinx version 14.5, Family: Virtex4, Device: xc4vlx200, Speed: −11, Package: ff1513. The results were analysed in Xilinx for 128-bit plain text and 128-bit secret key in AES algorithm. Further, DSA is employed to retrieve the key.

Table 2 presents the experimental results of Differential Scan Attack on basic AES, AES along with MISR time compactor and AES with Modular Exponentiation scheme. It contains the number of bits produced after one round of ciphering process with number of scan-chains and scan slices used in all three architectures. The performance analysis is carried out for all three schemes. It can be seen that all 16-key bytes and 9 key bytes are retrieved in case of AES and AES with MISR scheme respectively. Also, it is clearly indicated that ME-SS based secure scheme provides more security than the existing approaches at the cost of area and power overhead.

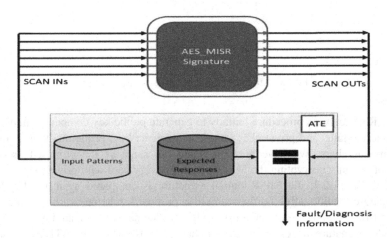

Fig. 4. Comparison of MISR signature against ATE golden signature

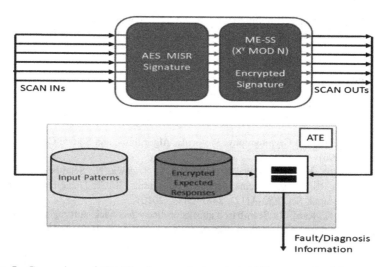

Fig. 5. Comparison of ME-SS scheme output against ATE encrypted golden response

Table 2. Performance analysis

Technique (Differential Scan Attack-DSA)	Number of output bits after first round	Number of scan chains	Number of scan slices	Number of key-bytes retrieved	Remaining key bytes to be retrieved by brute force attack	Security (%)	Threat (%)
AES	128-bits	1	128	16	0	0	100
AES MISR	16-bits	16	8	9	7	43.75	56.25
AES MISR ME-SS	16-bits	16	8	0	16	100	0

7   Conclusion and Future Work

This paper presents a study that explore three different implementation techniques security analysis. In these techniques, we have proposed one prevention mechanism namely, Modular Exponentiation based security scheme (ME-SS) that prevent the attacker to retrieve secret key. Further, the simulation of DSA in AES, AES with Time compactor (MISR) and the AES with the proposed countermeasures have led to different results. Based on experimentation, it is seen that the existing techniques provides poor performance results. Also, it was observed that the proposed mechanism, ME-SS provides more security compared to existing approaches. Security of crypto-hardware comes at the cost of area and power overhead. The future work deals with hardware implementation of the proposed scheme and comparing area & power overhead of the same with existing approaches.

Acknowledgment. We are thankful to Research Progress Committee members Dr. K.S. Dasgupta and Dr. Virendra Singh for their review, insightful comments and constructive suggestions.

References

1. Hurst, S.L.: VLSI Testing: Digital and Mixed Analogue/Digital Techniques. IEE, London (1998)
2. Schneier, B.: Applied Cryptography: Protocols, Algorithms, and Source Code in C. Wiley, Hoboken (1996)
3. Nara, R., Satoh, K., Yanagisawa, M., Ohtsuki, T., Togawa, N.: Scan-based side-channel attack against RSA cryptosystems using scan signatures. IEICE Trans. Fundam. Electron. Commun. Comput. Sci. **E93-A**(12), 2481–2489 (2010)
4. Liu, Y., Wu, K., Karri, R.: Scan-based attacks on linear feedback shift register based stream ciphers. ACM Trans. Des. Autom. Electron. Syst. (TODAES) **16**(2), 1–15 (2011)
5. Nara, R., Togawa, N., Yanagisawa, M., Ohtsuki, T.: Scan-based attack against ellipticcurve cryptosystems. In: 15th IEEE Asia and South Pacific Design Automation Conference (ASP-DAC10), pp. 407–412 (2010)
6. Yang, B., Wu, K., Karri, R.: Scan based side channel attack on dedicated hardware implementations of data encryption standard. In: Proceedings of IEEE International Test Conference, pp. 339–344 (2004)
7. Yang, B., Wu, K., Karri, R.: Secure scan: a design-for-test architecture for cryptochips. IEEE Trans. Comput. Aided Des. Integr. Circu. Syst. **25**(10), 2287–2293 (2006)
8. Kocher, P.C.: Timing attacks on implementations of diffie-hellman, RSA, DSS, and other systems. In: Koblitz, N. (ed.) CRYPTO 1996. LNCS, vol. 1109, pp. 104–113. Springer, Heidelberg (1996). https://doi.org/10.1007/3-540-68697-5_9
9. Kocher, P., Jaffe, J., Jun, B.: Differential power analysis. In: Wiener, M. (ed.) CRYPTO 1999. LNCS, vol. 1666, pp. 388–397. Springer, Heidelberg (1999). https://doi.org/10.1007/3-540-48405-1_25
10. Quisquater, J.-J., Samyde, D.: ElectroMagnetic analysis (EMA): measures and counter-measures for smart cards. In: Attali, I., Jensen, T.P. (eds.) E-smart 2001. LNCS, vol. 2140, pp. 200–210. Springer, Heidelberg (2001). https://doi.org/10.1007/3-540-45418-7_17
11. Kommerling, O., Kuhn, M.G.: Design principles for tamper-resistant smartcardprocessors. In: Proceedings of the USENIX Workshop on Smartcard Technology, p. 22. USENIX Association, Berkeley (1999)
12. Aumüller, C., Bier, P., Fischer, W., Hofreiter, P., Seifert, J.-P.: Fault attacks on RSA with CRT: concrete results and practical countermeasures. In: Kaliski, B.S., Koç, Ç.K., Paar, C. (eds.) CHES 2002. LNCS, vol. 2523, pp. 260–275. Springer, Heidelberg (2003). https://doi.org/10.1007/3-540-36400-5_20
13. Endo, S., Sugawara, T., Homma, N., Aoki, T., Satoh, A.: An on-chip glitchy clock generator for testing fault injection attacks. J. Cryptogr. Eng. **1**, 265–270 (2011)
14. Skorobogatov, S.: Low temperature data remanence in static RAM. University of Cambridge, Computer Laboratory, Technical Report UCAM-CL-TR-536, June 2002. http://www.cl.cam.ac.uk/techreports/UCAM-CL-TR-536.pdf
15. Skorobogatov, S.P., Anderson, R.J.: Optical fault induction attacks. In: Kaliski, B.S., Koç, Ç.K., Paar, C. (eds.) CHES 2002. LNCS, vol. 2523, pp. 2–12. Springer, Heidelberg (2003). https://doi.org/10.1007/3-540-36400-5_2

16. Schmidt, J.-M., Hutter, M.: Optical and EM fault-attacks on CRT-based RSA: concrete results. In: Karl, J.W., Posch, C. (eds.) Austrochip 2007, 15th Austrian Workhop on Microelectronics, 11 October 2007, Graz, Austria, Proceedings, pp. 61–67. Verlag der Technischen Universität Graz, Graz (2007)
17. DaRolt, J., Di Natale, G., Flottes, M.L., Rouzeyre, B.: Scan attacks and countermeasures in presence of scan response compactors. In: Sixteenth IEEE European Test Symposium, Trondheim, pp. 19–24 (2011)
18. Da Rolt, J., Di Natale, G., Flottes, M.L., Rouzeyre, B.: Are advanced DfT structures sufficient for preventing scan-attacks? In: IEEE 30th VLSI Test Symposium (VTS), Hyatt Maui, HI, pp. 246–251 (2012)
19. Ege, B., Das, A., Gosh, S., Verbauwhede, I.: Differential scan attack on AESwith X-tolerant and X-masked test response compactor. In: 2012 15th Euromicro Conference on Digital System Design (DSD), pp. 545–552. IEEE (2012)
20. Natale, G.D., Doulcier, M., Flottes, M.L., Rouzeyre, B.: Self-test techniques for crypto-devices. IEEE Trans. Very Large Scale Integr. (VLSI) Syst. **18**(2), 329–333 (2010)
21. Da Rolt, J., Di Natale, G., Flottes, M.L., Rouzeyre, B.: On-chip test comparison for protecting confidential data in secure ICS. In: 2012 17th IEEE European Test Symposium (ETS), p. 1, May 2012
22. Sengar, G., Mukhopadhayay, D., Roy Chowdhury, D.: An efficient approach to develop secure scan tree for crypto-hardware. In: International Conference on Advanced Computing and Communications, ADCOM 2007, pp. 21–26, December 2007
23. Das, A., Ege, B., Ghosh, S., Batina, L., Verbauwhede, I.: Security analysis of industrial test compression schemes. IEEE Trans. Comput. Aided Des. Integr. Circuits Syst. **32**(12), 1966–1977 (2013)
24. Kalaiselvi, K., Mangalam, H.: Power efficient and high-performance VLSI architecture for AES algorithm. J. Electr. Syst. Inf. Technol. **2**(2), 178–183 (2015)
25. Ahlawat, S., Vaghani, D., Tudu, J., Singh, V.: On securing scan design from scan-based side-channel attacks. In: 2017 IEEE 26th Asian Test Symposium (ATS), pp. 58–63. IEEE (2017)
26. http://csrc.nist.gov/publications/PubsFIPS.html

Optimization of Test Wrapper Length for TSV Based 3D SOCs Using a Heuristic Approach

Tanusree Kaibartta[1]([⊠]) and Debesh Kumar Das[2]

[1] Department of Computer Science and Engineering,
IIT (ISM) Dhanbad, Jharkhand, India
kaibartta.tanusree@gmail.com
[2] Department of Computer Science and Engineering,
Jadavpur University, Kolkata, India

Abstract. Core of an integrated circuit is supplied test stimulus generated by an external test source and then responses of the core are compared with expected responses. Test access mechanism (TAM) is a mechanism responsible for transporting test data to the cores. Core of a three-dimensional System on Chip (SOC) has various elements related to testing of the core, known as wrapper input cells, wrapper output cells and set of scan chains. These elements are to be interconnected to form wrapper chains. To perform this, the elements are connected in an order such that the wrapper chain begins with the wrapper input cells and then internal scan chains followed by the wrapper output cells. This paper aims to determine the placement of core elements in several layers of 3D SOC for a number of wrapper chains and interconnect the core elements using available number of TSV such that the length of the longest wrapper chain is minimized.

Keywords: Wrapper · TSV · TAM

1 Introduction

Generation to generation, there are high demands for electronic products to provide more functionalities and higher performance with less power consumption. SOC design consisting of a number of embedded cores is the solution to satisfy this market demand. Since embedded cores in a core-based SOC are not easily accessible via chip input and output pins, a special test infrastructure must be included in the chip to test them. According to IEEE 1500 in [1], the basic SOC test infrastructure of an embedded core is composed of - (1) test access mechanism (TAM) and (2) wrapper. Testing of a core can be described as follows-first, the test stimuli are sent to the particular core, and the test response is sent out. Then the test response is compared with the predefined correct response. Hence, TAM provides the way to transport test stimuli from the test pattern source to the core and core to the test response sink. Wrappers are also important components of the test access infrastructure in a core-based SOC. Detail of the wrapper design is discussed in Sect. 2.

S. Rajaram et al. (Eds.): VDAT 2018, CCIS 892, pp. 310–321, 2019.
https://doi.org/10.1007/978-981-13-5950-7_27

SOC design consisting of a number of embedded cores has become increasingly complex and interconnects has become the performance and power limiter for integrated circuits (ICs). Due to this, electronic system design technology has shifted from two dimensional integrated circuit (2D IC) to three dimensional integrated circuit (3D IC). Technological shift from 2D IC to 3D IC helps to resolve the interconnect related problem. Among various 3D integration technologies such as wire bonded, microbump based, contactless and through-silicon-via (TSV) interconnects, TSV based 3D integration method has the capability to provide the shorter interconnect length compared to 2D IC. Reduction in interconnect length reduces the interconnect energy and latency and thus increases the performance. According to report in [2], design transition of 2D to 3D architecture of arithmetic logic of barrel shifter helps to achieve 9% reduction in latency and 8% reduction in energy consumption. In spite of the above benefits, 3D SOC provides additional challenges on how to distribute the wrapper elements of a core in multi-layers such that wrapper length can be reduced. Number of works in wrapper optimization and test infrastructure design of 2D IC have been proposed in literatures [3–5]. Limited works exists in the domain of 3D SOC. Optimization of test infrastructure design under given number of TSV of 3D SOC has been proposed in [6, 7]. ILP and Genetic algorithm based approaches are used in [6] and [7] respectively.

Wrapper optimization of 3D SOC is presented in [8] and [9]. In [8], a heuristic method is used to reduce the wrapper chain length under the constrain of TSV. Same problem is resolved using genetic algorithm based approach in [9]. In this research work, we are dealing with 3D SOC, so wrapper elements i.e. input, output and scan chains has to be distributed in several layers. Main focus of our work is to create balanced wrapper chain to minimize the scan test time by distributing wrapper elements i.e. input, output and scan chains of the cores in different layers of 3D SOC under the constraint of given number of TSVs. The paper is organized as follows. Section 2 gives insight into wrapper architecture. Motivational example is discussed in Sect. 3. The wrapper optimization problem is formulated in Sect. 4. Proposed algorithm is discussed in Sect. 5. Experimental results on different benchmark SOC is discussed in Sect. 6. Finally, the paper concludes with observations in Sect. 7.

2 Wrapper Architecture

The striking feature of the 1500 standard is the provision of a wrapper on each core. A test wrapper is basically a layer of design-for-test (DFT) logic that connects a TAM to a core for the purpose of testing. According IEEE 1500 standard each wrapper consists of input, output and scan chain. Further, scan chain itself is the combination of scan-in and scan-out. In a wrapper chain at first, all the inputs are present either in one layer or in multiple layers. After input, scan-out follows scan-in. Scan chain is also distributed either in one layer or multiple layers depending upon the architecture. Same arrangement is followed in case of output. The element wise processing sequence of wrapper chain is first inputs then scan-in, which is followed by scan-out and finally output is achieved. The number of clock cycles depends on the length of the wrapper chain. Therefore to minimize the time, we must optimize the length of the longest wrapper chain.

The number of wrapper chain depends on the TAM width. The values of each cell indicate the layer number.

Table 1. Initial stage of wrapper design of the given example as mentioned in [9]

W_1			W_2			W_3			W_4		
I	Sc	O	I	Sc	O	I	Sc	O	I	Sc	O
	2			2				3		2	

Table 2. Final wrapper design of the given example as mentioned in [9]

W_1			W_2			W_3			W_4		
I	Sc	O	I	Sc	O	I	Sc	O	I	Sc	O
1	2	3	2	3	2	2	3	2	2	2	1
3	3	1		3	3		1	3			2
		1			3	1		1			1

3 Motivational Example

Consider, a core with 10 functional inputs, 10 functional outputs and 5 internal scan chains each of length 8, number of maximum available TSV_{max} 14, TAM width 4 and total number of layers 3. Objective is to distribute the wrapper elements over three layers of 3D SOC for a number of wrapper chains and interconnect the core elements using TSV_{max} such that the length of the longest wrapper chain is minimized. As the number of wrapper chains is equal to TAM width, 25 wrapper elements (i.e. 10 + 10 + 5) are to be distributed among 4 wrapper chains. A motivational example depicting solution for wrapper optimization problem is presented in Table 1 which is taken from [9]. W_1, W_2, W_3 and W_4 indicate four wrapper chains. For each wrapper chain I, SC and O indicate input, output and scan chain respectively. The value of each cell in Table 1 indicates the layer number.

According to [9], initially the wrapper elements are chosen randomly. That means chosen element can be of any type i.e. input, output or scan type. If the element type is scan type, no requirement check is needed and it can be placed at any wrapper, otherwise requirement check has to be performed because input and output affects the number of TSVs. According to [9], the input and output requirement over 4 wrapper chains W_1, W_2, W_3 and W_4 for the given problem is 3, 3, 2 and 2 and 2, 2, 3 and 3 respectively.

Based on this approach, suppose an element chosen randomly is of scan chain type and is placed randomly at layer 2 of wrapper chain W_1 as shown in Table 1. TSV requirement in this case is 2. Suppose, the next element is of input type, so it will be placed in the next wrapper i.e. W_2 and in the same way, the wrapper elements are assigned to the other two wrapper chains W_3 and W_4. At this point, each wrapper chain contains exactly one wrapper element as shown in Table 1, and the total number of

TSVs required up to this stage is 10 (i.e. 2 + 2 + 4 + 2). This is the completion of first cycle of assigning wrapper elements to every wrapper chains and in the next clock cycle, the next element will be assigned to the wrapper chain W_1. In this way, we obtain the final stage as shown in Table 2 in [9].

4 Problem to be Solved

Wrapper length optimization problem for TSV based 3D SOC core can be stated as follows - Given a 3D SOC core consisting of varying functional parameters such as number of functional inputs, number of functional outputs, set of scan chains, the length of each scan chains, TAM width and maximum number of available TSVs (TSV_{max}), we have to distribute the core elements over several layers of 3D SOC and interconnect the core elements using TSV_{max} such that length of the longest wrapper chain is minimized. This approach can be termed as wrapper design with available number of TSVs.

From the above discussion, it is clear that for a given TSVs (i.e. TSV_{max}) and given TAM width T, the goal of the proposed heuristic algorithm is to create some balanced wrapper chains whose maximum length is minimum. As the chip pins are at the lowest layer, so we assume the wrapper chain begins and ends at lowest layer and layer number starts from bottom to top and top to bottom (i.e. bottom layer number is 1, next layer number is 2 and so on). We also assume that TSVs internal to the scan chains are not considered for TSV calculation.

5 Our Algorithm

5.1 Data Structure

For a given core, wrapper elements are described as E = E_1, E_2, ..., E_n, TAM width T and maximum number of available TSVs (TSV_{max}). The proposed algorithm uses element and wrapper data structures.

The data structure of element is presented in Table 1. It contains the information about each core wrapper element E_i of the list E. The information includes the type of element (i.e. Input wrapper (I/P), Output wrapper (O/P) and Scan chain), layer number indicates in which it is placed and the length of the wrapper element. The wrapper data structure maintains three different lists using five variables corresponding to each type of wrapper element E_i. Information about the number of TSVs required at any instant of time, specifically before insertion of a wrapper element into the wrapper chain, is stored in the no_of_tsv.

The variables, length and no_of_elements are used to hold the length of the wrapper chain and the number of different types of wrapper elements contained by the wrapper chain respectively. Before starting of the algorithm, the length of wrapper chains are initialized with 0. The variable no_of_input and no_of_output indicate the total number of input and total number of output of the wrapper chain, respectively (Tables 3 and 4).

Table 3. Data structure of element

Type	Type of the element (I/P, Scan chain, O/P)
Layer	Layer no of the element
Length	Length of the element

Table 4. Wrapper data structure

no_of_tsv	Total no of TSVs required to connect all the elements for a particular wrapper chain
no_of_elemens	Total no of elements (input + scan chain + output) for a particular wrapper chain
no_of_input	Total no of input for a particular wrapper chain
no_of_output	Total no of output for a particular wrapper chain
Length	Length of a wrapper chain

If I/Ps are connected with scan-in in the same layer then the TSV requirement is 0. Hence the value of no_of_tsv is zero but if they are in different layers, the no-of-tsv holds a non-zero value. If scan-in is connected with scan-out either in same layer or different layers then the value of no_of_tsv is 0 as the internal TSVs are not counted. If scan-out is connected with other scan-in or with O/P in the same layer then the value of no_of_tsv is zero but if they are in different layers then no_of_tsv is considered. Hence, the no_of_tsv is some non-zero value. If O/P is connected with different O/P in the same layer, then TSV requirement is zero (i.e. no_of_tsv is 0) but if they are in different layers then TSV is considered (i.e. the value of tsv is some non-zero value).

5.2   Exact Algorithm

The proposed algorithm tries to create a set of balanced wrapper chain $W = W_1, W_2, W_3, W_4 \ldots \ldots W_T$ where T equals to maximum available TAM width and W_i is the i th wrapper chain. In wrapper length optimization problem, scan chain is the major contributor of increasing wrapper length. Therefore to reduce the wrapper length, the scan chain has to be placed properly such that the wrapper length gets minimized and TSV constraint (TSV_{max}) is satisfied.

Our algorithm is explained using the same problem discussed in Sect. 3, i.e. a core with 10 functional inputs, 10 functional outputs and 5 internal scan chains each of length 8, number of maximum available TSV_{max} 14, TAM width 4 and total number of layers 3. Objective is to distribute the wrapper elements over three layers of 3D SOC for a number of wrapper chains and interconnect the core elements using TSV_{max} such that the length of the longest wrapper chain is minimized.

Based on this, we implemented our algorithm and obtained the initial stage shown in Table 5. To get balanced wrapper chains, our first target is to place the scan chains among four wrapper chains. Hence, the scan chain requirements for four wrappers W_1, W_2, W_3 and W_4 are 2, 2, 3 and 2 respectively. These scan chains has to be placed in three layers in a way such that it satisfies TSV requirement (TSV_{max}). At first iteration, four scan chains are placed in four wrapper as shown in Table 5. According to Table 6 and Fig. 1, W_1 which spans across two layers, contains one input element, two scan chain elements and one output element and they are placed in layers 1, 2 and 1 respectively. Hence, the TSV requirement for W_1 is 2 and wrapper chain length is 18. Similarly, W_2 which spans across three layers, contains three input element, two scan chain elements and three output elements. Two input elements are placed at layer 1 and one input element is placed at layer 2, scan chain is placed at layer 2, two output elements are placed at layer 1 and one output element is placed at layer 2. Hence, the wrapper length is 14 and TSV requirement is 2.

Similarly W_3 which spans across three layers, contains three input elements, one scan chain element and three output elements. Two input elements are placed at layer 2 and one input element is placed at layer 3, scan chain element is placed at layer 3, three output elements are placed at layer 1. Hence, wrapper length is 14 and TSV requirement is 4.

Finally, W_4 which spans across three layers contains three input elements, one scan chain element and three output elements. Two input elements are placed at layer 2, one input element is placed at layer 1, one scan chain element is placed at layer 2, two output elements are placed at layer 2 and one output element is placed at layer 1. Hence, the wrapper length is 14 and TSV requirement is 2. Hence, the maximum wrapper length is 18 and TSV requirement is 10 (i.e. $2 + 2 + 4 + 2$).

Figure 1 shows the conceptual design of the given problem where 25 core elements are distributed on wrapper chains W_1, W_2, W_3 and W_4 over three layers. I, O written square boxes indicate input and output respectively and filled square box indicates scan chain.

Table 5. Initial stage of our solution for the problem

W_1			W_2			W_3			W_4		
I	Sc	O	I	Sc	O	I	Sc	O	I	Sc	O
	2			2			3			2	

6 Experimental Result

The proposed heuristics based algorithm is coded in C++ language and executed on a Intel Core 2 Duo processor having 1 GB RAM. Cores from ITC02 SOC test benchmarks are used for experiment. For experimental results, we have used cores 7, 5 and 4

Table 6. Final stage of our solution for the problem

W_1			W_2			W_3			W_4		
I	Sc	O	I	Sc	O	I	Sc	O	I	Sc	O
1	2	1	2	2	2	3	3	1	1	2	1
	2		1		1	2		1	2		2
			1		1	2		1	2		2

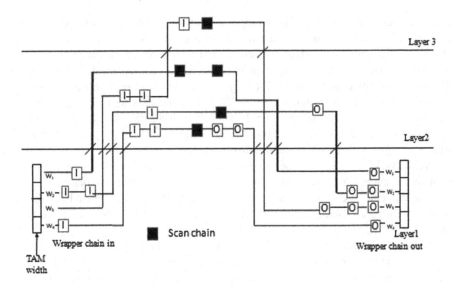

Fig. 1. Conceptual design of wrapper chain for the given example

of SOCs d281, h953 and p93791 respectively. We have restricted the number of layers to 3 for each simulation. The experimental result is presented in Tables 7, 8, and 9. Columns 1, 2, 3, 4, 5 and 6 indicate TAM width, maximum TSV, longest wrapper length obtained in [9], CPU time mentioned in [9], longest wrapper length in proposed method and CPU time in proposed method respectively. In these tables TAM width, maximum TSV, longest wrapper length and CPU time are abbreviated as TAM, TSV_{max}, LWL and Time respectively.

According to Table 7, we have achieved good results in 4 instances among 23 instances in all respect that is longest wrapper length wise and CPU time wise, though in remaining 19 instances our wrapper length is same as the wrapper length mentioned in [9].

Experimental result of core 5 of SOC Benchmark h953 is shown in Table 8. Compared to [9], our algorithm shows better result in 18 instances among 28 instances in all respect that is longest wrapper length wise and CPU time wise.

According Table 9, for core 4 of SOC Benchmark p93791, our algorithm performs better in 27 cases.

Algorithm 1

1: **Input:** E(Set of elements which follow the sequence n this order scan chain, input, output), TSV_{max}(Total available number of TSVs), L(Number of layers),T(TAM Width), V(Set of visited elements).

2: **Output:** : W_1, W_2, W_3, W_4 .... W_T(Wrapper chains).

3: **Begin**

4:     Set k=0, TSV_count=0, boolean tflag=0, pretsv=0, posttsv=0, v(set of vetex)=empty

5:     Set layer_number($E_i \in E$, for all i)=-1;

6:     For all k in T(W_k determine input output requirements R_i)

7:     **While**(E!=empty) /*Untill all the elements are unvisited*/

8:     **Begin**

9:         **if**(pretsv!=posttsv) **then**

10:            k=(k+1)modT;

11:        **if**(tflag==1) **then**

12:            shortest wrapper chain r;

13:            k=r;

14:        pickup an element $E_i \in$(E-V); /*pick up an unvisited element*/

15:        **if**(TSV_count==TSVmax) **then**

16:            tflag=1;

17:        set layer_number($E_i \in$(E-V))=1;

18:        **if**(length(W_k)==0) **then**

19:            set layer_number(E_i) $\in$2,3 ...L;

20:        **else**

21:            set layer_number(E_i) $\in$1,2,3 ...L;

22:        **if**(E_i.type==I) /*If element type is input*/ **then**

23:        **begin**

24:            **if**(W_k.no_of_input+1<=R_k) **then**

25:                r=k;

26:            **else**

27:                **begin**

28:                    **find** W_k((r!=k) &&

29:                        W_k.no_of_input <=R_k); /*find next wrapper chain to place the input elements*/

30:                    **End begin**

31:                W_k.no_of_input+=1;

32:        **End begin**

33:        **if**(E_i.type==O)

34:        **begin**

35:            **if**(W_k.no_of_output+1<=R_o) **then**

36:                r=k;

37:            **else**

38:                **begin**

39:                    **find** W_k((r!=k) &&

40:                        W_k.no_of_output$\leq R_o$);

41:                    **End begin**

42:                W_k.no_of_output+=1;

43:        **End begin**

44:        **if**(E_i.type==scanchain) **then**

```
45:              r=k;
46:              Add E_i to W_k list;
47:              no_of_elements+=1;
48:              pretsv=no_of_tsv;
49:              posttsv=Required TSV after insertion of new element E_i ;
50:              no_of_tsv_r=posttsv;
51:              W_r.wrapper_length+=E_i.length;
52:       V[i]=1;
53:          k=r;
54: End begin
55:          for all k in T(W_k check input availability) if(no_of_input==0)
56:          find maximum no_of_input wrapper W_r;
57:          node=delete(W_r.no_of_input=1);
58:          add(node,W_k);
59:          W_k.wrapper_length+=1;
60:          W_k.wrapper_length-=1;
61: End begin
62:          for all k in T(W_k check input availability) if(no_of_output==0)
63:          find maximum no_of_output wrapper W_r;
64:          node=delete(W_r.no_of_output=1);
65:          add(node,W_k);
66:          W_k.wrapper_length+=1;
67:          W_k.wrapper_length-=1;
68: End begin
```

Table 7. Result of problem I for benchmark d281 of core 7

TAM	TSV_{max}	LWL [9]	Time [9]	LWL	Time
2	10	1129	0.13	1064	0.002
	11	1223	0.08	1064	0.004
	10	1223	0.11	1064	0.002
	11	1095	0.1	1064	0.004
	12	710	0.1	710	0.001
3	14	710	0.1	710	0.001
	16	710	0.1	710	0.002
	15	784	0.13	710	0.002
	12	532	0.08	532	0.003
	14	532	0.06	532	0.015
4	16	532	0.1	532	0.003
	18	532	0.1	532	0.003
	22	532	0.11	532	0.015
	12	426	0.08	426	0.003
	14	426	0.08	426	0.003

(*continued*)

Table 7. (*continued*)

TAM	TSV_{max}	LWL [9]	Time [9]	LWL	Time
5	16	426	0.1	426	0.001
	18	426	0.11	426	0.003
	22	426	0.11	426	0.003
	12	355	0.11	355	0.002
	14	355	0.1	355	0.015
6	16	355	0.1	355	0.003
	18	355	0.08	355	0.002
	22	355	0.11	355	0.003

Table 8. Result of problem I for benchmark h953 of core 5

TAM	TSV_{max}	LWL [9]	Time [9]	LWL	Time
2	8	367	0.12	258	0.007
	10	375	0.1	258	0.003
	11	377	0.12	258	0.015
	11	377	0.1	258	0.015
	8	244	0.1	243	0.015
3	10	245	0.1	243	0.013
	12	252	0.12	245	0.013
	14	251	0.12	246	0.005
	8	129	0.08	129	0.015
4	10	246	0.1	129	0.015
	12	368	0.1	129	0.007
	16	250	0.133	129	0.008
	8	124	0.15	123	0.008
5	10	123	0.08	127	0.009
	12	246	0.1	123	0.009
	16	248	0.1	124	0.009
	8	123	0.1	123	0.027
6	10	126	0.1	126	0.013
	12	123	0.1	123	0.011
	16	243	0.06	126	0.011
	8	124	0.13	123	0.013
7	10	123	0.1	125	0.013
	12	124	0.08	123	0.013
	16	244	0.08	125	0.024
	8	123	0.15	123	0.015
8	10	123	0.1	124	0.036
	12	123	0.08	123	0.012
	16	123	0.1	124	0.016

Table 9. Result of problem I for benchmark p93791 core 4

TAM	TSV_{max}	LWL [9]	Time [9]	LWL	Time
2	11	85	0.1	77	0.01
	8	88	0.11	77	0.01
	12	91	0.13	77	0.01
	11	80	0.13	77	0.01
	11	96	0.11	77	0.01
	12	53	0.11	51	0.015
	13	53	0.1	51	0.015
3	14	52	0.08	51	0.013
	15	73	0.15	51	0.015
	13	64	0.08	51	0.015
	12	40	0.1	39	0.016
	13	39	0.1	39	0.014
4	14	40	0.08	39	0.015
	18	46	0.1	39	0.016
	20	54	0.11	39	0.014
	12	32	0.08	31	0.016
	13	31	0.08	37	0.015
5	14	32	0.1	31	0.015
	18	36	0.11	31	0.015
	20	31	0.08	31	0.015
	12	27	0.08	26	0.016
	13	27	0.13	32	0.015
6	14	28	0.15	26	0.015
	18	27	0.11	26	0.015
	20	31	0.11	26	0.015
	12	24	0.08	22	0.016
	13	24	0.1	25	0.015
7	14	24	0.08	22	0.015
	18	23	0.1	22	0.015
	20	24	0.13	22	0.015
	12	21	0.06	20	0.016
	13	21	0.11	25	0.015
8	14	21	0.1	20	0.015
	18	23	0.08	20	0.015
	20	21	0.06	20	0.015

7 Conclusion

We have presented an optimization technique for minimizing the wrapper length for 3D core-based SOCs under constraints on the number of TSVs and the TAM width. We have carried out a series of simulations for three ITC02 SOC test benchmarks by considering three layer in 3D IC. Simulation results show that the proposed method leads to lower wrapper length compared to the earlier work in [9]. We have also demonstrated a conceptual design to show the distribution of wrapper elements i.e. input, output and scan chain. This work is expected to pave the way for core-based testing of emerging 3D SOCs.

References

1. IEEE Std.1500: IEEE Standard Testability Method for Embedded Core based Integrated Circuits. IEEE, New York (2005)
2. Puttuswamy, K., Loh, G.H.: The impact of 3-dimensional integration on the design of arithmetic units. In: IEEE International Symposium on Circuits and Systems, pp. 4951–4954. IEEE, Greece (2006)
3. Iyengar, V., Chakrabarty, K., Marinissen, E.J.: Test wrapper and test access mechanism co-optimization for system-on-chip. J. Electron. Test. Theory Appl. **18**, 213–230 (2002)
4. Goel, S.K., Marinissen, E.J.: SOC test architecture design for efficient utilization of test bandwidth. ACM Trans. Des. Autom. Electron. Syst. **8**(4), 399–429 (2003)
5. Giri, C., Sarkar, S., Chattopadhyaya, S.: A genetic algorithm based heuristic technique for power constrained test scheduling in core-based SOCs. In: IEEE Proceedings of IFIP International Conference on Very Large Scale Integration, USA, pp. 320–323 (2007)
6. Wu, X., Chen, Y., Chakrabarty, K., Xie, Y.: Test-access mechanism optimization for core-based three-dimensional SOCs. Microelectron. J. **41**, 601–615 (2010)
7. Kaibartta, T., Das, D.K.: Testing of 3D IC with minimum power using genetic algorithm. In: 10th International Design and Test Symposium (IDT), pp. 112–117. IEEE, Jordon (2015)
8. Noia, B., Chakrabarty, K., Xie, Y.: Test-wrapper optimization for embedded cores in TSV-based three-dimensional SOCs. In: IEEE International Conference on Computer Design, pp. 70–77 (2009)
9. Roy, S.K., Giri, C., Rahaman, H.: Optimization of test wrapper for TSV based 3D SOCs. J. Elctron. Test. **32**, 511–529 (2016)

A Methodology to Design Online Testable Reversible Circuits

Mrinal Goswami$^{(\boxtimes)}$, Govind Raj, Aron Narzary, and Bibhash Sen

Department of Computer Science and Engineering,
National Institute of Technology Durgapur, Durgapur, India
mrinal.goswami21@gmail.com, govindraj564@gmail.com, aron596462@gmail.com,
bibhash.sen@cse.nitdgp.ac.in

Abstract. The bottleneck of high power consumption in VLSI circuits has attracted research community to explore a new low power computing era. Reversible computing is a pioneering step towards that direction. This paper proposes a methodology to design online testable (OT) reversible circuits which can be applied to any parity preserving logic circuit. An ancilla input (L) having constant value zero is augmented with the parity preserving circuit in order to make it online testable. To demonstrate the proposed method, an online testable Fredkin gate (TFR) and an online testable Feynman double gate (TF2G) are implemented. Cascading TFR and TF2G, a master-slave (MS) D flip-flop and a dual edge triggered (DET) D flip-flop are implemented which signify the efficacy of the proposed methodology. Comparison results report that the proposed flip-flops outperform the previous designs in terms of quantum cost, number of gates used, number of constant inputs and number of garbage outputs.

Keywords: Low power computing · Reversible logic ·
Online testable (OT) circuit · Sequential circuit ·
Testable block (TB)

1 Introduction

The main hurdle of all portable electronic devices is high power consumption. With the advancement of IOT, huge application of mobile/edge devices raises power crisis which in turn invites low power computing. The present state-of-the-art CMOS technology needs serious attention to control the high power dissipation of these electronic devices. CMOS based conventional circuits incur the loss of information in the form of heat.

According to [7], one bit of information loss dissipates KTln2 joules of energy where K represents the Boltzmann constant and T represents the absolute temperature at which operation is performed. Bennett showed that KTln2 joules of energy can be saved if the circuit realization is reversible [1]. Interestingly, it is quite possible to devise a reversible implementation of an irreversible computation using the overhead of garbage and ancilla inputs.

© Springer Nature Singapore Pte Ltd. 2019
S. Rajaram et al. (Eds.): VDAT 2018, CCIS 892, pp. 322–334, 2019.
https://doi.org/10.1007/978-981-13-5950-7_28

The faulty behaviour of reversible circuit demands efficient testing procedures. Online testing is preferable than the offline testing because of its ability to perform testing even if the circuit is doing its normal operation [3]. According to [5], all the online testable (OT) design methodologies found in literature can be grouped into two categories: design by modification [10] and design with testable gates [15]. However, all those OT circuits found so far in literature have huge hardware penalty.

Vasudevan et al. [15] proposed three reversible gates out of which two gates are utilized to construct the testable block. The remaining gate is used as a rail checker to test the parity of the testable blocks. However, this approach fails to detect faults which occur outside testable blocks [10]. In [10], a novel design methodology is proposed to construct OT reversible circuits. This method extends a Toffoli gate (Extended Toffoli Gate) to connect with party line with the help of CNOT gates. It can effectively detect any single bit fault at input-output lines including extra party line. However, this approach is only limited to Toffoli based network.

The research community is showing great interest to design OT reversible combinational circuits [2,3,8,10,14,15]. However, very limited attempts can be found to design OT reversible sequential circuits [6]. Hasan et al. [6] proposed the designs of OT reversible sequential circuits. However, the complexity of these designs is very high due to a huge number of cascading lines.

The major challenges of designing an OT circuit are high density of gates, variety of fault models, very low signal levels along with technological problems, like garbage output, ancilla input, fanout and feedback [5]. So, a systematic design methodology is essential to address all the aforesaid challenges. In this current work, an OT design methodology is proposed which can be applied to any parity preserving circuit. To show the significance of the proposed methodology, an OT master-slave D flip-flop and a dual edge triggered (DET) D flip-flop are implemented. Comparative analysis shows the supremacy of the proposed designs over the previous ones.

The article is organized as follows. In Sect. 2, background on the reversible circuit along with popular reversible gates are presented. In Sect. 3, previous attempts to design OT reversible circuits are presented. The proposed designs of OT reversible flip-flops are presented in Sects. 4, 5 and 6 respectively and Sect. 8 concludes the paper.

2   Basics of Reversible Circuits

A reversible logic function is a one-to-one and onto mapping (bijection) between inputs and outputs, i.e. each input pattern is mapped to a unique output pattern, while each output pattern has a unique input pattern mapped to it. A reversible circuit can be designed or constructed by cascading only reversible gates. Some popular reversible gates are:

Feynman Gate: The Feynman gate has two inputs (a, b) and two outputs $(p = a, q = a \oplus b)$ as shown in Fig. 1(a). If one of the input is zero, both the outputs will be same. Due to this property, it can be used as a fan-out gate. Alternatively, when one of the inputs is 1, the outputs will be the complement to each other. The quantum cost of the Feynman gate is 1.

Toffoli Gate: The Toffoli gate has three inputs (a, b, c) and three outputs $(p = a, q = b, r = a.b \oplus c)$ as shown in Fig. 1(b).

Fredkin Gate: It is one of the fundamental gates in reversible computing. Its inputs (a, b, c) and outputs $(p = a, q = \bar{a}b + ac, r = ab + \bar{a}c)$ are shown in the Fig. 1(c). When a = 1, Fredkin gate can be used as a swap gate or as a 2:1 multiplexer. The quantum cost of Fredkin gate is 5.

Feynman Double Gate: It is an extension of Feynman gate. Feynman double gate has three inputs (a, b, c) and three outputs $(p = a, q = a \oplus b, r = a \oplus c)$ as shown in Fig. 1(d).

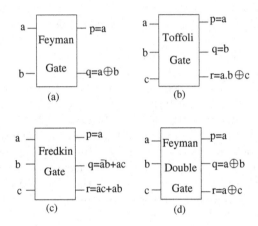

Fig. 1. Basic popular reversible gates (a) Feynman gate (b) Toffoli gate (c) Fredkin gate and (d) Feynman double gate

3   Related Work

The online testing of reversible circuit was first introduced in [15]. In [15], two reversible gates R1 and R2 are cascaded to construct the online testable (OT) block as shown in Fig. 2. A two-pair two-rail checker circuit is also proposed to test the parities of two testable blocks (TBs). However, it is not possible to detect all the single bit fault that occurs outside TBs [10]. On the otherhand, a complete new methodology to construct OT reversible circuit is proposed in [10]. In addition to make OT reversible circuit, an ancilla input (L) having constant value zero is augmented to the design as shown in Fig. 3. After adding the line L, CNOT gates are inserted to connect all the inputs $(c_1, c_2, c_3, c_4, c_5)$ and outputs $(c_6, c_7, c_8, c_9, c_{10})$ of the Toffoli gate. Moreover, the original gates (t_1, t_2, t_3, t_4) need to extend as (e_1, e_2, e_3, e_4) to connect the line L. The detail procedure is described in [10]. However, this technique is suitable for Toffoli network based circuits only.

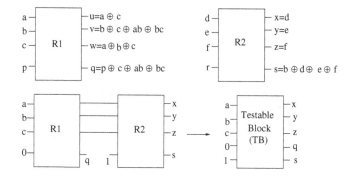

Fig. 2. Online testable block proposed in [15]

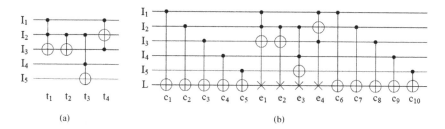

Fig. 3. Design by modification approach proposed in [10] (a) A Toffoli gate (b) An corresponding online testable circuit.

Following the principle proposed in [10,15], several other improved methods to design OT combinational circuits have proposed in [3,8,10,14,15]. However, a limited number of contribution has been found to design OT reversible sequential circuits [6]. In [6], an improved rail checker (IRC) circuit is implement by cascading both R1 and R2 gate. The IRC is used to implemented online testable D, T, SR and JK flip-flops. However, the design complexity of these flip-flops are huge and the proposed designs are implemented utilizing design by TBs methodology which fails to detect single bit fault that occurs outside testable blocks [10].

4   The Methodology and Proposed Designs

4.1   The Proposed Methodology

This section presents the proposed online testable design methodology. The proposed methodology can be applied to any parity preserving (PP) gate. An ancilla input line (L) is augmented with the PP gate and it is initialized to zero. After adding L, CNOT gates are employed to connect the inputs and outputs of the PP gate. The XOR of all the inputs and outputs of any PP gate results in zero. Thus, the initial and final value of the line L will be same i.e. zero which signifies there is no fault in the circuit. If any single bit fault occurs in any line (including L), the value of L changes from zero to one which indicates the presence of a fault else L remains zero in fault-free condition.

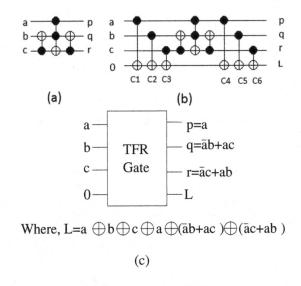

Where, L=a $\oplus$ b $\oplus$ c $\oplus$ a $\oplus$ (ab+ac) $\oplus$ ($\bar{a}$c+ab)

(c)

Fig. 4. Proposed online testable Fredkin gate (TFR) (a) Fredkin gate (b) Proposed TFR (c) Block diagram of TFR

To explain the detail procedure, we have employed two examples: Fredkin gate and Feynman double gate. First of all, in order to make Fredkin gate OT, an parity line (L) with initial value zero is appended with the Fredkin gate (Fig. 4(b)). After adding an extra line (L), three CNOT gates (c_1, c_2, c_3) are utilized to connect the input lines (a, b, c) with L. Similarly, output lines (p, q, r) and line (L) is connected with the help of another three CNOT gates. Therefore, the output of the line L is equal to zero (L = a $\oplus$ b $\oplus$ c $\oplus$ a $\oplus$ ($\bar{a}$.b + a.c) $\oplus$ ($\bar{a}$.c + a.b) = 0).

Here a, b, c are the inputs of the Fredkin gate. Fredkin gate is a parity preserving gate and if we take XOR of all the inputs and outputs then the result will be zero. It indicates that there is no fault in the circuit. The same methodology is utilized to construct the OT reversible Feynman double gate as exhibited in Fig. 5.

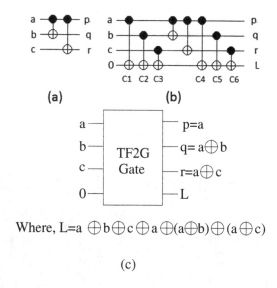

Fig. 5. Proposed online testable reversible Feynman double gate (TF2G) (a) Feynman double gate (b) Proposed TF2G (c) Block diagram of TF2G

4.2   Design of Online Testable Positive Enable D Flip-Flop

The process of applying the control signal to change the state of a flip-flop is called triggering. There are two types of triggering: level triggering and edge triggering. In level triggering, the flip-flop is affected by the input signal only if the clock is at logic 1 whereas, in edge triggering, the flip-flop is affected by the input signal only if they are present at the negative or positive edge of the clock pulse.

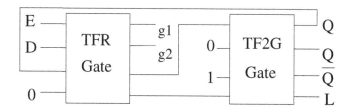

Fig. 6. Proposed online testable Positive Enable D Flip-Flop (OTPEDFF).

The characteristic equation of D flip-flop is Q^+ (next state) $= DE + \overline{E}Q$ where E is used as a clock. E (Enable) and clock are used interchangeably in the proposed work. In the positive enable D flip-flop, when E = 1, the output value is equal to the input value of the D flip-flop i.e., next state $(Q^+) = D$ whereas if E = 0, then the proposed D flip-flop retains its previous state, i.e.,

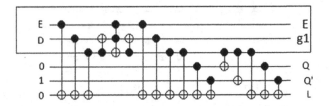

Fig. 7. Revkit [12] output of OTPEDFF

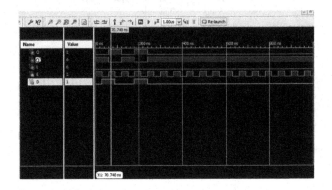

Fig. 8. Simulated behaviour of OTPEDFF

next state $(Q^+) = Q$. The proposed online testable (OT) positive enable D flip-flop is designed by cascading one TFR and one TF2G gate as shown in Fig. 6 and its corresponding quantum representation is shown in Fig. 7. In reversible logic, fan-out is restricted, so to tackle this issue a TF2G gate is cascaded with TFR gate. If any single bit error arises in any of the inputs as well as outputs (including L) then the output of L will be 1 otherwise it remains zero (fault-free). The functional correctness of the proposed OT positive enable D flip-flop is verified in XILINX ISE Design suit 14.7 using Verilog HDL. The corresponding simulated behaviour is shown in Fig. 8 which signifies correctness of the proposed logic. It is evident that every rising edge of the clock (E), the input data (D) is reflected at the corresponding output (Q) while the parity line L remains low.

4.3   Design of Online Testable Negative Enable D Flip-Flop

The characteristic equation of the proposed negative enable D flip-flop (Fig. 9) is $Q^+ = D\overline{E} + EQ$. In the negative enable D flip-flop, when E = 0, the output of the D flip-flop is equal to the input of the D flip-flop i.e., next state $(Q^+) = D$ and when E = 1, D flip-flop retains its previous state, i.e., next state $(Q^+) = Q$. If any single bit error occurs in the flip-flop then the value of the line L is changed to one otherwise it remains at zero. The quantum representation of the proposed OT negative enable D flip-flop is shown in Fig. 10. The functional correctness of the proposed negative enable D flip-flop is verified in XILINX ISE

Design suit 14.7 using Verilog HDL. The outcome of XILINX ISE Design suit 14.7 is presented in Fig. 11. Unlike positive enable D flip-flop, the corresponding input value (D) is visible in the output (Q) only at the falling edge of the clock (E). Moreover, the line L remains zero which specifies its fault-free behaviour.

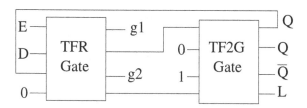

Fig. 9. Proposed online testable Negative Enable D Flip-Flop (OTNEDFF).

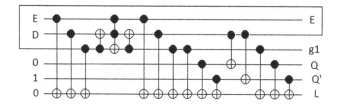

Fig. 10. Revkit [12] output of OTNEDFF

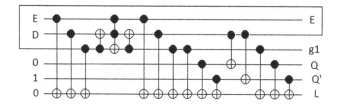

Fig. 11. Simulated behaviour of OTNEDFF

5 Design of Online Testable Master-Slave Flip-Flop

Master-slave (MS) flip-flop can be constructed by cascading two positive and negative enable D flip-flop where one flip-flop acts as master and the other one acts as a slave. In the proposed OT reversible master-slave D flip-flop (Fig. 12), positive enable D flip-flop works as a master flip-flop, and negative enable D flip-flop works as a slave flip-flop. Like positive and negative enable OT D flip-flop, the testable master-slave flip-flop can also detect any single bit error at any input or output lines (including L) just by checking the output of the line L. The Verilog HDL on XILINX ISE Design suit 14.7 is utilized to examine the logical correctness of the proposed online testable MS D flip-flop and their corresponding simulation outcome is shown in Fig. 13. The MS flip-flop changes its output (Q) only at the falling edges of the clock (E).

6   Design of Online Testable Dual Edge Triggered (DET) D Flip-Flop

The master-slave (MS) strategy is the most popular strategy to design any flip-flop. But, MS flip-flop can not sample data at both the edges and can sample data at only the falling edges [13]. To overcome this problem, DET flip-flops comes into the picture which can trigger the data at both the edges. In a single clock period, the DET flip-flops are able to sample double data values and this is the reason why the frequency of the clock in DET becomes half as compared to MS flip-flops while managing the equivalent data rate. The proposed DET flip-flop is constructed by cascading one positive enable and one negative enable flip-flop in parallel as exhibited in Fig. 14. As discussed earlier, fan-out is restricted in the reversible circuit, so to copy the input data (D) as d1 and d2, a TF2G gate as fanout is used. Finally, a TFR is used to generate the final output of the proposed online testable DET D flip-flop. The fault testing can be done just by looking at the line L. If the output of the line L = 0 then no fault is detected in the DET D flip-flop otherwise it is faulty. The proposed online testable DET flip-flop is coded by Verilog HDL on XILINX ISE Design suit 14.7 and their corresponding simulated result is shown in Fig. 15. As the name suggests, the DET D flip-flop triggers at both the rising and falling edges of the clock (E) which is evident from Fig. 15. The proposed flip-flop can be easily tested just by looking at the line L. If L = 0, there is no fault in the flip-flop.

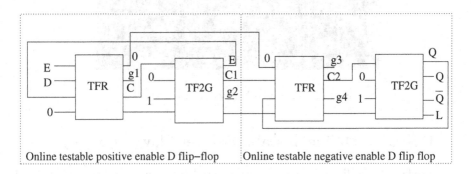

Online testable positive enable D flip–flop   Online testable negative enable D flip flop

Fig. 12. Proposed online testable Master-Slave Flip-Flop.

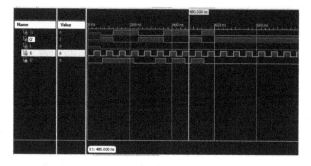

Fig. 13. Simulated behaviour of online testable Master-Slave Flip-Flop.

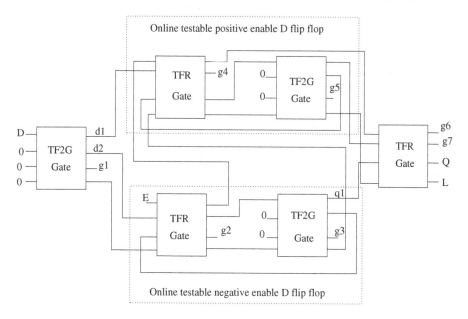

Fig. 14. Online testable DET Flip-Flop.

Fig. 15. Simulated behavior of online testable DET Flip-Flop.

7   Comparison Outcome

7.1   Online Testable Methodology

As stated in Sect. 1, all the previous online testable (OT) methodologies can be divided into two groups: (a) design by modification and (b) design with testable gates. Based on this assumption, the previous methodologies are arranged in Table 1. From Table 1, it is clear that the method designed with TBs has huge hardware requirements as well as is unable to handle the faults outsides the testable blocks (TBs). On the other hand, methods designed by modification requires less hardware as compared to methods designed with TBs. The major difference between the proposed methodology and the methodology proposed in [10] is that the proposed methodology is suitable for any parity preserving reversible circuit and there is no restriction of any logic synthesis and network-based design. Moreover, there is no extra overhead to extend the original gates which reduces the design complexity of the proposed method. On the contrary, the work proposed in [10] needs to extend its original gates and this methodology is suitable only for the Toffoli based networks.

7.2   Online Testable Flip-Flop

To the best of our knowledge, the work proposed in [6] is the only attempt to realize OT sequential circuit and thus it is taken into account for comparison. In [6], the authors have utilized the design by testable block methodology where a huge number of testable blocks are cascaded to construct OT designs. On the other hand, an efficient design by modification methodology is applied to construct our proposed designs. A comparison is shown in Table 2 between the proposed designs and prior reversible OT flip-flops [6] in terms of quantum cost, number of gates, number of constant inputs and number of garbage output. It is clear that the proposed designs outperform the existing reversible designs in all the aspects.

Table 1. Comparison of online testable methodologies

Method	Design by modification	Design by testable gates	Synthesis	Network	Parity preserving	Fault detection	Hardware requirement
In [15]	No	Yes	Any	Any	No	Single bit	High
In [14]	No	Yes	Any	Any	No	Single bit	High
In [8]	No	Yes	Any	Any	No	Single bit	High
In [4]	No	Yes	Any	Any	No	Single bit	High
In [9]	Yes	No	Any	Toffoli	No	Three faults	Moderate
In [11]	Yes	No	ESOP	Toffoli	No	Single bit	Low
In [10]	Yes	No	Any	Toffoli	No	Single bit	Low
Proposed	Yes	No	Any	Any	Yes	Single bit	Low

Table 2. Comparison of online testable Reversible Flip-Flop

Design ↓	Quantum cost			Number of gates			Number of constant inputs			Number of garbage output		
	In [6]	Proposed	Gain	In [6]	Proposed	Gain	In [6]	Proposed	Gain	In [6]	Proposed	Gain
PET D FF	28	19	32.14%	14	2	85.71%	25	3	88%	33	2	93.90%
MS D Flip-Flop	64	38	40.60%	32	4	87.50%	-	5	-	73	4	94.50%
DET D Flip-Flop	-	57		-	6		-	7		-	7	

Online testable Reversible DET D flip-flop is introduced for the first time in the literature
PET D FF = Positive edge triggered D FF
MS D FF = Master Slave D Flip-Flop

8   Conclusion

A methodology to design online testable (OT) reversible circuit is proposed which is suitable for any parity preserving circuit. The methodology is applied to the two most popular reversible gates (Fredkin and Feynman Double Gate) in order to make them OT. An OT positive edge triggered as well as a negative edge triggered D flip-flop is designed by cascading OT Fredkin and OT Feynman double gates. The OT positive edge triggered D flip-flop has achieved 32.14% improvement in terms of quantum cost, 85.71% improvement in terms of number of gates used, 88% improvement in terms of number of constant inputs and 93.90% improvement in terms of number of garbage output. A master-slave D flip-flop with 40.60% improvement in terms of quantum cost, 87.50% improvement in terms of number of gates used and 94.50% improvement in terms of number of garbage output is investigated in this work. Moreover, an OT reversible DET D flip-flop is also introduced.

Acknowledgment. This entire research has been carried out under the Visvesvaraya PhD scheme which is managed by the Media Lab Asia, India and is under the supervision of the Electronics and IT Department, Ministry of Communications and IT, Government of India.

References

1. Bennett, C.H.: Logical reversibility of computation. IBM J. Res. Dev. **17**(6), 525–532 (1973)
2. Bhoi, B., Misra, N.K., Pradhan, M.: Design and evaluation of an efficient parity-preserving reversible qca gate with online testability. Cogent Eng. **4**(1), 1416888 (2017)
3. Bose, A., Babu, H.M.H., Gupta, S.: Design of compact reversible online testable ripple carry adder. In: 2015 IEEE International WIE Conference on Electrical and Computer Engineering (WIECON-ECE), pp. 556–560, December 2015
4. Farazmand, N., Zamani, M., Tahoori, M.B.: Online fault testing of reversible logic using dual rail coding. In: 2010 IEEE 16th International On-Line Testing Symposium, pp. 204–205, July 2010

5. Gaur, H.M., Singh, A.K., Ghanekar, U.: A review on online testability for reversible logic. Procedia Comput. Sci. **70**, 384–391 (2015). Proceedings of the 4th International Conference on Eco-friendly Computing and Communication Systems

6. Hasan, M., Islam, A.K.M.T., Chowdhury, A.R.: Design and analysis of online testability of reversible sequential circuits. In: 2009 12th International Conference on Computers and Information Technology, pp. 180–185, December 2009. https://doi.org/10.1109/ICCIT.2009.5407143

7. Landauer, R.: Irreversibility and heat generation in the computing process. IBM J. Res. Dev. **5**(3), 183–191 (1961)

8. Mahammad, S.N., Veezhinathan, K.: Constructing online testable circuits using reversible logic. IEEE Trans. Instrum. Measur. **59**(1), 101–109 (2010). https://doi.org/10.1109/TIM.2009.2022103

9. Nashiry, M.A., Bhaskar, G.G., Rice, J.E.: Online testing for three fault models in reversible circuits. In: 2015 IEEE International Symposium on Multiple-Valued Logic, pp. 8–13, May 2015. https://doi.org/10.1109/ISMVL.2015.36

10. Nayeem, N.M., Rice, J.E.: Online fault detection in reversible logic. In: 2011 IEEE International Symposium on Defect and Fault Tolerance in VLSI and Nanotechnology Systems, pp. 426–434, October 2011. https://doi.org/10.1109/DFT.2011.55

11. Nayeem, N.M., Rice, J.E.: A simple approach for designing online testable reversible circuits. In: Proceedings of 2011 IEEE Pacific Rim Conference on Communications, Computers and Signal Processing, pp. 85–90, August 2011. https://doi.org/10.1109/PACRIM.2011.6032872

12. Soeken, M., Frehse, S., Wille, R., Drechsler, R.: RevKit: an open source toolkit for the design of reversible circuits. In: De Vos, A., Wille, R. (eds.) RC 2011. LNCS, vol. 7165, pp. 64–76. Springer, Heidelberg (2012). https://doi.org/10.1007/978-3-642-29517-1_6

13. Thapliyal, H., Ranganathan, N., Kotiyal, S.: Design of testable reversible sequential circuits. IEEE Trans. Very Large Scale Integr. (VLSI) Syst. **21**(7), 1201–1209 (2013)

14. Thapliyal, H., Vinod, A.P.: Designing efficient online testable reversible adders with new reversible gate. In: 2007 IEEE International Symposium on Circuits and Systems, pp. 1085–1088, May 2007. https://doi.org/10.1109/ISCAS.2007.378198

15. Vasudevan, D.P., Lala, P.K., Parkerson, J.P.: Online testable reversible logic circuit design using NAND blocks. In: 2004 Proceedings of 19th IEEE International Symposium on Defect and Fault Tolerance in VLSI Systems. DFT 2004, pp. 324–331, October 2004

Robust SRAM Cell Development for Single-Event Multiple Effects

Naga Raghuram CH[1]($\boxtimes$), D. Manohar Reddy[1],
Puli Kishore Kumar[1], and Gaurav Kaushal[2]

[1] Department of Electronics and Communication Engineering,
National Institute of Technology, Patna 800005, India
{naga.ece16,dmanoharreddy,pulikishorek}@nitp.ac.in
[2] Department of Electronics and Communication Engineering, ABV-IIITM,
Gwalior 800005, India
kaushal@iiitm.ac.in

Abstract. As the transistor size scales down exponentially to Nanometric dimensions, the susceptibility of electronic circuits to radiation increases drastically. Static-Random-Access Memories (SRAMs) are applicable in the areas of aerospace and space applications where their performance must meet the increased data rates and must be resilient to radiation exposures to guarantee reliability. Therefore, development of resilient SRAM is a challenging and demanding problem. In this paper a robust 10T SRAM (RHD10T) is proposed and compared with the existing radiation hardened (rad-hard) SRAM circuits. The proposed RHD10T SRAM is more robust towards Single Event Multiple Effects (SEME's) compared with the recently published literature. Further, it takes 29% lesser area with respect to the standard DICE cell. In contrast to latest rad-hard SRAM cells, the proposed RHD10T cell is delivering 99.8% less failure probability for the applied charge distribution. Process variations (PV) show least effects when compared to 6T SRAM cell.

Index Terms: Single event upset · Radiation hardening · Single-Event Multiple Effect (SEME) · Robust SRAM cell

1 Introduction

Soft errors induced by radiation, threats the basic functionality of logic cells. A high energetic ionized particle, when crashes with a memory cell, changes the stored logic resulting in the bit flip. This circumstance is defined as a Single Event Upset (SEU) [1]. Static Random-Access Memories (SRAMs) are more vulnerable to these radiations induced SEUs. As the CMOS technology scales down, there is an increase in the susceptibility of memory cells to the induced soft errors which kindles the new concerns like Single Event Multiple Effects (SEMEs) [2–4]. SEMEs are of serious issue in safety and critical applications like aerospace and space navigation [5]. In SEMEs when an ionized particle strikes the node of robustious SRAM like DICE cell [6], more than one node will get affected resulting in the bit flip. Different system level strategies like error detection and correcting codes have been suggested in the literature to get rid

© Springer Nature Singapore Pte Ltd. 2019
S. Rajaram et al. (Eds.): VDAT 2018, CCIS 892, pp. 335–347, 2019.
https://doi.org/10.1007/978-981-13-5950-7_29

of multi-bit flips [7], which doesn't highlight reason behind the bit-flip. In these system level techniques, authors have expected ionized particle hit results in one or more upsets and further they are not interested by what means a radiation hit results an upset in a SRAM cell. In circuit level strategies, design engineer, emphases on resilient memory cells in which a radiation strike hitting several nodes of the cell will not result in a bit flip. This work presents a circuit level strategy to tackle SEME. According to the recent research and study, little effort in design of SEME resilient SRAM cells was carried out [2, 8]. In cache memories where performance, power consumption and cell area are important features, SRAM cells are used. Using system level strategies like correcting codes and fault design of VLSI circuits [9] on the speed and power consumption of RHD10T and 6T SRAM cells. The paper outline is as follows: Sect. 2 comprises an explanation of model for a SEU and former rad-hard SRAM cells. In Sect. 3, working of robust rad-hard SRAM cell (RHD10T) is presented. In Sect. 4, analysis of SEU, SEME robustness of proposed and considered cells for comparison is presented. In Sect. 5, overheads of RHD10T SRAM cell in contrast to recently published rad-hard SRAM cells are presented. In Sect. 6 PV analysis and its discussion is presented. Finally, Sect. 7 consists of conclusion.

2   Introduction to of Radiation Effects

2.1   SEU and Critical Charge

The minimum charge needed to alter the stored state of any logic circuit is known as the Critical Charge (Qcrit) [4, 5]. The moment, charge at the radiation affected node of SRAM cell exceeds the Qcrit, an SEU occurs. The model of the charge induced by the radiation strike is double exponential current pulse [9] and applied by numerous researchers [2, 3, 5]. Equation (1) shows the mathematical equation of double exponential current pulse.

$$I_{inj}(t) = \frac{Q_{inj}}{T_1 - T_2}\left(e^{\frac{-t}{T_1}} - e^{\frac{-t}{T_2}}\right) \tag{1}$$

Here, the Qinj is the quantity of imparted charge in the hit area. In Eq. (1), $\tau 1$ as well as $\tau 2$ are material reliant time constants [9]. $1/\tau 1$ is the accumulation time constant of the node. We can calculate $\tau 1$ as shown in Eq. (2) [10]. It depends on doping concentration of silicon substrate (ND). We presumed the value of $\tau 2$ as 5×10^{-11} s in (1) and is insignificant in comparison to $\tau 1$ [5, 11, 12]. In (1), Iinj is the quantity of charge we injected as SEU for the targeted junction. To introduce the effect of ionized particle strike at a junction, we attach a current source [specified by (1)] to that junction.

$$\frac{1}{T_1} = \frac{K\varepsilon_0}{q\mu N_D} \tag{2}$$

Similar to [3, 4, 8, 13] for a radiation strike that disturbs two neighboring junctions, we used two current sources one at each junction.

2.2   Previous Work

Author in [14] showed RHD13T SRAM is more robust towards SEU's and SEME's than 13T and 11T in [8, 11] respectively. He also displayed low area overhead of RHD13T SRAM over dice cell [6], 13T and 11T. RHD13T cell has more shared critical charge over 13T SRAM cell. Still, the disadvantage of RHD13T is it cannot tolerate an SEME. Author in [15] proposed AS8 SRAM cell and displayed increase in its critical charge when compared to 6T SRAM. The disadvantage of AS8 is its inability to withstand radiation strikes in its two nodes. Authors in [6] proposed 12 transistors SRAM namely DICE cell, which is successful in with standing SEU but is unable to hold data in the presence of SEMEs. To address SEME we proposed a 10 transistors SRAM cell namely RHD10T in this paper. By understanding the withstanding ability of RHD10T SRAM over radiation induced current pulse we will be able to classify the difference between proposed and standard 6T SRAM.

3   RHD 10T SRAM Cell

As SRAM memories must be fast and consume small area, the radiation hardened SRAM cells that involve high penalty of area and performance would not be widely applicable. Also, until SRAM connects to power supply, it preserves the data stored in it. Working of the proposed RHD10T SRAM cell is same as conventional 6T-SRAM cell. Our proposed rad-hard SRAM cell consists of ten transistors. The basic latch of the circuit which preserves the data is the entire circuit, apart from transistors Xn5 and Xn6. The latch consists of four CMOS inverters whose arrangement is as shown in Fig. 1(a). Word Line (WL) is the control for access transistors Xn5 and Xn6. Figure 1 (a) shows the output of two inverters formed by Xn1, Xp1 and Xn2, Xp2 are at NODE1, their input at NODE2. And, output of another two inverters formed by Xn3, Xp3 and Xn4, Xp4 are at NODE2 and their input at NODE1. This forms a feedback, which strengthens the inverters to their respective states. The access transistors bit line (BL), bit line bar (BLB) and WL are used to read and write, from and to the cell. In idle state WL will be at low, making access transistors off, in this state NODE1 and stronger therefore they can switch the inverter transistors. Disabling access transistors concludes writing the SRAM. Figure 1(b) shows write '1' and write '0' operations performed for RHD10T SRAM cell. Pre-charging the BL and BLB to Vdd and applying a high pulse on WL begins reading the SRAM. A non-zero current starts flowing into BL or BLB through access transistor and ON state pull down transistors, (through a node which holds logic zero). This current leads to a voltage drop in the bit-line whose access transistor end is storing a logic low value. But, the bit-line whose access transistor other end stores Vdd, experiences no drop-in voltage from pre-charged voltage. This result in voltage difference in bit-lines, using which sense amplifier identifies the data stored. By running HSPICE simulations of proposed and recently published rad-hard SRAM cells and after analyzing the simulations, results are shown in next section. RHD10T SRAM cell is a SEU-resilient compared to other previously proposed rad-hard cells. However, like all other estimated SRAM cells, RHD10T SRAM cell could not with stand the radiation strikes affecting two junctions. If a high intensity radiation strike, disturbs the

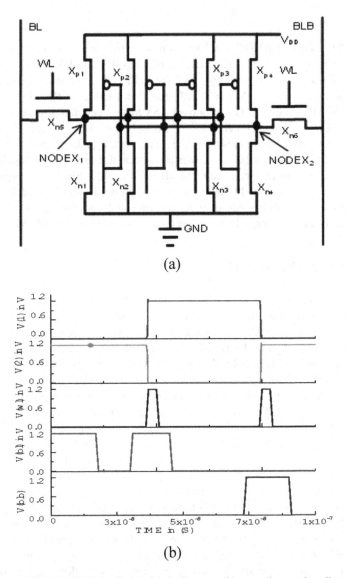

Fig. 1. RHD10T SRAM cell: (a) circuit diagram; (b) normal operation diagram.

junction pair X1–X2 the stored value could be altered. The next section is displaying that our proposed rad-hard SRAM cell on contrast to recently published rad-hard SRAM cells is delivering higher critical charge that is greater immunity to voltage variations and transient noise. It is also displaying that our proposed SRAM cell is more SEMU tolerant than DICE cell. For RHD10T SRAM cell an increase in read delay by 9:8% and an increase in write delay by 6:1% compared to 6T SRAM cell were observed. Critical charge of the proposed rad-hard SRAM is more than recently proposed SRAM and is achieved at the cost of higher power consumption (as explained in

Sect. 4). For assessing RHD10T SRAM and other important rad-hard cells, we made a set of simulations. HSPICE is used to perform simulations of SRAM cells with PTM libraries [16]. We set the temperature to 25 °C and source voltage to 1.2 V. The objective of RHD10T SRAM is to increase the internal resistance towards the current pulse induced by radiation strike. Proposed RHD10T SRAM cell consists of two extra CMOS inverters in parallel to the existing inverters of 6T SRAM as explained in Sect. 3. Because of added inverter the node's capacitance increases which strengthens to uphold stored data by dragging the signal back to the initial state [15]. The critical charge at the node increases because of charge sharing by gates of added transistors. Now consider if radiation strikes occur at any reverse biased drain junction of the inverter of SRAM. The current pulse formed at the drain node of the radiation affected set of inverters of SRAM. At this stage, output of first set of inverters strengthens the corrupted data until settling at certain inappropriate state. If the critical charge of the SRAM cell is higher than the injected charge because of a particle hit, the induced glitch will disappear after the strike and the cell holds its original state [15]. Our method is strengthening the feedback mechanism, resulting in radiation hardened design by mitigating the corrupting affect because of an ionized particle strike. Thus, the influence of ionized particle strikes on our proposed SRAM is unresponsive and limited by added inverters.

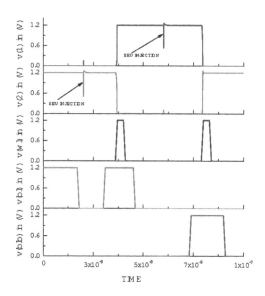

Fig. 2. SEU radiation strikes to nodes of RHD10 SRAM cell.

The smallest charge needed to alter the stored data will get increases in our proposed SRAM which boosts the resistance of SRAM cell against SE of inverters of SRAM. At this stage, output of first set of inverters strengthens the corrupted data until settling at certain inappropriate state. If the critical charge of the SRAM cell is higher

Table 1. Critical charge of various susceptive nodes

Technology	65 nm		
SRAM type	Node	SEU critical charge in femto coulomb	SEME critical charge in femto coulomb
6T	X1	18.729(1)	15.8156
	X2	18.729(1)	15.8156
AS8 [14]	X1	18.729	15.8156
	X2	35.7932	30.042
RHD13T [15]	X1	10.8212	8.831
	X3	24.5	19.43
	X4	26.63	20.049
Proposed	X1	37.0418(1)	31.215
	X2	36.6256(1)	31.215(1)
DICE [06]	X1	-	16.648(1)
	X2	-	16.648

than the injected charge because of a particle hit, the induced glitch will disappear after the strike and the cell holds its original state [15]. Our method is strengthening the feedback mechanism, resulting in radiation hardened design by mitigating the corrupting affect because of an ionized particle strike. Thus, the influence of ionized particle strikes on our proposed SRAM is unresponsive and limited by added inverters. The smallest charge needed to alter the stored data will get increases in our proposed SRAM which boosts the resistance of SRAM cell against SEU.

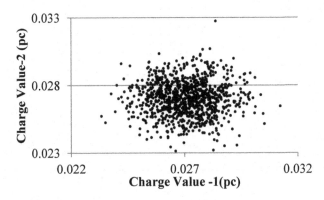

Fig. 3. 1000 randomly sample charge pairs used foe Monte Carlo simulation from normal distribution

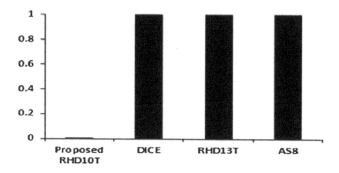

Fig. 4. Evaluation for probability of failure of SRAM cells in existence of SEME for charge distribution shown in Fig. 3.

4 Evaluation

4.1 Single Event Single Node Effect

To study SEU resilient ability of RHD10T SRAM and other rad-hard SRAM cells, we introduce transient faults (model discussed in Sect. 2.1) to drain nodes of inverter which holds logic high. Based on the displayed results in Fig. 2 we can state that, RHD10T SRAM is accepting high-power radiation hits to any of its junctions. Table 1 displays an assessment of critical charges of nodes of our proposed cell and other rad-hard SRAM's like RHD13T, RHD11T and DICE cell. We can identify from Table 1 that critical charge of RHD10T SRAM cell is higher compared to the recently proposed rad-hard cells.

4.2 Single Event Multiple Node Effects

To examine and compare the Single Event Multiple Effect tolerance ability of RHD10T SRAM cell with other RHD SRAMs, we introduce double exponential current pulses into two sensitive nodes (critical pair). We found the sensitive node pairs by introducing SEU injections to all probable junction pairs. Assessment of the critical charges of sensitive node pairs of RHD10T SRAM cell in contrast to other considered RHD SRAM cells is shown in Table 1. From Table 1. we can conclude that Dice cell is purely SEU tolerant but is not SEME tolerant. The critical charges for primary and secondary nodes of any other SRAM cell is clearly much lesser than RHD10T, which states that RHD10T cell is more robust towards SEMEs. As shown in simulation results, RHD10T SRAM cell displays significantly greater strength against SEME compared with former rad-hard SRAM cells. Also, our projected SRAM displays reasonably higher robustness than the RHD11T and RHD13T cells. We planned Monte Carlo (MC) simulations for a quantitative investigation for SEME tolerance ability of the rad-hard SRAM cells. 1000 randomly generated charge pairs from two normal distributions will be using as radiation strike induced deposited charges in MC simulations. A charge pair thus created is applied on identified sensitive nodes pairs

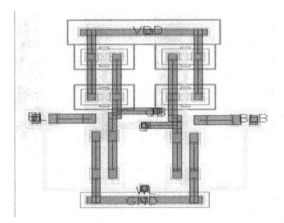

Fig. 5. Layout of RHD10T SRAM cell

(primary and secondary nodes) of SRAM cells. For the circuit under simulation, selecting the node pairs is done from the sensitive nodes identified in previous section. To find the Probability of Failure (POF) for the SRAM under simulation the numbers of bit flips for each simulation were counted. Figure 5 displays the layout of our aimed rad-hard RHD10T cell. In [17–19], particular approaches for increasing the robustness of the rad-hard SRAM cell with respect to SEMEs in layout level are recommended. Like in [17], by keeping enough distance among sensitive junction pairs, when the primary junction is struck by the radiation, possibility of consequential effects at secondary junction will be insignificant. Normal distributions displayed in Fig. 3. Were used for performing MC simulations. By noticing the MC simulation results, displayed in Fig. 4 for the applied charge distribution in Fig. 3 one can state that RHD10T delivers greater robustness to SEMEs when compared with former rad-hard SRAM cells. As in [17], the effects at secondary junctions can be minimized when a primary node is struck with a radiation hit, by keeping sufficient spacing between sensitive junction pairs. Figure 5 displays the layout of RHD10T cell. In [17–20], particular approaches for increasing the robustness of the rad-hard SRAM cell for SEMEs in layout level are recommended. Figure 6 shows the Static Noise Margins for SRAM's under simulation at various supply voltages. Static Noise margin is measure of SRAM's ability to tolerate noise voltages at the inputs of its inverters. RHD10T is delivering highest SNM than all the considered SRAMs after RHD13T. This indicates its noise withstanding ability. 1000 randomly generated charge pairs from two normal distributions will be using as radiation strike induced deposited charges in MC simulations. A charge pair thus created is applied on identified sensitive nodes pairs (primary and secondary nodes) of SRAM cells. For the circuit under simulation, selecting the node pairs is done from the sensitive nodes identified in previous section. To find the Probability of Failure (POF) for the SRAM under simulation the numbers of bit flips for each simulation were counted. Figure 5 displays the layout of our aimed rad-hard RHD10T cell.

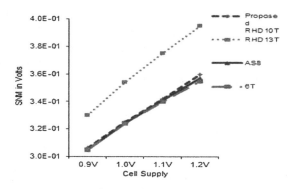

Fig. 6. SNM versus cell supply voltage

In [17–19], particular approaches for increasing the robustness of the rad-hard SRAM cell with respect to SEMEs in layout level are recommended. Like in [17], by keeping enough distance among sensitive junction pairs, when the primary junction is struck by the radiation, possibility of consequential effects at secondary junction will be insignificant. Normal distributions displayed in Fig. 3. Were used for performing MC simulations. By noticing the MC simulation results, displayed in Fig. 4 for the applied charge distribution in Fig. 3 one can state that RHD10T delivers greater robustness to SEMEs when compared with former rad-hard SRAM cells. As in [17], the effects at secondary junctions can be minimized when a primary node is struck with a radiation hit, by keeping sufficient spacing between sensitive junction pairs. Figure 5 displays the layout of RHD10T cell. In [17–20], particular approaches for increasing the robustness of the rad-hard SRAM cell for SEMEs in layout level are recommended. Figure 6 shows the Static Noise Margins for SRAM's under simulation at various supply voltages. Static Noise margin is measure of SRAM's ability to tolerate noise voltages at the inputs of its inverters. RHD10T is delivering highest SNM than all the considered SRAMs after RHD13T. This indicates its noise withstanding ability.

Table 2. Comparative factors of SRAM Cells for 65 nm Standardized to 6T SRAM

	AS8	RHD 13	Proposed
Power	1.211	1.7121	1.676
Write delay	1.326	1.9653	1.061
Read delay	0.986	0.9194	0.902
PDP	1.398	2.4822	1.676
Area	1.124	1.88	1.24

5 Comparative Analysis

Reliability may be achieved at the cost of drop in speed, increase in area, and increased energy consumption. Also, SRAM memories are applied in many small budget applications for example cache memories. That is, strict constraints for energy-consumption;

speed and area are our main concern. We examined the 6T, RHD11T, RHD13T, DICE and RHD10T SRAM cells. By the attained results displayed in Table 2 about area overhead, we will state that, RHD10T SRAM cell occupies low area compared with considered rad-hard SRAM cells. Along with simulations in 65 nm, various available technologies were used for assessment and comparison of power and delay factors. Figure 7 shows results for 32, 45, 65 nm technology simulations.

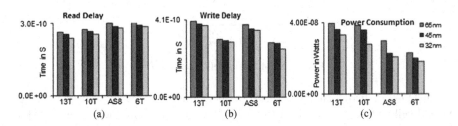

Fig. 7. Assessment for power and delay factors in different technologies: (a) read delay; (b) write delay; (c) power

6 Process Variations

The new challenge in design of VLSI circuits is their dependence on process variations. We assessed process variations effects on delay (average of write and read delays) and power consumption of RHD10T SRAM cell and compared with 6T SRAM cell. MC simulations were carried out on RHD10T SRAM cell and 6T to evaluate the process variation of design parameters. In the simulations performed, we applied a normal distribution for transistor dimensions (W/L) and threshold voltage (Vth. The performed simulations were carried out using Synopsys HSpice with 65-nm Predictive Technology Model (PTM) library [15]. Power consumption and delay (average of read and write delay) were evaluated for RHD10T and 6T SRAMs under process variations. We made 1000 MC simulations. 20% maximum deviation was allowed for W/L as well as for Vth. A normal distribution with maximum 20% deviation was allowed for each MC simulation, two values were allotted for every transistor for its Vth and W/L deviations. Figures 8 and 9 displays the effects of Vth and W/L variation on delay and power for 6T and RHD10T SRAM cells. In Fig. 8 the horizontal axis displays the variation of the maximum allowed deviation from original value. And vertical axis displays the effect of process variation on delay and power of the RHD10T and 6T SRAM cells in the associated set of MC simulations [21, 22]. Figures 8 and 9 determines that, process variation (on Vth and W/L) can impact both power consumption and delay of SRAM cells. Still, for all the circumstances, the sensitivities of RHD10T SRAM cells aren't higher compared to 6T SRAM cell.

In Fig. 8 average standard deviation of power consumption because of W/L variation, is 0.07 and 0.06 on 6T and RHD10T cells. This effect gets respectively 0.04 and 0.02 average standard deviation of delay for the mentioned cells. Also, in Fig. 9 the average standard deviation of power from the initial value resulted by Vth variation is

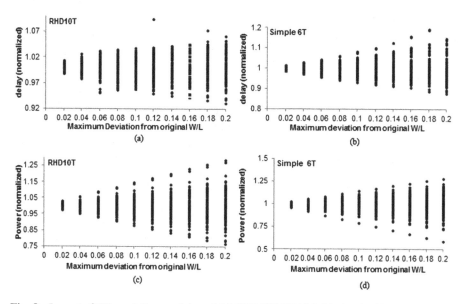

Fig. 8. Impact of WL variation on delay of (a) RHD10T SRAM, (b) simple 6T, and Impact of WL variation on power of (c) RHD10T SRAM, (d) simple 6T

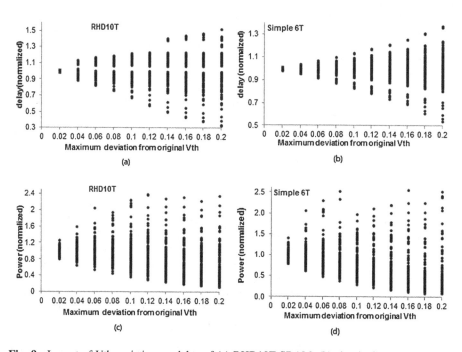

Fig. 9. Impact of Vth variation on delay of (a) RHD10T SRAM, (b) simple 6T, and impact of Vth variation on power of (c) RHD10T SRAM, (d) simple 6T

0.55 and 0.45 for 6T and RHD10T cells respectively. Also, the delay of 6T and RHD10T cells has an average deviation of 0.19 and 0.15 for Vth variations.

7 Conclusion

A new SRAM cell namely RHD10T is developed in this paper. After simulation, analysis and comparison of the proposed rad-hard SRAM cell and previous reported rad-hard SRAM cells we can conclude that our RHD10T cell is more robust towards SEU and SEMU by providing smaller area overhead.

References

1. Berkeley predictive technology model. http://www.eas.asu.edu/ptm/
2. Alouani, I., Elsharkasy, W.M., Eltawil, A.M., Kurdahi, F.J., Niar, S.: AS8-static random access memory (SRAM): asymmetric SRAM architecture for soft error hardening enhancement. IET Circuits Dev. Syst. **11**(1), 89–94 (2017)
3. Amusan, O.A., Massengill, L.W., Baze, M.P., Bhuva, B.L., Witulski, A.F., Black, J.D., Balasubramanian, A., Casey, M.C., Black, D.A., Ahlbin, J.R., et al.: Mitigation techniques for single-event-induced charge sharing in a 90-nm bulk CMOS process. IEEE Trans. Dev. Mater. Reliab. **9**(2), 311–317 (2009)
4. Calin, T., Nicolaidis, M., Velazco, R.: Upset hardened memory design for submicron CMOS technology. IEEE Trans. Nucl. Sci. **43**(6), 2874–2878 (1996)
5. Chengye, Z., Zhuangsi, W.: A novel reliable SEU hardened latch to mitigate multi-node charge collection. In: IET International Conference on Information Science and Control Engineering 2012 (ICISCE 2012), pp. 1–4, December 2012
6. Detcheverry, C., Dachs, C., Lorfevre, E., Sudre, C., Bruguier, G., Palau, J., Gasiot, J., Ecoffet, R.: SEU critical charge and sensitive area in a submicron CMOS technology. IEEE Trans. Nucl. Sci. **44**(6), 2266–2273 (1997)
7. Dodd, P.E., Massengill, L.W.: Basic mechanisms and modeling of single-event upset in digital microelectronics. IEEE Trans. Nucl. Sci. **50**(3), 583–602 (2003)
8. Duzellier, S., Ecoffet, R.: Recent trends in single-event effect ground testing. IEEE Trans. Nucl. Sci. **43**(2), 671–677 (1996)
9. Fazeli, M., Ahmadian, S.N., Miremadi, S.G., Asadi, H., Tahoori, M.B.: Soft error rate estimation of digital circuits in the presence of multiple event transients (METs). In: Design, Automation & Test in Europe Conference & Exhibition (DATE), pp. 1–6. IEEE (2011)
10. Heijmen, T., Giot, D., Roche, P.: Factors that impact the critical charge of memory elements. In: 12th IEEE International On-Line Testing Symposium, IOLTS 2006, p. 6. IEEE (2006)
11. Katsarou, K., Tsiatouhas, Y.: Soft error interception latch: double node charge sharing SEU tolerant design. Electron. Lett. **51**(4), 330–332 (2015)
12. Kelin, L.H.H., Klas, L., Mounaim, B., Prasanthi, R., Linscott, I.R., Inan, U.S., Subhasish, M.: Leap: layout design through error-aware transistor positioning for soft-error resilient sequential cell design. In: 2010 IEEE International Reliability Physics Symposium (IRPS), pp. 203–212. IEEE (2010)
13. Lin, S., Kim, Y.B., Lombardi, F.: A 11-transistor nanoscale CMOS memory cell for hardening to soft errors. IEEE Trans. Very Large Scale Integr. (VLSI) Syst. **19**(5), 900–904 (2011)

14. Lin, S., Kim, Y.B., Lombardi, F.: Analysis and design of nanoscale CMOS storage elements for single-event hardening with multiple-node upset. IEEE Trans. Dev. Mater. Reliab. **12**(1), 68–77 (2012)
15. Rajaei, R., Asgari, B., Tabandeh, M., Fazeli, M.: Design of robust SRAM cells against single-event multiple effects for nanometer technologies. IEEE Trans. Dev. Mater. Reliab. **15**(3), 429–436 (2015)
16. Rajaei, R., Tabandeh, M., Fazeli, M.: Low cost soft error hardened latch designs for nanoscale CMOS technology in presence of process variation. Microelectron. Reliab. **53**(6), 912–924 (2013)
17. Rajaei, R., Tabandeh, M., Fazeli, M.: Soft error rate estimation for combinational logic in presence of single event multiple transients. J. Circuits Syst. Comput. **23**(06), 1450091 (2014)
18. Rajaei, R., Tabandeh, M., Fazeli, M.: Single event multiple upset (SEMU) tolerant latch designs in presence of process and temperature variations. J. Circuits Syst. Comput. **24**(01), 1550007 (2015)
19. Reviriego, P., Maestro, J.A., Flanagan, M.F.: Error detection in majority logic decoding of euclidean geometry low density parity check (EG-LDPC) codes. IEEE Trans. Very Large Scale Integr. (VLSI) Syst. **21**(1), 156–159 (2013)
20. Seifert, N., Ambrose, V., Gill, B., Shi, Q., Allmon, R., Recchia, C., Mukherjee, S., Nassif, N., Krause, J., Pickholtz, J., et al.: On the radiation-induced soft error performance of hardened sequential elements in advanced bulk CMOS technologies. In: 2010 IEEE International Reliability Physics Symposium (IRPS), pp. 188–197. IEEE (2010)
21. Wang, W.: RC hardened FPGA configuration SRAM cell design. Electron. Lett. **40**(9), 525–526 (2004)
22. Yang, F.L., Saleh, R.A.: Simulation and analysis of transient faults in digital circuits. IEEE J. Solid-State Circuits **27**(3), 258–264 (1992)

Automation of Timing Quality Checks and Optimization

Dubakula Ketavanya[✉] and Anand D. Darji

Electronics Engineering Department,
S. V. National Institute of Technology, Surat, India
d.ketavanya@gmail.com, add@eced.svnit.com

Abstract. Due to the smaller geometries and increasing complexity, verification stage became critical phase. Development of CAD tools in every stage of design flow is necessary in technology growth. Each design quality check we can't check manually due to its more complexity. So, automating these checks leads to less effort and more productivity. The primary focus is on introducing auto fixer for weak driver and sequential loops to get better design quality in terms of timing so that the design will operate at required frequency in all corners and providing a utility to generate stage delay by providing constant slope at the input of the stage which is useful in case of p-shift (process shift).

Keywords: CAD · Optimization · Performance · Automation · Timing · Weak driver · Sequential loops

1 Introduction

In VLSI technology, the number of transistors integrated on a single chip is increasing drastically compared with the previous year designs. This number is still increasing in order to design a device which has small area, high speed and less power consumption. Due to the additional features from one generation to next generation the complexity of design increases. As going into the deep sub-micron regions (DSM) non ideal behavior will eventually occur which impacts the speed and leads to significant leakage and etc. This may impact the functional behavior of device. Therefore, these effects should be taken into account during the entire design flow in every stage [2]. Due to this considerations, chip design became very complex and it is far beyond human ability. So, computer aided design tools came into very large scale integrated technology design flow.

The design of complex circuit is simplified by CAD tools in different stages of design flow like to connect blocks together, check the functionality of circuit and layout, then optimize manually or by using automation techniques. We can find the critical issues in the design which may happen after manufacturing of device using CAD tools [9]. Performance is the main criteria based on which product quality depends. Performance verification of the design can be done in signoff stage by applying automation techniques. Here, Performance is in terms of speed/clock frequency. Now-a-days verification or testing phase of design takes most of the time. So, EDA CAD tools will take a main role to reduce the verification time and to increase the product life cycle.

© Springer Nature Singapore Pte Ltd. 2019
S. Rajaram et al. (Eds.): VDAT 2018, CCIS 892, pp. 348–356, 2019.
https://doi.org/10.1007/978-981-13-5950-7_30

1.1 Motivation

In semiconductor industry, productivity and demand is based on the device performance. So performance verification of any design before the manufacturing is advisable and necessary. Industries spent most of their effort in verification stage in order to achieve more productivity. Performance is measured in terms of speed, clock frequency mostly. To achieve required speed every timing path should met timing constraints and hence timing quality checks are needed before sign off of any design to prevent silicon failures. These are measured in terms of quality checks. Automation of design quality checks is necessary in industries as verifying at each sub-micron device manually is tedious [4]. In this paper, the focus is on weak driver auto fixer and sequential loop fixer. In addition to these auto fixers, need of additional information of design during process shift. Process shift means shifting the design from one process node to other process node (going to smaller nodes). This additional information provides the stage characteristics for some parameterized slope at the input of every stage.

1.2 Literature Review

Complex designs require greater design productivity to achieve reasonable costs, this is where EDA tools place a great role. Not only this, as the geometries are getting smaller and clock frequency increases on-chip interconnect issues will dominate. While generating EDA tools crucial factors which are to be considered are wiring congestion, routing, crosstalk and coupling noise, transmission line effects [7], power consumption, reliability, yield and their relation. It is noticed that automatic synthesis can make progress and improve design productivity. As the abstraction level increases verification tools, analysis tools, design entry and representation all progress, and to create a combined mature methodology a new design technology node is created. The gap between semiconductor productivity and design productivity is referred as productivity gap [8]. The main factor that has contributed to the gap is verification problem. To resolve this, design technology innovators will have to raise the abstraction of the specification language and they have to develop different methodologies to deal with new abstraction [3].

2 Proposed Method

In semiconductor industry, design starts with RTL code then synthesis and then checking the timing constraints i.e. setup checks and hold checks. If any checks fails apply some algorithms to meet timing.

2.1 Basic Block Diagram

One of the issue mostly seen in the design is sequential loops. When a signal traverses a transparent path and gets back to the same pin with the same mode and transitions it identifies a loop and stops the path propagation. A loop is considered as critical if the arrival time after the loop is worse than the arrival time at the beginning of the loop. So, fixing the critical loops should be done before fixing setup and hold checks. Process shift is referred as shifting the design to smaller process nodes which means one technology node to other technology node. According to Moore's law, the same silicon area would accommodate more and more number of transistors. To achieve this, transistor size is gradually getting reduced. A utility is developed to generate more information like what will be the characteristics of different nodes in the design if the slope at input node is some parameterized value. This will be useful in studying the design at every stage (Fig. 1).

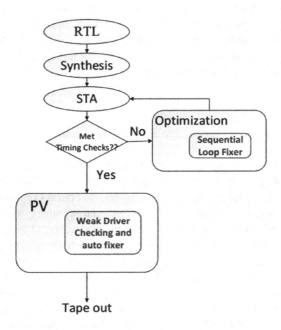

Fig. 1. Basic block diagram of proposed method

2.2   Design Checks and Auto Fixer

In digital designs, Sequential loops exists which can affect the performance of entire design. Sequential loop is defined as when a signal propagates through a transparent path and gets back to the same pin with the same mode and transitions. These loops can be critical if the arrival time after the loop is worse than the arrival time at the beginning of the loop. Need of fixing is necessary to achieve better performance. Other issue which frequently occurs is a weak driver issue. Based on driving strength of a cell we can define particular cell is weak driver or strong driver. Driving strength is the capacity of a cell to drive other cell which is connected to its output. Different sizes of standard cells have different parameters. The parameters which are affecting the timing are capacitance, size, slope, number of fan-outs, cells connected at output of driver.

3   Implementation

3.1   Weak Driver and Its Auto Fixer

This fixer is needed in order to avoid silicon failures. Weak Driver could not pass the signal when it has more output capacitance. Searching of weak drivers in a complex design is done by sourcing TCL script in the flow of STA tool. After getting the reports, auto fixer is applied on the design to eliminate weak drivers and flow is back annotated to STA to get updated reports. This is implemented in performance verification stage as a design quality check.

Algorithm to Get the Weak Drivers in a Design

- Load the design and get all the nets
- For each net, take the driver cell and get the capacitance value at its output node and z (width of the cell)
- Calculate c/z value. Make threshold limit separately for data nodes and clock nodes
- Check load capacitance (C_{eff}) and compare with threshold limit
- If it is greater than threshold limit then report those cells along with its properties like slope, margin, fan out

Algorithm of Weak Driver Auto Fixer

- Get the list of weak drivers in the design
- For each cell, based on its properties like fan-out and load capacitance select the standard cell from library
- Run partial timing analysis on that path
- Compare the results with previous reports and check if margin is improved or not

Figure 2 describes the algorithms to know about weak drivers in the design and its auto fixer to avoid weak drivers in the design.

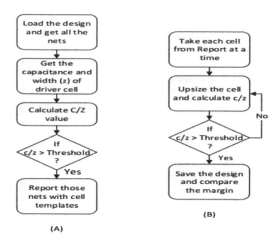

Fig. 2. Flowchart to (A) get weak drivers in the design (B) fix weak driver issue

3.2 Sequential Loop Fixer

Paths that go through critical loop (i.e. paths that have some common part with a loop) are not reported correctly in the setup report. Typically, if there are paths that go through a loop and cause negative margin at a sampling point, then at least one of them will be reported in the setup report but not necessarily the worst one. Also the report of this path will not have clear indication that it goes through a loop. Therefore it is recommended to first look at the critical loops report and fix the loops, and only then looks at the setup report.

Consider a sequential loop shown in Fig. 3 which has three latches and some combinational logic in between them. Due to the transparency of the latch, data should reach in 1.5 cycles as each latch takes half cycle to complete. Consider at first latch, the data captured just after transparency region and has 100 ps arrival time. In next iteration if the arrival time becomes 120 ps then it will consider worst case value as 120 ps and margin becomes more negative. It should be taken care first by reducing the delay of the cells in the path that means making data path is fasten which will leads to hold violation. So, fix should be done if high positive margin is present.

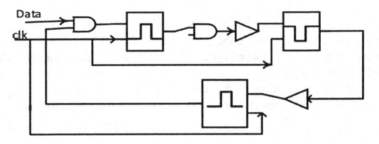

Fig. 3. Example of sequential loop circuit

Algorithm of Sequential Loop Fixer

- Get all the paths of sequential loops
- Check the hold margin at the sampling edge; if it has high positive margin then upsize the combinational cells in that path
- Do the partial analysis
- Repeat this process to all the critical paths
- Source the file which is generated after all the iterations
- Placement and Routing
- Save the design and perform STA (Fig. 4)

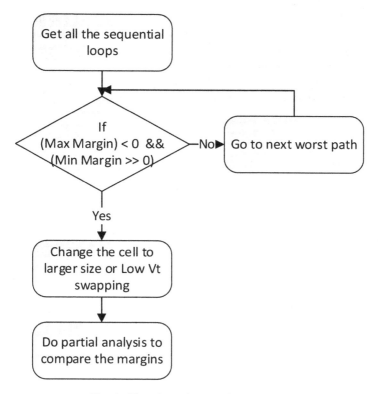

Fig. 4. Flowchart of sequential loop fixer

3.3 P-Shift Flow

As it is explained the proposed method section, If we consider a path, each and every element (RC, standard cell, etc.) needs to be scaled to get the required specifications in case of P-shift process. In addition to the setup and hold reports, stage report can be generated through automation. Stage report means cell delay and interconnect delay. At every node, it calculates the different properties like delay, number of fan-outs, receiver slope, p2p resistance and other properties for constant slope at input of the every stage. This will be helpful for designers to analyze different paths hence converging timing paths.

4   Results and Analysis

These auto fixers algorithm is sourced to STA tools by Tcl scripting and compares the results with reference reports. Each auto fixer is tested separately within the flow and results are in the favor of efficient design. We have tested this algorithms on a complex design and compared the margin and delay of different paths.

354   D. Ketavanya and A. D. Darji

Figure 5 shows the comparison results of setup margin check for all the paths in the design. In the Fig. 5, x-axis represents the range of margin in Nano seconds and y-axis represents number of paths in that margin range. From the Fig. 5, green color bars indicates the number of timing paths. We have noticed from Fig. 5(A) that number of paths which have margin from −40 ps to −20 ps are reduced from 2 to 0 and margin from −20 ps to −10 ps are reduced from 30 to 7 using the proposed algorithm in the flow (Fig. 6).

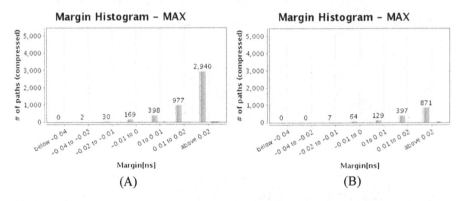

Fig. 5. Max margin report (A) without auto fixer (B) with auto fixer (Color figure online)

From the Fig. 5(B), it is shown that number of paths having negative hold slack are slightly reduced that means almost no change. Because this algorithm applied on the paths having positive hold slack. The number of paths having positive hold slack is drastically increased due to the usage of positive slack time in the algorithm. From the Fig. 5(B), the number of paths having hold slack more than 20 ps is decreased from 587 to 390 paths.

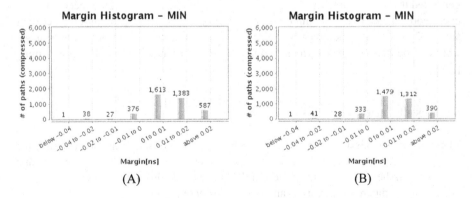

Fig. 6. Hold margin report (A) without auto fixer (B) with auto fixer

Table 1 contains No. of sequential loops in two different designs before sourcing the auto fixer and after fixing the auto fixer. Percentage of eliminating sequential loops is around 95% in execution block which contains approximately 15k cells and 55% in memory block which contains 16k cells approximately.

Table 1. Comparison of sequential loops before and after fixing

Design	No. of sequential loops before fixing	No. of sequential loops after fixing	Fix percentage	Execution time
Design 1	71	4	~95%	~10 min
Design 2	76	34	~55%	~5 min

5 Conclusions

In this paper, the timing closure of a design in various design stages and How the Static Timing Analysis is done for different timing paths are described. While using optimization techniques make sure that there is no effect on the overall design performance in terms of area and timing. The timing quality checks are very important, because as the complexity of the circuit increases, on chip variations and silicon failures can be seen. Automation algorithm described in this work has provided capability to the standard STA tool flow for resolving weak driver and sequential loop issues. It was seen that while fixing the sequential loops, there is a chance of getting hold violations due to fastening of data path, the proposed sequential loop auto fixer is robust enough to take care of such hold violations also. So, it will be very useful to the designers in fixing the hold violations and sequential loops simultaneously. The main constraints for this method is that the automation algorithm proposed is still dependent on the STA tool for the initial data base regarding weak drivers and sequential loops in the design. Thus, the quality of resolving the issues is dependent on STA tool to some extent. This can be resolved by carefully selecting the tool with better standards to start with.

References

1. Charles, J., Jassi, P., Ananth, N., Sadat, A., Fedorova, A.: Evaluation of the Intel Core i7 turbo boost feature. In: Proceedings of the IEEE International Symposium on Workload Characterization (IISWC), pp. 188–197, October 2009
2. Kim, J., Papaefthymiou, M.C., Neves, J.L.: Parallelizing post placement timing optimization. In: Proceedings of IEEE IPDPS, pp. 10–19 (2006)
3. Hemani, A.: Charting the EDA roadmap. IEEE Circuits Devices Mag. **20**(6), 5–10 (2004)
4. Farrahi, A.H., Hathaway, D.I., Wang, M., Sarrafiadeh, M.: Quality of EDA CAD tools: definitions, metrics and directions. In: Proceedings of the IEEE International Symposium on Quality Electronic Design, pp. 395–405, March 2000
5. Roy, J.A., Markov, I.L.: High-performance routing at the nanometer scale. IEEE Trans. Comput. Aided Des. Integr. Circuits Syst. **27**(6), 1066–1077 (2008)

6. Chen, H.-C., Du, D.C., Liu, L.-R.: Critical path selection for performance optimization. IEEE Trans. Comput. Aided Des. **12**(2), 185–195 (1993)
7. Deutsch, A., et al.: When are transmission-line effects important for on-chip interconnections? IEEE Trans. Microw. Theory Tech. **45**(10), 1836–1846 (1997)
8. Murai, Y., Ayala, C.L., Takeuchi, N., Yamanashi, Y., Yoshikawa, N.: Development and demonstration of routing and placement EDA tools for large scale adiabatic quantum-flux-parametron circuits. IEEE Trans. Appl. Supercond. **27**(6), 1–9 (2017)
9. Keshavarzi, A., et al.: Leakage and process variation effects in current testing on future CMOS circuits. IEEE Des. Test Comput. **19**(5), 36–43 (2002)
10. Sze, C.N., Alpert, C.J., Hu, J., Shi, W.: Path-based buffer insertion. IEEE Trans. Comput. Aided Des. Integr. Circuits Syst. **26**(7), 1346–1355 (2007)

Analog Circuits and Devices

Temperature Insensitive Low-Power Ring Oscillator Using only n-type Transistors

Nishtha Rai$^{(\boxtimes)}$ ⓘ, Vaibhav Agarwal ⓘ, Nishtha Wadhwa ⓘ, Bhawna Tiwari ⓘ, and Pydi Ganga Bahubalindruni ⓘ

Department of Electronics and Communication Engineering, Indraprastha Institute of Information Technology, New Delhi, India
{nishtha16101,vaibhav16119}@iiitd.ac.in

Abstract. A low-power five stage current starved ring oscillator which is robust against temperature variations is being presented in this work. The proposed work has been designed using only n-type transistors and therefore, can easily be adapted to amorphous oxide TFTs which have unstable p-type transistors. The ring oscillator uses temperature compensation biasing circuit, which contains a novel bootstrap op-amp. The biasing circuit generates constant bias voltage to make current starved ring oscillator insensitive to temperature variations. The proposed circuit simulations were done in Cadence Virtuoso on standard 180 nm CMOS technology with a supply voltage of 1.8 V. This circuit has shown a frequency of oscillation around 235.8 MHz and a power delay product of 0.139 pJ. The phase noise of designed ring oscillator is −98.532 dBc/Hz. It shows 3.73% variations in frequency over a temperature range from −40 °C to 125 °C. Since oxide TFT's are also n-type FET's (Field Effect Transistors), the proposed design can be directly adapted to this emerging post-silicon technology, which finds potential applications in smart packaging, bio-medical and wearable systems [1].

Keywords: TFT · Current starved ring oscillator · Temperature-insensitive circuit · Power delay product · Bootstrap opamp

1 Introduction

In the recent years, transparent TFT (thin-film transistor) technologies, such as a-GIZO [2] and ZnO [3] are gaining significant advances in several electronics and bio-medical applications. The attention is shifting towards these emerging technologies because of the ease of fabrication at room temperature [4]. These oxide TFT technologies show superior electrical characteristics compared to other low-temperature based TFTs, such as, a-Si:H and organic semiconductor based transistors [5]. Therefore they are gaining significant interest in flexible electronics [6]. Smart packaging is one of the interesting application of this technology as

Supported by IIIT Delhi.

S. Rajaram et al. (Eds.): VDAT 2018, CCIS 892, pp. 359–369, 2019.
https://doi.org/10.1007/978-981-13-5950-7_31

it allows direct integration of oxide electronics on the packaging material either glass or plastic to convey important information to the consumer, namely, storage conditions (temperature or pressure). In order to make this smart packaging compact and self contained to avoid external connections, all the required biasing voltages and clocks should be generated on-chip [7]. It is extremely important to design low-power circuits which are insensitive to temperature variations. As a first step a low-power temperature insensitive on-chip clock generator design is being addressed in this work. However, the major limitation for circuit design is the absence of a stable complementary (p-type) device, thus, they are confined only to n-type devices.

Oscillators are an inherent part of many analog and digital systems. The most commonly used oscillators are crystal oscillators, ring oscillators and LC tank oscillators. Crystal oscillators are well known for their precise clock frequency which is stable against process, voltage and temperature variations. Nevertheless, crystal oscillators lack the tuning capability and also have limited frequency range [8] which imposes limitation for on-chip integration. Another type of oscillators are LC tank oscillators, which have higher frequency range but they consume larger area on the chip due to inductors being bulky. LC oscillators also suffer from narrow frequency tuning range. Ring oscillators on the other hand are preferred due to their wide tuning range, compact design, and low power consumption [9].

One advantage of ring oscillators is that with the scaling of MOS devices, higher frequency operations can be easily achieved. Despite all the above mentioned advantages, ring oscillators suffer from poor frequency stability due to dependence of MOS transistors on temperature variations. As a result ring oscillators oscillate at different frequencies in different environments. This prohibits the use of ring oscillators as a frequency reference in analog and digital systems that have tight specifications of frequency accuracy. Therefore, it is necessary to compensate the effect of temperature on ring oscillators.

This work proposes a high-speed and temperature insensitive current starved ring oscillator. Due to unstable p-type transistors in TFT transistors, only n-type transistors are used throughout the design. In addition, these n-type TFT's exhibit almost similar like characteristics as those of n-type CMOS transistors, thus, the proposed work can be directly adapted to TFT technology for the afore mentioned applications. The ring oscillator is realized using current starved technique to lower the power consumption. In the current starved technique, current supplied to each inverter is restricted to promise low power consumption [10]. The inverter is realized using a NMOS driver and a diode connected NMOS load. A constant bias voltage circuit has also been proposed, which is insensitive to temperature variations that helps the ring oscillator to compensate against temperature variations. The complete circuit operates on 1.8 V supply voltage in 180 nm CMOS technology. Simulation results show only a 3.73% variation in frequency over a temperature range from $-40\,^\circ$C to $125\,^\circ$C.

The rest of the paper is organized as follows. Section 2 explains the proposed circuit design and its operating principle. Section 3 presents the simulation results along with the discussions. The conclusions are drawn in Sect. 4.

2 Design Concept and Circuit Techniques

A conventional ring oscillator consists of an odd number of inverting stages connected in a loop. The output of the last stage is fed as input to the first stage and then the chain continues. This violates the Barkhausen criteria for stability which causes the circuit to oscillate [11]. The frequency of oscillation, f_{osc} depends on the number of stages, 'n' and the delay time, 't_d' of each inverter. A factor of 2 is also there due to the fact that a complete cycle requires a high to low and low to high transitions.

$$f_{osc} = \frac{1}{2 * n * t_d} \qquad (1)$$

Thus, the frequency of oscillation of a n-stage ring oscillator can be set by varying the delay time of each stage of inverter and by varying the number of stages. To lower the power consumption of a ring oscillator, current starved technique is used in which the current is restricted and the transistors operate near sub-threshold region. In order to generate a precise frequency using ring oscillator which is insensitive to temperature variations, a temperature compensation bias technique has been proposed in this work that improves the ring oscillator's tolerance to temperature variations.

2.1 Ring Oscillator Using Current Starved Technique

As discussed in the previous paragraph that the frequency of oscillation of ring oscillator depends on the delay of each inverter stage which can be controlled by controlling the current flowing through the inverter. A controlled voltage (V_{bias}) decides the on-resistances of both driver and load of the inverter, which in turn controls the current, responsible for charging or dis-charging the capacitor looking at the output of each stage of inverter [12]. The current in inverter stage is proportional to V_{bias}, whereas, the delay of each stage is inversely proportional to V_{bias}.

The inverter stage comprising of only NMOS transistors is realized using a NMOS driver (T1) and a NMOS diode connected load (T2) shown in Fig. 1. The current starved technique uses current sink and current source, wherein current sink is realized with NMOS being controlled by V_{bias} while current source is a diode connected NMOS load. Thus, the current through the inverter is controlled by V_{bias}. Another advantage of using this technique is that the ring oscillator can be tuned for a wide range of frequencies by controlling the V_{bias}.

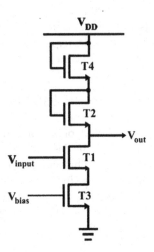

Fig. 1. Circuit schematic of single stage of current starved inverter.

2.2 Temperature Compensation Bias Circuit

As described in the previous section, the ring oscillator is triggered by a bias voltage. If that bias voltage is made constant with respect to temperature variations then a constant current will flow through the chain of inverters in the ring oscillator [11]. Since there is no or minimal dependence of delay on temperature variations because of the constant current, the ring oscillator will be stable at the desired frequency.

To generate a voltage that remains constant with temperature, two voltages having opposite temperature coefficients are averaged together with appropriate weights to generate zero temperature coefficient (ZTC) [11]. Desired reference voltage can be generated using (2), where both V_1 and V_2 vary in opposite direction with respect to temperature.

$$V_{bias} = \alpha_1 * V_1 + \alpha_2 * V_2 \tag{2}$$

In the above equation, α_1 and α_2 should be such that they follow below equation

$$\alpha_1 \frac{\delta V_1}{\delta T} + \alpha_2 \frac{\delta V_2}{\delta T} = 0 \tag{3}$$

For getting this type of behaviour, BJT's are mostly preferred but the proposed work consists of only NMOS transistors. To replicate the behaviour of BJT, NMOS transistors need to be operated in sub-threshold region so that their drain currents have exponential relation with the bias voltage, similar to BJT's or diodes. The circuit for generation of constant voltage is shown in Fig. 2, where T1 and n multiple copies of T2, all are always in sub-threshold region. Both T1 and T2 are unit sized transistors. Constant bias voltage for the circuit shown in

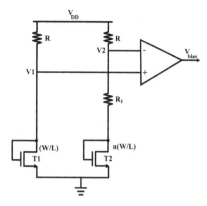

Fig. 2. Generation of temperature independent bias voltage

Fig. 2 is shown in (4), where $(V_T * \ln(n))$ is the difference between the V_{GS} voltages of the two transistors T1 and T2. To satisfy (3), $\delta V_{GS}/\delta T = -0.65$ mV/$^\circ$C and $\delta V_T/\delta T = +0.087$ mV/$^\circ$C.

$$V_{bias} = (V_{GS2}) + (\alpha_2 * (V_T * ln(n))(1 + \frac{R}{R_1})) \tag{4}$$

To satisfy (3), $(\alpha_2 \ln(n))(1 + \frac{R}{R1})$ value after solving the equation comes out to be 7.47 (where n is the number of multiple copies of T2 shown in Fig. 2 and V_T is the thermal voltage). Assuming n to be 4, R will be 4.38 times the value of R1. In this circuit, the op-amp senses the two voltages V_1 and V_2 and then drives the top terminals of the two resistors (R) to ensure that V_1 and V_2 are almost equal. The desired bias voltage insensitive to temperature variations is obtained at the output of the op-amp. The op-amp shown in Fig. 3 needs to have a high gain to ensure nearly equal voltages at the input of op-amp. To design a high gain op-amp with only NMOS transistors is a big challenge, so a novel technique has been proposed in this work.

A high-gain op-amp that uses capacitive bootstrapping is shown in Fig. 3. It has two stages, the first is a differential pair stage which has capacitive bootstrapping across each branch. The first stage also has common mode feedback (CMFB) that increases the common mode rejection ratio (CMRR) of the op-amp. For the op-amp to have high gain, single stage is not sufficient. Thus, to increase the gain of the op-amp and to get a single ended output, another stage is proposed, that provides gain as well as single ended conversion. At DC, transistors T5 and T6 are in cutoff, hence, their effective off resistances are significantly high. Due to the transistor intrinsic capacitance, T5(T6) can be viewed as a parallel combination of a resistor and a capacitor. Also, T1, T2, T3 and T4 should always be in saturation for the proper functionality of the op-amp.

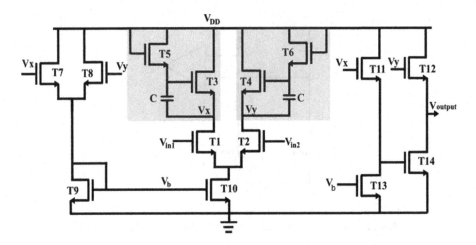

Fig. 3. Circuit schematic of op-amp with capacitive bootstrapping and common mode feedback used in Fig. 2.

For high frequencies, the capacitor (C) acts as a short circuit and the feedback factor (A_f) becomes one. However, A_f depends on the aspect ratio of transistor T5(T6) and C.

$$A_f = \frac{v1}{v0} = \frac{1}{1 + \frac{C_{off}}{C}} \tag{5}$$

From (5), it is clear that as C_{off} increases, A_f decreases, which leads to reduction in the overall amplifier gain.

$$A = -\frac{g_{m1}}{(1 - A_f)g_{m3} + g_{ds1} + g_{ds3}} * (\frac{1}{2}(\frac{g_{m14}}{g_{m12}} + 1)) \tag{6}$$

When A_f is approximately equal to one, high gain for the op-amp is achieved and in order to ensure a stable behavior, A_f must always be less than one. R_L value can be computed using (7).

$$R_L = \frac{1}{(1 - A_f)g_{m3} + g_{ds3}} \tag{7}$$

All the blocks described above are integrated and the overall proposed circuit is shown in Fig. 4. Temperature compensated bias circuit provides a constant V_{bias} voltage which is insensitive to temperature variations. This constant V_{bias} voltage is fed to the sink NMOS transistor of the current starved ring oscillator. Thus, a constant current flows through the inverter stages.

3   Simulation Results

Schematic of temperature insensitive current starved ring oscillator is shown in Fig. 4. The complete circuit uses only NMOS transistors and is implemented in Cadence Virtuoso in standard 180 nm CMOS technology. High-gain op-amp using only NMOS transistors has also been simulated in 180 nm with a supply voltage of 1.8 V.

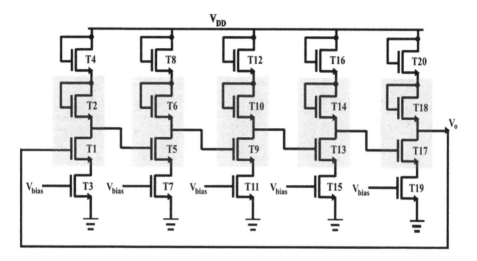

Fig. 4. Circuit schematic of proposed work where V_{bias} is generated by temperature compensation bias circuit.

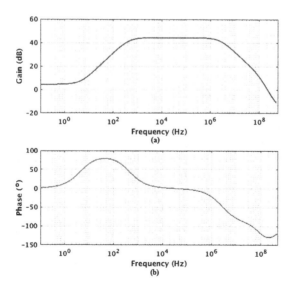

Fig. 5. Frequency response of proposed op-amp (a) Gain plot, (b) Phase plot.

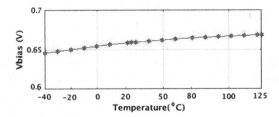

Fig. 6. Variations in bias voltage over a temperature range from $-40\,^{\circ}$C to $125\,^{\circ}$C.

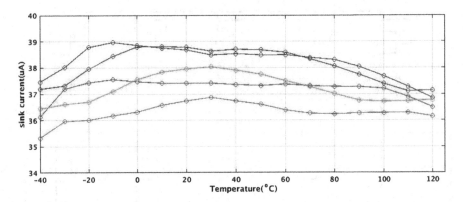

Fig. 7. Variations in NMOS sink (as depicted in Fig. 4) current over a temperature range from $-40\,^{\circ}$C to $125\,^{\circ}$C.

The op-amp is a two pole system such that for low frequencies, capacitor C acts as an open circuit and a low gain is achieved equivalent to any normal op-amp realized using only NMOS transistors. On the other hand as frequency increases, the same capacitor bootstraps the voltage at the load transistor and increases the gain significantly. The proposed op-amp has a gain of 44 dB with a unity gain bandwidth of 218 MHz and a phase margin of 52°, which can be seen from Fig. 5. The circuit uses CMFB and has a CMRR (common mode rejection ratio) of 83 dB. Thus, the op-amp has a very high gain and is stable at the same time using only NMOS transistors.

This op-amp is used in temperature compensation circuit which also has NMOS transistors instead of BJT's. The constant voltage generated using this circuit is 658.9 mV. When this circuit is simulated for a temperature range from $-40\,^{\circ}$C to $125\,^{\circ}$C, it is observed from Fig. 6 that the bias voltage varies by only 3.5% over the simulated temperature range. The constant bias voltage is fed to the current starved ring oscillator. Due to less variation in the bias voltage, the sink current flowing through the NMOS transistor of the current starved ring oscillator shows only 2.77% variation over the simulated temperature range, which can be seen from Fig. 7.

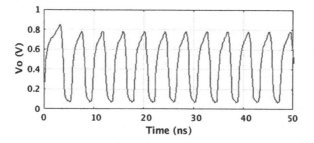

Fig. 8. Proposed ring oscillator oscillations.

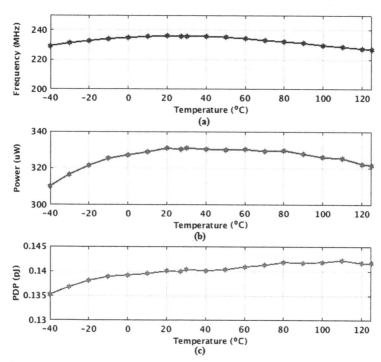

Fig. 9. (a) Frequency, (b) Power and (c) PDP variations with respect to temperature.

As a result, the variation in frequency of oscillation with this bias voltage with respect to temperature is 3.73%, which is very low and can be seen from Fig. 9(a). The variation in average power consumed by the circuit with respect to temperature is 6.06% and can be seen from Fig. 9(b). The variation in PDP (power delay product), defined as the product of average power and the gate delay t_d is 3.57% and can be seen from Fig. 9(c).

4   Conclusion

The proposed work presents a ring oscillator that uses current starved technique to lower the power consumption which is further integrated with a temperature compensated constant bias voltage circuit. Throughout the work only n-type transistors are used so that they can be easily adapted in a-GIZO TFT technology that doesn't support stable p-type transistors. Since both are FET's, it is expected that similar behaviour can be observed in TFT technology. Due to lack of TFT models that can predict temperature dependent behavior, the proposed work has been simulated using Cadence Virtuoso on standard 180 nm CMOS technology to show the successful operation of proposed work. Simulation results show that the ring oscillator is oscillating at 235.8 MHz frequency (Fig. 8) with a 3.73% variation of frequency over a temperature range from $-40\,°C$ to $125\,°C$. The current starved ring oscillator shows a power consumption of $330.2\,\mu W$ at 235.8 MHz. The phase noise of designed ring oscillator is $-98.532\,dBc/Hz$. The temperature-insensitive, low-power, and stable frequency design of the proposed ring oscillator, makes it a potential aspirant in several applications that include bio-medical applications and smart packaging.

Acknowledgment. The authors would like to thank everyone who helped with this work, including the project by early career research grant ECR/2017/000931.

References

1. Bahubalindruni, P., Tavares, V.G., Barquinha, P., Martins, R., Fortunato, E.: High-gain topologies for transparent electronics. In: Eurocon 2013, pp. 2041–2046, July 2013
2. Raiteri, D., et al.: A 6b 10MS/s current-steering DAC manufactured with amorphous Gallium-Indium-Zinc-Oxide TFTs achieving SFDR > 30dB up to 300kHz. In: 2012 IEEE International Solid-State Circuits Conference, pp. 314–316, February 2012
3. Bahubalindruni, G., et al.: Basic analog circuits with a-GIZO thin-film transistors: modeling and simulation. In: 2012 International Conference on Synthesis, Modeling, Analysis and Simulation Methods and Applications to Circuit Design (SMACD), pp. 261–264, September 2012
4. Kim, B., et al.: New depletion-mode IGZO TFT shift register. IEEE Electron Device Lett. **32**, 158–160 (2011)
5. Nomura, K., Ohta, H., Takagi, A., Kamiya, T., Hirano, M., Hosono, H.: Room-temperature fabrication of transparent flexible thin-film transistors using amorphous oxide semiconductors. Nature **432**(7016), 488–492 (2004)
6. Hwang, C., Bibyk, S., Ismail, M., Lohiser, B.: A very low frequency, micropower, low voltage CMOS oscillator for noncardiac pacemakers. IEEE Trans. Circuits Syst. I: Fundam. Theory Appl. **42**, 962–966 (1995)
7. Bahubalindruni, P., Tavares, V.G., de Oliveira, P.G., Barquinha, P., Martins, R., Fortunato, E.: High-gain amplifier with n-type transistors. In: 2013 IEEE International Conference of Electron Devices and Solid-state Circuits, pp. 1–2, June 2013

8. Yang, P., Xia, T., Li, H., Wang, X.: A temperature insensitive ring oscillator for low power RF communications. In: 2013 IEEE International Conference on Green Computing and Communications and IEEE Internet of Things and IEEE Cyber, Physical and Social Computing, pp. 1804–1809, August 2013
9. Zhang, X., Apsel, A.B.: A low-power, process-and- temperature- compensated ring oscillator with addition-based current source. IEEE Trans. Circuits Syst. I: Regul. Pap. **58**, 868–878 (2011)
10. Wang, Y., Chan, P.K., Li, K.H.: A compact CMOS ring oscillator with temperature and supply compensation for sensor applications. In: 2014 IEEE Computer Society Annual Symposium on VLSI, pp. 267–272, July 2014
11. Razavi, B., Rosa, J.: Design of Analog CMOS Integrated Circuits. Tsinghua University Press Co., Ltd, Beijing (2001)
12. Suman, S., Sharma, K.G., Ghosh, P.K.: Analysis and design of current starved ring VCO. In: 2016 International Conference on Electrical, Electronics, and Optimization Techniques (ICEEOT), pp. 3222–3227, March 2016

Low-Power Switched Operational Amplifier Using a-InGaZnO TFTs

Suprateek Shukla[1(✉)], Bhawna Tiwari[1], Nishtha Wadhwa[1],
Pydi Ganga Bahubalindruni[1], and Pedro Barquinha[2]

[1] Department of Electronics and Communication Engineering,
Indraprastha Institute of Information Technology, New Delhi, India
{suprateek16115,bpganga}@iiitd.ac.in
[2] CENIMAT/I3N, Departamento de Ciência dos Materiais,
Faculdade de Ciências e Tecnologia, FCT,
Universidade Nova de Lisboa and CEMOPUNINOVA, Caparica, Portugal

Abstract. This paper proposes a novel low-power operational amplifier (OPAMP) using amorphous indium-gallium-zinc-oxide thin-film transistors (a-IGZO TFTs). By introducing dynamic operation, power consumption of the proposed OPAMP has been significantly reduced without compromising with other design parameters like gain, slew rate etc. In addition, common mode feedback (CMFB) and internal frequency compensation have been used to ensure good common mode rejection ratio (CMRR) and stability of the OPAMP, respectively. In order to demonstrate the proposed idea, low power OPAMP is designed and simulated using in-house a-IGZO TFT model in Cadence Virtuoso. Circuit simulations have been carried out at a supply voltage and device channel length of 10 V and 20 μm, respectively. From simulations, a gain of 30 dB and unity gain bandwidth of 106.8 kHz with a phase margin of 63° were noticed. The power consumed by the proposed OPAMP is 146.8 μW, which is significantly lower compared to the OPAMPs implemented with various TFT technologies. The proposed OPAMP circuit would find potential applications in various real-world large area applications that need flexible electronics with low-power consumption like bio-medical and wearable devices.

Keywords: TFT · a-IGZO TFT · Low-power design · OPAMP · CMFB · CMRR

1 Introduction

Amorphous oxide semiconductor, mainly, amorphous indium-gallium-zinc oxide (a-IGZO) based thin-film transistors (TFTs) are gaining significant attention in various real-world applications [1–4]. This is because of its superior field-effect mobility, transparency and uniformity over large areas and better stability compared to other TFT technologies such as organic-TFT and a-Si:H. Due to its low temperature fabrication process, circuits can be fabricated on different substrates including glass [5–7], plastic [8,9] and paper [10] allowing flexible electronics which find potential applications in wearable technology, IOT (Internet of Things) [11] and NFCs (Near Field Communication) [12]. These applications demand low-power circuit design to enhance the life time of the circuits/systems. Many circuits including operational amplifiers [13–15], multipliers [6], data converters [16] and display driving circuits [17,18] have been reported with a-IGZO TFTs. However, very limited work has been reported to address low-power consumption [11].

Typically, a-IGZO TFTs based circuits require high supply voltages hence, consume significant power. One way to reduce power is to reduce bias current or keeping the devices in sub-threshold region of operation. However, that will limit the maximum gain in analog circuits and the switching speed in digital circuits. Another major limitation is lack of stable reproducible complimentary (p-type) device, which does not allow direct implementation of low-power CMOS design techniques. Therefore, new design schemes should be investigated that can counter act technology challenges (lack of stable p-type TFTs) and ensure low power consumption without compromising with circuit performance.

Operational amplifiers are critical blocks in most of the analog and mixed signal circuits. Though many amplifiers have been reported with a-IGZO TFTs [13–15], none of the designs attempt to minimize the power consumption. Then, this work presents a low power OPAMP whose power is significantly reduced by making the circuit dynamic. In the proposed OPAMP, the bias current is dynamically applied to the circuit using switches, which in turn, reduces the static power significantly. In addition, CMFB has been used to ensure good CMRR and control the output signal common-mode value against process variations. Moreover, stability of the OPAMP is maintained using internal frequency compensation. The low power operation of the proposed opamp is demonstrated using in-house a-IGZO TFT [19] model in cadence Virtuoso at a supply voltage and device channel length of $10\,V$ and $20\,\mu m$, respectively. It can be observed that the proposed circuit is able to provide low power consumption when compared to state of art work, without compromising with performance metrics.

Rest of the paper is organized as follows: Sect. 2 provides a brief description about a-IGZO TFT's principle of operation. Section 3 presents the proposed low power OPAMP. Results and discussion were shown in Sect. 4 and finally conclusions are drawn in Sect. 5.

2 *a*-IGZO TFT Technology

a-IGZO TFT is a three terminal device. The device structure used for designing and simulating OPAMP, in this work, follows the bottom staggered gate structure of a-IGZO TFT as shown in Fig. 1. As can be seen, the structure has gate, source and drain terminals, like MOS structure. But, here, a-IGZO semiconductor layer is deposited over dielectric, separately, which is responsible for channel formation and conduction. Since substrate is an insulator, body effect and bulk related capacitance can be neglected.

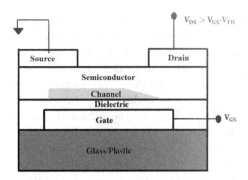

Fig. 1. Device structure of flexible a-IGZO TFT [20].

The device has $5\,\mu m$ overlap between source-gate and drain-gate layers. It has a threshold voltage of 1.6 V. With its operation being similar to MOSFET, Level-1 MOSFET model is used to approximate the a-IGZO TFT device behavior for circuit analysis purpose. However, since the semiconductor of the current device is amorphous in nature, charge carrier distribution and density of states in energy bands are different compared to the conventional crystalline silicon [21,22]. Therefore, an accurate in-house IGZO model has been used for circuit simulations [23,24].

3   Proposed Low Power OPAMP Design

One major limitation of a-IGZO technology in circuit design is absence of p-type TFTs. Another limitation is inferior electron mobility (approximately 10–$30\,cm^2/V.s$) compared to crystalline silicon, which makes the design of high-gain OPAMPs very challenging.

3.1   OPAMP with Positive Feedback Topology

In order to get high gain with amorphous oxide TFTs, differential amplifier formed by transistor $M0, M1, M2, M3$ and $M4$, and positive feedback load introduced by transistors $M5, M6, M7, M8$ and $M9$ (which is presented in the dotted box of Fig. 2) [25] is used as a first stage of the opamp. From small signal analysis, feedback gain of the positive feedback circuit is given by Eq. 1. Here, g_m is transconductance of transistors, and r_o is output impedance of active load transistors in saturation.

$$A_f = g_{m8}\left(\frac{1}{g_{m6}}\|r_{o8}\|r_{o6}\right) \approx \frac{g_{m8}}{g_{m6}} \tag{1}$$

$$R_{out} = r_{o3}\|\frac{1}{g_{m3}(1 - A_f)} \tag{2}$$

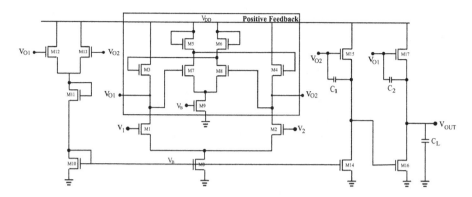

Fig. 2. Schematic of OPAMP with positive feedback topology.

R_{out} = effective active load impedance sensed by the driver transistors (M1 or M2).

As the gain of the feedback stage (A_f) becomes larger than unity, load provides a negative resistance as can be seen in Eq. 2. Thus, increasing gain while jeopardizing amplifier's stability. Therefore, there is a need to maintain the positive feedback gain slightly below unity, so that stability is maintained along with gain boosting. Effective voltage gain ($A_{v_{diff}, \, effective}$) of the differential pair is given by Eq. 3, which shows that the gain of the differential pair with positive feedback has been significantly improved in comparison with the gain ($A_{v_{diff}}$) of diode connected topology, given by Eq. 4.

$$A_{v_{diff}, \, effective} = g_{m1}\left(\frac{g_{m6}}{1 - A_f}\|r_{o1}\|r_{o3}\right) \approx g_{m1}(r_{o1}\|r_{o3}), \; For \; A_f < 1 \quad (3)$$

$$A_{v_{diff}} = g_{m1}\left(\frac{1}{g_{m3}}\|r_{o1}\|r_{o3}\right) \approx \frac{g_{m1}}{g_{m3}} \quad (4)$$

Further the differential to single ended conversion stage consisting of $M14, M15, M16$ and $M17$ transistors, is biased along with miller compensation in such a way that secondary pole is shifted away from the imaginary axis and phase margin is improved. In addition, a common mode feedback (CMFB) is introduced by $M0, M10, M11, M12,$ and $M13$, which improves the common mode rejection ratio (CMRR) of the circuit, without hampering the output voltage swing. $M12$ and $M13$ sense the change in output common-mode voltage and change the bias voltage V_B. This changes the bias current of differential amplifier and counteracts any change in output common-mode voltage. The voltage gain (A_v) of designed OPAMP is given by Eq. 5.

$$A_v = g_{m1}\left(\frac{g_{m6}}{1 - A_f}\|r_{o1}\|r_{o3}\right)\left(\frac{g_{m16}}{g_{m17}} + 1\right) \approx g_{m1}(r_{o1}\|r_{o3})\left(\frac{g_{m16}}{g_{m17}} + 1\right) \quad (5)$$

Device dimensions are mentioned in Table 1. The positive feedback stage introduced requires biasing, this increases the bias current requirement, thus increasing the power overhead. Moreover, if the bias current is reduced, slew rate of the OPAMP is significantly effected.

Table 1. Aspect ratios of transistors

Transistor	Aspect ratio (μm/μm)
M0	80/20
M1	160/20
M2	160/20
M3	160/20
M4	160/20
M5	160/20
M6	160/20
M7	200/20
M8	200/20
M9	40/20
M10	40/20
M11	40/20
M12	40/20
M13	40/20
M14	40/20
M15	80/20
M16	80/20
M17	160/20

3.2 Proposed Low Power Switched OPAMP

Proposed circuit ensures low-power consumption (i.e. negligible static power) through dynamic biasing. Schematic of the proposed low power switched OPAMP is shown in Fig. 3. The basic concept used by switched OPAMP is that we can switch an OPAMP by turning on/off its bias current using switch S_1 that is controlled by "*Clock*" signal. When "*Clock*" is high, switch S_1 pulls down V_B close to ground such that the bias transistors $M0, M9, M10$, and $M14$ are turned off, hence switching off the OPAMP. Apart from switching off the bias currents in OPAMP, Miller compensation capacitors, C_1 and C_2, might discharge through $M16$ in the off state. To avoid loss of charge, switch S_2 is placed such that load is isolated from the circuit. In addition, switch S_3 disconnects source terminal of $M16$ from ground to prevent possible discharging of the compensation capacitors in off state. Both switches S_2 and S_3 are controlled by "$\overline{Clock}$" signal which is 180° out off phase with "*Clock*" signal. However, switches S_1, S_2, and S_3 should be properly synchronized, if not, floating node will be created at the output terminal which might cause discharging of load capacitor through

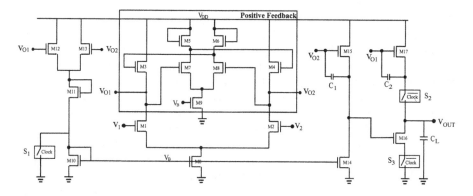

Fig. 3. Schematic of low power switched OPAMP.

transistor, $M16$. This can slow down the speed of operation. Thus, by maintaining proper synchronization between the switches, it is possible to reduce power consumption while maintaining the desired response of the OPAMP.

4   Simulation Results

To evaluate the proposed design, simulations have been carried out in Cadence Virtuoso Spectre simulator using in-house a-IGZO TFT model [19]. Power supply of 10 V and a load capacitance of 2 pF are used for simulations.

The frequency response of the switched OPAMP is shown in Fig. 4. The bode plot for gain shows a voltage gain of 30 dB and unity gain bandwidth of 106.8 kHz

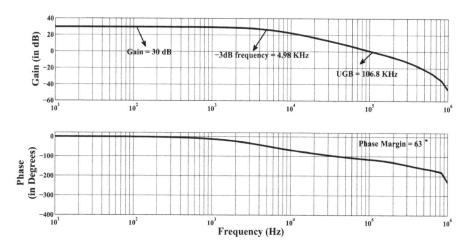

Fig. 4. Frequency response of switched OPAMP. A gain of 30 dB was observed with a phase margin of 63°, a 3 dB bandwidth of 4.98 kHz and unity gain bandwidth of 106.8 kHz.

with a 3 dB bandwidth of 4.98 kHz. A phase margin of 63° is observed from the phase plot. Transient response of the proposed circuit is shown in Fig. 5. The response is obtained for 100 Hz input sinusoidal signal, at a clock frequency of 1 kHz. Here we observe that output is following input as long as clock is low, which shows successful operation of proposed circuit.

Further, to find power consumption, rms value of transient current from the supply was calculated and subsequently multiplied by supply voltage. An rms power of 146.8 μW was observed. Since, we are switching on/off the circuit, dc power for this circuit is almost zero. A CMRR of 59.7 dB, PSRR of 39.64 dB were observed, with rising slew of 0.03534 V/μs and falling slew of 0.071 V/μs.

The performance of the proposed low power switched OPAMP using TFT is summarized in Table 2 and its compared with the already reported works in

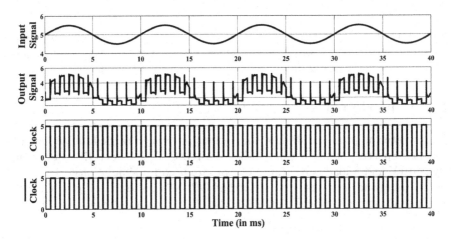

Fig. 5. Transient response of the switched OPAMP, for an input signal of frequency of 100 Hz.

Table 2. Performance metrics of OPAMP

Metrics	Values
DC Gain [dB]	30
BW [kHz]	4.98
Unity gain frequency [kHz]	106.8
PM [Deg.]	63
Power [μW]	146.8
Load [pF]	2
CMRR [dB]	59.7
PSRR [dB]	39.64
Rising slew rate [V/μs]	0.03534
Falling slew rate [V/μs]	0.07114

Table 3. Performance comparison

Circuit	[15]	[13]	[14]	[26]	[27]	This work
Technology	a-IGZO TFT	a-IGZO TFT	a-IGZO TFT	a-Si TFT	pMOS OFET	a-IGZO TFT
OPAMP topology	nMOS diode	Pseudo-CMOS	Positive feedback	Positive feedback	Positive feedback	Switched OPAMP with positive feedback
DC supply voltage [V]	5	5	6	25	15	10
Load [pF]	-	15	15	20	6	2
DC Gain [dB]	18.7	22.5	19	42.5	20	30
BW [kHz]	108	5.6	30.5	≈0.7	<0.03	4.98
Unity gain frequency [kHz]	472	31	450	30	2	106.8
PM [Deg.]	≈−19	≈20	88	-	65	63
Power [μW]	900	160	6780	3550	225	146.8

Table 3. From the table it can be concluded that proposed design has shown very low power consumption among all the designs. It should be noted that device models considered a total overlap of 10um from gate to source and drain. By scaling down the device dimensions and overlap area, frequency of operation can be improved further.

5 Conclusion

In this paper, we have presented TFT based low power switched OPAMP. The proposed switched OPAMP consumes less power, compared to other OPAMPs reported in the same TFT technology, without compromising on typical OPAMP design parameters. We have implemented OPAMP with positive feedback in the input differential pair to improve gain along with CMFB to improve CMRR, using a-IGZO TFT. The proposed OPAMP consumes 146.8 μW power, with 30 dB gain and a unity gain frequency of 106.8 kHz with 63° phase margin.

Acknowledgment. This work is supported by early career research grant with project ref. ECR/2017/000931. The publication is an outcome of the R&D work undertaken project under the Visvesvaraya PhD Scheme of Ministry of Electronics & Information Technology, Government of India, being implemented by Digital India Corporation.

References

1. Gong, N., et al.: 58.2: distinguished paper: implementation of 240Hz 55-inch ultra definition LCD driven by a-IGZO semiconductor TFT with copper signal lines. In: SID Symposium Digest of Technical Papers, vol. 43, pp. 784–787. Wiley Online Library (2012)
2. Kwon, J.Y., et al.: Bottom-gate gallium indium zinc oxide thin-film transistor array for high-resolution AMOLED display. IEEE Electron Device Lett. **29**(12), 1309–1311 (2008)

3. Lee, J.-H., et al.: 42.2: world's largest (15-inch) XGA AMLCD panel using IGZO oxide TFT. In: SID Symposium Digest of Technical Papers, vol. 39, pp. 625–628, Wiley Online Library (2008)
4. Riedl, T., Gorrn, P., Kowalsky, W.: Transparent electronics for see-through AMOLED displays. J. Disp. Technol. **5**(12), 501–508 (2009)
5. Bahubalindruni, P.G., et al.: Analog circuits with high-gain topologies using a-GIZO TFTs on glass. J. Disp. Technol. **11**(6), 547–553 (2015)
6. Bahubalindruni, P.G., et al.: InGaZnO thin-film-transistor-based four-quadrant high-gain analog multiplier on glass. IEEE Electron Device Lett. **37**(4), 419–421 (2016)
7. Tian, Y., et al.: Low-temperature fabrication of fully transparent IGZO thin film transistors on glass substrate. In: 2012 IEEE International Conference on Electron Devices and Solid State Circuit (EDSSC), pp. 1–3. IEEE (2012)
8. Mativenga, M., Choi, M.H., Choi, J.W., Jang, J.: Transparent flexible circuits based on amorphous-indium-gallium-zinc-oxide thin-film transistors. IEEE Electron Device Lett. **32**(2), 170–172 (2011)
9. Münzenrieder, N., et al.: Flexible a-IGZO TFT amplifier fabricated on a free standing polyimide foil operating at 1.2 MHz while bent to a radius of 5 mm. In: 2012 IEEE International Electron Devices Meeting (IEDM), pp. 5–2. IEEE (2012)
10. Steckl, A.J.: Circuits on cellulose. IEEE Spectrum **50**(2), 48–61 (2013)
11. Ozaki, H., Kawamura, T., Wakana, H., Yamazoe, T., Uchiyama, H.: 20-μw operation of an a-IGZO TFT-based RFID chip using purely NMOS "active" load logic gates with ultra-low-consumption power. In: 2011 Symposium on VLSI Circuits (VLSIC), pp. 54–55. IEEE (2011)
12. Köbler, F., Koene, P., Leimeister, J., et al.: Touch'n'Document-A nutrition management system on an NFC-tagged TFT-display (paper 117). In: 4th Proceedings of the International Conference on Health Informatics (2011)
13. Ishida, K., et al.: 22.5 dB open-loop gain, 31 kHz GBW pseudo-CMOS based operational amplifier with a-IGZO TFTs on a flexible film. In: 2014 IEEE Asian Solid-State Circuits Conference (A-SSCC), pp. 313–316. IEEE (2014)
14. Shabanpour, R., et al.: A 70° phase margin OPAMP with positive feedback in flexible a-IGZO TFT technology. In: 2015 IEEE 58th International Midwest Symposium on Circuits and Systems (MWSCAS), pp. 1–4. IEEE (2015)
15. Zysset, C., Münzenrieder, N., Petti, L., Büthe, L., Salvatore, G.A., Tröster, G.: IGZO TFT-based all-enhancement operational amplifier bent to a radius of 5 mm. IEEE Electron Device Lett. **34**(11), 1394–1396 (2013)
16. Raiteri, D., et al.: A 6b 10MS/s current-steering DAC manufactured with amorphous gallium-indium-zinc-oxide TFTs achieving SFDR>30dB up to 300kHz. In: 2012 IEEE International Solid-State Circuits Conference Digest of Technical Papers (ISSCC), pp. 314–316. IEEE (2012)
17. Kim, B., et al.: Highly reliable depletion-mode a-IGZO TFT gate driver circuits for high-frequency display applications under light illumination. IEEE Electron Device Lett. **33**(4), 528–530 (2012)
18. Kim, B., et al.: A depletion-mode In-Ga-Zn-O thin-film transistor shift register embedded with a full-swing level shifter. IEEE Trans. Electron Devices **58**(9), 3012–3017 (2011)
19. Bahubalindrun, P., Tavares, V., Barquinha, P., De Oliveira, P.G., Martins, R., Fortunato, E.: InGaZnO TFT behavioral model for IC design. Analog Integr. Circ. Sig. Process. **87**(1), 73–80 (2016)
20. Bahubalindruni, P.G.M.: Analog/Mixed signal circuit design with transparent oxide semiconductor thin-film transistors (2014)

21. Bae, M., et al.: Analytical models for drain current and gate capacitance in amorphous InGaZnO thin-film transistors with effective carrier density. IEEE Electron Device Lett. **32**(11), 1546–1548 (2011)
22. Ghittorelli, M., Torricelli, F., Colalongo, L., Kovács-Vajna, Z.M.: Accurate analytical physical modeling of amorphous InGaZnO thin-film transistors accounting for trapped and free charges. IEEE Trans. Electron Devices **61**(12), 4105–4112 (2014)
23. Bahubalindruni, P.G., et al.: Transparent current mirrors with a-GIZO TFTs: neural modeling, simulation and fabrication. J. Disp. Technol. **9**(12), 1001–1006 (2013)
24. Bahubalindruni, P.G., et al.: a-GIZO TFT neural modeling, circuit simulation and validation. Solid-State Electron. **105**, 30–36 (2015)
25. Calzolari, P., Masetti, G., Severi, M.: Integrated n.m.o.s. operational amplifier for c.c.d. transversal filters. Electron. Lett. **15**(1), 29–31 (1979)
26. Tarn, Y.-C., Ku, P.-C., Hsieh, H.-H., Lu, L.-H.: An amorphous-silicon operational amplifier and its application to a 4-bit digital-to-analog converter. IEEE J. Solid-State Circuits **45**(5), 1028–1035 (2010)
27. Marien, H., Steyaert, M.S., van Veenendaal, E., Heremans, P.: Analog building blocks for organic smart sensor systems in organic thin-film transistor technology on flexible plastic foil. IEEE J. Solid-State Circuits **47**(7), 1712–1720 (2012)

Threshold Voltage Investigation of Recessed Dual-Gate MISHEMT: Simulation Study

Preeti Singh[1], Vandana Kumari[2], Manoj Saxena[3],
and Mridula Gupta[1(✉)]

[1] University of Delhi South Campus, New Delhi, India
mridula@south.du.ac.in
[2] Maharaja Agrasen College, University of Delhi, New Delhi, India
[3] Deen Dayal Upadhyaya College, University of Delhi, New Delhi, India

Abstract. Simulation based investigation of Recessed Dual-Gate MISHEMT on sapphire substrate has been presented in this work using ATLAS simulation software. Various DC performance parameters such as: threshold voltage shift, drain current and transconductance has been compared for different gate combinations. Threshold voltage variation is observed to be nearly same if gate1 is recessed only or both gates are recessed. Positive shift in threshold voltage has been observed as the depth of gate recess is increased from 0 nm to 8 nm. Enhancement in negative junction depth from 10 nm to 18 nm results in the shift in threshold voltage towards positive i.e. -3.5 V to -2.45 V. This improvement in threshold voltage is due to the reduction in barrier thickness with increase in negative junction depth. DC performance has also been evaluated for the device with high-k gate dielectric such as HfO_2 and TiO_2 for non-recessed and recessed device. The parameters like gate oxide and work function variation results in the shift of threshold voltage from -3.5 V to 0 V in recessed Dual-Gate MISHEMT.

Keywords: Dual-Gate MISHEMT · TCAD simulation · Gate dielectric · Recessed gate

1 Introduction

Need for high power and high frequency solid state amplifiers for wireless communications have drawn interest of researchers to shift towards high-electron-mobility transistors [1]. The most suitable material for such application is AlGaN/GaN because of having distinct features like high saturation velocity, improved electron mobility and high blocking voltage [2]. However conventional AlGaN/GaN HEMTs are depletion mode devices while for reliable power-switching systems and to reduce circuit complexity, enhancement mode devices are preferred [3, 4].

Techniques generally used to achieve enhancement mode AlGaN/GaN HEMTs includes: (i) polarization charge engineering [5], (ii) gate workfunction engineering [6], (iii) amalgamation of back barrier [7], (iv) recessed gate [8] and (v) usage of fluorine ion implantation under the gate region [9, 10]. Altering the gate metallization leads to improved metal-semiconductor interface and hence small-signal performance [10, 11].

© Springer Nature Singapore Pte Ltd. 2019
S. Rajaram et al. (Eds.): VDAT 2018, CCIS 892, pp. 380–393, 2019.
https://doi.org/10.1007/978-981-13-5950-7_33

Double heterostructure results positive threshold voltage shift due to lower 2DEG charge density and negative polarization difference at channel/backbarrier interface but as a drawback drain current also decreases because of increased access resistance [10]. Fluorine ion implantation technique results in reduction of breakdown voltage if the device is exposed for longer duration [12]. Also, instability of fluorine ions result in performance deterioration when device is exposed to high-field or high temperature applications [13, 14]. Thus, out of various techniques, usage of recessed gate results in positive threshold voltage shift due to reduced barrier thickness under the gate and thus decreasing gate-to-channel separation [10, 15]. But as a tradeoff drain current of the device also deteriorates [16]. To enhance drain current as well as trans-conductance of the device, higher barrier thickness or mole fraction can be used. However, modulation efficiency decreases for larger barrier thickness and mobility of carriers is reduced due to increased scattering at higher mole fraction [17]. Also conventional AlGaN/GaN HEMTs exhibits high gate leakage current due to schottky gate contact. MISHEMTs results in lower gate leakage current but leads to negative shift of threshold voltage due to increased gate-to-channel separation and positive charge at the oxide-semiconductor interface [10]. To improve the power gain and RF characteristics of HEMTs after the insertion of gate dielectric, Dual-Gate MISHEMTs have been reported [18]. The subthreshold performance of Dual-Gate HEMTs with recessed gate having different barrier thicknesses have been studied experimentally by Yang et al. [19] and result shows positive shift of threshold voltage upto 1.2 V and improvement in gate control ability and reduction in off-state leakage current due to the introduction of second gate [19]. However the device used in this study is schottky gated with SiC substrate, without AlN nucleation layer and interface charge. Gate dielectric engineering is another technique to improve DC performance of the device. Recently, normally-ON AlGaN/GaN MIS-HEMT with HfON/SiON stack as gate dielectric have been reported with high I_{ON}/I_{OFF} ratio of order of 10^{11} and subthreshold slope of 77 mV/decade have been reported [20].

In present work Dual-Gate AlGaN/GaN MISHEMTs along with the recessed gate architecture have been explored to achieve positive threshold voltage. The depth of the recessed gate has been varied from 0 nm to 8 nm to optimize the device performance and also compared with non-recessed Dual-Gate MISHEMTs. Also, it has been observed that DC performance is almost identical for the devices having Gate1 recessed or both gates recessed. However, the amalgamation of recessed gate also results in slight reduction in drain current. It has been observed that using TiO_2 gate dielectric and platinum gate in Dual-Gate MISHEMT, 0 V threshold voltage is achieved.

2 Methodology

Device structure of Dual-Gate MISHEMT consists of AlGaN barrier (22 nm) with mole fraction of x = 25%, AlN layer as spacer layer and nucleation layer, GaN cap layer and sapphire substrate. For passivation layer and gate dielectric layer, silicon nitride has been used. Gate metal (Ni) with workfunction of 4.6 eV has been used while that of source/drain ohmic contacts (Ti) is 4.33 eV. ATLAS device simulator has been used for simulations [21]. Shockley Read Hall (SRH) model have been used for modeling low charge concentration and field dependent mobility model for modeling velocity saturation effect for the said device. Dual-Gate AlGaN/GaN MISHEMT structure used for simulation has been calibrated with the device structure that has been reported experimentally by Gao et al. [18]. The output characteristic of simulated device with field plates matches well with that of experimental results as shown in Fig. 1. Further it is shown in the same figure that drain current is almost identical if field plates were removed. So, for further study, device structure without field plates has been used for simulations.

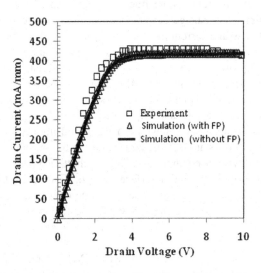

Fig. 1. Comparison of output characteristics of experimental data with simulation data (with Field Plates and without Field Plates) for Dual-Gate MISHEMT structures.

3   Results and Discussion

Figure 2(a)–(e) shows different gate combinations of Dual-Gate MISHEMT structure such as (i) Case I: Gate 1 and Gate 2 are connected, (ii) Case II: Gate 1 is connected to Source, (iii) Case III: Gate 2 is connected to Source, (iv) Case IV: Gate 1 is connected to Drain or (v) Case V: Gate 2 is connected to Drain.

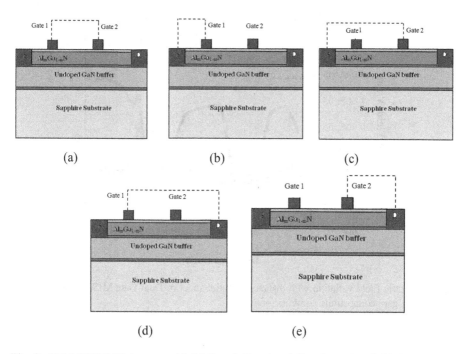

Fig. 2. DG-MISHEMT structure with (a) Case I: Gate 1 and Gate 2 connected, (b) Case II: Gate 1 connected to Source, (c) Case III: Gate 2 connected to Source, (d) Case IV: Gate 1 connected to Drain and (e) Case V: Gate 2 connected to Drain.

The distribution of electric field and electron velocity along channel region for different cases of gate combinations for DG-MISHEMTs is shown in Figs. 3 and 4. Electric field is higher for case I and case V near the drain side as compared to other cases. Case II, III and IV shows almost similar behavior of electric field and electron velocity.

Threshold voltages are almost identical in all five cases (i.e. varying from -4.4 V to -4.6 V) as shown by transfer characteristics in Fig. 5. But drain current is different for all the devices as gate position determines the drain-to-source resistance. This resistance is determined by gate-source distance (L_{GS}), gate-drain distance (L_{GD}) and channel resistance under the gate region [22]. Also electric field in source-gate region determines the injection electron velocity in the channel and thus impacts drain current [23]. Case I exhibits minimum g_{mpeak} due to lower electron velocity and high electric field as compared to all other cases resulting in reduced I_{ON} of 292 mA/mm.

Transconductance (g_{mpeak}) is nearly same for cases III and V (i.e. 117.27 mS/mm and 118.7 mS/mm respectively) but higher than other cases as shown in Fig. 6. This is because, Gate 1 is the controlling gate in these device structures and smaller L_{GS} results in reduced electric field in source-gate region leading to high electron velocity and thus higher drain current of 415 and 426 mA/mm respectively. In cases II and IV, smaller L_{GD} results in increase in electric field at gate-drain edge leading to reduction in I_{ON} and g_{mpeak}. Thus, by comparing all five cases, it is observed that case III is superior amongst all cases studied and has been used for further investigation in this work.

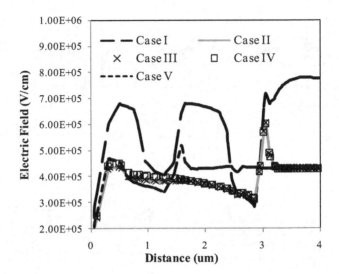

Fig. 3. Electric Field variation with distance along channel of Dual-Gate MISHEMT structures for different gate connections combinations.

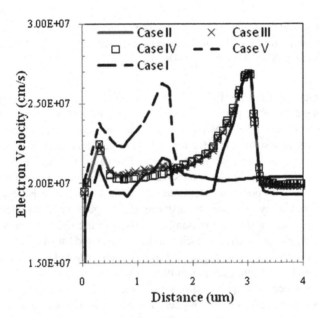

Fig. 4. Electron velocity variation with distance along channel of Dual-Gate MISHEMT structures for different gate connections combinations.

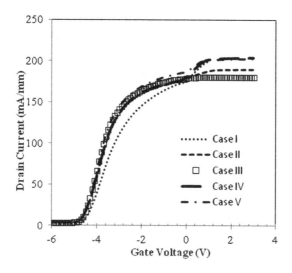

Fig. 5. Transfer characteristics for comparison of different gate combinations at $V_{DS} = 1$ V.

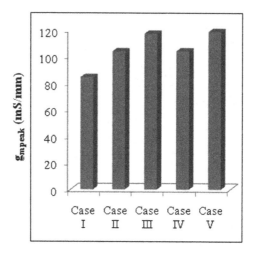

Fig. 6. Comparison of transconductance peak for DG-MISHEMT of different gate combinations at $V_{DS} = 1$ V.

Figure 7 demonstrates the I_D-V_{GS} plot for device with recessed and non-recessed gate at $V_{DS} = 1$ V. The non-recessed gate structure is the reference device with drain current and threshold voltage values calibrated with that of experimental results [18]. It is clearly shown that threshold voltage is shifted to -3.5 V for recessed Gate as compared to -4.6 V of reference DG-MISHEMT structure. Positive threshold voltage shift is due to reduced electron concentration in channel due to thinning of the barrier. Thus more gate bias is needed to start conduction and result in significant I_{ON}.

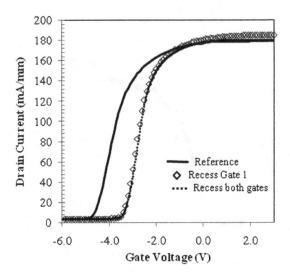

Fig. 7. I_D-V_{GS} plot for recessed and non-recessed gate for Dual-Gate MISHEMT at $V_{DS} = 1$ V.

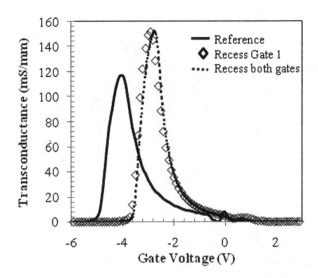

Fig. 8. Transconductance variation with V_{GS} for recessed and non-recessed gate for Dual-Gate MISHEMT at $V_{DS} = 1$ V.

Figure 8 shows transconductance variation with gate bias at $V_{DS} = 1$ V respectively of Dual-Gate MISHEMT with recessing only Gate 1 or both the gates and its comparison with reference structure. It has been observed that g_{mpeak} for recessing gate 1 only or both gates is 151 mS/mm (approximately) which is higher as compared to non-recessed structure. But there is reduction of 2DEG density of the channel after recessing the gate at higher drain bias and lower gate bias, which results in drain current reduction by 38% and 43% if only Gate1 is recessed or if both the gates are recessed respectively as compared to non-recessed device as shown in Fig. 9.

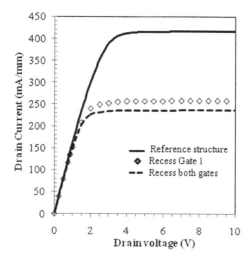

Fig. 9. I_D-V_{DS} plot for recessed and non-recessed gate for Dual-Gate MISHEMT at $V_{GS} = -2$ V.

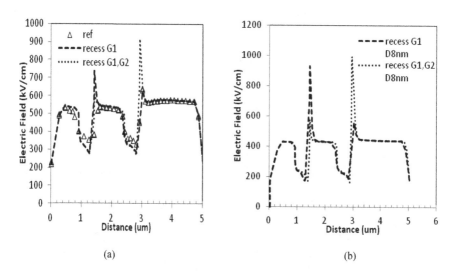

(a)   (b)

Fig. 10. Comparison of electric field distribution along channel for reference structure and devices with single recessed gate (G1) and both gates recessed having negative junction depth of (a) 10 nm and (b) 18 nm at $V_{DS} = 10$ V, $V_{GS} = -2$ V.

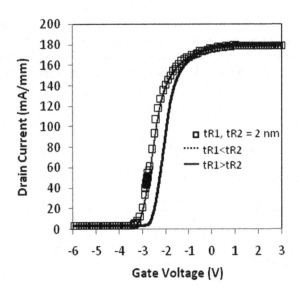

Fig. 11. Transfer characteristics for comparison of different gate depths for Gate1 (tR1) and Gate 2 (tR2) at V_{DS} = 1 V. (tR1 = recessed gate depth for gate 1; tR2 = recessed gate depth for gate 2).

Electric field distribution along the channel for non-recessed and recessed Dual-Gate MISHEMT having negative junction depths of 10 nm and 18 nm respectively is shown in Fig. 10(a) and (b) at V_{DS} = 10 V and V_{GS} = −2 V. It is evident that, recessing gate 1 (G1) results in electric field peak of 736 kV/cm at its gate-drain edge of G1 while recessing both the gates G1 and G2 results in electric field peak of 915 kV/cm at gate-drain edge of G2. Figure 11 shows the impact on transfer characteristics of DG-MISHEMT if recess depths for both the gates are same or different. It is observed that higher recess depth for gate 1 (i.e. tR1 = 6 nm and tR2 = 2 nm) results in improved performance in terms of higher threshold voltage shifts (i.e. V_{TH} = −2.7 V) as compared to the results for tR1 = 2 nm and tR2 = 6 nm and symmetric recess depth (i.e. tR1 = tR2 = 2 nm).

Figures 12 and 13 shows the performance comparison (i.e. drain current and transconductance respectively) of asymmetric gate length for gate1 (L_{G1}) and gate2 (L_{G2}) for Dual-Gate MISHEMTs. Three different cases are taken into consideration such as: *Case* (i) L_{G1} = 0.5 μm, L_{G2} = 1 μm; *Case* (ii) L_{G1} = 1 μm, L_{G2} = 0.5 μm; *Case* (iii) L_{G1} = 0.5 μm; L_{G2} = 0.5 μm. For all the cases, threshold voltage is nearly same i.e. −4.6 V, but the ON-current is slightly higher when L_{G1} = 1 μm. Transconductance of 110 mS/mm is achieved if gate length of either G1 or G2 is increased to 1 μm as compared to that of reference structure with L_{G1} and L_{G2} of 0.5 μm as 117 mS/mm. Although, if L_{G1} is increased to 1 μm, enhancement in drain current (by 13%) is observed as compared to reference structure i.e. L_{G1} = L_{G2} = 0.5 μm.

Now considering only gate 1 is recessed for further study and recess depth has been varied upto 8 nm in Fig. 14(a) and (b). Enhancement in negative junction depth leads to positive shift of threshold voltage from −3.5 V to −2.45 V as shown in Fig. 14(a)

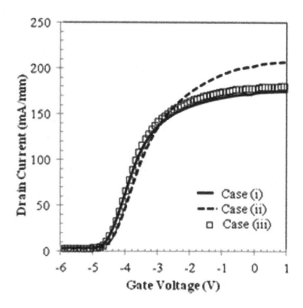

Fig. 12. Drain current variation with gate voltage for asymmetric gate lengths at $V_{DS} = 1$ V.

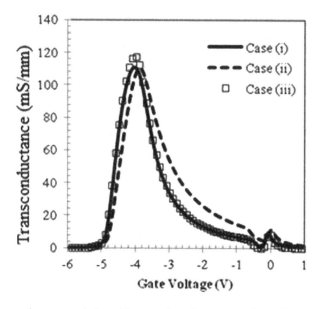

Fig. 13. Transconductance variation with gate voltage for asymmetric gate lengths at $V_{DS} = 1$ V.

i.e. an improvement of 47% (approximately) of threshold voltage as compared to non-recessed DG-MISHEMTs (reference structure). Also g_{mpeak} as shown in Fig. 14(b) is increased from 152 mS/mm to 182 mS/mm (approx.) for higher recess depth as the device is biased at lower drain bias i.e. $V_{DS} = 1$ V.

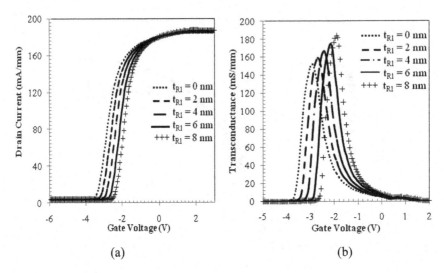

Fig. 14. (a) Transfer characteristics for recessing Gate 1 only for different gate depths for DG-MISHEMTs at $V_{DS} = 1$ V. (b) Transconductance variation with V_{GS} for recessing Gate 1 only for different gate depths for DG-MISHEMTs at $V_{DS} = 1$ V.

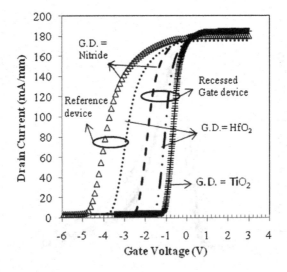

Fig. 15. I_D-V_{GS} plot for reference structure (non-recessed) and recessed gate device with different gate dielectric (G.D.) at $V_{DS} = 1$ V.

High-k gate dielectric is another method to improve the DC performance of the device further. Comparison of Dual-gate MISHEMT with HfO_2 gate insulator non-recessed and recessed is shown in Fig. 15. Positive shift in threshold voltage (nearly 24%) has been observed with HfO_2 gate dielectric for non-recessed MISHEMT as compared to reference structure. However, the shift in threshold voltage with Gate

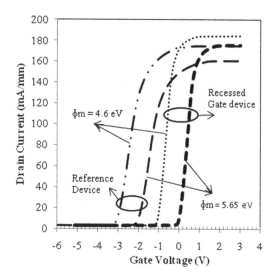

Fig. 16. I_D-V_{GS} plot to compare non-recessed (reference) device and recessed gate device with different workfunction values and TiO_2 as gate dielectric at $V_{DS} = 1$ V.

Dielectric (G.D.) permittivity is 38% in recessed gate DG-MISHEMT. Further improvement in device performance (shift in threshold voltage) has been achieved by using TiO_2 as gate dielectric. Thus, further optimization of gate work-function has been performed to achieve positive threshold voltage of the device in Fig. 16.

Figure 16 shows comparison of non-recessed and recessed device with TiO_2 as gate dielectric and different gate workfunction values. Positive shift of 1 V in threshold voltage has been achieved by using platinum gate instead of nickel in recessed gate DG-MISHEMT. Similar shift of threshold voltage has also been achieved with non-recessed gate device. But as a tradeoff drain current reduces by 9% (approximately) in non-recessed gate device which is only 5% in recessed gate DG-MISHEMT. Also the performance of the device is shifted from depletion mode to enhancement mode (i.e. 0 V threshold voltage) in recessed gate DG-MISHEMT by employing TiO_2 gate dielectric and platinum gate.

4 Conclusion

A simulation study is performed for Dual-Gate MISHEMT device structure using ATLAS device simulator. Device performance is optimized for different gate combinations. Recessing the gate upto depth of 8 nm results in positive threshold voltage shift of nearly 47% as compared to non-recessed device. Also it is observed that DC performance is almost identical if only Gate 1 is recessed or both the gates are recessed. Positive threshold voltage shift by 67% has been observed for recessed DG-MISHEMT with negative junction depth of 18 nm and HfO_2 as gate dielectric as compared to non-recessed device with nitride gate insulator. By using TiO_2 gate dielectric and platinum gate, threshold voltage of 0 V has been achieved through recessed Dual-Gate

MISHEMT. Also, the shift in the threshold voltage with gate dielectric and reduction in drain current with gate metallization is superior in recessed Dual-Gate MISHEMT compared to conventional Dual-Gate MISHEMT.

Acknowledgement. One of the authors, Preeti Singh, would like to thank Ministry of Science and Technology, Department of Science and Technology (SR/WOS-A/ET-143/2017), Government of India and University of Delhi for providing necessary financial assistance during the course of this research work.

References

1. Egawa, T., Zhao, G.Y., Ishikawa, H., Umeno, H., Jimbo, T.: Characterizations of recessed gate AlGaN/GaN HEMTs on sapphire. IEEE Trans. Electron Devices **48**(3), 603–608 (2001)
2. Ambacher, O., et al.: Two-dimensional electron gases induced by spontaneous and piezoelectric polarization charges in N- and Ga-face AlGaN/GaN heterostructures. J. Appl. Phys. **85**(6), 3222–3233 (1999)
3. Palacios, T., Suh, C.S., Chakraborty, A., Keller, S., DenBaars, S.P., Mishra, U.K.: High-performance E-mode AlGaN/GaN HEMTs. IEEE Electron Device Lett. **27**(6), 428–430 (2006)
4. Wu, J., Lu, W., Paul, K.L.: Normally-OFF AlGaN/GaN MOS-HEMT with a two-step gate recess. In: 2015 IEEE International Conference on Electron Devices and Solid-State Circuits (EDSSC), Singapore, pp. 594–596. IEEE (2015)
5. Hahn, H., et al.: First polarization-engineered compressively strained AlInGaN barrier enhancement-mode MISHFET. Semicond. Sci. Technol. **27**(5), 055004 (2012)
6. Jessen, G.H., et al.: Gate optimization of AlGaN/GaN HEMTs using WSi, Ir, Pd, and Ni Schottky contacts. In: 25th Annual Technical Digest 2003 Gallium Arsenide Integrated Circuit (GaAs IC) Symposium, San Diego, CA, USA, pp. 277–279. IEEE (2003)
7. Hilt, O., Knauer, A., Brunner, F., Bahat-Treidel, E., Würfl, J.: Normally-off AlGaN/GaN HFET with p-type Ga Gate and AlGaN buffer. In: 22nd International Symposium on Power Semiconductor Devices & IC's (ISPSD), Hiroshima, Japan, pp. 347–350. IEEE (2010)
8. Gregušová, D., et al.: Adjustment of threshold voltage in AlN/AlGaN/GaN high-electron mobility transistors by plasma oxidation and Al2O3 atomic layer deposition overgrowth. Appl. Phys. Lett. **104**(1), 013506 (2014)
9. Cai, Y., Zhou, Y., Chen, K.J., Lau, K.M.: High-performance enhancement-mode AlGaN/GaN HEMTs using fluoride-based plasma treatment. IEEE Electron Device Lett. **26**(7), 435–437 (2005)
10. Hahn, H., et al.: Threshold voltage engineering in GaN-based HFETs: a systematic study with the threshold voltage reaching more than 2 V. IEEE Trans. Electron Devices **62**(2), 538–545 (2015)
11. Hasegawa, H., Akazawa, M.: Interface models and processing technologies for surface passivation and interface control in III–V semiconductor nanoelectronics. Appl. Surf. Sci. **254**(24), 8005–8015 (2008)
12. Chong, W., et al.: Breakdown voltage and current collapse of F-plasma treated AlGaN/GaN HEMTs. J. Semicond. **35**(1), 014008 (2014)
13. Li, W., et al.: Design and simulation of a novel E-mode GaN MIS-HEMT based on a cascode connection for suppression of electric field under gate and improvement of reliability. J. Semicond. **38**(7), 074001 (2017)

14. Yi, C., Wang, R., Huang, W., Tang, W.C.W., Lau, K.M. Chen, K.J.: Reliability of enhancement-mode AlGaN/GaN HEMTs fabricated by fluorine plasma treatment. In: IEEE International Electron Devices Meeting (IEDM 2007), Washington, DC, USA, pp. 389–392. IEEE (2007)

15. Hahn, H., Lükens, G., Ketteniss, N., Kalisch, H., Vescan, A.: Recessed-gate enhancement-mode AlGaN/GaN heterostructure field-effect transistors on Si with record DC performance. Appl. Phys. Express 4(11), 114102 (2011)

16. Chan, C.Y., Lee, T.C., Hsu, S.S., Chen, L., Lin, Y.S.: Impacts of gate recess and passivation on AlGaN/GaN high electron mobility transistors. Jpn. J. Appl. Phys. 46(2R), 478–484 (2007)

17. Kordoš, P., Bernat, J., Marso, M.: Impact of layer structure on performance of unpassivated AlGaN/GaN HEMT. Microelectron. J. 36(3–6), 438–441 (2005)

18. Gao, T., et al.: Dual-gate AlGaN/GaN MIS-HEMTs using Si_3N_4 as the gate dielectric. Semicond. Sci. Technol. 30(11), 115010 (2015)

19. Yang, L., et al.: Improvement of subthreshold characteristic of gate-recessed AlGaN/GaN transistors by using dual-gate structure. IEEE Trans. Electron Devices 64(10), 4057–4064 (2017)

20. Hwang, I.H., et al.: High-performance E-Mode AlGaN/GaN MIS-HEMT with dual gate insulator employing SiON and HfON. Phys. Status Solidi (A) 215, 1700650 (2018)

21. Silvaco ATLAS TCAD tool, version 5.24.1.R

22. Rzin, M., et al.: Impact of gate-drain spacing on low-frequency noise performance of in situ SiN passivated InAlGaN/GaN MIS-HEMTs. IEEE Trans. Electron Devices 64(7), 2820–2825 (2017)

23. Russo, S., Di Carlo, A.: Scaling issues for AlGaN/GaN HEMTs: performance optimization via devices geometry modelling (2005). arXiv preprint: https://arxiv.org/abs/cond-mat/0510049

LEADER: Leakage Currents Estimation Technique for Aging Degradation Aware 16 nm CMOS Circuits

Zia Abbas[1]($\boxtimes$), Andleeb Zahra[2], and Mauro Olivieri[2]

[1] Center for VLSI and Embedded System Technologies (CVEST),
IIIT Hyderabad, Hyderabad, India
zia.abbas@iiit.ac.in
[2] DIET, Sapienza University of Rome, Rome, Italy
{andleeb.zahra,mauro.olivieri}@uniroma1.it

Abstract. Fast-computable and accurate leakage models for state of the art CMOS digital standard cells is one of the most critical issues in present and future nano-scale technology nodes. It is further interesting if such model can calculate leakage currents not only at initial circuit life but also over the years based on Bias Temperature Instability (BTI) aging mechanism, which increases the threshold voltage over the years – thus mitigating leakage – but in turn degrades circuit speed. A reliable quantification of such aging-induced leakage mitigation opens the way to effective trade-off techniques for compensating speed degradation while maintaining leakage within specification bounds. The presented logic level leakage characterization and estimation technique, currently implemented as VHDL packages, shows more than 10^3 speed-ups over HSPICE circuit simulation and exhibits less than 1% error over HSPICE. We report BTI aging aware leakage current estimation for ten years at 25 °C and 90 °C in 16 nm CMOS technology, and we analyze how such leakage reduction trend can be traded off to improve the degraded circuit speed over time.

Keywords: NBTI · PBTI · Leakage current · VHDL · CMOS

1 Introduction

The total power dissipation in digital circuits can be arranged in dynamic and static power dissipations. Dynamic power arises primarily from the currents needed to charge and discharge load capacitances during signal switching, and secondly from short circuit current in transitions when both the pull-up and pull-down networks of the circuits are simultaneously on. Conversely, static power occurs even there is no signal transition, due to leakage currents in the devices [1]. As per International Technology Road-map for Semiconductors (ITRS) for the trend of power dissipation with respect to technology progress, static power dissipation is expected to exceed dynamic power dissipations in the total power envelope [2] due to the continuous downscaling of MOS device dimensions. On the other side, the progressive downsizing of the devices is driven by the demand of semiconductor industry to meet the requirement of circuit complexity, i.e. higher number of functions in a single IC.

© Springer Nature Singapore Pte Ltd. 2019
S. Rajaram et al. (Eds.): VDAT 2018, CCIS 892, pp. 394–407, 2019.
https://doi.org/10.1007/978-981-13-5950-7_34

A number of fabrication technology strategies have been adopted in order to control the enormous increase in leakage currents, like the limitation of gate oxide leakage by high-K dielectrics [3], which are ubiquitous in present and future technologies. Yet, sub-threshold leakage is still a dominant source of power dissipation and the introduction of high-K dielectric material also invoke the Positive Bias Temperature Instability (PBTI) aging mechanism in nMOS devices, in addition to Negative Bias Temperature Instability (NBTI) which was already present in pMOS devices in earlier technologies based on SiO_2 dielectric. Both the NBTI and PBTI aging mechanism are primarily degrading the speed and secondarily the functional reliability of the circuit operation over time [4].

In the above context, it is interesting to estimate the leakage currents in digital circuits at initial circuit life (year = 0) as well as over the years under the influence of the BTI aging phenomena, and figure out the leakage behavior over time.

In general, aging phenomena tend to increase the threshold voltages of devices that cause a mitigation of sub-threshold leakage currents. This principle opens the way to the possibility of effectively trading-off leakage for the improvement of otherwise degraded speed performance in later years of circuit life. In principle, the trade-off can be obtained by ad-hoc design techniques such as supply voltage tuning and forward body biasing. A quantitative, reliable characterization and estimation model of the aging effect on leakage allows a clear early prediction of the effectiveness and feasibility of those countermeasures.

Early and accurate estimation of the leakage currents in the design flow has always been beneficial for allowing technology-based and design-based countermeasures [5, 6]. It is further helpful, if we have separate leakage currents due to different physical sources of leakage in a complex IC, which will allow us a more clear definition of countermeasure trade-offs [7, 15]. Generally, the most reliable source for the estimation of leakage currents is SPICE level simulations, which guarantees the highest accuracy. However, an heavy drawbacks of SPICE-level simulation is that it takes very long run time and therefore cannot considered as appropriate for estimating leakage currents in integrated circuit (IC) designs of medium-high complexity; even less when Monte Carlo iterations are required for the statistical analysis of technology variation effects on leakage currents. Secondly, SPICE-level simulation does not allow a straightforward distinction among the contributions of different physical sources of leakage in a complex IC.

On the other hand, logic level estimation models inherently have a large computational speed advantage over SPICE simulations and can be applied before getting to the circuit implementation of the design [7, 8], yet they may suffer from unreliable accuracy when considering all possible mechanisms affecting leakage current components. Many efforts have been done to develop logic level models for fast leakage power calculation with as high as possible accuracy [7, 8, 14]. In this regard, we have implemented a logic level leakage characterization and estimation technique, which supports the calculation of leakage currents not only at initial phase of design but also over the years, as affected by aging mechanisms. The technique supports separate calculation of gate leakage, sub-threshold leakage, and junction leakage, including input pattern dependence, stacking effects, and loading effects [5, 20]. In the proposed work, the technique is implemented by means of dedicated VHDL packages for a

16 nm CMOS standard cell library. However, the technique is equally valid for other real industry technology nodes and even for other switching devices such as by simply updating the appropriate characterization data and parameters in two VHDL packages.

2 Background and Methodology

NBTI takes place in negatively biased (VGS < 0 V) PMOS at elevated temperatures and is a consequence of an interface trap generation at the interface of Si/oxide [9, 10]. The traps increase the threshold voltage and reduce the channel mobility due to scattering. Overall, the drain current degrades. Interestingly, most of the effects of device aging mechanisms can be understood by the change in threshold voltage (Vt) only [11, 12]. ΔVth modelling equations are built-in within the MOS Reliability Analysis (MOSRA) tool in HSPICE (Synopsys) to model the BTI phenomenon [13], and are the basis for the characterization phase of the proposed work. MOSRA simulation is usually divided into pre-stress analysis (fresh simulations or at zero time) and post-stress analysis, which can be set up for several years with desired intervals of time.

Fortunately, aging-induced increment in Vth causes reduction in leakage power due to the relation between sub-threshold currents and threshold voltage; conversely, it causes an increase in propagation delays and can compromise system level performances [4, 17].

Figure 1 shows |ΔVth| versus time (in years) for DC stress in 16 nm pMOS (NBTI degradation) and nMOS devices (PBTI degradation) for 0.8 V supply voltage at 25 °C and 90 °C.

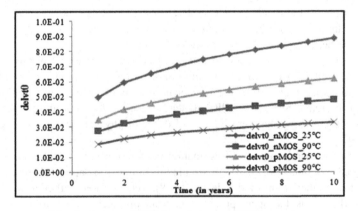

Fig. 1. Impact of BTI degradation on |ΔVT| over time

Broadly speaking, the basic idea of all logic-level leakage current estimation methods is based on the offline SPICE level simulation of the static currents in the cells, either by characterizing directly the total current, or by characterizing the currents flowing in single FET devices in static conditions and properly combining the obtained values to obtain the static current flowing in a cell [5, 14, 15]. The proposed work is based on the second type of approach. The second core idea of the approach is the characterization of voltage profiles at the internal nodes of the stacks inside the standard cells, which is very important in order to estimate accurate leakage currents. Both the characterization steps have been extended to include aging analysis.

All our SPICE level characterizations are performed in HSPICE simulator using Berkeley Short-channel IGFET Model (BSIM4) [16] for 16 nm CMOS High Performance Metal Gate/High-K model parameters from predictive technology model parameters (PTM) [18]. The aging analysis has been performed using the MOSRA in HSPICE for the same model parameters [19].

The characterization data of single FET device currents and of cell internal node voltages are stored separately in two VHDL packages (namely *AASMC.vhd* for 'Aging Aware Single MOS Current' and *AAINV.vhd* for 'Aging Aware Internal Node Voltage').

The *AASMC.vhd* package consists of data arrays of extracted leakage currents through drain, gate, source and body terminals in a single MOSFET for different voltages at each terminal, with BTI aging up to 10 years, at 25 °C and 90 °C temperatures. Overall, device level leakage current values (Idrain, Igate, Isource and Ibody) have been stored in the package in the form of matrices according to the following scheme for each device type:

- Multiple of minimum width (W, 2W, 3W, 4W, 6W and 8W), where W = 16 nm.
- Voltages ranging from 0 V to 1.2 V with 0.01 V step. 25 °C and 90 °C temperatures.
- Negative and positive BTI aging for 10 years.

In summary, the *AASMC.vhd* package contains 230400 static current values placed in 24 different matrices isolated on the basis of MOS type, MOS width, temperature and year, every matrix containing 240 values (120 values for each temperature) of each current at 120 V values.

Three functions have been implemented within the package in order to separately access the three major leakage components from the already built matrices, i.e. sub-threshold, gate and junction leakage respectively. The function declaration for sub-threshold leakage is shown below along with its parameter list. Other functions appear similarly.

```
Function Isub (Lmin         : in integer;
               Wmin         : in integer
               Vds          : in real;
               Temperature  : in integer;
               Year         : in integer  )
```

As an example, the minimum size 2-input NAND cell designed in 16 m CMOS technology has all nMOS and pMOS at 32 nm width (W = 2), as in Fig. 2. If we consider input pattern AB = "01", for the sub-threshold leakage current in the off-nMOS

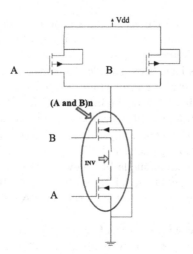

Fig. 2. Two input NAND cell

with gate connected to input A at 90 °C at 3rd year operation, the function I_{sub} will be invoked with the following parameter list:

$$\{Wmin,\ NWmin,\ Vds,\ temperature,\ year\} = \{16,\ 2,\ Vds,\ 90,\ 3\}$$

However, the exact voltage value (Vds) at internal node (INV in Fig. 2) is not *a priori* known. For the accurate calculation of sub-threshold current, the internal node voltage characterization for the required input combination is needed.

In this regard, the *AAINV.vhd* package has been implemented, containing the characterization of all the internal node voltages in pull-up and pull-down stacked

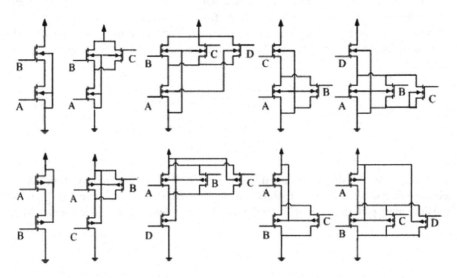

Fig. 3. Internal node voltage stacks of nMOS and pMOS (single internal nodes)

structures typically used in standard library cells. The data are organized in matrices, at the two temperatures and for aging degradation up to 10 years. Notably, the same pull-up and pull-down stacks often exists in different standard cells and have the same internal node voltage values. For example the same (A and B)n structure depicted in Fig. 2 for NAND2 cell also exists in full adder, XOR2, AND2, AO12, AO112 circuit and voltage values at INV will be same in all the cells for the respective input combination. The characterization of the internal node voltages (single internal node) covered all the basic structures shown in Fig. 3. Similarly other nMOS and pMOS stacks can be drawn for two or more internal nodes.

3 BTI Aging Aware Estimation of Leakage Currents and Accuracy Verification

The accuracy of aging aware leakage currents estimated technique has been tested with leakage values obtained from HSPICE (as reference) at both the temperatures. Thirteen combinational and sequential standard cell types of different fan-in and three multi stage complex cells are considered in this work to test the accuracy of the technique.

The presented leakage current estimation model at logic level sums up all leakage currents flowing to ground in each cell for each year and temperature separately, while in the referenced HSPICE simulations we directly measured the total static current flowing through the external voltage supply connected to the circuit under test using MOSRA for the required year and temperature. Table 1 reports the results for NOT cell, detailing pattern dependent leakage values for both the temperatures.

It appears evident from the reported values in Table 1 that leakage currents, as expected, reduce over the years due to BTI phenomenon at both the temperatures. Figure 4 depicts the leakage reduction trend over the 10 years at 25 °C and 90 °C in NOT cell for both input signal values.

Table 1. Aging aware leakage current comparison in NOT cell. (Currents values are estimated in nano-ampere.)

Cell	Year	Input	TEMP = 25 °C			TEMP = 90 °C		
			Model	Spice	Err%	Model	Spice	Err%
NOT	0	0	15.54	15.51	−0.22	32.10	31.84	−0.83
		1	35.90	35.72	−0.49	59.97	59.32	−1.10
	1	0	6.16	6.16	−0.11	20.93	20.80	−0.60
		1	9.30	9.29	−0.14	31.33	31.15	−0.61
	3	0	4.58	4.58	−0.09	18.26	18.17	−0.53
		1	6.02	6.01	−0.09	25.49	25.36	−0.50
	7	0	3.42	3.42	−0.06	15.97	15.90	−0.48
		1	3.91	3.90	−0.06	20.79	20.71	−0.42
	10	0	2.96	2.96	−0.06	14.96	14.89	−0.46
		1	3.16	3.16	−0.05	18.82	18.75	−0.38

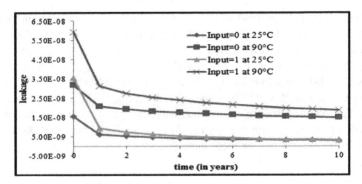

Fig. 4. Leakage reduction trend over 10 years under BTI phenomenon (in NOT cell)

Table 2. Aging aware leakage current comparison in NOR2 cell. (Currents values are estimated in nano-ampere.)

Cell	Year	Comb	TEMP = 25 °C			TEMP = 90 °C		
			Model	Spice	Err%	Model	Spice	Err%
NAND2	0	00	0.13	0.13	0.04	0.53	0.53	−0.03
		01	3.98	3.96	−0.35	9.95	9.92	−0.28
		10	24.12	23.89	−0.97	49.68	49.39	−0.60
		11	71.85	71.10	−1.07	119.99	119.04	−0.80
		Ave	25.02	24.77	−1.02	45.04	44.72	−0.71
	1	00	0.05	0.05	0.30	0.34	0.34	−0.03
		01	1.53	1.52	−0.71	6.41	6.39	−0.28
		10	9.60	9.54	−0.62	32.44	31.82	−1.94
		11	18.66	18.60	−0.30	62.72	62.87	0.22
		Ave	7.46	7.43	−0.42	25.48	25.35	−0.49
	3	00	0.04	0.04	0.79	0.29	0.29	0.16
		01	1.12	1.12	−0.39	5.57	5.56	−0.24
		10	7.16	7.11	−0.63	28.34	27.94	−1.43
		11	12.08	12.06	−0.19	51.03	50.45	−1.14
		Ave	5.10	5.08	−0.35	21.31	21.06	−1.17
	7	00	0.03	0.03	0.70	0.26	0.26	0.08
		01	0.84	0.83	−0.99	4.86	4.84	−0.34
		10	5.36	5.32	−0.65	24.79	24.69	−0.38
		11	7.86	7.85	−0.12	41.64	41.25	−0.94
		Ave	3.52	3.51	−0.37	17.89	17.76	−0.70
	10	00	0.02	0.02	0.66	0.24	0.24	0.04
		01	0.72	0.72	−1.33	4.55	4.53	−0.39
		10	4.65	4.62	−0.68	23.22	22.87	−1.53
		11	6.37	6.36	−0.09	37.70	37.38	−0.86
		Ave	2.94	2.93	−0.40	16.43	16.25	−1.06

Table 3. Cell library leakage estimation. (Reported leakage value is the average among all signal patterns)

Cell	Year	TEMP = 25 °C			TEMP = 90 °C		
		Model	Spice	Err%	Model	Spice	Err%
NOR2	0	31.34	31.62	0.89	54.95	54.84	−0.21
	1	9.40	9.36	−0.39	31.43	31.37	−0.20
	3	6.37	6.36	−0.18	26.18	26.26	0.30
	7	4.36	4.36	−0.06	21.89	22.04	0.70
	10	3.63	3.63	−0.03	20.48	20.23	−1.20
AND2	0	55.84	55.64	−0.35	98.05	97.44	−0.63
	1	15.98	15.96	−0.15	54.22	54.05	−0.32
	3	16.67	16.66	−0.03	45.00	44.88	−0.26
	7	11.29	11.29	0.00	37.48	37.40	−0.22
	10	6.06	6.04	−0.24	34.29	34.22	−0.21
XOR2	0	113.69	112.90	−0.70	204.64	201.01	−1.81
	1	33.75	33.57	−0.54	115.24	113.15	−1.84
	3	22.98	22.87	−0.49	96.29	94.69	−1.69
	7	15.78	15.72	−0.42	80.62	79.50	−1.40
	10	13.15	13.09	−0.41	73.93	73.00	−1.28
NAND3	0	26.76	26.60	−0.58	48.76	48.39	−0.78
	1	8.26	8.21	−0.65	28.21	27.82	−1.38
	3	5.70	5.67	−0.53	23.74	23.44	−1.29
	7	3.98	3.96	−0.57	20.00	19.82	−0.92
	10	3.34	3.32	−0.62	18.39	18.26	−0.75
NOR3	0	25.77	25.66	−0.43	44.58	44.06	−1.18
	1	7.70	7.61	−1.21	25.65	25.41	−0.96
	3	5.23	5.16	−1.26	21.48	21.29	−0.88
	7	3.56	3.53	−0.99	18.17	17.89	−1.54
	10	2.96	2.93	−0.89	16.68	16.43	−1.52
AND3	0	53.67	53.36	−0.58	93.49	92.82	−0.72
	1	15.14	15.09	−0.33	51.50	51.15	−0.67
	3	10.14	10.22	0.71	42.63	42.37	−0.59
	7	6.98	6.96	−0.25	35.41	35.23	−0.53
	10	5.79	5.78	−0.24	32.35	32.19	−0.50
MUX	0	117.21	116.87	−0.29	211.34	209.86	−0.71
	1	35.82	35.78	−0.08	120.98	120.44	−0.44
	3	24.69	24.67	−0.06	101.56	101.17	−0.39
	7	17.18	17.17	−0.05	85.58	85.29	−0.34
	10	14.40	14.40	−0.04	78.74	78.49	−0.32
AO12	0	64.14	63.74	−0.63	119.06	118.47	−0.49
	1	19.51	19.44	−0.36	68.31	67.79	−0.77
	3	13.41	13.37	−0.29	57.48	56.81	−1.18

(*continued*)

Table 3. (*continued*)

Cell	Year	TEMP = 25 °C			TEMP = 90 °C		
		Model	Spice	Err%	Model	Spice	Err%
	7	9.30	9.27	−0.23	48.22	47.77	−0.95
	10	7.78	7.77	−0.23	46.77	46.59	−0.39
FA	0	232.59	231.50	−0.47	412.04	408.53	−0.86
	1	67.33	67.57	0.35	229.59	229.56	−0.01
	3	45.55	45.75	0.43	191.15	191.29	0.07
	7	31.08	31.25	0.52	159.48	159.94	0.28
	10	25.82	25.96	0.55	146.01	146.56	0.37
LATCH	0	106.78	106.94	0.15	187.54	188.64	0.58
	1	30.90	30.93	0.10	104.25	104.72	0.45
	3	20.88	20.90	0.08	86.66	87.02	0.41
	7	14.24	14.25	0.06	72.32	72.59	0.37
	10	11.82	11.83	0.05	66.22	66.45	0.35
AO112	0	56.60	56.12	−0.85	100.61	100.37	−0.24
	1	17.68	17.55	−0.72	59.51	58.95	−0.95
	7	8.53	8.49	−0.49	42.71	42.16	−1.29
	10	7.16	7.13	−0.45	39.16	38.88	−0.73

Interestingly, the difference in the leakage associated to different input values tend to reduce, while the relative impact of temperature is amplified. For temperature rising from 25 °C to 90 °C, at 10 years we have (on average) a 262.2% leakage increase for input = '0' and 235.6% for input = '1'; at zero years, the same temperature rise causes an increase in leakage of only 105.3% for input = '0' and 66% for input = '1'. Correspondingly, the decrease in leakage current over the years is more abrupt at 25 °C than at 90 °C, which seems consistent from the ΔV_T versus time trend for the two temperatures in Fig. 1.

Table 2 illustrates the calculated leakage values for 2-input NAND cell computed through the logic level technique along with reference HSPICE results for all possible input pattern and for 10 years' operation at both the temperatures.

Table 3 reports the same results and the associated SPICE level accuracy verification, calculated as the average leakage with respect to all input patterns, in a larger set of non-trivial cells.

To calculate the leakage currents in multi-cell circuits at the logic-level, the leakage currents of all contributing cells are summed up, also considering the loading effects which affect output node voltages. Table 4 reports the calculated leakage in multi-cell circuits along with the comparison with HSPICE/MOSRA results. All cases show errors below 1%.

Table 4. Multi-cell multi-level logic leakage estimation

Cell	Year	TEMP = 25 °C			TEMP = 90 °C		
		Model	Spice	Err%	Model	Spice	Err%
4*4 Multiplier	0	2828.00	2815.88	−0.43	4836.08	4802.38	−0.70
	1	750.04	749.53	−0.07	2568.23	2561.00	−0.28
	3	489.84	489.85	0.00	2101.26	2097.00	−0.20
	7	322.05	322.11	0.02	1725.05	1722.63	−0.14
	10	262.34	262.40	0.02	1566.51	1564.75	−0.11
32-bit Adder	0	6009.35	5976.13	−0.56	10338.67	10239.25	−0.97
	1	1602.42	1598.88	−0.22	5511.96	5480.38	−0.58
	3	1048.74	1047.75	−0.09	4516.05	4493.25	−0.51
	7	691.24	690.23	−0.15	3712.93	3695.88	−0.46
	10	563.84	562.98	−0.15	3374.20	3359.25	−0.44
8-bit Parity Checker	0	797.41	790.04	−0.93	1427.77	1409.94	−1.27
	1	238.39	237.68	−0.30	814.26	806.91	−0.91
	3	122.92	122.44	−0.39	682.13	676.30	−0.86
	7	102.24	101.86	−0.37	572.38	568.62	−0.66
	10	93.99	93.80	−0.19	525.52	522.58	−0.56

Recognizing the most dominant leakage component (sub-threshold, gate and junction reverse body) in the total leakage budget clearly allow us to focus on counter-measures. Through the separate leakage component estimation capability of presented

Table 5. Separate leakage estimation of leakage component

Cell	Year	TEMP = 25 °C			TEMP = 90 °C		
		Isub	Ibody	Igate	Isub	Ibody	Igate
4*4 Multiplier	0	2824.7	0.67	2.62	4831.4	2.01	2.65
	1	747.2	0.40	2.49	2564.2	1.49	2.57
	3	487.0	0.35	2.45	2097.4	1.36	2.55
	7	319.3	0.30	2.41	1721.3	1.24	2.53
	10	259.7	0.29	2.40	1562.8	1.19	2.52
32-bit Adder	0	6002.15	1.58	5.61	10328.17	4.84	5.66
	1	1596.19	0.92	5.30	5502.89	3.58	5.49
	3	1042.75	0.79	5.20	4507.36	3.26	5.43
	7	685.44	0.69	5.12	3704.57	2.97	5.38
	10	558.12	0.65	5.07	3366.00	2.84	5.36
8-bit Parity Checker	0	796.71	0.09	0.60	1426.89	0.27	0.61
	1	237.77	0.06	0.56	813.47	0.21	0.59
	3	162.52	0.05	0.55	681.36	0.19	0.58
	7	111.96	0.05	0.54	571.63	0.17	0.57
	10	93.41	0.04	0.53	524.78	0.17	0.57

technique, we have calculated the contributions reported in Table 5 for multi-cell circuits. The data clearly illustrates the focus should be on sub-threshold leakage currents, which covers more than 99% of the total static consumption.

4 Trade-off Between Leakage and Delay

The leakage reduction trend over the years seems providing a room for trade-off between leakage and degraded propagation delays, through established techniques like adaptive supply voltage or forward body biasing (FBB) or the combination of two. Our methodology allows to quickly predict the effectiveness of such trade-off for a given design at logic level.

In order to evaluate the possible effectiveness of trade-off between leakage and delay, we characterized the low to high (tp_lh) and high-to-low (tp_hl) delay for the cells at zero years and over the years in HSPICE/MOSRA, at nominal 0.8 V supply in the given technology. At year zero, for the NOT cell we obtained tp_lh = 53.49 ps and tp_hl = 56.81 ps. Under the BTI aging mechanism, the tp_lh and tp_hl delays reach up to 68.11 ps and 69.35 ps respectively in 10 years.

Figure 5 shows the delays improvement over the years using an adaptive (increasing) supply voltage, aiming to maintain the delays equal to the values at year zero over the time, while also keeping the leakage current under control thanks to the aging effect, no higher than the values at zero years. As it can be clearly examined from Figs. 5 and 6, we keep increasing the supply voltage from V_{dd} = 0.8 V to V_{dd} = 0.95 V with the step of 0.05 V

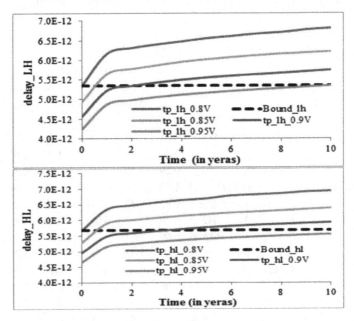

Fig. 5. Trade-off analysis using adaptive supply voltage (propagation delays)

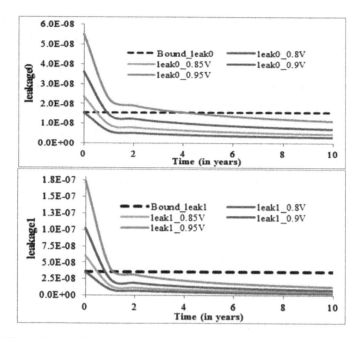

Fig. 6. Trade-off analysis using adaptive supply voltage (leakage currents)

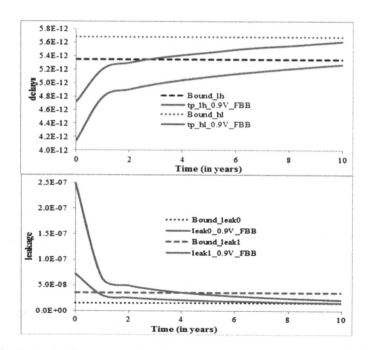

Fig. 7. Trade-off analysis jointly using adaptive supply voltage and body biasing

and correspondingly both the *tp_lh* and *tp_hl* delays start reducing. At $V_{dd} = 0.95$ V, both the delays are well within the bounds even at 10 years' operation. Correspondingly, the leakage gets increased but at 10 years it is within the values measured at year zero.

Similarly, Fig. 7 demonstrate the trade-off for delays improvement using the combination of supply voltage and forward body biasing technique. Figure 7 shows that the delays are in bound at $V_{dd} = 0.9$ V in conjunction with body biasing of VBp = 0.7 V and VBn = 0.1 V.

The above analysis assumes the possibility of adaptively adjusting the supply voltage during the life of the circuit, which is a procedure already demonstrated in previous works [4]. As the analysis can be performed at logic level, it allows predicting the actual effectiveness of such techniques in a specific design.

5   Conclusion

We have presented the principles of an aging aware approach for the accurate characterization and estimation of leakage currents in digital standard cell designs at the logic level. While implementing the technique in a complete tool is out of our scope, yet we have demonstrated the possibility of nearly SPICE accuracy with a run time speed-up of 103 over SPICE, in circuits composed of multiple cells. A specific contribution of the presented approach is that of early predicting the possible effectiveness of techniques for trading off speed degradation and leakage reduction over years by exploiting aging physical phenomena.

References

1. Bhunia, S., Mukhopadhya, S. (eds.): Low-Power Variation-Tolerant Design in Nanometer Silicon. Springer, New York (2011). https://doi.org/10.1007/978-1-4419-7418-1
2. International Technology Roadmap for Semiconductors. International SEMATECH, Austin, TX. http://public.itrs.net
3. Chau, R., et al.: Application of high-k gate dielectric and metal gate electrodes to enable silicon and non-silicon logic nanotechnology. Microelectron. Eng. **80**, 1–6 (2005)
4. Abbas, Z., Olivieri, M., Ripp, A.: Yield-driven power-delay-optimal CMOS full adder design complying with automotive product specifications of PVT variations and NBTI degradations. J. Comput. Electron. **15**(4), 1424–1439 (2016)
5. Abbas, Z., Olivieri, M.: Impact of technology scaling on leakage power in nano-scale bulk CMOS digital standard cell library. Elsevier Microelectron. J. **45**(2), 179–195 (2014)
6. Abbas, Z., Olivieri, M.: Optimal transistor sizing for maximum yield in variation aware standard cell design. Int. J. Circuit Theory Appl. **44**, 1400–1424 (2016)
7. Mukhopadhyay, S., Raychowdhury, A., Roy, K.: Accurate estimation of total leakage current in scaled CMOS logic circuits based on compact current modeling. In: Proceedings of IEEE/ACM Design Automation Conference (DAC 2003), pp. 169–174 (2003)
8. Rao, R., Burns, J., Devgan, A., Brown, R.: Efficient techniques for gate leakage estimation. In: Proceedings of International Symposium on Low Power Electronics and Design (ISLPED 2003), pp. 100–103 (2003)

9. Alam, M.A., Mahapatra, S.: A comprehensive model of PMOS NBTI degradation. Microelectron. Reliab. **45**(1), 71 (2005)
10. Schroder, D.K., Babcock, J.A.: Negative bias temperature instability: road to cross in deep submicron silicon semiconductor manufacturing. J. Appl. Phys. **94**(1), 1 (2003)
11. Chin, D., Pan, S., Wu, K.: Geometry effect on CMOS transistor stability under DC gate stress. In: IRPS, pp. 66–70 (1993)
12. Math, G., Benard, G., Ogier, J., Goguenheim, D.: Geometry effects on the NBTI degradation of PMOS transistors. In: Integrated Reliability Workshop Final Report, pp. 60–63 (2008)
13. Tudor, B., et al.: MOSRA: an efficient and versatile MOS aging modeling and reliability analysis solution for 45 nm and below. In: Proceedings of 10th IEEE International Conference on Solid-State Integrated Circuit Technology, pp. 1645–1647 (2010)
14. Abbas, Z., Genua, V., Olivieri, M.: A novel logic level calculation model for leakage currents in digital nano-CMOS circuits. In: Proceedings of IEEE 7th Conference PRIME, pp. 221–224, July 2011
15. Abbas, Z., Mastrandrea, A., Olivieri, M.: A voltage-based leakage current calculation scheme and its application to nanoscale MOSFET and FinFET standard-cell designs. IEEE Trans. Very Large Scale Integr. (VLSI) Syst. **22**(12), 2549–2560 (2014)
16. Dunga, M.W., et al.: BSIM 4.6.1 Mosfet model – user's manual. Technical reports, EECS Department, University of California, Berkeley (2007)
17. Abbas, Z., Zahra, A., Olivieri, M., Mastrandrea, A.: Geometry scaling impact on leakage currents in FinFET standard cells based on a logic-level leakage estimation technique. In: Anguera, J., Satapathy, S.C., Bhateja, V., Sunitha, K.V.N. (eds.) Microelectronics, Electromagnetics and Telecommunications. LNEE, vol. 471, pp. 283–294. Springer, Singapore (2018). https://doi.org/10.1007/978-981-10-7329-8_29
18. Predictive Technology Model. http://ptm.asu.edu/
19. HSPICE: MOS Reliability Analysis (MOSRA)
20. Abdollahi, A., Fallah, F., Pedram, M.: Leakage current reduction in CMOS VLSI circuits by input vector control. IEEE Trans. Very Large Scale Integr. (VLSI) Syst. **12**(2), 140–154 (2004)

Performance Optimization of FinFET Configurations at 14 nm Technology Using ANN-PSO

Srishti[✉] and Jasmeet Kaur

Department of Electronics and Communication Engineering, GNDEC,
Ludhiana, Punjab, India
srishtithukral7@gmail.com, jasmeetkr.90@gmail.com

Abstract. In this paper, device performance of 14 nm FinFETs have analyzed and electrical parameters like Ion, Ioff, Ion/Ioff, SS, DIBL and power dissipation are measured. These devices have also been analyzed in terms of V-I characteristics. Further, the effect of fin width on device performance was investigated by designing similar FinFETs with different top fin width at 14 nm technology. The designed structures have been simulated using drift diffusion model. In order to validate the results, same structures are also designed & simulated with 20 nm gate length. Also, the FinFETs' performance was optimized using ANN with the PSO algorithm. Both results i.e. optimization results and simulation results were closely matched with 0.48% error.

Keywords: Fin width · FinFET · SCEs · ANN and PSO

1 Introduction

To replace MOSFETs, FinFETs have occurred as they overcome SCEs and show better performance due to their simpler structure and easier fabrication [1–5]. Fin shape has huge impact on the performance of FinFET [6]. Also, there are some other parameters like fin height, fin angle, doping concentration, temperature which affects the device performance [7–11]. Literature shows that, with increment in fin width, drive current also increases. And the leakage current decreases with decrement in fin width [12]. In [13], FinFET structure proposed as nano CMOS device suppresses short channel effects at 17 nm technology. The authors in [14] compared rectangular and other shapes such as convex and concave at 10 nm technology. They concluded that fin with rectangle shape has better performance as compared to fin with non-rectangle shapes in terms of analog and digital parameters. They also observed that trapezoidal shape fin has advantage in low power applications due to low threshold voltage.

The researchers [15] used Sentaurus to compare DGMOSFET with FINFET. They noticed improvement in underlap gate length while optimizing underlap gate lengths in both cases. In [12], the simulation of rectangle fin and trapezoid fin FinFETs has been done. Using TCAD, the inclined fins effect and corner effect on performance has also been studied. The various parameters like field density, electron charge, electron mobility & threshold voltage were calculated. The authors concluded that there was less corner effect in case of trapezoidal FinFET and give better results. Other geometries like trapezium and

© Springer Nature Singapore Pte Ltd. 2019
S. Rajaram et al. (Eds.): VDAT 2018, CCIS 892, pp. 408–417, 2019.
https://doi.org/10.1007/978-981-13-5950-7_35

inverse trapezium partial cylindrical FinFET with different fin widths were designed and explored at 22 nm technology [16]. It was concluded that the FinFET with trapezium shaped acted as a better option and can be used for multi threshold applications. In [17], electrical performance of rectangular and trapezoidal FinFETs with 20 nm gate length was compared and was evaluated with various values of thickness of oxide and height of fin. The trapezoid fin shaped FinFET performed well as compared. This is because the channel's gate controllability was improved by thin fin.

In the work [18], the performance of tri-gate FinFET at 20 nm technology has been evaluated. The triangular fin shape FinFET has been optimized using genetic algorithm. It has been observed that there was reduction in DIBL of designed structure by 32.35% with GA optimization. In [19], the process parameters (i.e. doping concentration & fin height) variation in 20 nm triangular FinFET has been analyzed. The considerable improvement in performance was observed with 1 nm oxide thickness for fin height more than 15 nm whereas with 0.5 nm oxide thickness, fin height less than 15 nm showed better results.

In the present work, FinFETs have been designed with different top fin width keeping the other parameters (like fin height, gate oxide thickness, doping concentration etc.) constant to observe the exact effect of Wtop (top fin width) on the performance of device. The designed devices are simulated using TCAD (Technology Computer Aided Design) tool. The performance is calculated in terms of Ion, Ioff, Ion/Ioff, SS, DIBL and power dissipation. Further, the performance is optimized using artificial neural network (ANN) and particle swarm optimization (PSO) algorithm. PSO algorithm is basically based on fish schooling or the behavior of birds. Here, Levenberg-Marquardt method is used in the artificial neural network (ANN) training. The TCAD simulation results have been validated with the results of ANN and PSO.

In Sect. 2, methodology used for designing the device has been described. The discussion of the results is explained in the Sect. 3 and at last Sect. 4 includes the conclusion.

2 Device Design and Methodology

In this work, FinFET devices with 30 nm fin height have been designed using python script file and mask file taking four values of Wtop i.e. 11 nm, 7 nm, 3 nm & 0.1 nm separately. The bottom fin width is kept constant i.e. 15 nm, therefore, to study the

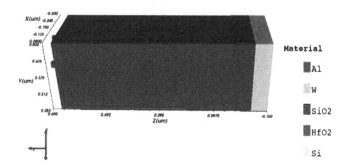

Fig. 1. Outer view of designed FinFET

impact of fin width, the selected top fin widths are in range between 0 to 15 nm. The 3D structures of FinFET devices with gate length 14 nm have been designed using Gds2Mesh 3D Modeller. The outer view of designed FinFET (see Fig. 1).

The designed device is simulated using drift diffusion model in TCAD. For the validation of above results, these same structures are also designed & simulated with 20 nm gate length. All the steps followed, Wtop & material used are kept similar as that of 14 nm FinFET devices. In this process, some parameters are kept constant to observe the top fin width effect. Those parameters are listed in Table 1.

Table 1. Parameters with their corresponding values.

Parameters	Description	Values (in μm)
Lmd	Design rule length unit lambda	0.007
Tsub	Thickness of the substrate region	0.1
Hfin	Height of the fin	0.03
Tox	Thickness of the gate oxide	0.001
Tpoly	Thickness of the poly-silicon gate	0.1
TM1	Thickness of Metal 1	0.3
off_Trap_fin	offset of trapezoidal fin, must be positive	0.005

The above designed FinFET shown is with the all layers (see Fig. 1). When we remove the outer insulating layer & other layers of contact, the internal view is obtained (see Fig. 2). The outer layer is the insulating layer of silicon dioxide material. The metal and active contact layers are of conductor type material aluminum and tungsten respectively. The source, drain, gate and substrate are of silicon material which is semiconductor in type. The insulating material used for the oxide layer is hafnium oxide.

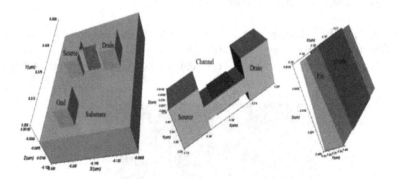

Fig. 2. Internal view of FinFET

The active fins of different top width i.e. 11 nm, 7 nm, 3 nm, and 0.1 nm by removing source, drain and substrate are shown (see Fig. 3).

Fig. 3. Trapezoidal fin FinFETs

The net doping of active region is shown (see Fig. 4). The doping parameters used for the structures are represented in Table 2.

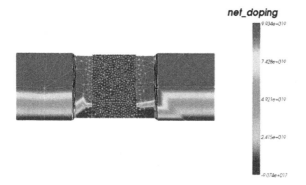

Fig. 4. Net doping of active region

Table 2. Doping parameters

Parameters	Description	Values (in cm^{-3})
Nsub	Doping concentration in p-type Substrate	1e + 17
Nwel_n	Well doping concentration (acceptor) for nMOS	1e + 18
Nwel_p	Well doping concentration (donor) for pMOS	1e + 18
Nsd_n	S/D doping concentration (donor) for nMOS	1e + 20
Nsd_p	S/D doping concentration (acceptor) for pMOS	1e + 20

The mesh of the designed device is shown (see Fig. 5). The meshing parameters used for the structures are represented in Table 3.

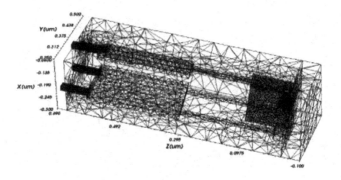

Fig. 5. Mesh of designed structure

Table 3. Mesh parameters

Parameters	Description	Values (in μm)
msz_sub	Mesh size constraint in the substrate region	0.1
msz_active	Mesh size constraint in the active region	0.05
msz_chn	Mesh size constraint in the transistor Channel	0.01

3   Results and Discussion

The results are calculated in terms of Ion, Ioff, Ion/Ioff, SS, DIBL and power dissipation. On-current is the drive current at gate voltage (Vg) = 1 V which depicts the device performance. Higher on-current signifies the better device performance. Off-current is the drive current at Vg = 0 V which is represents the leakage current. Therefore, off state means either zero Vg or no Vg is applied. Higher off current value represents higher leakage. Hence, less off current is required for better performance. On-Off ratio depicts that how well device performs as it is the figure of merit. Subthreshold Swing (SS) can be defined as the rate of change of gate voltage (Vg) per decade of drain current (Id) i.e. dVg/dlog(Id). SS and DIBL are short channel effects which degrades the performance. Drain Induced Barrier Lowering is abbreviated as DIBL which is a type of SCE. It is calculated with the transfer characteristic plots of linear drain voltage (taken as 1 V) and saturation drain voltage (taken as 0.05 V). Mathematically, drain current equation where transfer characteristics are measured is written as follows [20]:

$$I_d = \frac{W_{eff}}{L_g} \times 10^{-7} \tag{1}$$

where Weff = effective channel width & Lg = gate length.

$$W_{eff} = 2H_{fin} + W_{fin} \qquad (2)$$

$$W_{fin} = W_{top} + \left(W_{bottom} + W_{top}\right)\frac{\lambda}{\lambda + 1} \qquad (3)$$

$$\lambda = \frac{2W_{bottom} + W_{top}}{W_{bottom} + 2W_{top}} \qquad (4)$$

where Hfin = fin height, Wfin = fin width, Wtop = top fin width, Wbottom = bottom fin width. The comparison of results is discussed as below:

Table 4. Combined simulation results with 14 nm and 20 nm gate length

Parameters	L_g = 14 nm				L_g = 20 nm			
	W_{top} = 11 nm	W_{top} = 7 nm	W_{top} = 3 nm	W_{top} = 0.1 nm	W_{top} = 11 nm	W_{top} = 7 nm	W_{top} = 3 nm	W_{top} = 0.1 nm
I_{on} (A)	**1.71E–04**	1.52E–04	1.35E–04	1.12E–04	**1.698E–04**	1.572E–04	1.395E–04	1.175E–04
I_{off} (A)	4.22E–09	1.31E–09	4.53E–10	**2.633E–10**	6.191E–10	3.149E–10	1.822E–10	**1.195E–10**
Ion/Ioff	4.05E+04	1.17E+05	2.98E+05	**4.2385E+05**	2.74E+05	4.99E+05	7.66E+05	9.82E+05
SS (mV/dec)	82.3	75.2	70.3	**69.5**	72.3	69.6	67.7	**65**
DIBL (mV/V)	44.7	30.8	20.2	**18.1**	20.8	19.2	13.8	**12.7**
Power dissipation (W)	6.28E–05	5.56E–05	4.89E–05	**4.04E–05**	6.06E–05	5.58E–05	4.95E–05	**4.15E–05**

From the above Table 4, it can be observed that in case of 14 nm gate length, as top fin width decreases, the leakage current is decreasing but the drive current is also decreasing. Basically, the high on-current of device signifies the better current driving capacity. Among 14 nm FinFETs, the device with 11 nm Wtop have higher on-current i.e. 1.71E–04 A and among 20 nm FinFETs, the device with same Wtop have higher on-current i.e. 1.698E–04 A. The off-current represents the leakage current. So, its value should be less. In case of 14 nm FinFETs, the device with 0.1 nm top fin width have lesser off-current i.e. 2.633E–10 A and in case of 20 nm FinFETs, the device with same top fin width have lesser off-current i.e. 1.195E–10 A. It shows that the trend of 14 nm and 20 nm FinFET devices is similar. From the table it is evident that the decrement calculated is relatively less in drive current when compared with leakage current. Thus, there is improvement in on-off current ratio with both gate lengths. Its higher value indicates the device performance is better. SCEs like SS and DIBL which degrades the performance, are decreasing as Wtop is decreased. The power dissipation is also decreasing with decrease in Wtop. All over, this signifies that the performance of device is improved with the reduction in Wtop On comparing results at 14 nm and 20 nm technologies, leakage current and the values of DIBL and SS have increased with technology scaling down. It is also observed that at Lg = 14 nm, as the fin width is increased from 0.1 to 11 nm, the decrement in on current is relatively less in comparison to increment in off current when matched with the respective values at 20 nm. In other words, comparatively, the drive current is seen to be less degraded in geometries with thick fins while leakage current is degraded more. Though, the on-off current ratio is reduced by technology scaling down. But it can be observed that at 14 nm, a considerable improvement is seen in Ion/Ioff ratio on reducing fin width, i.e. maximum value obtained from simulation is 4.2385E+5. For the verification of results, present work is also compared with the results available in literature [17, 18] at same process node (i.e. 20 nm). In Table 5, the results of present work are compared with the results of rectangular, trapezoidal & triangular shaped fins available in literature.

Table 5. Comparison of results with literature at 20 nm technology

Parameter	L_g = 20 nm			L_g = 20 nm [17]		L_g = 20 nm [18]
	Trapezoidal	Trapezoidal	Trapezoidal	Rectangular	Trapezoidal	Triangular
	W_{top} = 14.5 nm	W_{top} = 10 nm	W_{top} = 0.1 nm	W_{top} = 15 nm	W_{top} = 10 nm	W_{top} = 0 nm
I_{on} (A)	**1.864E–04**	1.687E–04	1.175E–04	**2.95E–05**	2.73E–05	1.96E–05
I_{off} (A)	1.053E–09	5.059E–10	**1.195E–10**	2.63E–10	1.45E–10	**4.17E–11**
Ion/Ioff	1.77E+05	3.33E+05	**9.82E+05**	1.12E+05	1.88E+05	**4.71E+05**

Table 5 verifies the trend of present work. As compared to literature there is improvement in drive current of this work as shown in above table. But there is increment in leakage current also. As clear from the table, the increment in drive current is more as compared to the increment in leakage current. This fact leads to improvement in the on-off current ratio. High Ion/Ioff ratio indicates the better performance. The analysis discussed above shows that there is considerable improvement in present work on comparing with literature.

After this, artificial neural network i.e. ANN is trained. There is a method used in ANN called Levenberg-Marquardt where two layers feed forward back propagation network is created. It is a solution of the linear set of equations which is based on a search direction. It gives result in terms of average or mean of square errors which is known as Mean Square Error (MSE). For better device performance, its value should be less. Its less value indicates that device performs well with less error. The performance plot in which best, training & validating lines are connected at single point is shown (see Fig. 6). The regression plot for the analysis of accuracy of testing data is also shown (see Fig. 7). Basically the value of regression indicates the relationship of output & target data. The closer its value to 1 signifies more accuracy in expected and output data. The value of regression is quite closer to 1 i.e. 0.99994 (see Fig. 7). Thus, ANN training gives 99.9994% efficiency.

In combination with ANN, PSO algorithm is also applied to optimize the performance. To optimize the data, PSO algorithm is used combining with ANN. Particle Swarm Optimization (PSO) was first discussed by Dr. James Kennedy and Dr. Russell Eberhart in 1995 as a technique which is population based. This algorithm initiates with the generation of random values of Wtop. Then for each particle, it calculates the fitness value called pbest based upon the given fitness function. These values of pbest are compared at each step. If its current value is better than previous stored value of pbset, then it will update it with better value. Otherwise, it will keep the previous value. After this corresponding velocities are calculated using equations given to it. These steps will be repeated until its maximum iterations are achieved. At the end, the best value of pbest will be assigned as gbest which is maximum value or best value returned by objective function. The combination of ANN & PSO algorithm is simulated using MATLAB. After the repetitive simulations, the obtained value of on-off current ratio is 4.17E + 05 at the Wtop 0.034 nm. At last, FinFET structure with this top fin width (i.e. 0.034 nm) is simulated on TCAD for the verification of accuracy of MATLAB results. Table 6 shows the optimized & simulated results of MATLAB & TCAD.

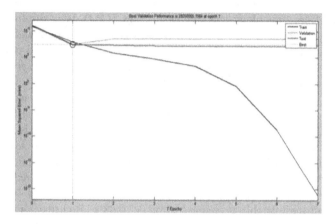

Fig. 6. Performance plot

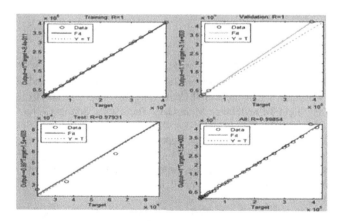

Fig. 7. Regression plot

Table 6. Optimized results

Parameters	Using MATLAB	Using TCAD
Optimum Width (nm)	0.034	0.034
Ion/Ioff	4.17E + 05	4.15E + 05

Above table shows that high on-off current ratio will be obtained at lesser value of Wtop. It shows that TCAD simulation results are closer with the optimized result. The calculated percentage error of simulation and optimized is 0.48%. From this, it becomes evident that the simulation results depicts good amount of accuracy.

4 Conclusion

In this work, FinFETs (with Wtop = 11 nm, 7 nm, 3 nm and 0.1 nm) have been designed at 14 nm technology and simulated using TCAD. With results, it was concluded that the performance is improved with the reduction of top fin width in terms of off-current, Subthreshold Swing, Drain Induced Barrier Lowering and power dissipation. As everything has pros & cons, there is some degradation also observed in case of on-current. If all over performance is considered, then the fin shape with lesser Wtop shows better performance when on-off current ratio is calculated and hence it is preferable. In order to validate these results, the same structures are also designed & simulated at 20 nm technology. It was observed that the drive current is less degraded in geometries with thick fins as compared to that in thinner ones while leakage current is degraded more. Further, the combination of ANN & PSO was simulated for the optimization of the device performance. When both the results (optimized results using MATLAB & simulated results using TCAD) were observed, they were in close agreement with the tolerable percentage error i.e. 0.48%. Both these results demonstrated better device performance in case of lesser Wtop as it gives higher on/off current ratio.

References

1. Bühler, R.T., Martino, J.A., Agopian, P.G.D., Giacomini, R., Simoen, E., Claeys, C.: Fin shape influence on the analog performance of standard and strained MuGFETs. In: Proceedings of IEEE International SOI Conference (SOI), pp. 1–2 (2010)
2. Colinge, J.P.: FinFETs and other Multi-Gate Transistors. Springer, New York (2008). https://doi.org/10.1007/978-0-387-71752-4. ISBN 978-0-387-71751-7
3. Dubey, S., Kondekar, P.N.: Fin shape dependent variability for strained SOI FinFETs. Microelectron. Eng. **162**, 63–68 (2016)
4. Gaynor, B.D., Hassoun, S.: Fin shape impact on FinFET leakage with application to multithreshold and Ultralow-Leakage FinFET design. IEEE Trans. Electron Device **61**(8), 2738–2744 (2014)
5. Bhattacharya, D., Jha, N.K.: FinFETs: From Devices to Architectures, Advances in Electronics, (2014). Hindawi Publishing Corporation, Article ID 365689. Available: http://dx.doi.org/10.1155/2014/365689. Accessed 09 June 2018
6. Tomida, K., et al.: Impact of Fin shape variability on device performance towards 10 nm node. In: Proceedings of International Conference on IC Design and Technology (ICICDT), pp. 1–4 (2015)
7. Yeh, W.K., Zhang, W., Shih, C.H., Yang, Y.L.: Effects of Fin width on performance and reliability for N- and P-type FinFETs. In: Proceedings of IEEE International Conference on Electron Devices and Solid-State Circuits (EDSSC), pp. 361–364 (2016)

8. Pradhan, K.P., Saha, S.K., Sahu, P.K.: Impact of Fin height and Fin angle variation on the performance matrix of Hybrid FinFETs. IEEE Trans. Electron Devices **64**(1), 52–57 (2017)
9. Li, Y., Hwang, C.H.: Effect of Fin Angle on electrical characteristics of NanoScale round-top-gate bulk FinFETs. IEEE Trans. Electrons Devices **54**(12), 3426–3429 (2007)
10. Zhangi, H., et al.: Temperature dependence of soft-error rates for FF designs in 20-nm bulk planar and 16-nm Bulk FinFET technologies. In: IEEE International Reliability Physics Symposium (IRPS), pp. 5C-3-1 – 5C-3-5 (2016)
11. Abraham, D., Gopinadh, D., George, A.: Effects of Fin shape on GIDL and subthreshold leakage currents. IJSTE- Int. J. Sci. Technol. Eng. **1**(10), 135–145 (2015)
12. Musalgaonkar, G., Chatterjee, A.K.: TCAD simulation analysis and comparison between triple gate rectangular and trapezoidal finfet. J. of Electron Devices **21**, 1881–1887 (2015)
13. Hisamoto, D.: FinFET-A self aligned double-gate MOSFET scalable to 20 nm. IEEE Trans. Electron Device **47**, 12 (2000)
14. Yu, Z., Chang, S., Wang, H., He, J., Huang, Q.: Effects of Fin Shape on sub-10nm FinFETs. J. Comput. Electron. **14**, 515–523 (2015)
15. Singh, D., Pradhan, K.P., Mohapatra, S.K., Sahu, P.K.: Optimization of underlap length for DGMOSFET and FinFET. Procedia Comput. Sci. **57**, 448–453 (2015)
16. Jyothi, A., Khan, T.E.A., Kuruvilla, N., Hameed, S.T.A.: Impact of Fin shape on FINFET performance. Int. J. Comput. Appl., Proceedings of International Conference on Emerging Trends in Technology and Applied Science (ICETTAS) (2015)
17. Gaurav, A., Gill, S.S., Kaur, N., Rattan, M.: Performance analysis of rectangular and trapezoidal TG Bulk FinFETs for 20 nm Gate Length. In: Proceedings of Annual IEEE India Conference (INDICON), pp. 1–5 (2015)
18. Gaurav, A., Gill, S.S., Kaur, N., Rattan, M.: Density gradient quantum corrections based performance optimization of triangular TG Bulk FinFETs using ANN and GA. In: 20th International Symposium on VLSI Design and Test VDAT (2016)
19. Shukla, S., Gill, S.S., Kaur, N., Jatana, H.S., Nehru, V.: Comparative simulation analysis of process parameter variations in 20 nm Triangular FinFET. In: Active and Passive Electronic Components, Hindawi, vol. 2017 (2017)
20. Fasarakis, N., Tassis, D.H., Tsormpatzoglou, A., Papathanasiou, K., Dimitriadis, C.A., Ghibaudo, G.: Compact modelling of nano-scaling trapezoidal cross-sectional FinFETs. In: Proceedings of International Semiconductor Conference Dresden-Grenoble (ISCDG), IEEE Conference Publications, pp. 1–4 (2013)

Performance Analysis of Graphene Based Optical Interconnect at Nanoscale Technology

Balkrishna Choubey[1]([✉]), Vijay Rao Kumbhare[2],
and Manoj Kumar Majumder[2]

[1] Chhattisgarh Swami Vivekanand Technical University,
Bhilai, Chhattisgarh, India
balkrishnachoubey1991@gmail.com
[2] Dr. S. P. Mukherjee International Institute of Information Technology,
Naya Raipur, India
{vijay,manojk}@iiitnr.edu.in

Abstract. In the modern technology era, interconnect is the key element for designing integrated circuits that provides on-chip and off-chip communication path for various systems. The primary challenges for modeling interconnect are reduced propagation delay, power dissipation, and its power delay product at advanced technology. This paper critically addresses the performance of optical interconnects using equivalent electrical model that comprises of different composite materials. Using industry standard HSPICE, the propagation delay and power dissipation characteristics of graphene nanoribbon have been compared with other composite materials. It has been observed that the propagation delay for graphene nanoribbon can be improved by 99.91% as compared to other composite materials. The power delay product of the proposed graphene based interconnect model is 59.73% lesser compared to other composite materials at 22 nm technology node.

Keywords: Optical interconnect · Graphene nanoribbons · Propagation delay ·
Power dissipation · Power delay product (PDP)

1 Introduction

In the modern technology, interconnect plays an important role in transferring the data for on-chip and off-chip communication. Copper (Cu) is the promising candidate for designing of interconnect due to its lower resistivity that reduces the propagation delay and hence increasing the speed of the integrated circuits (ICs) [1]. However, it has some major limitations such as grain boundaries generation and electron scattering [2] that makes the design of Cu interconnect challenging at advanced technology node. In order to mitigate these problems, optical interconnect (OI) is considered to be a novel candidate in recent research due to its extremely higher bandwidth density, high speed, less propagation delay, low power dissipation and minimum crosstalk noise for the ICs [3]. Recently, the OI is used in various circuits like Application Specific Integrated Circuits (ASIC), Advanced Optical Communication Systems and Satellite Communication Systems etc. for on-chip and off-chip communication that deals with Cu Interconnects.

© Springer Nature Singapore Pte Ltd. 2019
S. Rajaram et al. (Eds.): VDAT 2018, CCIS 892, pp. 418–429, 2019.
https://doi.org/10.1007/978-981-13-5950-7_36

Various composite materials like magnesium-doped lithium niobate (LN-Mg) [4], gold doped polydimethylsiloxane (PDMS-Au) [5], Cu doped polymethylmethacrylate (PMMA-Cu) [6] and graphene [7] have been proposed for optical interconnects. Among these diverse proposals, graphene has shown better performance and compatibility with optical interconnects. Graphene nanoribbon (GNR) is used due to its extraordinary high current carrying capability ($5 \sim 20 \times 10^8$ A/cm^2) [8], electrical conductivity, thermal conductivity and mechanical strength [9]. It has two-dimensional monolayer structure in which atoms are closely packed and the atoms of carbon on GNR are arranged in honeycomb lattice structure [10]. Previously, Watson *et al.* [12] presented three-layer stack characteristics utilizing an optical waveguide that specifies the frequency response without considering the effect of inductance at low frequency. Liu *et al.* [13] demonstrated the comparison between electrical and optical on-chip interconnects but not specified the behavior of OI at advanced technology node. Consider these research works [12, 13], the primary contribution of the paper includes:

1. The electrical model of OI is presented for various composite materials.
2. The investigation is made on the parasitics (Resistance, Inductance, and Capacitance) of OI at advanced technology nodes based on PTM.
3. The propagation delay and power dissipation of various composite materials are compared with GNR by using CMOS driver.

The paper is organized as follows: Sect. 1 presents the introduction and properties of composite material and GNR. Section 2 briefs about the geometry and electrical modeling and simulation setup of various materials. Section 3 presents performance comparison of OIs. A brief summary is drawn in Sect. 4.

2 Geometry and Modeling of OI

This section presents the basic geometry and its electrical modeling of composite materials and GNR based equivalent single conductor model (ESC).

2.1 Modeling of Composite Materials

Figure 1(a) and (b) shows the geometry and its electrical model for optical interconnect, respectively. The rectangular OI consists of core, cladding and contact material. The Core contains composite materials *i.e.* host and dopant material. The silicon dioxide (SiO_2) is used as cladding material due to its remarkable properties such as large resistivity (Since its conductivity is zero), dielectric, refractivity and insulation. For SiO_2 insulator, ε_r, μ_r, ρ and n represent the dielectric constant, relative permeability, resistivity and refractive index, respectively. It is assumed that the effect of SiO_2 is negligible on the electrical model of OI. The gold (Au) is used as contact material that has resistance (R_{el}) 0.1 Ω such that the functionality and frequency response of the OI works properly [12].

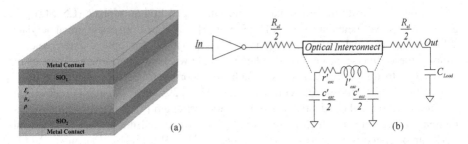

Fig. 1. (a) Geometry of OI (b) electrical model of OI

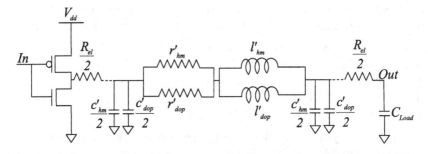

Fig. 2. Equivalent electrical model of CMs with parallel dopant resistance

The resistivity of material increases with technology node due to change in width of OI. Therefore the resistivity of material is calculated using Fuchs-Sondheimer model at 65 nm, 45 nm, 32 nm, and 22 nm technology node and can be expressed as

$$\frac{\rho}{\rho_0} = 1 + \frac{3}{4}(1-p)\frac{l_d}{w} \tag{1}$$

where ρ_0, p, l_d and w is the resistivity at room temperature, fraction of electron scattered specularly at the surface (*i.e.* assumed as 0.6 for each material [14]), mean free path of material, and width of interconnect, respectively. The electrical model for composite material is presented in Fig. 2.

To reduce the resistivity of OI materials such as Lithium Niobate (LN), Poly Dimethyl Siloxane (PDMS), and Polymethyl methacrylate (PMMA), are doped with magnesium (Mg), Gold (Au), and Copper (Cu) to increases its conductivity. The parasitics of dopant and host material is taken parallel to each other. The resistivity (ρ), and dielectric constant (ε_r) of host and dopant material at room temperature are summarized in Table 1 [15–17].

The composite material core parasitics are calculated by following relationship [18]

$$r'_{esc} = \frac{r'_{hm} \cdot r'_{dop}}{r'_{hm} + r'_{dop}}, \quad l'_{esc} = \frac{l'_{hm} \cdot l'_{dop}}{l'_{hm} + l'_{dop}}, \quad \text{and } c'_{esc} = c'_{hm} + c'_{dop} \tag{2}$$

where r'_{esc}, r'_{hm}, r'_{dop}, l'_{esc}, l'_{hm}, l'_{dop}, c'_{esc}, c'_{hm} and c'_{dop} is the resistance of core material in per unit length, resistance of host material, resistance of dopant material, inductance of core material in per unit length, inductance of host material, inductance of dopant material, capacitance of core material in per unit length, capacitance of host material and capacitance of dopant material, respectively.

Table 1. Summarize the quantitative values of host and dopant materials at room temp.

Physical parameter	Core material			Dopant material		
	LN	PDMS	PMMA	Mg	Au	Cu
ε_r	28	2.8	2.6	1	1	1
ρ ($t\Omega$-m)	10	40	1	–	–	–
ρ ($n\Omega$-m)	–	–	–	43.9	22.14	16.78

2.2 Modeling of MLGNR

This sub-section presents the geometry of multi-layered graphene nanoribbon (MLGNR) as shown in Fig. 3. A coupled MLGNR with a spacing S is placed above the ground plane with a distance H. The MLGNR is separated by using dielectric medium ($\varepsilon_r = 2.2$) with a width (w) and thickness (t). The distance $\delta = 0.34$ nm represents the separation between two neighboring layers, that is also known Van der Waal gap [11]. The near and far end of interconnect has fixed resistance that is equally distributed at

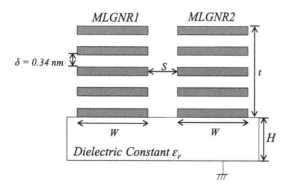

Fig. 3. Geometry of MLGNR interconnect above the ground plane

the ends with the value of $T_{tot} = R_{el} + R_q = 100.4 \ m\Omega$, where R_{el} is the contact electrode resistance and R_q is the quantum resistance of graphene nonoribben. The total number of layers can be obtained using thickness t and interlayer separation δ as

$$N = 1 + int \left(\frac{t}{\delta}\right) \tag{3}$$

Each layer of MLGNR primarily consists of a number of conducting channels associated with electrons and holes and can be expressed as [19]:

$$N_{ch} = \sum_{j=0}^{n_c} \left[\left(e^{\frac{(E_j - E_f)}{k_B T}} + 1\right)\right]^{-1} + \sum_{j=0}^{n_v} \left[\left(e^{\frac{(E_j + E_f)}{k_B T}} + 1\right)\right]^{-1} \tag{4}$$

where $j = 1, 2, 3\ldots$ is a positive integer, n_c and n_v is the number of conduction and valence sub-band, respectively. E_j is the fermi energy level, k_B is the Boltzmann's constant, T is temperature in kelvin and E_j is the jth sub-band energy in conduction (n_c) and valance (n_v) band.

In MLGNR, R_q is the quantum resistance and for N-layers it is given by the following expression [9]

$$R_q = \frac{\left(\frac{h}{2e^2}\right)}{N_{ch} N} \tag{5}$$

where h, e, N_{ch} and N are the planks constant, the charge of electron, the number of conducting channel and the number of layers. In this work, The ESC model of zigzag (zz) MLGNR is considered at $E_f = 0.6$ eV as shown in Fig. 4. Using expression (5) the number of layers have been analytically obtained as 470, 457, 339 and 236 at 65 nm, 45 nm, 32 nm and 22 nm technology node, respectively. The scattering resistance per unit length (p.u.l.) is given as [9]

$$r'_s = \frac{\left(\frac{h}{2e^2}\right)}{N_{ch} l_d} \tag{6}$$

where l_d is the mean free path (419 nm for MLGNR [11]). Figure 4 represents the kinetic energy stored in each conducting channel and the density of electronic states, respectively. The p.u.l. l'_k and c'_q primarily depends on the total number of conducting channels associated with each layer of MLGNR and can be expressed as [11]

$$l'_k = \frac{\left(\frac{h}{4e^2}\right)}{N_{ch} v_f}, \quad \text{and } c'_q = \frac{4e^2 N_{ch}}{h v_f} \tag{7}$$

where v_f is the Fermi velocity $i\ e.\ 8 \times 10^5\ ms^{-1}$ [11]. The p.u.l magnetic inductance $\left(l'_e\right)$ and electrostatic capacitance $\left(c'_e\right)$ primarily depends on the MLGNR width (w) and distance (H) above the ground plane of the OI and can expressed as [11]

$$l'_e = \frac{\mu_0 H}{w}, \quad \text{and } c'_e = \frac{\varepsilon_0 \varepsilon_r H}{w} \tag{8}$$

Figure 4 represents the ESC model of MLGNR and the equivalent scattering resistance for N-layers of MLGNR can be calculated in *p.u.l.* as

$$r'_{s,esc} = \frac{r'_s}{N} \tag{9}$$

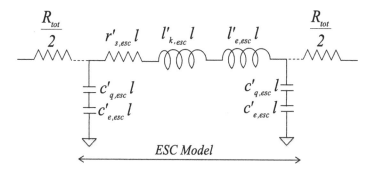

Fig. 4. A distributed ESC model of MLGNR

However, the equivalent kinetic inductance $\left(l'_{k,esc}\right)$, magnetic inductance $\left(l'_{e,esc}\right)$ and the total equivalent inductance $\left(l'_{esc}\right)$ for N-layers of MLGNR in *p.u.l.* is expressed as

$$l'_{k,esc} = \frac{l'_k}{N}, \quad l'_{e,esc} = l'_e, \quad \text{and } l'_{esc} = l'_{k,esc} + l'_{e,esc} \tag{10}$$

The equivalent capacitance can be obtained using the series combination of equivalent quantum and coupling capacitance. The *p.u.l.* can be expressed as

$$\frac{1}{c'_{esc}} = \frac{1}{c'_{q,esc}} + \frac{1}{c'_{e,esc}}, \quad c'_{q,esc} = c'_q.N, \quad \text{and } c'_{e,esc} = c'_e \tag{11}$$

In order to reduce the computational effort, the equivalent ESC model is presented in Fig. 4. It accurately measures the propagation delay and power dissipation of MLGNR at different technology nodes of 65 nm, 45 nm, 32 nm and 22 nm, respectively.

Table 2. Quantitative values of parasitics of composite materials

Technology node	65 nm				45 nm				32 nm				22 nm			
Parasitics	CMs															
	LN-Mg	PDMS-Au	PMMA-Cu	GNR	LN-Mg	PDMS-Au	PMMA-Cu	GNR	LN-Mg	PDMS-Au	PMMA-Cu	GNR	LN-Mg	PDMS-Au	PMMA-Cu	GNR
Contact resistance (Ω)	0.1	0.1	0.1	0.58	0.1	0.1	0.1	0.64	0.1	0.1	0.1	1.17	0.1	0.1	0.1	2.43
Resistance ($\Omega/\mu m$)	4.15	2.21	1.69	1.26	4.61	2.47	1.89	1.40	9.05	4.95	3.79	2.67	20.7	11.71	9.01	5.67
Inductance (pH/100 μm)	72.59	72.59	72.59	297	73.01	73.01	73.01	313	76.1	76.12	76.12	359	79.8	79.8	79.8	450
Capacitance (aF/μm)	451.2	451.2	451.2	12.23	416.3	416.3	416.3	10.46	378	378	378	8.85	339	339	339	7.38

Table 3. Quantitative values of physical parameter

Technology node	At global level			
	65 nm	45 nm	32 nm	22 nm
Width (nm)	72.5	67.5	48	32
Thickness (nm)	159.5	155.25	115.2	80
H (nm)	152.25	148.5	110.4	76.8
Dielectric constant (ε_r)	2.9	2.6	2.3	2.0

Using the expression (1) through (11), the parasitic values (as in Table 2) for various composite materials and GNR are obtained for different interconnect lengths 100 µm, 200 µm, 500 µm, 800 µm and 1000 µm based on the physical parameters provided in Table 3 [20].

3   Result and Discussion

Propagation delay and power dissipation of the OI is affected by parasitics R, L and C that degrade the system performance. In this paper, the electrical model is proposed for propagation delay and power dissipation analysis for different interconnect lengths and technology nodes. The propagation delay and power dissipation comparison of various materials LN-Mg, PDMS-Au, PMMA-Cu and GNR at different technology nodes are shown in Fig. 5(a), (b), (c) and (d), respectively. It is observed that the propagation delay increases and the power dissipation reduces as lowering the technology node for optical interconnect. This is due to the fact that the resistivity of other composite materials is higher than the GNR, thereby high speed and low PDP characteristics can be obtained.

Table 4. Quantitative value of percentage change in PDP at 22 nm technology node *w.r.t.* 65 nm technology node

Length (µm)	% change in PDP at 22 nm technology node *w.r.t.* 65 nm technology node for			
	LN-Mg	PDMS-Au	PMMA-Cu	GNRs
100	64.39	63.86	64.52	50.71
200	63.89	61.53	62.26	46.87
500	61.41	60.21	62.17	44.51
800	56.22	57.97	56.12	22.59
1000	46.72	48.69	51.39	18.81

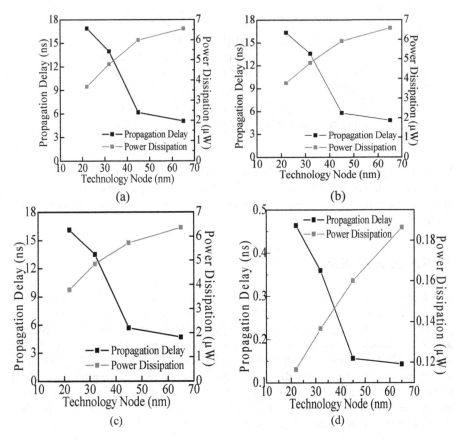

Fig. 5. The propagation delay and power dissipation comparison at different technology node for various materials (a) LN-Mg (b) PDMS-Au (c) PMMA-Cu (d) GNR

This study also shows that a negligible increase in propagation delay of GNR compared to the other composite materials. The advancement of technology node also influenced the power delay product. The PDP for various materials are shown in Fig. 6 (a), (b), (c) and (d), respectively. However, the PDP increases for reduced technology nodes but this study presents the a negligible increase in PDP of GNR compared to other composite materials. The percentage change in PDP at 22 nm technology *w.r.t.* 65 nm on GNR compared to other composite materials are summarized in Table 4. The analysis also shows the improved behavior of GNR over other composite materials *w.r.t.* performance characteristics at different technology nodes.

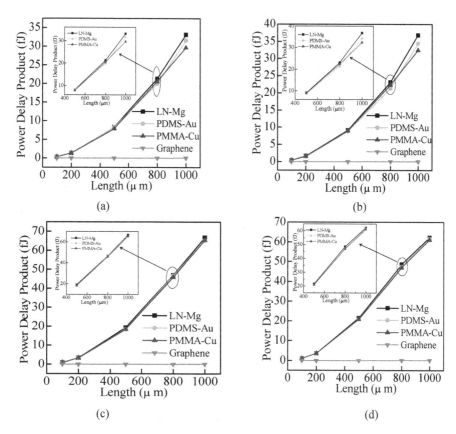

Fig. 6. The power delay product comparison at different interconnect length for various technology node (a) 65 nm (b) 45 nm (c) 32 nm (d) 22 nm

4 Conclusion

In this paper, the impact of various composite materials with varying interconnect length at different technology node are critically examined using the proposed ESC model for future nanoscale technology. Among various proposed materials, the MLGNR possesses improved performance in comparison to the other composite material in terms of propagation delay and power dissipation characteristics. Using industry standard HSPICE, the propagation delay and power dissipation characteristics of graphene nanoribbon have been compared with other composite materials. It can be observed that the propagation delay for graphene nanoribbon can be improved by 99.91% as compared to other composite materials. The power delay product of proposed model at 22 nm technology is 59.73% lesser compared to other composite materials *w.r.t.* 65 nm technology.

References

1. Majumder, M.K., Kumar, J., Kaushik, B.K.: Process-induced delay variation in SWCNT, MWCNT, and mixed CNT interconnects. IETE J. Res. **61**(5), 533–540 (2015)
2. Kaushik, B.K., Majumder, M.K., Kumar, V.R.: Carbon nanotube based 3-D interconnects - a reality or distant dream. IEEE Circuits Syst. Mag. **14**(4), 16–35 (2014)
3. Sallah, S.S.B., Ali, S.H.M., Menon, P.S., Juhari, N., Islam, S.: Implementation of on-chip optical interconnect in high speed digital circuit: two-stage CMOS buffer. Asian J. Sci. Res. **10**(1), 50–55 (2017)
4. West, A.R.: Magnesium doped Lithium Niobate: some comments on stoichiometry, structure and property. Jpn. J. Appl. Phys. **31**(5), 1424–1425 (1992)
5. Cataldi, U., Cerminara, P., De Sio, L., Caputo, R., Umeton, C.P.: Fabrication and characterization of stretchable PDMS structures doped with Au Nanoparticles. Mol. Cryst. Liq. Cryst. **558**(1), 22–27 (2012)
6. Ma, X., Su, X., Zhou, B., Zhao, X., Tian, Y., Wang, Z.: Synthesis and friction properties of Copper/PMMA composites by soapless emulsion polymerization. J. Appl. Polym. Sci. **122**, 2837–2842 (2011)
7. Li, X., et al.: Graphene and related two-dimensional materials: structure-property relationships for electronics and optoelectronics. Appl. Phys. Rev. **4**, 021306–021331 (2017)
8. Morozov, S.V., et al.: Giant intrinsic carrier mobilities in graphene and its bilayer. Phys. Rev. Lett. **100**(1), 01662–01664 (2008)
9. Xu, C., Li, H., Banerjee, K.: Modeling, analysis, and design of graphene nano-ribbon interconnects. IEEE Trans. Electron Devices **56**(8), 1567–1578 (2009)
10. Li, H., Xu, C., Srivastava, N., Banerjee, K.: Carbon nanomaterials for next-generation interconnects and passives: physics, status, and prospects. IEEE Trans. Electron Devices **56**(9), 1799–1821 (2009)
11. Cui, J.P., Zhao, W.S., Yin, W.Y., Hu, J.: Signal transmission analysis of multilayer graphene nano-ribbon (MLGNR) interconnects. IEEE Trans. Electromagn. Compat. **54**(1), 126–132 (2012)
12. Watson, M.D., Ashley, P.R., Guenthner, A.J., Abushagur, M.A.G.: Modeling of electrooptic polymer electrical characteristics in a three-layer optical waveguide modulator. IEEE J. Quantum Electron. **41**(4), 589–595 (2005)
13. Liu, W., Wang, Y., Feng, X., Huang, Y., Yang, H.: Exploration of electrical and novel optical chip-to-chip interconnects. IEEE Design Test **31**(5), 28–35 (2014)
14. Steinhogl, W., Schindler, G., Steinlesberger, G., Engelhardt, M.: Size-dependent resistivity of metallic wires in the mesoscopic range. Phys. Rev. B **66** (2002). 075414–4
15. Tong, X.C.: Advanced Materials for Integrated Optical Waveguides. Springer Series in Advanced Microelectronics, vol. 46, 1st edn. Springer, Heidelberg (2014). https://doi.org/10.1007/978-3-319-01550-7
16. Mark, J. E.: Polymer Data Handbook. Oxford University press, (1999)
17. Gall, D.: Electron mean free path in elemental metal. J. Appl. Phys. **119**, 085101–085105 (2016)
18. Grote, J.G., Jetts, J.S., Nelson, R.L., Hopkins, F.K.: Effect of conductivity and dielectric on the modulation voltage for optoelectronic devices based on nonlinear polymers. Opt. Eng. **40**(11), 2464–2473 (2001). Society of Photo-Optical Instrumentation Engineers

19. Nasiri, S.H., Faez, R., Moravvej-Farshi, M.K.: Compact formulae for number of conduction channels in various types of graphene nanoribbons at various temperatures. Mod. Phys. Lett. B **26**(1) (2012). 1150004–5
20. Gupta, P., Kumar, G.: Analysis of single wall carbon nanotubes interconnect & comparison with copper interconnects at different technology nodes. Int. J. Sci. Eng. Res. **5**(5), 579–583 (2014)

Network-on-Chip

Heuristic Driven Genetic Algorithm for Priority Assignment of Real-Time Communications in NoC

Ajay Khare[✉], Chinmay Patil[✉], Manikanta Nallamalli,
and Santanu Chattopadhyay

Indian Institute of Technology Kharagpur, Kharagpur, West Bengal, India
khareajay03@gmail.com, chinmaympatil@gmail.com, manin1220@gmail.com,
santanu@ece.iitkgp.ac.in

Abstract. Network-on-chip (NoC) is a paradigm shift for communication of cores in Multi-Processor System. Task mapping and priority assignment of communications is one of the critical aspects in Real-Time NoC design. Fixed priority pre-emptive arbitration is most widely used in worm-hole switched NoCs. Flow priorities, used in this arbitration, determine the network latency and are therefore crucial in guaranteeing deadline satisfaction of real-time communications. Earlier work presented in literature for flow priority assignment uses a heuristic based exhaustive search algorithm (HSA). HSA is faster but non optimal, in terms of number of priority assignments explored. Two graph-based priority assignment techniques, the GESA and the GHSA which improved on HSA also have been explored. These techniques reduce search space significantly by exploiting the interference dependencies of flows in the NoC. In this paper a search based exploratory solution to the flow priority assignment problem is proposed with a Genetic Algorithm (GA) whose evolution is guided by experimentally determined heuristics. It is compared with existing techniques and is found to give a better or equal solution in lesser computation time in most of the cases. Execution time of tasks is also considered while assigning flow priorities to make the algorithm practically applicable to real-time systems.

Keywords: Real-time · Network-on-chip · Priority assignment ·
Schedulability · Heuristics · Genetic Algorithm

1 Introduction

Embedded Systems are normally real-time systems that are designed to meet application specific requirements. Multiprocessor systems are commonly used for the development of these real-time embedded systems. Designers are integrating complex heterogeneous functional elements into a single device, known as a System on Chip (SoC) [22]. In SoC, different components need on chip communication. SoC design work started with point to point communication and

© Springer Nature Singapore Pte Ltd. 2019
S. Rajaram et al. (Eds.): VDAT 2018, CCIS 892, pp. 433–445, 2019.
https://doi.org/10.1007/978-981-13-5950-7_37

bus based architecture. But as the number of communicating elements increased, these solutions suffered from problems of scalability and performance due to communication bottleneck [7]. In the last decade, the Network on chip (NoC) has gained a lot of traction as the scalable and reliable communication paradigm for on chip communication [2,3]. A NoC connects all the IP (Intellectual Property) cores with a layer of inter-connected routers that use these links for communication between any two cores. A NoC based multiprocessor system can have a real-time communication requirement, where the correctness relies not only on the communication result but also on the completion time bound [21].

NoCs having a large number of cores predominantly use packet switching techniques. Wormhole switching, specifically, is popular and widely used in NoCs because of its reduced buffer usage [15]. A packet transmitted over the network has a time bound to reach the destination, denoted by the packet network latency. For hard real-time communications (flows), it is necessary that all the packets generated by the flows must be delivered before their deadlines to ensure correct execution. Employing such architectural considerations, combining response-time equations for tasks with latency equations for flows [20], it is possible to execute a feasibility analysis over the system in order to achieve temporal guarantees [5].

In NoC based multi-core system design, one of the crucial steps is to find priority assignments of flows of an application. Fixed priority pre-emptive arbitration in the routers of a NoC is a major factor in determining flow latencies. This arbitration causes packet latencies to be non-deterministic as a result of contentions causing delay and jitter in packet delivery. Prediction of these latencies at design time is therefore important to guarantee a certain degree of deadline satisfaction i.e. schedulability of the application.

As shown in Fig. 1, a task graph is mapped onto a 3×3 NoC, and three flows have been highlighted with colours. These flows will have to contend for common links on their paths, and the higher priority flow will block the lower priority one. If priorities of f_1, f_2, and f_3 are such that $f_1 > f_2 > f_3$, f_1 can block f_2 which in turn can block f_3, leading to indirect interference. Higher the interference, more will be the network latency of the flow, and greater are its chances of missing its deadline. Assigning optimal priorities to flows so that maximum number of flows are schedulable is thus crucial in real-time NoC design.

The contribution of this paper is in experimentally finding optimal heuristics for priority assignment of flows accounting for execution of tasks. These heuristics are then used to converge a Genetic Algorithm faster. These priority assignment heuristics use different aspects derived from task graphs to guide the optimization process.

This paper is organized as follows. Section 2 describes the literature Review and related work. Section 3 discusses the system model used and the mathematical foundation of schedulability analysis for real-time NoC. Section 4 gives brief information about Genetic Algorithms (GA) and its implementation. Section 5 establishes experimental work covering details of the derived heuristics and their

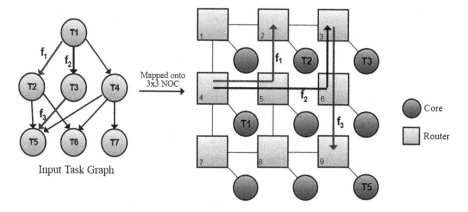

Fig. 1. The flow priority assignment problem. (Color figure online)

use in the evolution of GA. Section 6 presents the results and comparisons with existing techniques. Conclusions and future work are discussed in Sect. 7.

2   Related Work

This section presents a review of literature on priority assignment and scheduling in the domain of NoC based MPSoC. Worst Case Schedulability analysis, used widely for mapping and priority assignment, was first established in the base work of Shi and Burns [20]. Separate end-to-end schedulability tests were designed in [5]. The state-of-the-art analysis model for real-time communication of [20] is revisited in [23]. Xiong et al., in [23], show that the model may provide pessimistic or even incorrect network delay upper-bound. Revised analysis in [6] corrects the flaws in the previous model by classifying interference into upstream and downstream according to the relative positions of traffic flows. Simulated evaluations show that revised model provides tighter and correct network delay upper-bound compared with the state-of-the-art model.

When an application is mapped over cores, selection of appropriate processing elements for the execution of tasks is decided by the mapping [17]. Main objective of the mapping in non-real-time domain is to reduce consumption of energy and minimize the delay. With increased scope of embedded systems having real-time requirements [4,14], task mapping and flow priority assignment with schedulability analysis has become quite important. Several mapping algorithms that consider real-time NoC constraints have been explored. Discussion and development of different heuristics for improving task mapping in the context of Genetic Algorithms has been considered in previous work [11–13,16]. In [16], Racu et al. used a Genetic Algorithm for mapping a real-time application. The GA explores both the mapping as well as priority ordering of the task set so that all tasks and communications meet their deadlines.

Priority assignment for tasks to be executed on single processor systems is a quite well known problem and many solutions of that exist. Rate Monotonic and Deadline Monotonic priority assignment are some of them [8,9]. Audsley's optimal priority assignment algorithm, which guarantees to find a priority assignment in a polynomial number of schedulability tests, is not optimal for NoC [1].

In [19], it has been presented that none of the earlier priority assignment policies work well for assigning priorities to communications in wormhole switched networks. A heuristic based branch and bound search algorithm (HSA) was introduced to find a possible priority ordering for flows. In comparison to the traditional exhaustive algorithm which has exponential complexity, the HSA is much faster with the drawback of missing certain schedulable cases. In [10], two graph based priority assignment algorithms, the Graph Exhaustive Search Algorithm (GESA) and the Graph Heuristic Search Algorithm (GHSA) have been presented. Compared to HSA, it reduces the search space significantly by exploiting the interference dependencies of flows in the NoC. The results in their paper show that the GESA can always achieve higher schedulability ratios than the HSA, but may require longer processing time. On the other hand, the GHSA has the same performance as the HSA regarding the schedulability, but can significantly improve the efficiency.

The contributions made in this paper are as follows:

- Focus on priority assignment of flows considering execution time of tasks and worst case latency within its deadline bound.
- A search based exploratory solution to the priority assignment problem is proposed with a Genetic Algorithm (GA) that uses experimentally determined heuristics for converging faster and with a better solution.
- The proposed solution is evaluated on synthetic applications and compared with existing techniques of GESA and GHSA. Results clearly show that the proposed technique performs better than GESA in terms of schedulability as well as time taken to converge. The proposed technique has better or equally good solution as the GHSA in almost the same computation time.

3   Mathematical Foundation and System Model

The system model used here consists of a set of tasks and flows. Each task has attributes, task $= \{d, t, p, c\}$ where d is deadline, t is period, p is task priority and c is task execution time. Order of tasks picked up for execution on a core is assumed to be arbitrary. A traffic flow is a series of packets sent over the NoC from a source task to a destination task. Each flow has the following attributes, flow $= \{D, T, P, C, J^R\}$, where, D is the flow deadline, T is the time interval between successive releases of flow, P is the flow priority, C is the basic network latency, for the flow to reach destination from source in zero contention situation. J^R is the release jitter which is the deviation encountered while releasing flow from task. A flow is sent only after the source task completes execution. All packets in a flow inherit priority level from the flow. A fixed priority preemptive model is assumed for the routers, with as many VCs as there are flows in the network. Execution of tasks, and the resulting response time is considered for determining flow schedulability. The deadline of a flow is assumed to be equal to that of its sending task and not greater than its period. Time bound response is the main objective in Real-time NoCs. With regards to this, predicting reliable end-to-end packet transmission latencies has been a major challenge. The pioneering work in this direction done by Shi and Burns [20] proposes a design time worst-case schedulability analysis considering inter-dependencies between data flows. The worst case network latency (R), defined in [20], is the latency encountered by the flow assuming maximum contention in the network. Xiong et al. in [23], pointed out drawbacks in [20] when buffering effects are considered. Indrusiak et al. in [6], considered the problem created by buffering and back pressure and extended [20] by improving the worst case latency given in (1).

$$R_i^{n+1} = C_i + \sum_{\forall \tau_j \in S_i^D} \left\lceil \frac{R_i^n + J_j^R + J_j^I}{T_j} \right\rceil \cdot (C_j + I_{ji}^{down}) \tag{1}$$

Here interference from all directly interfering flows is considered with J^I being the effect of other flows indirectly interfering $flow_i$ through $flow_j$. I_{ji}^{down} is the downstream interference given in (2).

$$I_{ji}^{down} = \sum_{\forall \tau_k \in S_{I_i}^{down_j}} \left\lceil \frac{R_j + J_k}{T_k} \right\rceil \cdot bi_{ij} \tag{2}$$

In this paper, task execution is also considered within the flow deadlines, and thus the response time analysis for tasks defined in [18], is used. The response time of a task is given in (3).

$$r_i^{n+1} = c_i + \sum_{\forall Task_j \in hp(i)} \left\lceil \frac{r_i^n}{t_j} \right\rceil \cdot c_j \tag{3}$$

Given that r_i and d_i are the response time and deadline of a $task_i$, the task is schedulable if,

$$r_i \leq d_i \tag{4}$$

On the other hand, if r_i is the response time of the source task of $flow_i$ and R_i is the worst case latency of that flow, then $flow_i$ is schedulable if its sending task completes execution as well as the flow reaches its destination, all within the deadline of the flow, i.e.

$$r_i + R_i \leq d_i \tag{5}$$

4   Implementation of Genetic Algorithm

Genetic Algorithm (GA) is an evolutionary meta-heuristic useful in cases where complex relationships have to be modelled and optimized. A population of candidate solutions is evolved over generations to find the fittest solution. Evolution of particles is done using the usual genetic operators of cross-over and mutation.

Typically, the type of the quantity to be optimized, and its formulation defines the structure of the chromosome. For optimizing the priority assignment the chromosome structure, shown in Fig. 2 is an ordering of priorities where each number in the array represents priority level, and index of the array represents flow to which it is assigned.

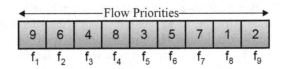

Fig. 2. Chromosome structure.

For the problem of optimizing priority assignment, the mapping is assumed fixed, and has been obtained from previous techniques presented in [16]. Fitness function for each particle is the worst-case schedulability obtained using the priority assignment in the chromosome and the fixed mapping that is assumed beforehand. In the evolution of GA, operators like crossover and mutation are applied along with fitness based parent selection and elitism.

5   Experimental Work

5.1   Heuristics Derived from Task Graph and Mapping

The priority assignment that we get from a usual GA formulation does not typically use all the information at hand. In order to make the optimization relevant to the task at hand, information from the task graphs is used to guide the evolution of particles. Task graphs give information about the volume of communication flows, task and flow deadlines, and the dependency of tasks. The following heuristics were derived and used in the evolution of GA:

Hop Heuristic: The mapping of a task graph on a NoC gives a very intuitive approach for prioritizing flows. When each task is mapped on the platform, we can easily get the number of hops that a particular flow has to travel to get to its destination. These number of hops can help in assigning priority to each flow based on the fact that higher the number of hops, more time will the flow take to travel, and more probable would it be to miss its deadline. Hence, flows with higher number of hops are given precedence over those having smaller hops.

Volume Heuristic: Each flow is assigned a particular volume of data that it is supposed to transmit from one task to another. A simple way of prioritizing flows is to allow flows having larger volume to have higher priority. A flow with a larger volume would occupy links along its path for a longer time than a flow having the same path but smaller volume. Higher the time a flow occupies links, higher is its probability of interfering with other flows and missing deadline.

Deadline Heuristic: This is same as Earliest Deadline First, and although quite fundamental, makes a lot of sense to prioritize flows according to deadline. Flows that have earliest deadline, have to reach the destination in the least amount of time compared to other flows.

Response Heuristic: When multiple tasks are mapped to the same core, the task that is picked up last for execution has to wait for the other tasks to finish execution so that it can start sending packets to another task. In general, a flow has a time proportional to the difference of response time and the flow deadline to reach the destination. So it follows that a flow having lesser time to travel (greater source task response time) has to be prioritized ahead of the flows having lesser response time.

5.2   Experimental Observations for Applying Heuristics

Although all the above heuristics are logical at first glance, no single heuristic works best for all cases, for all task graphs, for all platform sizes. This is no surprise as the flow priority assignment problem is quite complicated to be solved by such simple heuristics. It was clear that some combination of these heuristics had to work for all cases. To investigate this, the mapping was fixed to a reasonably good one, and a large set of particles stuck at local maxima (98% fitness) were compared to particles at global maxima (100% fitness). The particles were sorted in different order of heuristics to see if a pattern was visible in the data that would differentiate between the fully schedulable particles from the ones at local maxima.

As shown in Fig. 3, it was found that when hops, response time, deadline, and volume heuristics are applied in that particular order, the top 15 priorities of all fully schedulable particles clustered to the top whereas the same priorities were scattered in the local maxima particles. The particles having 100% fitness showed maximum consistency when sorted in this order. Hence this particular order was used in the evolution of GA for obtaining better results.

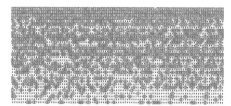 

Fig. 3. On the left is a set of chromosomes stuck in local maxima (98%), while those on the right are in global maxima (100%). Distinguishing pattern is observed after sorting in a particular order.

5.3   Evolution of GA with Heuristics

As observed before, heuristics help in obtaining fully schedulable solution. In this paper, we present the Heuristic Driven Genetic Algorithm (HDGA) that makes use of these heuristics. Initially, four particles having their priority assignment sorted according to hops, deadline, volume and response time difference were obtained. Along with this, as we saw, a particular order of heuristic sorting is found to perform better. Hence, three particles were created with small changes in that experimentally determined order applied from left to right for priority assignment:

- Deadline, Hop, Response, Volume
- Hop, Deadline, Response, Volume
- Response, Hop, Deadline, Volume

The point of having multiple orders was that, a single order did not work best on all task graphs, for all platform sizes. If we call these orders, O_1, O_2 and O_3, then the particles that we obtain using them would be P_1, P_2, and P_3. In each generation, along with crossover and mutation, these particles P_1, P_2 and P_3, and their simple mutations were added into the current population. Crossover helps in exploring solutions near the maximum fitness, whereas mutations help in converging the optimization. So, mutating heuristic particles would make the GA explore solutions somewhere near them in the search space.

In order to make the GA exploratory in nature, a part of the population was refreshed with random particles every few generations. Whenever population was refreshed, each time, P_1, P_2, P_3, and their mutations were inserted at random points in the population so that refreshing does not take the GA much further away from heuristic guided search space.

To see the effect of these heuristics, the performance of a simple GA without heuristics was compared with HDGA. As shown in Fig. 4, it was found that the heuristics improved convergence of the HDGA and that too with better global fitness than the simple GA. The combination of heuristics in a particular order did help in improving performance of the GA.

5.4   Validating Worst-Case Analysis

In order to find out how tight the worst-case bound in [6] is, a real time simulator was needed that could simulate a task graph, given its mapping and priority assignment. This simulator could give us the actual number of schedulable tasks and flows, which could be compared to that predicted by worst-case analysis.

A two-phase design was implemented for the simulator consisting of an evaluation phase and an updation phase. Flit movement of each flow was evaluated first for all routers. Updation started with header flit of highest priority flow in the network, and the movement of flits was achieved by consequent updation. During updation whenever a flit is blocked by another higher priority flit, updation is stopped for that flow. A router-cycle accurate simulator was thus designed to obtain real-time latencies of flows.

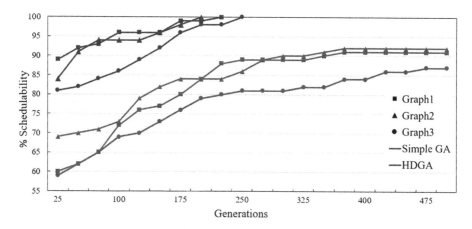

Fig. 4. Effect of heuristics on GA evolution.

For a fixed set of parameters, the simulator was run for 50 ms of execution of the application. The average schedulability in every 10 ms was observed and plotted as shown in Fig. 5.

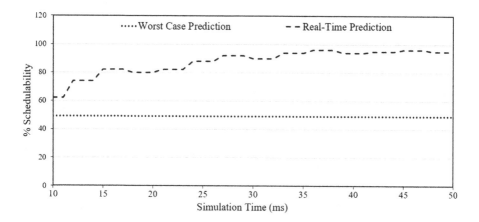

Fig. 5. Comparing real-time schedulability with worst-case schedulability.

This was seen to be well above the schedulability predicted by worst-case analysis. The worst-case upper bound was thus validated by ensuring that the simulated real-time latencies are really upper bounded by the worst case predictions.

6 Results

HDGA was tested on four synthetic graphs, two of them communication intensive (first two) and two computation intensive (last two). To evaluate the proposed algorithm, it was compared with the previous state-of-the-art graph-based

Table 1. Performance evaluation of priority assignment techniques[abc]

Task graph	NoC size	Avg. % schedulability			Avg. time taken (sec)		
		HDGA	GHSA	GESA	HDGA	GHSA	GESA
Comm25	3 × 3	80.34	*	*	10.43	15	3600
	3 × 4	89.95	*	*	8.44	15	3600
	4 × 4	94.9	89.55	94.81 (9)	10.22	4.71	3600
	4 × 5	99.1	97.29	96.58	2.87	4.59	3085
	5 × 5	99.66	98.61	98.40	2.03	2.18	2571
Comm30	4 × 4	84.44	*	69.23 (1)	16.49	15	3600
	4 × 5	88.08	87.1 (1)	*	16.95	15	3600
	5 × 5	95.68	94.3 (9)	93.4 (9)	12.73	8.96	3200
	5 × 6	98.88	96.11	96.7 (4)	4.28	3.44	3600
	6 × 6	98.97	97.53	95.6 (13)	4.99	3.87	3046
Comp25	3 × 3	65.12	*	*	11.13	15	3600
	3 × 4	74.18	*	*	10.35	15	3600
	4 × 4	86.06	77.6 (1)	75.3 (2)	7.89	6.84	3600
	4 × 5	90.6	81.66	83.46	12.67	6.75	3600
	5 × 5	91.2	88.48	85.89	8.39	8.44	3600
Comp30	4 × 4	65.87	*	*	12.31	15	3600
	4 × 5	77.71	*	*	9.52	15	3600
	5 × 5	92.81	91.8 (9)	92.7 (8)	4.54	3.67	3600
	5 × 6	100	100 (9)	99.71	3.06	1.21	761
	6 × 6	100	100(12)	99.91	1.95	0.83	257

[a]'*' is marked in cases where algorithm was not able to converge in allocated time limit
[b]CommX - Communication intensive; CompX - Computation intensive; X - # tasks
[c]Figure in round brackets indicates number of times out of 15 where technique converged

priority assignment algorithms [10]. Liu et al. proposed two algorithms in [10], one graph heuristic based (GHSA), and one graph exhaustive based (GESA). GHSA, according to the authors, gave quicker but not always optimal results, whereas, GESA took larger amount of time, but came up with the best possible solution. As obtaining best schedulability was the main criterion, HDGA was compared with GESA. In order to compare both, GESA was modified to consider task response times within the flow deadline. They were both tested on the same task graphs with 15 different mappings of good quality. GESA was allowed to execute for a maximum of 1 h, and after that, the maximum obtained till then, was taken as the result. A core-i5 CPU clocked at 3.2 GHz was used as the evaluation platform. For observing trends and making inferences, each task graph was mapped onto 5 different NoC sizes. The average schedulability of both techniques and their respective computation times are reported in Table 1.

In cases where the NoC size was small with respect to the number of tasks, neither GESA nor GHSA was able to converge to a priority assignment within the allotted time. When number of available cores for mapping was almost 50 to 60% of the number of tasks to be mapped, more than one task will be mapped onto a core. As described in the system model, the flow deadlines have to account for sending task response time and worst case network latency of the flow. In cases where GESA failed to converge, the response time of the sending task was larger than the flow deadline itself. HDGA, in this case, assigned lowest priority to this flow because other flows have a better chance of being schedulable than this particular flow.

GESA, on the other hand, has to assign priority levels to all flows one by one. It keeps on progressing and backtracking till it exhausts all possible priority assignments, because it can never assign priority to that one flow which has sending task response time greater than its deadline. GESA is designed to find a fully schedulable priority assignment, and when that does not occur, it does not converge. The computation time for GESA thus depends on how long it is allowed to explore. To account for this, while reporting average schedulability values, the number of times GESA could converge in the allocated time, is mentioned in round brackets () beside the average. In cases where GESA could not converge even once for all the mappings, a '*' is indicated.

The following observations can be made from the results:

- HDGA could converge to a solution logarithmically faster than GESA, and in almost the same time as GHSA with better schedulability.
- HDGA converges ≈ 9.7% faster for communication intensive task graphs compared to computation intensive ones, because in these cases, the number of flows as well as communication volumes is high. So the heuristics which are largely flow based will have a significant effect in improving fitness of the population.
- GESA and GHSA both converged only when number of available cores was comparable to number of tasks.
- HDGA obtained a 3.2% increase compared to GHSA, and a 5% increase compared to GESA on the basis of percentage schedulability.
- GHSA converges ≈ 20% faster than HDGA in cases where the platform size is larger. But, its schedulability is still 4% lesser than HDGA.
- GHSA obtained better schedulability than GESA in some cases because GHSA takes greedy decisions at each priority level, whereas GESA explores all possible solutions. So, GESA might reach the same schedulability as GHSA, just not in the allotted time.
- Increasing no of available cores drastically increases schedulability for both techniques in computation intensive task graphs because availability of a core provides an extra resource for execution, making response times smaller thus reducing impact on flow deadlines.

– Computation intensive tasks cause response time to be higher, reducing time available for flows to travel to destination. Hence schedulability for smaller NoCs is almost 14% lower compared to larger NOCs in HDGA.

7   Conclusion and Future Work

In this paper, we have presented a genetic algorithm (HDGA) for priority assignment of communications in real-time NoC. Using experimentally derived heuristics from input task graphs, the GA converged much faster, with better results. This formulation considers task execution along with flow transmission while assigning flow priorities which makes it more practical for real-time applications. Results show that the proposed technique obtains 5% better schedulability than the existing graph-based priority assignment algorithms (GESA, GHSA). HDGA was observed to converge logarithmically faster than GESA and within similar computation times as GHSA. It was also found that the existing techniques failed to converge in cases of small NoC platforms where a fully schedulable solution was not possible. In such cases our technique obtained $\approx 80\%$ schedulability on average.

The proposed algorithm optimizes priority assignment assuming a predetermined mapping of good quality. The current algorithm can be modified to evolve both mapping and priority assignment together. Also, when mapping multiple tasks onto the same core, an arbitrary task is picked up for execution in the current system model. These task priorities can be optimized along with flow priorities to get the best schedulability.

References

1. Audsley, N.C.: Optimal priority assignment and feasibility of static priority tasks with arbitrary start times. Citeseer (1991)
2. Benini, L., De Micheli, G.: Networks on chips: a new SoC paradigm. Computer **35**(1), 70–78 (2002)
3. Dally, W.J., Towles, B.: Route packets, not wires: on-chip interconnection networks. In: Proceedings of Design Automation Conference 2001, pp. 684–689. IEEE (2001)
4. De Dinechin, B.D., Van Amstel, D., Poulhiès, M., Lager, G.: Time-critical computing on a single-chip massively parallel processor. In: Proceedings of the Conference on Design, Automation & Test in Europe, p. 97. European Design and Automation Association (2014)
5. Indrusiak, L.S.: End-to-end schedulability tests for multiprocessor embedded systems based on networks-on-chip with priority-preemptive arbitration. J. Syst. Architect. **60**(7), 553–561 (2014)
6. Indrusiak, L.S., Burns, A., Nikolic, B.: Analysis of buffering effects on hard real-time priority-preemptive wormhole networks. arXiv preprint arXiv:1606.02942 (2016)
7. Lee, H.G., Chang, N., Ogras, U.Y., Marculescu, R.: On-chip communication architecture exploration: a quantitative evaluation of point-to-point, bus, and network-on-chip approaches. ACM Trans. Design Autom. Electron. Syst. (TODAES) **12**(3), 23 (2007)

8. Leung, J.Y.T., Whitehead, J.: On the complexity of fixed-priority scheduling of periodic, real-time tasks. Perform. Eval. **2**(4), 237–250 (1982)
9. Liu, C.L., Layland, J.W.: Scheduling algorithms for multiprogramming in a hard-real-time environment. J. ACM (JACM) **20**(1), 46–61 (1973)
10. Liu, M., Becker, M., Behnam, M., Nolte, T.: Improved priority assignment for real-time communications in on-chip networks. In: Proceedings of the 23rd International Conference on Real Time and Networks Systems, pp. 171–180. ACM (2015)
11. Mesidis, P., Indrusiak, L.S.: Genetic mapping of hard real-time applications onto NoC-based MPSoCs-a first approach. In: 2011 6th International Workshop on Reconfigurable Communication-centric Systems-on-Chip (ReCoSoC), pp. 1–6. IEEE (2011)
12. Mitchell, M.: An Introduction to Genetic Algorithms. MIT Press, Cambridge (1998)
13. Mohd Sayuti, M., Indrusiak, L.S., Garcia-Ortiz, A.: An optimisation algorithm for minimising energy dissipation in NoC-based hard real-time embedded systems. In: Proceedings of the 21st International Conference on Real-Time Networks and Systems, pp. 3–12. ACM (2013)
14. Nélis, V., et al.: The challenge of time-predictability in modern many-core architectures. In: 14th International Workshop on Worst-Case Execution Time Analysis (2014)
15. Ni, L.M., McKinley, P.K.: A survey of wormhole routing techniques in direct networks. Computer **26**(2), 62–76 (1993)
16. Racu, A., Indrusiak, L.S.: Using genetic algorithms to map hard real-time on NoC-based systems. In: 2012 7th International Workshop on Reconfigurable Communication-Centric Systems-on-Chip (ReCoSoC), pp. 1–8. IEEE (2012)
17. Sahu, P.K., Chattopadhyay, S.: A survey on application mapping strategies for network-on-chip design. J. Syst. Architect. **59**(1), 60–76 (2013)
18. Sayuti, M.N.S.M., Indrusiak, L.S.: A function for hard real-time system search-based task mapping optimisation. In: 2015 IEEE 18th International Symposium on Real-Time Distributed Computing (ISORC), pp. 66–73. IEEE (2015)
19. Shi, Z., Burns, A.: Priority assignment for real-time wormhole communication in on-chip networks. In: Real-Time Systems Symposium 2008, pp. 421–430. IEEE (2008)
20. Shi, Z., Burns, A.: Real-time communication analysis for on-chip networks with wormhole switching. In: Second ACM/IEEE International Symposium on Networks-on-Chip 2008. NoCS 2008, pp. 161–170. IEEE (2008)
21. Sparsø, J.: Design of networks-on-chip for real-time multi-processor systems-on-chip. In: 2012 12th International Conference on Application of Concurrency to System Design (ACSD), pp. 1–5. IEEE (2012)
22. Wolf, W.: Multiprocessor system-on-chip technology. IEEE Signal Process. Mag. **26**(6) (2009)
23. Xiong, Q., Lu, Z., Wu, F., Xie, C.: Real-time analysis for wormhole NoC: revisited and revised. In: 2016 International Great Lakes Symposium on VLSI, pp. 75–80. IEEE (2016)

A Novel Fault-Tolerant Routing Algorithm for Mesh-of-Tree Based Network-on-Chips

Monil Shah[1], Mohit Upadhyay[1], P. Veda Bhanu[1(✉)], J. Soumya[1], and Linga Reddy Cenkeramaddi[2]

[1] Birla Institute of Technology and Science - Pilani, Hyderabad Campus, Hyderabad 500078, Telangana, India
shahmonil1996@gmail.com, mupadhyay09@gmail.com, vedabhanuiit2010@gmail.com, soumyatkgp@gmail.com
[2] University of Agder, postboks 422, 4630 Kristiansand S, Norway
linga.cenkeramaddi@uia.no

Abstract. Use of bus architecture based communication with increasing processing elements in System-on-Chip (SoC) leads to severe degradation of performance and speed of the system. This bottleneck is overcome with the introduction of Network-on-Chips (NoCs). NoCs assist in communication between cores on a single chip using router based packet switching technique. Due to miniaturization, NoCs like every Integrated circuit is prone to different kinds of faults which can be transient, intermittent or permanent. A fault in any one component of such a crucial network can degrade performance leaving other components non-usable. This paper presents a novel Fault-Tolerant routing Algorithm for Mesh-of-Tree (MoT) topology in presence of stem faults. The proposed technique is compared with routing technique already in the literature. The results show improvements in terms of number of packets reaching destination routers from any source routers in MoT network in presence of faults, by scaling the topology size.

Keywords: System-on-Chip · Network-on-Chip · Fault-Tolerance · Mesh-of-Tree Topology · Routing

1 Introduction

With advances in integrated circuits (IC) manufacturing, more and more transistors are placed on single chip, in an attempt to improve resource utilization and efficiency [6]. This has lead to increased communication complexities in existing System-on-chip (SoC) communication architecture [1]. Decreased signal integrity, cross talk effects and increased delay due to coupled capacitances degrade the efficiency of the network further [9]. Network-on-Chip (NoC)

This work is partially supported by the research project No. ECR/2016/001389 Dt. 06/03/2017, sponsored by the SERB, Government of India.

ⓒ Springer Nature Singapore Pte Ltd. 2019
S. Rajaram et al. (Eds.): VDAT 2018, CCIS 892, pp. 446–459, 2019.
https://doi.org/10.1007/978-981-13-5950-7_38

was thus found to be a modular and scalable alternative architecture to the increased inter-core communication demands [2]. NoCs employ router based packet switching network [3]. Processing elements in a NoC are namely network interfaces(NIs), Routers or switches, and links.

In deep sub-micron technology, ICs are prone to defects that cannot be entirely eliminated even with the best technology available. This leads to three different kinds of faults namely permanent, intermittent and transient [7]. Most of the routing techniques reported in the literature are for standard topologies like Torus and Mesh. A review of different routing algorithms in NoC with advantages and disadvantages has been summarized in [8], but a potential topology, Mesh-of-Tree (MoT), has not been addressed. The MoT based topology has many advantages like small router degree, small diameter, large bisection width along with a symmetric and recursive structure when compared to the direct network topologies like Torus or Mesh [5]. This has motivated us to design an efficient fault-tolerant routing technique for MoT topology based NoC while considering permanent faults in the stem routers. Same addressing scheme is used as given in [4]. The rest of the paper is organized as follows. Section 2 gives an overview of the MoT topology and its addressing scheme. Section 3 describes the existing fault-free routing algorithm. Section 4 describes the proposed fault-tolerant routing algorithm. Section 5 presents a comparison of both the algorithms with examples. Section 6 shows the experimental results by varying size of topology and number of faults, followed by conclusion in Sect. 7.

2   Overview

This section gives a brief overview of MoT topology and its advantages. Section 2.1 discusses the properties of MoT network and Sect. 2.2 discusses the addressing scheme used.

2.1   Mesh-of-Tree Structure

The MoT topology is a hybrid interconnect network. The properties of MoT topology [8] have been described below. Considering an $A \times B$ MoT structure (where A and B denotes the number of row trees and column trees respectively) has the following properties:

- Number of Routers = 3 * (A * B) − (A + B).
- Diameter = $2 * (log_2 A) + 2 * (log_2 B)$.
- Bisection width = min (A, B).
- Symmetric and recursive structure.

For an $A \times B$ MoT structure, the number of routers are as follows:

- Number of leaf routers = A * B.
- Number of level 1 stem routers = $2^N * (A + B)$.
- Number of level 2 stem routers = $2^{N-1} * (A + B)$.
- Number of level 3 stem routers = $2^{N-2} * (A + B)$.

Similarly,

- Number of level N stem routers = 2 * (A + B).
- Number of root routers = A + B.

The Fig. 1 shows an 4 × 4 MoT structure, having 4 row trees and 4 column trees. The leaf routers are attached to both the trees. Two cores are connected to each of the leaf router.

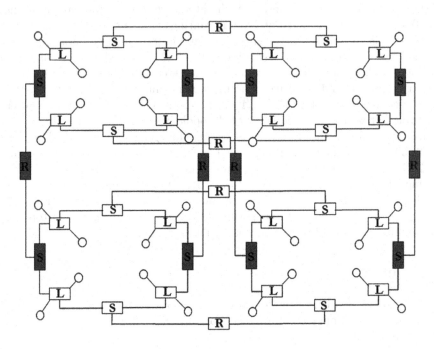

Fig. 1. 4 × 4 MoT Structure along with the cores attached

2.2 Addressing Scheme

In a MoT, each router address consists of four different fields: (i) Row Number (R^N) (ii) Column Level (C^L) (iii) Column Number (C^N) (iv) Row Level (R^L). For every row tree, the value of R^N is fixed; thus, for a 4 × 4 MoT, R^N values are 00,01,10 and 11. The R^L values are gradually incremented by 1 from the leaf level to the root level of a row tree. In a row tree, C^L is 00 for all the routers. C^N is assigned as 00,01,10 and 11 for the column trees. For a column tree, the C^L values are incremented by 1 from the leaf level to the column level. The R^L values for all column tree routers is equal to 00. The R^L values for all column tree routers is equal to 00. An additional Core-ID bit is introduced for each core at the same leaf router as they have the same R^N,C^L,C^N,R^L. For example the address for the top-left leaf router cores are 0-00-00-00-00 or 1-00-00-00-00 based on the core bit ID , the bottom-right router has addresses 0-11-00-11-00 and 1-11-00-11-00

3 Routing Algorithm

The routing algorithm follows a deterministic approach. This ensures that the data packet reaches the destination through the shortest path, and is always live-lock free. This algorithm has been proposed in [4]. The following abbreviations are used to describe the algorithm.

- addrs_curr : to denote current router address
- addrs_dest : to denote the destination router address

Algorithm is executed by the leaf and stem routers only, top level root routers are simply First In First Out (FIFO) Buffers and hence do not execute the algorithm. The routing algorithm is given as Algorithm 1

Algorithm 1. Non-FTR Algorithm

Input: Address of the Source router (R^N, C^L, C^N, R^L), and the Destination router (R^N, C^L, C^N, R^L).
Output: Shortest Path from Source Router (R^N, C^L, C^N, R^L) to Destination Router (R^N, C^L, C^N, R^L).
    if R^N of addrs_curr $\neq$ R^N of addrs_dest **then**
        Route to the Column Parent;   **Part I**
    else if C^L of addrs_curr $\neq$ C^L of addrs_dest **then**
        Route to the Column Child having equal R^N as addrs_dest;
    else if C^N of addrs_curr $\neq$ C^N of addrs_dest **then**
        Route to the Row Parent;   **Part II**
    else if R^L of addrs_curr $\neq$ R^L of addrs_dest **then**
        Route to the Row child having equal C^N as addrs_dest;
    else if Destination Core-ID = 0 **then**
        Route to Core 1;   **Part III**
    else
        Route to Core 2;
    end if

The Algorithm is divided into 3 stages. The first stage is responsible for routing the packet to same R^N as that of destination, second stage for routing packet to same C^N as that of destination and the final stage forwards the packet to the required core.In the *Part I* of the algorithm, if R^N of current and destination addresses are not equal, then it signifies that the current and the destination routers are at different row trees. Thus the packet is routed to the root of column tree and then to the respective leaf to equate the R^N and the C^L. For example, as shown in Fig. 2, if router address of the source router and the destination router are 01-00-00-00 and 11-00-10-00 respectively. The path traversed by the packet is 01-00-00-00, then 0X-01-00-00 then XX-10-00-00 then 1X-01-00-00 and finally 11-00-00-00. Therefore, after the first stage the packet will be at the same row tree as the destination router.

In *Part II* of the algorithm, if the C^N of current and destination addresses is not equal, then it signifies that the current and the destination routers are at different column trees. Thus the packet is routed to the root of row tree and then to the respective leaf to equate the C^N and R^L. For the above example, the path traversed by the packet is 11-00-00-00, then 11-00-0X-01 and then 11-00-XX-10 then 11-00-1X-01 and finally 11-00-10-00. Therefore, after the second stage the packet will reach the destination router where the destination core is present. In *Part III*, the packet is forwarded to the destination core based on the Core-ID bit of the destination core. This routing algorithm does not take into account the faults, hence it fails to route the packet to the destination in presence of faults in the specified path.

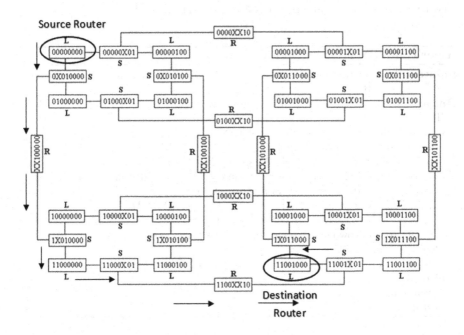

Fig. 2. Source Router at 01000000, Destination Router at 11001000

4   Proposed Fault-Tolerant Routing Algorithm

The proposed fault-tolerant algorithm also follows the deterministic approach. It uses the same addressing scheme as proposed in Sect. 2.2. The proposed algorithm is given as Algorithm 2.

– Algorithm 2 uses four functions namely adjust-for-row (addrs_curr), adjust-for-col (addrs_curr), equate-row (addrs_curr, addrs_dest) and equate-col (addrs_curr, addrs_dest).

Algorithm 2. FTR Algorithm

Input: Address of the Source router (R^N, C^L, C^N, R^L), Address of the Destination router (R^N, C^L, C^N, R^L) and Address of the Faulty router (R^N, C^L, C^N, R^L)
Output: Possible Shortest Path from Source router (R^N, C^L, C^N, R^L) to Destination router (R^N, C^L, C^N, R^L) .

  if C^N of addrs_curr = C^N of addrs_fault **then**
    if C^N of addrs_dest - C^N of addrs_curr = 0 **then**
      adjust-for-col (addrs_curr);
      equate-row (addrs_curr, addrs_dest);
    else
      equate-row (addrs_curr, addrs_dest);
      equate-col (addrs_curr, addrs_dest);
    end if
  else if R^N of addrs_curr = R^N of addrs_fault **then**
    if R^N of addrs_dest - R^N of addrs_curr = 0 **then**
      adjust-for-row (addrs_curr);
      equate-col (addrs_curr, addrs_dest);
    else
      equate-row (addrs_curr, addrs_dest);
      equate-col (addrs_curr, addrs_dest);
    end if
  else
    if R^N of addrs_dest - R^N of addrs_curr = 1 and R^N of addrs_dest = R^N of addrs_fault **then**
      equate-col (addrs_curr, addrs_dest);
      adjust-for-row (addrs_curr);
    else
      equate-row (addrs_curr, addrs_dest);
      if R^N of addrs_dest = R^N of addrs_fault **then**
        adjust-for-row (addrs_curr);
        equate-col (addrs_curr, addrs_dest);
        adjust-for-row (addrs_curr);
      else
        equate-col (addrs_curr, addrs_dest);
      end if
    end if
  end if
  if Destination Core-ID = 0 **then**
    Route to Core 1;
  else
    Route to Core 2;
  end if

– The function adjust-for-row (addrs_curr) is a user defined function which
adjusts the row number based on presence of fault in destination row and
routes the packet to the R^N where there is no fault.
– The function adjust-for-col (addrs_curr) is a similar function which adjusts
the col number based on presence of fault in destination col and routes the
packet to the C^N where there is no fault.
– The function equate-row (addrs_curr, addrs_dest) represents Part I mentioned
in the Algorithm 1. It brings the packet from the current router to the same
row tree as destination router.
– The function equate-col (addrs_curr, addrs_dest) is the Part II mentioned in
Algorithm 1. It brings the packet from the current tree to the same column
tree as addrs_dest. The final part is forwarding of packet to the core based
on core-ID bit in the packet.

There are two main parts in the algorithm proposed in [4]. Initial part will equate
row numbers (R^N) between current router and destination router. Similarly in
the second part of the algorithm [4] it will equate column numbers (C^N) between
current router and destination router. Our algorithm uses these two parts independently depending upon the fault present. In Algorithm 2, it checks whether
the fault is in row tree or column tree. If the fault is in a column tree i.e.,
same column tree as the current router, the algorithm first makes the column
numbers(C^N) equal and then it makes the row number(R^N) equal. This simply
means that the packet is routed to go through the row tree first and later on
to column tree. If the fault is in a row tree i.e., same row tree as the current
router, the algorithm works like the Algorithm mentioned in [4]. If the fault is in
destination row tree, the packet is re-routed to the adjacent row tree and then
the packet is passed to the adjacent row root router.

In the next section, we give a brief comparison between Algorithm proposed
in [4] and our proposed algorithm. We will demonstrate the working of our
algorithm by using a few examples.

5   Comparison of Proposed Algorithm with Algorithm proposed in [4]

In this section we compare Algorithms 1 and 2 by using few examples. The
example shown in Fig. 3 is the case when the source router address is 00-00-00-
00, the destination router address is 11-00-11-00. The faulty router address is
taken to be 0X-01-00-00, then the C^N of the current/source router and the faulty
router are the same. So, the packet will now go through the row tree and then
the column tree. According to our proposed algorithm the path traversed by the
packet will be 00-00-00-00, 00-00-0X-01, 00-00-XX-10, 00-00-1X-01, 00-00-11-00,
0X-01-11-00, XX-10-11-00, 1X-01-11-00, 11-00-11-00.

Algorithm proposed in [4] which is non fault-tolerant (non-FTR) fails at the
stem level. According to the Algorithm 1, the packet starts at the leaf router
00-00-00-00, and then goes on to equate R^N by routing on to the stem router

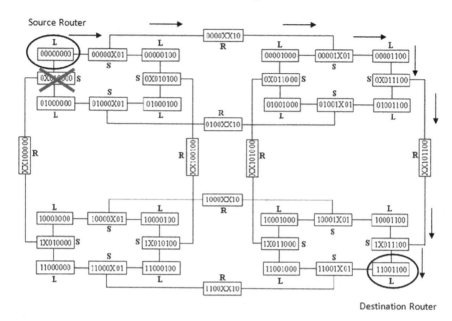

Fig. 3. Source Router at 00000000, Destination Router at 11001100 and Fault Router at 0X010000

whose address is 0X-01-00-00. But, in this example this particular stem is faulty. Hence, it cannot go further, thus failing to reach the destination. We take another example shown in Fig. 4 where the source, destination and the faulty router addresses are 00-00-00-00, 11-00-11-00 and 11-00-0X-01 respectively. In this case according to Algorithm 2, the packet follows the path 00-00-00-00, 0X-01-00-00, XX-10-00-10, 1X-01-00-00, 10-00-00-00, 10-00-0X-01, 10-00-XX-10, 10-00-1X-01, 10-00-11-00, 1X-01-11-00, 11-00-11-00.

In the example shown in Fig. 4, we can observe that the algorithm proposed in [4] fails after it reaches the row tree root. According to the algorithm, the packet starts at the router 00-00-00-00, then it moves to 0X-01-00-00, then to XX-10-00-00 and then to 1X-01-00-00 and moves on to 11-00-00-00. Here the algorithm in [4] fails as it will try to move the packet towards to 11-00-0X-01, but this is not possible as this stem root is faulty. Hence, the algorithm cited in [4] fails at the stem level.

Similarly, the example shown in Fig. 5 is a case when the source router address is 00-00-00-00, the destination router address is 11-00-00-00. The faulty router address is taken to be 1X-01-00-00, then the C^N of the source router and the fault router are the same. According to our algorithm the packet will select the adjacent column tree of the fault column tree. Figure 5 shows the path traversed by the packet using our algorithm will be 00-00-00-00, 00-00-0X-01, 00-00-01-00, 0X-01-01-00, XX-10-01-00, 1X-01-01-00, 11-00-01-00,11-00-0X-01 and finally 11-00-00-00 whereas the algorithm proposed in [4] fails at the row stem router near the destination router (1X-01-00-00) itself. It will route the packet

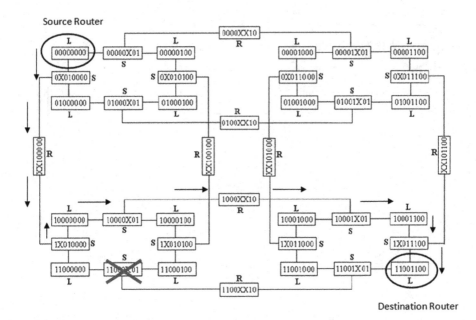

Fig. 4. Source Router at 00000000, Destination Router at 11001100 and Fault Router at 11000X01

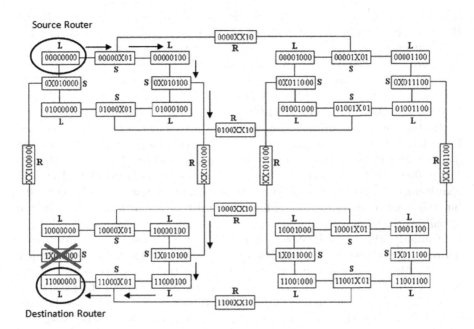

Fig. 5. Source Router at 00000000, Destination Router at 11000000 and Fault Router at 1X010000

to 00-00-00-00, and then to 0X-01-00-00 and then to the row root 1X-01-00-00. But, in this case the stem router near destination (1X-01-00-00) is faulty.

Similarly, the example shown in Fig. 6 is the case when the source router address is 00-00-00-00, the destination router address is 01-00-11-00. The faulty router address is taken to be 01-00-1X-01, then the R^N of the dest router and the fault router are the same. According to our algorithm the packet will select the adjacent row tree of the fault row tree. Figure 6 shows the path traversed by the packet using our algorithm will be 00-00-00-00, 00-00-0X-01, 00-00-XX-10, 00-00-1X-01, 00-00-11-00, 0X-01-11-01, 01-00-11-00, whereas the algorithm proposed in [4] fails at the row stem router near the destination router (01-00-1X-01) itself. It will route the packet to 00-00-00-00, and then to 0X-01-00-00 and then to the row root 01-00-00-00. But, in this case the stem router near destination (01-00-1X-01) is faulty.

As we can observe from the examples shown in Figs. 2, 3, 4, 5 and 6 our algorithm routes the packets even in the presence of stem faults by reaching the destination successfully.

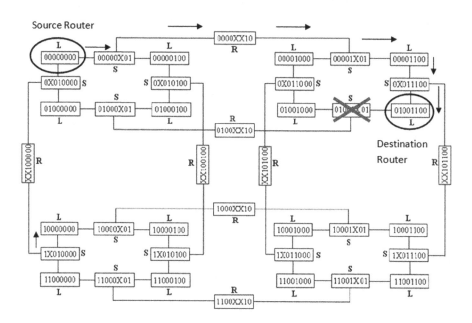

Fig. 6. Source Router at 00000000, Destination Router at 11000000 and Fault Router at 01001X01

6   Experimental Results

This section compares the performance of both the routing algorithms by varying the size of MoT network, no of stem faults present and the level of stem fault present in the network. For a 4×4 MoT, there is one level of stem routers, for

8 × 8 MoT there are 2 levels of stem routers, for 16 × 16 there are 3 levels of stem routers. Here, we have assumed that the fault can occur only in stem routers. We have compared algorithm [4] and our algorithm by varying the number of faulty routers in the MoT network and observing the percentage of packets reaching the destination in the presence of faults. In all those examples shown in Figs. 2, 3, 4, 5 and 6 algorithm proposed in [4] simply stalls due to a fault in its way, whereas our proposed algorithm could provide a path to reach the destination successfully. As we can observe from Figs. 7, 8 and 9, when the number of faults are increased, more number of packets have reached their respective destination routers when they are routed using our algorithm.

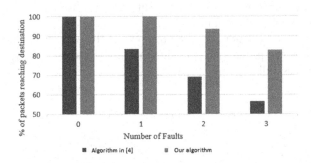

Fig. 7. Performance Variation on varying the number of faults in 4 × 4 Mesh-of-Tree Structure

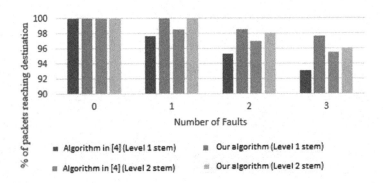

Fig. 8. Comparison of percentage of packets reached destination while varying the number of faults in 8 × 8 MoT structure

The scalability of our algorithm is demonstrated in Figs. 10, 11 and 12, where it can be seen that the algorithm can be scaled up to 4 × 4, 8 × 8 and 16 × 16 structures. We can also observe that our algorithm is able to route packets when there are faults in the stem level shown in Fig. 3. Figure 10 shows the case where only one router fails in the network, there is no loss of packet using our algorithm.

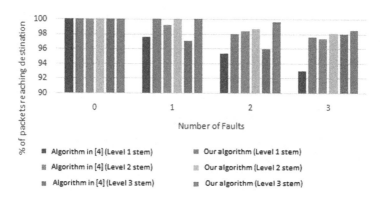

Fig. 9. Comparison of percentage of packets reached destination while varying the number of faults in 16×16 MoT structure

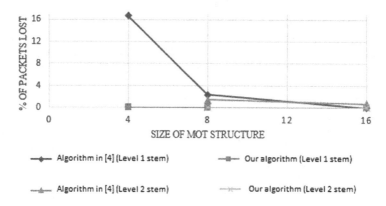

Fig. 10. Comparison of percentage of packets lost to size of MoT network with 1 faulty router

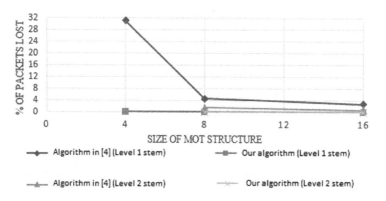

Fig. 11. Comparison of percentage of packets lost to size of MoT network with 2 faulty routers

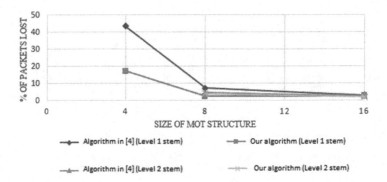

Fig. 12. Comparison of percentage of packets lost to size of MoT network with 3 faulty routers

This shows the superiority of our algorithm compared to the algorithm proposed in [4]. Similarly from the Figs. 11 and 12 we can observe that when the packets are routed using our algorithm, the loss of packets is significantly lower in comparison to the packets which are routed using the routing algorithm proposed in [4]. The percentage of packets lost reduces as the size of the MoT network increases. This is due to the fact that faults are assumed only at one level. As the size of the network is increased, the communication between the leaf router increases as algorithm routes the packet to non faulty path, so this leads to increase in the communication between the leaf router because the packets are transmitted using the lower level routers. This reduces the packet loss with increase in MoT network size using our algorithm.

7   Conclusion

We have presented a fault-tolerant routing algorithm for MoT topology based NoC in presence of stem router fault. The results show significant improvement in terms of the number of packets reaching the destination using our routing algorithm compared to the routing algorithm proposed in the literature. Our future work includes extending our algorithm to leaf and root routers.

References

1. International technology roadmap for semiconductors. Technical report (2015)
2. Benini, L., Micheli, G.D.: Networks on chips: a new SoC paradigm. Computer **35**(1), 70–78 (2002). https://doi.org/10.1109/2.976921
3. Dally, W.J., Towles, B.: Route packets, not wires: on-chip interconnection networks. In: Proceedings of the 38th Design Automation Conference (IEEE Cat. No. 01CH37232), pp. 684–689 (2001)
4. Kundu, S., Chattopadhyay, S.: Network-on-chip architecture design based on mesh-of-tree deterministic routing topology. Int. J. High Perform. Syst. Archit. **1**(3), 163–182 (2008)

5. Leighton, F.T.: Introduction to Parallel Algorithms and Architectures, 1st edn. MorganKaufmann, San Mateo (1992)
6. Moore, G.E.: Cramming more components onto integrated circuits. In: IEEE Solid-State Circuits Society Newsletter, vol. 11, no. 3, pp. 33–35, September 2006. Reprinted from electronics, vol. 38, no. 8, pp. 114 ff, 19 April 1965
7. Radetzki, M., Feng, C., Zhao, X., Jantsch, A.: Methods for fault tolerance in networks-on-chip. ACM Comput. Surv. 46(1), 8:1–8:38 (2013)
8. Rantala, V., Lehtonen, T., Plosila, J.: Network on chip routing algorithms (2006)
9. Tsai, W.C., Lan, Y.C., Hu, Y.H., Chen, S.J.: Networks on chips: structure and design methodologies. J. Electr. Comput. Eng. 2012, 15 (2011)

Performance Enhancement of NoCs Using Single Cycle Deflection Routers and Adaptive Priority Schemes

K. S. Midhula[1(✉)], Sarath Babu[1], John Jose[2], and Sangeetha Jose[1]

[1] Government Engineering College Idukki, Idukki, Kerala, India
midhulaks01@gmail.com, sarathbabu0410@gmail.com, sangeethajosem@gmail.com
[2] Indian Institute of Technology Guwahati, Guwahati, Assam, India
johnjose@iitg.ernet.in

Abstract. It is important to design an energy efficient underlying communication framework for multicore systems. The communication framework must satisfy the requirements of NoC (Network on Chip) such as minimum latency and minimum critical path delay. Routing on multicore framework help to compute the route to which the flit wants to reach its destination. Buffered routing consumes more power and area of the chip due to the presence of in-router buffers and buffer-less routing causes more number of deflections due to unavailability of productive port on contention. Hence, design of a minimally buffered deflection router having reduced power consumption and deflection rate is critical. There are minimally buffered deflection routers, which are characterized with minimum buffering and reduced latency. Nevertheless, limitations still exist such as higher flit latency, deflection rate. In this paper, we propose a single cycle minimally buffered deflection router with a good prioritization mechanism which leads to minimum latency and reduced deflection rate than conventional minimally buffered deflection router (MinBD). This improves the quality of NoC by prioritizing aged flits which are side buffered, redirected and re-injected in the router pipeline.

Keywords: Network on Chip · Minimally buffered deflection router ·
Single cycle minimally buffered deflection router

1 Introduction

A processor is an electronic circuitry integrated inside a chip that resides in a computer. The processor fetches, decode, execute instructions and give back its appropriate results. Based on the number of cores inside the processor, there are two different types of processors known as, unicore processor and multicore processor. Unicore processors have single processing element which can handle single thread at a time. Whereas, multicore processors contain multiple processing elements inside a processor and can process different tasks simultaneously. The process allocation to multiple cores is done by the operating system.

© Springer Nature Singapore Pte Ltd. 2019
S. Rajaram et al. (Eds.): VDAT 2018, CCIS 892, pp. 460–472, 2019.
https://doi.org/10.1007/978-981-13-5950-7_39

The multicore processor can reduce power consumption which leads to its performance enhancement. Hence, the need for faster processors is become more and more apparent and these multicore processors are popular in the world.

Network on Chip (NoC) is the communication paradigm for the underlying communication framework of integrated circuits. This communication subsystem consists of a number of cores connected with a network of routers. Routers are used to connect the channels at junctions in the multicore processor. Each router having 'p' number of input channels and output channels. Normally, the number of channels, 'p' is five. It is important to design energy efficient router micro-architecture for communication.

There are many situations where flits from different input ports request the same output port simultaneously. It can be handled by using either buffering or deflection. A buffered router can store and forward the flits using buffers. However, in most of the cases, low injection rate application uses only less than 25% of the buffers [15]. This exposes the over provisioning of buffers in the router. This causes wastage of the die area and static power. Buffer-less deflection router save the power and die area over the buffered router. However, buffer-less deflection router increases the number of flits which get deflected at high injection rate. Hence, minimally buffered deflection router is the best choice for energy efficient router design. Minimally buffered deflection router incorporates the advantages of both buffered and buffer-less router. This consists of a minimum buffer which act as 'side buffer' to store some deflected flits in order to reduce the deflection rate and thereby also reduces the average latency.

In this paper, we propose a single cycle minimally buffered deflection router with different prioritizations concerns at different stages. Experiments on an 8×8 mesh with synthetic traffic patterns [3] show that single cycle MinBD performs better than the existing Minimally Buffered Deflection router (MinBD) in terms of average flit latency and deflection rate.

2   Buffer-less Deflection Router: Related Work

Traditionally routers are designed with buffers (buffered routers) to store and forward the incoming flits to the next output router. However, these routers are power hungry routers as they consume more power and reduces the performance. Buffer-less deflection routers are introduced to address the limitations of buffered routers and reduces the die area. Buffer-less routers can handle the contention in network links with two mechanisms such as, drop one mechanism and deflection mechanism [3]. Drop one mechanism has a negative impact on re-transmission of the dropped flit. There is no guarantee for the source, which is near to the contention router. Hence, the complexity increases. In the case of deflection mechanisms, some amount of network traffic is sent to another link instead of using a buffer to store the traffic. The deflected flit will reach the destination with extra link traversal [9].

The first buffer-less deflection router introduced in BLESS [8] by Moscibroda et al., with sequential port allocation for all the incoming flits. It increases the critical path latency of flit in the router. Fallin et al. introduced CHIPPER [10] with parallel port allocation and golden packet prioritization in buffer-less deflection router. It did not reduce the deflection rate despite of the use of golden packet prioritization scheme. The golden packet prioritization scheme is only beneficial for a single flit with in specific period of time. There is no effective impact on ordinary flits for reducing its chances of deflection.

Minimally buffered deflection router (MinBD) is a promising solution which effectively combines the best features of both buffered and buffer-less routers. Rather than using in-router buffers, MinBD uses a simple side buffer. The side buffer is used to store only one flit among the deflected flits in a single cycle and the side buffered flit will be re-injected into the pipeline again in subsequent cycles.

The best available two-stage deflection router is DeBAR [15] by Jose et al. have better prioritization scheme, hybrid ejection and parallel execution of independent operations. SLIDER [12] by Nayak et al. is also, a two-stage deflection router with smart late injection and selective flit pre-emption features.

There have been prior works on single cycle router architecture. However, their design methodologies and intentions are different. SCARAB [17] by Hayenga et al. is the buffer-less adaptive single cycle router architecture. Minimally buffered single cycle deflection router (MinBSD) [13] by Jose et al. is the single cycle deflection router having an innovative module, which is capable of handling all the operations in a single cycle. While these architectures have structural limitations and latency problems.

3   Motivation

MinBD [11] is the two-cycle deflection router with different modules of core injection, redirection, re-injection, 2-stage ejection etc shown in Fig. 1. Injection from the core occurs only if there is an empty port and core injection module is placed after the re-injection module. Re-injection module is used for the re-injection of side buffered flits from the side buffer. Ejection of flit from the router to the local port is handled by a two-stage ejection unit. Redirection module is used for the pre-emption of flits from input ports when the four input ports and side buffer are busy. The side buffer can re-inject the side buffered flit to the empty port. The second stage of the MinBD pipeline starts with 'silver flit selection' module followed by permutation deflection stage. Silver flit selection is the prioritization scheme [16] used in MinBD. MinBD randomly selects a flit as silver, which is the most prioritized flit for the local router. Permutation deflection network used for the parallel allocation of output ports. This module checks all the four incoming flits for the presence of silver marking in order to give higher prioritization. We identify four performance limitations in the MinBD design that motivated us for the proposed work. We analyse these limitations and its after effects, and suggest suitable solutions.

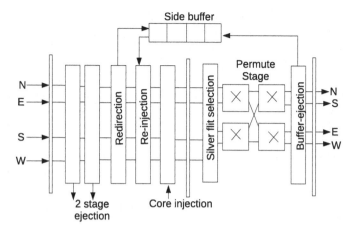

Fig. 1. MinBD pipeline architecture

3.1   The Lifetime of a Flit in a Router

In MinBD, an incoming flit will take two-cycles to complete its traversal within a router. Average flit latency is very much related with this time spent by flit in the router. Flit delay can be reduced by reducing the router delay and the router delay can be reduced by designing a single-cycle deflection router. The average flit latency can be reduced with single cycle deflection router by reducing the time taken by the flit for completing its operations within the router.

3.2   Aged Flits are Side Buffered

The purpose of side buffer in MinBD is to store some flits which otherwise would be deflected. The selection of those flits are random and side buffering reduces the deflection rate. However, the problem is that flit from the side buffer is re-injected only if there is an empty port. Otherwise, it is side buffered for a long time. Also, there is no guarantee for getting productive port after re-injection of the buffered flit. Our experiments with uniform traffic at pre-saturation load in 8×8 mesh network employing MinBD show that 49% of aged flits are side buffered. This problem arises due to the random flit selection among those flits for side buffering.

3.3   Aged Flits are Deflected

As per the silver flit prioritization in MinBD, only one silver flit gets prioritized over other flits in the corresponding router locally. The possibility for aged flit as silver flit is 25% only. The aged flits get deflected in most of the cases. Our experiments using uniform traffic at pre-saturation load on 8×8 mesh network employing MinBD show 48% deflected flits are aged ones. This increases the average flit latency and degrades the overall performance.

3.4   Aged Flits are Pre-empted/Redirected

Based on the prioritization scheme used in MinBD, silver flit gets prioritization over other flits. Consider the case when all the four input ports of the router are busy with incoming flits and none of the flits are destined to be ejected, injection or re-injection of flits from respective input queue or side buffer is not possible. However, the aged flit in the side buffer get freezes and re-injection is not possible. This situation can be handled by redirection/pre-emption of a random flit from an input channel to side buffer. Since redirected flit selected randomly, there is a chance for aged flit redirection. Our experiments using uniform traffic at pre-saturation load on 8 × 8 mesh network employing MinBD gives a significant number of redirected flits are aged. Figure 2 shows that the intensity of these limitations are increases with injection rate.

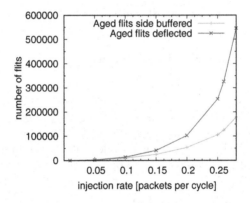

Fig. 2. Statics of aged flit side buffered and aged flits deflected for varying injection rates using uniform traffic in 8 × 8 mesh with MinBD.

Our experimental studies on various synthetic traffics show that the metric that decides when and whether deflect a flit or side buffer a flit has a significant impact on the average flit latency and overall performance. To overcome above mentioned limitations, we suggest a modification in the design of MinBD that brings in a major improvement in performance by achieving reduction in average latency and in deflection rate. We can solve all the problems by changing the silver flit prioritization scheme for permutation stage, and random flit selection for side buffering and pre-emption. We propose a single cycle minimally buffered deflection router with enhanced adaptive prioritization schemes to improve performance.

4 Single Cycle Minimally Buffered Deflection Router Architecture

Our proposed system is an advancement of minimally buffered deflection router (MinBD). A block diagram of various stages of the router pipeline of single cycle minimally buffered deflection router is shown in Fig. 3. Single cycle minimally buffered deflection router differs from MinBD as the following ways:

- Total cycles used by the flit in a router is reduced to one in single cycle minimally buffered deflection router. Conventional MinBD works as a two-cycle deflection router.
- The priority scheme used for routing is modified such a way that the flit with nearest destination among the four flits will get highest priority. This will avoids deflection of flit which is have nearest destination.
- The priority scheme used for the selection of flit for side buffering is changed from random flit selection to least aged flit selection. This scheme helps to save the aged flits from side buffering and it will reduces the latency.
- Introduces a prioritization scheme which selects flit with minimum deflection for redirection. This scheme avoids the chances of redirection of highly deflected flits to side buffer.
- The priority scheme provides high priority for redirected flits than other flits. This gives importance to the flits which are either side buffered or redirected.

Internal architecture of the proposed system as follows.

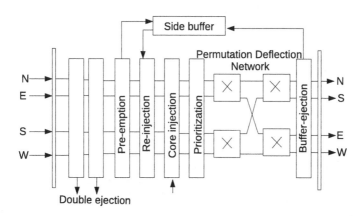

Fig. 3. Proposed architecture

4.1 Double Ejection Unit

Double ejection unit is used for the ejection of flits from the router to local port. Flits stored in the pipeline are passed through the double ejection unit. This module have separate two stages of ejection. Double ejection unit can eject up to two locally destined flits in a cycle. Otherwise, a locally addressed flit would be deflected rather than ejected if only one ejection unit used in a single cycle. One of the significance of this module is, it helps to make empty ports in the router by router ejection. That empty ports are used by the core for injecting flits to the router. Double ejection unit will avoid the ejection bottleneck in the network.

4.2 Injection Unit

Injection unit is used to inject flits from the injection queue. Local node can only inject flit to an empty port. This unit can push only one flit per cycle to the router pipeline.

4.3 Prioritization Unit

Prioritization unit is used for fixing the priority of each incoming flit based on hop-to destination value. Prioritization unit computes the priority value by extracting the destination address from each incoming flit and assigns its priority. This prioritization unit gives high priority to the flit with nearest destination address.

4.4 Permutation Deflection Network (PDN)

The PDN is the two-stage arbitration circuit used for the parallel allocation of output ports. Arbitration circuit has four arbiters which check the priority and output port of each incoming flit. Comparing the priority value assigned by prioritization unit, the arbiter will allocate to productive port or non-productive port (deflected) for every flit.

4.5 Buffer Ejection Unit

Buffer ejection unit is used for storing the flits to the side buffer. This module reduces the deflection rate by selecting the least aged flit for side buffering among the deflected flits. It avoids side buffering of aged flits gently.

4.6 Side Buffer

Side buffer stores the flit and reduces the deflection rate. It only side buffers least aged flit that otherwise should have been deflected to non-productive port. In later time, the flit will be re-injected into the router pipeline, when there is an empty port.

4.7 Re-injection Unit

Re-injection unit is used to re-inject the flits from side buffer. Re-injection operation only occur when there is a free port. This unit is placed prior to the injection unit and it makes the re-injected flit with the highest priority among all other flits in the arbitration.

4.8   Pre-emption Unit

NoC at higher injection rate experiences penalization of flits by all input ports busy with neighbouring flits and no flit ejection. This situation prevents the injection of flit from injection queue and re-injection of flit from side buffer. The pre-emption unit picks minimum deflected flit among the incoming flits and places it in the side buffer. This flit will returned to the router pipeline by re-injection with highest priority.

5   Experimental Analysis

5.1   Simulation Setup

We modified the traditional VC based, cycle accurate input buffered NoC simulator Booksim [3] to model the single-cycle minimally buffered deflection router microarchitecture mentioned in CHIPPER [10]. We considered flits with necessary header information for independent routing of flits used for deflection routing. We made changes on the microarchitecture of baseline deflection router simulator to model MinBD router and proposed single cycle minimally buffered deflection router, and conducted the experimental result analysis.

We evaluated the performance of MinBD and proposed router in an 8×8 mesh network using four synthetic traffic patterns: *uniform, transpose, tornado, and bit-complement*. We captured the results on the behalf of average flit latency, deflection rate, count of aged flits deflected, redirected and side buffered by varying the injection rate from very low load till saturation and analyze the results. We also examined the results of the proposed system in detail with the MinBD using multiprogrammed SPEC CPU2006 benchmark mixes.

We model 64-core CMP setup with cache hierarchy and coherent protocols using gem5 [18] simulator. Each core be composed of an out-of-order x86 processing unit with a 64 KB, dual ported, unified, private L1 cache. We use 4-way associative L1 cache with block size of 32B and a shared distributed 16-way associative L2 cache with block size of 64B.

SPEC CPU2006 benchmark applications are used to run on each core for the evaluation. Based on the *misses per kilo instructions* (MPKI) on L1 cache, benchmarks are classified into *Low* (less than 5), *Medium* (between 10 and 20), and *High* (greater than 25) as shown in Table 1.

Table 1. Classification of applications based on MPKI

Percentage miss rate	Benchmarks
Low MPKI (less than 5)	specrand, sjeng, calculix, namd
Medium MPKI (between 10 and 20)	aster, sphinx, libquantum, bzip2
High MPKI (greater than 25)	lbm, soplex, mcf, leslie3d

We create 15 multiprogrammed workloads, each having 64 applications chosen from the SPEC CPU2006 benchmark suite. Based on the network injection intensity (*Low/Medium/High*), the workloads are categorized into 3 mixes (M1 to M3) as shown in Table 2. Consider mix 1 (M1); where out of 64 cores that we model, 16 cores run specrand, 16 cores run sjeng, 16 cores run calculix and last 16 cores run namd benchmark. Similarly, other workload mixes (M2 and M3) can also be described.

Table 2. Workload constitution

Workload#	SPEC 2006 Benchmarks			
M1	specrand(16)	sjeng(16)	calculix(16)	namd(16)
M2	aster(16)	sphinx(16)	libquantum(16)	bzip2(16)
M3	lbm(16)	soplex(16)	mcf(16)	leslie3d(16)

5.2   Results and Discussions

We compared the performance of proposed single cycle minimally buffered deflection router with conventional two-cycle MinBD with 4-flit side buffer. We use xy-routing with adaptive prioritization schemes.

Effect on Number of Aged Flits Side Buffered, Redirected and Deflected

While changing the prioritization scheme used in MiBD to an adaptive prioritization, the percentage of conflicts against aged flits are reduced. By reverting the aged flits from deflection, redirection and side buffering will help to reduce the average latency and deflection rate. Figure 4 shows the reduction in number of aged flits side buffered, deflected and redirected in proposed system with respect to MinBD in *uniform* traffic.

Effect on Average Latency

The Latency of a flit is defined as the total amount of time taken by the flit from its source to reach its ultimate destination. Figure 5 shows the plots of injection rate vs average flit latency for various synthetic patterns of an 8×8 mesh network. Average latency increases with injection rate and at a specific point (saturation point) in each synthetic traffic, average latency will increase exponentially. Proper flit management in terms of side buffering, redirection and deflection for right flit extends the saturation point further, which gives the network more load handling capacity than MinBD.

We observed that for all synthetic traffic patterns, the single cycle minimally buffered deflection router having an extended saturation point and low average latency than MinBD during pre-saturation load. This is due to the techniques applied for selecting the flits for side buffering, deflection and redirection.

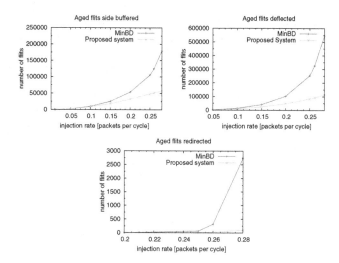

Fig. 4. Reduction in number of aged flits side buffered, deflected and redirected in proposed system with respect to MinBD in *uniform* traffic.

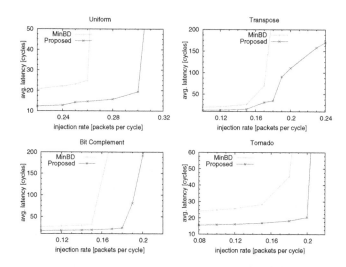

Fig. 5. Average flit latency comparison for various synthetic traffic patterns in 8×8 mesh network.

Figure 6 shows the latency results using multiprogrammed workloads with low (M1), medium (M2), high (M3) and average (Avg) network intensity workloads. The plot shows the percentage reduction in average latency with respect to MinBD for SPEC CPU 2006 benchmark mixes. The values ploted in the graph are calculated using the equation:

$$\begin{aligned} Percentage\ Reduction\ w.r.t\ MinBD = (Latency\ of\ MinBD\ - \\ Latency\ of\ Proposed\ system)/Latency\ of\ MinBD \end{aligned} \quad (1)$$

We observed that proposed system in all the workloads shows reduction in average flit latency.

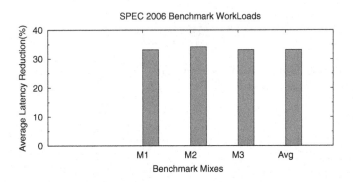

Fig. 6. Reduction in average flit latency rate for proposed system with respect to MinBD for multiprogrammed workloads.

Effect on Deflection Rate

Deflection rate is defined as the average number of deflections per flit. Reduction in deflection rate not only reduces the network activity but also reduces the dynamic power consumption. Figure 7 shows deflection rate comparison for various synthetic traffic patterns. When the injection rate is low, then deflection rate is also less because there are not many conflicts occurring between flits for the output port or chances for contention is very less. But at higher injection rate, chances for contention is high. The proposed system will check the deflected flit and gives more preference for older flits.

Figure 8 shows normalized deflection rate of proposed system with respect to MinBD for SPEC CPU 2006 benchmark mixes. M1 indicates low network intensity workload, M2 indicates medium network intensity workload, M3 indicates high network intensity workload and Avg indicates average of all. In every workloads, the proposed system maintains a significant reduction in deflection rate. Proposed system only deflects the flit with less priority based on the hop to destination prioritization scheme. Hence, deflection rate shows decrement than MinBD with random deflection flit selection.

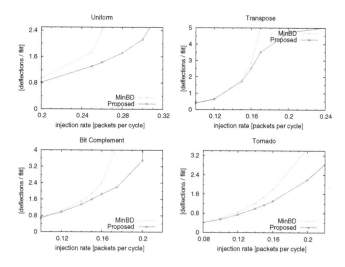

Fig. 7. Deflection rate comparison for various synthetic traffic patterns in 8×8 mesh network.

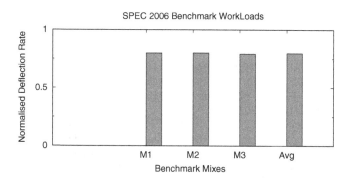

Fig. 8. Normalized deflection rate for proposed system with respect to MinBD for multiprogrammed workloads.

6   Conclusion

In this work, we analyzed the existing state-of-the-art MinBD and identified few drawbacks due to insufficient prioritization schemes and improper consideration of aged flits at several stages of the pipeline with multiple cycles. Since, aged flits are the main cause of increased average latency, it is important to give attention for those flits. We provided an efficient single cycle minimally buffered deflection router with adaptive prioritization schemes that reduces the average latency and deflection rate to a significant extent. We further showed that the NoCs using single cycle minimally buffered deflection router can operate and achieve a considerable improvement in the network level performance.

References

1. Rantala, V., Lehtonen, T., Plosila, J.: Network on chip routing algorithms. TUCS, Technical report No 779, pp. 10–12, (2006)
2. Muralidharan, D., Muthaiah, R.: Bufferless routing algorithms: a survey. Int. J. Appl. Eng. Res. **11**(6), 3811–3813 (2016)
3. Dally, W.J., Towles, B.: Principles and Practices of Interconnection Networks. Morgan Kaufmann Publishers, San Francisco (2004)
4. Peh, L.-S., Keckler, S.W., Vangal, S.: On-chip networks for multicore systems. In: Keckler, S.W., Olukotun, K., Hofstee, H.P. (eds.) Multicore Processors and Systems. ICIR, pp. 35–71. Springer, Boston (2009). https://doi.org/10.1007/978-1-4419-0263-4_2
5. Stojanovic, I., Jovanovic, M., Djosic, S. Djordjevic, G.: Improved deflection routing method for bufferless networks-on-chip. IEEE (2013)
6. Baran, P.: On distributed communications networks. IEEE Trans. Commun. Syst. **12**(1), 1–9 (1964)
7. Cai, Y., Mai, K., Mutlu, O.: Comparative evaluation of FPGA and ASIC implementations of bufferless and buffered routing algorithms for on-chip networks. In: 16th International Symposium on Quality Electronic Design (ISQED) (2015)
8. Moscibroda, T., Mutlu, O.: A case for bufferless routing in on-chip networks. In: Proceedings of the Fourth International Symposium on Networks-on-Chip, pp. 9–16 (2010)
9. Fallin, C., Nazario, G., Yu, X., Chang, K., Ausavarungnirun, R., Mutlu, O.: Bufferless and minimally-buffered deflection routing. In: Palesi, M., Daneshtalab, M. (eds.) Routing Algorithms in Networks-on-Chip, pp. 241–275. Springer, New York (2014). https://doi.org/10.1007/978-1-4614-8274-1_10
10. Fallin, C., Craik., Mutlu, O.: CHIPPER: a low-complexity bufferless deflection router. In: International Symposium on High Performance Computer Architecture (HPCA), pp. 144–155 (2011)
11. Fallin, C., Nazario, G., Yu, X., Chang, K., Ausavarungnirun, R., Mutlu, O.: MinBD: minimally-buffered deflection routing for energy-efficient interconnect. In: International Symposium on Networks-on-Chip (NOCS), pp. 1–10 (2012)
12. Nayak, B., Jose, J., Mutyam, M.: SLIDER: smart late injection deflection router for mesh NoCs. In: International Conference on Computer Design (ICCD), pp. 377–383 (2013)
13. Jose, J., Jonna, G.R., Radhakrishnan, R., Mutyam, M.: Minimally buffered single-cycle deflection router. In: Design, Automation and Test in Europe (DATE) (2014)
14. Michelogiannakis, G., Sanchez, G.D., Dally, W.J., Kozyrakis, C.: Evaluating bufferless flow-control for on-chip networks. In: Proceedings of the Fourth International Symposium on Networks-on-Chip, pp. 9–16 (2010)
15. Jose, J., Nayak, B., Kumar, K., Mutlu, O.: DeBAR: deflection based adaptive router with minimal buffering. In: Design, Automation and Test in Europe (DATE), pp. 1583–1588 (2013)
16. Atagoziyev, M.: Routing algorithms for on chip networks. M. Sc. Thesis, Middle East Technical University (2007)
17. Hayenga, M., Jerger, N. E., Lipasti, M.: SCARAB: a single cycle adaptive routing and bufferless routing. In: Proceedings of the 42nd Annual IEEE/ACM International Symposium on Microarchitecture, MICRO 42, pp. 244–254 (2009)
18. Binkert, N., et al.: The gem5 Simulator. ACM SIGARCH Computer Architecture News, vol. 39, no. 2, pp. 1–7 (2011)

3D LBDR: Logic-Based Distributed Routing for 3D NoC

Ashish Sharma[1,2]([✉]), Manish Tailor[1], Lava Bhargava[3], and Manoj Singh Gaur[1]

[1] Department of Computer Science and Engineering,
Malaviya National Institute of Technology, Jaipur, India
ashishsharma.fitt@gmail.com, gaurms@gmail.com
[2] Swami Keshvanand Institute of Technology Management & Gramothan,
Jaipur, India
[3] Department of Electronics and Communication Engineering,
Malaviya National Institute of Technology, Jaipur, India
lavab@mnit.ac.in

Abstract. A Network-on-Chip (NoC) is a new design in a complex system on chip (SoC) designs that provide efficient on-chip communication between networks. The design of router in NoC must be an efficient one with a lower latency and higher throughput. As the size of on-chip network grows, the distance between the cores increases in 2D NoC so the area has created the necessity to seek alternatives to the existing 2D NoCs. Exploiting the vertical dimension and migrating to 3D NoCs introduces novel structures that enable significant performance improvements over the conventional solution. So here it is the necessity of routing algorithms implementation for 3D NoCs. Using the routing table for routing in 3D NoC will increase the area of NoC because it needs memory for routing purpose. LBDR is an implementation method which is a solution of this area overhead problem. LBDR implements the routing logic without the using of routing tables at each port. LBDR enable the distributed implementation of any routing algorithm. Proposed 3D LBDR support all the algorithm which provides the minimal paths. Our proposed 3D LBDR routing implementation logic show the better handling of internal switch restriction using R_{xx} bits than [6]. We are getting the throughput, average latency, and power regarding the conventional deterministic algorithm. We have also analyzed the area and power of both 2D-LBDR and 3D LBDR through hardware logic.

Keywords: Network-on-Chip · LBDR · 3D · Routing · Restriction bits

1 Introduction

Network-on-Chip (NoC) is the most efficient on-chip communication architecture for System on Chip (SoC) where computational, and storage blocks are designed

Supported by organization x.

on a single chip. Network-on-Chip is proficient for communication between cores on shared bus design [5]. Routing algorithm and implementation play a major role in the performance of NoC [9]. Previously for routing implementation routing table were used. As the number of cores is increasing, the size of the routing table is also increasing which is creating area overhead problem. So the design of chip expanding in 3 dimension which is a solution of area overhead.

Routing can be two types one is source routing and distributed routing. Source routing is the routing in which route is stored in the head flit [2]. From the node where the packet is originated the route is fixed in source routing. In distributed routing the path is calculated at per node itself where the packet is going. Implementation of all the algorithm can be done in two types one is look up table and second is FSM based approaches. In look-up a table, there is a table, which contains that if the packet is generated at this node and want to go at that node then what path has to be followed throughout the destination. In FSM based approach the state machine will decide that what is the initial state and now what is the input. The new concept comes here in implementation stage which is knows as LBDR means Logic Based Distributed Routing. For distributed algorithm implementation LBDR is a solution. LBDR in 2 dimension relies on three bits per output port at every switch and a little logic of several gates. LBDR can implement a combination of topology and routing algorithm with some characteristics. It relies on the use of only three bits per switch output port. Also, for routing purposes, LBDR is preferred to reduce latency, power and area requirements for NoCs.

Here we are presenting LBDR mechanism for 3D supposing that every core is also connected from its upper layer and lower layer if they are present. Proposed 3D LBDR support all the algorithm which provide the minimal paths. The 3D LBDR also guarantees deadlock freedom. Like 2D LBDR it also uses restriction bits and connectivity bits. Here additional T bits are used in acquiring the proper solution for 3D LBDR. 3D LBDR requires T bits and restriction bits like R_{xy}. T_{xy} at any switch indicates whether turn towards Y dimension is allowed or not when some distance in X still needs to be covered to reach the destination. Both bits present the significant meaning in 3D.

The remaining paper is organized as follows. The LBDR for 2D is discussed in Sect. 2. In Sect. 3. We discuss the proposed work based on our methods. In Sect. 4, we have concluded experimental setup and result analysis. Finally, conclusions are derived in Sect. 5.

2   Related Work

LBDR stands for logic based distributed routing. LBDR uses all the possible minimal paths provided by the basic routing algorithm. LBDR is a logic by which we can implement all minimal path routing algorithm [1]. LBDR is not bounded to any particular routing algorithm. It means it applies to any routing algorithm [8]. The underlying routing algorithm guarantees deadlock freedom, If packets do not cross any routing restriction, then no cycle can be formed.

LBDR implements distributed routing mechanism using some bits. These bits can be categories in two types of bits, routing bits and connectivity bits [3,4,8]. Routing bits indicate which routing option can be taken, and connectivity bits indicate whether a switch is connected with its neighbors.

In 2D, there are two sets of channels North, South and East, West by which routing restrictions are made. In 2D per port, three bits are used in which there are two restriction bits and one connectivity bit [3]. Therefore, total 12 bits required per switch. The values of these bits decided by topology and the routing algorithm. By setting the routing restriction, the algorithm for routing implemented. The routing restriction is used to set the direction of the packet. Connectivity bit indicate whether a switch is connected with its neighbors.

Restriction bits like R_{nw}, R_{ne}, R_{sw}, R_{se}, R_{en}, R_{es}, R_{wn}, R_{ws} decides the path for packet. Here R_{nw} (North-West) means that you can not take west after taking north it is restricted. For XY deterministic algorithm R_{nw}, R_{ne}, R_{sw} and R_{se} bits assign to 0. The remaining bits R_{en}, R_{es}, R_{wn} and R_{ws} set to 1.

LBDR can be a divide into two parts. The first part is comparators [4] that will give the information regarding the relative distance between current node and destination. Second part calculates the routing direction for next hop with the help of restriction bits and connectivity bits. A very few work address the 3D LBDR [6] but they are laking on internal switch restriction bits. Here, we proposed the novel 3D LBDR with consider internal switch restriction bits.

2.1 Equation for 2 Dimension LBDR

$n' = n \cdot \bar{e} \cdot \bar{w} + n \cdot e \cdot R_{ne} + n \cdot w \cdot R_{nw}$ $s' = s \cdot \bar{e} \cdot \bar{w} + s \cdot e \cdot R_{se} + s \cdot w \cdot R_{sw}$
$e' = e \cdot \bar{n} \cdot \bar{s} + e \cdot n \cdot R_{en} + e \cdot s \cdot R_{es}$ $w' = w \cdot \bar{n} \cdot \bar{s} + w \cdot n \cdot R_{wn} + w \cdot s \cdot R_{ws}$
$N = n' \cdot C_n$ $S = s' \cdot C_s$ $E = e' \cdot C_e$ $W = w' \cdot C_w$.

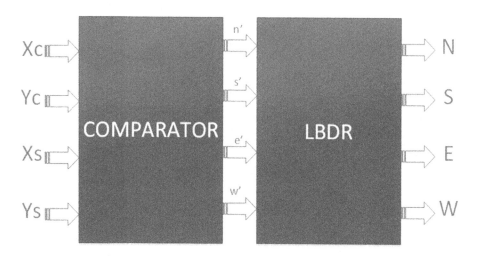

Fig. 1. Block diagram of 2D LBDR

2.2   Block Diagram for Dimension LBDR

According to the Fig. 1, first part comparator will take the input of current port and destination port then gives the difference output as n', s', e', w'. LBDR block contains the logic gates which take input of restriction bit and connectivity bit. Then LBDR block calculate the actual direction of packet which has to be taken. In LBDR block there are combination of gates which actually calculate the direction. Then after getting the direction the packet will route to its path.

3   Proposed Work

As we know, that technology is going towards 3D ICs to sustain the performance improvement. In 3D integration, the layers are connected from the bottom layer and upper layer using TSV (Through Silicon Via). For 3D till now no fully adaptive algorithm designed. Like in 2D we have implemented LBDR for 3d. It supports all algorithms which will give minimal path from source to destination. It also supports partial adaptive algorithm for 3D. Its completely deadlock free due to the combination of restriction bits. The Fig. 2 shows how the layers will be present in 3D design. This is a regular mesh design in 3D. The layer 1 is connected to layer 2. Each node is connected on it's lower layer node or it's upper layer node if present [10]. Based on this connectivity the connectivity bits are configured.

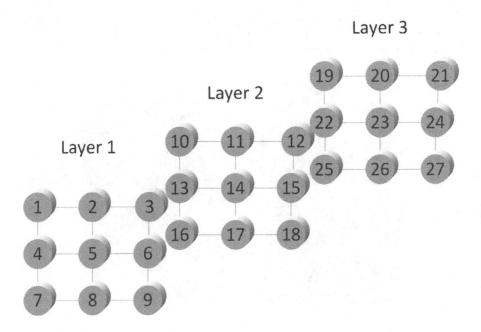

Fig. 2. 3D Layers in Network-on-Chip

For 3d, there are six directions North, South, East, West, Up and Down as shown in Fig. 3. In 3d LBDR along with routing restriction bits (R_{xy}) and connectivity bits (C_x), will be require few more bits like T_{xy} bits.

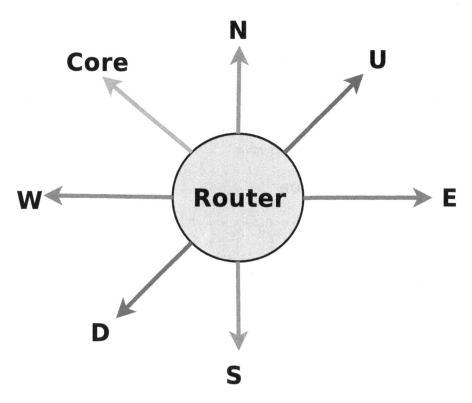

Fig. 3. Directions at each port

Routing Logic: T bit is used to indicate whether turn from dimension 1 to dimension 2 is allowed when few more distance in dimension 1 needs to cover to reach the destination. For example T_{xy}, at any switch it, indicates whether turn towards Y dimension is allowed or not when some distance in X still needs to be covered to reach the destination. For XYZ routing, T_{xy} bit would be set to zero. The Reason is that in XYZ when X is completely covered then only turn from X dimension to Y is allowed. When the destination is only in XY quadrant, this case would be captured by existing routing bits only. However, when the destination is in XYZ quadrant, then we need to check T_{xy}, T_{xz} bits along with routing bits.

Following T bits will be used:

1. T_{xy}: Turn from X to Y dimension is allowed or not when some distance in X is remaining to reach the destination.
2. T_{xz}: Turn from X to Z dimension is allowed or not when some distance in X is remaining to reach the destination.
3. T_{yx}: Turn from Y to X dimension is allowed or not when some distance in Y is still remaining to reach the destination.
4. T_{yz}: Turn from Y to Z dimension is allowed or not when some distance in Y is still remaining to reach the destination.
5. T_{zx}: Turn from Z to X dimension is allowed or not when some distance in Z is still remaining to reach the destination.
6. T_{zy}: Turn from Z to Y dimension is allowed or not when some distance in Z is remaining to reach the destination.

3.1   Equation of 3D LBDR

$$N2 = N1 \cdot \bar{u} \cdot \bar{d} \cdot \bar{e} \cdot \bar{w} + n \cdot \bar{u} \cdot \bar{d} \cdot \bar{e} \cdot \bar{w} \cdot R_{nn} + n \cdot e \cdot \bar{u} \cdot \bar{d} \cdot R_{ne} + n \cdot w \cdot \bar{u} \cdot \bar{d} \cdot$$
$$R_{nw} + n \cdot u \cdot \bar{e} \cdot \bar{w} \cdot R_{nu} + n \cdot d \cdot \bar{e} \cdot \bar{w} \cdot R_{nd} + n \cdot e \cdot u \cdot R_{ne} \cdot T_{xy} \cdot T_{zy} + n \cdot e \cdot u \cdot$$
$$R_{nu} \cdot T_{xy} \cdot T_{zy} + n \cdot w \cdot u \cdot R_{nw} \cdot T_{xy} \cdot T_{zy} + n \cdot w \cdot u \cdot R_{nu} \cdot T_{xy} \cdot T_{zy} + n \cdot e \cdot d \cdot$$
$$R_{ne} \cdot T_{xy} \cdot T_{zy} + n \cdot e \cdot d \cdot R_{nd} \cdot T_{xy} \cdot T_{zy} + n \cdot w \cdot d \cdot R_{nw} \cdot T_{xy} \cdot T_{zy} + n \cdot w \cdot d \cdot R_{nd} \cdot T_{xy} \cdot T_{zy}$$

$$S2 = S1 \cdot \bar{u} \cdot \bar{d} \cdot \bar{e} \cdot \bar{w} + s \cdot \bar{u} \cdot \bar{d} \cdot \bar{e} \cdot \bar{w} \cdot R_{ss} + s \cdot e \cdot \bar{u} \cdot \bar{d} \cdot R_{se} + s \cdot w \cdot \bar{u} \cdot \bar{d} \cdot$$
$$R_{sw} + s \cdot u \cdot \bar{e} \cdot \bar{w} \cdot R_{su} + s \cdot d \cdot \bar{e} \cdot \bar{w} \cdot R_{sd} + s \cdot e \cdot u \cdot R_{se} \cdot T_{xy} \cdot T_{zy} + s \cdot e \cdot u \cdot$$
$$R_{su} \cdot T_{xy} \cdot T_{zy} + s \cdot w \cdot u \cdot R_{sw} \cdot T_{xy} \cdot T_{zy} + s \cdot w \cdot u \cdot R_{su} \cdot T_{xy} \cdot T_{zy} + s \cdot e \cdot d \cdot$$
$$R_{se} \cdot T_{xy} \cdot T_{zy} + s \cdot e \cdot d \cdot R_{sd} \cdot T_{xy} \cdot T_{zy} + s \cdot w \cdot d \cdot R_{sw} \cdot T_{xy} \cdot T_{zy} + s \cdot w \cdot d \cdot R_{sd} \cdot T_{xy} \cdot T_{zy}$$

$$E2 = E1 \cdot \bar{u} \cdot \bar{d} \cdot \bar{n} \cdot \bar{s} + e \cdot \bar{u} \cdot \bar{d} \cdot \bar{n} \cdot \bar{s} \cdot R_{ee} + e \cdot n \cdot \bar{u} \cdot \bar{d} \cdot R_{en} + e \cdot s \cdot \bar{u} \cdot \bar{d} \cdot$$
$$R_{es} + e \cdot u \cdot \bar{n} \cdot \bar{s} \cdot R_{eu} + e \cdot d \cdot \bar{n} \cdot \bar{s} \cdot R_{ed} + e \cdot n \cdot u \cdot R_{en} \cdot T_{yx} \cdot T_{zx} + e \cdot n \cdot u \cdot$$
$$R_{eu} \cdot T_{yx} \cdot T_{zx} + e \cdot s \cdot u \cdot R_{es} \cdot T_{yx} \cdot T_{zx} + e \cdot s \cdot u \cdot R_{eu} \cdot T_{yx} \cdot T_{zx} + e \cdot n \cdot d \cdot$$
$$R_{en} \cdot T_{yx} \cdot T_{zx} + e \cdot n \cdot d \cdot R_{ed} \cdot T_{yx} \cdot T_{zx} + e \cdot s \cdot d \cdot R_{ed} \cdot T_{yx} \cdot T_{zx} + e \cdot s \cdot d \cdot R_{es} \cdot T_{yx} \cdot T_{zx}$$

$$W2 = W1 \cdot \bar{u} \cdot \bar{d} \cdot \bar{n} \cdot \bar{s} + w \cdot \bar{u} \cdot \bar{d} \cdot \bar{n} \cdot \bar{s} \cdot R_{ww} + w \cdot n \cdot \bar{u} \cdot \bar{d} \cdot R_{wn} + w \cdot s \cdot \bar{u} \cdot$$
$$\bar{d} \cdot R_{ws} + w \cdot u \cdot \bar{n} \cdot \bar{s} \cdot R_{wu} + w \cdot d \cdot \bar{n} \cdot \bar{s} \cdot R_{wd} + w \cdot n \cdot u \cdot R_{wn} \cdot T_{yx} \cdot T_{zx} + w \cdot n \cdot$$
$$u \cdot R_{wu} \cdot T_{yx} \cdot T_{zx} + w \cdot s \cdot u \cdot R_{ws} \cdot T_{yx} \cdot T_{zx} + w \cdot s \cdot u \cdot R_{wu} \cdot T_{yx} \cdot T_{zx} + w \cdot n \cdot d \cdot$$
$$R_{wn} \cdot T_{yx} \cdot T_{zx} + w \cdot n \cdot d \cdot R_{wd} \cdot T_{yx} \cdot T_{zx} + w \cdot s \cdot d \cdot R_{wd} \cdot T_{yx} \cdot T_{zx} + w \cdot s \cdot d \cdot R_{ws} \cdot T_{yx} \cdot T_{zx}$$

$$U2 = U1 \cdot \bar{e} \cdot \bar{w} \cdot \bar{n} \cdot \bar{s} + u \cdot \bar{e} \cdot \bar{w} \cdot \bar{n} \cdot \bar{s} \cdot R_{uu} + u \cdot n \cdot \bar{e} \cdot \bar{w} \cdot R_{un} + u \cdot s \cdot \bar{e} \cdot \bar{w} \cdot$$
$$R_{us} + u \cdot e \cdot \bar{n} \cdot \bar{s} \cdot R_{ue} + u \cdot w \cdot \bar{n} \cdot \bar{s} \cdot R_{uw} + u \cdot n \cdot e \cdot R_{un} \cdot T_{yz} \cdot T_{xz} + u \cdot n \cdot e \cdot$$
$$R_{ue} \cdot T_{yz} \cdot T_{xz} + u \cdot s \cdot e \cdot R_{us} \cdot T_{yz} \cdot T_{xz} + u \cdot s \cdot e \cdot R_{ue} \cdot T_{yz} \cdot T_{xz} + u \cdot n \cdot w \cdot$$
$$R_{un} \cdot T_{yz} \cdot T_{xz} + u \cdot n \cdot w \cdot R_{uw} \cdot T_{yz} \cdot T_{xz} + u \cdot s \cdot w \cdot R_{us} \cdot T_{yz} \cdot T_{xz} + u \cdot s \cdot w \cdot R_{uw} \cdot T_{yz} \cdot T_{xz}$$

$D2 = D1 \cdot \bar{e} \cdot \bar{w} \cdot \bar{n} \cdot \bar{s} + d \cdot \bar{e} \cdot \bar{w} \cdot \bar{n} \cdot \bar{s} \cdot R_{dd} + d \cdot n \cdot \bar{e} \cdot \bar{w} \cdot R_{dn} + d \cdot s \cdot \bar{e} \cdot \bar{w} \cdot$
$R_{ds} + d \cdot e \cdot \bar{n} \cdot \bar{s} \cdot R_{de} + d \cdot w \cdot \bar{n} \cdot \bar{s} \cdot R_{dw} + d \cdot n \cdot e \cdot R_{dn} \cdot T_{yz} \cdot T_{xz} + d \cdot n \cdot e \cdot R_{de} \cdot$
$T_{yz} \cdot T_{xz} + d \cdot s \cdot e \cdot R_{ds} \cdot T_{yz} \cdot T_{xz} + d \cdot s \cdot e \cdot R_{de} \cdot T_{yz} \cdot T_{xz} + d \cdot n \cdot w \cdot R_{dn} \cdot T_{yz} \cdot$
$T_{xz} + d \cdot n \cdot w \cdot R_{dw} \cdot T_{yz} \cdot T_{xz} + d \cdot s \cdot w \cdot R_{ds} \cdot T_{yz} \cdot T_{xz} + d \cdot s \cdot w \cdot R_{dw} \cdot T_{yz} \cdot T_{xz}$

$$N = N2 \cdot C_n \quad S = S2 \cdot C_s \quad E = E2 \cdot C_e \quad W = W2 \cdot C_w \quad U = U2 \cdot C_u \quad D = D2 \cdot C_d$$

The First part of equations calculate the temporary direction in terms on N2, S2, E2, W2, U2, D2. Then these signals and connectivity bits decide the finally in which direction the packet will go. If connectivity bit is 0, then the respective signal will be 0 so that the final output of direction signal mapped as 0. The final direction is calculated by N, S, E, W, U, D signals.

3.2   Block Diagram of 3D LBDR

Comparator: This will compare the source and destination coordinates. Then it generates 12 signals, n, e, s, w, u, d and N1, E1, S1, W1, U1, D1. First six signals give the distance in a particular direction, and last six signals are used to indicate that destination is only one hop away means next switch in particular direction.

3D LBDR: In this block, the actual hardware is present which generated by the equation and takes the input of restriction bits, connectivity bits and "T" bits. After this, it will calculate the direction in which packet the packet will be routed.

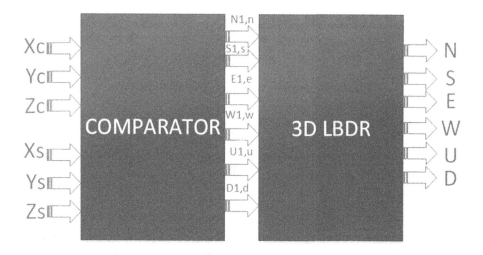

Fig. 4. Block diagram of 3D LBDR

4   Experimental Setup and Result Analysis

The LBDR3D is implemented on NIRGAM [7] simulator, which is a cycle accurate systemC based simulator. NIRGAM calculates the throughput, average latency, and power for routing algorithm. We have added new routing LBDR3D in routing section. We have changes the source code according to the instruction for adding the new routing mechanism in NIRGAM. There we have taken XYZ and ZXY routing algorithm for comparison. Here we are getting the satisfactory result. Because the output port direction is calculated for only one cycle, so the parameters are same as defined algorithm. We have taken different topologies for the experiment. There is maximum 16 * 16 * 4 mesh type topology is allowed in NIRGAM. The throughput and delay graph shows the same statistics for same algorithms while their implementation scheme are different like 3DLBDR implementation and simple routing based.

For hardware logic first, we have done synthesis on Xilinx ISE. Then after power and area is calculated through Synopsis Design vision on 90 nm technology. This result is compared with 2D LBDR (Table 1).

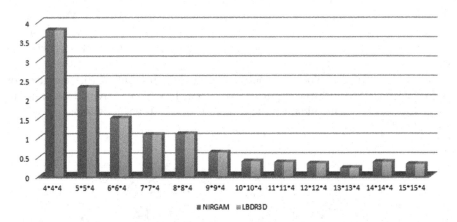

Fig. 5. Throughput of regular XYZ and LBDR3D

Table 1. NoC power (mW) comparison

Routing type	Static power	Dynamic power	Total power
LBDR 2D	158.35	161.18	319.52
LBDR 3D	158.28	157.05	315.33

In table based routing the size of the table (area) and its power depends on the topology size. The power and area both are increase with increasing topology size. In 3D LBDR the configuration bits are fixed for each router hence increasing in topology size have no impact on router area and power to capture the routing algorithm.

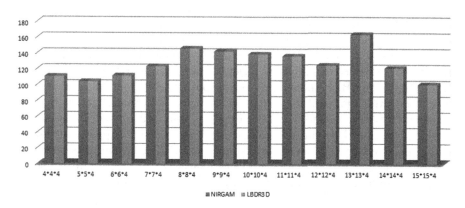

Fig. 6. Average latency of regular XYZ and LBDR3D

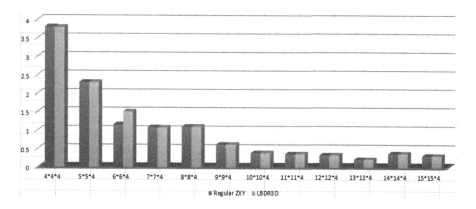

Fig. 7. Throughput of regular ZXY and LBDR3D

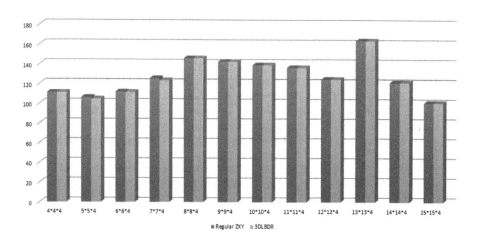

Fig. 8. Average latency of regular ZXY and LBDR3D

5 Conclusion

In this paper, the extended LBDR for 3D is presented. 3D LBDR is a routing mechanism which can implement deterministic and partial adaptive routing algorithm. Using LBDR there is no need of routing table, so it efficiently regards area when we go for multi-core 3D architecture. It uses restriction bits and connectivity bits to decide the path of packets from source to destination. The routing algorithm determines by restriction bits values. It supports all routing algorithm which gives minimal path from source to destination. It is also deadlocked free if the routing algorithm using a constraint for it. Here we can see we have successfully implemented the routing algorithm like XYZ, ZXY.

References

1. Bishnoi, R., Laxmi, V., Gaur, M.S., Flich, J.: d^2 LBDR: distance-driven routing to handle permanent failures in 2D mesh NOCs. In: 2015 Design, Automation Test in Europe Conference Exhibition, pp. 800–805, March 2015
2. Bolotin, E., Cidon, I., Ginosar, R., Kolodny, A.: Routing table minimization for irregular mesh NOCs. In: 2007 Design, Automation Test in Europe Conference Exhibition, pp. 1–6, April 2007. https://doi.org/10.1109/DATE.2007.364414
3. Flich, J., Duato, J.: Logic-based distributed routing for NOCs. IEEE Comput. Archit. Lett. **7**(1), 13–16 (2008). https://doi.org/10.1109/L-CA.2007.16
4. Gupta, N., Kumar, M., Laxmi, V., Gaur, M.S., Zwolinski, M.: σLBDR: congestion-aware logic based distributed routing for 2D NOC. In: 2015 19th International Symposium on VLSI Design and Test (VDAT), pp. 1–6, June 2015. https://doi.org/10.1109/ISVDAT.2015.7208058
5. Jerger, N.E., Peh, L.S.: On-Chip Networks. Morgan & Claypool Publishers, San Rafael (2009)
6. Niazmand, B., Azad, S.P., Flich, J., Raik, J., Jervan, G., Hollstein, T.: Logic-based implementation of fault-tolerant routing in 3D network-on-chips. In: 2016 Tenth IEEE/ACM International Symposium on Networks-on-Chip (NOCS), pp. 1–8, August 2016. https://doi.org/10.1109/NOCS.2016.7579317
7. NIRGAM
8. Rodrigo, S., Medardoni, S., Flich, J., Bertozzi, D., Duato, J.: Efficient implementation of distributed routing algorithms for NOCs. IET Comput. Digit. Tech. **3**(5), 460–475 (2009). https://doi.org/10.1049/iet-cdt.2008.0092
9. Singh, J.K., Swain, A.K., Reddy, T.N.K., Mahapatra, K.K.: Performance evaluation of different routing algorithms in network on chip. In: 2013 IEEE Asia Pacific Conference on Postgraduate Research in Microelectronics and Electronics (PrimeAsia), pp. 180–185, December 2013. https://doi.org/10.1109/PrimeAsia.2013.6731201
10. Zhou, J., Li, H., Wang, T., Li, X.: LOFT: a low-overhead fault-tolerant routing scheme for 3D NOCs. Integr. VLSI J. **52**, 41–50 (2016). https://doi.org/10.1016/j.vlsi.2015.08.002

Parameter Extraction of PSP MOSFET Model Using Particle Swarm Optimization - SoC Approach

Amit Rathod[1(✉)] and Rajesh Thakker[2]

[1] Government Engineering College, Bhavnagar 364002, Gujarat, India
amitcrathod@gmail.com
[2] Vishwakarma Government Engineering College, Chandkheda 382424,
Gujarat, India
rathakker2008@gmail.com

Abstract. System on Chip (SoC) architecture offers performance acceleration by offloading compute-intensive functions in FPGA logic together with application specific instruction set processor (ASIP). In this paper, we report a novel approach of SoC implementation for MOSFET parameter extraction. Xilinx's Zynq 7000 SoC supplied with AVNET Zedboard[TM] is used in this work. Extraction of PSP MOSFET Model parameters for 65 nm technology devices has been carried out using Particle Swarm Optimization (PSO) algorithm. PSP MOSFET Model code is executed by ARM Cortex A9 processor available on Zynq 7000 SoC. Parameter extraction of PSP MOSFET model is carried out for two different cases of implementations of PSO algorithm using: (1) ARM Cortex A9 and (2) FPGA. In both cases, excellent agreement between measured data of 65 nm technology MOSFET devices and PSP MOSFET model is observed. We have measured time taken by PSO algorithm in both cases for its execution. Implementation of PSO algorithm using FPGA is found to be 3.71 times faster on average compared to that on ARM Cortex A9. In both cases, the RMS error between measured and PSP MOSFET model is found to be less than 10%.

Keywords: System on chip · MOSFET parameter extraction ·
Particle swarm optimization · PSP MOSFET model · Zynq 7000soc

1 Introduction

Circuit Simulator is one of the most useful Integrated Circuit (IC) design tool that provides extensive understanding of a circuit with fine details of its operation. Manufacturer and designer can quickly evaluate the circuit performance before actual costly fabrication prototype, providing linkage between circuit designers and silicon foundries. However, trustworthy of the simulator outcome is solely depends on the accuracy of the circuit element model used inside the IC tool. MOSFET (Metal–Oxide Semiconductor Field Effect Transistor) models are vital for the correct analysis, design, and simulation of MOS circuits. Complexity of the MOSFET model has increased with downscaling technology of the MOSFET device. MOSFET models have many device specific parameters to solve mathematically in order to express the behavior of the

© Springer Nature Singapore Pte Ltd. 2019
S. Rajaram et al. (Eds.): VDAT 2018, CCIS 892, pp. 483–494, 2019.
https://doi.org/10.1007/978-981-13-5950-7_41

MOSFET. Model parameters need to be precisely extracted such that model can imitate the behavior of MOSFET circuit accurately. Therefore, parameter extraction process is corresponding to obtaining a appropriate set of parameter values for which the measured characteristics and model generated data exhibits good agreement.

Difficulties in determining the values for the model parameters arise because of either the approximations used to derive the device model are far from reality or the accurate determination of a given parameter sometimes depends on the value of another parameters which is not accurately known. Need of efficient optimization algorithm for the best fit to the actual device is arise because of the complex and multi dimensional characteristics of MOSFET model.

1.1 Related Work

Parameter extraction of various compact MOSFET models is addressed by many researchers by way of various optimization techniques and algorithms. The effect of optimization on parameter extraction is discussed in [1]. They strongly emphasis the role of the optimizer by concluding that optimizer dominates accuracy of the MOSFET model. Parameter extraction of PSP MOSFET model has been addressed by Zhou, Yao, Wu, Li, Zhu, and Gildenblat [2] where Levenberg-Marquardt (LM) algorithm is used for optimization of 65 nm CMOS device. LM is a combination of gradient decent and Gauss Newton method which requires good initial guess. They validate the results with Genetic Algorithm (GA) and found GA consuming large computational time than LM. Meanwhile, Thakker [3] explored PSO algorithm and its variants to extract PSP MOSFET model parameters for 65 nm MOS devices. They have proposed modified Hierarchical PSO by including memory loss (ML) operation and other features which provides better matching. Levenberg-Marquardt (LM) algorithm is used for parameter extraction of EKV-MOSFET model in the work carried out by Arabas, Bartnik, Szostak, Tomaszewski [4] and Le, Pham and Nguyen [5]. Hybrid Genetic Algorithm is applied to optimize BSIMPD MOSFET model parameters in [6]. while PSO is successfully used as an optimization algorithm for the task parameter extraction of MOS MODEL11 Level 1100 (MM11) in [7].

Zynq 7000 SoC platform is used for acceleration of various process in diverse field of application. In [8], Zynq SoC platform is used for motion estimation in video to accelerate the process and found to be reliable. In [9], Boyer Moore algorithm is implemented as a hardware accelerator in Zynq 7000 SoC for on-line pattern search in TCP packets for Deep Packet Inspection (DPI) network monitoring application. Three different FPGA co-processor design is presented for Long Sort Term Memory (LSTM) architecture of Recurrent Neural Network (RNN) by Chang in [10], and shown Zynq 7000 implementation been 23 times power efficient than Tegra X1 development board.

1.2 Contribution

MOSFET model library code is a perplexing code which requires sensibly expensive measure of CPU time to execute. System on Chip (SoC) architecture is a great design alternative in this perspective as it has efficient combination of software advantages such as easy implementation and hardware parallelism. This paper is focused on a SoC implementation of PSP MOSFET parameter extraction applying PSO as an optimizer. Best of our knowledge, hardware realization of parameter extraction of PSP MOSFET model is attempted for the first time. Measurement of various characteristics of 65 nm technology MOS devices, which is used by Thakker et al. [3] is considered in this work.

The paper is organized as follows. In Sect. 2, parameter extraction problem along with extraction strategy and PSO algorithm as an optimizer is discussed. The proposed SoC Hardware architecture is described in Sect. 3. Experimental results and discussion are provided in Sect. 4. Conclusion and future scope is presented in Sect. 5

2 MOSFET Parameter Extraction and Optimization Algorithm

Device parameter extraction process is method of finding optimized set of model parameters to match the model generated output with measured set of data for various device characteristics. Block level functional diagram is shown in Fig. 1. Optimization algorithm is fed with measurement data and parameters to be extracted along with algorithm termination criteria. Iteration by iteration, optimization algorithm matches the model responses (generated by model equations) with measurement values. Role of the optimization algorithm is to extract the model parameters, such that model provides best matching output for various measured characteristics (I–V, C–V, Gm–V). Extracted model parameters must be consistent and compatible with the process technology and device physics. Hence, parameter extraction is a global optimization issue.

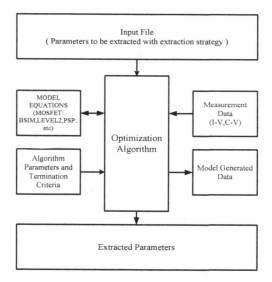

Fig. 1. Block level functional diagram of parameter extraction process

In this paper, PSO is used as an optimization algorithm being very simple and applied for many practical applications including MOSFET parameter extraction. It is briefly explained in the following.

2.1 Particle Swarm Optimization (PSO) Algorithm

Particle swarm optimization (PSO) is a population based stochastic optimization technique developed by Dr. Eberhart and Dr. Kennedy in 1995 [11]. This algorithm is inspired by social behaviour of bird flocking or fish schooling in search of food. In the beginning, PSO algorithm is initialized with a group of particles which are randomly assigned position (x) and velocity (v) within the search space. It then searches for optimum solution by updating particles' position after every iteration. Particle holding the best solution among all other particles is referred as globally best particle (X_{Gbest}). The best position attained by particle along its trajectory is called personal best (X_{best}). Velocity and position of each particle is calculated by Eqs. (1) and (2).

$$v(t + \Delta t) = w * v(t) + p1 * r1(x_{best} - x(t)) + p2 * r2(x_{Gbest} - x(t)) \qquad (1)$$

$$x(t + \Delta t) = x(t) + v(t + \Delta t) \qquad (2)$$

where w is particle's inertia parameter, and $p1$ and $p2$ are acceleration coefficients. The commonly used value of w is 0.7298, and 1.4798 for $p1$ and $p2$. $r1$ and $r2$ are random numbers holding value between 0 to 1. t represents iteration number and Δt (increment in iteration) is 1.

In the case of model parameter extraction task, the objective function (F) is formulated as summation of mean square error calculated between model generated value and experimental measured value at every measured test point, represented by Eq. (3).

$$F = \sqrt{\frac{1}{\mathsf{T}_p} \sum_{i=0}^{\mathsf{T}_p} \left(\frac{y_i^{exp} - y_i^{model}}{y_i^{exp}} \right)^2} \qquad (3)$$

where T_p represents total number of measured points in a given characteristics. y_i^{exp} and y_i^{model} represent experimental measured value and model generated value at given test point, respectively.

2.2 PSP MOSFET Model and Parameter Extraction Strategy

The PSP MOSFET model is based on surface potential and jointly developed by Gildenblat and Philips NXP. It is a combination of various features of SP (Surface Potential) model and MM11 Model [12]. It has 70 parameters to capture the behaviour of a single device (bulk-source and bulk-drain diodes not considered). These 70 parameters can be grouped into three different types: (a) Geometry independent parameters, (b) Geometry-dependent (called as local) parameters, and (c) Interpolation parameters.

As the current–voltage (I–V) characteristics of MOSFET in different regions are influenced by different sets of parameters, it is difficult to extract all of the desired parameters in one optimization step. Therefore, the parameters must be extracted in a successive steps referred to as the "parameter extraction strategy". The *I–V* and C_g–V_g measured data used in this exercise permits to extract 32 parameters of PSP MOSFET mode (Table 1).

Table 1. List of parameters and concerned measured characteristic for extraction.

Step	Measurement characteristics		Model parameters
Step1	$C_g - V_g$		VFB, NEFF
	V_{bs}	0 v	NP, DPHIB
	V_{ds}	0 v	
	V_{gs}	−1.5 v to 1.5 v with 25 mv step	
Step2	$I_d - V_g$		BETN, VNSUB DNSUB, NSLP CS,
	V_{bs}	[0, −0.45, −0.9 v]	XCOR
	V_{ds}	[0.05, −0.45, −0.9 v]	MUE, THEMU FETA, RS, RSG, CT
	V_{gs}	0 to 0.9 v with 25 mv step	
Step3, 5	$Gm - V_{gs}$		CFB, CF ALP2
	V_{bs}	[0 ,0.45, 0.9 v]	
	V_{ds}	0.05 v	
	V_{gs}	0 to 0.9 v with 25 mv step	
Step4	$I_d - V_d$		THESAT, THESATB THESATG,
	V_{bs}	[0, −0.45, −0.9 v]	ALP1
	V_{ds}	0 to 0.9 V with steps of 25 mV	ALP, VP, AX
	V_{gs}	[0.4, 0.65, 0.9 v]	
Step6	$I_g - V_g$		NOV, IGOV GC2, GC3
	V_{bs}	0 v	TOXOV
	V_{ds}	[0.05, −0.45, −0.9 v]	GCO, IGINV
	V_{gs}	0 to 0.9 v with 25 mv step	

3 Hardware Architecture

3.1 Zynq SoC Design

Using parallel architectural structure of reconfigurable hardware, optimization process of the PSP parameter extraction can be accelerated. The Zynq-7000 All programmable SoC is one of the popular Xilinx's SoC which integrates Processing System (PS) having a dual-core ARM Cortex-A9 APU (Application Processing Unit) and Programmable Logic (PL) in a single device [13]. Advanced Microcontroller Bus Architecture (AMBA), which is an open standard on-chip interconnect, is provided along with memory mapped master/slave AXI (Advanced eXtensible Interface) protocol. It serves as a bridge between ARM Cortex-A9 and FPGA. Detailed performance analysis of Zynq SoC is presented in [14].

Complete SoC architecture for parameter extraction using PSO algorithm is shown in Fig. 2. PSO algorithm is implemented in Zynq 7000 PL FPGA fabric. PSP MOS Model file is compiled and run by ARM Cortex A9 in PS part of Zynq 7000 SoC. AXI Interconnect manages transfer of data among the processing elements.

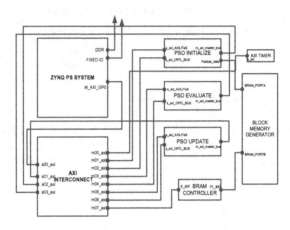

Fig. 2. Zynq SoC architecture for parameter extraction using PSO algorithm

FPGA implementation of PSO is partitioned in following hardware blocks:

(a) *PSO INITIALIZE:* This hardware block provides initial randomly generated values for each particles' position and velocity. Proficiency of optimization algorithm relies upon how well the swarm is initialized. Random Number Generator plays a very important roles in PSO initialization. Mersenne Twister Random number generation scheme is used and implemented in this block. This block also provides initial velocity of each of the particles which decides the exploration speed of the algorithm. Particle's information are stored in block memory so that ARM APU can access this information.

(b) *PSO EVALUATION:* The Task of this block is to perform fundamental PSO operation and calculate the next position of particles. It uses standard PSO algorithm Eqs. (1) and (2) to move every particles. This block also bounds the particle within the search space. ARM Cortex A9 processor, which is located in the PS part run the model library and calculate the rms error between measured data and model generated data. Hence, provides fitness value of every particles.

(c) *PSO UPDATE:* This block identifies personal best position for each particle with reference to its own trajectory, referred to as Xbest and globally best particle (XGbest) among all particles. Swarm is follow these pilot particles in the next iteration. Particles information such as position, velocity, Xbest, globally best (XGbest) best etc. are stored in Block RAM available inside the FPGA which is also visible to ARM Cortex A9 PS.

(d) *BLOCK RAM:* Block RAM is the fastest accessible memory to FPGA. Zynq7000 comes with 560 Kb of BRAM organised with 140 units. 102 Kb of 25.5 unit is used in this design. This memory stores particles information which is also accessible to PS as well as other blocks of PSO.

(e) *AXI INTERCONNECT:* The 4th generation AXI protocol is used as a means of communication between FPGA IP cores. One of the important feature of AXI4 protocol is burst-based transactions which allows stream data transfer in a single strobe. AXI masters can be connected to AXI slaves through an AXI interconnect.

3.2 Processing Flow Demonstrating PS-PL Interface

Rapid and correct-by-construction design of complex processing system can be implemented using modern EDA [Electronic Design Automation] tools such as Xilinx's Vivado^{TM}. In this SoC implementation, Xilin'x Vivado^{TM} platform is used to construct hardware acceleration on Avnet Zedboard^{TM} board. AXI4 stream interface is used to connect the Artix-7 FPGA (PL) part to PS (i.e. ARM CorTex A9). PSP MOSFET model C library code, known as SiMKit [12] is compiled and executed on ARM Cortex A9 processor. Zynq programmable system holds the control and configure the Programmable Logic (PL) FPGA fabric. The flow diagram is demonstrated in Fig. 3.

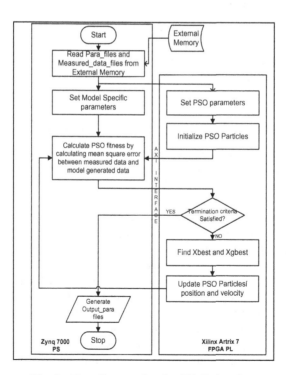

Fig. 3. Flow diagram showing PS-PL interface

Measured data files and parameter files are stored in SD memory. ARM APU reads these data files and accordingly, initiate the extraction process stepwise. At the beginning, PSO algorithm parameters and process parameters are set. PSO particles are initialized randomly within the search space in PL block. Particles' fitness is measured by applying set of parameter values holding by each particles to model library and comparing the model generated response with experimental measured values. PS is providing fitness values of each particles to PSO algorithm in PL. On the basis of fitness values, particles' personal position (Xbest) and globally best particle (Xgbest) are identified and updated. After that every particle's position and velocity are updated. This iterative process continues until the termination criteria is satisfied. In this work termination criteria is set as per three conditions: (1) max number of iteration is 1000, (2) improvement in solutions not observed continuously for 100 iterations and (3) solution reaches minimum min square error (i.e. $1e^{-6}$). If either of these conditions being satisfied, algorithm stops and ARM processor generates the output parameter file associated to the best solution achieved by the PSO algorithm.

4   Results and Discussion

4.1   Experimental Data

In this work, we have used measurements used and reported previously in Thakker [3]. It includes (I–V) and C_g–V_g characteristics of different devices with W ranging from 175 nm to 10 μm, and L from 70 nm to 1 μm. PSP Model parameter extraction are carried out in several consecutive steps as per the extraction strategy discussed earlier in Sect. 2.2.

4.2   PSO Algorithm Parameters and Performance Measures

PSO has several algorithm parameters which is to be set at the beginning. Swarm size is kept as 40 particles and maximum iterations is taken as 1000. PSO inertia weight (w) and acceleration coefficients (p1, p2) used in Eqs. (1) and (2) are set to 0.7298 and 1.49618, respectively.

As PSO is an evolutionary algorithm, reliability of the algorithm is checked by taking **10** independent runs (trials). In each run, the same parameter extraction strategy was used to extract parameters in successive steps. Results are compared with two various implementation: SW implementation - in which whole process is running on ARM Cotrex APU, and HW-SW implementation in which optimizer task (PSO algorithm) is accelerated on FPGA hardware. For both short channel (L = 70 nm) and long channel (L = 1um) NMOS device, rms error statistics (minimum, maximum, average, and standard deviation over 10 runs) is measured and shown in Table 2. It can be seen in both the implementation that rms error in all the steps are achieved below 10% which proves the capability of PSO algorithm to optimize and extract the PSP model parameters.

Table 2. Mean square error report (S = Short Channel L = 70 nm, W = 10 μm, L = Long Channel L = 1 μm, W = 10 μm)

Characteristic	Device	SW implementation				HW-SW implementation			
		ε_{rms}^{max}	ε_{rms}^{min}	ε_{rms}	δ_ε	ε_{rms}^{max}	ε_{rms}^{min}	ε_{rms}	δ_ε
I_d-V_d	S	0.0519	0.0371	0.0429	0.0050	0.0552	0.0296	0.0407	0.0075
($V_{gs} = 0.4$; 0.65; 0.9 V; $V_{bs} = 0, -0.45; -0.9$ V)	L	0.1603	0.0405	0.0795	0.0396	0.0771	0.0318	0.0556	0.0146
I_d-V_g	S	0.1164	0.0619	0.0813	0.0190	0.0880	0.0599	0.0758	0.0081
($V_{ds} = 0.05$ V $V_{bs} = 0, -0.45, -0.9$)	L	0.1297	0.0888	0.1081	0.0162	0.0995	0.0607	0.0796	0.0123
I_d-V_g	S	0.1010	0.0639	0.0789	0.0108	0.0975	0.0660	0.0785	0.0100
($V_{ds} = 0.9$ V; $V_{bs} = 0$; -0.45; -0.9)	L	0.1421	0.0450	0.0845	0.0302	0.0957	0.0414	0.0692	0.0195
I_d-V_g	S	0.1745	0.0936	0.1358	0.0270	0.1577	0.1351	0.1467	0.0073
($V_{ds} = 0.45$ V; $V_{bs} = 0$; -0.45; -0.9)									
I_g-V_g	L	0.0268	0.0120	0.0180	0.0050	0.0362	0.0120	0.0223	0.0091
($V_{ds} = 0.05, -0.45, -0.9$ v, $V_{bs} = 0$ v)									

Figures 4 and 5 shows - (linear and log scale), $-_d$, and $_g$-$_g$ plots comparing the experimental data with the results obtained with the SoC implementation. These plots show a good matching between measured and model values in various regions for both L = 1 μm and L = 70 nm channel length devices. The good matching can even be observed for $_g$-$_g$ data. Both the implementation are performing similar with respect to the mean square error. It was observed that in the beginning iterations, PSO performs better and error reduces at a faster rate. But, then the rate of error reduction reduces. Finally, model generated data shows a matching with measured data. However, in some cases, it has been observed that PSO struggles to regain exploration and algorithm stuck at local minima.

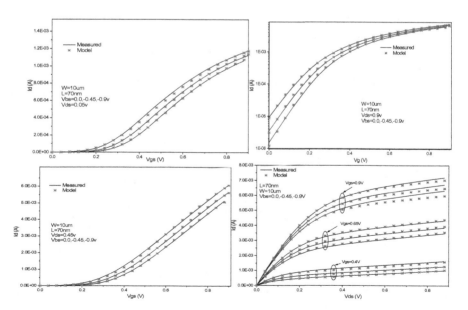

Fig. 4. Measured and model generated characteristics of short channel (L = 70 nm) NMOS device with parameter extracted using PSO: (a) $I_d - V_g$ at $V_{ds} = 0.05$ V, (b) logarithmic plot of $I_d - V_g$ at $V_{ds} = 0.9$ V, (c) $I_d - V_g$ at $V_{ds} = 0.45$ V and (d) $I_d - V_{ds}$.

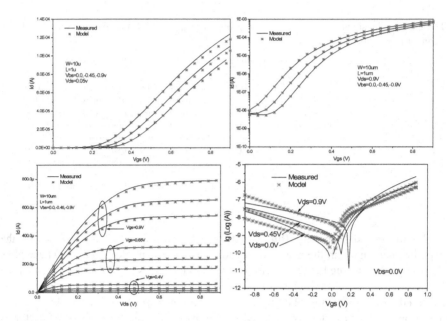

Fig. 5. Measured and model generated characteristics of short channel (L = 1 μm) NMOS device with parameter extracted using PSO: (a) $I_d - V_g$ at V_{ds} = 0.05 V, (b) logarithmic plot of $I_d - V_g$ at V_{ds} = 0.9 V after extraction of gate current parameters, (c) $I_d - V_d$ and (d) $I_g - V_g$

4.3   Hardware Acceleration Measurement

As mentioned earlier, we have tested two different implementations: SW implementation - in which PSO optimizer is running on ARM Cotrex APU, and HW-SW implementation - in which optimizer task (PSO algorithm) is accelerated on FPGA hardware. Comparison with respect to software implementation and hardware realization is shown in Table 3. As PSO is the stochastic algorithm, number of iterations are vary with each run which can be observed from this comparison. In the process of parameter extraction optimization process, the time taken by PSO algorithm as compared to SiMKiT model

Table 3.   Hardware acceleration report

	PSO implementation	Short channel L = 70 nm, W = 10 μm	Long channel L = 1 μm, W = 10 μm	Total
Avg. iteration	SW	2482.2	2381.1	4863.3
	HW-SW	2315.0	2659.6	4974.6
Avg. time (sec)	SW	3473.5	4333.6	7807.2 s
	HW-SW	3485.5	4324.0	7809.6 s
PSO execution time (sec)	SW	3.8802	4.1167	7.9964 s
	HW-SW	1.0439	1.1110	2.1542 s

library code execution time has the minor effect on the total process time. However, average 3.71 fold speedup is measured in the execution of PSO algorithm while implemented on FPGA hardware as compared to the PSO running in ARM APU. Table 3 represents the FPGA resource utilization of PSO implementation.

5 Conclusion

To the best of authors' knowledge, this is the first attempt of implementation of MOSFET parameter extraction process at hardware level. We have extracted PSP MOSFET model parameters using PSO implementation on Xilinx's Zynq 7000 SoC for 65 nm technology NMOS device. ARM Cortex A9 is proven proficient to execute PSP Model library SiMKit. Further, SoC implementation provides an opportunity to run MOSFET parameter extraction process in OS(Operating System) free platform. Offloading key functions from the processor to the FPGA can increases system performance in the form of execution time. Average 3.71 fold speedup is measured in the execution of PSO algorithm while implemented on FPGA hardware as compared to the PSO running in ARM APU.

The SoC implementation has provided very good agreement between measured data and model generated characteristics. The mean square error between measured and model generated data is found to be less than 10%. The average computational time in the proposed testing of parameter extraction process is approximately 130 min.

Acknowledgment. The authors are thankful to Gujarat Council for Science and Technology (GUJCOST) for providing financial support to this project under Minor Research Project [Grant no: GUJCOST/MRP/15-16/1091].

References

1. Balodi, D., Saha, C., Govidacharyulu, P.A.: Effect of parameter optimization effort over MOSFET models' performances in analog circuits' simulation. In: International Conference on Devices, Circuits and Systems (ICDCS), pp. 389–394 (2012)
2. Zhou, Q., Yao, W., Wu, W., Li, X., Zhu, Z., Gildenblat, G.: Parameter extraction for the PSP MOSFET model by the combination of genetic and Levenberg-Marquardt algorithms. In: IEEE International Conference on Microelectronic Test Structures, pp. 137–142 (2009)
3. Thakker, R.A., Patil, M.B., Anil, K.G.: Parameter extraction for PSP MOSFET model using hierarchical particle swarm optimization. sci. Dierct J. Eng. Appl. Artif. Intell. **2**, 317–328 (2009)
4. Arabas, J., Bartnik, L., Szostak, S., Tomaszewski, D.: Global extraction of MOSFET parameters using the EKV model: some properties of the underlying optimization task. In: International Conference Mixed Design of Integrated Circuits Systems, pp. 67–72 (2009)
5. Le, D.-H., Pham, C.-K., Nguyen, T.T.T., Bui, T.: Parameter extraction and optimization using Levenberg-Marquardt algorithm. In: Fourth International Conference on Communications and Electronics (ICCE), pp. 434–437 (2012)

6. Wu, T., et al.: Model-adaptable MOSFET parameter extraction with a hybrid genetic algorithm. In: International Conference on Solid-State and Integrated Circuit Technology Proceedings, pp. 1299–1302 (2006)

7. Chopde, A.M., Khandelwal, S., Thakker, R.A., Patil, M.B., Anil, K.G.: Parameter extraction for mos model 11 using Particle Swarm Optimization. In: International Workshop on Physics of Semiconductor Devices, pp. 253–256 (2007)

8. Makryniotis, T., Dasygenis, M.: Implementation of a motion estimation hardware accelerator on Zynq SoC. In: 6th International Conference on Modern Circuits and Systems Technologies (MOCAST), pp. 1–4 (2017)

9. Domínguez, A., Carballo, P.P., Núñez, A.: Programmable SoC platform for deep packet inspection using enhanced Boyer-Moore algorithm. In: International Symposium on Reconfigurable Communication-Centric Systems-on-Chip (ReCoSoC), pp. 1–8 (2017)

10. Chang, A.X.M., Culurciello, E.: Hardware accelerators for recurrent neural. In: IEEE International Symposium on Circuit and Systems (ISCAS), pp. 1–4 (2017)

11. Kennedy, J., Eberhart, R.C.: Particle Swarm Optimization. In: Proceedings of the IEEE International Conference on Neural Networks, pp. 1942–1948 (1995)

12. Gildenblat, G., et al.: PSP: an advanced surface-potential-based MOSFET model for circuit simulation. IEEE Trans. Electron Devices **53**, 1979–1993 (2009)

13. Crockett, L.H., Elliot, R., Enderwitz, M.: The Zynq Book: embedded Processing with the arm Cortex-A9 on the Xilinx Zynq-7000 All Programmable SoC. Strathclyde Academic Media (2016)

14. Powell, A., Silage, D.: Statistical performance of the ARM Cortex A9 accelerator coherency port in the xilinx zynq SoC for real-time applications. In: International Conference on ReConFigurable Computing and FPGAs (ReConFig), pp. 1–6 (2015)

Implementation of a Novel Fault Tolerant Routing Technique for Mesh Network on Chip

Akshay B. P.[1(✉)], Ganesh K. M.[1], Thippeswamy D. R.[1], Vishnu S. Bhat[1], Anitha Vijayakumar[1], Ananda Y. R.[2], and John Jose[2]

[1] Department of ECE, Dayananda Sagar College of Engineering, Bengaluru, India
akshaybp456@gmail.com, ganesh.km.n7@gmail.com, dr.thippu@gmail.com,
vishnu.s.bhat@gmail.com, anithavijaya@gmail.com
[2] MARS Research Lab, Department of CSE,
Indian Institute of Technology Guwahati, Guwahati, India
yrananda@gmail.com, johnjose@iitg.ac.in

Abstract. The continuous advancements in the Network on Chip technology emphasizes the need for fault tolerant designs. In this work, we propose a routing technique that handles multiple link faults. We use flit parameters to handle the fault in the routing path. Experimental analysis show that the proposed routing technique is capable of routing packets even with two fault locations and the packets are received in the destination router without any error. In addition, hardware implementation done using ZedBoard Zynq FPGA hardware kit shows that our design is having minor area overhead compared to the standard XY routing and it's a significantly better choice than the other fault tolerant algorithms.

Keywords: Router micro-architecture · Double faults

1 Introduction

As technology increases, design and scalability issues associated with multi-core processors become evident. In addition, increasing number of transistors on a single chip has invaded the concept of system on chip [12] that scales up deep sub-micron effects like cross-talk and interference. Network on chip (NoC) design paradigm has been proposed to replace traditional bus-based interconnect. Here data communication takes place through data packets with the help of routing algorithm and packet switching technology. Figure 1 shows the basic two-dimensional mesh NoC. It is a 16-core tiled chip-multiprocessor (CMP) architecture. Each router has 5×5 crossbars with 4 virtual channels per port.

Each processing element (PE) consists of an L1 cache block, a shared L2 cache block and also connected to a router. Usually, a source core generates packets and divides them into smaller units called as flits. Each packet is segmented into head flit, single or multiple body flits and a tail flit. Head flit carries routing

© Springer Nature Singapore Pte Ltd. 2019
S. Rajaram et al. (Eds.): VDAT 2018, CCIS 892, pp. 495–506, 2019.
https://doi.org/10.1007/978-981-13-5950-7_42

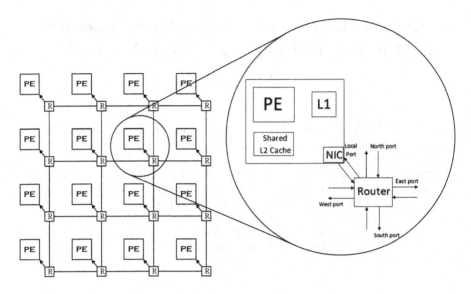

Fig. 1. Basic two-dimensional mesh NoC

information of the packet, body flit has the required data and tail flit performs bookkeeping to close the connection between the nodes. These flits are injected into local router when an L1 miss occurs. Wormhole virtual channel switching occurs between the source and the destination routers for all flits of a packet. Packets follow an embedded routing algorithm. The rapid growth in the NoC framework for multi-core systems demands fault-tolerant architecture. Generally, the quality of chip is directly influenced by its fault tolerance limit. Faults are categorized into two types in NoC, namely transient faults and permanent faults. The former occurs due to bit error in the transmitted flit and the latter occurs due to electron-migration, temperature instability and oxide break down [13]. The aforementioned faults are a threat to the reliability of Network on Chip. To address these issues researchers are focusing on building a fault tolerant NoC. As the Standard XY routing is known for its better traffic management and network latency, we build our fault tolerant algorithm on top of traditional XY routing. In this paper, we propose a fault-tolerant adaptive XY routing algorithm that can handle one or more faults in the routing path with minimal traffic management and area overhead. To evaluate the effectiveness of our algorithm, we model our proposed algorithm on BookSim2.0 simulator. In addition, we validated our algorithm on ZedBoard Zynq-7000 FPGA hardware kit [15] using Xilinx Vivado HLS 2016.2. The rest of the paper is organized as follows. Section 2 discusses about the related work. Section 3 presents about the motivation of our work. Section 4 addresses our proposed mechanism, Sect. 5 describes the experimental setup, Sect. 6 depicts our experimental results and findings, and finally Sect. 7 concludes the paper with future work.

2   Related Work

In an approach given by Wang et al. [1], the authors consider two types of faults, one is node fault and another one is link fault. The algorithm aims at bypassing this node fault and the link fault with the help of new paths that passes through the neighbouring nodes. This new path strategy across all the neighbouring nodes results in increased hops to destination and high traffic conditions across corners.

An approach given by Wu et al. [2], uses the XY algorithm as their default routing function to make a fault tolerant routing algorithm. When the fault is detected, if the faulty router is not the edge router, then it bypasses the fault by north last routing algorithm. If it is an edge router, then routing list information (table) is stored in the edge router. This approach requires a larger hardware and latency overhead.

DeOrio et al. [3], explains fault tolerant architecture and a routing algorithm called VICIS. This algorithm can address permanent faults with its features like BIST (Built In Self Test) units, fault diagnosis and reconfiguration of router architecture. Fault diagnosis is carried out with the help of error correcting codes (ECC). This approach adds many hardware components like port swapper, ECC units and FIFO buffers which increases the area overhead. This approach may also become susceptible to deadlock in some pathological cases.

It includes a detection mechanism with the help of Error Correcting Codes, followed by a diagnosis phase which determines the fault location. In short VICIS includes a reconfigurable router architecture and a routing algorithm. VICIS explores in finding solution through changing the architecture and also changing the routing algorithm that may incur high performance overhead. A Built-In Self-Test (BIST) at each router is also employed for diagnosis. Architecture features including error correction a crossbar bypass bus and port swapping result in overall increase in the latency.

Schonwald et al. [4], explains a fully adaptive and fault tolerant routing algorithm for NoC's called force directed wormhole routing (FDWR). FDWR mainly concentrates on distributing the traffic across the entire network using wormhole routing principle. In order to adapt to different network topologies, FDWR uses a routing table concept which updates the number of hops to the destination. This in turn increases the memory overhead.

An approach given by Fukushima et al. [5], consists of fault tolerant implementation for both regular and irregular network due to permanent link failures. The technique is deadlock free and guarantees a path between every pair of nodes. The segment routing is used for irregular topology. In this approach, three sets of bits are used for each of the switch. First set of bits are used to represent routing option and are called routing bits, second set of bits are used to capture the connection pattern and are called connectivity bits and the last set of bits are used to capture the faulty routing options and are called faulty bits. Routing logic has two phases and are termed as comparator phase and computation phase. In the comparator phase, comparing of the x and y coordinates takes place while the appropriate routing is computed in the computation stage.

The algorithm is deadlock free, but it restricts switch design and also loads the communication traffic by extra messages. This approach guarantees the connectivity without additional hardware overhead. It provides high performance for a regular network, but degrades performance for an irregular network.

A unique approach by Chatterjee et al. [13], presents a fault tolerant reconfigurable NoC architecture using router redundancy. In this paper, a double router is implanted in all the nodes of a mesh, instead of a single router, one active router and a spare router. Both routers use the same links with the help of a multiplexer. In case of failure of a router the routing algorithm remains the same since the faulty router is replaced by spare router and the topology is not affected. This type of approach increases area overhead. In this architecture a controller is designed, it has a look up table for storing individual router information. Therefore, this approach requires additional memory with increased complexity.

An approach by Zhang et al. [14], have considered 4 main neighbours and 4 indirect-neighbours. As in an 8×8 2-D mesh a router can fit into 9 different contours i.e., four borders, four corners and one in the center. The NE router of center contour is not said to be deadlock-free as there will be two complete cycles formed due to the turn-based algorithm. In-order to overcome that aforementioned problem, the authors have come up with a solution that is to remove two turns at the NE router of the contour, thus reducing these cycle count from two to one. The authors have also proposed another approach by completely replacing the turn-based algorithm with some unique paths for every contour at the expense of increased area overhead.

3   Motivation

With the increase in the number of cores on a chip, the hardware complications arising due to link failures are significant. As the links between each router in the network is very small in size, there might be a case in which these links get down permanently. Then this may lead to discarding the entire chip, which is not an economical solution. This signifies the need for fault tolerant algorithms.

In earlier discussed approaches [1–3, 5, 14], the fault tolerant routing algorithms involve a complex hardware design with various limitations and requires an additional memory space for routing table information [13]. This motivates us to design a fault tolerant algorithm which should be minimal in implementation as well as efficient enough to by-pass up to two faults in the entire network without any hardware complexities.

4   Proposed Design

In our proposed fault-tolerant algorithm (Algorithm 1), we are considering permanent faults. For the explanation purpose let's consider a single router. We include two extra fields in the packet header to implement our proposed algorithm they are *valid bit* and *fault bits* Whenever a flit arrives at the router, the *valid bit*, *fault bits* and *destination ID* is extracted. If the *valid bit* is set, *fault bits* are checked first before applying the routing logic. If the *fault bits* are '00' it is considered as normal flit which is following its natural path, and the flit is XY routing. When the *fault bits* are '01', the flit is deflected before coming to the present router, due to an X-axis fault. Then that flit has to be re-routed by resetting the source as the current router; i.e., that is the path starts freshly from the current router. If the *fault bits* are '10', then the flit is deflected to the current router because of a Y-axis fault, then that type of flits are re-routed by pushing such flits through east port. This is done in all type of routers in a network except last column router. In last column router these Y-axis deflected flits are re-routed by pushing them through west-port. If continuous parallel faults are observed, the flits are moved to columns aside according to the algorithm and further decision is taken depending on the destination router location. We had analysed various cases for our algorithm as given below.

Algorithm 1. Proposed Fault-Tolerant Algorithm

---

if *validbit* == 1 then
  if *faultbits* == 00 then
    Calculate the output port using XY routing
  else if *faultbits* == 01 then
    Based on destination address apply XY routing
  else if *faultbits* == 10 then
    Based on destination row, calculate north or south port
  end if
  if Calculated port is not faulty then
    Calculated port is assigned
    Reset *faultbits* to 00
  else
    if East or West port is faulty then
      Based on destination row, calculate north or south port
      Set *faultbits* to 01
    end if
    if North or South port is faulty then
      East port is assigned
      Set *faultbits* to 10
    end if
  end if
else
  Invalid input
end if

Case 1 (Single X-Axis Fault): Consider Fig. 2, where for a packet source is 9 and destination is 45, and a fault in the east port of router 11 (marked as 'x'). The algorithm first checks the *destination ID*, if the destination row is above or same as that of the current row, then the algorithm deflects the flit to north.

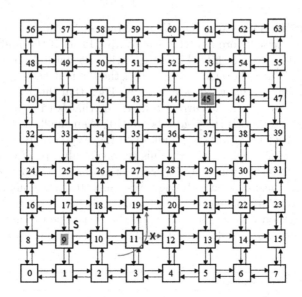

Fig. 2. 8 × 8 mesh NoC architecture with one X-axis fault

If the destination row is below the current row, then the algorithm deflects the flit to south. In both the cases, before deflecting the flit we set the *fault bits* to '01'. When a flit arrives at a particular router with the *fault bits* set as '01', this means that the flit was deflected due to an X-axis fault and has reached the current router from a north or south port. The current router resets the *fault bits* to '00' and routes the packets as normal XY routing.

Case 2 (Single Y-Axis Fault): Consider Fig. 3, where for a packet source is 9 and destination is 45, and a fault in the north port of router 21 (marked as 'x'). Whenever this type of fault occurs, it means that the flit has arrived its destination column. According to standard XY routing, a flit has to take Y turn only when the destination column is reached. We deflect such flit to east. Before deflecting the flit we set the *fault bits* to '10'. When a flit arrives a particular router with the *fault bits* set as '10', it means that the flit was deflected due to a Y-axis fault and has arrived the current router from a west port. The current router resets the *fault bits* to '00' and routes the packets to north if the destination row is above the current row or to south if the destination row is below the current row. In the case of the right most column, such flits are pushed to the network through west port as there will be no more east port available. Then the immediate next router will guide that flit to reach it's destination. In our example, the flit is pushed to east port from router 21 and sets the *fault bits* '10', it will be taken back to the destination column through a new path i.e., 21-22-30-29. Once it reaches the router 29 it is treated separately as explained before.

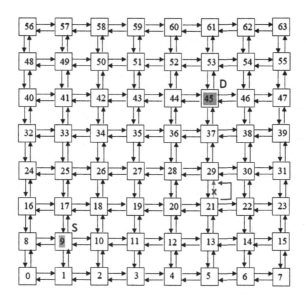

Fig. 3. 8 × 8 mesh NoC architecture with one Y-axis fault

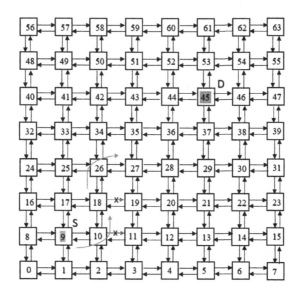

Fig. 4. 8 × 8 mesh NoC architecture with two X-axis faults

Case 3 (Double X-Axis Faults): Consider Fig. 4, where for a packet source is 9 and destination is 45, and a fault in the east port of router 10 (marked as 'x') and in the east port of router 10 (marked as 'x'). Whenever this type of fault occurs, if the destination row is above or in the same row as that of the current row, then we deflect the flit to north. If the destination row is below the current row, then we deflect the flit to south. In both the former and latter cases before deflecting the flit we set the *fault bits* to '01' in that particular flit. If the next router also has an X-axis fault, the *fault bits* are kept as it is that is '01' and again deflected based on the destination row. When a flit arrives a particular router either from north or south port with the *fault bits* set as '01', the current router resets the *fault bits* to '00' and routes the packets as normal XY routing. In our example, the routing follows the path 10-18-26 then from 26 it starts afresh and routes the packet according to XY-routing.

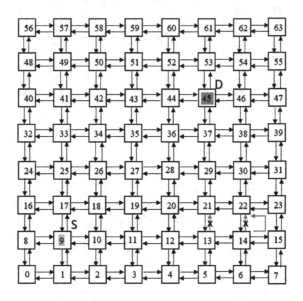

Fig. 5. 8×8 mesh NoC architecture with two Y-axis faults

Case 4 (Double Y-Axis Faults): Consider Fig. 5, where for a packet source is 9 and destination is 45, and a fault in the north port of router 13 (marked as 'x') and in the east port of router 14 (marked as 'x'). Whenever this type of fault occurs, it means that the flit has arrived its destination column, we deflect the flit to the east, before deflecting the flit we set the *fault bits* to '10' in that particular flit. If the next router also has a Y-axis fault, the *fault bits* are kept as it is (i.e. '10') and again deflected to east. When a flit arrives a particular router with the *fault bits* set as '10', this means that the flit was deflected due to a Y-axis fault and has arrived the current router from a west port. The current router resets the *fault bits* to '00' and routes the packets to north if the destination row is above the current row or to the south if the destination row is below the current row. In our example, the routing takes the path 13-14-15-23-22-21 then it takes its final turn.

5   Experimental Setup

5.1   Simulation Setup

We use Booksim2.0, the cycle accurate NoC simulator for modelling 8×8 CMP with 2D topology [11]. Booksim supports various kinds of routing algorithms, traffic patterns and network topologies. It can generate NoC traffic from real traffic traces in addition to the synthetic traffic patterns. We incorporate an algorithm which handles the traffic in the entire NoC. The simulation is carried out in latency mode, in which the simulation is carried out by injecting batch of packets. The simulation is run till the average network latency is calculated for the current network configuration. A flit history is taken out to trace the flit traffic path, which will reflect the entire path taken by a particular flit. We verify the fault bypassing strategy by this flit-tracing file.

5.2   Hardware Implementation Setup

We use Vivado tool from Xilinx to implement an NoC router architecture with and without fault tolerant routing technique on a FPGA kit. In our case we have used ZedBoard Zynq-7000 XC7Z020CLG484-1 [15]. The design and the synthesised code is flashed on to the board, with the help of an IP catalogue VIO. This IP catalogue helps in creating a top module VIO wrapper which can directly be flashed on the board, and verified successfully.

6   Result and Analysis

Figure 6 contains the injection rate vs average packet latency plot for normal XY algorithm without fault and proposed fault tolerant algorithm with single and double faults. As expected normal XY performs better. Our fault tolerant algorithm due to flit deflections around the fault location takes more number of hopes to reach the destination. This increases the latency of such flits. Due to the additional hops and hence the extra packet movement in the network with fault tolerant routing, it saturates easily. Our approach guarantees packet delivery at destination at the additional overhead of higher average packet latency.

We also analyse the count of such deflections flit due to our algorithm. Figure 7 contains the number of deflected flits. Higher the traffic higher the number of deflected flits. We also observe that the result for single X fault and single Y fault cases are almost same. Hence they are not separately plotted. Same is the case with double X fault and double Y fault. Our algorithm cannot ensure guaranteed delivery of packets if one fault is in X and other is in Y links. We could address this at the expense of additional fault bits. We reserve that part for a future extension.

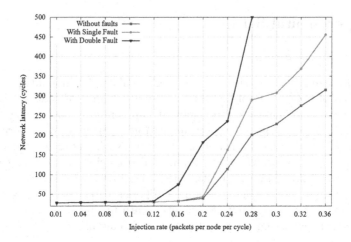

Fig. 6. Injection rate versus average packet latency for single and double fault

Table 1. Area overhead comparision

Routing-algorithm	LUTs-used (count)	BUFGs-used (count)	Power consumption (mW)
Basic-XY	493	3	120
Fault-tolerant	718	3	125

Terms used:- LUTs - Look Up Tables and BUFG - Buffer Gates

For the hardware implementation, we have considered a single router with five ports (north, south, east and west along with a local port) representing links of a node in the network. The Verilog design of the proposed routing module is done and the synthesized RTL was dumped on ZedBoard Zynq-7000 FPGA hardware kit [15].

We use Virtual Input Output (VIO) to realise our implementation as there is a need of more than 40 input pins as well as nearly 80 output pins. Since these many pins are not available physically on the board. VIO in the Vivado tool for pin virtualization. The area overhead is calculated by looking at the increase of number of LUTs and BUFGs as listed in Table 1. Even though the routing logic takes 1.45 times the LUTs than basic XY routing. The overall router area overhead is approximately 4%. Power is one of the major factors to be considered in NoC architecture. For our proposed algorithm the power consumption increase is about 5 mW more than the standard XY algorithm. These numbers are taken for ZedBoard Zynq-7000 FPGA hardware kit [15] and may vary from one FPGA chip to other.

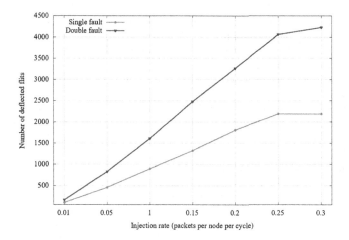

Fig. 7. Injection rate versus deflected flits for single and double fault

7 Conclusion

In this paper we proposed a new algorithm for guaranteed delivery of packets in an NoC with faulty links. In the proposed algorithm we re-routed a packet approaching a faulty link, by deflecting it to the direction closer to the destination. There are different cases considered such as a fault in x-axis, a fault in y-axis, parallel faults and others. The proposed algorithm is efficient for all the types of faults present in the network. The output for different types of faults are explained. The various statistical analysis and graphs are shown and a number of parameters compared between single and double faults can be observed. The proposed algorithm is adaptive to any type of faults in the network, saves a large number of flits from getting discarded in the network due to faulty links by deflecting it to a new path and is hardware implementable. Few disadvantages such as increase in average latency, congestion and heat dissipation is also seen which can be minimised. We hope that the proposed fault tolerant algorithm can ensure NoC design with higher reliability.

Acknowledgement. This work is supported in part by a grant from DST Government of India, SERB-ECR scheme (project number ECR/2016/212)

References

1. Wang, J., Fu, F., Zhang, T., Chen, Y.: A small-granularity solution on fault-tolerant in 2D-mesh network-on-chip. In: 10th IEEE International Conference on Solid-State and Integrated Circuit Technology (2010)
2. Wu, J., Cai, H., Qu, F., Yang, Y.: The reconfigurable fault tolerance routing algorithm in mesh topology structure. In: 10th International Conference on Wireless Communications, Networking and Mobile Computing (WiCOM 2014) (2014)

3. DeOrio, A., et al.: A reliable routing architecture and algorithm for NoCs. IEEE Trans. Comput.-Aided Des. Integr. Circ. Syst. **31**(5), 726–739 (2012)
4. Schonwald, T., Zimmermann, J., Bringmann, O., Rosenstiel, W.: Fully adaptive fault-tolerant routing algorithm for network-on-chip architectures. In: 10th Euromicro Conference on Digital System Design Architectures, Methods and Tools (DSD 2007) (2007)
5. Fukushima, Y., Fukushi, M., Yairi, I., Hattori, T.: A hardware-oriented fault-tolerant routing algorithm for irregular 2D-mesh network-on-chip without virtual channels. In: IEEE 25th International Symposium on Defect and Fault Tolerance in VLSI Systems (2010)
6. Ebrahimi, M., Daneshtalab, M., Plosila, J.: High performance fault-tolerant routing algorithm for NoC-based many-core systems. In: 2013 21st Euromicro International Conference on Parallel, Distributed, and Network-Based Processing (2013)
7. Pirretti, M., Link, G., Brooks, R., Vijaykrishnan, N., Kandemir, M., Irwin, M.: Fault tolerant algorithms for network-on-chip interconnect. In: IEEE Computer Society Annual Symposium on VLSI (ISVLSI) (2004)
8. Fick, D., DeOrio, A., Chen, G., Bertacco, V., Sylvester, D., Blaauw, D.: A highly resilient routing algorithm for fault-tolerant NoCs. In: Design, Automation and Test in Europe Conference and Exhibition (DATE) (2009)
9. Jojima, Y., Fukushi, M.: A fault-tolerant routing method for 2D-mesh network-on-chips based on components of a router. In: IEEE 5th Global Conference on Consumer Electronics (2016)
10. Gu, X., Cai, H., Zhang, Y., Huang, N., Yang, Y.: Research on network fault tolerance method on chip. In: 2016 9th International Congress on Image and Signal Processing, BioMedical Engineering and Informatics (CISP-BMEI) (2016)
11. Dally, W., Towles, B.: Route packets, not wires: on-chip interconnection networks. In: Design Automation Conference (2001)
12. Yan, P., Jiang, S., Sridhar, R.: A novel fault-tolerant router architecture for network-on-chip reconfiguration. In: 28th IEEE International System-on-Chip Conference (SOCC) (2015)
13. Chatterjee, N., Chattopadhyay, S., Manna, K.: A spare router based reliable network-on-chip design. In: IEEE International Symposium on Circuits and Systems (ISCAS) (2014)
14. Zhang, Z., Greiner, A., Taktak, S.: A reconfigurable routing algorithm for a fault-tolerant 2D-mesh network-on-chip. In: Proceedings of the 45th Annual Conference on Design Automation (DAC) (2008)
15. Zedboard.org Zedboard. http://www.zedboard.org/product/zedboard

Memory

Efficient and Failure Aware ECC for STT-MRAM Cache Memory

Keerthi Sagar Kokkiligadda$^{(\boxtimes)}$, Yogendra Gupta, and Lava Bhargava

Department of Electronics and Communication,
Malaviya National Institute of Technology, Jaipur, Jaipur, Rajasthan, India
ks.kokkiligadda@gmail.com, yogen.571@gmail.com, lavab@mnit.ac.in

Abstract. Spin Transfer Torque Magnetoresistive Random Access Memory (STT-MRAM) is a favorable memory technology for on-chip cache hierarchies in multi-core processors. STT-MRAM offers scalability, near zero leakage power, non-volatility, high density, etc. which makes it a good candidate for on-chip cache memory. However, write operation in STT-MRAM is asymmetric which causes multiple errors in single line of cache (up to 70 bits of errors). For this usually error control codes are used. In this paper, we focus on analyzing the effectiveness of BCH codes in rectifying the write errors of STT-MRAM. So in the current work (1216, 512) BCH encoder and decoder are designed and verified at the RTL level using Verilog HDL. For encoder, the conventional linear feedback shift register (LFSR) structure is used and for decoding Meggitt decoder is used which also requires 2 LFSR one for first-time syndrome calculation and another for spontaneous recalculation of the syndrome. In our proposed technique, we have reused the syndrome calculator as spontaneous calculator thereby reducing the area. It is practically impossible to manually write Verilog code for designing large architectures such as the (1216, 512) BCH decoder. We have solved this problem by writing a Matlab script which takes the code and data sizes as input, gives the Verilog code as output. We have synthesized the BCH encoder and decoder at 32 nm technology using synopsis design compiler and estimated area, power and delay of the encoder and decoder.

Keywords: STT-MRAM · Error control coding (ECC) ·
BCH encoder and decoder · Meggitt decoder

1 Introduction

The downscaling of CMOS technology puts some serious challenges on traditional SRAM memories, such as scaling and leakage limitations [1]. Below 40 nm SRAM cells are faced with several scalability challenges such as high leakage power and unreliability [5]. Among the emerging memories STT-MRAM can be a very good replacement to SRAM because of its features like scalability, low read time, high density and low leakage power. It is expected that STT-MRAM is scalable upto the 22-nm node and also below [12]. Since STT-MRAM can potentially enable

© Springer Nature Singapore Pte Ltd. 2019
S. Rajaram et al. (Eds.): VDAT 2018, CCIS 892, pp. 509–520, 2019.
https://doi.org/10.1007/978-981-13-5950-7_43

high-capacity on-chip nonvolatile data storage with relatively high access speed and very low leakage power consumption, many recent computer architecture research efforts have explored the potential and demonstrated appealing possible advantages of using STT-MRAM to implement low-level on-chip caches in microprocessors [4]. Because of these properties STT-MRAM can replace SRAM as cache memory [2,18]. We have simulated 1MB of STT-MRAM and SRAM as cache memory using the nvsim tool [17] at 45 nm and the comparision is given in Table 1. As we can see the read latency and energy of STT-MRAM is almost equal to its SRAM counterpart but the write energy and write latency and energy of STT-MRAM is greater than SRAM based cache memory.

Table 1. Comparision of 1 MB STT MRAM and SRAM cache features at 45 nm.

Device	STT-MRAM	SRAM
Area	$1.170\,\text{mm}^2$	$3.59\,\text{mm}^2$
Read latency	2.744 ns	2.610 ns
Write latency	7.039 ns	2.610 ns
Read energy per access	0.368 nJ	0.320 nJ
Write energy per access	0.768 nJ	0.350 nJ
Leakage power	25 mW	631 mW

STT-MRAM suffers from many failures like high write latency, poor reliability and high write energy. The write operation in STT-MRAM is probabilistic in nature with the write latency following a distribution with long tail which results in high latency and thereby high energy. This asymmetry in write operation causes the reliability issue in STT-MRAM based cache memories which results multiple bit errors in single line of cache.

The common solutions for addressing these problems can be classified into two types, one at device level and the other at architectural level. At device level the thermal stability factor (Δ) can be lowered to reduce the switching delay. At architectural level for reducing the bit error rate due to these failures, error control coding (ECC) is used [7–9]. The architectural level solutions are easier to implement compared to the device level solutions because changing the thermal stability factor (Δ) may improve the writing time but at the same it also reduces the retention time as explained in detail in the section Write failure in STT-MRAM. In the current work we have focussed on the architectural level solution of using ECC to reduce the write error rate (WER) in STT-MRAM.

There are many ECC like Hamming, BCH, Turbo, Reed Solomon, Golay etc. Since linear block codes offer low power consumption and can be implemented easily with simple design they are preferred. Cyclic codes are a special class of linear block codes which require only simple operations like multiplication and division for their implementation. BCH codes are a type of cyclic codes which can correct multiple errors. The current work focuses on Register Transfer level (RTL) design of BCH encoder and decoder and their overhead evaluation in terms of area and power and delay metrics using Synopsis Design Vision tool. Conventional serial lfsr approach mentioned in [11] is used for encoder. For decoder the Meggitt decoding approach mentioned in [6,10] is followed. But the current work improvises on the decoder mentioned in [6,10] by using the principle of hardware re-utilization. The syndrome calculator is reused as spontaneous calculator there by reducing the area and power without loosing any efficiency in the error correcting capability of the code.

The rest of the paper is organized as follows. In Sect. 2 some basic concepts of STT-MRAM and its write failure are given. In Sect. 3 BCH encoder and decoder designs which we have implemented are discussed. In Sect. 4 the results are given and Sect. 5 concludes the paper.

2 Spin Transfer Torque Magnetoresistive Random Access Memory

STT-MRAM is an emerging resistive memory technology that uses the magneto-resistance property for storing the bits. The storage element of STT-MRAM is Magnetic Tunnel Junction (MTJ) as shown in Fig. 1. The MTJ is made up of two ferromagnetic layers, with an MgO layer sandwiched between them as a tunnel barrier. Among the two ferromagnetic layers, the magnetization of one layer is fixed which is located at the bottom called reference layer or pinned layer. The magnetization of the upper layer called free layer is changed by applying appropriate current through the fixed layer.

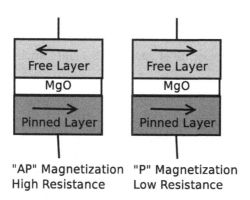

Fig. 1. Magnetic tunnel junction cell.

STT-MRAM cell consists of an MTJ and an access transistor as shown Fig. 2. The data storage element in STT-MRAM cell is Magnetic Tunnel Junction device. The most common STT-MRAM cell is one access Transistor, one MTJ structure. The direction of the two magnetized FM films can be 'low resistance

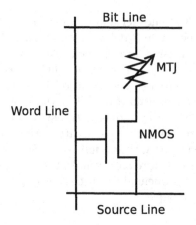

Fig. 2. Spin transfer torque MRAM cell.

state' (Parallel) or 'high resistance state' (Anti-Parallel) which are used to specify electrical signals. MTJ is accessed by turning on the Word-Line by using the gate terminal of NMOS transistor. We generally mention MTJ as a current dependent resistor in the circuit. In Fig. 1 a high resistance (Anti-Parallel) state is designated by '1' and for writing a positive voltage is applied between the source line and the bit line and on the other hand a low resistance (Parallel) state is designated by '0'. The difference between the value of parallel and anti-parallel resistance is important in sensing circuit operations. This is called as TMR ratio and the equation is:

$$TMR = \frac{R_{AP} - R_P}{R_P} \tag{1}$$

R_{AP} and R_P are the resistance of Anti-Parallel and Parallel states respectively.

2.1 Write Failure in STT-MRAM

As mentioned in the previous section the write operation in STT-MRAM is probabilistic in nature and the switching time varies between successive write accesses. But in any digital system all the operations between different components must be synchronized. So we cannot have varying write time and it is usually limited to a finite value t_W. Because of this limiting of write time sometimes the write current will be terminated before the STT-MRAM switches and the data to be written will fail to be stored correctly which results in a write failure. The write error rate (WER) in a single bit STT-MRAM cell varies with the write time as given below [13].

$$WER_{bit}(t_W) = 1 - exp[\frac{-\pi^2 \cdot (I-1) \cdot \Delta}{4(I \cdot e^{(C(I-1)t_W)} - 1)}], I = \frac{I_W}{I_C} \tag{2}$$

where C is a technology dependent parameter, Δ is the thermal stability factor and I is the ratio of write current (I_W) to the critical current (I_C). It can be seen from Eq. 1 that increasing the write current reduces the write time for a given write error rate. But this results in high power and energy. The write current is also limited by the oxide breakdown. Alternatively the thermal stability factor Δ can be lowered. However the average retention time given as $\tau \cdot e^{\Delta}$ decreases by lowering the Δ. The probability of retention failure for a given retention time t_{RF} also increases by decreasing Δ as given below [14].

$$P_{RF} = 1 - exp[-\frac{t_{RF}}{\tau \cdot e^{\Delta}}] \tag{3}$$

From the above discussion it can be seen that the device level solutions are not very effective. This is where the architectural level solution of using ECC comes into play.

3   Failure Aware ECC for STT-MRAM

3.1   BCH Encoder

The Bose-Chaudhuri-Hocquenghem codes are a class of cyclic codes invented independently in 1960 by Bose and Ray-Chaudhuri and in 1959 by Alexis Hocquenghem [15,16]. The BCH codes can correct multiple bits of errors and can be implemented with simple hardware. Because of these features BCH codes are one of the suitable error control codes for correcting write errors in STT-MRAM.

In an (n, k) binary BCH code k bits of message is encoded into n bits of code by padding (n − k) parity bits. In any cyclic code the codeword of n bits is treated as a degree n − 1 polynomial and the message of k bits is treated as a degree k − 1 polynomial. Then the non-systematic BCH code c(x) can be obtained by multiplying the message polynomial m(x) with a predefined polynomial of degree n − k called g(x). But in non-systematic coding the original message bits may not appear in the codeword. For this reason usually systematic encoding of BCH codes is preferred. In systematic encoding the k bit message is padded with n − k parity bits. This simplifies the design of the decoder as the message bits can be directly obtained from the corrupted codeword after correcting it.

Systematic encoding involves finding the n − k parity bits and appending them to the message of k bits to form the n-bit codeword. The parity bits are nothing but the remainder obtained after dividing the message polynomial by the generator polynomial. Before the division the message polynomial must be padded with n − k zeros. The steps involved are summarized below [11].

1. The message polynomial m(x) of degree k − 1 is multiplied with x^{n-k} to pad with n − k zeros.
2. Divide (m(x) · x^{n-k}) by g(x) to obtain the remainder
   (i.e. [x^{n-k}·m(x)] mod g(x)).
3. Form the code word by appending this remainder to m(x).

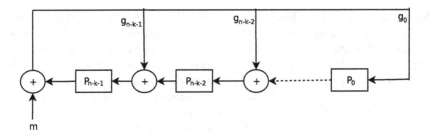

Fig. 3. BCH encoder [3].

All these steps can be implemented by the simple LFSR structure [3] shown Fig. 3 which basically performs division and obtains the remainder. In Fig. 3 all the registers are initialized to zero and the message 'm' is fed serially bit by bit starting from MSB. $g_{n-k}, g_{n-k-1}, g_{n-k-2}, \ldots, g_0$ are the bits of the generator polynomial. The first bit g_{n-k} is always going to be 1 because if it is zero it is no longer a degree $n-k$ polynomial. In Fig. 3 for any register p_i $(0 \leq i \leq n-k-1)$ if the corresponding g_i bit value is one then it means that particular vertical connection before the register is present. If it is zero then the connection is not present. After k clock cycles the parity bits are available in the registers p_{n-k-1} to p_0 which can be appended to the message.

As we are trying to use STT-MRAM as cache memory the designed BCH code should be able to correct upto 70 [1] bits of errors in a block of size 512 [4,5] bits. Using Matlab it is found that it is possible in $GF(2^{11})$ field with $n-k$ value equal to 704. So we need to pad 704 bits to 512 bits making a total code size of 1216 bits. The generator polynomial of degree 704 (i.e. 705 bits) is also calculated using Matlab.

Since it is hard to verify the working of (1216, 512) BCH encoder, first BCH codes of smaller length are implemented using the structure shown in Fig. 3. We have implemented the (7, 4), (15, 7) and (15, 5) BCH codes which are single bit, two bit and three bit error correcting codes respectively. After verifying and testing their operation the same Verilog code has been extended to design the (1216, 512) BCH encoder. This ensures the correctness of the design. They are synthesized in Synopsis Design Vision tool at 32 nm technology. Their corresponding area, power, delay overhead estimates are shown in Table 1 of the results section.

3.2 BCH Decoder

Any conventional cyclic decoding scheme involves the following steps.

1. Calculate the syndrome polynomial s(x) by dividing the corrupted codeword polynomial r(x) by g(x) and obtain the remainder (i.e. s(x) = r(x) mod g(x)).
2. Do a look up table operation in the syndrome table pre-stored in ROM to obtain the error vector.
3. Add the error to the corrupted codeword to obtain the original codeword c(x).

The operation of Meggitt decoder differs slightly from the above approach. Instead of correcting all the erroneous bits at once it attempts to correct one bit at a time. This has some advantages when it comes to hardware implementation which will become obvious by the end of this section. The actual steps involved in Meggitt decoder are elaborated below.

Step 1: This step is same as step one of the conventional approach mentioned above. First the syndrome must be calculated from the corrupted codeword as mentioned above. As it involves only division operation it can be implemented by the simple LFSR division circuit shown in Fig. 4 which is very similar to the one used in encoder (Fig. 3) [6,10]. All the registers are initialized to zero and the corrupted codeword polynomial r is fed serially bit by bit at the XOR gate before register s_0. Simultaneously r is also fed into an n-bit buffer (not shown in diagram) as it will be required again later in step 2. After n clock cycles the syndrome is available in the registers $s_{n-k-1}, s_{n-k-2}, \ldots, s_0$. As in the encoder circuit of Fig. 3 g_i indicates the ith bit of generator polynomial and the value of bit indicates whether the corresponding vertical connection is present or not.

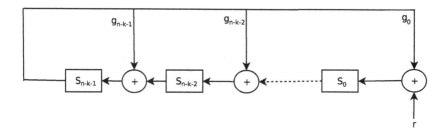

Fig. 4. Syndrome calculator circuit [6,10].

Step 2: After calculating the syndrome the decoder tries to detect if an error is present in the MSB of codeword stored previously in n-bit buffer. If there is an error the MSB is flipped. If there is no error the MSB is kept as it is. Then the corrupted codeword is cyclic shifted so that the next bit comes into the MSB position of n-bit buffer and again it tries to detect the error in this bit and corrects it if it is present. This process is repeated until all the bits are covered.

In order to detect the error present in the MSB it is sufficient for the decoder to store only those syndromes corresponding to error patterns which have a 1 in the MSB. This reduces the length of the syndrome table to a good extent. Further as the error correction involves only the flipping of the MSB bit there is no need to store the error pattern along with its corresponding syndrome in memory. It is sufficient to store only the syndrome. This reduces the width of the syndrome table by n bits.

But one problem this approach poses is that every time the codeword is shifted its syndrome has to be recalculated which adds to the delay. But this problem is overcome as the Meggitt decoder uses the following property which is inherent to cyclic codes.

Property 1. If $s(x)$ is the syndrome of $r(x)$ and $r'(x)$ is the codeword obtained by cyclic shifting $r(x)$ then the syndrome $s'(x)$ of $r'(x)$ is given by

$$s'(x) = (x.s(x)) \bmod g(x) \tag{4}$$

From this property it can be understood that once the syndrome of a codeword is calculated the syndrome of its cyclic shifted version can be obtained by simply cyclic shifting the current syndrome and dividing it with generator polynomial and taking the remainder. This entire step can be executed in one clock cycle using the spontaneous calculator circuit shown in Fig. 5 [6,10]. Hence this step can be executed in parallel while shifting the codeword in the n-bit buffer so that it doesn't add any extra delay.

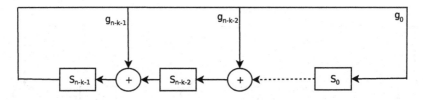

Fig. 5. Spontaneous calculator circuit [6,10].

In Fig. 5 the registers $s_{n-k-1}, s_{n-k-2}, \ldots, s_0$ are initialized with the syndrome value calculated by the syndrome calculator circuit in the previous step. For every clock cycle the corrupted codeword stored in the n-bit shift register is cyclic shifted once and simultaneously the registers of the spontaneous calculator circuit are also shifted once, thereby obtaining the new value of syndrome, corresponding to the shifted corrupted codeword. This process is repeated for n clock cycles i.e. until all the bits of the corrupted codeword are covered. It should also be noted that whenever an error is detected in the MSB of codeword, while correcting it, the current syndrome should also be corrected to match the syndrome of codeword with the MSB corrected. For this the current syndrome should be added with the syndrome of error pattern which has a single bit in MSB. This operation is not shown in Fig. 5 for the sake of simplicity.

It can be seen from Figs. 4 and 5 that the structures of syndrome calculator and spontaneous calculator are very similar. The only difference is that in syndrome calculator the input to the LSB of the register is obtained by XOR operation of the corrupted codeword bit and MSB whereas in spontaneous calculator the MSB of the register is directly connected to the LSB of the register. Also the syndrome calculator is used in step 1 and the spontaneous calculator is used in step 2 which don't occur simultaneously. We used this to our advantage and used the same circuit for syndrome calculation and spontaneous calculation. All that is required is an extra control signal which is equivalent to a switch to identify whether we are in step 1 or step 2.

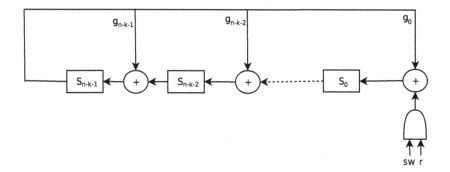

Fig. 6. Syndrome-spontaneous calculator circuit.

The modified syndrome-spontaneous calculator is shown in Fig. 6. As it can be seen Fig. 6 the input 'r' passes into the circuit only when 'sw' is high in which case it works like syndrome calculator. When 'sw' is low the input 'r' is not passed in which case it works like a spontaneous calculator. This approach of hardware reutilization will surely reduce the area overhead of the BCH decoder as compared to the approach followd in [6,10] where separate circuits are used for syndrome and spontaneous calculations. The same can be observed in Table 4 of the results section.

Step 3: This step occurs in parallel with step 2. The value of the syndrome in syndrome-spontaneous calculator is constantly fed to the ROM which is pre-stored with all the syndromes corresponding to error patterns within the error correction capability of the code, which have a 1 in the MSB. Whenever the syndrome of spontaneous calculator matches with any of these syndromes the ROM outputs an error signal which flips the MSB of the codeword. The design of this ROM becomes critical for codes of larger size, because the size of syndrome table increases exponentially with increase in code size. Manually determining the contents of the syndrome table and writing it to the ROM is an impractical task. We have solved this problem by making a Matlab script which not only calculates the values of the syndrome table but also writes the entire table to the ROM. This Matlab function takes the code size and message size as input and directly gives the Verilog file of ROM as output.

All the above steps involved in the working of Meggitt decoder are summarized in the block diagram of Fig. 7. Similiar to approach followed in encoder design first BCH decoders of smaller size such as (7, 4), (15, 7) and (15, 5) are implemented and then the same structure has been extended to implement the

(1216, 512) BCH decoder. They are synthesized in Synopsis Design Vision tool at 32 nm technology and their area, power, delay overhead estimates are given in Table 3 of the results section.

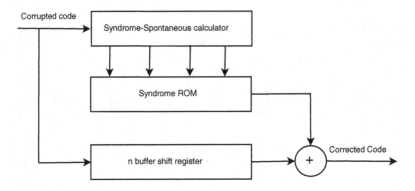

Fig. 7. Operational block diagram of Meggitt decoder.

4   Results

We have modelled the proposed encoder and decoder in Verilog and synthesized using Synopsys Design Compiler at 32 nm technology node to estimate the area and power overhead. As seen in Table 4 the proposed method has improved the area by around 15–17% in the decoder. This is because we have reused the syndrome calculator circuit (Fig. 4) as spontaneous calculator circuit (Fig. 5) as shown in Fig. 6. For an (n, k) binary BCH code this reduces $n - k$ registers in the decoder. In case of $(7, 4)$ code it reduces 3 registers and in case of $(15, 7)$ code it reduces 8 registers. This will surely reduce area and power as observed in Tables 4 and 5.

Table 2. Overhead required for BCH encoder at 32 nm.

Code size	Area (um^2)	Power (uW)	Critical path delay (ns)
(7, 4, 1)	136.24	13.58	0.16
(15, 7, 2)	260.45	22.83	0.10
(15, 5, 3)	269.69	23.86	0.09
(1216, 512, 70)	17326.63	1.20×10^3	0.28

Table 3. Overhead required for BCH decoder at 32 nm.

Code size	Area (um^2)	Power (uW)	Critical path delay (ns)
(7, 4, 1)	236.00	20.43	0.22
(15, 7, 2)	495.39	49.96	0.33
(15, 5, 3)	671.80	70.98	0.41
(1216, 512, 70)	54909.54	3.44×10^3	0.72

Table 4. Comparision of improvement in area between the proposed method and the method used in [6, 10].

Code size	Area of proposed method	Area in [6, 10]	Percentage improvement
(7, 4, 1)	236.00	277.94	15.09
(15, 7, 2)	495.39	601.03	17.58

Table 5. Comparision of improvement in power between the proposed method and the method used in [6] and [10].

Code size	Power of proposed method	Power in [6] and [10]	Percentage improvement
(7, 4, 1)	20.43	23.69	13.77
(15, 7, 2)	49.96	50.19	0.46

5   Conclusion

In this paper we have proposed an efficient and failure aware ECC technique for STT-MRAM based cache memory. Our proposed ECC technique has less overhead in terms of area and power as compared to state of the art techniques. In future we will apply this technique in multicore cache hierarchies using full system simulation framework (gem5).

Acknowledgement. This work is partly supported by SMDPC2SD project, sponsored by Ministry of Electronics & Information of Technology, Government of India.

References

1. Sayed, N., Oboril, F., Bishnoi, R., Tahoori, M.B.: Leveraging systematic unidirectional error-detecting codes for fast STT-MRAM cache. In: 2017 IEEE 35th VLSI Test Symposium (VTS), Las Vegas, NV, pp. 1–6 (2017)
2. Sun, G., Dong, X., Xie, Y., Li, J., Chen, Y.: A novel architecture of the 3D stacked MRAM L2 cache for CMPs. In: 2009 IEEE 15th International Symposium on High Performance Computer Architecture, Raleigh, NC, pp. 239–249 (2009)

3. Meggitt, J.: Error correcting codes and their implementation for data transmission systems. IRE Trans. Inf. Theory **7**(4), 234–244 (1961)
4. Sun, H., Liu, C., Min, T., Zheng, N., Zhang, T.: Architectural exploration to enable sufficient MTJ device write margin for STT-RAM based cache. IEEE Trans. Magn. **48**(8), 2346–2351 (2012)
5. Azad, Z., Farbeh, H., Monazzah, A.M.H., Miremadi, S.G.: AWARE: adaptive way allocation for reconfigurable ECCs to protect write errors in STT-RAM caches. IEEE Trans. Emerg. Top. Comput. **PP**(99), 1 (2017)
6. Nguyen, V.T., Dao, V.L., Phan, T.T.D.: Hardware implementation of cyclic codes error correction on FPGA. In: 2016 3rd National Foundation for Science and Technology Development Conference on Information and Computer Science (NICS), Danang, pp. 97–100 (2016)
7. Chen, T.J., Li, J.F., Tseng, T.W.: Cost-efficient built-in redundancy analysis with optimal repair rate for RAMs. IEEE Trans. Comput.-Aided Des. Integr. Circ. Syst. **31**(6), 930–940 (2012)
8. Kang, W., et al.: A low-cost built-in error correction circuit design for STT-MRAM reliability improvement. Microelectron. Reliab. **53**, 1224–1229 (2013)
9. Lu, S.K., Huang, H.H., Huang, J.L., Ning, P.: Synergistic reliability and yield enhancement techniques for embedded SRAMs. IEEE Trans. Comput.- Aided Des. Integr. Circ. Syst. **32**(1), 165–169 (2013)
10. Li, Y., Shi, D., Xia, P.: Cyclic codes error correction system based on FPGA. In: 2014 7th International Congress on Image and Signal Processing, Dalian, pp. 212–216 (2014)
11. Jun, Z., Zhi-Gong, W., Qing-Sheng, H., Jie, X.: Optimized design for high-speed parallel BCH encoder. In: Proceedings of 2005 IEEE International Workshop on VLSI Design and Video Technology, pp. 97–100 (2005)
12. Kim, K., Jeong, G.: Memory technologies for sub-40nm node. In: Proceedings of IEEE International Electron Devices Meeting (IEDM), pp. 27–30, December 2007
13. Munira, K., et al.: A quasi-analytical model for energy-delay-reliability tradeoff studies during write operations in a perpendicular STT-RAM cell. Electron Dev. **59**(8), 2221–2226 (2012)
14. Smullen, C.W., et al.: Relaxing non-volatility for fast and energy-efficient STT-RAM caches. In: HPCA, pp. 50–61 (2011)
15. Hocquenghem, A.: Codes correcteurs d'erreurs. Chiffres **2**, 147–156 (1959). in French
16. Bose, R.C., Ray-Chaudhuri, D.K.: On a class of error correcting binary group codes. Inf. Control **3**(1), 68–79 (1960)
17. Dong, X., Xu, C., Xie, Y., Jouppi, N.P.: NVSim: a circuit-level performance, energy, and area model for emerging nonvolatile memory. IEEE Trans. Comput.- Aided Des. Integr. Circ. Syst. **31**(7), 994–1007 (2012)
18. Gupta, Y., Bhargava, L.: Write energy reduction of STT-MRAM based multi-core cache hierarchies. Int. J. Electron. Lett. (2018). https://doi.org/10.1080/21681724. 2018.1482005

A Novel Design Approach to Implement Multi-port Register Files Using Pulsed-Latches

T. S. Manivannan[(⊠)] [iD] and Meena Srinivasan

Department of ECE, Government College of Technology,
Coimbatore 641013, India
manivannan1992.salem@gmail.com,
meenasrinivasan@gct.ac.in

Abstract. Pulsed-latches provide high performance with low power consumption by taking the advantages of both flip-flops and latches and thus, they are targeted in implementing different kinds of memory devices in various applications. One such memory device is the register files, which is traditionally being realized using SRAMs. To implement n READ/WRITE multi-ports in SRAM register file design, the transistors that forms READ/WRITE ports must be replicated n times. Thus, there exist a proportionality between the number of transistors required per cell and the number of READ/WRITE ports per cell. This relationship is completely eliminated in the proposed pulsed-latches based register file design. The proposed pulsed-latches requires only 10 transistors per cell for any number of READ/WRITE ports. The proposed pulsed-latches based multiport register files consumes low power, area efficient and performs multi-read and multi-write operations. Hence, to implement n READ/WRITE ports in pulsed-latches based register files, n individual non-overlapping pulses are required, thereby making the number of transistors required per cell to be unchanged. These register files showed significant decrease in area as well as power consumption when compared to the SRAM based register files. An 8-bit (1X8), 64-bit(8X8), 128-bit(16X8) and a 256-bit(32X8) 4-READ and 2-WRITE (4R2W) pulsed-latches based multiport register files were designed and simulated in cadence 180 nm technology.

1 Introduction

Multiport-register files are highly preferred for multi/many core processing units, as the register units (cache memory) needs to be shared among all the processing cores. These multiport-register files are currently being implemented in SRAM based architectures. The accessing transistors should be replicated to implement additional READ/WRITE ports in an 6T-SRAM. Thus, to have four READ ports per cell, four sets of accessing transistors should be added to that cell. Hence in an SRAM based multiport register files, the area increases quadratically on implementing 4R2W register-file sizes of beyond 128 KB. This overall area of the multiport-register files can be reduced by two common techniques namely array duplication and time multiplexing or double pumping. Although these techniques tend to reduce the area of the register files, the pulsed-latches based multiport register files produced better results in terms of area and power consumption.

© Springer Nature Singapore Pte Ltd. 2019
S. Rajaram et al. (Eds.): VDAT 2018, CCIS 892, pp. 521–537, 2019.
https://doi.org/10.1007/978-981-13-5950-7_44

2 SRAM Based Register Files

There are many versions of SRAM based registers [1] and [2]. Generally, a typical SRAM register consists of a cross-coupled inverters, which serves as a storage cell and the accessing transistors which is used for READ/WRITE operations. A 6T-SRAM cell is the simplest form of SRAM-based register, which consists of six transistors of which four of them are used to construct the cross-coupled inverters and the remaining two is used as access transistors. The two access transistors serve as READ port as well as WRITE port. The SRAM based register files are used as cache memories because of their high-speed static behaviour. There are various advanced versions of SRAMs, each composed of different number of transistors from one another. The SRAMs that are targeted towards the FPGAs and ASICs are area efficient, rather than offering high performances.

2.1 6T-SRAM Cell

A typical 6T SRAM cell consists of six transistors in total, that includes four NMOS and two PMOS transistors as shown in Fig. 1. The two NMOS and two PMOS are used to form the cross coupled inverter, which holds the data stored in it. The remaining two NMOS transistors are used as accessing transistors. The gates of the two accessing transistors are connected together to create the word-line port. These two accessing transistors are used for both READ and WRITE operation. Hence, the wordline has to be enabled for both the operations. Since the SRAM based registers possesses array architectures, the wordline is common for the cells in column wise and by using the BITline, the corresponding cell is accessed. Apart from the address decoders, which includes row and column decoders, they require sense amplifiers for every column. To avoid losing the data through discharge from the cross coupled inverter while performing the READ operation, sense amplifiers are used.

2.2 8T and 9T-SRAM Cell

Unlike the 6T-SRAM cell where the accessing transistors serves for both READ and WRITE operations, the 8T-SRAM cell as shown in Fig. 2, has two more additional transistors than the 6T-SRAM cell. Thus, it has a dedicated READ and WRITE ports, where two transistors contribute for READ port and the other two for WRITE port. The storage cell design remains the same as it was in the 6T-SRAM cell. It was suggested to be power efficient than the 6T-SRAM cell because of its individual READ and WRITE port design. Another low power design of SRAM, which includes the 8T-SRAM cell [2] with an additional PMOS transistor called 9T-SRAM cell [2] was shown in Fig. 3. This PMOS transistor is connected between the global supply voltage and the cross coupled inverter.

Hence, the supply voltage of the cross coupled inverter is controlled by this additional transistor.

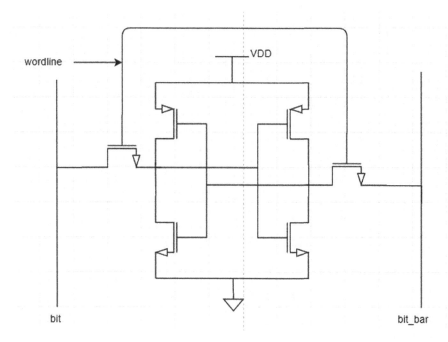

Fig. 1. 6T SRAM cell

3 Multiport SRAM Register Files

The mentioned 6T, 8T and 9T-SRAM cells are better in terms of performance only when they are implemented with single READ and WRITE port. In an 6T-SRAM cell for each additional READ/WRITE port requires one set of accessing transistors (for bit and bit bar) individually. For a register file with 4-READ port requires 12 transistors in total of which, 8 transistors contribute to the 4-READ ports and the rest 4 transistors forms the storage cell as shown in Fig. 4. These additional access transistors will impact the area consumption greatly when the register size is increased beyond 128 KB. The power efficient design of 8T- SRAM cell which has two transistors dedicated for READ port and two for WRITE port, along with the 4 transistors that form the storage cell. Even though it is more power efficient than the 6T-SRAM cell, the multiport implementation of register files using 8T-SRAM cell will demand more area than the 6T-SRAM cell type. Also, the advanced multiport SRAMs designs [5, 6] that uses multi-pumping and similar techniques were area efficient, in only register files consisting of sizes less than 128 KB.

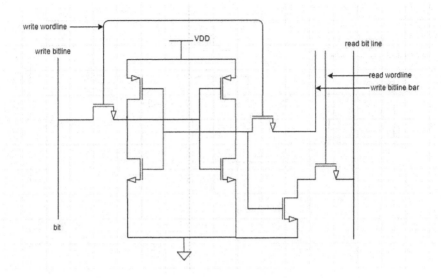

Fig. 2. 8T SRAM cell [2]

4 Pulsed-Latches

In recent years, pulsed latches have gained more importance in high performance ASICS (Application Specific Integrated Circuits) designs [4]. A pulsed latch consists of a latch and a pulse generator or pulsar. They can be considered as the best alternative to the conventional Flip-Flops as they offer high performance, low area and low power consumption. The pulse generator is an independent circuit that converts the global clock signal into pulse, that has a very short pulse-width. The timing model of the latch is simplified by using pulses of very short pulse-width instead of clock signal, hence they require a dedicated pulsar circuit to trigger the latch. This pulsing technique will enable the latch to exhibit the characteristics of the Flip-Flops. Thus, the pulsed latches have both the advantages of Flip-Flops and latches. That is, the simple timing model characteristic of the Flip-Flops as well as the high data transfer rate feature of the latchs together. Hence in a way, it fills the gap that exists between the Flip-Flops and latches [4].

4.1 The Pulse Generator Unit

The pulse generator [4] or simply pulser, which is shown in Fig. 5 has a two input NAND gate with a delay unit attached to one of its input end. The clock signal is given as input to the NAND gate, thus the difference between the clock and the delayed clock forms a pulse signal at the NAND gates output. Hence, the delay unit decides the width of the pulse. The NAND gate will produce the pulse with respect to the rising/positive edge of the clock. Similarly, the pulse can be obtained at the negative edge by replacing the NAND with the NOR and to have dual pulse, EX-OR gate is used.

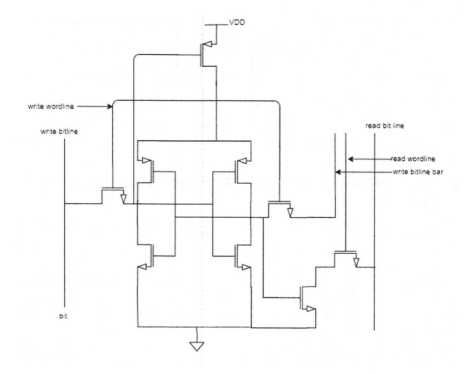

Fig. 3. 9T SRAM cell [2]

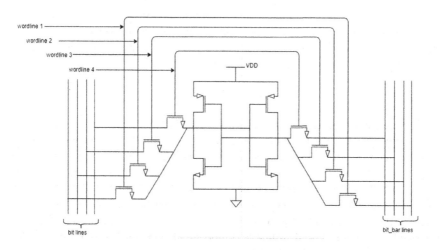

Fig. 4. 4-port 6T-SRAM cell

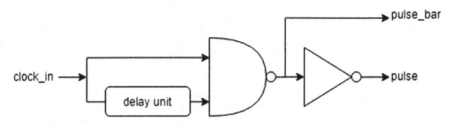

Fig. 5. NAND based pulser

5 Proposed Multiport Register File Design Using Pulsed-Latches

The pulsed-latches techniques are not efficient in implementing 1-READ and 1-WRITE register files. Hence their advantages come to light, in implementing multiport register files [3]. Multiple pulses can be accommodated in one clock cycle to enable multiple READ on the same cell. The proposed design includes two new logic blocks namely READ logic and WRITE logic, which enables the register file to perform multiple multi-READ and multi-WRITE operations. The READ logic is coupled to the MUX unit, while the WRITE logic is coupled to the decoder unit. For every additional port, a separate pulsar is required. Hence each port is associated with a unique pulse. The latches will only be active for the WRITE pulses, also called as register pulse. The WRITE pulse A and B are added with an OR gate to get the register pulse. A full schematic block diagram of the proposed design to implement m-WRITE n-READ ports is shown in Fig. 6. Also Fig. 7 shows the 8-bit 4-READ 2-WRITE multiport register file in the proposed design approach. The mentioned 8-bit register has eight register cells of each holding exactly one bit(1X8), hence only one MUX is used. A 32X8 register file has 32 registers of each holding the data of 8-bits. Thus, 8 32X1 MUX is needed to extract the eight bit output from the register file. The complete design includes the following sub-blocks/units.

5.1 The Latch Unit

To use the latch as an register, an AND gate is coupled to every latch unit in the register file. The inputs to the AND gate are the register pulse and the corresponding output data of the decoder. The 1:8 DE-MUX has eight outputs, D0–D7 respectively. Hence, starting from D0, where it goes to the first latch unit, D1 to the second and so on. The data in is common to all the latch registers. For the WRITE address 001, only D1 is enabled at the decoders output side, which makes the corresponding latch active, while all other latches are inactive. Thus, only the active latch reads the data. A single latch-register cell is shown in Fig. 8, which is comprised of 2X1 MUX and a 2-input AND gate. The MUX is constructed using transmission gates, which requires four transistors and the AND gate is from CMOS logic, which requires six transistors. Thus a single latch cell requires ten transistors (10T) in total. However, this latch design (10T) remains the same for any level of multi-port register design.

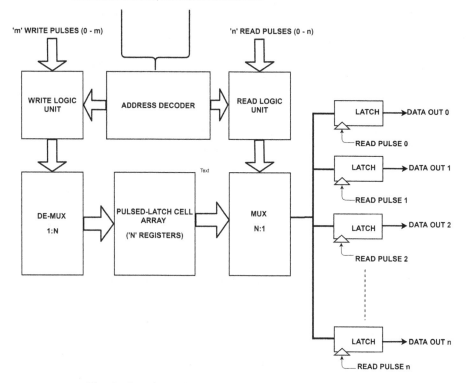

Fig. 6. Complete schematic of the proposed design approach

5.2 The Pulser Units

A total of six non-overlapping (out-off phase) pulse signals are required to perform the 4-READ 2-WRITE operations in one clock cycle. Hence, six pulse generators are used, where each pulse generator receives the delayed clock input from the previous pulse generator unit. Figure 9 shows the six pulse generators that are required for the 4-READ 2-WRITE multiport register.

5.3 READ Logic

The READ logic as shown in Fig. 10 is comprised of two input AND gates followed by the OR gates. An 8-BIT register will have the address data of 3-BITs. A two READ operation on the 8-BIT register requires two sets of address bits (address A and address B). Hence six AND gates and three OR gates are needed. Also a two READ operation requires two unique pulse signals (pulse A and pulse B). The address A BITs are AND-ed with pulse A and address B are AND-ed with pulse B. When pulse A is logic 1 and

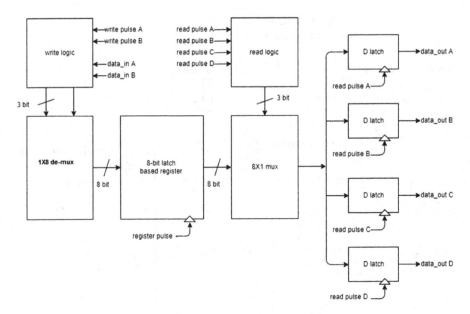

Fig. 7. 4-READ 2-WRITE pulsed-latches based multi-port register file design

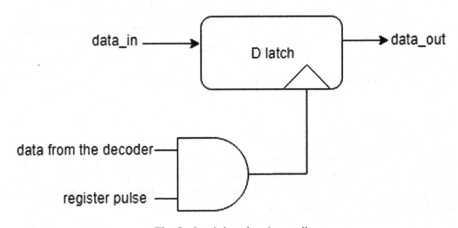

Fig. 8. Latch based register cell

pulse B is logic 0, only the data BITs of address A will be present at the OR gates. And, for pulse A is logic 0 and pulse B is logic 1, the data BITs of address B will be present in the OR gate. The purpose of the READ logic is to select the addresses and making them to be present for a particular duration within the clock period. This duration time is decided by the relevant pulse signal.

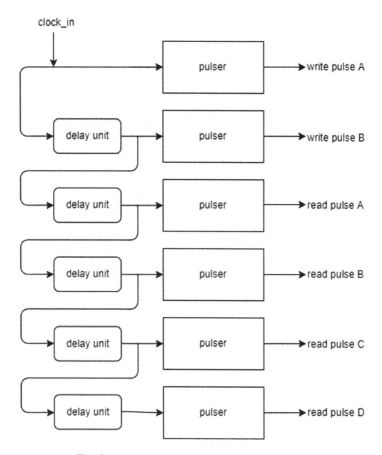

Fig. 9. READ and WRITE pulse generator units

5.4 WRITE Logic

The logic design used here is similar to that of the READ logic. The READ logic, where the address A and address B can have same data BITs to have two reads on the same register. This case is not valid in the WRITE logic section, since a register cant be written with two datas at a time. Hence, an EX-OR logic is used to eliminate the situation, where two or more write addresses have identical write address BITs. Figure 11 shows the WRITE logic for performing two write operations.

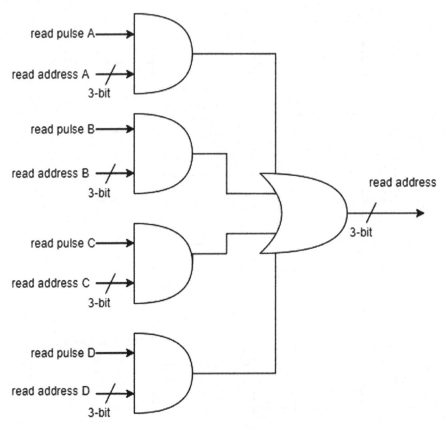

Fig. 10. Read logic for 4-READ

6 Result and Analysis

The entire proposed design was implemented by using cadence analogue virtuoso simulator in 180 nm technology. The transient analysis was done to verify the WRITE and READ operations of the register file. Also in addition, the input/output delay, average power consumption and power-delay product were calculated for varying supply voltage (VDD 0.85–1 V) by using the parametric analysis. Table 1 shows the average power consumption (Avg.pwr.), delay and power-delay product (p-d product). Figure 12 shows the transient response of the implemented 8-bit register with respect to the read operation. Also, the arrangement of the WRITE and READ pulses can be seen from Fig. 12. The WRITE pulses should be accommodated before the READ pulses in the overall arrangement, so as to READ the updated data in the same clock cycle. The detailed average power consumption of the 1X8, 8X8, 16X8 and 32X8 register files are tabulated in Table 2. It is found that the power consumption of the pulse generator unit are almost similar for register files having various sizes that are tested. Also, around 20–30% of the total power are consumed by the READ and WRITE logic alone. Figures 13 and 14 shows the effect of VDD variation on READ and WRITE delay and

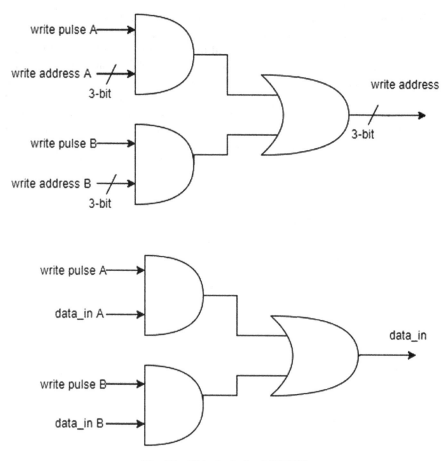

Fig. 11. Write logic for 2-WRITE

average power consumption. The product of delay and the power graphs yields the power-delay graph. Figures 15 and 16 shows the power- delay product graph of READ and WRITE delays, respectively. Figures 17 shows the 8X8 register design which is designed and simulated in cadence virtuoso in 180 nm technology. From the obtained results, it is concluded that the supply voltage has a huge impact on the delay, that is introduced by the delay units. Since, all the six operations (4 read and 2 write) are done by using time multiplexing, the considerable amount of change in delay of the delay units will make the operations to overlap with one another. Hence, it is advised to have enough space/delay between each time-slot/pulse-signal, that way we can reduce the possibility of overlap. From the power-delay plot as shown in Figs. 15 and 16, it is shown that the trade-off between the delay and the average power consumption are efficient in the range, for VDD = 0.85 to 1 V.

The number of transistors required per cell to implement 4-READ 2-WRITE multi-port register by using 8T sram cell is 16(4 for two WRITES, 8 for 4-READS and remaining 4 contributing to the cross coupled inverter) and for 4-READ 4-WRITE, it requires 20 transistors. Thus the transistor count per cell in sram based multiport registers will increase as the multi-READ/WRITE operations per clock cycle are increased. where as the proposed latch cell is comprised of only 10 transisitors, which remains the same for any level of multi-READ/WRITE operations. A comparison of 8T-sram cell based multi-port register versus the 10T-pulsed latches based multi-port register files for 8X8, 8X16 and 8X32 register sizes are shown below in the bar graphs respectively.

Table 1. VDD vs average power and delay

VDD (V)	Avg.pwr. (μW)	delay (ns)	p-d product (f)
0.85	40.78	581.183	23.69
1	63.23	407.583	24.43

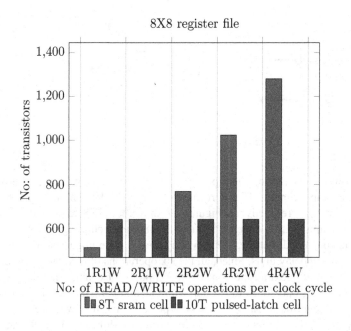

8X16 register file

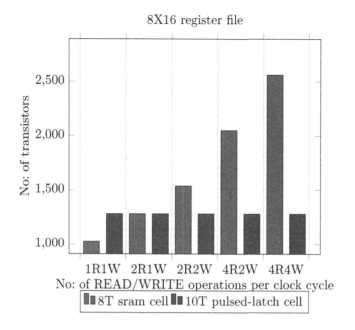

8X32 register file

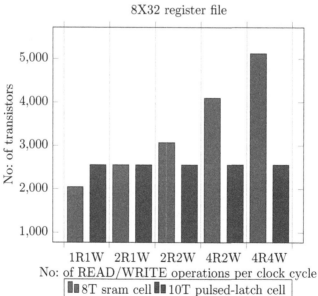

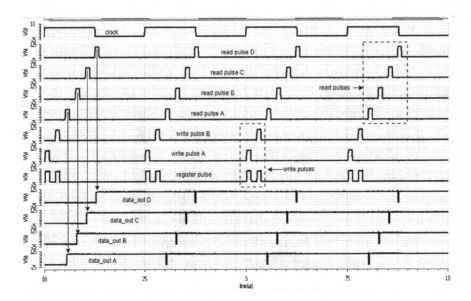

Fig. 12. Transient analysis of 4-READ operation

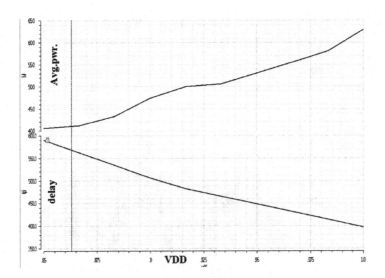

Fig. 13. VDD vs average power consumption and READ-delay plot

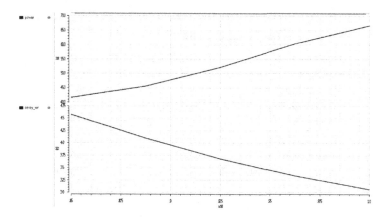

Fig. 14. VDD vs average power consumption and WRITE-delay plot

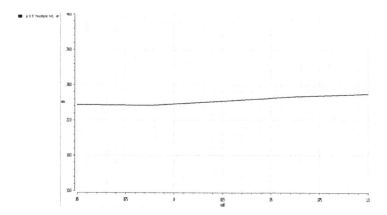

Fig. 15. Power-delay (READ) product

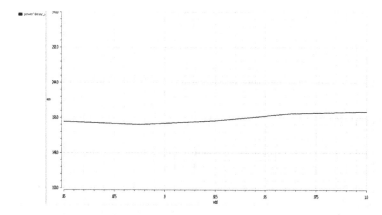

Fig. 16. Power-delay (WRITE) product

Table 2. Average power consumption of individual units for one clock cycle at vdd = 1 v

Average power consumption μW				
Register size	1X8	8X8	8X16	8X32
Latch units	4.538	10.27	19.18	33.44
READ logic unit	5.787	12.32	30.467	47.72
WRITE logic unit	2.005	18.25	22.44	30.43
DE-MUX	1.037	7.62	11.59	15.31
READ MUX units	2.447	17.1	37.39	57.16
Pulser generator	44.066	56.08	56.6	56.8
Pulse driver for latch cells	3.36	10.27	19.18	33.44
Total Avg.power	63.23	131.92	196.847	274.3

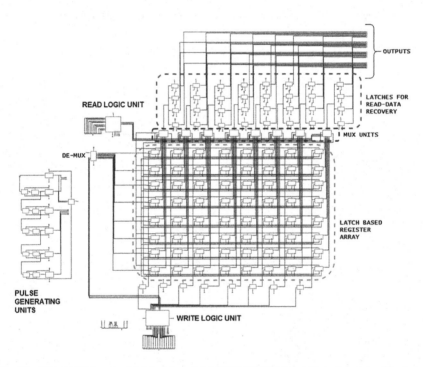

Fig. 17. 64-bit (8X8) pulsed-latches based 4-READ 2-WRITE multi-port register file design

7   Conclusion

The average power consumption of the 8-bit register unit which includes 8 D-latch and 8 two input AND gates for 2-WRITE and 4-READ is 4.538 μW at VDD = 1 V in 180 nm technology, which is less when compared to the other multiport register file designs. Here the D-latch is constructed using the transmission gate logic style, which requires two NMOS and two PMOS in total. The AND gate is realized in CMOS logic style requires 6 transistors and thus, for a single latch register cell, 10 transistors are required, which is less than the number of transistors in a 4-port 6T-SRAM. Also, the number of logic gates required for the READ/WRITE logic will remains the same for any size of the register file, unless the number of READ/WRITE ports are varied. But at higher register sizes (beyond 512 KB or so), the decoder and the MUX sizes will be much larger, which not only consumes more area but also requires more power and introduces a huge delay across them. This kind of issue is very less in case of SRAM based register files, where they follow array type architecture. The analysis shows that the proposed pulsed-latches based multiport register is suitable for L3-cache.

References

1. Teman, A., Visotsky, R.: A fast modular method for true variation-aware separatrix tracing in nanoscaled SRAMs. IEEE Trans. Very Large Scale Integr. (VLSI) Syst. **23**, 2034–2042 (2015)
2. Teman, A., Pergament, L., Cohen, O., Fish, A.: A 250 mV 8 kb 40 nm ultra-low power 9T supply feedback SRAM (SF-SRAM). IEEE J. Solid-State Circ. **46**(11), 2713–2726 (2011)
3. Elsharkasy, W.M., Yantir, H.E., Khajeh, A.: Efficient pulsed-latch implementation for multiport register files. ACM (2017)
4. Elsharkasy, W.M., Khajeh, A., Eltawil, A.M., Kurdahi, F.J.: Reliability enhancement of low-power sequential circuits using reconfigurable pulsed latches. IEEE Trans. Circ. Syst. **64**, 1803–1814 (2017)
5. Sarfraz, K., Chan, M.: A 1.2 V-to-0.4 V 3.2 GHz-to-14.3 MHz power- efficient 3-port register file in 65-nm CMOS. IEEE Trans. Circ. Syst. **64**, 360–372 (2016)
6. Hsiao, S.F., Wu, P.C.: Design of low-leakage multi-port SRAM for register file in graphics processing unit. IEEE (2014)
7. Li, S., Li, Z., Wang, F.: Design of a high-speed low-power multipart register file. IEEE (2009)

Low Leakage Noise Tolerant 10T
SRAM Cell

Vinay Gupta, Pratiksha Shukla[✉], and Manisha Pattanaik

Indian Institute of Information Technology and Management, Gwalior, Gwalior, India
vinny7536@gmail.com, pratiksha38884@gmail.com, manishapattanaik@iiitm.ac.in

Abstract. This paper presents a low leakage noise tolerant (LL10T) SRAM cell. The proposed SRAM cell has high read static noise margin and low leakage power in contrast to the conventional 6T (C6T) SRAM cell. LL10T isolates the read circuitry through read decoupling technique to improve the read static noise margin by reducing the disturbance in read operation. The proposed cell also prevents false discharging of read bitline while reading high logic using data dependent charge pump circuit. Further, a sleep transistor is used in read circuitry that remains off in hold and write operation to reduce the leakage power consumption in proposed SRAM cell. A separated write circuitry is suggested to enhance the write operation. Simulation results show that LL10T SRAM cell offers 2.1x higher read static noise margin and 5.9x less leakage power over C6T SRAM cell. The proposed SRAM cell is also compared with low power (LP8T) SRAM cell. LL10T SRAM cell offers 33.6x higher hold static noise margin and 4.7x less leakage power. However it has 4x and 2.9x longer delay over C6T and LP8T SRAM cells respectively due to single read bitline and increased node capacitance in read path. Simulations were performed using HSPICE at 32-nm PTM technology at supply voltage of 900 mV. So, this SRAM cell may be suitable for applications which demand low power noise tolerant, enhanced stability and moderate speed SRAM cell at sub-micrometer technology.

Keywords: Charge pump circuit · Stacking effect · Static leakage ·
Write ability · Sleep transistor

1 Introduction

Static random access memory (SRAMs) is an integral part of system-on-chip, network-on-chip and microprocessors. Applications such as satellites, biomedical instruments like pacemaker, wireless sensors and many battery operated devices require low power and less area SRAM cells [13]. Amongst area and power semiconductor industry is facing a major problem of static leakage power consumption. According to the international roadmap for semiconductors (ITRS) with technology scaling (below 65 nm) the leakage power consumption increases [5]. This leakage power dictates the density of SRAM cells in memory at sub-micrometer technology, so leakage power must be reduced. To reduce dynamic

© Springer Nature Singapore Pte Ltd. 2019
S. Rajaram et al. (Eds.): VDAT 2018, CCIS 892, pp. 538–550, 2019.
https://doi.org/10.1007/978-981-13-5950-7_45

power low supply voltage can be used, as dynamic power is directly proportional to square of supply voltage and to reduce the static power threshold voltage can be increased [5] but this will degrade the speed hence performance, other methods to reduce the leakage power are power gating technique [4], stacking effect etc. [12]. Further, SRAMs suffer from stability issues (read and write failure) [15,16] at such small scale technology, to increase the stability during read operation read decoupled circuit can be used which will isolate the core circuitry from read circuitry in read operation and to increase the write ability of a write assist circuit can be used that will enhanced its write ability. In this paper a SRAM cell is suggested that consumes low leakage power and is highly stable as compared to other SRAM cells.

The rest of the paper is arranged as follows. Section 2 gives the background of state of the art SRAMs and associated work. Section 3 elaborates the proposed design and its operation. Section 4 gives various design metrices of SRAMs with the simulated results. The results and tabular comparative analysis are discussed in Sect. 4. Section 5 concludes the paper.

2 Background and Related Work

In C6T SRAM cell read and write failures are serious issues at low operating voltages [3]. At such low voltages write access transistors cannot beat the strong feedback of cross coupled transistors [9] for instance initially let node Q is at logic 0 (left pull down transistor MN1 is on), while writing logic 1 transistor MN1 tries to bring down the voltage of node Q to logic 0 and transistor M4 tries to increase the voltage of the node Q to logic 1, due to this fight between write access transistor M4 and pull down transistor MN1, write failure occurs (Fig. 1) similarly for writing logic 0. However this problem of write ability can be resolved by weakening of pull up and pull down transistors. While performing read operation especially reading logic 0 bitline (BL) discharges through transistors M4 and MN1, due to this high voltage is developed across pulldown transistor (higher than the switching voltage of other inverter storing logic 1) which flips the stored data and causes read failure (Fig. 1). So there is a tradeoff between read stability and write ability in C6T SRAM cell, as no mechanism is present to reduce leakage current in C6T SRAM cell, it has high leakage power. In LP8T SRAM cell read circuit consists of two discharging paths as shown in Fig. 2 so its read access time is minimum among the compared SRAM cells. In this SRAM cell to reduce the leakage power a stacking transistor (MN7) that is turned off and a control signal WWLB set to logic 1 in hold mode are used to reduce the leakage power but this increases the voltage of node storing logic 0. So this SRAM cell is more prone to noise compared to other SRAM cells due to this the hold stability of this SRAM cell is poor as compared to C6T and LL10T SRAM cells. To reduce the leakage power and enhancing the stability of SRAM cell, a read decoupled circuit with a sleep mode transistor in read circuitry is used in proposed LL10T SRAM cell. Further, a new write assist circuit is proposed to enhance the write operation.

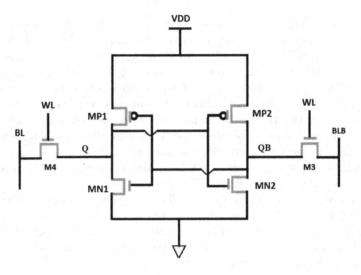

Fig. 1. Conventional 6T SRAM cell [7]

3   Proposed Design and Contribution

In this paper a low leakage SRAM cell is proposed as shown in Fig. 3. In order
to get better read noise margin a read decoupled circuit is used for read operation, here the read circuitry is separated from rest of the circuit through buffer
transistor (M3). A sleep transistor [4] (M4) is used to minimize the leakage current during hold and write operations along with a charge pump circuit (M2) to

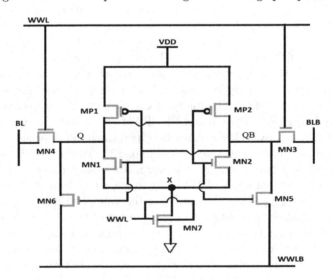

Fig. 2. LP8T SRAM cell [8]

prevent false discharging of read bitline while reading logic 1. Due to this charge pump circuit bitline leakage reduces which results in increased sense margin of SRAM cell. Also a new write circuit is proposed for write operation. In C6T SRAM cell better RSNM can be obtained at the cost of degraded WSNM only and viceversa [9,10]. In C6T for acceptable RSNM and WSNM sizing should be done properly. So for C6T SRAM β_{ratio} should be between 1.2 and 3 and γ_{ratio} should be kept less than or equal to 1.2 [8] so transistors sizing for C6T SRAM is selected considering these ratios in account. Although in proposed SRAM cell minimum sizing can be used but for fair comparison size of all other transistors (except C6T portion of cells) are kept 1.5 times than the size of transistors used for C6T SRAM cell. The operations are explained below.

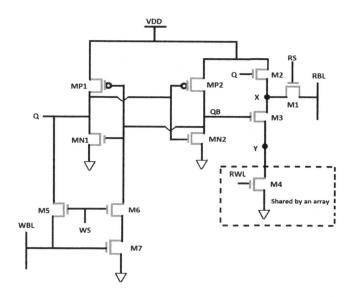

Fig. 3. Proposed LL10T SRAM cell

3.1 Read Operation

In read operation read bitline (RBL) is precharged to VDD and control signals RWL (read word line) and RS (read select) are set to logic 1 and WS (write select) is set to logic 0. As control signals RS and RWL are set to logic 1, read access transistor M1 and sleep transistor M4 are turned on. For instance if node Q holds logic 0 and QB logic 1 the buffer transistor M4 is turned on and transistor M2 (Charge pump circuit) is turned off leading to discharging of RBl through transistors M1, M3 and M4 to logic 0. Likewise if node Q holds logic 1 and node QB holds logic 0, buffer transistor M3 is turned off and charge pump transistor M2 is turned on, due to this voltage of node X is increased (due to stacking effect) to logic high preventing the false discharging of read bitline, retaining its voltage at VDD, performing read operation properly.

3.2 Write Operation

In write operation control signals RS (read select) and RWL (read word line) are forced to logic 0 due to this read access transistor M1 and sleep transistor M4 are turned off. As two transistors of read circuitry are off during write operation leakage power is reduced to large extent. Further, control signal WS (write select) is forced to logic 1 due to this write access transistors M5 and M6 are switched on. For instance let the write bit line (WBL) is precharged to VDD forcing the transistor M7 to be turned on, if node Q stores logic 0 and node QB logic 1, the node Q now charges to logic 1 through write access transistor M5 and pull down transistor MN1 and node QB discharges to logic 0 through transistors M6 and M7. Likewise if node Q stores logic 1 and QB logic 0 and if WBL is at logic 0 transistor MN7 is turned off and the node Q now discharges through transistor M5 towards logic 0, as the voltage of node Q reduces to value less than the switching voltage of right half cell the output QB switches to logic 1. So the desired data is written in storage nodes Q and QB properly.

3.3 Hold Operation

In hold operation of SRAM cell the read and write bit lines are precharged to VDD and control signals RS, RWL and WS are raised to logic 0, forcing the write access transistors (M5, M6) and read access transistor (M1) to be in off state also the sleep transistor M4 is turned off (as RWL is at logic 0). The reason for keeping sleep transistor off is to minimize the leakage current through read circuitry in hold state and write mode of operation. The leakage current in proposed LL10T SRAM cell is less than LP8T and C6T SRAM cells due to two transistors (M1, M4) which are kept off in idle mode. Table 1 shows the level of WBL, RBL, WS, RS and RWL signals along with the mode of operations of LL10T SRAM cell.

Table 1. Operation table of proposed LL10T SRAM cell.

Signals	Write 1	Write 0	Hold	Read
WBL	VDD	0V	VDD	0V
RBL	0V	0V	VDD	VDD
WS	VDD	VDD	0V	0V
RS	0V	0V	0V	VDD
RWL	0V	0V	0V	VDD

4 Simulation Results and Discussion

This section presents different design metrices for proposed LL10T SRAM cell and are compared with C6T and LP8T SRAM cells. Synopsys HSPICE 2016 is used for simulation and circuits are designed using 32 nm PTM model [1].

4.1   Read Access Time (T_{RA})

Read access time/read delay (T_{RA}) determines how fast the read operation can be performed. It is calculated during read mode of operation. For differential read bitline read access time is expressed as the time duration between read control signal (RS) activation to the time at which 50 mV voltage difference is set up between two bitlines, BL and BLB [6,8]. But for single read bitline it is measured as the difference between the time instant at which control signal (RS) is forced to VDD to the time instant at which voltage of read bitline (RBL) decreases by 50 mV [2]. Read access time is minimum for the LP8T as two discharging paths are available for discharging of read bitline. For proposed LL10T SRAM cell the read access time is more than LP8T and C6T SRAM cells due to increased bitline capacitance during discharging of read bitline as shown in Fig. 4.

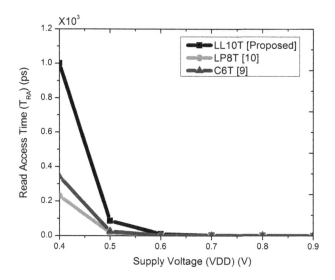

Fig. 4. Read access time of C6T, LP8T and LL10T SRAM cells at various supply voltages

4.2   Write Access Time (T_{WA})

Write access time/write delay determines how fast the write operation can be performed in SRAM cell. It is determined while accessing the SRAM cell for write operation. T_{WA} for writing logic 0 is defined as the difference between time instant at which write control signal (WS) is activated to the time instant at which logic 1 storing node discharges to 10% of VDD. Likewise write access time for writing logic 1 is defined as the difference between the time instant at which control signal WS is activated to time instant at which logic 0 storing node charges to 90% of VDD [2,8]. For differential write bitline write access time for both writing logic 0 and logic 1 is same. But for single bitline write access time mainly depends on data to be written. Write access time of LL10T SRAM is higher as shown in Fig. 5 than LP8T and C6T SRAM cells due to large storage node capacitance.

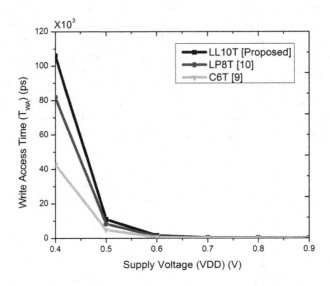

Fig. 5. Write access time of C6T, LP8T and LL10T SRAM cells at various supply voltages

4.3   Leakage Power Dissipation

With the scaling of technology the size of transistor is also shrinking. Low threshold voltage to achieve better performance results in high leakage current due to short channel effects. As explained in introduction a major portion of memory remains idle for large period of time, so high leakage current is becoming the major source of power dissipation in memory [8,10]. There are three basic components of leakage current in any SRAM cell through various transistors, subthreshold current (I_{SUB}), gate current (I_{GATE}) and junction current (I_{JN}) [5] (ignoring minor leakage currents like drain induced barrier leakage, punch through leakage etc.). Amongst these current components the most important and dictating leakage current in any SRAM cell is subthreshold current [5].

Subthreshold leakage current in 6T, LP8T and LL10T SRAM cells [8].

$$I_{SUB,LL10T} = I_{SUB_{MN1}} + I_{SUB_{MP2}} + I_{SUB_{M1}} + I_{SUB_{M2}} \\ + I_{SUB_{M3}} + I_{SUB_{M4}} \tag{1}$$

$$I_{SUB,LP8T} = I_{SUB_{MP1}} + I_{SUB_{MN1}} + I_{SUB_{M2}} + I_{SUB_{M3}} \\ + I_{SUB_{M5}} + I_{SUB_{M7}} \tag{2}$$

$$I_{SUB,6T} = I_{SUB_{MN1}} + I_{SUB_{MP2}} + I_{SUB_{M3}} \tag{3}$$

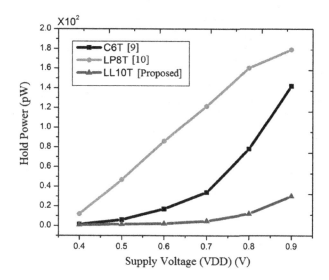

Fig. 6. Hold power of C6T, LP8T and LL10T SRAM cells at various supply voltages

From the above equations of subthreshold current for compared cells the current components in C6T is less than the current components in LL10T and LP8T SRAM cells so leakage current in C6T is less than LP8T SRAM cell but due to two series transistors in read circuitry of proposed LL10T SRAM cell (M1 and M4) the sum of current components $I_{SUB_{M1}} + I_{SUB_{M2}} + I_{SUB_{M3}} + I_{SUB_{M4}}$ is less than the current component $I_{SUB_{M3}}$ of C6T SRAM cell.

$$I_{SUB,LP8T} > I_{SUB,6T} > I_{SUB,LL10T}$$

So total subthreshold leakage current in LL10T SRAM cell is less than the LP8T and C6T SRAM cells. Hence total leakage current in LL10T SRAM cell is less than the conventional 6T and LP8T SRAM cell. Figure 6 shows the variation of leakage power at various supply voltages.

4.4 Read Stability

To measure the stability of SRAM cell in read state, read static noise margin (RSNM) is used. It is elaborated as the maximal amount of static noise that SRAM cell can withstand in read operation without changing its stored data [3,14]. To measure RSNM traditional butterfly curve is used. It is calculated by fitting maximum length square in the smaller lobe of voltage transfer curves (VTCs) [11]. RSNM of LL10T SRAM cell is more than C6T and LP8T SRAM cells as shown in Fig. 7 due to the use of read decoupled circuit that removes any possibility of disturbance in data storing node while performing read operation. So read noise margin of proposed LL10T SRAM cell is more than the C6T and LP8T SRAM cells. RSNM of different SRAM cells at various supply voltages is plotted as shown in Fig. 8.

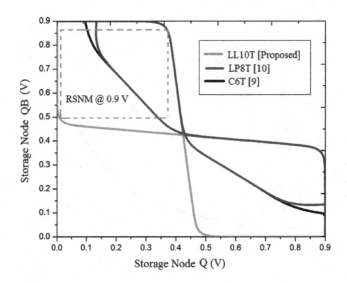

Fig. 7. VTCs of C6T, LP8T and LL10T SRAM cells during read operation @ 0.9 V

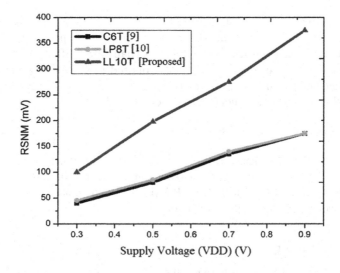

Fig. 8. Read SNM of C6T, LP8T and LL10T SRAM cells at various supply voltages

4.5 Hold Stability

The stability of SRAM cell in idle or hold state is determined by the hold static noise margin (HSNM). It is elaborated as the maximal amount of static noise that SRAM cell can withstand in idle state without changing its stored data [2,13]. To determine HSNM traditional butterfly curve is used. It is calculated by fitting maximum length square in the smaller lobe of VTC curves [14]. The HSNM of proposed SRAM cell is comparable to C6T and larger than LP8T as shown in

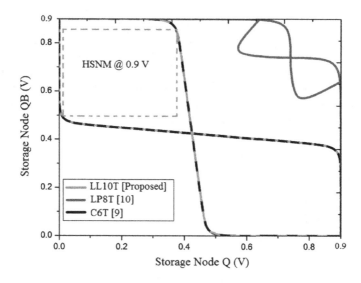

Fig. 9. VTCs of C6T, LP8T and LL10T SRAM cells during hold operation @ VDD = 0.9 V

Fig. 9. The less HSNM for LP8T is due to the transistor MN7 that is switched off during idle state, which results in, increased voltage of node storing logic 0 to some positive value, due to this LP8T is more prone to noise than proposed SRAM cell in hold state. Thus LP8T has poor hold noise margin compared to proposed LL10T and C6T SRAM cells. Hold noise margin for different SRAMs is plotted at various supply voltages as shown in Fig. 10.

4.6 Write-Ability

To determine the write-ability of SRAM cell, write static noise margin (WSNM) is used. WSNM determines the ability of SRAM cell to degrade the voltage of

Table 2. Comparision of design metrics among C6T, LP8T and LL10T SRAM cells @ VDD = 0.9 V

Design metrics	C6T	LP8T	LL10T
Average read power	45 nW	3.36 mW	29 nW
Average write power	511 nW	3.36 mW	2.5 nW
Write '0' delay	17 ps	27 ps	34 ps
Write '1' delay	43 ps	85 ps	98 ps
Read delay	200 fs	200 fs	400 fs
HSNM	370 mV	110 mV	370 mV
RSNM	175 mV	180 mV	370 mV
WSNM	380 mV	375 mV	375 mV

node storing logic 1 to a voltage less than the triping voltage of other inverter storing logic 0 [8]. It is determined during write operation of SRAM cell using butterfly curve [11]. WSNM of any SRAM cell is the length of minimum size square that can be embodied within the two VTCs of cross coupled inverters. The proposed LL10T SRAM has WSNM comparable to C6T and LP8T SRAM cells as shown in Fig. 11. Table 2 compares the noise margins mainly RSNM, WSNM, HSNM and various design metrices.

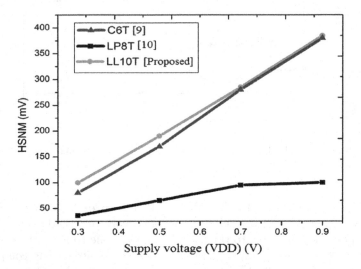

Fig. 10. Hold SNM of C6T, LP8T and LL10T SRAM cells at various supply voltages

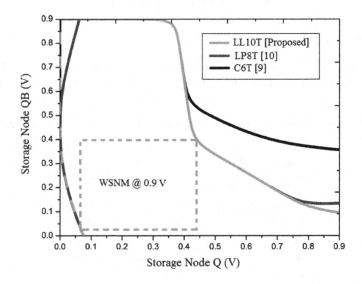

Fig. 11. VTCs of C6T, LP8T and LL10T SRAM cells during write operation @ VDD = 0.9 V

5 Conclusion

In this paper, a low leakage noise tolerant 10T SRAM cell is proposed which is suitable for low power applications. The proposed SRAM cell improves leakage power along with RSNM over state of the art SRAM cells. The proposed cell has 2x higher RSNM over C6T and LP8T cells. Further, an improvement of 3.36x in HSNM is observed over LP8T cell. Furthermore, LL10T SRAM cell shows 5.96x/4.7x low leakage power at the cost of increased area over compared SRAM cells. Although, the read and write circuitry in LL10T presents longer delay, the proposed cell may be suitable for applications which demand low leakage noise tolerant 10T SRAM Cell at sub-micrometer technology.

References

1. http://ptm.asu.edu
2. Ahmad, S., Gupta, M.K., Alam, N., Hasan, M.: Low leakage single bitline 9T (SB9T) static random access memory. Microelectron. J. **62**, 1–11 (2017)
3. Grossar, E., Stucchi, M., Maex, K., Dehaene, W.: Read stability and write-ability analysis of SRAM cells for nanometer technologies. IEEE J. Solid-State Circ. **41**(11), 2577–2588 (2006)
4. Jiao, H., Kursun, V.: Power gated SRAM circuits with data retention capability and high immunity to noise: a comparison for reliability in low leakage sleep mode. In: 2010 International SoC Design Conference, pp. 5–8 (2010)
5. Kim, N.S., et al.: Leakage current: Moore's law meets static power. Computer **36**(12), 68–75 (2003)
6. Kulkarni, J.P., Kim, K., Roy, K.: A 160 mV robust Schmitt trigger based sub-threshold SRAM. IEEE J. Solid-State Circ. **42**(10), 2303–2313 (2007)
7. Nabavi, M., Sachdev, M.: A 290-mV, 3.34-MHz, 6T SRAM with pMOS access transistors and boosted wordline in 65-nm CMOS technology. IEEE J. Solid-State Circ. **53**, 656–667 (2017)
8. Pal, S., Islam, A.: Variation tolerant differential 8T SRAM cell for ultralow power applications. IEEE Trans. Comput.-Aided Des. Integr. Circ. Syst. **35**(4), 549–558 (2016)
9. Pasandi, G., Fakhraie, S.M.: A new sub-threshold 7T SRAM cell design with capability of bit-interleaving in 90 nm CMOS. In: 2013 21st Iranian Conference on Electrical Engineering (ICEE), pp. 1–6 (2013)
10. Pasandi, G., Fakhraie, S.M.: A 256-kb 9T near-threshold SRAM with 1k cells per bitline and enhanced write and read operations. IEEE Trans. Very Large Scale Integr. (VLSI) Syst. **23**(11), 2438–2446 (2015)
11. Qiu, H., et al.: Statistical write stability characterization in SRAM cells at low supply voltage. IEEE Trans. Electron Devices **63**(11), 4302–4308 (2016)
12. Roy, K., Mukhopadhyay, S., Mahmoodi-Meimand, H.: Leakage current mechanisms and leakage reduction techniques in deep-submicrometer CMOS circuits. Proc. IEEE **91**(2), 305–327 (2003)
13. Samandari-Rad, J., Guthaus, M., Hughey, R.: Confronting the variability issues affecting the performance of next-generation SRAM design to optimize and predict the speed and yield. IEEE Access **2**, 577–601 (2014)
14. Seevinck, E., List, F.J., Lohstroh, J.: Static-noise margin analysis of MOS SRAM cells. IEEE J. Solid-State Circ. **22**(5), 748–754 (1987)

15. Yadav, N., Shah, A.P., Vishvakarma, S.K.: Stable, reliable, and bit-interleaving 12T SRAM for space applications: a device circuit co-design. IEEE Trans. Semiconductor Manuf. **30**(3), 276–284 (2017)
16. Yang, Y., Jeong, H., Song, S.C., Wang, J., Yeap, G., Jung, S.O.: Single bit-line 7T SRAM cell for near-threshold voltage operation with enhanced performance and energy in 14 nm FinFET technology. IEEE Trans. Circ. Syst. I: Regul. Papers **63**(7), 1023–1032 (2016)

A Write-Improved Half-Select-Free Low-Power 11T Subthreshold SRAM with Double Adjacent Error Correction for FPGA-LUT Design

Vishal Sharma[1]([envelope])[iD], Pranshu Bisht[1], Abhishek Dalal[1],
Shailesh Singh Chouhan[2], H. S. Jattana[3], and Santosh Kumar Vishvakarma[1]

[1] Nanoscale Devices, VLSI Circuit and System Design Lab, Electrical Engineering,
Indian Institute of Technology Indore, Indore 453552, M.P., India
phd1501102022@iiti.ac.in
[2] EISLAB, Department of Computer Science, Electrical and Space Engineering,
Lulea University of Technology, Lulea, Sweden
[3] SCL Mohali, Department of Space, Govt. of India, Ajitgarh, Punjab, India

Abstract. This work presents a new bit-interleaving low-power 11T subthreshold SRAM cell with the Data-Dependent Partial-Feedback Cutting to improve the write ability. The isolated read path of 11T enhances the read static noise margin (RSNM) which is equivalent to that of its hold SNM (HSNM), while the incorporated PMOS stacking in each of the inverter helps to reduce the leakage power of the cell. The half-select free behavior of the proposed 11T cell facilitates the bit-interleaving architecture of memory array that reduces the multi-bits error occurrence in a single word of data, and thus enhance the soft error tolerance. Using the proposed cell, a four-input FPGA lookup table (LUT) has been implemented working on 0.4V supply, which consumes $0.59\times$ less leakage power as compared to that of 6T LUT. Finally, a two adjacent bits error correction technique is also suggested to incorporate with the proposed bit-interleaving 11T array, so that the effect of soft error can almost be neglected. It consumes comparable leakage and read access energy to that of one-bit error correcting conventional hamming code.

Keywords: Static Random Access Memory (SRAM) ·
Static noise margin (SNM) · Leakage power ·
Field Programmable Gate Array (FPGA) · Soft error correction

1 Introduction

With the aggressive growth of semiconductor market, low power Static Random Access Memory (SRAM) has been an important research area. Moreover, the

Supported by Special Manpower Development Program for Chips to System Design (SMDP-C2SD) research project of Department of Electronics and Information Technology (DEITY), Government of India.

S. Rajaram et al. (Eds.): VDAT 2018, CCIS 892, pp. 551–564, 2019.
https://doi.org/10.1007/978-981-13-5950-7_46

Field Programmable Gate Arrays (FPGA) based devices are steadily becoming the preferred platform to implement the modern embedded applications due to their high reconfigurability, massive parallelism, and rapid prototyping capability [1,2]. The SRAM based FPGA manufactured by Xilinx and Altera occupy the largest fraction of the overall FPGA market, in which the SRAM memory cells are the basis to provide the configurability feature of FPGA through the use of different configurable logic blocks (CLBs). A typical CLB consists of an LUT, multiplexers (MUX) and flip-flops, as shown in Fig. 1. Within a CLB, LUT is used to store all the possible combination of data that determines the functionality of that particular CLB. For example, a 4-input LUT contains 16 SRAM memory cells, as can be seen in Fig. 1. Therefore, with the increasing complexity of today's FPGAs, most of the chip area and therefore the overall power is dominated by the on-chip SRAM. Also, most of the time a large portion of this on-chip memory stay in standby mode and thus the leakage power becomes the imperative concern in the SRAM memory design [3].

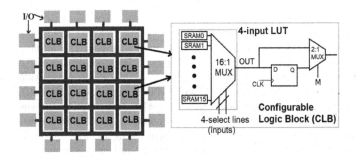

Fig. 1. A typical FPGA architecture

Supply voltage scaling always seems a preffered choice to offer the exponential and quadratic reduction in leakage and dynamic power respectively [4,5]. However, the conventional 6T SRAM cell prevents to be operated at ultra-low voltage ($<2V_{TH}$) due to its degraded read static noise margin (RSNM) [6]. It is because of the internal read disturbance created by the potential divider formation between the access and pull down devices of 6T cell [7]. Moreover, at the scaled technology nodes the Random Dopant Fluctuations (RDF) during lithography increases the threshold voltage (V_{TH}) variability [8], and the exponential dependence of V_{TH} with the static noise margin (SNM) leads to functional loss of on-chip SRAMs at ultra-low voltage [3,7]. Read and write conflict is another major issue for conventional 6T SRAM cell.

To address the above mentioned issues, several SRAM cells have been proposed in the literature. Chang et al. [9] proposed an 8T to improve the RSNM by isolating the storage nodes from the read path, known as read decoupling approach. However, the half-select issue, which is related to the cells of selected row and unselected column or the unselected row and selected column, is not addressed by the 8T cell. SRAM cells proposed in [10] improve both the write ability and read stability, but the feedback cutting of cross coupled inverters through the NMOS devices results in floating storage nodes, which could easily be affected by the leakage current and noise occurrence. A multi-V_{TH} 9T SRAM was proposed in [11] for the energy efficiency, but it demands of additional boosted supply and extra processing steps. A PPN10T cell [12] proposed a robust low leakage design based on the P-P-N devices connected in each of the inverter, but the cells has lower write ability. In [13], a 12T cell incorporate the data aware feedback cutting to assist the write improvement, but the use of data dependent word line signals need additional signal generating circuitry, and thus may result in area and power overhead for the overall memory array. Another 12T SRAM has been proposed in [14] claiming the improved write margin, but there is no consideration of half-select issue. Therefore, there is still a lot of research needed which can simultaneously improve the read-write stability, control the leakage power and handle the half-select issue against the process-voltage-temperature (PVT) variations at lower supply voltage.

Furthermore, the effect of energetic alpha particles induced soft error becomes critical in the subthreshold region, as compared to the superthreshold region. It is due to the reduced critical charge (Q_{crit}) at scaled supply voltage in the nanometer regime [15, 16]. Moreover, it is reported that the soft error rate (SER) increases by 18% for every 10% reduction in V_{DD} [17]. Furthermore, the SRAM cell becomes susceptible to the soft errors at the advance technology nodes due to the reduced storage node capacitance, and thus there are high probability for the multi-bits error occurrence. Bit-interleaving memory architecture is a popular approach to reduce such multi-bits error in SRAM memory. So, many SRAM cells have been proposed to support the bit-interleaving architecture [10, 13, 18, 19], but either those cells have degraded write performance, larger area overhead or they need extra peripheral circuitry for their successful operation.

Therefore, in this work we propose a new low power 11T SRAM cell with enhanced write ability and increase read stability without any half-select issue. The contribution of this work is as follows:

1. Data dependent partial feedback cutting of cross coupled inverters enhances the write ability. The row and column wise write selection of each individual cell removes the half-select issue and supports to bit-interleaving architecture.
2. Read decoupling approach provides the increased RSNM value, equivalent to that of HSNM.
3. Two stacked PMOS devices in each of the inverter reduces the leakage current.
4. A double adjacent bits error checking and correction (ECC) is proposed with the lower area and power requirement as compared to the conventional ECC technique.

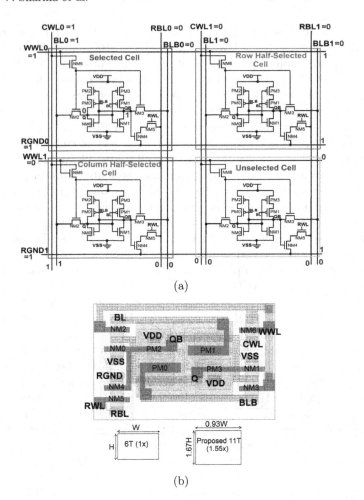

Fig. 2. (a) A 2×2 SRAM array of proposed 11T cell during write 1 operation (b) Layout of proposed 11T and its area normalized to conventional 6T

2   Proposed PPN11T SRAM Cell and Device Sizing

As shown in Fig. 2(a), the proposed 11T consists of P-P-N devices in each of its inverter pair. Two stacked PMOS devices of the inverter increase the equivalent resistance of the path, and therefore controls the current flowing through it which ultimately reduces the overall power. In our proposed cell, all the devices of minimum size have been used. However, we have doubled the size of the pull up devices PM0 and PM1 to compensate the conductivity degradation of stacked connection, which help to contribute a good Hold SNM [12]. The layout design of the proposed cell is shown in Fig. 2(b), while the Table 1 exhibits the status of its control signals during read, write and hold condition.

Table 1. Status of control signals for proposed 11T SRAM cell

	Hold	Read	Write 1/0
WWL	0	0	1
CWL	0	0	1
RWL	0	1	0
RGND	1	0	1
BL	0	0	1/0
BLB	0	0	0/1
RBL	0	1	0

2.1 Write Operation using Cross-Point Selection

The write operation is performed only when both the signals column word line (CWL) and row sharing write word line (WWL) high are enabled high, as can be seen from Fig. 2(a). It forms a cross-point (row and column wise selection) and thus doesn't allow to change the stored data of any other SRAM cell sharing the same row or column. Therefore, the write operation of proposed 11T doesn't face any half-select issue.

For the write 1 operation, bit lines BL and BLB are connected to logic 1 and 0 respectively, which turns off PM1 and isolates the path of QB node from V_{DD}. Therefore, BLB can easily discharge the node QB to 0 through NM3, with the increased write ability of the proposed 11T. It consequently turns on PM2 and thus connects the node Q to supply voltage V_{DD} through the path PM2-PM0. This path additionally help to write 1 being performed at the storage node Q through BL using NM2. Hence, the write ability of the cell is significantly increased, that has been expressed in terms of write trip point (WTP) which is the difference between the supply voltage V_{DD} and the word line voltage (WWL) voltage required to flip the stored data. Similarly the write 0 operation for the proposed cell is explained.

2.2 Read Operation with the Read Buffer

For the read operation, read word line (RWL) is enabled high with the help of row decoder, and read ground (RGND) is forced to logic 0 using a read buffer, while the read bit line (RBL) is precharged at 1, as shown in Table 1. Now for the read 0 operation when QB stores 1, both the devices NM4 and NM5 are turned on. It facilitates the RBL to get a quick discharge to 0 which can easily be sensed by the sense amplifier. For the read 1 operation, NM4 remain turned off and doesn't allow RBL to discharge, which is reflected by the sense amplifier as logic 1 at the output.

The isolated read path of the cell from its storage nodes offers the independent optimization of read path to provide the RSNM equivalent to that of its HSNM value without affecting the write operation. Because of this decoupled read path, there are very less chances to flip the stored data due to any noise occurrence in the read path.

2.3 Hold Operation

During hold mode of the proposed cell, WWL, CWL and RWL are kept at logic 0, and all the bit lines also remain at 0 as demonstrated in Table 1. In this condition, the intermediate PMOS transistors PM0 and PM1 remain turned on and thus enable the operation of two simple cross coupled inverters similar to that of 6T cell.

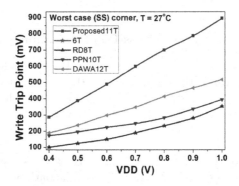

Fig. 3. WTP comparison of proposed 11T with the state of art SRAM cells at worst process (SS) corner

3 Simulation Results

To validate the proposed cell, the post layout simulation has been performed using a standard CMOS 180 nm technology node. The 180 nm node was chosen due to the requirement of ongoing project work.

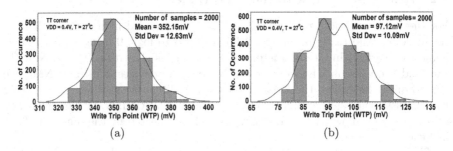

Fig. 4. Statistical distribution of WTP for (a) proposed 11T and (b) conventional 6T at 0.4 V and TT corner using 2000 Monte Carlo samples with 6σ variations

As described in section II(A), the write ability has been calculated in terms of WTP and compared with the conventional 6T and other state-of-art SRAM cells considered in this work which are read decoupled 8T (RD8T) [9], PPN10T [12] and data aware write assist 12T (DAWA12T) [13] SRAM cells. A comparative analysis of WTP at worst process (SS) corner is provided in Fig. 3, and it shows that the proposed 11T exhibits the highest WTP value for both subthreshold and the superthreshold regions of operation. WTP is 2.84 ×, 2.84×, 1.65× and 1.5× at 0.4 V and 2.53×, 2.53×, 2.27× and 1.73× higher at 1 V supply as compared to that of 6T, RD8T [9], PPN10T [12] and DAWA12T [13] respectively. The statistical analysis of WTP was also performed using 2000 Monte Carlo (MC) samples with 6σ variations for the V_{TH_n} and V_{TH_p} values, which is shown in Fig. 4. The Monte Carlo simulation result shows that the WTP mean (μ) value is much higher than that of 6T which is 3.63× at 0.4 V. The WTP variability (σ/μ) is another important parameter which should be as low as possible to exhibits the less variation and it is 0.34× lower for the 11T than that of 6T at 0.4V, where σ represents the standard deviation.

Read stability for the SRAM cell can easily be determined from the butterfly curve, and expressed as the side length of the largest square that can best fit into the smaller lobe of the butterfly curve [20]. Figure 5(a) exhibits the comparison of read butterfly curves, at the worst process (FS) corner with various V_{DD} values, for the proposed cell and the conventional 6T. It demonstrates that the proposed 11T has a good enough read stability down to a supply of 0.2V, while the 6T cell is prone to be read unstable even at 0.4 V for FS corner. The statistical distribution curves for the RSNM is also given in Fig. 5(b), according to which the RSNM mean (μ) value for 11T cell is 1.95× larger and the variability (σ/μ) is 0.408× lower as compared to that of 6T.

Although, the read current for the 11T SRAM cell is 1.67× less than that of the 6T SRAM cell due to the minimum sized devices used in the read path which may cause the 11T cell to exhibit the slower read operation. However, the bit line (RBL) leakage of 11T is 5.98× less than that of 6T cell, as shown in Fig. 6. Therefore, a read bit line of memory array can afford more memory cells using the 11T cell than the 6T SRAM during the read operation. which ultimately offers the improved array density. As the read path is isolated for the 11T SRAM cell, the read speed of 11T can also independently be improved by increasing its read devices size without affecting the read or write ability.

To justify the half-select removal of the proposed cell, the Monte Carlo simulations using 2000 samples have been performed, and the results are illustrated in the Fig. 7 for the selected and column half-selected cell (see Fig. 2) during the write 1 operation at 0.4 V supply. It can be seen that the selected cell successfully stores the data by flipping the storage node's values, while the column half selected cell rigidly preserves its previous data with the help of turned off device NM6 due to the logic 0 at WWL.

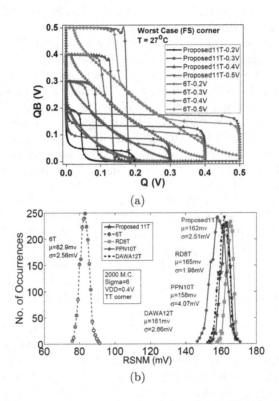

Fig. 5. (a) Read butterfly comparison for the proposed 11T SRAM and 6T SRAM cell at worst process (FS) corner at V_{DD} values (b) Statistical distribution of RSNM for different SRAM cells using 2000 Monte Carlo samples with 6σ variations and 0.4 V supply

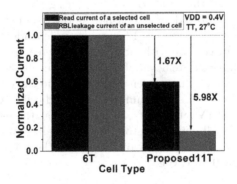

Fig. 6. Simulated RBL leakage and read current comparison

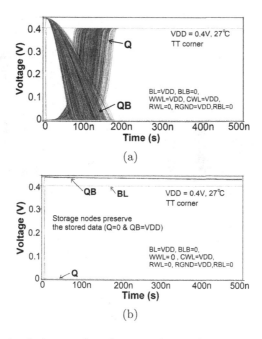

Fig. 7. Transient simulation results of proposed 11T during write 1 operation using 2000 Monte Carlo samples, 0.4 V supply and 27 °C temperature for the (a) Selected and (b) Column half-selected cell

It is observed that the leakage power increases with the temperature, so we have compared the leakage power of 11T with that of 6T at 85 °C, as illustrated in Fig. 8(a), and it shows that the 11T consumes 1.67 × and 1.79 × less power at 0.4 V and 1 V respectively. Read-write power-delay product (PDP) comparison, which is normalized in terms of PDP values for 6T, is also depicted in Fig. 8(b) for 0.4 V supply.

4   Four-Input LUT for FPGA

As SRAM based FPGAs utilize SRAM to implement the routing and core computational functions with the help of LUT and MUXs, the reprogrammability feature of it leads to high logic density for SRAM memory [1]. Therefore, the power efficient and high stability SRAM cells are highly required, otherwise the bit flip of any memory cell in the LUT may damage the functionality of the FPGA. To ensure the validity of proposed 11T cell for such applications, a four-input LUT, using this 11T cell, has been implemented as shown in Fig. 9 and the leakage power has been compared with the 6T SRAM based LUT. The simulation results show that the 11T SRAM based LUT consumes only 0.59× leakage power as compared to that of 6T based LUT.

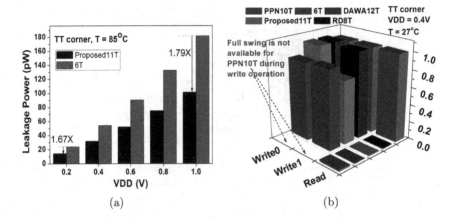

Fig. 8. (a) Leakage power for different V_{DD} at $80\,^{\circ}$C temperature (b) Read-Write power-delay product (PDP) normalized to those of 6T at 0.4 V

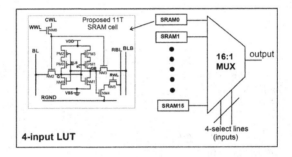

Fig. 9. 4-input LUT architecture using the proposed 11T SRAM cell

Table 2. A comparison between proposed two-bits and conventional one-bit correction approach

	Proposed method (two-bits correction)		Conventional approach (one-bit correction)	
	Encoder	Decoder	Encoder	Decoder
Leakage power	93.41×10^{-12} W	413×10^{-12} W	102.17×10^{-12} W	296.5×10^{-12} W
Read access PDP	9.6×10^{-21} J	25.44×10^{-21} J	10.30×10^{-21} J	27.5×10^{-21} J

5 Error Detection and Correction for Bit-Interleaving Architecture

Moving towards the deep-submicron region, a number of physical events can create error for the data stored in the memory arrays. The shared word line array architecture, where all the bits of a word are placed adjacent to each other (as shown in Fig. 10(a)), has high probability of multi-bits upsets (MBUs) due

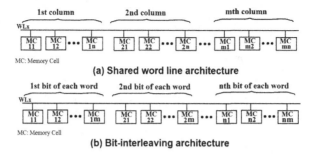

(a) Shared word line architecture

(b) Bit-interleaving architecture

Fig. 10. Memory array architecture having m no. of columns with word size of n

to such events. The bit-interleaving architecture is commonly used to solve the issue by placing the nth bit of each word adjacent to each other, as illustrated in Fig. 10(b). But it faces another challenge of half-select issue [7]. The proposed half-select free 11T cell can effectively be used in bit-interleaving architecture, and therefore any single event upset (SEU) caused by the soft error can affect atmost a single bit of a data word at a given time.

Moreover, a Double Adjacent Error Detection and Correction (DAEDC) is proposed if somehow the soft error affects two adjacent bits of the 11T SRAM bit-interleaved architecture. The basic block diagram for the DAEDC is shown in Fig. 11, where the ECC encoder generates the parity bits based on the input data which are stored in the memory array along with the given input data. At the receiver side, the syndrome decoder receives the data (data bits+parity), and based on the detailed process as shown in Fig. 12 it can correct the two adjacent bits error. The H-matrix used in this work is based as suggested in [21], while

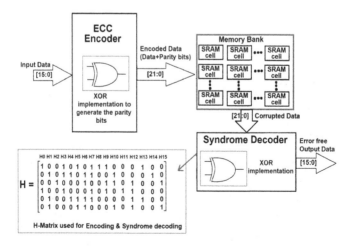

Fig. 11. Block level architecture for two adjacent bits error detection and correction

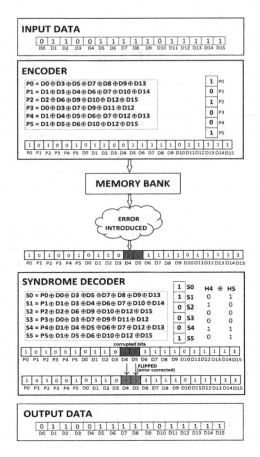

Fig. 12. Detailed process of encoding and decoding for two adjacent bits error correction

the number of parity bits required has been determined by the relation [22]: $[n \leq 2^{n-k} - 1]$ and $[(2n-1) \leq 2^{n-k} - 1]$. A comparison of proposed technique for two bits error and conventional hamming code for single bit error for the leakage power and read access PDP is given in the Table 2.

6   Conclusion

In this paper, a P-P-N based half-select free subthreshold 11T SRAM has been proposed to facilitate the reliable SRAM operation. Half-select issue is completely removed by the cross point formation during the cell write operation, and thus it successfully utilizes the bit-interleaved architecture to remove the multi-bits upset. The proposed 11T also removes the read-write trade-off for the 6T, and individually improves the read and write ability which is 1.95× and

2.84× larger respectively when compared to that of 6T at 0.4 V. Furthermore, the statistical analysis (Monte Carlo simulation) of proposed cell confirms its robustness against the process-voltage-temperature (PVT) variations. The leakage power of the cell is also improved which has been verified by implementing a four-input FPGA lookup table (LUT) and compared with that of 6T based LUT. The proposed double adjacent error correction technique associated with the bit-interleaving architecture for 11T offers an attractive soft error free SRAM memory design.

Acknowledgment. The authors would like to thank Special Manpower Development Program for Chips to System Design (SMDP-C2SD) research project of Department of Electronics and Information Technology (DEITY) under Ministry of Communication and Information Technology, Government of India to provide the lab facilities.

References

1. Safarulla, I.M., Manilal, K.: Design of soft error tolerance technique for FPGA based soft core processors. In: 2014 International Conference on Advanced Communication Control and Computing Technologies (ICACCCT), pp. 1036–1040. IEEE (2014)
2. Ullah, Z., Jaiswal, M.K., Cheung, R.C.: Z-TCAM: an SRAM-based architecture for TCAM. IEEE Trans. Very Large Scale (VLSI) Integr. Syst. **23**(2), 402–406 (2015)
3. Sharma, V., Gopal, M., Singh, P., Vishvakarma, S.K.: A 220 mV robust read-decoupled partial feedback cutting based low-leakage 9T SRAM for Internet of Things (iot) applications. AEU-Int. J. Electron. Commun. **87**, 144–157 (2018)
4. Roy, K., Prasad, S.C.: Low-power CMOS VLSI Circuit Design. Wiley, Hoboken (2009)
5. Sharma, V., Kumar, S.: Design of low-power CMOS cell structures using subthreshold conduction region. Int. J. Sci. Eng. Res. **2**(2), 29–34 (2011)
6. Chang, M.-F., et al.: A sub-0.3 V area-efficient l-shaped 7T SRAM with read bitline swing expansion schemes based on boosted read-bitline, asymmetric read-port, and offset cell VDD biasing techniques. IEEE J. Solid-State Circuits **48**(10), 2558–2569 (2013)
7. Pal, S., Islam, A.: 9-T SRAM cell for reliable ultralow-power applications and solving multibit soft-error issue. IEEE Trans. Device Mater. Reliab. **16**(2), 172–182 (2016)
8. Andrei, P., Oniciuc, L.: Suppressing random dopant-induced fluctuations of threshold voltages in semiconductor devices. J. Appl. Phys. **104**(10), 104508 (2008)
9. Chang, L., et al.: An 8T-SRAM for variability tolerance and low-voltage operation in high-performance caches. IEEE J. Solid-State Circuits **43**(4), 956–963 (2008)
10. Chang, M.-F., Chang, S.-W., Chou, P.-W., Wu, W.-C.: A 130 mV SRAM with expanded write and read margins for subthreshold applications. IEEE J. Solid-State Circuits **46**(2), 520–529 (2011)
11. Wang, B., Nguyen, T.Q., Do, A.T., Zhou, J., Je, M., Kim, T.T.-H.: Design of an ultra-low voltage 9T SRAM with equalized bitline leakage and cam-assisted energy efficiency improvement. IEEE Trans. Circuits Syst. I: Regul. Pap. **62**(2), 441–448 (2015)

12. Lo, C.-H., Huang, S.-Y.: PPN based 10T SRAM cell for low-leakage and resilient subthreshold operation. IEEE J. Solid-State Circuits **46**(3), 695–704 (2011)

13. Chiu, Y.-W., et al.: 40 nm bit-interleaving 12T subthreshold SRAM with data-aware write-assist. IEEE Trans. Circuits Syst. I: Regul. Pap. **61**(9), 2578–2585 (2014)

14. Kim, J., Mazumder, P.: A robust 12T SRAM cell with improved write margin for ultra-low power applications in 40 nm CMOS. Integr. VLSI J. **57**, 1–10 (2017)

15. Jahinuzzaman, S.M., Rennie, D.J., Sachdev, M.: A soft error tolerant 10T sram bit-cell with differential read capability. IEEE Trans. Nucl. Sci. **56**(6), 3768–3773 (2009)

16. Lage, C., et al.: Soft error rate and stored charge requirements in advanced high-density SRAMS. In: International Electron Devices Meeting, 1993. IEDM 1993 Technical Digest, pp. 821–824. IEEE (1993)

17. Hazucha, P., et al.: Neutron soft error rate measurements in a 90-nm CMOS process and scaling trends in sram from 0.25-/spl mu/m to 90-nm generation. In: IEEE International Electron Devices Meeting, 2003. IEDM 2003 Technical Digest, p. 21.5. IEEE (2003)

18. Chang, I.J., Kim, J.-J., Park, S.P., Roy, K.: A 32 kb 10T sub-threshold SRAM array with bit-interleaving and differential read scheme in 90 nm CMOS. IEEE J. Solid-State Circuits **44**(2), 650–658 (2009)

19. Wen, L., Duan, Z., Li, Y., Zeng, X.: Analysis of a read disturb-free 9T sram cell with bit-interleaving capability. Microelectron. J. **45**(6), 815–824 (2014)

20. Seevinck, E., List, F.J., Lohstroh, J.: Static-noise margin analysis of MOS SRAM cells. IEEE J. Solid-State Circuits **22**(5), 748–754 (1987)

21. Li, J., Reviriego, P., Xiao, L., Argyrides, C., Li, J.: Extending 3-bit burst error-correction codes with quadruple adjacent error correction. IEEE Trans. Very Large Scale Integr. (VLSI) Syst. **26**(2), 221–229 (2018)

22. Li, J., Xiao, L., Reviriego, P., Zhang, R.: Efficient implementations of 4-bit burst error correction for memories. IEEE Trans. Circ. Syst. II: Express Briefs **65**(12), 2037–2041 (2018)

Low Leakage Read Write Enhanced 9T SRAM Cell

Pratiksha Shukla$^{(\boxtimes)}$, Vinay Gupta, and Manisha Pattanaik

Indian Institute of Information Technology and Management, Gwalior, India
pratiksha38884@gmail.com, vinny7536@gmail.com,
manishapattanaik@iiitm.ac.in

Abstract. In deep submicrometer technology (below 65 nm), SRAM designs suffer from high leakage and low stability issues. This paper presents a low leakage highly stable SRAM cell with read-write enhanced circuitry. The proposed SRAM performs read-write operation through single bitline and have separate read-write circuitry. It consists of a sleep transistor (shared by an array) in the read path, that remains OFF during hold and write mode to suppress the bitline leakage. It shows enhanced write ability and low leakage due to stacking effect in left inverter. Additionally, one data dependent charge pump circuit is used to prevent read bitline leakage while reading logic '1' thereby improving the sense margin of bitline. Various design parameters such as read static noise margin (RSNM), read access time (T_{RA}), write access time (T_{WA}), leakage power and write ability of differential 6T (D6T), single bitline 9T (SB9T) and proposed (RWE9T) SRAM cell have been discussed. HSPICE simulations are performed using 32 nm PTM (LP). The proposed SRAM shows 2.14x improvement in RSNM as compared to D6T. Also, it shows an improvement of 2x and 1.38x in write '1' margin as compared to D6T and SB9T and 1.38x in write '0' margin than SB9T SRAM cell. An improvement of 1.75x in T_{RA} and 3.62x in write '0' access time as compared to SB9T is shown at a penalty of write '1' access time. RWE9T consumes 4.5x and 4.12x less leakage power as compared to D6T and SB9T at VDD = 0.9 V.

Keywords: Low leakage · Stacking effect · Write margin ·
Read stability · Random Access Memory (SRAM)

1 Introduction

Static Random Access Memory (SRAM) occupies an important part of system-on-chip (SoC), network-on-chip (NoC) and processors. It finds its application in wireless sensors, biomedical devices, portable electronic circuits etc. As SRAM occupies a major portion of these devices so, low power SRAMs are in high demand today. With the technology scaling leakage current is also increasing, about 40% of the total active power consumed by processors is due to leakage current. As large no of transistors are used in on-chip cache memory, SRAM cell

© Springer Nature Singapore Pte Ltd. 2019
S. Rajaram et al. (Eds.): VDAT 2018, CCIS 892, pp. 565–577, 2019.
https://doi.org/10.1007/978-981-13-5950-7_47

array is a basic source of leakage current in processors. Therefore, low power SRAMs are very much required for high performance processors. Many methods were proposed to reduce the leakage current. One method is scaling of supply voltage, leakage power reduces linearly with voltage scaling while dynamic power reduces quadratically [12]. Therefore, low power SRAM can be obtained by operating the cell in the subthreshold region. But at such low voltage, performance of an SRAM is highly affected so, some other methods were proposed to minimize the leakage current such as power gating technique, stacking etc. [4]. In deep submicrometer technology (below 65 nm) read stability and write ability becomes crucial at lower supply voltages. To overcome the read stability issue, read circuitry is isolated from cross coupled inverters, this increases the stability of an SRAM cell during read operation [9]. To increase the write ability various techniques were proposed. One technique is to make write access transistor more stronger so that it can overcome the strong feedback of cross coupled inverters and another is to reduce the strength of feedback of cross coupled inverters while performing write operation [6]. In this paper, a noval SRAM (RWE9T) cell is proposed that is highly stable and consumes low leakage power.

This paper is organized as follows. Section 2 gives the background of existing SRAMs and related work. Section 3 presents the proposed design and its operation. Section 4 presents various design metrices of SRAMs with their simulated results. The graphical and tabular comparative analysis are presented in Sect. 4. Section 5 concludes the paper.

2   Related Work

The differential 6T (D6T) SRAM cell (as shown in Fig. 1) suffers from read upset and write ability issues at low supply voltages. Since access transistor M4 and driver transistor MN1 associated with '0' storing node act as voltage divider. This voltage division raises the voltage of logic '0' storing node and if this voltage becomes greater than the tripping voltage of the other inverter storing logic '1' than the stored data can get flipped and read failure occurs. Similarly for proper write '0' operation access transistor M4 should be stronger than pull up transistor MP1 and for writing '1' it should be stronger than MN1. Therefore, for proper read stability there occurs degradation in write ability and vice versa [14]. For proper read-write operation transistor sizing is done depending on β_{ratio} and γ_{ratio} [11,14]. At deep submicrometer technology transistor sizing becomes very difficult and hence read stability becomes worse. Several SRAM cells have been proposed to overcome the stability issues of D6T SRAM cell. Single ended designs consumes almost half of active power as compared to differential designs at the cost of increased read/write access time and exhibits poor write '1' ability. SB9T cell (as shown in Fig. 2) [3] uses single bitline for read/write operation using transmission logic. SB9T shows improved write '1' ability due to virtual ground concept [10] and low write '0' ability. It offers low leakage as compared to differential 6T SRAM cell. In this paper a noval SRAM cell (RWE9T) have been proposed that overcomes the difficulties of D6T SRAM with low leakage and better read/write performance.

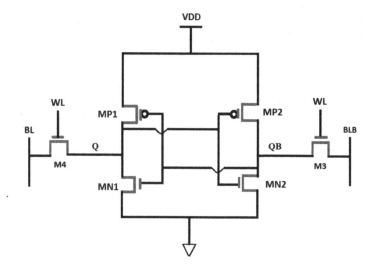

Fig. 1. Differential 6T (D6T) SRAM cell [12].

3   Proposed RWE9T Design

The proposed SRAM cell (RWE9T) has separate read-write circuitry (as shown in Fig. 3). Read circuitry comprises of access transistor MR1, buffer transistor MR2, charge pump transistor MR3, sleep transistor MR4 and read

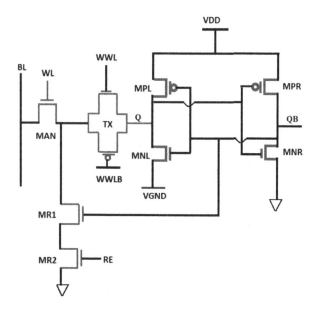

Fig. 2. SB9T SRAM cell [3].

bitline RBL whereas write circuitry includes access transistor MW and bitline BL. Writing logic '1' in an SRAM through single bitline is very challenging [3]. In differential SRAM cell writing of logic '1' is achieved by writing logic '0' on the other side of storage cell. Therefore, writing of logic '1' in single bitline is done using write assist technique. In the proposed RWE9T SRAM cell transistor M5 is kept OFF during write mode which eliminates the contention current produced by transistor M2 and weakens the storage node Q to be pulled to ground thus, facilitating the transfer of logic '1' to the cell [9]. Since RWE9T has separate read-write circuitry there is no sizing conflict, minimum sized transistors can be used for proper read-write operation.

3.1 Hold Mode

During hold mode signals WS (write select) and RS (read select) are maintained at 0 V so that transistors MR1, MR4 and MW are in OFF state whereas transistors MR2 and MR3 will be ON/OFF depending on the data stored in storage nodes Q and QB. Transistor MR4 is kept OFF during hold mode to suppress the RBL (read bitline) leakage current. Transistor M5 is kept ON so that cross coupled inverters experience full power supply during hold mode for storing data properly.

3.2 Read Mode

During read operation signals RS and WS are maintained at VDD and 0 V respectively, read bitline (RBL) is charged to VDD and BL (write bitline) is kept at 0 V. Read access transistor MR1 and sleep transistor MR4 are tuned

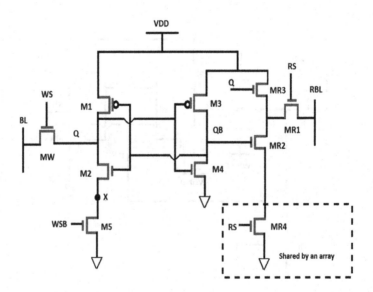

Fig. 3. Proposed RWE9T SRAM cell.

ON (as RS is high). Also buffer transistor MR2 and transistor MR3 are turned ON/OFF depending on data stored in cross coupled inverters. For instance let us assume that node Q is storing logic '0' and node QB logic '1' which turns ON transistor MR2 and RBL discharges through MR1, MR2 and MR4 to ground. When node Q is storing logic '1' and QB logic '0' then, MR2 will be turned OFF whereas MR3 is ON which acts as a charge pump circuit to prevent RBL from discharging during read '1' operation.

3.3   Write Mode

During write mode signal WS is raised to VDD and RS is maintained at 0V. Therefore, the complementary of WS (i.e WSB) is pulled down. Because of high WS and low WSB transistor MW is turned ON and M5 is turned OFF. Write bitline BL is kept at VDD or 0 V depending upon the data to be written into the cell and RBL is maintained at 0 V. For instance let initially node Q is storing logic '0' and QB logic '1'. Now to write logic '1' in SRAM cell , BL is maintained at VDD due to which node Q charges to logic '1' through write access transistor MW and node QB is pulled to logic '0' through feedback mechanism of cross coupled inverters. Similarly if BL is maintained at 0 V and node Q initially stores logic '1' and QB logic '0' then, the storage node Q discharges through MW and as voltage of node Q becomes less than the tripping voltage of inverter storing logic '0', the data of node QB flips to logic '1'. Table 1 shows the control signals and its value at various mode of operation of RWE9T SRAM cell.

Table 1. Operation table of proposed RWE9T cell.

Signals	Write 1	Write 0	Hold	Read
BL	VDD	GND	VDD	GND
RBL	GND	GND	VDD	VDD
WS	VDD	VDD	GND	GND
RS	GND	GND	GND	VDD

4   Simulation Results and Analysis

HSPICE and 32 nm Predictive Technology Model (LP) [1] is used for analysis and comparison of RWE9T, SB9T and D6T SRAM cells. Transistor sizing is an important factor in order to achieve proper functionality of D6T SRAM cell therefore, sizing for D6T is kept same as suggested in [12]. As there is no sizing issue in SB9T and proposed design (RWE9T) minimum transistor sizing can be used to reduce leakage power. But for fair comparison same transistor sizing is used in D6T portion of all SRAM cells. Also, in RWE9T the width of transistors MR1, MR2, MW is increased to 1.5 times of length to reduce the delay. Table 2 shows the comparison of various design parameters of D6T, SB9T and RWE9T SRAM cells.

4.1 HSNM

Hold static noise margin (HSNM) measures the stability of an SRAM cell during hold mode. It is defined as the maximum DC noise voltage that can be tolerated by an SRAM cell without disturbing the stored data in the hold mode. Graphically HSNM of an SRAM cell is measured using butterfly curve method [8]. In hold mode cross coupled inverter is kept isolated from read/write circuitry. Therefore, the hold capability of an SRAM cell basically depends on the cross coupled inverters. Since D6T, SB9T and RWE9T SRAM uses same inverter therefore, they all have almost same HSNM (as shown in Fig. 4). HSNM at various supply voltages is shown in Fig. 5, difference in hold noise margin at low voltage is due to different bitline capacitance.

4.2 RSNM

Read stability of an SRAM cell is measured in terms of read static noise margin (RSNM). Graphically RSNM is measured as the side length of the largest square that can be inserted inside the smaller lobe of the butterfly curve [5,8]. RWE9T SRAM cell fully decouples the data storing node Q from read bitline instead the voltage of node Q is sensed through the gate of buffer transistor MR2. Thus, the read stability of RWE9T is improved as compared to D6T (as shown in Fig. 6). RSNM for different SRAM cells have been compared at 0.9 V supply voltage. Read noise margin of various SRAM cells at different supply voltages is shown in Fig. 7.

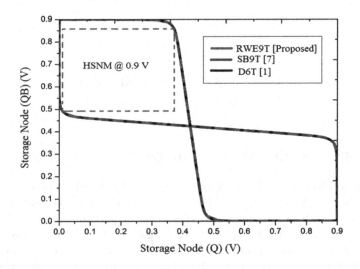

Fig. 4. HSNM of D6T, SB9T and RWE9T SRAM cells @ VDD = 0.9 V.

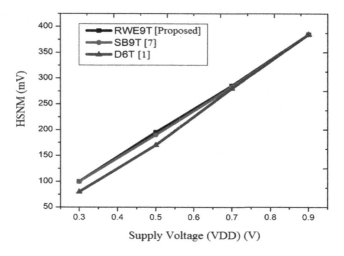

Fig. 5. Variation of HSNM at various supply voltages.

4.3 Write Ability

Write ability of an SRAM cell is defined as the ability to flip the value of node storing logic '0' to logic '1' and vice versa. Write ability of an SRAM cell can be represented in terms of write margin. This method of write margin is more appropriate then conventional butterfly curve method. In this method BL (write bitline) is loaded with data to be written into the cell and then, write select signal (WS) is swept from 0 V to VDD. The write margin is defined as the difference between VDD and the WS voltage at which Q or QB flips [7] its stored

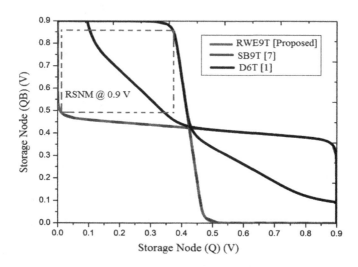

Fig. 6. RSNM of D6T, SB9T and RWE9T SRAM cells @ VDD = 0.9 V.

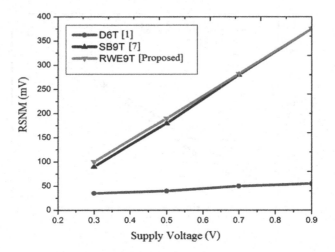

Fig. 7. Variation of RSNM at various supply voltages.

data. RWE9T has highest write '1' margin (as shown in Fig. 9) as compared to SB9T and D6T. Transistor M5 is kept OFF during write operation due to which potential of node "X" is raised to a voltage greater than 0 V which assist in writing '1' into the SRAM cell. SB9T exhibits poor write '0' margin when compared to RWE9T and D6T (as shown in Fig. 8).

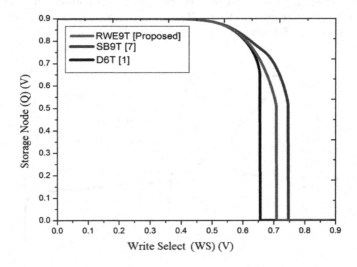

Fig. 8. Write '0' margin of D6T, SB9T and RWE9T SRAM cells @ VDD = 0.9 V.

4.4   Leakage Power Dissipation

In cache memory SRAM cells remain in idle mode for most of the time. As technology is scaling down, leakage power is becoming almost equal to dynamic power. Total Leakage current in any SRAM cell is due to gate leakage (I_G), junction leakage (I_{JN}) and subthreshold leakage (I_{sub}) current. For low leakage SRAM cell, I_{sub} should to be reduced, as it dominates all leakage components. Therefore, in the proposed SRAM cell left inverter consists of three transistors in series which reduces the subthreshold leakage current I_{sub} due to stacking effect [6]. During hold condition most of the leakage power dissipation is due to bitline leakage therefore, it is very important to suppress it. To suppress bitline leakage transistors MR4 and MR1 are kept OFF during hold mode which reduces leakage current in proposed SRAM cell. Also, MR2 and MR3 is controlled by node voltage Q and QB. Due to which transistors MR2 and MR3 remain in ON state for unselected cells which contribute to large leakage current. But since during hold mode either MR2 or MR3 will be ON. Therefore, three transistors will remain in OFF state which reduces the bitline leakage [13]. RWE9T has least leakage power dissipation than D6T and SB9T (as shown in Fig. 10).

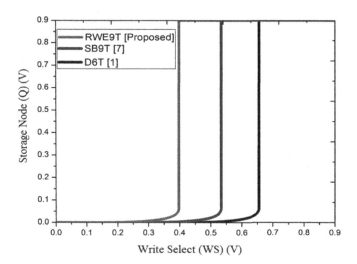

Fig. 9. Write '1' margin of D6T, SB9T and RWE9T SRAM cells @ VDD = 0.9 V.

4.5   Read Access Time (T_{RA})

Read access time/read delay (T_{RA}) determines the speed of an SRAM cell while performing read operation. For differential bitline T_{RA} is defined as the time duration from the instant when the wordline (WL) is activated to the time when 50 mV difference is build between the two bitlines. For single bitline, T_{RA} is defined as the time duration from the instant when the read select signal (RS) is activated to the time when RBL (read bitline) discharges to 50% of its initial

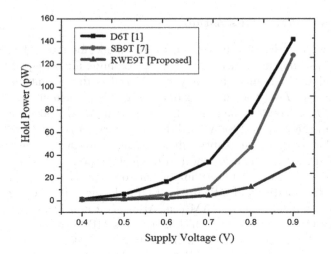

Fig. 10. Variation of hold power at various supply voltages.

high value [2]. For fair comparison the T_{RA} of single bitline is measured as the time duration from RS activation to the time when bitline (RBL) voltage drops to 50 mV from its initial high value [13]. It can be seen that D6T is fastest among SB9T and RWE9T (as shown in Fig. 11) since it has smaller bitline capacitances. RWE9T shows improvement in read delay as compared to SB9T. Read access time for various SRAM cells at different supply voltages is shown in Fig. 11.

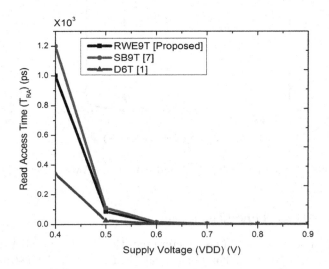

Fig. 11. Variation of read access time at various supply voltages.

4.6   Write Access Time (T_{WA})

Write access time/write delay determines how fast the write operation can be performed by an SRAM cell. It is calculated while accessing the SRAM cell for write operation. T_{WA} for writing logic '0' is defined as the time duration from the instant when the write select signal (WS) is activated to time at which node storing logic '1' discharges to 10% of VDD [3]. Likewise T_{WA} for writing logic '1' is defined as the time duration from the instant when the write select signal (WS) is activated to time at which node storing logic '0' charges to 90% of VDD [3]. For differential SRAMs write access time for writing logic '0' or '1' will be same. But for single bitline write access time mainly depends on data to be written. Write '1' access time of proposed SRAM cell is higher than SB9T and D6T

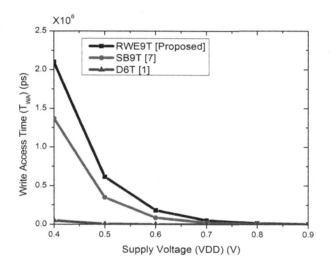

Fig. 12. Variation of write access time at various supply voltages.

Table 2. Comparison of design parameters among D6T, SB9T and RWE9T SRAM cells @ 0.9 V.

Design metrics	D6T	SB9T	RWE9T
Average read power	45 nW	42 nW	29 nW
Average write power	511 nW	4.45 nW	6.4 nW
Write '0' delay	17 ps	134 ps	37 ps
Write '1' delay	43 ps	1.8 ns	4.6 ns
Read delay	200 fs	700 fs	400 fs
HSNM	370 mV	370 mV	370 mV
RSNM	175 mV	370 mV	370 mV
Write '0' margin	250 mV	150 mv	198 mV
Write '1' margin	250 mV	360 mV	500 mV

(as shown in Fig. 12) due to large bitline capacitance of SRAM cell. Proposed SRAM cell (RWE9T) shows improvement in write '0' delay when compared to SB9T. Write access time for various SRAM cells at different supply voltages is shown in Fig. 12.

5   Conclusion

This work presents a low leakage read-write enhanced single bitline 9T SRAM cell (RWE9T) which is suitable for low power applications. Various design parameters have been studied and compared with previously proposed SRAM designs. RWE9T shows 2.14x improvement in RSNM as compared to D6T. Further, it shows improvement of 2x/1.38x in write '1' margin as compared to D6T/SB9T and 1.38x in write '0' margin than SB9T SRAM cell. Furthermore, an improvement of 1.75x in T_{RA} and 3.62x in write '0' access time as compared to SB9T is shown at a penalty of write '1' access time. RWE9T consumes 4.5x/4.12x less leakage power as compared to D6T/SB9T SRAM cells. So this SRAM cell is suitable for applications requiring high stability and low power with moderate speed.

References

1. http://ptm.asu.edu/modelcard/LP/32nm.pm
2. Ahmad, S., Gupta, M.K., Hasan, M.: Single ended schmitt trigger-based robust low-power SRAM cell. IEEE Trans. Very Large Scale Integr. VLSI Syst. **24**(8), 2634–2642 (2016)
3. Ahmad, S., Gupta, M.K., Alam, N., Hasan, M.: Low leakage single bitline 9T (SB9T) static random access memory. Microelectron. J. **62**, 1–11 (2017)
4. Bikki, P., Karuppanan, P.: Sram cell leakage control techniques for ultra low power application: a survey. Circuits Syst. **8**(02), 23 (2017)
5. Grossar, E., Stucchi, M., Maex, K., Dehaene, W.: Read stability and write-ability analysis of SRAM cells for nanometer technologies. IEEE J. Solid-State Circuits **41**(11), 2577–2588 (2006)
6. Pasandi, G., Fakhraie, S.M.: An 8T low-voltage and low-leakage half-selection disturb-free SRAM using bulk-CMOS and FinFETs. IEEE Trans. Electron Devices **61**(7), 2357–2363 (2014)
7. Qiu, H., et al.: Statistical write stability characterization in SRAM cells at low supply voltage. IEEE Trans. Electron Devices **63**(11), 4302–4308 (2016)
8. Islam, A., Hasan, M.: A technique to mitigate impact of process, voltage and temperature variations on design metrics of SRAM cell. Microelectron. Reliab. **52**(2), 405–411 (2012). Low Temperature Processing for Microelectronics and Microsystems Packaging
9. Jiao, H., Qiu, Y., Kursun, V.: Low power and robust memory circuits with asymmetrical ground gating. Microelectron. J. **48**, 109–119 (2016)
10. Tu, M.H., Lin, J.Y., Tsai, M.C., Jou, S.J., Chuang, C.T.: Single-ended subthreshold SRAM with asymmetrical write/read-assist. IEEE Trans. Circuits Syst. I Regul. Pap. **57**(12), 3039–3047 (2010)

11. Verma, N., Kwong, J., Chandrakasan, A.P.: Nanometer MOSFET variation in minimum energy subthreshold circuits. IEEE Trans. Electron Devices **55**(1), 163–174 (2008)
12. Pal, S., Islam, A.: Variation tolerant differential 8T SRAM cell for ultralow power applications. IEEE Trans. Comput. Aided Des. Integr. Circuits Syst. **35**(4), 549–558 (2016)
13. Pasandi, G., Fakhraie, S.M.: A 256-kb 9T near-threshold SRAM with 1k cells per bitline and enhanced write and read operations. IEEE Trans. Very Large Scale Integr. VLSI Syst. **23**(11), 2438–2446 (2015)
14. Pal, S., Islam, A.: 9T SRAM cell for reliable ultralow-power applications and solving multibit soft-error issue. IEEE Trans. Device Mater. Reliab. **16**(2), 172–182 (2016)

A Novel March C_{2RR} Algorithm for Nanoelectronic Resistive Random Access Memory (RRAM) Testing

H. Sribhuvaneshwari[1]([⊠])[iD] and K. Suthendran[2][iD]

[1] Department of Electronics and Communication Engineering, Kalasalingam Academy of Research and Education, Krishnankoil, Tamilnadu, India
sribhuvaneshwari.h@klu.ac.in
[2] Department of Information Technology, Kalasalingam Academy of Research and Education, Krishnankoil, Tamilnadu, India

Abstract. Promising nanoelectronic memories such as PCRAM, STT-RAM, Ferroelectric FET Memory and Resistive Random Access Memory (RRAM) are capable of substituting the conventional memory technologies such as SRAMs, DRAMs and flash memory in future computers. Among all these nanoelectronic memories RRAM results in higher density, lower power consumption, higher speed and better scalability which can fulfill the requirements of massive data growth as well as storage. But it is expected to go through numerous faults that reduce the reliability of the system. These faults may arise at any element of the memory system which includes the marginal circuits, inter junction and memory cell array. Read 1 Disturbance (R1D) fault is one among the main faults in RRAM that occurs, if the read value is 0 when 1 is the actual result which is kind of low resistance defect. In RRAM SET voltage (V_{SET}), bit line voltage, restricted thermal stability and accumulated read current pulse leads to read disturbance faults and also when maximum current is applied for a read operation that immediately induces the read disturbance fault. As the read current and write current have the same path, read disturbance faults makes a bit flip. The accumulated effect of this read '1' disturbance degrades the memory reliability. This kind of fault changes the value stored in a particular memory cell which leads to consequent inaccurate read values that keep on propagates till a new logic value is written in the same cell. Read disturbance lies between the read operation and read disturbance fault which is a major concern of today's NVM since it directly affects the performance of the system. According to march C* test algorithm HfO_2 based 1T1R RRAM's R1D faults can be sensitized by ensuring the presence of '1' (read 1) after the write '1' operation and detected by another read 1 operation. In this article a novel March C_{2RR} algorithm is proposed, here read operation is repeated twice in the second, fourth memory element (R3, R4 in M3 and R5, R6 in M4) and 100% fault coverage is achieved by the proposed method that detects R1D faults and all the random faults effectively.

Keywords: Nanoelectronic memory · RRAM · R1D fault · SET · RESET operation · Fault coverage · Test complexity

S. Rajaram et al. (Eds.): VDAT 2018, CCIS 892, pp. 578–589, 2019.
https://doi.org/10.1007/978-981-13-5950-7_48

1 Introduction

The memory chip is the fundamental unit for every electronic system to store the data. The massive growth of data and various blooming electronic technologies require huge data storage capacity. This requirement is achieved by CMOS miniaturizations, the future resolution is to integrate CMOS and non-CMOS technologies such as spintronics, magnetic tunneling junctions, carbon nanotubes and memristors in a single memory chip. This hybrid memory technology is referred as nanoelectronic memories [9–14]. Due to the fiery expansion of digital data in the latest technology of Internet of Things (IoT), quick and scalable memory technologies are being researched for data storage and data-driven computation. 1T1R RRAM is one of the most promising candidates where the transistor is used to limit the pulse current that avoids the hard breakdown (HBD) in resistor [21, 22]. It can be applied in many fields like medical healthcare devices [24] and in system-on-chip (SoC) applications such as wireless sensor networks (WSNs) [23]. Various materials are used as resisitive switching element [18, 20] since 2007 HfO_2 has been selected as "standard" gate dielectric material in modern CMOS transistors [25] due to its compatibility with the current semiconductor fabrication process hence HfO_2 based 1T1R RRAM is tested with various existing algorithms and march C$_{2RR}$ algorithm is proposed for R1D fault detection.

2 Importance of Testing

Defect is the physical abnormality materialized by manufacturing process that was not originally defined in the design circuit. Due to the contaminations, unintended particles like an additional or misplaced materials results in hard defects. Moreover, the slight progression variations lead to latent defects like source/drain dislocation, inadequate doping and via pinholes that are much crucial in nanoelectronic memories. The fault is the symptom of defects and an exterior conflict. Exterior conflicts are due to environmental sources such as cosmic rays, alpha particles and temperature fluctuations that will result in three types of faults they are hard faults, intermittent faults, and transient faults. Hard faults arise with determination, intermittent faults that occur over and over again (i.e., appears, disappears and reappears repeatedly) which is caused by hidden defects or older elements. Transient faults appear and disappear shortly that is caused by exterior instability. The error is the outcome of fault at the output of a circuit and failure is the incapability of a circuit to carry out its intentional task due to errors. The capability of the system to handle the failure can be manifested as either an incorrect result, no result or delayed results (e.g., an exact result that delays from the intended time). Quality is the term used to quantify the defective devices that escape manufacturing tests but are returned back to the manufacturer by customers. Similarly reliability is the term used to quantify the ability of a system to operate correctly for a specified period of time under certain conditions. The longer a system operates correctly corresponds to higher reliability. However, faults due to latent defects and external disturbances affect the reliability. Since the applications of RRAM are deployed in various multidimensional applications, it has to be tested well for the proficient outcome. The principle behind the memory test is to authenticate that each storage site in a memory device is functionally correct. In case, if we fetch the arithmetical value 18 at a specific address, we look forward to tracing that particular value stored in a specific address until a new value is written to that address. i.e., the memory test is an act of writing some sequence of data to each and every address in the memory device and verifying the presence of that written data by reading back. At when all the values retrieved are the one which was written previously then the memory device is fault free. The expenditure, moment in time and the worth of the test are the considerations that require being weighed for every device in each company. But no issue what methodology is taken or how decisive consistency is for a meticulous purpose. All of this needs to be done earlier than ever before. The test is moving more rapidly to design any electronic system as quality is a key metric. As it does, it is moving much further to the left of the design through industrialized flow. Various factors involved in RRAM testing are reactive ion etching [3], thermal stability [15], thermal crosstalk [16] and more importantly various internal processing faults.

3   Operational Characteristics of RRAM

RRAM is fabricated on a p-type silicon substrate and a 3 nm Ti layer was deposited over the silicon layer as an adhesion promoting layer followed by the deposition of 100 nm of Ru depositions using RF magnetron sputtering. After the deposition process, the temperature was increased to 300 °C, a 6 nm thick HfO_2 was layered by reactive sputtering of Hf within 20% oxygen and 150 nm thickness of TiO_x was deposited by the same method of Ti within 10% oxygen. RRAM is a passive device where both top and bottom layers are electrically conducting electrodes, insulating switching layer is located in-between the electrodes [1]. By applying external bias voltage the resistance can be changed. If a memristive element has a high resistance, then it is represented as HRS (High Resistance State). Similarly for low resistance state LRS. RON and ROFF are the maxima and the minimum CRS resistances respectively. Based on the bias voltage applied to RRAM write '0' and write '1' operations are carried, data '0' low resistance state and data '1' stands for by high resistance state (Fig. 1).

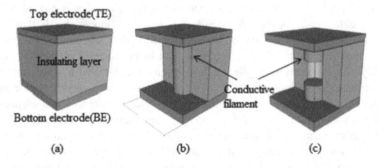

Fig. 1.   (a) Initial state (b) Set operation (c) Reset operation

The connection between the top electrode layer and bottom electrode layer by means of the conductive layer results in SET operation (from HRS to LRS) which is responsible for a write operation and similarly subsequent application of voltage returns the resistance to the HRS in the RESET process. Reproducible resistive switching is achieved by repeating these processes. The disconnection between (HRS, LRS) them results in RESET operation (from LRS to HRS), which is responsible for read operation. RON = R(LRS) + R(LRS), ROFF = R(HRS) + R(LRS) (Figs. 2 and 3).

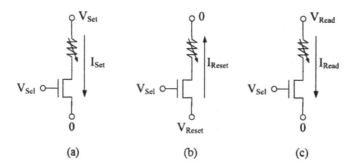

Fig. 2. (a) Set: Write 0 (b) Reset: Write 1 (c) Read

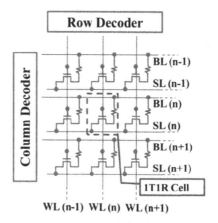

Fig. 3. 1T1R RRAM structure

To accomplish forming and SET operation, a positive voltage is given to the bottom electrode (BE), whereas for the RESET operation top electrode (TE) was positively biased [2]. In the case of 1T1R RRAM structure which is used here, the forming/SET and RESET were programmed by the source line (SL) and bit line (BL), respectively. By applying SET voltage (V_{SET}) to the bit line and connecting the source line to the ground, resistive device can be changed from HRS to LRS. This process is called as SET operation similarly RESET operation can be made by applying RESET voltage V_{RESET} to the source line and connecting bit line to the ground [19]. All the conditions are summarized in Table 1.

Table 1. Functional conditions for Forming, SET and RESET

	VBL	VSL	VG
Forming	GND	+	+
SET	GND	+	+
RESET	+	GND	+

4   RRAM: Fault Occurrence and Its Notation

The deviated behavior of particular write/read operation is called as a fault. It can be identified by basic two fault models (i) Fetching a sequence of operation to a specific memory function (ii) Observing Resultant behavior. The sequence which results in faulty behavior is called sensitizing sequence (S). Following faults can occur in 1T1R RRAM. If the fault f is observed within the memory element by applying the sensitizing sequence (S), for example when S is applied to M1 by enabling write logic 1 and stuck at 0 is noted in M1 then it is called self-fault (SF). In controversy, if the sensitizing sequence 'S' is applied to a particular cell M1 and a fault is observed in another cell M2 then it is called as coupling fault (CF). Here M1 is aggressor cell and M2 is victim cell. During the doping process, the effect of over doping results in stuck at 1 fault (SA1). In the functional process, if the column or memristor is connected to Vdd SA1 occurs. This fault is manifested as <0/1>, here logic '1' is the output when logic '0' is expected output. When there is a lack of oxygen vacancies in memristor or due to an open circuit in row/column that will create stuck at 0 fault (SA0), here logic '0' is the output when logic '1' is expected output and it is denoted by <1/0>. Even there is a minimum increase in impurities that will lead to slow write 1fault (SW1). Similarly, the decrease in a deficiency in oxygen vacancies results in slow write 0 (SW0). Increase in length 'L' and shrink in the cross-sectional area 'A' results in deep-0 fault and if the length decrease with the increase in cross-sectional area deep-1 fault occurs. Undefined output occurs due to excessive doping and increases in cross-sectional length which leads to unknown read (UR), it is manifested as <-/x> . Based on the resistance all faults are occurring in RRAM, that may be high resistance or low resistance applied HRS and LRS. In order to make RRAM with a fault-free state, various test algorithms are introduced. Each algorithm will focus specifically some kind of faults. Based on the reason of fault occurrence the operation of RRAM testing algorithm is designed. The effectiveness of testing algorithms assessed by parameters like test time, test complexity and fault coverage. In order to improve the overall performance of RRAM some soft computing techniques are incorporated [7] some unique bias schemes are used to improve the power utilization and read margin [17].

5 Existing Testing Methodologies

5.1 March Algorithm

March algorithms are used in most of the memory testing schemes. Its write and read actions are done through unchangeable patterns that thoroughly checks the memory with a certain number of faults in series manner i.e., at a time one memory element can be tested. So large memristor based memories take protracted test time using this march testing algorithm. The conventional march test just detects the predictable faults like stuck-at fault 1, stuck-at fault 0, transition fault 1, transition fault 0, coupling faults and address decoder faults and the sequence of march test is given below.

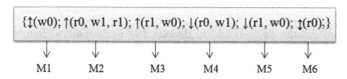

$$\{\updownarrow(w0); \uparrow(r0, w1, r1); \uparrow(r1, w0); \downarrow(r0, w1); \downarrow(r1, w0); \updownarrow(r0);\}$$

| M1 | M2 | M3 | M4 | M5 | M6 |

The notations of the march algorithm are as follows:
$\uparrow$:   Address sequence changes in ascending order
$\downarrow$:   Address sequence changes in descending order
$\updownarrow$:   Address sequence can change either way
r0:   Reading 0 from the particular memory cell
r1:   Reading 1 from the particular memory cell
w0:   Writing 0 to a particular memory cell
w1:   Writing 1 to a particular memory cell
M: Memory element

5.2 Modified March Algorithm

Chen et al. [5] has developed a modified march algorithm in order to detect dynamic write disturbance fault (DWDF) and write disturbance fault (WDF). In this method for an N-bit memristor memory $(1 + 2a + 2b)$ N write operations and 5N read operations are required where 'a' is the number of consecutive Write-1 and 'b' is the Write-0 operations.

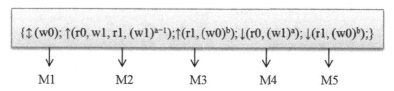

$$\{\updownarrow(w0); \uparrow(r0, w1, r1, (w1)^{a-1}); \uparrow(r1, (w0)^b); \downarrow(r0, (w1)^a); \downarrow(r1, (w0)^b);\}$$

| M1 | M2 | M3 | M4 | M5 |

5.3   Fast March Algorithm

Mozaffari et al. [8] has proposed fast march algorithm to reduce the time dominance created by w0 and r0. Here two new writes and read are used rather than time intense w0 and r0 that can be applied to sneak path testing [6] also, the proposed fast march test can trace out undefined state fault (USF) with 97% of reduced test time.

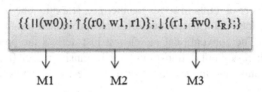

$$\{\{ \,\| (w0)\}; \uparrow\{(r0,\ w1,\ r1)\}; \downarrow\{(r1,\ fw0,\ r_R\};\}$$

↓	↓	↓
M1	M2	M3

Here, fw0 denotes fast w0 and r_R denotes fast r0 operations. Symbol $\|$ denotes parallel operation.

5.4   March C-Algorithm

Since RRAM architecture is comparable to the traditional RAMs, the majority of the practical fault models frequently utilized for testing RAMs including the Transition Fault (TF), Address Decoder Fault (AF), Stuck-At Fault (SAF) and inter-word Coupling Fault (CF) are found to be helpful for testing RRAM. The March C- is a testing algorithm similar to March C with reduced complexity that detects the abovementioned faults in the RRAM array. But in RRAM 'R1D' fault will flip the cell data before the read operation that results in corrupted read data. It can be detected by the March C-test, however, it cannot be predicted accurately whether the activator of R1D fault is read operation or an earlier write operation. Hence, it simply defines the R1D as the fault that occurs after the read operation. So a read-1 operation is introduced in front of a random read-1 operation, which can be an individual element or one more read-1 operation in M3 (r1, w0) as shown in the two algorithms below:

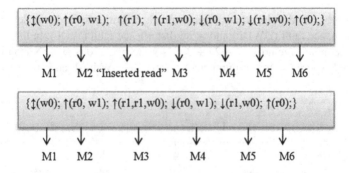

$$\{\updownarrow(w0);\ \uparrow(r0,\ w1);\ \ \uparrow(r1);\ \ \uparrow(r1,w0);\ \downarrow(r0,\ w1);\ \downarrow(r1,w0);\ \uparrow(r0);\}$$

↓	↓	↓	↓	↓	↓	↓
M1	M2	"Inserted read"	M3	M4	M5	M6

$$\{\updownarrow(w0);\ \uparrow(r0,\ w1);\ \uparrow(r1,r1,w0);\ \downarrow(r0,\ w1);\ \downarrow(r1,w0);\ \uparrow(r0);\}$$

↓	↓	↓	↓	↓	↓
M1	M2	M3	M4	M5	M6

5.5 March C* Algorithm

Chen et al. [4] has proposed March C*-1T1R algorithm for 1T1R RRAM that detects all known modeled faults. This method accomplishes 100% fault coverage with less test time for 4 MB HfO_2 based RRAM.

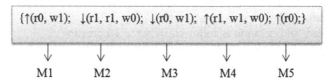

$$\{\uparrow(r0, w1); \ \downarrow(r1, r1, w0); \ \downarrow(r0, w1); \ \uparrow(r1, w1, w0); \ \uparrow(r0);\}$$

M1   M2   M3   M4   M5

6 Proposed Algorithm for RRAM Testing

Enhanced March C algorithm is introduced in this paper that detects most of the random faults. Due to the bidirectional flexibility of RRAM's I-V characteristics read 1 fault, read 0 fault occurs, read 1 disturbance fault can be detected effectively by using the proposed algorithm. During the read operation or after that, there is a probabilistic occurrence of read disturbance fault. This modifies the value in the particular cell which is going to be read that will result in faulty read data. The confusion between whether the fault is due to a previous write operation or presence of read disturbance occurs here if the read value is 0 when 1 is the actual result than it is "Read 1 Disturbance" fault (R1D) which is kind of low resistance defect. Here a couple of read 1 operation is followed to detect such R1D fault. In order to ensure the presence of '1' after the write '1' operation in 1st march element, two repeated read '1' operation is performed in 2nd march element which is proposed in march C* algorithm [4]. At the same time there is a probability of R1D fault after the write '1' operation in 3rd march element also therefore in 4th march element two repeated read '1' operation is performed to ensure the presence of '1', so that R1D fault is detected fully by using such repeated read '1' operation after write '1' operation rather than making lengthy march sequence. It is effective when repeating the main march element for a particular fault detection that improves the diagnosing resolution that is the basic idea proposed here. Since the read operation is repeated for two times, the proposed algorithm is named as March C_{2RR}.

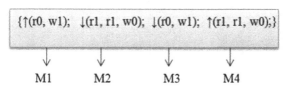

$$\{\uparrow(r0, w1); \ \downarrow(r1, r1, w0); \ \downarrow(r0, w1); \ \uparrow(r1, r1, w0);\}$$

M1   M2   M3   M4

Steps involved in the proposed algorithm:

Step 1: Initially write '0' operation is performed (Write '0' operation is neglected since the RRAM is fabricated and initially fetched with 0 [4])

Step 2: Corresponding read operation and write '1' operation is performed

Step 3: Equivalent read operation is repeated twice and write '0' operation is also performed

Step 4: Read '0' operation is followed by write 1 operation

Step 5: Again Equivalent read operation is repeated twice and write '1' operation is also performed.

7 Fault Detection in 1T1R RRAM

Stuck-at 0 (SA0) faults are sensitized by write 1 operation and detected by read 1 operation. Here these faults are sensitized by R2, R3 in M2 or R5, R6 in M4. Stuck-at 1 (SA1) are sensitized by 'write 0 operations' and detected by 'read 0 operations'. Here these faults are sensitized by R1 in M1, R4 in M3 and detected by M2 and M4.

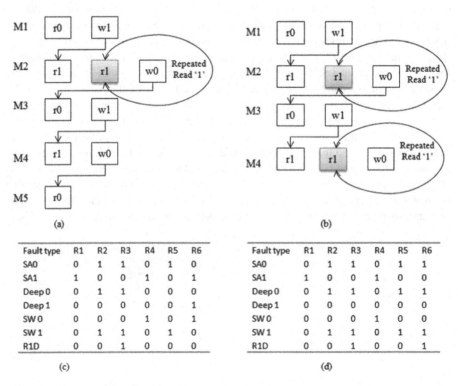

Fig. 4. (a) March C* test algorithm (b) Proposed March C_{2RR} algorithm (c) Fault dictionary of March C* test algorithm (d) Fault dictionary of Proposed March C_{2RR} algorithm

Deep-0 faults are initialized by two write 0 operations that are sensitized by write 1 operation and detected by read 1 operation, as the memristor of 1T1R cross-bar goes through a forming process, where all the memristors are started into LRS and all 1T1R cells are in logic 0 states (Fig. 4).

After the forming process, initial write 0 operations are carried and M1 initializes the faults in the cross-bar as the second write 0 operations. M2 sensitizes the faults then the faults are detected by R2, R3 in M2 or R5, R6 in M4. Deep-1 faults are initialized by two write 1 operation, be sensitized by write 0 operations and detected by read 0 operations. M4 initializes the faults as the first write 1 operation. M5 initializes the faults as the second w1. M5 also sensitizes the faults. Deep-1/0 faults consist the characteristics of both Deep-1 and Deep-0 faults. Hence, the test method of either Deep-1 or Deep-0 is also effective in detecting these faults. Slow Write 0 (SW0) faults are initialized by write 1 operations, sensitized by write 0 operations, and detected by read 0 operations. M2 or M5 initializes the faults. M3 sensitizes the faults and it is detected by R4 in M4. Slow Write 1 (SW1) faults are initialized by write 0 operations, be sensitized by write 1 operation and detected by read 1 operation. M1 or M3 initializes the faults. M2 or M4 sensitizes the faults. Then, the faults can be detected by R2, R3 in M2 or R5, R6 in M5. Read 1 Disturbance (R1D) fault occurs during the read operation the data stored in a particular cell will be flipped to logic 0 from logic 1. This kind of faults can be sensitized by read 1 operation and detected by another succession of read 1operation. In the proposed March C$_{2RR}$ algorithm R3, R6 in M3 and R5, R6 in M4 detects the R1D faults.

8   Experimental Result

An 8-Mb RRAM with eight 1-Mb macros and each macro has 1,024 rows and 1,024 columns (with 512K words and 8 bits in each word) have been designed. March C$_{2RR}$ test is applied to the first macro and the test follows. The test time for RRAM is formulated by the set time, Tset, reset time, Treset, and read time, Tread as well. As a result, the test time complexity of the proposed March C$_{2RR}$ test algorithm is 2N. Treset + 2N.Tset + 6N.Tread (N is a number of addresses). Though the complexity of March C$_{2RR}$ algorithm is higher than fast march algorithm it is less than march algorithm and march C-algorithm. March C$_{2RR}$ has linear complexity, which is scalable with respect to the memory size (Table 2).

Table 2. Complexity of various existing test algorithm and the proposed algorithm

Test algorithm	Complexity
March algorithm	2 N.Treset + 3N.Tset + 6N.Tread
Modified march algorithm	2N.Treset + 2N.Tset + 6N.Tread
Fast march algorithm	1N.Treset + 2N.Tset + 4N.Tread
March C-Algorithm	2N.Treset + 3N.Tset + 7N.Tread
Proposed March C$_{2RR}$	2N.Treset + 2N.Tset + 6N.Tread

9 Conclusion

An HfO$_2$ based 8 MB 1T1R RRAM is tested with various existing algorithms and the proposed march C$_{2RR}$ algorithm is designed to trace all the random faults and main focus in this work is directed to detect all the R1D faults which lead performance degradation. In the proposed march C$_{2RR}$ algorithm read operation is repeated twice in the second memory element and also in the fourth memory element (R3, R4 in M3 and R5, R6 in M4) 100% fault coverage is achieved by the proposed method that detects R1D faults and all the random faults effectively. In future, such proposed method of testing can be designed for all kinds of fault in RRAM.

References

1. Ielmini, D.: Resistive switching memories based on metal oxides: mechanisms, reliability, and scaling. Semicond. Sci. Technol. **31**(6), 063002 (2016)
2. Lv, H., et al.: Evolution of conductive filament and its impact on reliability issues in oxide-electrolyte based resistive random access memory. Sci. Rep. **5**, 7764 (2016)
3. Beckmann, K., Holt, J., Olin-Ammentorp, W., Alamgir, Z., Van Nostrand, J., Cady, N.C.: The effect of reactive ion etch (RIE) process conditions on ReRAM device performance. Semicond. Sci. Technol. **32**(9), 095013 (2017)
4. Chen, C.Y.: RRAM defect modeling and failure analysis based on march test and a novel squeeze-search scheme. IEEE Trans. Comput. **64**(1), 180–190 (2015)
5. Chen, Y.X., Li, J.F.: Fault modeling and testing of 1T1R memristor memories. In: 33rd VLSI Test Symposium (VTS), pp. 1–6. IEEE (2015)
6. Kannan, S., Rajendran, J., Karri, R., Sinanoglu, O.: Sneak-path testing of crossbar-based nonvolatile random access memories. IEEE Trans. Nanotechnol. **12**(3), 413–426 (2013)
7. Sribhuvaneshwari, H.: A novel feed forward back propagation technique for online resistive random access memory testing. Int. J. Pure Appl. Math. **118**(12), 13909–13915 (2018)
8. Mozaffari, S.N., Tragoudas, S., Haniotakis, T.: Fast march tests for defects in resistive memory. In: 2015 IEEE/ACM International Symposium on Nanoscale Architectures (NANOARCH), pp. 88–93. IEEE (2015)
9. The International Technology Roadmap for Semiconductors (2011). http://www.itrs.net/Links/2011ITRS/Home2011.htm
10. Strukov, D.B., Likharev, K.K.: Prospects for terabit-scale nanoelectronic memories. Nanotechnology **16**(1), 137–148 (2004)
11. Likharev, K.K.: Hybrid CMOS/nanoelectronic circuits: opportunities and challenges. J. Nanoelectron. Optoelectron. **3**(3), 203–230 (2008)
12. Mishra, M., Goldstein, S.C.: Defect tolerance at the end of the roadmap. In: Shukla, S.K., Bahar, R.I. (eds.) Nano, Quantum and Molecular Computing, pp. 73–108. Springer, Boston (2004). https://doi.org/10.1007/1-4020-8068-9_3
13. Chung, A., Deen, J., Lee, J.S., Meyyappan, M.: Nanoscale memory devices. Nanotechnology **21**(41), 412001 (2010)
14. Fujisaki, Y.: Current status of nonvolatile semiconductor memory technology. Jpn. J. Appl. Phys. **49**(10R), 100001 (2010)
15. Lai, Y.F., Chen, F., Zeng, Z.C., Lin, P., Cheng, S.Y., Yu, J.L.: Thermal stability and data retention of resistive random access memory with HfO x/ZnO double layers. Chin. Phys. B **26**(8), 087305 (2017)

16. Sun, P., et al.: Thermal crosstalk in 3-dimensional RRAM crossbar array. Sci. Rep. **5**, 13504 (2015)
17. Sun, W., Choi, S., Shin, H.: A new bias scheme for a low power consumption ReRAM crossbar array. Semicond. Sci. Technol. **31**(8), 085009 (2016)
18. Wang, X.F., Zhao, H.M., Yang, Y., Ren, T.L.: Graphene resistive random memory - the promising memory device in next generation. Chin. Phys. B **26**(3), 038501 (2017)
19. Xie, Y.: Emerging Memory Technologies Design, Architecture, and Applications. Springer, New York (2014). https://doi.org/10.1007/978-1-4419-9551-3
20. Waser, R., Aono, M.: Nanoionics-based resistive switching memories. Nat. Mater. **6**(11), 833–840 (2007)
21. Walczyk, C., et al.: Impact of temperature on the resistive switching behavior of embedded HfO$_2$-based RRAM devices. IEEE Trans. Electron Devices **58**(9), 3124–3131 (2011)
22. Zangeneh, M., Joshi, A.: Design and optimization of nonvolatile multibit 1T1R resistive RAM. IEEE Trans. Very Large Scale Integr. (VLSI) Syst. **22**(8), 1815–1828 (2014)
23. Zhang, K.: Embedded Memories for Nano-Scale VLSIs, 1st edn. Springer, New York (2009). https://doi.org/10.1007/978-0-387-88497-4
24. Micheloni, R., Campardo, G., Olivo, P.: Memories in Wireless Systems, 1st edn. Springer, Heidelberg (2008). https://doi.org/10.1007/978-3-540-79078-5
25. Mistry, K., et al.: A 45nm logic technology with high-k+ metal gate transistors, strained silicon, 9 Cu interconnect layers, 193nm dry patterning, and 100% Pb-free packaging. In: Electron Devices Meeting, IEDM 2007, pp. 247–250. IEEE (2007)

Quantum Computing and NoC

A Heuristic Qubit Placement Strategy for Nearest Neighbor Realization in 2D Architecture

Anirban Bhattacharjee, Chandan Bandyopadhyay$^{(\boxtimes)}$,
Laxmidhar Biswal, and Hafizur Rahaman

Indian Institute of Engineering Science and Technology, Shibpur,
Howrah 711103, West Bengal, India
anirbanbhattacharjee330@gmail.com,
chandanb.iiest@gmail.com, laxmidhar.cvrce@gmail.com,
rahaman_h@yahoo.co.in

Abstract. Recently, quantum computing has received massive attention of the researchers due to the advantages it offers in solving some problems efficiently compared to conventional computing. But there are several design challenges that need to be satisfied for various quantum technologies to perform reliable quantum operation. One such essential requirement demands to maintain the neighborhood organization of the operating qubits, referred to as the nearest neighbor (NN) constraint. This can be settled through insertion of SWAP gates which helps to synthesize a NN-compliant design by exchanging the positions of the qubits. Consequently, the cost overhead of the circuit enhances due to SWAP gate insertion as the number of gates in the circuit increases, thereby exploitation of various approaches to address this issue has turned out to be essential of late.

In this regard, here we have introduced an improved heuristic design approach for the synthesis of a two dimensional NN-compliant circuit with reduced cost overhead. The approach has been executed in three phases of qubit selection, qubit placement and SWAP gate insertion. Initially, the qubits have been chosen for placement based on some cost metric estimation and then organized them on the grid locations in a specific order in the second phase. Lastly, SWAP gate insertion phase has been exercised to make qubits adjacent. It has been observed that our method has performed comparatively better than the previous works after carrying out experimental evaluations over a wide range of benchmark specifications.

Keywords: Quantum circuit · Quantum gates · Nearest neighbor ·
SWAP gate · 2D architecture

1 Introduction

Quantum computing has made a tremendous landmark in the computing paradigm because of its capability of solving some specific problems in polynomial time. Some of the applications that have turned out to be beneficial for quantum computation are

© Springer Nature Singapore Pte Ltd. 2019
S. Rajaram et al. (Eds.): VDAT 2018, CCIS 892, pp. 593–605, 2019.
https://doi.org/10.1007/978-981-13-5950-7_49

factorization in RSA cryptosystem [1], database search [2], discrete logarithm etc. over conventional computation. Subsequently, a massive interest has been generated among the researchers for the development of a small scale quantum computer in the last decade. In this conjecture, design of quantum algorithms for the practical realization of quantum computer in terms of quantum circuits has turned out to be significant. Quantum circuits manipulate quantum information represented in the form of qubits than as bits used in the conventional computing paradigm. Qubits are similar to bits except that it can also exist in multiple states that can be considered as the linear combination of the basis states. In quantum circuit, a sequence of quantum gates basically operates on the qubits and subsequently transforms it into a different state during quantum information processing. It has been witnessed through experimental observations that the qubits are susceptible to changes due to environmental disturbances or noises that might result in computational errors. In order to overcome this issue, the interactions between the interacting qubits should be made adjacent so as to ensure the computational accuracy. This has been considered as the necessary criteria for the synthesis of several quantum technologies like ion trap [3], nuclear magnetic resonance [4], quantum dots [5] and superconducting qubits [6]. In order to bring the interacting qubits close to each other, a standard way of applying SWAP gates in the original circuit has been followed to satisfy the design constraints for the quantum technologies. Basically, SWAP gate exchanges the states of the qubits rather than its magnitude to bring the non-adjacent qubits close to each other. Consequently, such an operation induces some circuit design issues in the form of increase in circuit depth and quantum cost of the resultant NN based circuit. As a result, optimizing the NN based design by using less number of SWAP gates has turned out an essential design challenge for the researchers. They have attempted to fulfil this design issue by exploiting several design methodologies as discussed next.

Several design strategies have been suggested for linear arrangement of qubits in 1D format, where they can communicate with at most two adjacent neighbours. In [7], the authors mapped the NN based design problem into a task assignment one and applied harmony based search technique to solve the equivalent problem. To obtain a better design, a unique technique based on 1D arrangement of qubits has been introduced in [8], which emphasized on using limited number of SWAP gates. By mapping the qubits on a lattice structure not only reduces the SWAP gate count but also the technique becomes feasible for large benchmarks that have been undertaken in the work [9]. In [10], an NN based design has been optimized by constructing an interaction graph for the corresponding problem and then subsequently optimized it by employing a look-ahead policy. A graph-partitioning based approach has been presented in [11] to realize an NN based circuit with reduced cost overhead. An improved NN based design has been synthesized by employing an efficient conversion technique is discussed in [12]. As heuristic approach does not provide an optimal solution, so an exact approach based on SAT solvers has been implemented by *Robert et al.* [13] to synthesize an optimal NN based design but consumed substantial amount of time to process large benchmark circuits. A much improved design compared to the optimal one can be achieved by transforming the circuit representation from 1D format to 2D structure. As the number of interacting neighbours rises from 2 to 4, has resulted in a better cost effective design. Several works pertaining to 2D representation has been declared of late.

To realize an improved NN based design compared to the linear based designs, a mixed integer programming approach for mapping the qubits on a grid has been reported in [14]. *Lye et al.* [15] exercised an exact search strategy to derive an optimal solution for small sized benchmarks as it was not applicable for larger benchmarks due to extensive computational cost. In [16], the authors presented a meta-heuristic approach for the realization of an efficient NN-compliant design. To obtain an improved and scalable design, a heuristic qubit placement scheme has been employed for mapping the qubits on a grid location based on the degree of interactions has been summarized in the work [17]. To optimize the NN design further, another heuristic approach based on look-ahead policy has been introduced by *Robert et al.* [18], where SWAP gates have been reduced extensively. For better placement of qubits in the grid structure, a priority based ordering strategy has been followed by the authors of [19]. In addition to 2D design synthesis, mapping of circuits in 3D configuration has been demonstrated in one of the recent works [19]. Although representation of circuits in 3D platform provides a better cost-effective design than in 2D format as the number of adjacent neighbours of qubits escalates to 6 but at the same time controlling of such qubit representation becomes a cumbersome problem compared to 2D orientation of qubits.

In this work, we have presented a design synthesis approach for 2D representation of any quantum circuit. The primary intention of the design strategy is to obtain a cost effective NN based design by reducing the SWAP gate count. In this conjecture, our design policy has been executed in three phases for the realization of a 2D NN-complaint circuit. We have conducted a comprehensive experimental analysis over a number of different benchmarks and the resulting observations are recorded in the result tables, which suggest that our strategy has performed reasonably well than the reported 2D works regarding NN based optimization of 2D quantum circuits.

The remaining portion of the paper has been organized as follows. Section 2 dis-cusses about the preliminaries of quantum computation and nearest neighbour criteria. Discussion of our design methodology and experimental evaluations has been pre-sented in Sects. 3 and 4 respectively. Finally, we conclude the paper in Sect. 5.

2 Background

A qubit represents the basic unit of information acted upon by a set of elementary quantum gates constituting a quantum circuit. These quantum information units can be found in either one of the basis states of $|0\rangle$, $|1\rangle$ or in other states which can be expressed as the combination of the basis states by means of a state vector as

$$|\varepsilon\rangle = \alpha|0\rangle + \beta|1\rangle \tag{1}$$

where α and β represents the probability amplitudes of the basis states $|0\rangle$ and $|1\rangle$ satisfying the condition $\alpha^2 + \beta^2 = 1$. To have a better interpretation about the concepts, we have introduced some fundamental terminologies related to quantum computing and nearest neighbor constraint.

Definition 1: *A quantum circuit consists of a set of elementary quantum gates that perform manipulation on qubits to implement a specific function.*

Generally, quantum gates from various quantum gate libraries are exercised to implement a quantum algorithm. Some of the most commonly used libraries are NCV, NCVW, Clifford +T group [20–23] for the logical representation of any specific function. However, in the present work we have restricted our investigation only on gate level representations from NCV library. Basically, the quantum gate operations can be represented as $2^n \times 2^n$ transformation matrices. These transformation matrices are all unitary in nature that operates on the states of the input qubits. Table 1 represents some of the basic quantum gates along with their corresponding symbolic representation as summarized below.

Table 1. Some basic quantum gates and their symbolic representations

Gates	Notation	Gates	Notation
NOT	⊕	Control led -V	● — V
CNOT	● ⊕		
V	V	Control led -V†	● — V†
V†	V†		

Despite, quantum circuits are used to realize the Boolean functions in their gate level representation but there are some physical constraints that need to be fulfilled for the realization of such circuits. One such major criterion is to accomplish the neighborhood arrangement of qubits to enable the so-called nearest neighbor property. This is considered as one of the essential design criteria for the synthesis of efficient quantum circuit representation. To address this design challenge, a solution of SWAP gate insertion (diagrammatically represented in Fig. 1) is being followed to attain the nearest neighbor property.

Definition 2: *The interaction distance between the positions of the control (c) and target (t) qubits of any 2-qubit gates (G) represents the nearest neighbor cost (NNC) and it can be expressed mathematically as $NNC_G = |c - t| + 1$, where NNC_G denotes the NNC of any 2-qubit gate.*

To determine the NNC for the entire circuit (NNC_C), an overall sum for all the 2-qubit gates in the given circuit (C) is computed. A quantum gate is said to satisfy the nearest neighbor constraint if it is either a 1-qubit gate or for 2-qubit gates the NNC, $NNC_G = 0$.

Definition 3: *SWAP gate is a 2-qubit gate that acts on qubits q_a, q_b and interchanges the states than values of these qubits. For instance it acts on qubits q_7, q_9 and transforms them from the state $(q_1, q_2, ..., q_7, q_8, q_9, ..., q_{20})$ to $(q_1, q_2, ..., q_9, q_8, q_7, ..., q_{20})$.*

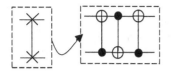

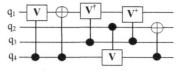

Fig. 1. SWAP gate representation   **Fig. 2(a).** Original circuit with NNC = 7

Example 1: *The circuit depicted in Fig. 2(a) does not satisfy the NN design criteria as the interaction distance of all the 2-qubit gates is having a positive numeral (interacting qubits are not placed adjacent). The corresponding NN based design of Fig. 2(a) has been obtained by adding SWAP gates before each of the non-adjacent gates as shown in Fig. 2(b). It is evident from Fig. 2(b) that 14 SWAP gates have been incorporated to accomplish the NN-compliant design of the circuit of Fig. 2(a).*

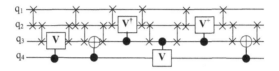

Fig. 2(b). NN based design of Fig. 2(a)

Though we have attained the equivalent NN design of the original circuit by means of SWAP insertion but still a room for improving the design further exists by projecting the entire circuit representation into 2D platform. Such higher dimensional representation facilitates to obtain a better design compared to 1D platform as less SWAP gates are required to derive the equivalent NN design of the given circuit.

A quantum circuit can be projected into a 2D format by organizing the qubits on a grid structure rather than organizing in a linear fashion. In way, the communication between the neighbors in such a representation enhances due to higher number of adjacent neighbors results in a lesser use of SWAP gates. Several possible 2D configurations exist in which the qubits can be mapped on the grid structure. Lets consider the circuit of Fig. 2(a) where the qubits are arranged linearly but several choices exists to represent the corresponding circuit in 2D format is represented in Fig. 3. Different configurations may influence the neighborhood organization of the qubits that in turn affects the nearest neighbor criteria.

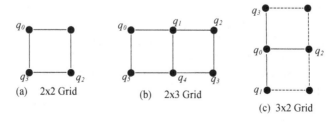

Fig. 3. Possible grid configurations for qubit mapping in 2D layout

The circuit in Fig. 2(a) has been transformed into a 2D structure by positioning the qubits in a 2 × 2 grid structure as depicted in Fig. 4(a) and the corresponding NN based design is shown in Fig. 4(b). We observe that only a single SWAP gate is required to obtain the NN design in 2D platform compared to 14 SWAP gates needed for the same circuit in 1D representation.

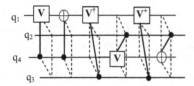

Fig. 4(a). Quantum circuit of Fig. 2 (a) is represented in 2D layout

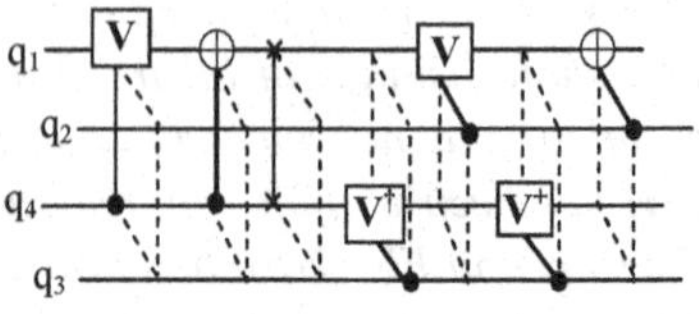

Fig. 4(b). 2D NN-compliant realization of Fig. 4(a)

3 Proposed Technique

Here, we have discussed about our proposed approach exercised for the purpose of designing of NN-compliant quantum circuit in 2D configuration. In order to attain the NN-compliant nature of any given circuit, the method initially arranges the qubits in the grid locations and then finally applies SWAP gates to bring any two non-neighboring interacting qubits operating over a quantum gate close to each other. In this context, we have implemented a qubit selection and placement strategies followed by SWAP gate insertion method to achieve the NN-compliant design of a given circuit are described next.

3.1 Qubit Selection Approach

In the present section, we have applied a heuristic technique that determines the sequence in which the qubits are preferred for placement in the grid location. In this regard, we have performed a number of calculations to derive the order in which the qubits are to be placed in a grid structure. Initially, we have estimated the time interval of interactions for each qubit by estimating the difference between the start and end time instants and recorded the same in a time span table (see Table 2) for the given circuit (see Fig. 5). From the time span table, we have computed the cost impact table (see Table 3) in which the cost factor of each qubit over their respective time intervals (obtained from the time span table) has been determined. In other words, the total nearest neighbor costs contributed by each qubit has been estimated. For instance, qubit q_1 interacts at the first, fourth, sixth and seventh time units of the given circuit (see Fig. 5) and contributes a cost of 2, 1, 1 and 2 (Total cost = 2 + 1 + 1 + 2 = 6) at the respective gate positions. Finally, the cost impact table has been sorted in a descending order based upon the cost factors and stored in a qubit order table (see Table 4) that determines the order in which the qubits are to be selected for placement in a 2D grid. It has been observed that the qubits q_1, q_4 have same cost factor but q_1 has been given higher priority for selection over q_4 (see Table 4) as q_1 has the least time interval compared to the one of q_4. Therefore, q_1 has been placed before q_4 in the qubit order table.

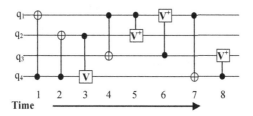

Fig. 5. Quantum circuit

Table 2. Time span table

Qubits	Start time	End time	Time interval
q_1	1	7	6
q_2	2	5	3
q_3	4	8	4
q_4	1	8	7

Table 3. Cost impact table

Qubits	Time interval	Cost factor
q_1	6	6
q_2	3	2
q_3	4	2
q_4	7	6

Table 4. Qubit order table

Qubits	Time interval	Cost factor
q_1	6	6
q_4	7	6
q_2	3	2
q_3	4	2

3.2   Qubit Placement Technique

In this phase, a qubit placement strategy has been executed after determining the order in which the qubits are to be arranged in a grid structure obtained in the previous phase. In way, the placement strategy organizes the qubits in a grid in the order in which they appear in the qubit order table. After obtaining the qubit order table, the placement strategy places the highest priority qubit in the centre of the grid. Then the rest of the qubits are selected from the order table and placed them around the location of the highest priority qubit by following the order viz. right, top, left, bottom depending upon the availability of space as explained in Algorithm 1. In our case, the qubit q_1 has been chosen for placement in a 2D grid as it is having the highest priority for selection compared to other qubits (see Table 4) and placed it in the centre of the grid (see Fig. 6 (a)). Then, the next qubit q_4 is chosen from Table 3 and placed it on the right of the location of q_1 since it is empty (see Fig. 6(b)). Now, we select the qubit appearing after q_4 viz. q_2 from the order table and checks whether the cell on the top of q_1 is available or not. Due to its availability, qubit q_2 has been allocated on the top of the location of q_1 (see Fig. 6(c)). Similarly, the last occurring qubit q_3 has been placed on the left of q_1 (see Fig. 6(d)).

After allocating all the qubits from the qubit order table on the grid locations, finally SWAP gates are incorporated to bring the positions of any two interacting qubits close to each other to enable the nearest neighborhood property for the given circuit is illustrated next.

600 A. Bhattacharjee et al.

Fig. 6(a). Placing qubit q_1 in the center of the grid

Fig. 6(b). Placing qubit q_4 on the right of q_1

Fig. 6(c). Placing qubit q_2 on the top of q_1

Fig. 6(d). Placing qubit q_3 on the left of q_1

Algorithm 1 describes about the process of arrangement of qubits in a 2D grid by selecting qubits from the qubit order table.

Algorithm 1: qubit placement strategy
Input: qubit order table, OT
Output: qubits arranged in a grid, GD_{2D}
begin
  | **for** $((q_i \in OT))$ **do**
      if (q_i is the highest priority qubit) **then**
          $q_{high\_order} = q_i$;
          row_centre = $GD_{2D}/2$;
          column_centre = $GD_{2D}/2$;
      else
          row_num = *retrieve_row*(q_{high_order});
          column_num = *retrieve_column*(q_{high_order});
          if (GD_{2D}(row_num, column_num+1) is empty) **then**
            place the next qubit in GD_{2D}(row_num, column_num+1);
          else if (GD_{2D}(row_num-1, column_num) is empty) **then**
            place the next qubit in GD_{2D}(row_num-1, column_num);
          else if (GD_{2D}(row_num, column_num-1) is empty) **then**
            place the next qubit in GD_{2D}(row_num, column_num-1);
          else if (GD_{2D}(row_num+1, column_num) is empty) **then**
            place the next qubit in GD_{2D}(row_num+1, column_num);
          else
          place the next qubit close to the location of the highest priority qubit q_i in one of the empty locations;
          end if
      end if
  end for
  return GD_{2D};
end

3.3 SWAP Gate Insertion

Here, SWAP gates are being utilized to obtain the NN-compliant design for the quantum circuit represented in Fig. 5.

For this purpose, we have examined each individual gate in the circuit to investigate whether its operating qubits are placed adjacent or not and subsequently inserted SWAP gates to alter the positions of the qubits of the corresponding non-adjacent gate in such a manner so that its interacting qubits approach towards each other and finally becomes adjacent. We have considered the grid obtained in the previous phase (see Fig. 6(d)) as input of this phase and applied SWAP gates wherever we find any gate whose qubits are not adjacent by traversing the circuit from the left. The entire process of SWAP gate insertion for the circuit of Fig. 5 is represented in Fig. 7.

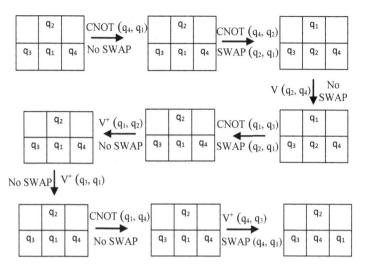

Fig. 7. SWAP gate insertion process

To understand the methodology more clearly, we have further illustrated the entire transformation process by considering a benchmark circuit as discussed next (Fig. 8(a), 8(b) and 8(c)).

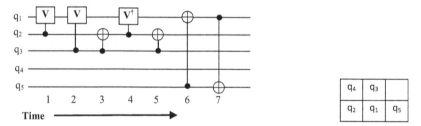

Fig. 8(a). Example benchmark (4gt11_84)

Fig. 8(b). Placement of qubits from qubit order table

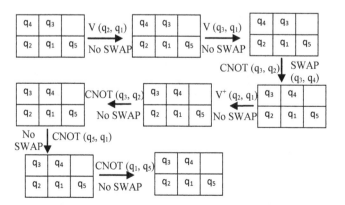

Fig. 8(c). SWAP gate insertion

Example 2: *Let's consider the NN-complaint transformation process of a benchmark circuit "4gt11_84" in this example. All the associated computational stages have also been summarized* (Tables 5, 6 and 7).

Table 5. Time span table

Qubits	Start time	End time	Time interval
q_1	1	7	6
q_2	1	5	4
q_3	2	5	3
q_4	-	-	-
q_5	6	7	1

Table 6. Cost impact table

Qubits	Time interval	Cost factor
q_1	6	7
q_2	4	0
q_3	3	1
q_4	-	-
q_5	1	6

Table 7. Qubit order table

Qubits	Time interval	Cost factor
q_1	6	7
q_5	1	6
q_3	3	1
q_2	4	0
q_4	-	-

4   Experimental Results

We have implemented the proposed method in C and executed on a system with configurations of intel5 processor, 3.30 GHz clock and 4 GB RAM. Experimental analysis has been carried out on various benchmark functions available on [24] as shown in Tables 8 and 9 respectively. Table 8 represents the experimental evaluations performed over small and medium size benchmarks (up to 16 qubits) while Table 9 represents the results carried out over large size benchmarks (more than 16 qubits).

Table 8. Improvements in SWAP gates over existing 2D works

Benchmarks	No. of qubits	Prop. work		Prev. work [17]	Joint scheme [18]	Iterative scheme [18]	Prev. work [14]	% Improv. over			
		Grid	SWAP count	SWAP count	SWAP count	SWAP count	SWAP count	[17]	[18]	[18]	[14]
4gt10-v1_81	5	2 × 3	12	15	15	22	16	20	20*	83.33*	25
4gt11_81	5	2 × 3	1	2	-	-	2	50*	-	-	50*
QFT7	7	3 × 3	13	14	13	22	18	7.14	0.0	40.90	27.77
QFT8	8	3 × 3	16	23	17	25	18	30.43	5.88	36	11.11
QFT9	9	3 × 3	24	36	22	27	34	33.33	−9.09	11.11	29.41
QFT10	10	4 × 3	36	51	37	43	53	29.41	2.70	16.27	32.07
aj-e11_165	5	3 × 3	14	22	16	37	24	36.36	12.5	62.16	41.66
3_17_13	3	2 × 2	5	3	5	8	6	−66.6	0.0	37.5	16.66
4gt5_75	5	3 × 3	8	10	-	-	8	20	-	-	0.0
mod5adder_128	6	3 × 3	31	36	33	45	41	13.88	6.06	31.11	24.39
mod8-10_177	6	3 × 3	34	43	-	-	45	20.93	-	-	24.44
hwb4_52	4	2 × 3	7	9	-	-	9	22.22	-	-	22.22
hwb5_55	5	3 × 3	30	49	37	64	45	38.77	18.91	53.12	33.33
hwb6_58	6	3 × 3	53	76	59	85	79	30.26	10.16	37.64	32.91

(*continued*)

Table 8. (*continued*)

Benchmarks	No. of qubits	Prop. work		Prev. work [17]	Joint scheme [18]	Iterative scheme [18]	Prev. work [14]	% Improv. over			
		Grid	SWAP count	SWAP count	SWAP count	SWAP count	SWAP count	[17]	[18]	[18]	[14]
alu-v4_36	5	2 × 3	9	11	-	-	10	18.18	-	-	10
4mod7-v0_95	5	3 × 3	10	14	-	-	13	28.57	-	-	23.07
rd53_135	7	3 × 3	26	40	30	47	39	35	13.33	44.68	33.33
ham7_104	7	3 × 3	32	45	37	53	48	28.88	13.51	39.62	33.33
rd73_140	10	4 × 3	31	43	-	-	37	27.90	-	-	16.21
rd84_142	15	5 × 3	56	62	-	-	54	9.67	-	-	−3.70
cnt3-5_180	16	3 × 6	63	84	-	-	69	25	-	-	8.69
Average improvement over SWAP gate count								*21.87*	*9.39*	*41.12*	*24.59*

Note: The values marked with * represents the improvement in best case over the related works.

Table 9. Results for large size benchmarks

Benchmarks	No. of qubits	Gate count	Grid	SWAP
ac_21_1	21	129	4 × 6	90
ac_21_2	21	67	6 × 4	52
ac_21_3	22	42	6 × 4	48
QFT_17	17	136	5 × 4	199
QFT_18`	18	153	5 × 4	238
QFT_19	19	171	5 × 4	258
hm_20	20	73	5 × 4	77
hm_21	21	79	4 × 6	70
hm_22	22	85	6 × 4	82

We have performed a detailed evaluation over SWAP gate count and compared the results with some of the related 2D works as represented in the result table. After analyzing the result table, we observe that our methodology organizes the qubits in an efficient manner such that less number of SWAP gates is used than the ones used in existing works.

5 Conclusion

Here, we have implemented a heuristic design strategy for arranging qubits in a 2D structure so as to obtain the NN based design of a given circuit. To this end, we have segmented the design strategy into three phases of qubit selection followed by qubit placement and lastly applying SWAP insertion technique. Such application of heuristic policy for determining a suitable qubit placement leads to faster execution. We have evaluated the SWAP gate count for different benchmark functions and witnessed significant improvements over the related works.

Though, we have achieved better results over the reported works, but these are far from optimal due to the application of heuristic based design policy thereby we would investigate better design policies so as to obtain optimal or near optimal results in the future.

References

1. Shor, P.W.: Polynomial-time algorithms for prime factorization and discrete logarithms on a quantum computer. SIAM J. Comput. **26**(5), 1484–1509 (1997)
2. Grover, L.K.: A fast quantum mechanical algorithm for database search. In: Symposium on the Theory of Computing, pp. 212–219 (1996)
3. Kielpinski, D., Monroe, C., Wineland, D.J.: Architecture for a largescale ion-trap quantum computer. Nature **417**(6890), 709–711 (2002)
4. Criger, B., Passante, G., Park, D., Laflamme, R.: Recent advances in nuclear magnetic resonance quantum information processing. Philos. Trans. R. Soc. Lond. A: Math. Phys. Eng. Sci. **370**(1976), 4620–4635 (2012)
5. Taylor, J., Petta, J., Johnson, A., Yacoby, A., Marcus, C., Lukin, M.: Relaxation, dephasing, and quantum control of electron spins in double quantum dots. Phys. Rev. B **76**(3), 035315 (2007)
6. Blais, A., et al.: Quantum information processing with circuit quantum electrodynamics. Phys. Rev. A **75**(3), 032329 (2007)
7. Alfailakawi, M., Alterkawi, L., Ahmad, I., Hamdan, S.: Line ordering of reversible circuits for linear nearest neighbor realization. Quant. Info. Proc. **12**(10), 3319–3339 (2013)
8. Saeedi, M., Wille, R., Drechsler, R.: Synthesis of quantum circuits for linear nearest neighbor architectures. Quant. Info. Proc. **10**(3), 355–377 (2011)
9. Perkowski, M., Lukac, M., Shah, D., Kameyama, M.: Synthesis of quantum circuits in linear nearest neighbor model using positive Davio lattices (2011)
10. Shafaei, A., Saeedi, M., Pedram, M.: Optimization of quantum circuits for interaction distance in linear nearest neighbor architectures. In: Design Automation Conference (2013)
11. Chakrabarti, A., Sur-Kolay, S., Chaudhury, A.: Linear nearest neighbour synthesis of reversible circuits by graph partitioning. arXiv preprint arXiv:1112.0564 (2011)
12. Hirata, Y., Nakanishi, M., Yamashita, S., Nakashima, Y.: An efficient conversion of quantum circuits to a linear nearest neighbor architecture. Quantum Info. Comput. **11**(1), 142–166 (2011)
13. Wille, R., Lye, A., Drechsler, R.: Exact reordering of circuit lines for nearest neighbour quantum architectures. IEEE Trans. CAD **33**(12), 1818–1831 (2014)
14. Shafaei, A., Saeedi, M., Pedram, M.: Qubit placement to minimize communication overhead in 2D quantum architectures. In: Proceedings of ASP Design Automation Conference, pp. 495–500, January 2014
15. Lye, A., Wille, R., Drechsler, R.: Determining the minimal number of swap gates for multi-dimensional nearest neighbor quantum circuits. In: Proceedings of ASP Design Automation Conference, pp. 178–183, January 2015
16. Alfailakawi, M.G., Ahmad, I., Hamdan, S.: Harmony-search algorithm for 2D nearest neighbor quantum circuits realization. Expert Syst. Appl. **61**, 16–27 (2016)
17. Shrivastwa, R., Datta, K., Sengupta, I.: Fast qubit placement in 2D architecture using nearest neighbour realization. In: IEEE International Symposium on Nanoelectronic and Information Systems, pp. 95–100, December 2015

18. Wille, R., Keszocze, O., Walter, M., Rohrs, P., Chattopadhyay, A., Drechsler, R.: Look-ahead schemes for nearest neighbor optimization of 1D and 2D quantum circuits. In: Proceedings of ASP Design Automation Conference, pp. 292–297, January 2016

19. Kole, A., Datta, K., Sengupta, I.: A new heuristic for N-dimensional nearest neighbour realization of a quantum circuit. In: IEEE Trans. Comput.-Aided Des. Integr. Circuits Syst. **12** (2017). https://doi.org/10.1109/tcad.2017.2693284

20. Barenco, A., et al.: Elementary gates for quantum computation. APS Phys. Rev. **52**, 3457–3467 (1995)

21. Sasanian, Z., Miller, D.Michael: Transforming MCT circuits to NCVW circuits. In: De Vos, A., Wille, R. (eds.) RC 2011. LNCS, vol. 7165, pp. 77–88. Springer, Heidelberg (2012). https://doi.org/10.1007/978-3-642-29517-1_7

22. Miller, D., Wille, R., Sasanian, Z.: Elementary quantum gate realizations for multiple-control Toffolli gates. In: Proceedings of International Symposium on Multiple-valued Logic, pp. 217–222 (2011)

23. Sasanian, Z., Wille, R., Miller, D.M.: Realizing reversible circuits using a new class of quantum gates. In: Proceedings of Design Automation Conference, pp. 36–41 (2012)

24. Wille, R., Große, D., Teuber, L., Dueck, G.W., Drechsler, R.: RevLib: an online resource for reversible functions and reversible circuits. In: International Symposium on Multi-Valued Logic, pp. 220–225 (2008). RevLib is available at http://www.revlib.org

Quantum Domain Design of Clifford+T-Based Bidirectional Barrel Shifter

Laxmidhar Biswal[✉], Anirban Bhattacharjee, Rakesh Das,
Gopinath Thirunavukarasu, and Hafizur Rahaman

Indian Institute of Engineering Science and Technology Shibpur,
Howrah 711103, India
laxmidhar.cvrce@gmail.com,
anirbanbhattacharjee330@gmail.com,
rakesh.0689@gmail.com, gopinath23t@gmail.com,
hafizur@vlsi.iiests.ac.in

Abstract. The prime objective behind the synthesis of quantum circuits in the field of quantum computing is to obtain so-called quantum supremacy where many intractable problems can be solved with high accuracy and fidelity for which no classical algorithm exists as of now. To suppress inherent noise, the fault tolerant circuit becomes an unavoidable feature. Fault tolerant quantum circuit demands high threshold quantum error correction code, such as surface code. The Clifford+T group with surface code provides universal gates to design quantum circuits.

On the other hand, many key computational operations like arithmetic and logical operation, address decoding and indexing requires shifting, rotating of data in unidirectional as well as bidirectional way, which can be achieved by using shift resistor with multiple cycles. However, the barrel shifter can be used to shift or rotate multiple bits in one cycle that leads to faster computation. In this conjecture, we have proposed a fault tolerant quantum barrel shifter using Clifford+T which will be relevant to quantum computing. Towards the end of this research paper, we have also evaluated some cost parameters like T-depth and T-count associated with the performance of quantum circuit.

Keywords: Barrel shifter · T-count · T-depth

1 Introduction

In digital circuit, the shifter has been used extensively for shifting and rotating of bits either from left to right; as well as in floating-point arithmetic. Basically, the shifter means shift register which shifts a bit of information per cycle. However, the barrel shifter [1] did all these tasks in unit cycle without including any sequential circuit. Due to faster computation and robust architecture the barrel shifter is embedded in DSP, Microprocessor and ALU. Even though the barrel shifter has several features but the trend to increase by overall performance of the circuit is going to cease beyond the atomic limit as no more further miniaturization of transistor is allowed in CPU [2] and results in enormous errors as quantum effect starts to dominate. So there are only two options available to design a high computational machine beyond atomic limit that

© Springer Nature Singapore Pte Ltd. 2019
S. Rajaram et al. (Eds.): VDAT 2018, CCIS 892, pp. 606–618, 2019.
https://doi.org/10.1007/978-981-13-5950-7_50

either to suppress the internal quantum effects or to accept quantum information processing.

Quantum computer has emerged as computational machine in alternation to classical computer for the ability to solve problems [3] like database search in polynomial time and discrete logarithm for which no classical algorithms exists which demonstrates quantum supremacy. Furthermore, the recent developments in the field of physical implementation over technologies like Ion trap [4], NMR [5], and quantum dot which aspires to contribute idea to achieve so-called quantum supremacy. Apart from these, zero power dissipation is another novel feature of quantum computing over classical computing for use of reversible logic [6]. But, the quantum computing has several design constraints, viz., fan-out and close loop circuits are not allowed. Quantum computing considers qubit rather than bits for computational purpose.

One of the major constraints is that all the quantum hardwires have high affinity towards noise which requires fault tolerant circuit. The fault tolerant property of the circuit can be achieved by using Quantum error correction code (QEC). In this regard, several QEC have been developed such as Steane code [7], source code [8], 2-D NN complaint promising Surface code [9]. It is fact that all the QEC has successful implementation of CNOT gates. However, the fault tolerant circuit requires transversal quantum gates in its design so that the each error can be handled independently within the encoded block of QEC which demand one qubit quantum gate. Several quantum gate libraries are there to design quantum circuits like NCV, NCVW [10], NCV$|1\rangle$ [14], Clifford+T [11].

The Clifford+T is a universal gate set of transversal quantum gates CNOT, H, T, S gates along with surface code which provides platform for the design of fault tolerant quantum circuit. Furthermore, the computational speed of the quantum circuit is another essential feature for the design architecture of high scalable quantum circuit. However, the speed of the Clifford+T based quantum circuit becomes significant lower due to the random presence of wide spectrum of high latency non-Clifford T gate which warrants reduction of T-depth of the circuit globally. The parallelism of T-gate is one way to reduce T-depth and can be achieved by using extra ancillary lines [12, 13]. The addition of ancillary not only increases the qubit size of the circuit but also increases the space and cost of the circuit.

There are several parameters associated with the performance of the quantum circuit, *viz.* quantum cost, delay, qubit size, garbage bits, and ancillary inputs which are needed to be optimized.

In this conjecture, we are going to design a Clifford+T based universal bidirectional quantum barrel shifters which will be compatible to QIP and will also show the distinguished property of fault tolerant.

1.1 Preliminaries

In preliminaries, we have introduced reversibility, reversible quantum circuit, fault tolerant, and barrel shifter.

Definition 1: A quantum circuit is a sequence of quantum gates used for quantum computation in quantum information theory and based on reversible logic known as reversible quantum circuit. The quantum circuit takes qubit as input and provides qubit as output instead of bit in classical computing.

a. **Qubit**: it is abbreviated from **Quantum Bit**. Like bit, the Qubit represents the state of information in quantum computing. Mathematically, it is represented by *ket* notation with superposition of two orthogonal basis states through complex probability amplitudes as $|\psi\rangle = a|0\rangle + b|1\rangle$, where $a, b \in \mathbb{C}$, $|a|^2 + |b|^2 = 1$.

b. **Quantum gate**: This is the basic building block of quantum circuit operating on a small number of qubits. Basically all quantum gates are unitary in nature and order of its transformation matrix is either 2×2 or 4×4. In Table 1, we have shown some basic elementary gates and their respective properties.

c. **Reversible gate and Reversible circuit**: Gate that has bijective mapping between the vectors of inputs and outputs are known as reversible gate. Reversible circuit is formed by combining reversible logic gates. It is very useful in the design of zero-power dissipated computation due to zero entropy. One drawback is that the reversible gate does not allow fan-in and fan-out. For better understanding, we have shown some reversible gate.

Feynman Gate (FE): The FG gate is also called as controlled-NOT gate (CNOT) which is a reversible gate with the mapping from input (A, B) to output (P = A, Q = A ⊕ B). The CNOT gate is used to address the fan-out problem as reversible circuit does not allow fan-out. The FE gate is shown in Fig. 1(a).

Toffoli Gate (TG): The reversible TG maps the input vector (A, B, C) into output vector (P = A, Q = B, R = C ⊕ AB). It is also called double controlled-NOT gate.

Fredkin Gate (FR): The mapping function between the input and output vector of **(FR)** are $(A, B, C) \leftrightarrow (P = A, Q = A' \cdot B + AC, R = A' \cdot C + AB)$. The FR gate is also called as controlled SWAP gate and the FR gate is shown in Fig. 1(c).

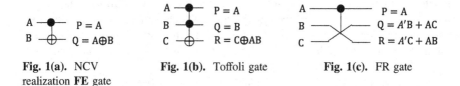

Fig. 1(a). NCV realization **FE** gate

Fig. 1(b). Toffoli gate

Fig. 1(c). FR gate

Clifford+T group: It is a universal set of transversal quantum gates (CNOT, H, S, T) used in the synthesis of quantum circuit. The Clifford+T group becomes de-facto quantum gate library in the field of synthesis of quantum circuit as it provides fault tolerant circuit Table 2.

The Clifford+T-based Toffoli gate presented in [13] is shown in Fig. 1(d).

Performance of the Quantum Circuit

There some well known parameters like quantum cost, T-count, T-depth, circuit depth, Garbage output, ancillary input are associated with the performance of quantum circuit.

Quantum Cost (QC): It is defined as the minimum number of elementary quantum gate used in the realization of a quantum circuit.

Table 1. Elementary quantum gates and properties

Type (symbol)	Matrix	Diagram	Properties
NOT (X)	$\begin{bmatrix} 0 & 1 \\ 1 & 0 \end{bmatrix}$	$\oplus$	$X\vert 0\rangle = \vert 1\rangle$ $X\vert 1\rangle = \vert 0\rangle$
CNOT (**CN**)	$\begin{bmatrix} 1 & 0 & 0 & 0 \\ 0 & 1 & 0 & 0 \\ 0 & 0 & 0 & 1 \\ 0 & 0 & 1 & 0 \end{bmatrix}$	$c \quad\bullet\quad c$ $t \quad\oplus\quad t\oplus c$	$t_{out} = t\oplus c$
Hadamard (**H**)	$\frac{1}{\sqrt{2}}\begin{bmatrix} 1 & 1 \\ 1 & -1 \end{bmatrix}$	$\boxed{C}$	$H\vert 0\rangle = \frac{1}{\sqrt{2}}(\vert 0\rangle + \vert 1\rangle)$ $H\vert 1\rangle = \frac{1}{\sqrt{2}}(\vert 0\rangle - \vert 1\rangle)$
Z-gate	$\begin{bmatrix} 1 & 0 \\ 0 & -1 \end{bmatrix}$	$\boxed{Z}$	$Z\vert 0\rangle = \vert 0\rangle$ $Z\vert 1\rangle = -\vert 1\rangle$
S-gate	$\begin{bmatrix} 1 & 0 \\ 0 & i \end{bmatrix}$	$\boxed{S}$	$S\vert 0\rangle = \vert 0\rangle$ $S\vert 1\rangle = i\vert 1\rangle$
S⁺-gate	$\begin{bmatrix} 1 & 0 \\ 0 & -i \end{bmatrix}$	$\boxed{S^+}$	$S^+\vert 0\rangle = \vert 0\rangle$ $S^+\vert 1\rangle = -i\vert 1\rangle$
T-gate	$\begin{bmatrix} 1 & 0 \\ 0 & e^{i\pi/4} \end{bmatrix}$	$\boxed{T}$	$T\vert 0\rangle = \vert 0\rangle$ $T\vert 1\rangle = e^{i\pi/4}\vert 1\rangle$
T+-gate	$\begin{bmatrix} 1 & 0 \\ 0 & e^{-i\pi/4} \end{bmatrix}$	$\boxed{T^+}$	$T+\vert 0\rangle = \vert 0\rangle$ $T+\vert 1\rangle = e^{-i\pi/4}\vert 1\rangle$

Table 2. Clifford+T-group representation CV/CV⁺

NCV Quantum gate library	Equivalent fault tolerant circuit using Clifford+T	NCV Quantum gate library	Equivalent fault tolerant circuit using Clifford+T
$\boxed{V}$	$\boxed{H}\ \boxed{T}\oplus\boxed{T^+}\oplus\boxed{H}$ with $\boxed{T}$ controls	$\boxed{V^+}$	$\boxed{H}\ \boxed{T^+}\oplus\boxed{T}\oplus\boxed{H}$ with $\boxed{T^+}$ controls
$\boxed{T}\bullet$ $\oplus$	$\bullet\ \boxed{T}$ $\oplus$	$\boxed{T}$ $\vert 0\rangle \text{———} \vert 0\rangle$	$\bullet\ \bullet$ $\vert 0\rangle\text{-}\oplus\boxed{T}\oplus\text{-}\vert 0\rangle$

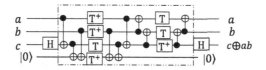

Fig. 1(d). Clifford+T representation of Fig. 1(b)

T-count: The minimum number of T-gate implemented in the optimized quantum circuit.

T-depth: The minimum number of T-cycle required in the execution of the quantum circuit.

Circuit Depth: The minimum number of clock cycles required to get faithful output with respect to input in quantum circuit.

Barrel Shifter:
Barrel shifter is a shift register which shifts/rotates the bits from the MSB end to LSB end and *vice-versa* for any desired number of positions in a single cycle. There are two kinds of barrel shifter according to the architecture namely array shifter and logarithmic shifter. Due to use of decoder circuit the array shifter is not used widely. The operations performed by the universal barrel shifter are as follows:

Left Logical Shift (LLS): This operation moves the position of each bit in register to the left by one. The vacant right most position (**LSB**) is filled with zero and the left most bit (**MSB**) is discarded.

Right Logical Shift (RLS): The RLS is a similar operation like LLS and moves the position of each bit to the right by one. The right most bit (**LSB**) is discarded and the vacant left most bit (**MSB**) is filled with zero.

Left Arithmetic Shift (LAS): The operation LAS moves the position of the each bit to the left by one like LLS. The vacant LSB is filled with zero and the most significant bit (MSB) is discarded. It is identical to Left Logical Shift.

Right Arithmetic Shift (RAS): The operation RAS moves the position of the each bit to the right by one like RLS. The vacant MSB is filled with sign bit instead of 0 and the least significant bit (LSB) is discarded. It is identical to Right Logical Shift.

Left Rotation (LR): In this operation, the position of each bit in the register moves to left by one bit. The vacant LSB is filled with previous MSB and the MSB is filled with its succeeding MSB.

Right Rotation (RR): In RR, the position of each bit moves by one into right. The MSB is filled by the previous LSB and the LSB is filled with its succeeding LSB.

For better comprehension, an illustration to explain shift and rotate operation by one bit is given in Fig. 1(e).

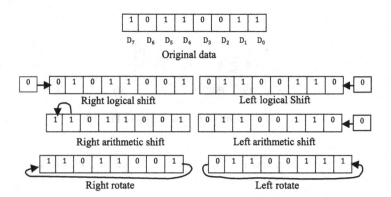

Fig. 1(e). Rotation of left/right, shifting of logical and arithmetic operations on 8-bit data i.e. D_7 to D_0

Logarithmic Barrel Shifter (n, k): A logarithmic barrel shifter is composed of 2:1 MUX in $k = \log_2(n)$ stages, where n is the input data length and k selector lines. The number of bit position to be shifted/rotated in either direction will be encoded into k- binary data bit and then sent into k-different stages of the shifter. The MSB of the encoded bit attached with the sequence MUX which shifts maximum number of positions and is always exponent of 2 at a time. For example in 32 bit shifter the MSB of encoded bit will connect to the sequence of MUXs which shifts 16 bits at a time. Unlike the array shifter, in Barrel shifter the input and output are separated by more than one gate.

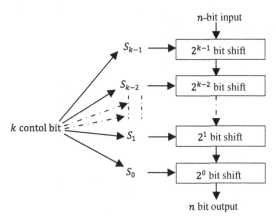

In this paper, we focus on the universal barrel shifter which perform bi-directional logical and arithmetic of shifting and rotating.

1.2 Previous Work and Contribution

In quantum mechanics, every linear observable Hamiltonian is a unitary operator which leads to reversibility for which reversible logic is used in the synthesis of quantum circuit. In this regard, several approaches have been proposed to design reversible barrel shifter.

In 2007, Kaivani et al. [15] designed barrel shifter in reversible logic using Fredkin gate as MUX to shift data bits and Feynman's gate (CNOT) to address fan-out problem. That each MUX generates one extra garbage output and each Feyman's gate need an extra ancillary input for copying operation which increases the number of garbage output as well as ancillary input that needs further optimization. In 2010, a generalized architecture had been proposed by Hashmi et al. [16] with reduced number of Feyn-man's gates. Both these two approaches are able to act as unidirectional barrel shifter and also performed rotation operation only, but it couldn't do arithmetic and logical shifting operations. Kotiyal et al. proposed reversible barrel shifter in the year of 2011 which performed both logical and arithmetic shift operation in bi-directional way. In 2011, Koushandeh et al. [17] proposed fault tolerant reversible barrel shifter using Feynman Double gate and Fredkin gate. Though this approach provides fault tolerant property in reversible logic but provides more number of garbage outputs in the design.

Anjaneyulu et al. [18] proposed a compact architecture for the design of bi-directional barrel shifter which can perform arithmetric, logical rotating as well as shifting operations by using four control bits *viz left*, *rot*, *sra*, and *sla*. In 2013, Shamsujjoha et al. [19] proposed a compact design of reversible barrel shifter where number of gate and garbage outputs has been minimized but able to act the arithmetic shifting as well as rotation operation in one direction only for which this approach treated as an incomplete one. In 2013, a fault tolerant design for barrel shifter had been proposed by Thapliyal et al. [20] using super conservative reversible gate which required excess number of Fredkin gates. In 2015, Sanjib et al. proposed [21] an optimized logarithmic barrel shifter in reversible logic which perform bidirectional arithmetic and logical shifting, including rotation operation and also shown the property of fault tolerance behavior in reversible logic.

Contribution: The approach proposed in [19, 20, and 21] provides fault tolerant reversible barrel shifter by using extra ancillary inputs being added to the circuit and that affects the performance of the circuit. However, the mapping of any circuit into Clifford + T group is fault tolerant due to transversal quantum gates which does not require any extra ancillary inputs. Here, we have extended the approach of [13] and proposed a fault tolerant quantum bi-directional barrel shifter (8,3) with reduced T-depth. We have used the approach in the literature [18] as an intermediate. Finally, the main goal of this work is to design a fault tolerant quantum bi-directional barrel shifter which will be compatible to a quantum computation.

The remainder of this paper has been organized as follows. Section 2 discusses about our design approach and the experimental results have been presented in Sect. 3. Finally, we conclude the paper in Sect. 4.

2 Proposed Technique

Here, we have discussed about our approach to design fault tolerant bi-directional barrel (n, k) shifter using Clifford+T mapping. In this design, we have taken the approach used in the design of bi-directional reversible barrel shifter introduced in the literature [18] and its final architecture for (8, 3) is depicted in Fig. 2(a) as in the literature [18]. That architecture performs all tasks by using four control bits *viz left*, *rot*, *sra*, and *sla*. In Table 3, the relation between control bit and task of the barrel shifter is illustrated.

Table 3. Operation performed by a (n, k) reversible bidirectional Barrel shifter

Operation performed	Control signal values			
Logical right shift	Left = 0	Rot = 0	Sra = 0	Sla = 0
Arithmetic right shift	Left = 0	Rot = 0	Sra = 1	Sla = 0
Rotate right	Left = 0	Rot = 1	Sra = 0	Sla = 0
Logical left shift	Left = 1	Rot = 0	Sra = 0	Sla = 0
Arithmetic left shift	Left = 1	Rot = 0	Sra = 0	Sla = 1
Rotate left	Left = 1	Rot = 1	Sra = 0	Sla = 0

The bi-directional Barrel shifter composes different parts:

1. Data Reversal Control Unit-I
2. Arithmetic Right Shift Control Unit
3. Shifter or Rotation Unit
4. Rotation Unit
5. Arithmetic Left Shift Control Unit
6. Data Reversal Control Unit II

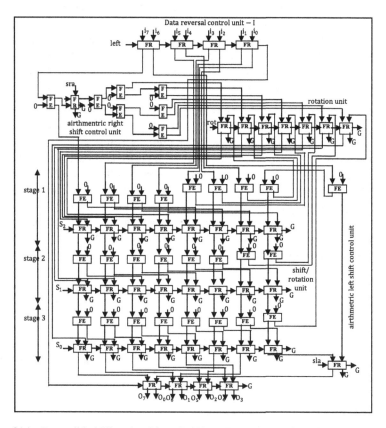

Fig. 2(a). Reversible bidirectional barrel shifter **FE**: Feynman Gate **FR**: Fredkin Gate

Further all these six units are composed of reversible Fredkin gate as MUXes and reversible Feyman gate for copying circuit. According to the quantum paradigm, if each small unit/block of a large quantum circuit exhibits property of fault tolerant then overall circuit enables the property of fault tolerant behavior. To design a fault tolerant bi-directional barrel shifter, we mapped each unit of that barrel shifter into Clifford+T group followed by cancellation of redundant gates. The entire mapping approach has been decomposed into two phases.

In phase 1: each unit of that bi-directional barrel shifter has been mapped into Clifford+T based quantum circuit so that each small unit will show the property of fault tolerant. In phase 2: replacement of each unit of the bi-directional barrel shifter by its equivalent Clifford+T representation.

2.1   Phase1: Mapping of Small Block of Reversible Circuit into Fault Tolerant Circuit

Each small block/unit of the bi-directional shifter is composed of Fredkin gate and Feynman gate only. The Clifford+T based circuit for each unit of bi-directional barrel shifter can be synthesized by replacing each Fredkin and Feynman gate with its equivalent Clifford+T circuit. So, prior to mapping of each small unit of that barrel shifter into the Clifford+T, here we have used two template functions that are the Clifford+T-based Fredkin gate and Feynman gate. As the Feynman gate does not contain any phase gate other than CNOT gate so there is hardly any change in the circuit while mapping process to its corresponding Clifford+T representation.

Template1 (Clifford+T-based Fredkin gate): The reversible architecture of the Fredkin gate is presented in Fig. 1(c) and its NCV based Fredkin gate is depicted in Fig. 2(b). The dotted portion of the Fig. 2(b) represents Toffoli gate. There was already three different kinds of architecture proposed by the researchers using the Table 2 with significant advantages i.e. no ancillary line with three T-depth in [22, Fig. 13], [23] four ancillary line with T-depth one in [12, Fig. 1], one ancillary line with T-depth two in [13, Fig. 3]. However, we used the approach as in the literature [13] even though low T-depth in [12] as the entire Fredkin gate in each unit block works concurrently in Fig. 2(a). So, there is hardly any chance that the same ancillary line will be used by other Fredkin gates also.

The resultant Clifford+T based circuit for 3 × 3 Fredkin gate is presented in Fig. 2(c).

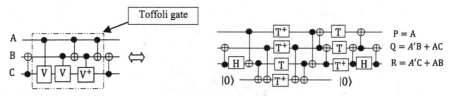

Fig. 2(b). NCV realization of FR gate

Fig. 2(c). Clifford+T circuit of Fig. 2(b)

Here, the Clifford+T mapping of the block diagram that presents FR gate in Fig. 2(a) is depicted below (Fig. 2d):

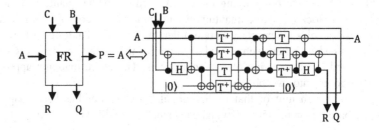

Fig. 2(d). Clifford+T circuit of **Template-1**

Template 2 (Clifford+T mapping of Feynman Gate): This template does not contain any phase gate other than one CNOT gate (Fig. 1(a)), hence, there is no change in the architecture of the Feynman gate. In other way we can say that Feynman gate remains unaltered in Clifford+T mapping and the Fig. 1(a) presents itself the Clifford+T architecture of own. The block diagram, which presents the Clifford+T representation of FE gate which is represented by Fig. 2(a), is depicted in Fig. 2(e):

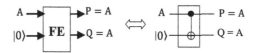

Fig. 2(e). Clifford+T circuit of **Template-2**

Clifford+T Mapping of Reversible Data Reversal Control Unit-I: This unit used for reversing the sequence of data where the MSB bit takes the position of LSB and *vice-versa*. It is used at the input and output to reverse incoming sequences as well as outgoing sequences. The **data reversal control unit** is controlled by control bit (*left*). When *left* = 1, barrel shifter performs the shift operation in the left direction. The reversal control unit-I did this task by using classical n/2 number of 2:1 MUX in classical computing and by 3×3 Fredkin gates. eg., 8-bits data sequence reversed by using four numbers of 3×3 Fredkin gates. The Clifford+T based circuit for data reverse control unit-I can be designed by replacing each FR and FE gate by its equivalent template as defined earlier.

Clifford+T Mapping of Reversible Arithmetic Right Shift Control Unit: The arithmetic right shift control unit controls the arithmetic right shift operation. This unit composed of a single Fredkin gate controlled by the control signal *sra*, and preserves the sign bit of input data. When the control signal *sra* = 1 then arithmetic right shift operation is performed, otherwise it simply passes the data to the next module. Its Clifford+T architecture can be well designed by replacing each FR and FE gate with its equivalent Clifford+T circuit as defined in templates.

Clifford+T Mapping of Reversible Shifter or Rotation Unit: The amount of shift operation that has to be performed is done by the shifter unit in the design of reversible bidirectional barrel shifter. This unit is controlled by the control signals S_{k-1}, S_1 and S_0. This unit can be divided into k-stages. Depending on the value of control signal S_i and $0 \leq i \leq k - 1$, the first, second and the third stages of this unit right shifts the input data by 2^2, 2^1 and 2^0 bits respectively. For 8-bit barrel shifter, the number of stages is three and designed using the chain of 8 Fredkin gates controlled by the control signals S_2, S_1, and S_0. The Feynman gates are used in the design to avoid the fan-out problem. The Clifford+T based reversible Shifter is designed by replacing Clifford+T based Fredkin gate.

Clifford+T Mapping of Reversible Rotation Unit: The rotation operation is controlled by the rotation unit. Like shift unit, the rotation unit consists of n-Fredkin gate. For 8-bit barrel shifter, the **Rotation Unit** is consist of chain of 8 Fredkin gates and controlled by the control signal *rot*, and performs the rotation operation of input data when *rot* = 1. Otherwise, it simply passes the data to the next module. Like the previous, Clifford+T circuit for rotation unit can be designed by simply replacing the all the FR and FE gate by its template.

Clifford+T Mapping of Reversible Arithmetic Left Shift Control Unit: Likewise in arithmetic right shift, the arithmetic left shift is designed by using single Fredkin gate. This control unit is controlled by the control signal *sla*. The barrel shifter performs the arithmetic left shift operation when *sla* = 1, else it simply passes the LSB of the shifter or rotation unit. Its Clifford+T architecture can be designed by replacing all FR and FE gate with its predefined template as like design of other blocks.

Clifford+T Mapping of Reversible Data Reversal Control Unit II: The data reversal control unit is controlled by the control signal left. If the value of control signal left is 1, this unit reverses its input data to generate a left shifted result else it simply passes the input data to its outputs. The data reversal control unit II reverses its 8 bit input which consists of 1 bit from the output of the arithmetic left shift control unit and 7 bits from the outputs of the shifter unit. The Clifford+T design of this unit is shown in Fig. 2(a) which is same as explained for data reversal control unit I.

2.2   Phase 2: Mapping of Reversible Bidirectional Universal Barrel Circuit into Clifford+T Group

From the phase1, it is observed that all six unit of bidirectional reversible barrel shifter composed of either FE or FR gate or both. The architecture of the bidirectional barrel shifter can be mapped into Clifford+T very easily by replacing the internal part of each unit (FR gate and FE gate) with its equivalent Clifford+T realization as defined in two Templates. For better appreciation of the entire design approach, we illustrate an example, where the design of universal Cliffort+T-based quantum barrel shifter (8, 3) has been explained.

Example 1: Initially a classical universal barrel shifter with order (8,3) has been considered for the design of fault tolerant universal reversible barrel shifter in quantum domain using Clifford+T group. The architecture has been introduced in reversible logic in [18] as an intermediate step and is depicted in Fig. 2(a) where the entire architecture is composed of six units and each unit presents either 2x2FE gate or 3x3FR gate. In phase 1 by all the FR and FE gates have been replaced by template-1 and template-2 respectively. In phase-2, the entire six units have been replaced by its equivalent Clifford+T representation. The final architecture can be illustrated as Fig. 2 (a) where each FE has been replaced with template 2 and FR gate is being replaced with template 1.

3   Experimental Result

We have implemented the proposed method in the design of universal bidirectional barrel shifter (8, 3) in quantum domain using Clifford+T. The resultant circuit not only shows the property of fault tolerant behavior but also exhibits the reversibility nature. Table 4 represents the experimental evaluations performance parameter that is associated with quantum circuit (T-count, T-depth, ancillary input) for higher order barrel shifter.

We have performed a detailed evaluation of performance (T-count, T-depth, ancillary input) over various approaches.

Table 4. Fault tolerant quantum bidirectional barrel shifter

Dimension of the barrel shifter (n, k)	Cost metrics obtained using technique [18] followed by [13]			Cost metrics obtained using technique [18] followed by [12]			Cost metrics obtained using technique [18] followed by [22]		
	T-count	T-depth	Number of ancillary line	T-count	T-depth	Number of ancillary line	T-count	T-depth	Number of ancillary line
(4, 2)	119	2	30	119	1	81	119	3	13
(8, 3)	287	2	74	287	1	197	287	3	33
(16, 4)	735	2	186	735	1	501	735	3	81
(32, 5)	1687	2	620	1687	1	1157	1687	3	193
(64, 6)	3805	2	994	3805	1	2629	3805	3	449
(n, k)	$\left[\sum_{m=0}^{k-1} 2^m + n*(k+1) + 2\right]*7$	2	$\sum_{m=0}^{k-1} 2^m + 2^k + 2n*(k+0.5) + 3$	$\left[\sum_{m=0}^{k-1} 2^m + n*(k+1) + 2\right]*7$	1	$4\sum_{m=0}^{k-1} 2^m + 2^k + 5n*(k+0.8) + 9$	$\left[\sum_{m=0}^{k-1} 2^m + n*(k+1) + 2\right]*7$	3	$2^k + n*k + 1$

4   Conclusion

In this paper, we have implemented a bidirectional universal barrel shifter in quantum domain. Our design approach deals with the tradeoff between T-depth and number ancillary line. Our approach also provides fault tolerant architecture with high performance in quantum domain for which none of the existing state-of-the-art methods [15–21] possess the features of bi-directionality, rotation capability and fault-tolerance in their designs and that will be compatible to quantum information processing for which our approach is emerging one.

References

1. Tharakan, G.M., Kang, S.M.: A new design of a fast barrel switch network. IEEE J. Solid-State Circuits 28(2), 217–221 (1992)
2. Moore, G.E.: Cramming more components onto integrated circuits. Electronics, 19 April 1965. Accessed 01 July 2016
3. Farhi, E., Harrow, A.W.: Quantum supremacy through the quantum approximate optimization algorithm. arXiv preprint arXiv:1602.07674 (2016)

4. Haffner, H., et al.: Scalable multiparticle entanglement of trapped ions. Nature **438**, 643–646 (2005)
5. Laforest, M., et al.: Using error correction to determine the noise model. Phys. Rev. A **75**(1), 133–137 (2007)
6. Bennett, C.H.: Logical reversibility of computation. IBM J. Res. Develop. **17**, 525 (1973)
7. Steane, A.: Quantum Computing and Error Correction. Decoherence and its implications in quantum computation and information transfer. In: Gonis, Turchi (eds.) pp. 284-298. IOS Press, Amsterdam (2001). quant-ph/0304016
8. Yoder, T.J., Kim, I.H.: The surface code with a twist. Quantum **1**, 2 (2017)
9. Fowler, A.G., Mariantoni, M., Martinis, J.M., Cleland, A.N.: Surface codes: towards practical large-scale quantum computation. Phys. Rev. A **86**, 032324 (2012)
10. Biswal, L., Bandyopadhyay, R., Wille, R., Drechsler, R., Rahaman, H.: Improving the realization of multiple-control Toffoli gates using the NCVW quantum gate library. In: 29th International Conference on VLSI Design (VLSID), pp. 573–574 (2016)
11. Buhrman, H., et al.: New limits on fault tolerant quantum computation. In: Proceedings of the 47th Annual IEEE Symposium on Foundations of Computer Science, pp. 411–419 (2006)
12. Selinger, P.: Quantum circuits of T-depth one. Phys. Rev. A **87** (2013). Article ID 042302
13. Amy, M., Maslov, D., Mosca, M.: Polynomial-time T-depth optimization of Clifford+T circuits via Matroid Partitioning. e-print arXiv: 1303.2042, March 2013
14. Sasanian, Z., Wille, R., Miller, D.M.: Realizing reversible circuits using a new class of quantum gates. In: Proceedings of Design Automation Conference, pp. 36–41 (2012)
15. Gorgin, S., Kaivani, A.: Reversible barrel shifters. In: Proceedings of 2007 International Conference on Computer Systems and Applications, Amman, May 2007, pp. 479–483 (2007)
16. Hashmi, I., Babu, H.: An efficient design of a reversible barrel shifter. In: 2010 23rd International Conference on VLSI Design, VLSID 2010, January 2010, pp. 93–98 2010
17. Koushandeh, E., Haghparast, M.: A beginning in the design of nanometric fault tolerant reversible barrel shifter. Aust. J. Basic Appl. Sci. **7**(9), 1110–1115 (2011)
18. Anjaneyulu, O., Pradeep, T., Reddy, K.: Design of an efficient reversible logic based bidirectional barrel shifter. Int. J. Electron. Signals Syst. **2**, 48–53 (2012)
19. Shamsujjoha, M., Babu, H.M.H., Jamal, L., Chowdhury, A.R.: Design of a fault tolerant reversible compact unidirectional barrel shifter. In International Conference on VLSI Design, pp. 103–108 (2013)
20. Thapliyal, H., Bhatt, A., Ranganathan, N.: A new CRL gate as super class of Fredkin gate to design reversible quantum circuits. In: International Midwest Symposium on Circuits and Systems, pp. 1067–1070 (2013)
21. Mitra, S.K., Chowdhury, A.R.: Optimized logarithmic barrel shifter in reversible logic synthesis. In: 28th International Conference on VLSI Design and 2015 14th International Conference on Embedded Systems (2015)
22. Amy, M., Maslov, D., Mosca, M., Roetteler, M.: A meet-in-the-middle algorithm for fast synthesis of depth-optimal quantum circuits. IEEE Trans. CAD Integr. Circuits Syst. **32**(6), 818–830 (2013)
23. Soeken, M., Miller, M., Drechsler, R.: On quantum circuits employing roots of the Pauli matrices. Phys. Rev. A **88**, 042322 (2013)

Source Hotspot Management in a Mesh Network on Chip

Ajay S[1], Satya Sai Krishna Mohan G[1], Shashank S Rao[1],
Sujay B Shaunak[1(✉)], Krutthika H K[1], Ananda Y R[2], and John Jose[2]

[1] Department of ECE, Dayananda Sagar College of Engineering, Bengaluru, India
ajaysrinivasa96@gmail.com, sai.krishna521@gmail.com,
shashankrao729@gmail.com, sujayshaunak@gmail.com,
krutthika.hk09@gmail.com
[2] MARS Lab, Department of CSE, Indian Institute of Technology Guwahati,
Guwahati, India
yrananda@gmail.com, johnjose@iitg.ac.in

Abstract. Network-on-Chip helps to accomplish greater throughput in multi-core chips. In a multi-core chip, each core parallelly processes multiple applications thereby increasing the overall processing capability of the chip. One of the major concern in this field is managing congestion on the network. There are many reasons for congestion, one of them is hotspots, which has been considered in this paper. The applications on a multi-core architecture that operates on large amount of data and computation may create hotspots. These hotspots introduce congestion on the network and increase the latency of packets that pass through them. Our solution to hotspots, identify the source hotspots and decrease inflow of packets into the hotspots, thereby reducing the network pressure where hotspots are present. The congestion control scheme is a threshold based approach that dynamically evaluates the presence of hotspots on the network and a routing algorithm to effectively route the packets away from the hotspots. Our experimental results show that the packets are routed away from the source hotspots and the packet latency of the network is effectively reduced.

Keywords: Congestion management · Odd-Even routing · Threshold

1 Introduction

The necessity for better performance is satisfied by increasing the number of processing cores on the chip. These multi-cores upon connecting on the conventional bus architecture lead to scalability issues. The time required for each core to be bus master and complete their transaction on the bus, would increase exponentially with increase in the number of cores. To tackle this issue and to simultaneously increase the number of cores on a chip, the concept of Network on Chip (NoC) was introduced [12]. There are many network topologies like mesh, torus, hypercube, octagon and fat-tree [13]. Using NoC architectures, the cores

S. Rajaram et al. (Eds.): VDAT 2018, CCIS 892, pp. 619–630, 2019.
https://doi.org/10.1007/978-981-13-5950-7_51

address cache misses and coherence transactions. Each router has a connection to one or many cores which routes the various packets of cache misses and coherency issues, concurrently. A router is a device that comprises of input/output ports along with buffers to hold packets and the logic used to route the packets through the network. The packets that are generated follow a certain path to reach its destination core through the network of routers. The routing algorithm takes into consideration the information present in the packet and determines the next router a packet has to hop to depending on the routing algorithm. In classical XY routing algorithm, the packet first travels in the X (Horizontal) direction, then travels in the Y (Vertical) direction.

A major concern with any algorithm is that, as the traffic on the network increases the latency of the packets also increase. Latency is the time taken for the traversal of the packet from its initialization, till it's retirement. There is also a high possibility that the packet can be deadlocked: the packet cannot make for progress from a router because it is unable to obtain a buffer space in the downstream router. There is also a problem of livelock of the packets: the packet is continuously hoping from router to router but making no progress towards the destination. To overcome livelocks, the implementation of priority-based routing shows promising results. To avoid deadlocks, different routing algorithms with turn restrictions like North-last or East-first, odd-even are proposed.

In a real-time multi-core environment many applications can run simultaneously on different processing cores. Depending on the application, the number of cache misses generated by a single core may vary. When there are very few of those packets generated, most routing algorithm will be able to handle these packets without any deadlocks or livelocks. But, when there is an increase in the number of packets generated, traffic on the network increases which creates congestion. Congestion can be characterized by burstiness, injection distribution and hop distance. Burstiness is characterized by the rate of packet generation from a specific processing core (High, Moderate or Low). Injection distribution is characterized by the localization of traffic (Hot-Spot or Evened-Out). Hop distance is characterized by the proximity of the destination to the source (Local or Global) [1].

Our novel research proposal is trying to address source hotspot traffic. In source hotspot traffic, one or more routers produce a higher number of packets in comparison to others routers in the network. This results in higher traffic through a certain router. If the packets are routed through these routers, the congestion increases causing higher latency of the packets. Unless the only path for a packet is through the hotspot, the packet should be routed to any of the other possible paths to reach its destination. Thus, the latency of the deflected packets is improved. To validate our work, we are simulating our algorithm on cycle accurate simulator BookSim2.0 [14]. The benchmark suite we are using to support our test results is SPEC CPU 2006 benchmark. In addition, hardware implementation has been done for the proposed algorithm by using Zedboard hardware FPGA kit and Xilinx Vivado 2016.2.

The paper is organized as follows. Section 2 discusses the related works. Section 3 describes the motivation. Section 4 discusses the proposed algorithm and implementation details. Section 5 gives the result and analysis. At the end, Sect. 6 concludes the work.

2 Related Works

Link et al. [3] proposes to dynamically reconfigure the hotspot inducing computations to different cores periodically so as to even-out the thermal impact of the hotspots on the chip. Though the dynamic shifting of the hotspot does even-out the temperature, this technique cannot be applied to multithreaded applications as the resources needed for the applications cannot be split off to another core [4].

Kakoulli et al. [7], proposed an Artificial Neural Network to predict where a hotspot might occur and using DOR-XY routing to resolve the hotspot. They claim that their algorithm works with an accuracy ranging from 65% to 92% with the overhead of the neural network not exceeding 5.06%. [6] provides an improvement to their previous paper [7] by reducing the network latency and enhancing the throughput by 81% for an overall hardware overhead of 11.4%.

Gupte et al. [8] proposed hot modules being swapped with cool modules to decrease the thermal effect on the chip. This method employs swapping of a hot module with any cool module available on the design under the consideration of only a single hotspot. [5] introduces Weighted Order Toggle which assigns weights to the links and sets the source-destination pairs as XY or YX routed to minimize network capacity for certain routing algorithms. They claim to balance the load on the links by repeated reconfiguration.

3 Motivation

Congestion that is encountered in single set turn restriction algorithms, such as north-last and east-first are non-existent in Odd-Even algorithm [11]. Due to the above reason we choose Odd-Even algorithm. Considering a single set turn restriction algorithm like north-last, when traffic increases on the network the number of packets converging at a single router to travel north as their last turn increases. This in turn increases the congestion along that column which affects the latency of the packets traversing through or along that column. Just with turn restrictions that are present in Odd-Even routing algorithm, the problem of deadlock is avoided.

Alfaraj et al. [9] proposed HOPE (HOtspot PrEvention) algorithm which throttles packets at the source if the packet is destined to a destination hotspot. The hotspot is measured by checking if the destination router is receiving more flits than a certain threshold and then flags it as a hotspot. In [2] the hotspot mitigation proposed addresses destination hotspots. The technique used to calculate if a router is a hotspot or not is to use a single counter per port (four counters per router) and increment the counter if the packet is destined for that router or not. This counter value is compared to a fixed value and the router is flagged as a hotspot if the value is greater than the fixed value. The drawback in these techniques is, if the injection rate of the packets increases, then the number of packets on the network and the packets destined to a single router would significantly increase, thereby always flagging the router as a hotspot. This would cause a major problem on the network.

We have come up with a new approach to address the hotspot problem. This provides motivation to find a solution effectively to avoid hotspots in the path of the packet and decrease the latency thereby decreasing the network latency.

4 Proposed Work

The conventional method we consider is minimal Odd-Even routing algorithm [10]. In this algorithm the packet is always routed to take a minimal path from source to destination, adhering to the turn restrictions. This algorithm does not take into account the presence of source hotspots when routing a packet. This causes the packets to pass through a hotspot, thereby increasing the latency of those packets unnecessarily. This problem can be solved by identifying the source hotspots and rerouting the packets away from the hotspots. These approaches form the basis of our algorithm.

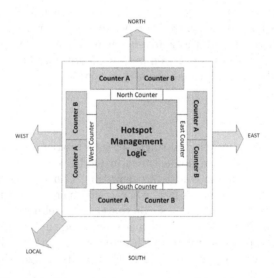

Fig. 1. Architectural changes proposed in the router.

Our simple approach proposes the usage of two counters for every port of each router as shown in Fig. 1, one to count the number of incoming packets originating from the neighboring router (Counter A) and the other to count the number of incoming packets that do not originate from the neighboring router (Counter B). We use 2 conditions to flag a router as a hotspot. If both the

---

Algorithm 1. Algorithm for HAV (Hotspot AVoidance)

Input: Current core (cur) (C_x, C_y), Destination core (dest) (D_x, D_y), Source core (src), incoming packets from neighboring cores, CW = cycle window, HT = hotspot threshold, RT = ratio threshold, C_A [E/W/N/S] = Counter A, C_B [E/W/N/S] = Counter B and inport = input port packet came through
Output: Destination core router for all the incoming packets
  if src is from one of the immediate neighbor routers **then**
    Increment C_A for (east/west/north/south) the respective port
  else
    Increment C_B for (east/west/north/south) the respective port
  end if
  Calculate possible output ports from Algorithm 2
  if (cur_cycle % CW == 0) **then**
    if $C_A \geq$ HT AND $(C_A : C_B) \geq$ RT **then**
      Flag that neighbour as hotspot
    end if
  end if
  if Number of output ports in *Outputs* > 1 AND hotspot is present **then**
    Mask the hotspot in *Outputs*
  end if

---

conditions are satisfied only then the router is flagged as a hotspot. Firstly, we use a fixed value (hotspot threshold; HT) to check if Counter A is greater than HT. Secondly, we use a ratio of Counter A to Counter B which if exceeds a fixed ratio (ratio threshold; RT), flag that router as hotspot.

In reference to Fig. 2a and b, the following situations have been considered and the routes taken in the proposed and conventional algorithm have been explained.

1. **Packet 1 (Src: 4, Dest: 23):** Follows $4 \rightarrow 5 \rightarrow 6 \rightarrow 7 \rightarrow 15 \rightarrow 23$ in the conventional method. As there is a hotspot in router 6 the proposed method avoids it by taking $4 \rightarrow 5 \rightarrow 13 \rightarrow 14 \rightarrow 15 \rightarrow 23$ which still has a minimal number of hops.
2. **Packet 2 (Src: 11, Dest: 8):** Follows $11 \rightarrow 10 \rightarrow 9 \rightarrow 8$ in the conventional method. As there is a hotspot in router 9 the proposed method avoids it by taking $11 \rightarrow 10 \rightarrow 2 \rightarrow 1 \rightarrow 0 \rightarrow 8$ which takes 2 more hops than the minimal number of hops.
3. **Packet 3 (Src: 18, Dest: 42):** Follows $18 \rightarrow 26 \rightarrow 34 \rightarrow 42$ in the conventional method. As there is a hotspot in router 34 the proposed method avoids it by taking $18 \rightarrow 26 \rightarrow 25 \rightarrow 33 \rightarrow 41 \rightarrow 42$ which takes 2 more hops than the minimal number of hops.
4. **Packet 4 (Src: 44, Dest: 47):** Follows $44 \rightarrow 45 \rightarrow 46 \rightarrow 47$ in the conventional method. As there is a hotspot in router 46 the proposed method avoids it by taking $44 \rightarrow 45 \rightarrow 37 \rightarrow 38 \rightarrow 39 \rightarrow 47$ which takes 2 more hops than the minimal number of hops.
5. **Packet 5 (Src: 56, Dest: 52):** Follows $56 \rightarrow 57 \rightarrow 58 \rightarrow 59 \rightarrow 51 \rightarrow 52$ in the conventional method. As there is a hotspot in router 58 the proposed method avoids it by taking $56 \rightarrow 57 \rightarrow 49 \rightarrow 50 \rightarrow 51 \rightarrow 52$ which still has a minimal number of hops.

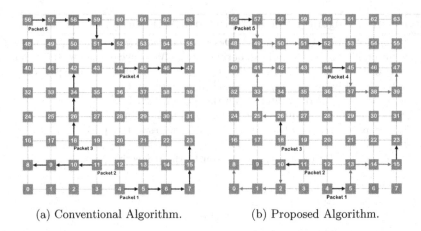

(a) Conventional Algorithm.   (b) Proposed Algorithm.

Fig. 2. Comparison of paths taken by proposed and conventional algorithm.

At low injection rates even if Counter A and Counter B is less in number and satisfies the ratio threshold (RT), the router is not flagged as hotspot due to not meeting with the hotspot threshold (HT) constraint, which means that the overall traffic on the network is not high enough for the router to become a hotspot. Whereas, at high injection rate, considering the hotspot threshold (HT) condition being satisfied, if the ratio of the counters is not met, which effectively tells us that the congestion on the network is evened-out, the router is not flagged as a hotspot. We observe the network for a fixed number of cycles which is defined as cycle window (CW) and at the end of every cycle window we evaluate the counters and flag routers as hotspots if necessary conditions are met. While checking for the hotspot, we normalize the counters so as to not lose the history of the packet count. The periodicity of this check and identification of hotspot depends on the number of cycles we monitor the network (cycle window; CW). The hotspot routers that were flagged remain in the same state till the next cycle window, when the conditions are checked again. Using this method, we can accurately identify source hotspots.

Utilizing Odd-Even turn restrictions we have modeled our algorithm to function minimally and actively avoid hotspots if present in the path of the packet. On encountering a hotspot, the algorithm makes the packet consider the non-minimal paths. Our routing algorithm calculates the possible output ports and assigns priority based on the minimality of the port with respect to the destination. By default the packet will take the minimal path following the Odd-Even turn restrictions. If the minimal path has a hotspot the packet takes an alternative path. In the case of only one available path, that single path is taken irrespective of a hotspot existing in that path or not. *Outputs* in Algorithm 2 is a set of the possible output ports a packet can take from a given router.

Algorithm 2. Algorithm for route calculation

---

if cur == dest **then**
  The current node is the destination node
else if $C_y == D_y$ **then**
  if not $(inport == west$ and $(C_x\%2) == 0)$ **then**
    Add (north/south) appropriately to the set of *Outputs*
  end if
  Add west to the set of *Outputs*
else if $C_x == D_x$ **then**
  Add (east/west) appropriately to the set of *Outputs*
  if not $((inport == west$ AND $(C_x\%2) == 0)$ OR $(D_y > C_y$ AND $(D_y\%2) == 0)$
  OR $(D_y < C_y$ AND $(C_y\%2) == 1)$ **then**
    Add (north/south) appropriately to the set of *Outputs*
  end if
else if $(D_x > C_x$ AND $D_y > C_y)$ **then**
  if not $((D_y - C_y) == 1$ AND $(C_y\%2) == 1)$ **then**
    Add east to the set of *Outputs*
  end if
  if not $(inport == west$ and $(C_x\%2) == 0)$ **then**
    Add north to the set of *Outputs*
  end if
  Add west to the set of *Outputs*
else if $(D_x > C_x$ AND $D_y < C_y)$ **then**
  if not $(D_y < C_y$ AND $(C_y\%2) == 1)$ **then**
    Add (north/south) appropriately to the set of *Outputs*
  end if
  Add west to the set of *Outputs*
else if $(D_x < C_x$ AND $D_y > C_y)$ **then**
  if not $((D_y - C_y) == 1$ AND $(C_y\%2) == 1)$ **then**
    Add east to the set of *Outputs*
  end if
  if not $(inport == west$ and $(C_x\%2) == 0)$ **then**
    Add south to the set of *Outputs*
  end if
  Add west to the set of *Outputs*
else if $(D_x < C_x$ AND $D_y < C_y)$ **then**
  if not $(D_y < C_y$ AND $(C_y\%2) == 1)$ **then**
    Add north to the set of *Outputs*
  end if
  if not $(C_y\%2) == 1)$ **then**
    Add south to the set of *Outputs*
  end if
  Add west to the set of *Outputs*
end if

Note: For a concise representation, the algorithm we have mentioned above does not include boundary conditions. The algorithm also does not include the logic for not sending a packet back through the same port it came in through. Both these conditions are considered and included in our simulation setup and results.

---

5   Experimental Work

5.1   Simulation Setup and Workload Details

We implement our proposed algorithm on BookSim 2.0, a cycle accurate Network on Chip simulator. This software is versatile in configuring routing algorithm, router functionality, and flow control. We have run our simulations on an 8 × 8 mesh NoC with Hotspot injection. Hotspot injection is the type of synthetic injection of packets. This injection selects a set of routers randomly, which is flagged as hotspot. These routers inject a large number of packets for a set duration of time. This process is repeated to simulate sustained source hotspot formation. We use a uniform random traffic pattern to decide a destination for the packet which has been created by hotspot injection. The conventional method we have considered is Odd-Even minimal routing algorithm [10].

We compared our method with a set of multi-programmed workloads. We have used Gem5 simulator [15] to model the 64 core (8 × 8 mesh) CMP setup with CPU cores, cache hierarchy, and coherence protocols. Each core contains an out-of-order x86 processing unit with 64 KB, dual ported, unified and private L1 cache. There is a shared L2 cache with a total size of 32 MB. The block size of L1 and L2 are 32 bytes and 64 bytes, respectively.

We built 25 multi-programmed workloads, each with 64 applications selected from the SPEC CPU 2006 benchmark suite on gem5 simulator. We classified these workloads into 5 mixes (WL1 to WL5) based on the type of network injection intensity. The L1 cache misses that generate NoC packets are fed into BookSim2.0 simulator to simulate the operations on the network.

In our setup WL1 consists of applications (*bwaves* and *bzip2*) which have less number of hotspot events. Workloads WL2 and WL3 contains applications with low hotspot events (*bzip2* and *gcc*) and applications with high number of hotspot events (*mcf* and *leslie3d*). Lastly, WL4 and WL5 comprises of applications with solely high hotspot events (*lbm*, *mcf*, *leslie3d* and *calculix*).

5.2   Analysis Under Synthetic Workloads

In Fig. 3 we can see the comparison of our algorithm to the conventional algorithm in BookSim2.0. We consider the predefined hotspot threshold (HT) as 16, 32 and 64 while keeping the ratio threshold (RT) constant at 2:1 in Fig. 3a. In Fig. 3b we consider the ratio threshold (RT) as 1:1, 2:1 and 4:1 while maintaining the predefined hotspot threshold (HT) value at 32. In Fig. 3a, the latency values for different hotspot thresholds are relatively similar. At higher injection rates, the latency for HT at 16 increases drastically due to false detection of hotspots. Similarly, the latency for HT at 64 increases by a small margin due to false hotspot identification. The threshold of 32 gives us the optimal result of lower latency. In Fig. 3b, the latency for RT at 2:1 is the highest while the RT at 1:1 and 4:1 give an optimal result.

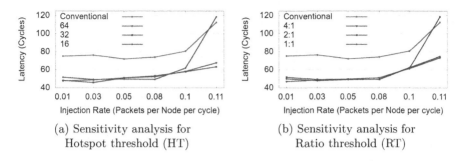

(a) Sensitivity analysis for
Hotspot threshold (HT)

(b) Sensitivity analysis for
Ratio threshold (RT)

Fig. 3. Sensitivity analysis

In both the scenarios of changing the ratio threshold and hotspot threshold value, our algorithm provides better average latency in all the conditions. The difference between latencies when the ratios and thresholds change, is negligible. But, it can be observed that different ratios and different thresholds perform better at different injection rates.

5.3   Analysis Under Real Workloads

Figure 4 shows the simulation results of our algorithm on SPEC CPU 2006 benchmark using BookSim2.0. Figure 4a shows the overall average packet latency. It can be seen that the average latency of our algorithm is lesser than the average latency of the conventional algorithm. Figure 4b shows the latency of flits that pass through the hotspot in the conventional algorithm and latency of flits that are deflected in the proposed algorithm. Figure 4c shows the average number of hops of the flits that are affected. Comparing Fig. 4b and c it is clear that while the latency of affected flits decreases, there is an increase in average number of hops. This is due to the fact that packets are taking a longer path to avoid the hotspots and since the hotspots are avoided the latency is decreased. Figure 4d shows the number of flits that are deflected in the proposed algorithm.

In workload 1 (WL1), the average latency of the conventional method and proposed method is similar and also less, in comparison with the other workloads. The number of hotspots in this workload is also less along with the injection rate. The latency of affected flits is lower in the proposed algorithm as the hotspots are detected and avoided. For the low number of flits that are on the network at any point in time, the hotspots are correctly being identified and avoided.

In workload 2 (WL2), the number of hotspots increase and in turn the number of flits deflected increases. The same pattern in workload 1 (WL1) can be seen in the latency of deflected flits. The latency of affected flits in the proposed algorithm is lesser since it does not pass through hotspots whereas the average hops of affected flits increases and non-minimal paths are taken occasionally.

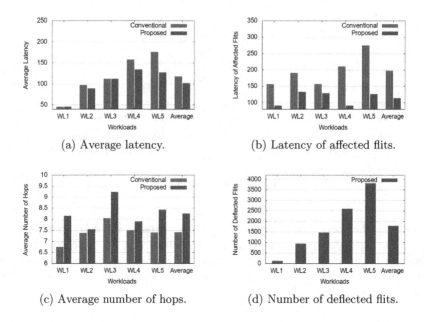

(a) Average latency.

(b) Latency of affected flits.

(c) Average number of hops.

(d) Number of deflected flits.

Fig. 4. Performance parameters for SPEC CPU 2006 benchmark.

In workload 3 (WL3), the average latency between conventional and proposed method is almost equal. This is due to the drastic increase in the average number of hops. Due to this, the latency of the affected flits shows minimal change as compared to other workloads.

In workload 4 and 5 (WL4 and WL5), the difference in latency of affected flits between conventional and proposed algorithm is high since our algorithm gives the most optimal result. The injection rate in these workloads allows the algorithm to run at its best as the number of false detection of hotspot and undetected hotspots is the least compared to other workloads.

5.4   Hardware Analysis

With improvement in latency and throughput, the need to estimate the area and power overheads is essential. We calculate the area and power of our algorithm by modelling a router on Zedboard FPGA development kit [16] using Xilinx Vivado 2016.2 [17]. The data and control flows of the proposed router design is as follows. First, the packets received in the input buffers are checked. We then calculate the possible outputs ports using our routing algorithm with Odd-Even turn restrictions (Algorithm 2). We apply our hotspot aware counting algorithm (Algorithm 1). We assign input priority to all the packets from all the different directions by choosing one output port. Finally, we assign the output priority of the packets based on age. We implement the above logic in Verilog, synthesize and run the implementation of the design on Xilinx simulator. We then generate the bitstream and run our design on the Zedboard FPGA. We generate the area and power reports of both our design and the conventional methodology. We compare the area and power overheads below (Table 1).

Table 1. Hardware implementation details

	Look Up Tables (LUTs)	Flip-Flops (FF)	Power Consumed (mW)
Conventional method	580	155	124
Proposed method	722	195	126

We obtain a clock cycle time of 10ns with 50% duty cycle for our algorithm. We have compared the area and power values with the minimal Odd-Even router. Our algorithm has an overhead of 1.61% in power, 11.82% in Look-Up Tables and 2.96% in Flip Flops. This is because of the additional counters and combinational logic used for detection and avoidance of hotspot routers.

6   Conclusion and Future Works

Our paper proposed a method to manage the congestion created by the source hotspots. We explained the need for two check parameters for effective hotspot detection. We further discussed the problems that are encountered using a single check parameter and how our two check parameters of fixed hotspot threshold and fixed ratio threshold actively combats them. The proposed algorithm yielded better latency performance with mostly same number of hops but at the expense of a slight area and power increase. The benchmark simulation results showed that the latency of the packets that pass through the hotspot are improved, along with the overall average latency.

Our design can be extended to accommodate a variable threshold value and variable ratio threshold for the counters to more effectively and adaptively recognize hotspots. The results of the proposed algorithm implementation depend highly on the location of the hotspot. The conventional method works similar to ours when the location of hotspots is not critical but fails when the location of the hotspots is critical. Odd-Even routing algorithm has a few conditions where the turn restrictions prevent the packets from avoiding the hotspot. Improvements can be made in respect of changing the routing algorithm to a better deadlock free algorithm with turn restrictions that favours hotspot avoidance.

Acknowledgement. This work is supported in part by a grant from DST Government of India, SERB-ECR scheme (project number ECR/2016/212).

References

1. Wang, C., Hu, W., Bagherzadeh, N.: Scalable load balancing congestion-aware network-on-chip router architecture. J. Comput. Syst. Sci. **79**(4), 421–439 (2013)
2. Reshma Raj, R.S., Das, A., Jose, J.: Implementation and analysis of hotspot mitigation in mesh NoCs by cost-effective deflection routing technique. In: IFIP/IEEE International Conference on Very Large Scale Integration (VLSI-SoC), Abu Dhabi, pp. 1–6 (2017)
3. Link, G.M., Vijaykrishnan, N.: Hotspot prevention through runtime reconfiguration in network-on-chip. In: Design, Automation and Test in Europe (DATE), pp. 648–649 (2005)
4. Huang, W., et al.: HotSpot: a compact thermal modeling methodology for early-stage VLSI design. IEEE Trans. Very Large Scale Integr. (VLSI) Syst. **14**(5), 501–513 (2006)
5. Gindin, R., et al.: NoC-based FPGA: architecture and routing. In: International Symposium on Networks-on-Chip (NOCS), pp. 253–264 (2007)
6. Kakoulli, E., et al.: HPRA: a pro-active hotspot-preventive high-performance routing algorithm for networks-on-chips. In: International Conference on Computer Design (ICCD), pp. 249–255 (2012)
7. Kakoulli, E., et al.: Intelligent hotspot prediction for network-on-chip based multicore systems. IEEE Trans. Comput.-Aided Des. Integr. Circuits Syst. **31**(3), 418–431 (2012)
8. Gupte, A., Jones, P.: Hotspot mitigation using dynamic partial reconfiguration for improved performance. In: International Conference on Reconfigurable Computing and FPGAs (ReConFig), pp. 89–94 (2009)
9. Alfaraj, N., et al.: HOPE: hotspot congestion control for Clos network on chip. In: International Symposium on Networks-on-Chip (NOCS), pp. 17–24 (2011)
10. Tang, M., Lin, X., Palesi, M.: The repetitive turn model for adaptive routing. IEEE Trans. Comput. **66**(1), 138–146 (2017)
11. Tsai, W.-C., Chu, K.-C., Hu, Y.-H., Chen, S.-J.: Non-minimal, turn-model based NoC routing. Microprocess. Microsyst. **37**(8, Part B), 899–914 (2013). ISSN 0141-9331
12. Benini, L., De Micheli, G.: Networks on chips: a new SoC paradigm. Computer **35**, 70–78 (2002)
13. Tatas, K., Siozios, K., Soudris, D., Jantsch, A.: Designing 2D and 3D Network on-Chip Architectures, 1st edn, p. 265. Springer, New York (2014). https://doi.org/10.1007/978-1-4614-4274-5
14. Jiang, N., et al.: A detailed and flexible cycle-accurate network-on-chip simulator. In: International Symposium on Performance Analysis of Systems and Software (ISPASS), pp. 86–96 (2013)
15. Binkert, N., et al.: The gem5 simulator. ACM SIGARCH Comput. Arch. News **39**(2), 1 (2011)
16. Zedboard.org Zedboard. http://www.zedboard.org/product/zedboard
17. Xilinx.com Xilinx. http://www.xilinx.com/products/design-tools/vivado

An Energy-Efficient Core Mapping Algorithm on Network on Chip (NoC)

B. Naresh Kumar Reddy$^{(\boxtimes)}$ and Sireesha

Intel Technology India Pvt Ltd., Bangalore, India
naresh.nitg@gmail.com

Abstract. In Nano scale technology, Network on Chip (NoC) is recommended as a solution for increasing communication difficulties of System-on-Chip (SoC) design. Network-on-Chip (NoC) has better reliability and scalability compared to on-chip interconnects. An important phase in the NoC design with mesh based topologies requires core mapping for a given application. This paper proposes an energy efficient mapping algorithm (EMAP) that maps the cores onto the NoC under communication rate constraints to minimize the total communication energy. The EMAP algorithm has been applied and calculated for randomly generated benchmarks. Experimental results demonstrate that the EMAP algorithm can deal with large number of task graphs and significant saving communication energy when compared to existing algorithm. The proposed EMAP algorithm was simulated and verified on Kintex-7 (KC705) FPGA board. Which reduces hardware utilization and power consumption compared to existing mapping algorithms.

Keywords: System on Chip · MPSoC · Core · Network on Chip

1 Introduction

Semiconductor technology has advanced towards System on Chip (SoC), in which every one of the functions required a specific product, it is incorporated into a single chip [1]. SoC tools is capable of developing cycle while increasing the performance and usefulness. At the end of the day, previous processors memory and interfacing devices are separately. SoC based processors are reduce the complexity and cost [2].

Systems on Chip (SoC) are planned utilizing prior components, for example, processors, memory clusters and DSPs. These are cores. In these cores have communication problem because cores are not scalable in present technology, can be solved through concurrent communication and point to point communication using Network on Chip (NoC). It can be composed various ways, according to the system design [3]. A generic NoC architecture consist of several cores, Routers (R) and Network Interface (NI). The cores in NoC generally resembles the mesh, which is clearly depicted in Fig. 1. These cores can be homogeneous i.e. central processing unit, or heterogeneous i.e. audio-video cores, wireless transmitter and

© Springer Nature Singapore Pte Ltd. 2019
S. Rajaram et al. (Eds.): VDAT 2018, CCIS 892, pp. 631–640, 2019.
https://doi.org/10.1007/978-981-13-5950-7_52

receiver, etc. In NoC every core is linked with local router through Network Interface. In the similar fashion, every router is consequently associated with neighboring router, establishing a packet based NoC [4].

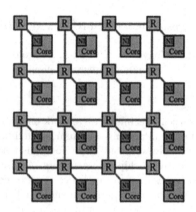

Fig. 1. NoC architecture

In this paper, we confine our contemplation to mesh topology and data transferred in the form of packets. Take note of that our work are not restricted to mesh topologies, but rather we adhere to this confinement to be more particular in this paper. Researchers have observed around communication energy issues and proposed different strategies to the optimal parallelization of the mapping. Our paper deals with the obtained issue of task allocation onto the parallel processors, by proposing an elective way to deal with above mentioned systems. We model energy efficient mapping (EMAP) algorithm, main goal of EMAP is saving communication energy.

The remaining part of this paper is organized as follows. Section 2 presented Literature review, Sect. 3 explained our Methodology and Mapping algorithm is elaborated with example in Sect. 4. Experimental results and hardware verification are presented in Sects. 5 and 6, followed by conclusion in Sect. 7.

2   Previous Work

We refer the reader to a few recent surveys on core mapping NoCs for pointers to modern research and improvement. Nectarios Koziris and et al., proposed Physical Mapping of Clustered Task Graphs onto Multiprocessor Architectures. Map the task graphs on nodes of the processor network with respect low complexity [5]. In [6] Srinivasan Murali and et al., presented NMAP algorithm, which maps the cores onto NoC architectures with respect to bandwidth and it is presented both single minimum-path routing and split traffic routing. It contains three phases, initial one is mapping generation, based on a which module has highest number of communication, next one is find shortest path using

Dijkstr's algorithm and finally iterative improvement, by changing pairs of modules and recomputing shortest paths. A simple technique for low energy mapping and routing in Network-on-Chip architectures. This problem projected in the occurrence of bandwidth and latency explained Krishnan Srinivasan and Karam Chatha [7]. In [8], described mapping algorithm which consequently maps a given set of property onto a NoC and builds a deadlock-free deterministic routing function for performance and minimize the communication energy.

Wein-Tsung Shen et al., proposed a well-organized binomial core mapping and optimization algorithm (BMAP) to reduce the hardware cost of on-chip network (OCN) infrastructure. BMAP complexity is O(N2log(N)) and provides more economical when compared to traditional mapping techniques and it is a fast and efficient technique when compared to NMAP [9]. Wei Hu et al., [10] discussed fast algorithm, which maps the cores onto a WK-Recursive NoC under Performance Constraints. A new energy efficient and bandwidth aware topological core mapping on NoC platform. Which is significant reduction in execution time presented Saurabh Agrawal et al., [11]. Nithin Michael et al., proposed map the applications on network on chip nodes (processors) with respect to communication cost. The idea is that minimizing communication cost translates to minimizing dynamic power and leads to better energy-efficiency [12]. They have done incredible work and gave an excellent guideline for this paper. The commitments of this paper are to propose mapping algorithm with respect to communication energy.

3   Methodology

We assume to have an application that should be mapped onto the NoC platform. Every application has multiple parallel tasks. By method for static analysis, it is probably regulate the data traded among cores. Which indicates how frequently a packet is sent between the source to destination in the network. Our problem is to map the cores onto the mesh based NoC Platform. This paper illustrates energy efficient mapping on NoC under communication rate constraints, which minimize the total communication energy. It is formalized in the next section.

3.1   Mathematical Formulation of the Mapping Problem

The communication rate between the vertices is denoted by the core graph:

Definition 1: An Application Core graph is a directed graph ACG(V, E), V represents Vertex $(\forall V_i \in V, \forall V_j \in V)$ E represents communication rate between the two vertices $\forall e_{ij} \in E, e_{ij}$ denoted by rate, signifies the communication rate from V_i to V_j [13,14].

The connectivity and communication of the NoC is represented by topology graph:

Definition 2: NoC preferred mesh topology, this topology graph can be uniquely described TG(N, D) is a directed graph. N representing a node or tile in the topology $\forall t_{xy} \in N, t_{xy}$ represents x^{th} row and y^{th} column of tile. D represents communication distance $\forall N_{ij} \in D$, N_{ij} denotes distance between node (N_i) and node (N_j) [15].

Problem 1: Given an Application Core Graph (V, E) and NoC Topology Graph (N, D); Find a mapping function
$\Omega : V \rightarrow N$ have $\forall V_i \in V$, $\forall V_j \in V$ and total communication energy.

   such that : $\forall V_i \in V$, $\forall N_i \in N$.
        $\text{map}(V_i) \in N$,
        $\forall V_i \neq \forall V_j \in V$, $\text{map}(V_i) \neq \text{map}(V_j)$
in definition 1
        $\forall e_{ij} \in E$
in definition 2
        $\forall N_{ij} \in D$ energy is calculated in terms of distance(hops) and communication rate using [16].

$$\text{WMD}(V_i, V_j) = e_{ij} \text{ X MD } (\text{MAP}(V_i), \text{ MAP}(V_j))$$

$$\text{MD } (\text{MAP}(V_i), \text{MAP}(V_j)) = |x_1 - x_2| + |y_1 - y_2|$$

here V_i parameters are (x_1, y_1) and V_j parameters are (x_2, y_2). Let $\text{map}(V_i) = (x_1, y_1)$ and $\text{map}(V_j) = (x_2, y_2)$. The parameters MD(MAP($V_i$), MAP($V_j$)) represents the Manhattan distance between cores. More preciously the resulting communication energy is

$$CE_{ij} = e_{ij} \text{ x } N_{ij}$$

N_{ij} denotes distance between node (N_i) and node (N_j). e_{ij} signifies the communication rate from V_i to V_j.

Total communication energy $= \sum_{\forall (i,j)} e_{ij} \text{ x } N_{ij}$

Problem 2: Given an Application Core Graph (V, E) and NoC Topology Graph (N, D); Find a mapping function and minimum communication energy. Which

$$CE = \sum_{\forall (i,j)} e_{ij} \text{ x } N_{ij}$$

such that : Using these definitions, the problem of mapping can be formulated as follows. Given an ACG and an NoC topology that satisfy

   size (ACG) $\leq$ size (NoC Topology)
   $\text{map}(V_i) \in N$,

Problem 1 clearly explained mapping and communication energy. For solution of minimum communication energy is

$$f(CE) = \left\{ \begin{array}{ll} \min CE & : \text{intial mapping} \\ \min \{ce: ce \in CE\} & : \text{changing mapping} \end{array} \right\}$$

4   EMAP Algorithm

In this section, we present the energy efficient mapping algorithm (EMAP), which have little complexity and gives ideal results. Which minimize the total communication energy. In proposed algorithm pseudo code as shown in Fig. 2. It explains map the first vertex, which has maximum communicate rate and select node which has maximum free neighbouring nodes. Map the vertex on nodes. Same procedure repeated for mapping of all vertices and it should be minimum communication energy, otherwise mappings with pairwise swapping of vertices are calculated to find the mapping with the minimum communication energy.

```
Mapping with minimum communication energy
(ACG(V, E), TG(N,D))
{
initialize(S(A,B), TG(N,D));
S(A,B) = map(ACG(V,E));
{
select vertex ∀V_i ∈ V
V_i should be max e_{ij}
{
select node ∀t_{xy} ∈ N
t_{xy} should be communicate maximum number of nodes.
}
map (V_i) →t_{xy}
}
map (V) → N
CE = ∑_{∀(i,j)} e_{ij} x N_{ij}
if(CE < min CE)
CE = min CE
return (Mapping with minimum communication energy)
}
```

Fig. 2. EMAP algorithm

Figure 3, shows an EMAP algorithm example. A simple Application core graph is shown in Fig. 3(a) and Mesh NoC graph for a 25-node is shown in Fig. 3(b). In our example 8 vertices mapped to the 25 nodes ($8 << 25$) EMAP is shown in Fig. 3(c) based on mapping algorithm. Selection of nodes based on maximum communication and communication energy.

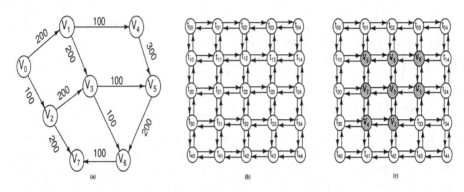

Fig. 3. Mapping of core graph onto NoC graph (a) an example core graph (b) NoC graph (c) Mapping

5   Evaluation

We simulated the our energy efficient core mapping algorithm (EMAP) using Noxim simulator [17] for synthetically generated random traffic patterns as well as for common benchmark patterns like MPEG4 decoder, MWD, Video Object Plane Decoder (VOPD) and Dual Screen Display (DSD) shown in Table 1. Figure 4, shows the communication energy for the applications with the same communication rate for all algorithms. As seen from the figure, MMAP algorithm perform well for all applications when compared to the other algorithms (NMAP [6], BMAP [9] and PMAP [5]).

In order to compare algorithm domain and optimization is shown in Table 2. NMAP algorithm is mainly based on iteration of vertices and path optimization, BMAP algorithm mainly based on greedy binomial merge, PMAP algorithm is

Table 1. Benchmarks

Benchmarks	# of tasks	# of flows	Mesh size
MPEG4	8	12	5 X 5
MWD	8	12	5 X 5
VOPD	12	16	5 X 5
DSD	6	10	5 X 5

Table 2. Characteristics of different algorithms and optimization algorithm

	NMAP [6]	BMAP [9]	PMAP [5]	EMAP
Algorithm	Intialization & iteration	Greedy binomial merge	NN- embedded algorithm	Efficient mapping & swapping
Optimization	Shortest path	Low cost	Low complexity	Low communication energy

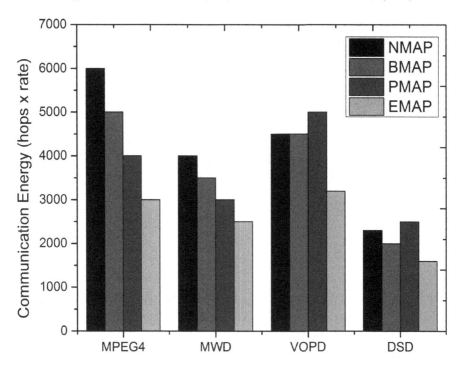

Fig. 4. Communication energy of different mappings for benchmarks (normalized)

mainly based on nodes of the processor network with respect to low complexity and EMAP algorithm efficient mapping by swapping nodes in the network. Finally we can see that EMAP algorithm gives better mapping with minimum communication energy.

6   FPGA Implementation and Verification Environment

The energy efficient mapping (EMAP) algorithm was simulated, synthesized and verified on Kintex 7 FPGA provided by Xilinx [18]. The 7 series FPGAs offered by Xilinx has 4 FPGA families that address a wide range of system requirements that spans from cost sensitive - small form factor requirements to ultra-high-end connectivity bandwidth for high volume applications, and signal processing architectures for high speed applications. Kintex 7 FPGA, which is a part of the cutting edge FPGA family from Xilinx has special features such as high-speed transceivers, clock management timers, and DSP blocks. Because of the advanced architecture and technology, Kintex 7 has a high frequency of operation. Moreover because of the smaller process technology, the power consumption is very less. The advantages of such a platform are not only providing logic resources to emulate real communications but also to carryout the performance evaluation in a short time. The main clock frequency of the platform is 66 MHz. Its maximum bandwidth can reach 62.94 MByte/s [19].

The energy efficient mapping (EMAP) algorithm was designed using Verilog hardware description language. The design was simulated on Vivado 2016.4 tool provided by the Xilinx [20].

Table 3. Hardware utilization of different mapping algorithms

Site type	Availble	NMAP [6]		BMAP [9]		PMAP [5]		EMAP	
		Used	Util (%)	Used	Util (%)	Used	Util (%)	Used	Util (%)
Slice	32340	3638	11.25	2263	7	1940	6	608	1.88
LUT as logic	157840	15150	9.6	9780	6.2	7570	4.8	2520	1.6
LUT as memory	51000	0	0	0	0	0	0	0	0
LUT as distributed RAM	–	0	–	0	–	0	–	0	–
LUT as shift register	–	0	–	0	–	0	–	0	–
LUT as flip-flop pairs	157840	8204	5.2	6002	3.8	4584	2.9	1421	0.9
fully used LUT- FF pairs	–	129	–	104	–	90	–	64	–

The proposed energy efficient mapping (EMAP) algorithm was implemented on Kintex 7 FPGA platform using Verilog HDL. Table 3 shows the hardware utilization for different mapping algorithms.

Table 4 shows the power utilization for EMAP on Kintex 7 FPGA family. It is seen that the proposed mapping shows reduced the power consumption when compared to the different mapping algorithms.

Table 4. Power consumption for existing and proposed mapping algorithm

Parameter	Power (mW) for NMAP	Power (mW) for BMAP	Power (mW) for PMAP	Power (mW) for EMAP
Total on chip power	157.202	151.9	94.6	64.8
Dynamic	144.7	142	86	52.7
Device static	4.2	3.8	2.9	1.6

7   Conclusion

In this paper presented an energy efficient core mapping algorithm onto the mesh NoC platform. We have accessible mapping algorithm that maps the cores onto the NoC under communication rate constraints to minimize the total communication energy. EMAP algorithm evaluated for random generated benchmarks. There is a significant saving communication energy when compared to existence algorithm. An experimentation environment was developed for simulating the proposed approach and the simulation was verified on FPGA board (Kintex-7 FPGA housed on KC705 evaluation kit).

References

1. Benini, L., De Micheli, G.: Networks on chips: a new SoC paradigm. IEEE Comput. **35**(1), 70–78 (2002)
2. DiTomaso, D., Morris, R., Kodi, A.K., Sarathy, A., Louri, A.: Extending the energy efficiency and performance with channel buffers, crossbars, and topology analysis for network on chips. IEEE Trans. Very Large Scale Integr. Syst. **21**(11), 2141–2154 (2013)
3. Naresh Kumar Reddy, B., Vasantha, M.H., Nithin Kumar, Y.B., Sharma, D.: Communication energy constrained spare core on NoC. In: 6th International Conference on Computing, Communication and Networking Technologies (ICCCNT), pp. 1–4 (2015)
4. Naresh Kumar Reddy, B., Vasantha, M.H., Nithin Kumar, Y.B., Sharma, D.: A fine grained position for modular core on NoC. In: IEEE International Conference on Computer, Communication and Control, pp. 1–4 (2015)
5. Koziris, N., Romesis, M., Tsanakas, P., Papakonstantinou, G.: An efficient algorithm for the physical mapping of clustered task graphs onto multiprocessor architectures. In: Proceedings 8th Euromicro Workshop on Parallel and Distributed Processing (2000)
6. Murali, S., De Micheli, G.: Bandwidth-constrained mapping of cores onto NoC architectures. In: Proceedings Design Automation and Test in Europe Conference and Exhibition (2004)
7. Srinivasan, K., Chatha, K.S.: A technique for low energy mapping and routing in network-on-chip architectures. In: International Symposium on Low Power Electronics and Design, pp. 387–392 (2005)
8. Rahmati, D., Murali, S., Benini, L., De Micheli, G., Sarbazi-Azad, H.: Computing accurate performance bounds for best effort networks-on-chip. IEEE Trans. Comput. **62**(3), 452–467 (2013)
9. Shen, W.-T., Chao, C.-H. Lien, Y.-K., Wu, A.-Y.: A new binomial mapping and optimization algorithm for reduce complexity mesh based on chip-networks. In: Proceedings of the First International Symposium on Networks-on-Chip (2007)
10. Hu, W., Du, C., Yan, L., Tianzhou, C.: A fast algorithm for energy-aware mapping of cores onto WK-recursive NoC under performance constraints. In: International Conference on High Performance Computing (HiPC) (2009)
11. Agrawal, S., Sant, D., Sharma, G.K.: An efficient energy- and bandwidth- aware mapping algorithm for regular NoC architectures. In: International Symposium on Networks-on-Chip (2010)
12. Michael, N., Wang, Y., Suh, G.E., Tang, A.: Quadrisection-based task mapping on many-core processors for energy-efficient on-chip communication. In: International Symposium on Networks-on-Chip (2013)
13. Beechu, N.K.R., Harishchandra, V.M., Balachandra, N.K.: High-performance and energy-efficient fault-tolerance core mapping in NoC. Sustain. Comput.: Inform. Syst. **16**, 1–10 (2017)
14. Beechu, N.K.R., et al.: An energy-efficient fault-aware core mapping in mesh-based network on chip systems. J. Netw. Comput. Appl. **105**, 79–87 (2018)
15. Beechu, N.K.R., et al.: Energy-aware and reliability-aware mapping for NoC-based architectures. Wirel. Pers. Commun. **100**(2), 213–225 (2017)
16. Reddy, B.N.K., Vasantha, M.H., Nithin Kumar, Y.B.: A Gracefully degrading and energy-efficient fault tolerant NoC using spare core. In: 2016 IEEE Computer Society Annual Symposium on VLSI (ISVLSI 2016), Pennsylvania, USA, pp. 146–151 (2016)

17. Noxim the NoC simulator. http://noxim.sourceforge.net/
18. http://www.xilinx.com/products/boards-and-kits/ek-k7-kc705-g.html
19. Beechu, N.K.R., et al.: System level fault-tolerance core mapping and FPGA-based verification of NoC. Microelectron. J. **70**, 16–26 (2017)
20. Beechu, N.K.R., et al.: Hardware implementation of fault tolerance NoC core mapping. Telecommun. Syst. **68**(4), 621–630 (2017)

Sensors and Interfaces

Fabrication and LBM-Modeling of Directional Fluid Transport on Low-Cost Electro-Osmotic Flow Device

T. Pravinraj$^{(\boxtimes)}$ and Rajendra Patrikar

Center for VLSI and Nanotechnology, Nagpur, Maharashtra 440010, India
pravinraj1711@gmail.com

Abstract. In this work, we have presented a low-cost fabrication and modeling of an electro-osmotic flow (EOF) device. The presented fabrication approach eliminates the need of expensive UV lithography and plasma setups. The polydimethylsiloxane (PDMS) microfluidic device for EOF is fabricated using simple printed circuit board (PCB) as a mold. The device is bonded with glass using adhesive bonding technology hence eliminates the need for plasma. The in-house low cost microfluidic characterization setup is used for experimental study. The obtained characteristics are modeled by the mesoscopic lattice Boltzmann method (LBM) in which the Poison Boltzmann equations is successfully coupled to capture the electrical double layer (EDL) physics. From the obtained results, it is shown that the directional transport of a bulk fluid can be achieved by EOF mechanism by suitably switching the electrodes. The experimental velocity characteristics show good agreement with the simulated results. Thus, easy coupling of LBM can be used as a tool to design and investigate such MEMS devices.

Keywords: Electro-osmotic flow · Microfluidics · PCB mold · Lattice Boltzmann method · Poison-Boltzmann equation

1 Introduction

Due to advancements in micro and nano engineering, the manipulation of fluids in micro and nano scale has now emerged as the interesting research problem. Controlling the smaller volume of fluid is preferable in many useful applications such as lab-on-chip (LOC) [1, 2]. Usually, the fluid is transported in the microchannel either by pressure driven flow, capillary forces, vibrational or electro kinetic forces. To pressure driven flow is the popular method to transport the fluid. But, it is not easy to achieve the precise control and often not a good option as it results in leaking and breaking. Electro-kinetic transport plays an important role in the microfluidics systems which can be used in variety of MEMS devices [3]. A controlled Electro-osmotic flow (EOF) can be produced by the application of external electric field. Unlike pressure driven flow, the electro-osmotic flow (EOF) is generated uniformly along the length of the micro channel as a plug-like flow [4]. So irrespective of their cross-sectional position in the micro-channel all of the molecules experience the same velocity component. Therefore, the electro-osmotic flow is being explored for various applications such as a micro-pumping device [5], micro-mixer, a micro-injector etc.

© Springer Nature Singapore Pte Ltd. 2019
S. Rajaram et al. (Eds.): VDAT 2018, CCIS 892, pp. 643–656, 2019.
https://doi.org/10.1007/978-981-13-5950-7_53

Generally, for fabrication of micro and nano devices, UV-lithography offers tremendous advantages like low-feature size, batch fabrication [6] etc. But the establishment and maintenance of such a setup demands higher resources. Moreover most clean room environment prevents the usage of materials other than CMOS compatible process [7]. As an alternative to the above case, printed circuit Board (PCB) based platform is being adopted as an emerging alternative [8]. Recently, polydimethylsiloxane (PDMS) [9] is evolved as a most preferable material for the fabrication of lab-on-a-chip (LOCs) devices due to its biocompatibility along with better optical and interesting surface properties. The PDMS channels can be formed by techniques such as replica molding, stamping, and other soft lithographic techniques [10]. In most of the case, PDMS-microchannels need to be tightly sealed. The bonding step usually is a time-consuming and fault-prone, requiring skill and careful control. Oxygen plasma enhanced bonding [11] is a popular solution for bonding PDMS channels with glass. But it is possible only within the clean room. Characterization of microfluidics device is a challenging one. Especially EOF devices require electrical, mechanical and optical characterization. Equipment which offers all above features are generally expensive and delicate. In this work, we focused on fabrication and characterization of PDMS based electro osmotic flow device using in house developed low cost microfluidics characterization system in a semi-clean room lab environment.

Usually, to model such a low dimension microfluidic problem, molecular dynamics (MD) simulation [12] is a straight forward approach. But it consumes enormous time in solving complex geometry and physics. So, it is not feasible for microfluidics problems. Recently a mesoscopic lattice Boltzmann method (LBM) is effectively proved alternative due to its tremendous advantages like massive parallelism and easy incorporation of multi physics [13, 14]. The lattice Boltzmann method (LBM) has proven successful in investigation of complex fluid flows, including multi-phase flow, particle suspension flow, binary mixtures, liquid crystals, blood flow, and microchannel and nano channel flows [15–17]. The method solves Boltzmann equation from scratch and allows the particles to move on discrete lattices. The mass and momentum are locally conserved by streaming and collision among particles. The objective of this work is to present a low-cost approach to fabricate an electro-osmotic flow device and model the electro-osmotic flow in a microfluidic device using LBM.

2 Theoretical Background

In general, even in the absence of chemical reactions, any surface that comes in direct contact with a polar solution will build a static surface charge along the wall. This is due to different chemical mechanisms, such as ionization of surface groups, specific ionic absorptions on the wall etc. [18–20]. This static surface charge will attract the solution ions that have the opposite charge. The ions of same charge as the wall will be repelled. This phenomenon also neutralizes the surface charge at wall. The region close to the wall where the wall surface charge is affecting the solution ions is called the electric double layer (EDL). EDL has two distinct regions: stern layer (a region containing immobile ions), and the diffuse layer. In stern layer the ions are firmly attracted to the wall hence they are immovable. But in diffuse layer, the ions have some mobility of motion, such as diffusion, while still being affected by the wall charge. The thickness of the EDL is confined by Debye length (k^{-1}) which can be approximated as the

$$k^{-1} = \left(\frac{\varepsilon k_b T}{2e^2 z_i^2 n_{i,\infty}} \right) \tag{1}$$

where ε is solution permittivity, k_b is Boltzmann constant, T is absolute temperature, e is the electron charge, z_i is the valence of the species i and $n_{i,\infty}$ is ionic concentration at natural state. Usually it is assumed that the ionic distribution for a certain species follows a Boltzmann distribution as given by

$$n_i = n_{i,\infty} \sinh\left(-\frac{z_i e \phi}{k_b T} \right) \tag{2}$$

where n_i is the ionic concentration of species and φ is the electrostatic potential distribution from the wall which can be determined by solving Poison's equation. Whenever an external electrical body force is applied tangentially to EDL, the mobile ions in the diffuse region of the EDL will move with a non uniform velocity distribution proportional to the Poison-Boltzmann profile in opposite direction across the EDL thickness. This movement of ions causes a plug like electro osmotic flow of a bulk fluid. The strength of EOF depends on the ionic concentration across EDL. Along with it, an electrophoretic flow of charged particles also developed in a system. This electrophoretic flow is the accumulation of net positive charged particles moving in the direction of EOF and net negative charged particle moved in the opposite direction along with non-charged particles. Usually, an average EOF velocity is expressed as

$$u_{eo} = \left(\frac{\varepsilon \tau}{\eta} \right) E_x \tag{3}$$

where τ is the zeta potential of EDL, η is the fluid viscosity and E_x is the electric flied applied across the length of the channel.

3 Experimental Details

3.1 Fabrication

An EOF microfluidic device is fabricated by mold replica process. Generally, a UV-lithography based transferred pattern on SU-8 will be used as a mold for fabrication of such devices. But we skipped the expensive UV-lithography step by using a simple PCB Cu-layer as a mold as shown in Fig. 1. But the limitation of this method is the higher feature size due to PCB technology. In our case the minimum width of the micro channel is 250 μm and depth is 70 μm which still can be exploited for many Bio-MEMS applications.

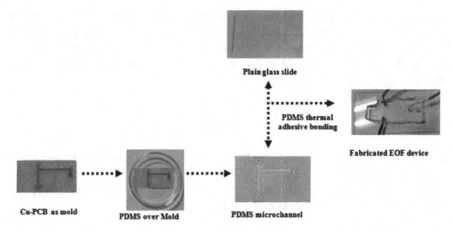

Fig. 1. Fabrication flow.

To fabricate an EOF device, an elastomer precursor (sylgard 184) and its curing agent are mixed in 10:1 ratio and degassed using desiccators. The solution is then poured over PCB-mold on flat surface and cured at 80 °C for 40 min. After the replica is peeled off from mold, the reservoir holes were punched. The PDMS channels are then bonded to a glass slide using an adhesive bonding technique [21]. For adhesive bonding, a fresh PDMS solution is uniformly spin coated on glass slide at 8000 rpm for 8 min. As a result, an uncured PDMS thickness of 1–1.5 μm is obtained on a glass substrate. Then, the previously fabricated PDMS micro channel is gently placed on the freshly coated glass surface without trapping air. Finally, the device altogether then kept flat at 90 °C for 15 min to cure the adhesive bonding layer. For applying external electric field, we simply inserted a Cu-electrode from above into reservoir after bonding. The microchannel is fabricated in T-shape to investigate a directional transport of fluid. Thus, an EOF device with three reservoirs and electrodes are fabricated in a low-cost approach as shown in Fig. 2.

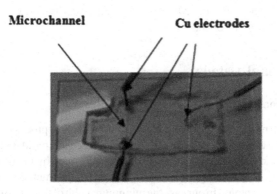

Fig. 2. Fabricated EOF device.

3.2   Characterization Set-up

An in-house developed Microfluidics characterization set-up [22] is used for characterization of the fabricated EOF device. The system is developed to provide high actuation DC voltage (0 to 400 V) using Arm7 architecture board (R-pi) which is programmed to control the electromagnetic relays. A DC Boost converter is used for the supply of high DC voltage. The setup also consists of a sample holder in XYZ directions and a USB digital camera for capturing video in real time along with a standard HDMI display as shown in Fig. 3. The complete system is designed in real time embedded Linux platform with Qt GUI interface. To characterize the fabricated device, the fluid is filled with completely in a channel as shown in Fig. 4. Then voltage is applied by our characterization set up through Cu electrode. To measure velocity, a video is captured at 30 fps. Experimentally, velocity is measured using a kymograph image processing technique using characterization set-up.

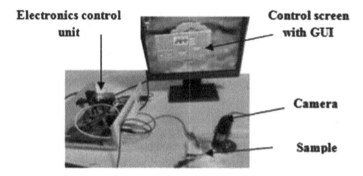

Fig. 3. Microfluidics characterization set-up for EOF device.

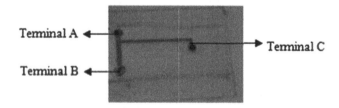

Fig. 4. Fluid flow in the fabricated channel.

4   Modeling Technique

The dynamics of the fluid transport are usually analyzed with a multiphase lattice Boltzmann method. The LBM solves the probability of the particle distribution f_i in discrete space (x) at discrete time (t) [23].

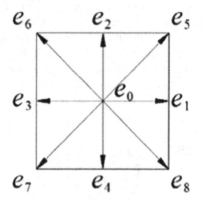

Fig. 5. Discrete velocity set of 2 dimension 9-velocity (D2Q9) LBM model.

4.1   Governing Equation

For the implementation of 2D lattice Boltzmann study, the choice of the lattice is very important because it decides the accuracy as well as computation time required for the simulations. In this work, we have used a most accurate and standard D2Q9 (2 dimension 9 velocity vector) model [24] as shown in Fig. 5.

The LBM solves the probability of the particle distribution f_i in discrete space (x) at discrete time (t). This discrete Boltzmann equation can be rigorously derived from the Boltzmann equation [25]. The equilibrium distribution function (f^{eq}) and the discretization strategy are based on the choice of the LBM model. The basic vectors of D2Q9 model are given by

$$\bar{e}_i = \bar{c}_i \Delta t = \overline{(e_1, e_2, e_3, e_4, e_5, e_6, e_7, e_8, e_9)}$$
$$= \left\{ \begin{matrix} 0 & 1 & 0 & -1 & 0 & 1 & -1 & -1 & 1 \\ 0 & 0 & 1 & 0 & -1 & 1 & 1 & -1 & -1 \end{matrix} \right\}$$

Now, the streaming and collision are two major process which leads to the evolution of particle distribution function in the above nine predefined direction. This process is described by

$$f_i(\vec{x} + \vec{e_i}\delta_t, t + \delta_t) - f_i^t(\vec{x}, t) = -\frac{f_i^t(\vec{x}, t) - f_i^{eq}(\vec{x}, t)}{\tau} \quad (4)$$

where i = 0, 1, .. 9 and τ is the dimensionless relaxation time of Bhatnagar-Gross-Krook (BGK) collision operator [26] which is related to kinematic viscosity of the fluid. Using the above distribution function, the macroscopic density and velocity are defined as

$$\rho(\vec{x}, t) = \sum_{i=0}^{e_i} f_i^t(\vec{x}, t) \quad (5)$$

For a linear elastic collision, a local equilibrium distribution function is defined as only the function of locally conserved mass and momentum density. It is given by

$$\vec{u}(\vec{x}, t) = \frac{1}{\rho} \sum_{i=0}^{e_i} f_i \vec{e_i} \quad (6)$$

$$f_i^{eq}(\vec{x}, t) = w_i \rho (1 + \frac{3\vec{e_i}\vec{u}}{c^2} + \frac{9(\vec{e_i}\vec{u})^2}{2c^4} - \frac{3(\vec{u})^2}{2c^2}) \quad (7)$$

where c is the lattice pseudo-speed of sound ($c = 1/\sqrt{3}$). The lattice weights (w_i) for D2Q9 model are predefined as

$$w_i = \begin{cases} 4/9 & i = 0 \\ 1/9 & i = 1, 2, 3, 4 \\ 1/36 & i = 5, 6, 7, 8 \end{cases}$$

In LBM, the physical quantities must be converted into dimensionless lattice units. The macroscopic velocity is then updated with respect to the body force at the lattice point as

$$\vec{u}(\vec{x}, t) = u' + \frac{\tau}{\rho_x} F_x \quad (8)$$

where u' is the velocity obtained earlier and F_x is the body force which can be pressure driven or electrostatic. In this case the flow is driven only by electrical field (F_E) and the pressure gradient is zero.

4.2   Governing Equations for Electro Hydrodynamics

As per the above EDL theory, the applied electrostatic potential is related to the distribution of ions in the bulk solution using the Poisson's equation [27]

$$\nabla^2 \psi = -\frac{\rho_e}{\varepsilon \varepsilon_0} \tag{9}$$

where Ψ is electrostatic potential, and $\mathcal{E}_0$ is permittivity of the vacuum and ρ_e is the net charge density. By Nernst-Planck equation, the net charge density distribution can be described by the equilibrium Boltzmann distribution function by neglecting the sizes and interactions of ions. Generally, for symmetric electrolyte, $z_i = z$ and $n_{i,\infty} = n_\infty$

$$\rho_e = -2zen_\infty \sinh\left(\frac{ze}{k_BT}\psi\right) \tag{10}$$

Substituting the above Eq. 9 in Eq. 8 gives the Poison-Boltzmann equation for electrical potential in electrolyte solution.

$$\nabla^2 \psi = -\frac{1}{\varepsilon \varepsilon_0} \sum_i zen_\infty \sinh\left(-\frac{ze}{k_BT}\psi\right) \tag{11}$$

For most of the low surface electric potential, the Debye-Huckel approximation $\sinh\left(\frac{ze}{k_BT}\psi\right) = \left(\frac{ze}{k_BT}\psi\right)$ is applied to linearization of the PB equation as

$$\nabla^2 \psi = \frac{2n_\infty z^2 e^2}{\varepsilon \varepsilon_0 k_b T}\psi = k^2 \psi \tag{12}$$

where $k = \sqrt{\frac{2n_\infty z^2 e^2}{\varepsilon \varepsilon_0 k_b T}}$ and its reciprocal k^{-1} is denoted as Debye length as discussed earlier in the Eq. 1. The above PB equation is also solved in 1D using LBM frame work to obtain net ionic potential distribution in same D1Q3 model with $e_0 = 0$, $e_1 = 1$, $e_2 = -1$. $w_0 = 2/3$, $w_1 = w_2 = 1/6$.

$$h_i(\vec{x} + \vec{e_i}\delta_t, t + \delta_t) - h_i^t(\vec{x}, t) = -\frac{h_i^t(\vec{x}, t) - h_i^{eq}(\vec{x}, t)}{\tau} + \omega_i \partial_t (1 - \frac{0.5}{\tau})\frac{\rho_e}{\varepsilon \varepsilon_0}$$

$$h_i^{eq} = \left\{ \begin{array}{ll} (w_0 - 1)u(x, t) & i = 0 \\ w_i u(x, t) & i = 1, 2. \end{array} \right\} \tag{13}$$

Here, the time-step is $\partial_{t,\psi} = \frac{\partial_x}{c_\psi}$. Here c_ψ is the pseudo-speed of sound. The steady state solution of the evolution has been proved consistent with Eq. 9 with the applied boundary conditions $u(0) = 1$ and $u(nx) = 1$.

So, for electro kinetic flows, the body force together as a large electrical force (E) and small ionic potential is given by

$$F_E = \rho_e E = F_X \tag{14}$$

4.3 Algorithm of Computation

The computational algorithm can be summarized as

Step 1: Initialize velocities (e_i), weights (w_i), relaxation time (τ),densities ρh, ρl,,'.

Step 2: Define a periodic boundary condition, no-slip bounce back condition on the required walls.

Step 3: Solve the PB equation for electrodynamics using Eq. (13).

Step 4: Compute the particle distribution function for streaming and collision using Eq. (4).

Step 5: Compute macroscopic density and macroscopic velocity using Eqs. (5) and (6) respectively.

Step 6: Update the velocity using Eq. (8).

Step 7: Advance one time step and return to Step 4.

5 Results and Discussion

5.1 Experimental Results

The EOF device of 70 μm depth and 300 μm width is fabricated by the above method. The fabricated device is filled with fluid (0.1 M KCL mixed with ink) then the voltage is applied by our characterization set up through Cu electrode. We observed the pattern of maximum fluid flow happened across the path where the potential difference is maximum. Figure 6 shows the directional movement of bulk fluid for the two cases. In case A, the electrode is supplied by A = 300 V; B = 0 V; C = 100 V and in case B, the electrodes are switched to A = 300 V; B = 100 V; C = 0 V. In case A, the direction of maximum fluid motion is observed from electrode A to electrode B. During that time, a negligible less flow from electrode A to electrode C. Similarly in case B, the direction of maximum fluid motion is observed from the electrode A to electrode C. In general, the directional transport of fluid from higher potential reservoir to lower potential reservoir is observed.

652   T. Pravinraj and R. Patrikar

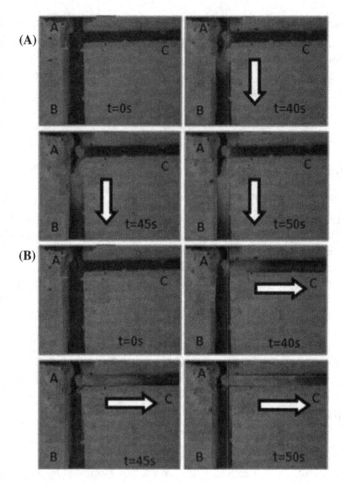

Fig. 6. Experimental results of directional fluid flow in the fabricated sample for various time steps for (A) A = 300 V, B = 0 V, C = 100 V (B) A = 300 V, B = 100 V, C = 0 V

5.2   Simulation Results

To model, this phenomenon using LBM frame work as explained above, the following simulation parameters are chosen which are suitable for 0.1 M KCl solution with ink. Bulk ionic number concentration values c_∞ = 0.1 M, N_A = 6.02 × 10^{23}, valence of the ions $|z|$ = 1, absolute proton charge e = 1.6201 × 10^{-19} C, Boltzmann constant k_b = 1.3805 × 10^{-23}, absolute temperature T = 273 K, dielectric constant $\varepsilon\varepsilon_0$ = 6.95 × $10^{-10}C^2/Jm$, zeta potential ξ = −10 mV. For this case, the analytical solution can be solved theoretically [28] as k = 27.79

$$u(x) = \frac{e^k - 1}{e^k - e^{-k}} e^{-kx} + \frac{1 - e^{-k}}{e^k - e^{-k}} e^{kx} \tag{15}$$

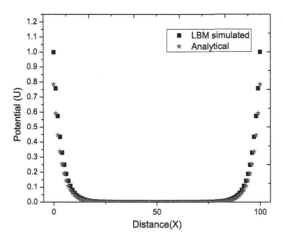

Fig. 7. Validation of PB-LBM simulation

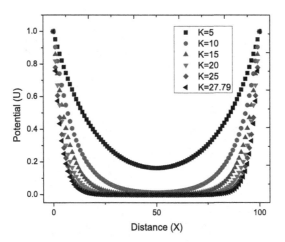

Fig. 8. Effect of K on potential U

Figure 7 shows the comparison of LBM simulation and analytical solution of the poison Boltzmann equation. The plot shows the excellence agreement of the theory with the model. We then analyzed the effect of Debye length on the potential by varying K. Increase in K, resulted in more plug-like profile which agreed with the similar studies done earlier [11]. This effect of K on potential U is plotted in Fig. 8. Figure 9 shows the comparison analysis of average velocity for different voltages. The plot shows good agreement with the simulation and experiment. Thus, LBM simulations are proved its effectiveness. Finally as discussed in experimental results, directional transport from terminal A to terminal B and terminal A to terminal C respectively for case A and case B as shown in Fig. 10.

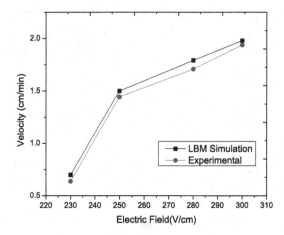

Fig. 9. Comparison of average velocity of simulated and experimental result for various electric filed

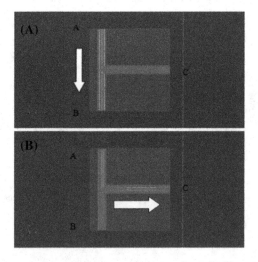

Fig. 10. LBM simulation results of directional fluid flow in the fabricated sample for various time steps for (A) A = 300 V, B = 0 V, C = 100 V (B) A = 300 V, B = 100 V, C = 0 V

6 Conclusion

In this work we presented the theory, experiment and simulation of electro-osmotic flow device. As a low-cost approach, we have presented a PCB mold technology as an alternative for UV lithography and plasma bonding for EOF device is presented. In-house developed microfluidics characterization system is used for characterization. The fabricated device is also simulated for better understanding of the flow and potential distribution. The Poison-Boltzmann equation is successfully coupled with the LBM hydrodynamics equations. Simulation and experimental results show good agreement with each other. The fabricated device can be further explored for EOF pumping and EOF micro mixer.

References

1. Luka, G., et al.: Microfluidics integrated biosensors: a leading technology towards lab-on-a-chip and sensing applications. Sensors **15**(12), 30011–30031 (2015)
2. Srinivasan, V., Pamula, V.K., Fair, R.B.: An integrated digital microfluidic lab-on-a-chip for clinical diagnostics on human physiological fluids. Lab Chip **4**(4), 310–315 (2004)
3. Stone, H.A., Stroock, A.D., Ajdari, A.: Engineering flows in small devices: microfluidics toward a lab-on-a-chip. Annu. Rev. Fluid Mech. **36**, 381–411 (2004)
4. Kirby, B.J.: Micro-and Nanoscale Fluid Mechanics: Transport in Microfluidic Devices. Cambridge University Press, Cambridge (2010)
5. Nguyen, N.T., Huang, X., Chuan, T.K.: MEMS-micropumps: a review. J. Fluids Eng. **124**(2), 384–392 (2002)
6. Friend, J., Yeo, L.: Fabrication of microfluidic devices using polydimethylsiloxane. Biomicrofluidics **4**(2), 026502 (2010)
7. Howard, J.L., Hanssen, A.D.: Principles of a clean operating room environment. J. Arthropl. **22**(7), 6–11 (2007)
8. Kontakis, K., Petropoulos, A., Kaltsas, G., Speliotis, T., Gogolides, E.: A novel microfluidic integration technology for PCB-based devices: application to microflow sensing. Microelectron. Eng. **86**(4–6), 1382–1384 (2009)
9. Mata, A., Fleischman, A.J., Roy, S.: Characterization of polydimethylsiloxane (PDMS) properties for biomedical micro/nanosystems. Biomed. Microdevices **7**(4), 81–293 (2005)
10. Lam, E., Ngo, T.: Manufacturing a PDMS microfluidic device via a Silicon Wafer Master. Harvard-MIT Div. Health Sci. Technol. HST. J., **400** (2007)
11. Bhattacharya, S., Datta, A., Berg, J.M., Gangopadhyay, S.: Studies on surface wettability of poly (dimethyl) siloxane (PDMS) and glass under oxygen-plasma treatment and correlation with bond strength. J. Microelectromech. Syst. **14**(3), 590–597 (2005)
12. Phillips, J.C., et al.: Scalable molecular dynamics with NAMD. J. Comput. Chem. **26**(16), 1781–1802 (2005)
13. Gupta, A., Matharoo, H.S., Makkar, D., Kumar, R.: Droplet formation via squeezing mechanism in a microfluidic flow-focusing device. Comput. Fluids **100**, 218–226 (2014)
14. Chen, S., Doolen, G.D.: Lattice Boltzmann method for fluid flows. Annu. Rev. Fluid Mech. **30**(1), 329–364 (1998)
15. Pravinraj, T., Patrikar, R.: Splitting and transport of a droplet with no external actuation force for lab on chip devices. In: Kaushik, B.K., Dasgupta, S., Singh, V. (eds.) VDAT 2017. CCIS, vol. 711, pp. 707–717. Springer, Singapore (2017). https://doi.org/10.1007/978-981-10-7470-7_66
16. Pravinraj, T., Patrikar, R.: Modelling and investigation of partial wetting surfaces for drop dynamics using lattice Boltzmann method. Appl. Surf. Sci. **409**, 214–222 (2017)
17. Aidun, C.K., Clausen, J.R.: Lattice-Boltzmann method for complex flows. Annu. Rev. Fluid Mech. **42**, 439–472 (2010)

18. Herr, A.E., Molho, J.I., Santiago, J.G., Mungal, M.G., Kenny, T.W., Garguilo, M.G.: Electroosmotic capillary ow with nonuniform zeta potential. Anal. Chem. **72**(5), 1053–1057 (2000)
19. Li, D.: Electrokinetics in Microfluidics. Elsevier, New York (2004)
20. Mohammadipour, O.R., Niazmand, H.: Numerical simulation of a at electroosmotic driven flow in the presence of a charged mid-plate. Int. J. Mod. Phys. C **26**(7), 1550078 (2015)
21. Wu, H., Huang, B., Zare, R.N.: Construction of microfluidic chips using polydimethyl-siloxane for adhesive bonding. Lab Chip **5**(12), 1393–1398 (2005)
22. Jain, V., Raj, T.P., Deshmukh, R., Patrikar, R.: Design, fabrication and characterization of low cost printed circuit board based EWOD device for digital microfluidics applications. Microsyst. Technol. **23**(2), 389–397 (2017)
23. Hecht, M., Harting, J.: Implementation of on-site velocity boundary conditions for D3Q19 lattice Boltzmann simulations. J. Stat. Mech. Theory Exp. **1**, P01018 (2010)
24. Li, L., Mei, R., Klausner, J.F.: Lattice Boltzmann models for the convection diffusion equation: D2Q5 vs D2Q9. Int. J. Heat Mass Transf. **108**, 41–62 (2017)
25. He, X., Luo, L.S.: Theory of the lattice Boltzmann method: from the Boltzmann equation to the lattice Boltzmann equation. Phys. Rev. E **56**(6), 6811 (1997)
26. Bhatnagar, P.L., Gross, E.P., Krook, M.: A model for collision processes in gases. I. small amplitude processes in charged and neutral one-component systems. Phys. Rev. **94**(3), 511 (1954)
27. Wang, J., Wang, M., Li, Z.: Lattice Poisson Boltzmann simulations of electro-osmotic flows in microchannels. J. Colloid Interface Sci. **296**(2), 729–736 (2006)
28. Chai, Z., Shi, B.: A novel lattice Boltzmann model for the Poisson equation. Appl. Math. Model. **32**(10), 2050–2058 (2008)

Fully Digital, Low Energy Capacitive Sensor Interface with an Auto-calibration Unit

Chintanika Chothani and Biswajit Mishra[✉]

VLSI and Embedded System Research Lab, DA-IICT, Gandhinagar 382007, India
biswajit_mishra@daiict.ac.in

Abstract. This paper presents an all-digital Capacitive Sensor Interface (CSI) implemented in 0.18 µm CMOS technology. The circuit consists of two blocks: a Capacitance to Time Converter (CTC) and a Time to Digital Converter (TDC). The CTC block uses a Capacitive Controlled Oscillator (CCO) in addition to a Calibration Unit with a dummy capacitor bank for estimating the capacitance value. The TDC consists of a ring delay line and an edge combiner. The CTC generates a pulse width according to the sensing capacitance (C_{sense}) and passes the generated pulse to the TDC that provides the coarse and fine counts according to the pulse width. The range of the C_{sense} is varied from 0.1 pF to 36 pF that can cover a wide range of applications. Energy efficiency of this circuit is 53.28 pJ and average power consumption is 28.08 nW with 5.72 bit accuracy at an operating voltage of 1.8 V at 10 Hz sampling frequency and can measure a minimum change in capacitance of 298.92 fF. At a lower voltage of 0.3 V, the CSI consumes 1.26 nW with 7.81 bit accuracy for the same sampling frequency.

Keywords: Capacitive Sensor Interface · Calibration · CCO · CTC · TDC · Low power

1 Introduction

Bladder pressure monitoring devices suffer from limited accuracy and have a short lifetime as they are battery powered [1]. For long lasting battery, lower power consumption is required and can be accomplished by novel capacitive sensor interfaces [1–4]. Capacitive sensors are used to measure flow, pressure, liquid level, temperature and humidity [5]. They dissipate less power and offer high sensitivity [2] compared to resistive ones. However such circuits suffer from non–linearity. To remove such discrepancies, calibration is often employed to increase the accuracy. Analog data is processed using power hungry analog pre–conditioning circuits within ADC [6]. To overcome certain problems in analog designs as they are more prone to noise and higher power consumption, capacitive sensor with digital interface circuits are often employed [1–4,7].

Thanks to SAC - ISRO for support under grant ISRO/RES/3/717/2016-17.

© Springer Nature Singapore Pte Ltd. 2019
S. Rajaram et al. (Eds.): VDAT 2018, CCIS 892, pp. 657–669, 2019.
https://doi.org/10.1007/978-981-13-5950-7_54

Most of the sensor applications use the conventional ADC in their design that is the main source of the power consumption. Also ADCs are less prone to technology scaling and have a less noise immunity at lower supply. To overcome these problems a digital architecture of sensor interfaces are often employed [6]. Digital CSI have lower power, better system performance in terms of Figure of Merit (FoM), Effective no. of bits (ENOB) as compared to the analog designs [3]. In this paper we discuss a fully digital CSI architecture and compare with the state of the art designs. The proposed design is simulated for FoM, ENOB and lower power and the results are discussed. We conclude that proposed design can be useful for low rate, low power and low voltage applications. The architecture is described in Sect. 2. Detailed architecture of the circuit blocks and description are given in Sect. 3. Analysis and simulation results are given in Sect. 4. We conclude in Sect. 5.

2 Capacitive Sensor Interface (CSI)

Figure 1 shows the block diagram of the capacitive sensor interface (CSI) in which the conventional ADC is replaced with a Capacitance to Time Converter (CTC) followed by a Time to Digital Converter (TDC) [7,8]. CTC consists of CCO and a calibration unit. The CTC module generates a pulse width that varies with the change in sensor capacitance. TDC consists of Ring Delay Line, an edge combiner and a counter with storing registers. Generated pulse width from CTC is fed to the TDC that produces coarse and fine pulses and provides a digital code from a counter.

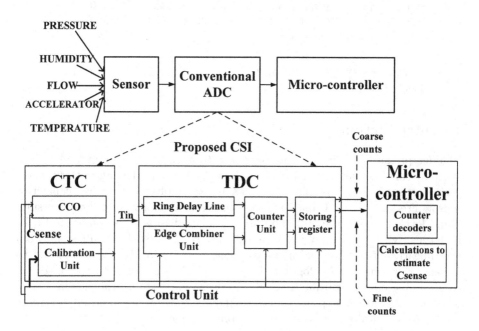

Fig. 1. Proposed Capacitive Sensor Interface

The important parameters for the CSI are the capacitive and the TDC resolution. The capacitive resolution (C_{LSB}) is the minimum change in sensor capacitance that can be measured by the TDC and is a measured period of the smallest pulse (fine pulse) duration that measures the value of C_{LSB}. The TDC resolution is a minimum change in pulse width T_{in} that can be measured by the TDC. The minimum change in T_{in} is measured by fine counter and the period of one fine pulse is TDC resolution.

3 Proposed Capacitive Sensor Interface

3.1 Capacitive Controlled Oscillator (CCO) — Pulse Width (T_{in}) Generator

As shown in Fig. 2, the CCO generates a pulse width Tin based on a variable capacitance C_{sense} where the charging and discharging time depends on the value of C_{sense}. A NAND gate forms the input of CCO followed by four inverters along with their dummy capacitors. En_CCO is used for enabling the CCO where the duty cycle is dependent on the conversion time i.e. En_CCO signal should remain high at least upto conversion time.For the same reason the sampling time should be greater than the conversion time to avoid incorrect output.

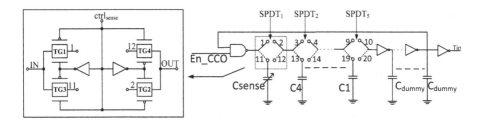

Fig. 2. Capacitive Controlled Oscillator

The value of dummy capacitor in Fig. 2 is very small and is taken as 1 pf to lower both the power consumption and conversion time. It should be noted that the change in T_{in} should be greater than one fine pulse period. Hence the four inverters with dummy capacitors are kept to adjust the pulse width T_{in}. The TDC in our proposed design can measure C_{sense} varying from 0.1 pF to 36 pF. An extra inverter at the end ensures false counting in TDC.

There are four capacitors placed through the single pole double throw switch–pair (SPDT$_1$ to SPDT$_5$) in between C_{sense} and C_{dummy}. Each of these capacitors has one control signal for connecting or disconnecting them from the circuit as shown in Fig. 2. Capacitors C4, C3, C2, C1 are disconnected all the time from the circuit except initially during the calibration and is explained in the next section.

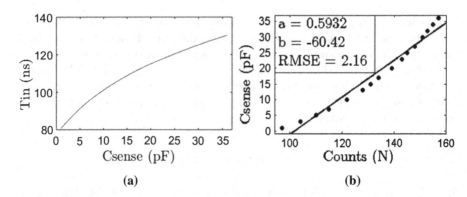

Fig. 3. (a) Sensitivity curve – T_{in} vs. C_{sense} (b) Linear approximation of curve C_{sense} vs. counts

Figure 3(a) shows the T_{in} vs. C_{sense} sensitivity curve. As can be seen, the slope of the sensitivity curve is proportional to the capacitive resolution (C_{LSB}) and is not linear. As the TDC provides the counts, the C_{sense} is estimated through a linear approximation Eq. (1) as following:

$$C_{sense} = a \times N + b \tag{1}$$

Where N is the value of the count, a and b are constants. Based on the above equation, the RMSE is plotted in Fig. 3(b) and is found to be 2.16.

3.2   Time to Digital Converter

Ring Delay Line — Coarse Pulse Generator: Inside the TDC, Ring Delay Line (RDL) generates the coarse pulses. The Delay Line provides this to the Roll Back Logic and if the condition $T_{in} > T_d$ is satisfied then it inverts the signal till pulse width T_{in} is high (T_d is total delay of the Delay Line).

As shown in Fig. 4 the Delay Line consists of sixteen buffer stages followed by an inverter and a 2:1 MUX where the pulse width T_{in} provides the control of the multiplexer. For T_{in}='1', the inverted output of Delay Line is provided back to the input of Delay Line and for '0' the output of Delay Line is forced to zero. Input of the Delay Line generates the coarse pulses only when T_{in} is high as shown in Fig. 4.

Edge Combiner – Fine Pulse Generator: Following the RDL, the edge combiner performs EX–ORing of the output. The eight EX–OR gates in the combiner produces a single pulse. These individual pulses are combined in the OR stages to get a series of pulses for fine count. Due to symmetrical structure,

Roll back logic

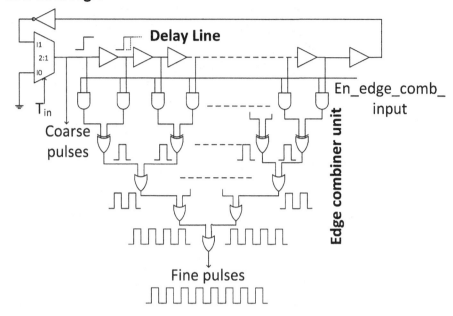

Fig. 4. Generation of coarse and fine pulses

one period of coarse pulse comprises of 16 fine pulses. The period of coarse pulse and fine pulse is denoted by T_{coarse} and T_{fine} respectively. If x and y are stored coarse counts and fine counts respectively then time T_{in} is given by,

$$T_{in} = x \times T_{coarse} + y \times T_{fine} \tag{2}$$

Where T_{in} is the time pulse denoting the capacitance value.

Counter Unit and Storing Registers: At the onset of T_{in}, the 4–bit synchronous coarse counter starts counting and is sufficient to accommodate the range of the capacitance. Lowering the supply voltage than 1.8 V needs an additional bit in the synchronous counter as T_{in} increases.

Fine pulses are generated from the Edge Combiner and is enabled after the last coarse pulse. Due to this, the power consumption in the circuit is also reduced. In the absence of such a control, the fine pulses will be generated throughout T_{in} as shown in Fig. 5 and contribute to power. An 8–bit fast Johnson counter is used for counting the fine pulses.

Control Unit: The control unit is used for interfacing and generation of T_{in}, coarse pulses, fine pulses, and fine counter clock as shown in Fig. 5.

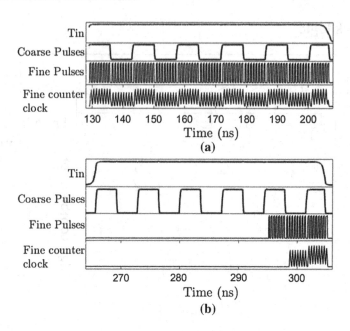

Fig. 5. (a) Coarse and Fine pulses before control unit (b) Coarse and Fine pulses after control unit

3.3 Calibration Unit

Calibration is a technique to reduce errors while estimating sensor capacitance. In Fig. 3(a), the curve is not linear throughout the entire range of capacitance varying from 0.1 pF to 36 pF but is piecewise linear. This provides an opportunity to apply a five point calibration technique on the curve in Fig. 3(a) into capacitance ranging from 0 pF$-$5 pF, 5 pF$-$13 pF, 13 pF$-$20 pF, 20 pF$-$27 pF, and 27 pF$-$36 pF. These durations can be perceived as almost linear where RMS error are 0.125, 0.203, 0.106, 0.229, and $1.83\,e^{-14}$ respectively so each of the duration is to be considered as a slope.

The RMS error is calculated from the Eq. (1) where a,b are constants and have values shown in Figs. 6(a) and (b). For a better estimation, a more precise model is developed and is described in the following section. The calibration for both hardware and software is discussed.

Hardware Calibration: Already shown in Fig. 2, the capacitor bank besides the sensor capacitance provides different capacitance through the switches at input of CCO. For a known capacitance the corresponding digital value will be stored inside a μcontroller. Total five pair of single pole double throw switches are used for selecting desire valued combinations of capacitors. For example, when control signal of corresponding switch–pair goes high, the lower terminal of that switch–pair will get connected to each other. If control signal corresponding to C_{sense} goes high then terminals 11 and 12 will get connect to each other. In this

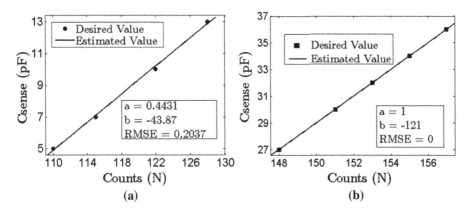

Fig. 6. Estimated value of C_{sense} and RMS error for (a) $5\,\mathrm{pF}-13\,\mathrm{pF}$ (b) $27\,\mathrm{pF}-36\,\mathrm{pF}$

case other control signals are low and the circuit provides counts corresponding to C_{sense} only. While making control signal of C_{sense} low and providing other combinations to the four controls provides the counts corresponding to desired capacitance.

The new equation for the sensor capacitance C_{sense} can be expressed as following:

$$C_{sense} = C_L + \left(\frac{N_{sense} - N_1}{N_2 - N_1}\right) \times (C_H - C_L) \tag{3}$$

Where C_L is assumed to be the lowest value and C_H be the highest value of capacitance. N_1, N_2, N_{sense} are total counts corresponding to C_L, C_H, C_{sense} respectively.

A 4–bit control signal ctrl[3:0] corresponding to C4, C3, C2, C1 and ctrl_{sense} is corresponding to C_{sense}. C1, C2, C3 and C4 values are taken as $2\,\mathrm{pF}$, $4\,\mathrm{pF}$, $8\,\mathrm{pF}$ and $16\,\mathrm{pF}$ respectively to get the capacitance value according to the above given slopes. From the given values all required combinations of capacitance can be generated shown in Table 1.

Table 1. Control signals for different modes

Control signals	Value	Mode/Equivalent input capacitance
ctrl_{sense}	1	Sensing mode
ctrl_{sense}	0	Calibration mode
ctrl[3:0]	0000	$0\,\mathrm{pF}$
	0011	$6\,\mathrm{pF}$
	0110	$12\,\mathrm{pF}$
	1010	$20\,\mathrm{pF}$
	1101	$26\,\mathrm{pF}$
	1111	$30\,\mathrm{pF}$

The digital count corresponding to capacitors are read out from TDC. Further the counts are decoded and stored inside the controller. *e.g.* if C_{sense} is 18 pF then N_{sense} is generated and will be later compared with stored calibrated counts.

Software Calibration: The calibration can be done by using a set of equations and can be processed offline by a μcontroller. It is done in two phases: First step is is for calculating the total count N by decoding the count values coming from an interface circuit from the equation $N = x \times 16 + y$ where x and y are stored coarse counts and fine counts respectively. The values of x and y differ according to C_L, C_H and C_{sense} and corresponding N_1, N_2, and N_{sense} are obtained. In the second step, calculations are done as per Eq. (3) using a commercially available PIC μcontroller. All quantities given in that equation are known, which gives the sensor capacitance value within fixed error margin.

4   Analysis and Simulation Results

In addition to improving the resolution, simulations are performed to study the error due to the effect of temperature on the design.

4.1   Temperature Effect

Effect of temperature on counts at $V_{DD} = 1.8\,V$ and at $V_{DD} = 1\,V$ is shown in Fig. 7(a). It can be seen that variation in counts is minimal at 1.8 V as compared to error at 1 V. The graph is linear from $-25\,°C$ to $85\,°C$ with RMS error of 0.3621 at $V_{DD} = 1.8\,V$ (Fig. 7(b)). The approximation of the results at different temperature can be expressed by the following equation,

$$N = a \times T + b \tag{4}$$

Where T denotes temperature and N denotes fine counts, and a, b are the coefficients and their values are obtained from Fig. 7(b).

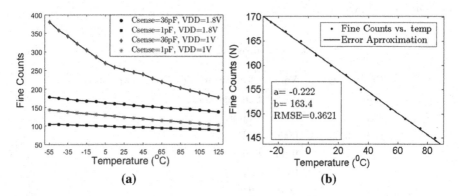

(a)   (b)

Fig. 7. (a) Variation in fine counts vs. temperature (b) Curve fitting approximation for counts vs. temperature

4.2   Importance of the Slope of the Sensitivity Curve

As stated earlier, the capacitive resolution is proportional to slope of the sensitivity curve. To improve the resolution of the interface circuit (C_{LSB}), value of the slope of the curve should be higher and can be increased by —

- Decreasing Wp/Wn ratio (sizing) of the CCO
- Increasing the number of inverters in CCO
- Decreasing the Supply Voltage
- Increasing the Value of C_{dummy}.

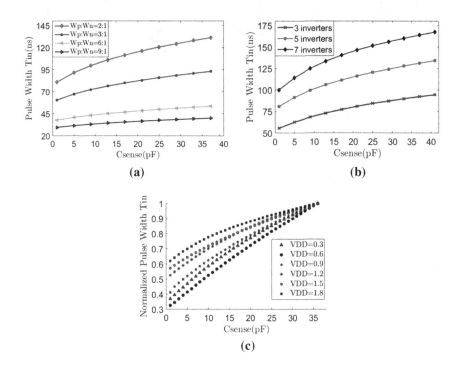

Fig. 8. Slope of the sensitivity curve at – (a) different Wp/Wn ratio (b) different number of inverters in CCO (c) different supply voltage

It can be seen from Fig. 8 that resolution is improved for a constant TDC resolution. Figures 8(a) and (b) shows the increment in slope with increment in Wp/Wn ratio and with number of inverters respectively. Figure 8(c) shows the curve to have more linear relationship with decrement in supply voltage. The highest accuracy achieved is 8.28 bits at 0.6 V. Moreover at this voltage the curve is highly linear with maximum slope among other supply voltages. Values for slope of the curve shown in Fig. 8(c) at different supply voltages are given in Table 2.

Slope can be increased by increasing the C_{dummy} value, but power consumption and conversion time is almost doubled with the increase in the number of inverters in the CCO shown in Figs. 9(a) and (b). Hence This is not preferable when the design is aimed for low power applications.

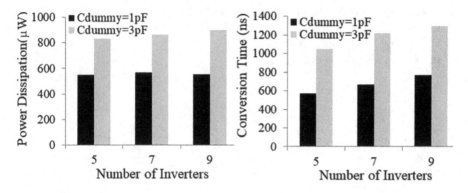

Fig. 9. (a) Power dissipation (b) Conversion time for different number of inverters in CCO at C_{dummy}=1 pF and C_{dummy}=36 pF

4.3 Simulation Results

The design is envisaged to be useful for low power applications discussed in [1,3,4]. We observed that for a low sample bladder pressure monitoring system, the change in pressure is usually between 0.5 s to 2 s [9]. Additionally sampling frequency of approximately 10 Hz is adequate for such applications. Hence proposed CSI can fit into above specifications well.

To find out the performance of the CSI, the design metrics in ENOB, Power and FoM are obtained. Further sampling time is obtained where the total sampling time T_{total} is given by:

$$T_{total} = T_{sample} = T_{ON} + T_{OFF} \tag{5}$$

T_{ON} equals to the conversion time, T_{OFF} is the off period. From this T_{sample} to be 0.1 s (10 Hz). Maximum C_{sense} is 36 pF and minimum C_{sense} is 0.1 pF for our proposed design. The average power consumption and FoM can be calculated from the following equations [2, 10]:

$$P_{avg} = \frac{P_{ON} \times T_{ON} + P_{OFF} \times T_{OFF}}{T_{total}} \tag{6}$$

$$FoM = \frac{P_{avg} \times T_{sample}}{2^{ENOB}} \tag{7}$$

Where P_{ON} is on time power consumption during the on period T_{ON} and P_{OFF} is off time power consumption due to leakage current during the off period T_{OFF}. $P_{ON} = 550.7\,\mu\text{W}$ during on period $T_{ON}=570\,\text{ns}$ and $P_{OFF}=24.95\,\text{nW}$ during off period $T_{OFF}=0.1\,\text{s}$ for $C_{sense}=36\,\text{pF}$ then From Eq. (6), $P_{avg}=28.088\,\text{nW}$. ENOB is required to find the FoM from Eq. (7). For that, ENOB [7] is calculated from the Eq. (8) and required values can be found from Table 2.

Table 2. Capacitive resolution and ENOB at different supply voltage

V_{DD}	TDC resolution (Tr)	Slope of the sensitivity curve (S)	$C_{LSB}=\frac{Tr}{S}$	ENOB [bits]
0.3 V	2.7 μs	24.3845 μs/pF	130.35 fF	7.81
0.6 V	14.48 ns	153.896 ns/pF	94.089 fF	8.28
0.9 V	2.53 ns	14.281 ns/pF	179 fF	7.36
1.2 V	1.4 ns	3.987 ns/pF	351.14 fF	6.38
1.5 V	989.44 ps	2.014 ns/pF	491.16 fF	5.90
1.8 V	828 ps	1.486 ns/pF	556.89 fF	5.72

$$ENOB = \frac{20log\left(\frac{maxC_{sense}-minC_{sense}}{C_{LSB}}\right) - 1.76}{6.02} \tag{8}$$

Where maximum and minimum values of C_{sense} is the upper and lower limit of the sensitivity curve in Fig. 3(a). From Table 2, TDC resolution and slope of the sensitivity curve are carried out from simulation. Hence FoM$=\frac{28.088\,nW\times0.1s}{2^{5.72}}=53.28\,\text{pJ}$ for $C_{sense}=36\,\text{pF}$ at 1.8 V.

The graph of ENOB vs. supply voltage (V_{DD}) is plotted from Table 2. As can be seen that maximum number of bits is achieved at 0.6 V shown in Fig. 10(a). The conversion time at different supply is shown in Fig. 10(b) where the increment in time is observed at lower supply voltage.

Figures 11(a) and (b) shows the ON and OFF power of the circuit design at different supply voltages. The power consumption of the circuit is decreasing by lowering the supply. Average power consumption is due to obvious dominant leakage current in the off state.

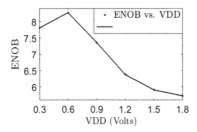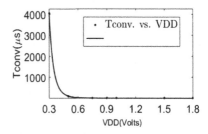

Fig. 10. (a) ENOB vs. V_{DD} (b) Conversion time vs. V_{DD}

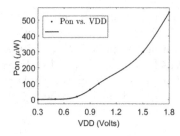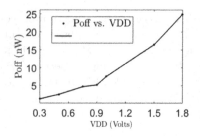

Fig. 11. (a) ON power vs. supply (b) OFF power vs.t supply

As can be seen in Table 3, the proposed design has an improved Power, ENOB and FoM at 1.8 V and 0.3 V compared to similar designs discussed in Literature.

Table 3. Performance comparison of this design with other designs

Ref	This work		[7]		[2]	[3]
Application	Pressure monitoring		-		Pressure monitoring	Pressure Monitoring
Output	Digital		Digital		Digital	Digital
Tech.	0.18 μm		0.18 μm		0.5 μm	0.13 μm
V_{DD}	1.8 V	0.3 V	1.8 V	0.3 V	0.3 V	2.7 V – 3.3 V
ENOB	5.72 bits	7.81 bits	6.19 bits	6.1 bits	6.1 bits	8 bits
$T_{conv.}$	570 ns	4 ms	<278.43 ns	<792 μs	1 ms	2 ms
P_{ON}	550.7 μW	4.64 nW	883.8 μW	12 nW	-	-
P_{OFF}	24.95 nW	1.29 nW	-	-	-	-
P_{avg}	28.08 nW	1.26 nW	-	-	270 nW	7 μW
FoM	53.28 pJ	0.56 pJ*	<1.675 pJ	<80.82 fJ	2.1pJ	2.7 nJ
fs	10 Hz		-		-	10 Hz

*Result given in the table is calculated by considering sampling time, whereas in paper [7] conversion time is considered, according to conversion time in this work FoM=22 fJ

5   Conclusion

This paper presents the all-digital, low power capacitive sensor interface using UMC 0.18 μm CMOS technology. Average power consumption of the proposed capacitive sensor interface is 28.08 nW at 1.8 V supply with a 10 Hz sampling frequency. The design proposed is shown to exhibit accuracy of 7.81 bits and lower power consumption of 1.26 nW at 0.3 V supply. For temperature stability purpose, output counts are checked from −55 °C to 125 °C and observed a linear variation in the counts by decreasing the temperature range. It is concluded that for lower range of C_{sense}, a higher resolution with an improved linearity can be obtained. We conclude that the low power and improved design metric obtained could be useful for low data rate, low power health monitoring applications.

References

1. Coosemans, J., Puers, R.: An autonomous bladder pressure monitoring system. Sens. Actuators, A **123**, 155–161 (2005)
2. Bracke, W., Merken, P., Puers, R., Hoof, C.V.: Ultra-low-power interface chip for autonomous capacitive sensor systems. IEEE Trans. Circuits Syst. I Regul. Pap. **54**(1), 130–140 (2007)
3. Danneels, H., Coddens, K., Gielen, G.: A fully-digital, 0.3 V, 270 nW capacitive sensor interface without external references. In: Proceedings of the ESSCIRC (ESSCIRC), pp. 287–290. IEEE (2011)
4. Jourand, P., Puers, R.: An autonomous, capacitive sensor based and battery powered internal bladder pressure monitoring system. Procedia Chem. **1**(1), 1263–1266 (2009)
5. Puers, R.: Capacitive sensors.: when and how to use them. Sens. Actuators, A **37**, 93–105 (1993)
6. Hou, Y., Watanabe, T., Miyahara, M., Matsuzawa, A.: An all-digital reconfigurable time-domain ADC for low-voltage sensor interface in 65 nm CMOS technology. IEICE Trans. Fundam. Electron. Commun. Comput. Sci. **98**(2), 466–475 (2015)
7. Savaliya, A., Mishra, B.: A 0.3 V, 12 nW, 47 fJ/conv, fully digital capacitive sensor interface in 0.18 μm CMOS. In: 2015 International Conference on VLSI Systems, Architecture, Technology and Applications (VLSI-SATA), pp. 1–6. IEEE (2015)
8. Pokhara, A., Agrawal, J., Mishra, B.: Design of an all-digital, low power time-to-digital converter in 0.18 μm CMOS. In: 2017 7th International Symposium on Embedded Computing and System Design (ISED), pp. 1–5. IEEE (2017)
9. Chapple, C.R.., Hillary, C.J., Patel, A., MacDiarmid, S.A.: Urodynamics Made Easy E-Book (2018)
10. Omran, H., Muhammad, A., Khaled, S.N.: 7.9 pJ/step energy-efficient multi-slope 13-bit capacitance-to-digital converter. IEEE Trans. Circuits Syst. II Express Briefs **61**(8), 589–593 (2014)

An Angular Steiner Tree Based Global Routing Algorithm for Graphene Nanoribbon Circuit

Arindam Sinharay[1], Subrata Das[2], Pranab Roy[3(✉)], and Hafizur Rahaman[1]

[1] Department of Information Technology,
Indian Institute of Engineering Science and Technology, Shibpur, Howrah, India
arindam.sinhray@gmail.com, rahaman_h@yahoo.co.in
[2] Department of Information Technology, Academy of Technology, Hooghly, India
dsubrata.mt@gmail.com
[3] School of VLSI Technology,
Indian Institute of Engineering Science and Technology, Shibpur, Howrah, India
ronmarine14@yahoo.co.in

Abstract. Graphene nanoribbon (*GNR*) based circuit and interconnects are now an emerging research interest. *GNR* based interconnect is now coming out as good alternative of copper as interconnect due to its excellent thermal and electrical behavior. Due to the geometrical and physical properties of *GNR*, it can be routed only along 0°, 60°, and 120° angles. Of these three routing angles cost due to 120° bending is three times than that of 60° bending. Hence for routing the use of 120° bending should be as minimum as possible. In this paper, we propose an algorithm for the construction of global routing tree for Graphene nanoribbon interconnect using computational geometry approach.

Keywords: Graphene nanoribbon · Global routing · Steiner tree ·
Angular steiner tree · Voronoi diagram

1 Introduction

Due to excellent electronic and thermal properties of *graphene nanoribbon* (*GNR*) it is now motivating research topic for VLSI designer. Conventional CMOS devices are facing several challenges such as surface and grain boundary scattering, increased leakage power, large dopant fluctuation, significant mobility degradation and more [2]. Moreover interconnects are not scale down at the same rate as that of semiconductor. *Graphene nanoribbon* can be used as both transistor and interconnects. *Graphene* is a flat two-dimensional (2D) single atomic layer sheet of carbon atoms packed into a honeycomb lattice [3,6]. *Graphene Nanoribbon* can be formed by cutting a ribbon out of *graphene*. Figure 1 shows the schematic cross section of the *graphene nanoribbon* transistor. Thin ribbons of *graphene* is used as the channel material. Two dimensional special structure of *graphene* is favorable for the construction of *graphene transistor*. The use of

© Springer Nature Singapore Pte Ltd. 2019
S. Rajaram et al. (Eds.): VDAT 2018, CCIS 892, pp. 670–681, 2019.
https://doi.org/10.1007/978-981-13-5950-7_55

GNR as interconnect has several advantages over traditional interconnects such as copper interconnect. *GNR* interconnect shows less power dissipation and less delay in comparison to that of copper interconnect.

There are two types of *GNR*: Armchair and zigzag. Armchair and zigzag *GNR* are respectively classified by number of dimer lines (N_a) and the number of zigzag chains (N_z) along the width [7]. Figure 2 shows the structure of Armchair and zigzag *GNR*. *Graphene nanoribbon* with zigzag edges are metallic and that with armchair edges are semiconducting [2]. From Fig. 2 we can see that, metallic *GNR* are oriented at 30°, 90° and 150° angles and semiconducting *GNR* are oriented at 0°, 60° and 120° angles. But due the bending in 0°, 60° and 120° metallic of *GNR* remains metallic and semiconducting *GNR* remains semiconducting [2].

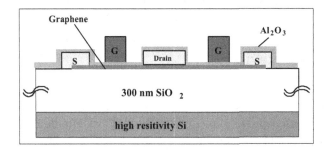

Fig. 1. Schematic Cross section of the graphene nanoribbon [1,2]

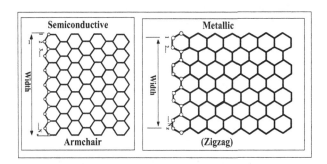

Fig. 2. Structure of Armchair and zigzag GNR.

In this paper we focus on GNR routing problem for single source and multiple sinks.

The process of finding geometric layouts of all the nets is called routing. *Graphene nanoribbon* based interconnect can be bent only in 0°, 60° and 120° angles. The underlying routing grid of *GNR* based circuits is aligned in the above mentioned degrees only. This type of routing mesh is known as triangular routing mesh. Natural way for multi-terminal nets is steiner tree approach. *GNR* routing problem can be solved with special kind of steiner tree known as angular steiner tree. The metallic *GNR* wire can be bent only in 0°, 60° and 120° angles. Hence the routing of *GNR* based circuits is different than that of traditional VLSI routing. The construction of angular steiner tree is much more complex than that of rectilinear steiner tree. In this paper we computational geometry based approach namely concepts of voronoi diagram to the problem of *GNR* routing.

The rest of the paper is organized as follows. Section 2 discusses the recent literatures of *graphene nanoribbon*. Section 3 describe the basic concept of *GNR* routing. The problem is described in Sect. 4. Proposed methodology and algorithm for routing of *GNR* based circuits are discussed in Sect. 5. Construction mechanism for Angular Steiner Tree (AST) is described in Sect. 6. Explanation of the proposed method with motivating example is given in Sect. 7. Experimental result is given in Sect. 8. Finally, Sect. 9 conclude the paper.

2   Literature Review

A comprehensive conductance and delay analysis of graphene nanoribbon (GNR) interconnects was presented in [4]. The performance of multilayer GNR interconnects with both copper interconnects and SWCNT bundle interconnects was compared in [3,9] and the simulation results shows multi-layer GNR interconnects superior than conventional copper interconnects for small widths (<15 nm). The first integration of graphene interconnects with standard CMOS technology was demonstrated in [5]. Gigahertz operation frequency was observed for graphene interconnects as long as 80 nm. *GNR* routing problem between pair of source and sinks was first introduced as a minimum *hybrid-cost shortest path problem* in [1]. The idea then modified in [2]. Graph expansion technique followed by shortest path algorithm on the expanded graph was used to formulate GNR routing problem. In [8] a *GNR routing tree* is constructed for single source and multiple sinks. The relative accuracy is measured in terms of Spearman rank correlation coefficient with Elmore delay and delay measured in that paper.

3   GNR Routing Problem

As metallic *GNR* wires remains metallic due to 0°, 60°, and 120° bending, hence routing occurs along these degrees only. The routing mesh of *GNR* are aligned 0°, 60°, and 120° angles so that *GNR* can be bent in these angles only. Such a routing mesh is known as *triangular mesh*. *GNR routing* problem for a pair of source and sink terminals was discussed in [1,2]. Construction of routing tree with single source and multiple sink terminals is a popular problem in VLSI design. In a triangular mesh, a source and multiple sink terminals are given and we have to interconnect them with metallic *GNR* wire in such a way so that total *hybrid-cost* is minimized.

The cost due to 120° bending is three times than that of 60° bending. Hence 120° bending path should be as minimum as possible. Length cost and bending cost constitute the total *hybrid cost* of *GNR* wire. The cost due to length is basically the length of the wire times the weight w_L if the length is greater than the mean free path length. The cost due to length is small constant if the length is within mean free path [2,3,8]. Let A_{60} and A_{120} respectively represent the cost due to 60° and 120° angles. If l, n_{60} and n_{120} are respectively represent the length of metallic *GNR* wire, number of 60° bending and number of 120° bending then *hybrid cost* is given by following formula

$$Hybrid\ cost = lw_L + n_{60}A_{60} + n_{120}A_{120} \qquad (1)$$

Figure 3 shows triangular routing mesh for *GNR* routing path. Here length of metallic *GNR* wire is 11, number of 60° bending is 3 but no 120° bending. Hence total hybrid cost is

$$Hybrid\ cost = 11w_L + 3A_{60} \qquad (2)$$

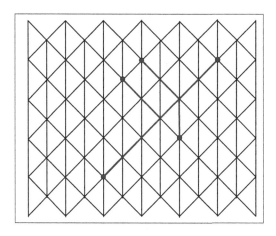

Fig. 3. Triangular Routing mesh for GNR Routing path.

4   Problem Description

In this paper we deal with global routing problem in context of *Graphene nanoribbon* circuit. The routing grid of *GNR* is triangular mesh. To explore the shortest path in this triangular mesh one has to find out *minimum hybrid cost* of the path. The problem is addressed in [1,2] for single source and sink pairs and is known as *MHCP* problem. We also consider *MHCP* model for single source and many sinks. It has difference with the traditional IC routing problem. In traditional IC routing problem is to find out minimum edge cost from source to sink. In *GNR* routing we have to find out minimum hybrid cost in a triangular mesh. The uniqueness in the *MHCP* problem over all the available standard routing techniques is that maze routing will not work here. In the next section we describe a method to solve the problem.

5   Proposed Method

Consider a triangular mesh M, as shown in Fig. 3, with finite number of terminals. Also we consider the intersection of six lines as a node and the shortest possible segment between two consecutive intersection point as edge. Hence our primal job is find a connected graph G. Each terminal will be consider as a node of the graph G. The entire paths between two terminals represents the routing path between the corresponding terminals. By attaching a cost W_L, we can compute the total length cost. So far we are not consider the bending cost to the cost function.

5.1   Computation of Bending Cost

To compute the bending cost, [2] has proposed a geometric model. We follow the method in this paper. Now we briefly describe the method.

We expand the nonterminal node. Initial six edges that coincide with each other are now coincide with six different nodes. These six nodes are connected by star topology. The cost of such edge is computed by the angle of bending from one node to the other. The edge cost the bending is given in the Table 1 and shown in Fig. 4a.

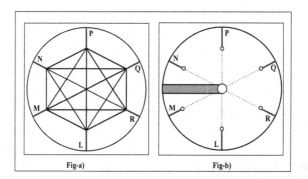

Fig. 4. Expanded node with terminal.

If the terminal node is the center node then the cost of bending from semiconducting GNR to metallic GNR is given by Table 2 and shown in Fig. 4b.

Table 1. Edge Cost of determining node

Edge	Cost	Edge	Cost	Edge	Cost
PQ	60°	QR	120°	RM	120°
PR	120°	QL	120°	RN	0°
PL	0°	QM	0°	LM	60°
PM	120°	QN	120°	LN	120°
PN	60°	RL	60°	MN	60°

Table 2. Edge Cost of terminal node

Edge	Cost	Edge	Cost	Edge	Cost
TN	30°	TQ	150°	TL	90°
TP	90°	TR	150°	TM	30°

To find out the shortest global routing path, we do the following computation.

1. We compute a Voronoi diagram on the triangular mesh grid with terminal points as the site points of the Voronica diagram. We name it by *Triangular Grided Voronoi Diagram (TGVD)*.
2. We extract boundary line of *TGVD*.
3. We connect the terminal nodes considering minimum cost Algorithm to form *Angular Steiner Tree (AST)*.

5.2 Computation of Triangular Grided Voronoi Diagram (TGVD)

The construction of *Triangular Grided Voronoi Diagram (TGVD)* is a significant study of this work. We have found that *Vornoi Diagram* has been extensively used in decomposition of spatial domain [10]. To construct the *Vornoi Diagram* effectively, first scan all the terminal nodes with their triple ordinates (α, β, γ). If there are n terminals, then the triplet ordinate of the ith terminal will be $(\alpha_i, \beta_i, \gamma_i)$, $i = 1, 2, \ldots, n$.

Before further proceeding, we consider the following definitions and properties of *Voronoi Diagram*.

Definition 1. *Given a set of terminal set $T = \{t_1, t_2, \ldots, t_n\} \subset R^2$, $2 < n < \infty$, when $i \neq j$, $t_i \neq t_j$. Voronoi region is given by the formula $V_R = \{s \mid D(s, t_i) \leq D(s, t_j)\}$. Here $D(s, t_i)$ is the minimum distance between t_i and s. The t_i is the generation points of the* Voronoi Diagram *and the* Voronoi Region $VR(t_i)$ *determined by t_i is called* Voronoi Polygon.

Voronoi Polygon edges are denoted as $VPE(t_i)$. The diagram defined by $VD(R) = \{VR(t_1), \ldots, VR(t_n)\}$ is called Voronoi diagram.

Property 1. [10] The distance between any terminal point s in a *Voronoi Polygon* $VP(t)$ and t is less than the distance between s and any other *Voronoi* generation point.

Definition 2. *Given a two dimensional terminal point set t and a query point s, the nearest neighbor query is to find a subset of the $NN(s, t)$:*

$$NN(s, t) = \{t \in T \mid \bigvee p \in T : D(s, t) \leq S(s, p)\} \tag{3}$$

5.3   Generating Method of Triangular Grided Vornoi Diagram (TGVD)

In order to enhance the efficiency of constructing *TGVD* dynamically, we search the terminal point dynamically. As the grid is triangular mesh, therefore, there will be three reference links and accordingly construct three set of parallel lines. They are as follows

1. set of horizontal lines
2. set of 60° inclined line
3. set of 120° inclined line.

Therefore, every terminal node as well as non terminal intersections will have three different values like the following data structure as shown in Table 3. The specific steps of the algorithm are as follows.

Table 3. Different Edge Cost of terminal node

	t_1	t_2	$\ldots$	t_{n-1}	t_n
H.L.	x_1	x_2	$\ldots$	x_{n-1}	x_n
60°. L.	y_1	y_2	$\ldots$	y_{n-1}	y_n
120°. L.	z_1	z_2	$\ldots$	z_{n-1}	z_n

6   Construction Mechanism for Angular Steiner Tree (AST)

To construct a triangular Steiner Tree first we have to form a Triangular Grided Voronoi Diagram (TGVD). The formal description of the formation of Triangular Grided Voronoi Diagram (TGVD) is given in Fig. 5. Now we see that the connected boundary edges of the TGVD forms an equilateral triangle grided graph. Our next problem is to connect all the terminal points in such a way that the hybrid cost is minimum. After that we construct the AST out of the above said graph. The *Steiner Tree problem* in a graph is much studied combinatorial problem in computer science. The well known Steiner tree problem can be summarized as follows: *In the Euclidian d-dimensional space, let there be n points* $\{t_1, t_2, \ldots, t_n\}$. *The task is to find out the shortest connected set containing these points.* Theoretically, a *steiner tree problem* is well understood, a solution always exists, often it may not be unique. The graph which optimize the problem domain, is collection of segments which terminates at the terminal points t_i's or in the intermediate Steiner points. The Steiner tree problem in graph theory is a NP-complete problem [11, 12].

In this paper, we introduce a similar variant of rectangular grided Steiner tree i.e. *Rectilinear Steiner Tree (RST)*. Instead of constructing a Steiner tree on the rectangular grid, we take triangular mesh grid as discussed before. The Steiner tree formed on this grid is defined as *Angular Steiner Tree (AST)*. The leaf node of *AST* will be a member of the set of terminals, T. Intermediate junction points are Steiner points of *AST*. Now we present the computational procedure of construction of *AST* from *TGVD*. We have followed the following steps.

A formal description for the construction of angular steiner tree is described in Fig. 6.

After the operations of Algorithm 1, we get Fig. 7. The final output is given by Fig. 10 which comes after the execution of Algorithm 2.

7   Explanation with Motivating Example

Consider Fig. 7. This figure shows voronoi diagram of single source and 11 sink terminals. Now we have to interconnect these source and sink terminals in such a way that *hybrid cost* is minimized. These source and sink terminals are basically placed in triangular mesh. Figure 8 shows the actual positions on of source and sink terminals in the triangular grid. Now if we apply technique for Formation of Triangular Grided Voronoi Diagram as shown in Fig. 5, then we get Fig. 9.

Algorithm 1 : Formation of Triangular Grided Voronoi Diagram

1. Consider the t_1 terminal point.
2. Find out is nearest neighbor terminal say t_i
3. Find out the differences of three-ordinate values t_1 & t_i. In general for any referential ordinate line it can be of the following types
i) On the same line
ii) On one line apart
ii)On more than one line apart
In case iii) there can be two types of differences as follows
a) Odd number of lines apart such as 3, 5 and so on
b) Even number of lines apart such as 2, 4 and so on
We do the same type of computation for all three types of referential lines.
4. We discard first and second cases for impossibility of drawing Voronoi edge on the triangular grided lines.
5. Compute the values for the third case for all three reference line which has the minimum difference.
6. If the minimum difference is n and $n = 2m$=even draw the triangular grided Voronoi edge temporarily through the equal distant apart.
If $n = 2m + 1$ i.e odd then draw the same edge line through the m distant apart from the current terminal. More to the next terminal.
7. Repeat this process from step 2 until all terminals are exhausted.
8.We only retain the edges (boundary edges on triangular grid) for nearest neighbor only. Now we get all the terminals are bounded by the triangular polygonal plane or triangular grided polygonal planes.
The calculation set of all of the above regions(planes and half planes) form the *Triangular grided Voronoi Diagram(TGVD)*.

Fig. 5. Formation of Triangular Grided Voronoi Diagram

Algorithm 2: Construction of Angular Steiner Tree

---

step 1. By construction of TGVD, every Voronoi edge is situated on the shortest distance from two neighboring terminal nodes. We add each of the terminal node with the Voronoi edge satisfying the following constraints:-

1. Connection should be through minimum possible unit distance (i.e. mean free path of the triangular grid).
2. If the terminal point form 0° bending angle with the Voronoi edge at the junction point then perform it.
3. If the terminal point form 60° bending angle with the Voronoi edge at the junction point then perform it.
4. If the terminal point form 120° bending angle with the Voronoi edge at the junction point then do not perform the join operation. In this case, perform an extra 60° angle bending to deviate from the shortest path constraint (1). Join the path to the to the Voronoi edge.

step 2. Find out the Voronoi edges which have no connection with the terminal nodes.

1. If there is/are such edge(s), delete them in such a way that
   (a) Circuit should not persist.
   (b) The graph should remain connected.
2. If there is no such edge or still remain at least one circuit, the find out the Voronoi edge which has minimum terminal node connected to it.Go to step 3.
3. If there is no circuit and the graph is connected, then it forms a tree and go to step 4.

step 3. Omit the connection and perform the operations of step 2 to find out alternative connection.
step 4. Put a Steiner node at each junction of the tree (i.e. internal junction points) and return the Angular Steiner Tree (AST).

Fig. 6. Constructing Angular steiner tree

Now after converting this to Angular steiner tree as described in method of Constructing Angular steiner tree (Fig. 6). In Fig. 6, total length of the *GNR* wire is $l = 31$, number of 60° and 120° are respectively $n_{60} = 8$ and $n_{120} = 2$. Hence total *hybrid cost* for this routing tree is 171 as shown in Fig. 10.

8   Experimental Result

There is no existing data for routing of *graphene nanoribbon* based circuits. In Ma et al. [2] shows a test case (ex3) with pair of source and sink terminals. We take terminal as source and the remaining terminals as sinks. The routing of these set of terminals is shown in Fig. 11. As in [2] in this paper also we assume the cost due to unit interconnect length is unity. The cost due to 60° and 120° are respectively bending are respectively 10 and 30. From Fig. 11 we find that total interconnection length is 148. The number of 60° and 120° are 43 and 6 respectively. Hence total *hybrid cost* is 758.

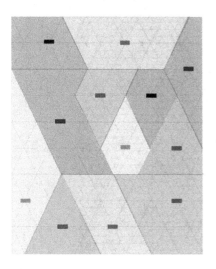

Fig. 7. Voronoi Diagram with single source and 11 sink terminals

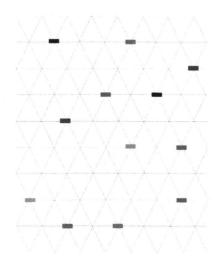

Fig. 8. Single source and 11 sink terminals in triangular grid

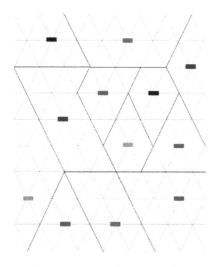

Fig. 9. Formation of Triangular Grided Voronoi Diagram

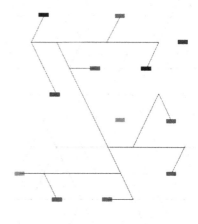

Fig. 10. Global Routing Tree between source and sink terminals

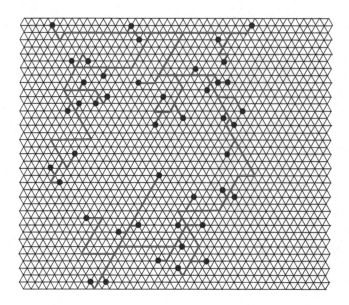

Fig. 11. Angular steiner tree for GNR routing, terminals are taken form ex3 [2]

9 Conclusion

In this paper we have studied the routing problem of *graphene nanoribbon*. The routing of *GNR* is possible only in triangular routing grid and *GNR* wire cane be bent only in 0°, 60° and 120° angles. Hence The routing of *GNR* different than that of traditional VLSI routing. We have proposed algorithm based on computational geometry approach to interconnect single source and multiple sink terminals so that *hybrid cost* is minimized. We have tested the algorithm on random data. The work can be improved by simulating the experiment in some practical simulation tool.

References

1. Yan, T., Ma, Q., Chistedt, S., Wong, M.D.F., Chen, D.: Routing for graphene nanoribbons. In: Proceedings of the 16th Asia and South Pacific Design Automation Conference. IEEE, pp. 323–329 (2011)
2. Yan, T., Ma, Q., Chistedt, S., Wong, M.D.F., Chen, D.: A routing algorithm for graphene nanoribbon circuit. ACM Trans. Des. Autom. Electron. Syst. **18**(4), 61:1–61:18 (2013). Article-61
3. Ragheb, T., Massoud, Y.: On the modeling of resistance in graphene nanoribbon (GNR) for future interconnect applications. In: IEEE/ACM International Conference on Computer-Aided Design, pp. 593–597 (2008)
4. Xu, C., Li, H., Banerjee, K.: Graphene Nano-Ribbon (GNR) interconnects: a genuine contender or a delusive dream? In: IEEE International Electron Devices Meeting (IEDM 2008) (2008)

5. Chen, X., et al.: Fully integrated graphene and carbon nanotube interconnects for gigahertz high-speed CMOS electronics. IEEE Trans. Electron Devices **57**(11), 3137–3143 (2010)
6. Anderson, P.D., Subramania, G.: Unidirectional edge states in topological honeycomb-lattice membrane photonic crystals. Opt. Express **2**(11), 23293 (2017)
7. Yamijala, S.S., Bandhyopadyay, A., Pati, S.K.: Electronic properties of zigzag, armchair and their hybrid quantum dots of graphene and boron-nitride with and without substitution: a DFT study. https://arxiv.org/pdf/1405.4605
8. Das, S., Das, S., Majumder, A., Dasgupta, P., Das, D.K.: Delay estimates for graphene nanoribbons: a novel measure of fidelity and experiments with global routing trees. In: ACM GLSVLSI 2016, pp. 263–268 (2016)
9. Dhillon, G., Raghu, N.: Performance analysis of single-wall carbon nanotubes and copper as VLSI interconnect. Indian J. Sci. Technol. **9**(S1) (2016). https://doi.org/10.17485/ijst/2016/v9iS1/106892
10. Reitsma, R., Trubin, S., Mortensen, E.: Weight-proportional space partitioning using adaptive Voronoi diagrams. GeoInformatica **11**(3), 383–405 (2007)
11. Dobrin, A.: A Review of Properties and Variations of Voronoi Diagrams. Whitman College (2005)
12. Santuari, A.: Steiner tree NP-completeness proof, Technical report, University of Trento, May 2003

A Complete Hardware Advent on IEEE 802.15.4 Based Mac Layer and a Comparison with Open-ZB

Ammu Lakshmy Rajesh[(✉)], Sanket V. Kadam, and Rajendra Patrikar

Center for VLSI and Nanotechnology, Visvesvaraya National Institute of Technology, Nagpur 440010, India
ammulakshmy91@gmail.com, asanket.05@gmail.com, rajendra@computer.org

Abstract. In this era of IoT, everything settles down to low power implementation. As the communication between different IoT Wireless Sensor Nodes are considered, the major way of communication is via Zigbee transceiver that has been built on the foundation laid by IEEE 802.15.4 standard specified physical layer and Mac Layer. In this work, major efforts are being focused on the Mac Layer to reduce power consumption in the node by converting this module into hardware. One of the main reasons for this is that the power consumed in this module is large compared to physical layer. The comparison of power consumption with software implementation Open-ZB shows that there is a substantial power saving in hardware implementation.

Keywords: MAC · Power · Hardware · Open-ZB · Micaz

1 Introduction

Short range wireless communication is a major research area. One of the evident reasons for this is the growth of Wireless Personal Area Networks (WPAN) in Internet of Things (IoT) applications. Zigbee is a low power consumption, low cost technology targeted towards these kind of applications. The complete stack is given in Fig. 1. IEEE 802.15.4 standard [1] delivers a robust description of specifications for the Physical Layer as well as Medium Access Control (MAC) Layer of Zigbee.

The MAC Layer handles the access grant to the channels which are used by multiple devices. For a full function device (FFD), the functions include network beacon generation (if it acts like a coordinator), executing CSMA-CA algorithm for channel access, PAN association and dissociation, synchronization with arriving beacon, security maintenance etc. As there are a lot of functions involved, when the whole WSN is considered, MAC Layer consumes the major share of power. And it is justified for the effort too. A detailed analysis of power consumption can be found in [3].

Even though there are many implementations available, never it had found an optimal solution in terms of area and power. Like the implementation provided

S. Rajaram et al. (Eds.): VDAT 2018, CCIS 892, pp. 682–694, 2019.
https://doi.org/10.1007/978-981-13-5950-7_56

in [1], all implementations take the aid of software atleast for the frame building. Involvement of a microcontroller or a processor for these purposes will increase the power consumption to a considerable amount.

Attempts and analysis like the one provided in [4] were promising for power reduction. A more hardware approach can be found in [2,8] but a comparison with the software is missing in both cases. A comparison provides a very solid idea about the extend of achievement in the results. It makes more sense than a mere implementation and calculation on an existing technology. Here is an attempt to find a complete hardware solution for the same and analyse it by comparing with the already implemented software counterpart.

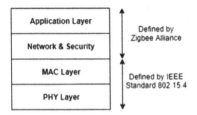

Fig. 1. Zigbee stack

Hardware implementation is done from scratch beginning from the basic transmission-reception functionality and advances through incorporating the frame formats, CSMA-CA mechanism, beacon management etc. It gives the freedom of separating the overall functionality as different entities unlike the software. Even then software is used in most cases due to its ease of use.

Hardly a few implementations can be seen as a complete software approach too. At least the CRC part or security part will be hardware defined due to power concerns and design comfort. Designs like Open-ZB, TIMAC, TKN15.4 are the examples for this type of co-design. Their design and comparison are worked out in [7].

From the existing results, it is evident that involving the processor along with the hardware consumes a lot of power if not properly designed. Designing everything in hardware is quite a hard job too. However, it gives a better option to track the signals and bugs through the behavioural simulation.

Rest of the paper is organized as follows. The description of hardware and software aspects of MAC is discussed in Sect. 2. The implementation aspects are discussed in Sect. 3. Simulation results are presented in Sect. 4 followed by implementation in FPGA and ASIC in Sect. 5. A set-up for software implementation is discussed in Sect. 6 including the discussions on the results obtained followed by the conclusions in the Sect. 7.

2   Hardware and Software Implementation

2.1   Hardware

A device in a PAN can work as a FFD or a Reduced Function Device (RFD).
The three modes of operation of a FFD are as a PAN coordinator or as a coordinator or as a device. An RFD can operate only in device mode. Here, we have
implemented a FFD and analysed the behaviour as a coordinator and a device.
The design is done referring to the standards mentioned in IEEE 802.15.4 [1].
The following functionality has been implemented using VHDL and behavioural
simulation is done using Xilinx Integrated Synthesis Environment (ISE).

(1) Beacon frame building, transmission and reception.
(2) Synchronized transmission using Superframe structure.
(3) CSMA-CA execution for channel access.
(4) Transmission and Reception of data frames.
(5) FCS generation (while transmission) and check (while reception) using serial
    CRC module.
(6) Acknowledgement transmission and reception.

The top level logic of the functionality is given in Fig. 2.

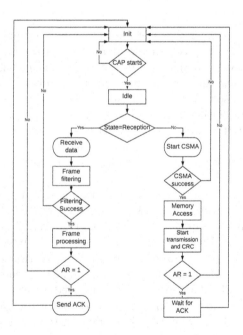

Fig. 2. Basic flow of Hardware MAC

2.2   Software

For the comparison with a software implementation, Open-ZB stack has been selected. It is implemented on Crossbow Micaz. As the stack is written in NesC language, Tiny-OS is selected as the platform for code compilation.

Tiny-OS and NesC. Tiny-OS is an event driven embedded operating system designed for low power wireless applications such as WSNs [13]. It has component based execution model which provides modularity in turns helps designing complex functionalities. The tasks run non-preemptively and for time consuming operations, asynchronous calls with callbacks are used. As a result Tiny-OS have non-blocking event trigged models which provides concurrency.

Tiny-OS is written in NesC programming language which is a dialect of C language. NesC uses interfaces to connect the components together. Interfaces dictate the functional connections between the components. The interfaces are of two types (1) *provided* and (2) *used* interfaces. Component providing Interface implements the functionality of that interface which can be used by user component. Used interfaces represent the functionalities needed for performing the job. The interfaces are bidirectional and work as commands and events. Interface user calls commands from user to the Interface provider whereas Interface provider signals events from provider to interface user. Normally commands are called from upper layers to the lower layers close to hardware and events from lower layers to the upper layers like interrupts. The interfaces are wired to bind the components together functionally using the configuration files. Native NesC and ncc compilers along with AVR binutils are used for compiling the Tiny-OS applications.

Open-ZB. Open-ZB is a software version of IEEE 802.15.4. The code is open and it defines the Zigbee stack having MAC and PHY layers written in NesC language [9,10].

The stack works over the Tiny-OS operating system and mainly uses the scheduler and the system libraries from Tiny-OS for working of the stack. For communicating between the two layers Zigbee defines the Service Access Points (SAPs), interfaces are used to wire the components and functions as the SAPs between layers. The stack does not interact with hardware directly instead it relies on the hardware specific components provided by the Tiny-OS. The stack is implemented on hardware platform Crossbow Micaz mote which contains IEEE.802.15.4 compliant 2.4 GHz Zigbee transceiver and provides 250 kbps data rate and Atmel ATMega128L processor. Micaz hardware specific drivers are provided by the Tiny-OS operating system.

For implementation of the stack on hardware, Tiny-OS-1.x installed on Ubuntu 12.04 along with the NesC and ncc compilers and required binutils. The stack then ported over Tiny-OS and then complete stack ported on Micaz mote using MIB520 board.

3   Design and Implementation

The main modules and functions are described below.

3.1   Transceiver

The transceiver module takes care of the transmission and reception of data frames by giving proper control signals to the memory access module. It is designed as a controlpath which becomes enabled when the beacon transmission is done and when the Active period begins. Transmit and receive ports are designed as serial as mentioned in the standard. It acts as the main module which consistently watches the Superframe periods, CSMA-CA mechanism, Sequence Number generation, Interframe Spacings (IFS) etc. (Fig. 3).

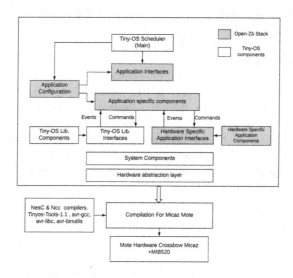

Fig. 3. Block diagram of Open-ZB

3.2   CSMA-CA

As superframe is used in this design, slotted CSMA-CA algorithm is adopted for channel access. Once the beacon has been sent and transmission request happens, this FFD will run this algorithm to check if the channel is free or not. If the channel is free, success flag becomes high else asserts the failure flag. This algorithm is employed before transmitting a data frame or MAC Command frame and not used before acknowledgement and beacon frames. Also, it is used only in the Contention Access Period (CAP) and not in the Contention Free Period (CFP). The algorithm used is as shown in Fig. 4. In the design, flag for success or failure is received as input to the main module and transmission happens based on this. Random number generators are employed for generating random back-off periods. The algorithm given is strictly followed in every CAP slots.

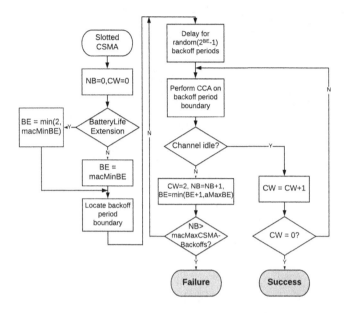

Fig. 4. CSMA-CA algorithm

3.3 Superframe

All Low Rate (LR)-WPAN networks have an option to work in two modes (1) beacon-enabled mode or (2) non-beacon enabled mode. Superframe format is used for beacon enabled networks. It is bounded by two beacons and in between there is the active period as well as the inactive period. Active period amounts to the CAP and the CFP. A total of 16 slots are there in Active period and CFP can occupy zero or more slots leaving aside aMinCAPLength for CAP (Fig. 5).

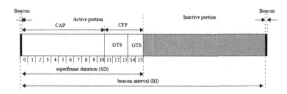

Fig. 5. Superframe format. All periods can be variable as mentioned in [1]

3.4 Memory Access Module

There is a RAM file provided which can accommodate one complete frame at a time. From the general frame format mentioned in the standard [1], the number of bytes in a frame can be upto 143 maximum. Hence the memory is given the maximum size with the first byte comes at the top and the first bit of that byte comes first as shown in Fig. 6.

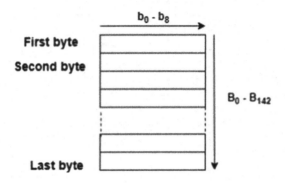

Fig. 6. RAM memory to store one frame

Beacon frame is handled separately as it can overwrite the data otherwise. It has a maximum of 145 bytes.

3.5 Frame Check Sequence

The last two bytes of all types of frame is dedicated for FCS which is generated by the serial Cyclic Redundancy Check (CRC) module. Parallel CRC is not used here as the frames are of variable size and it also increases the amount of hardware. Although serial CRC takes more calculation time than parallel CRC, it is compensated by simultaneously calculating the CRC bits along with the serial transmission and reception. Hence it do not require an additional clock cycle. The standard CRC-16 generator polynomial is used and the implementation is done as shown in Fig. 7.

Fig. 7. Serial CRC implementation

4   Simulation Results

The behavioural simulation is done using Xilinx ISE and below given is the simulation result for the main module.

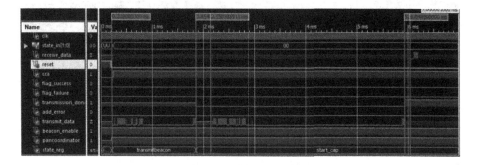

Fig. 8. Transmission of one data frame

4.1   Transmission

One of the transmission scenarios is shown in Fig. 8. There are five markers provided to indicate the flow of actions taking place while transmission. The relevant signals and working are as follows.

1. *transmit_data, state_reg*: Beacon transmission begins.
2. *transmit_data, state_reg*: Beacon transmission ends.
3. *flag_success, transmit_data*: Just after the third marker, flag_success becomes high indicating the channel is free and immediately the data frame transmission begins.
4. *transmit_data, transmission_done*: Data transmission ends.
5. *receive_data*: Acknowledgement reception begins as Acknowledgement Request (AR) bit of the transmitted frame is set to '1'.

4.2   Reception

One of the reception scenarios is shown in Fig. 9. There are five markers provided to indicate the flow of actions taking place while reception. The relevant signals and working are as follows.

1. *transmit_data, state_reg*: Beacon transmission begins.
2. *transmit_data, state_reg*: Beacon transmission ends.
3. *receive_data*: Starts to receive data.
4. *receive_data, reception_done*: Ends receiving data.
5. *send_ack, transmit_data*: As the received frame requires an acknowledgement (AR = '1'), acknowledgement transmission happens.

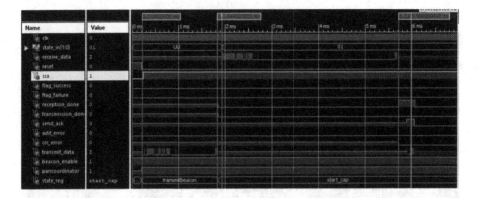

Fig. 9. Reception of one data frame

5   FPGA and ASIC Implementation

The RTL Design has been synthesized for device XC7K325T of Kintex 7 FPGA family. 4% of the available LUTs are used to implement the design. Device utilization summary is given in Table 1. Hence only a small portion of the resource is utilized. The highest clock frequency acquired is 87.79 MHz which is found to be higher than that mentioned in [2] which is an improvement in our design. For the complete design, ASIC platform is opted and rest is carried out as described in the next section.

Table 1. Device utilization summary

Logic utilization	Utilization
Number of slice registers	1%
Number of slice LUTs	4%
Number of bonded IOBs	11%
Number of DSP48E1s	0%

Complete front end and backend flow of ASIC design is done using Cadence tools. The Register Transfer Level (RTL) code is synthesized to a netlist using Genus Synthesis Tool from Cadence. This is done using the SCL 180 nm technology libraries. Power, area and timing reports are extracted and the results are given in Table 2. Clock frequency is set as 64 MHz.

For comparison purposes, this power is calculated with security feature disabled. In the total power, 0.8 mW is consumed by the main transceiver module, 0.2 mW by the superframe module (along with all beacon functionalities and synchronizations) and the rest is split between the other modules. Two frame memories are provided with 143 and 145 bytes capacity each which are considered in the synthesis.

Table 2. ASIC synthesis results

Power (mW)	Area (mm^2)	Slack
1.1	0.5	Met

Backend flow is done using Innovus Implementation System, a physical implementation tool from Cadence. Place and route of the complete design is done and other physical design steps are also carried out to get the final GDS file. Layout diagram of the design is shown in Fig. 10.

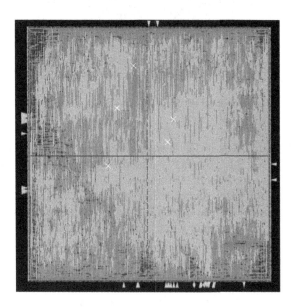

Fig. 10. ASIC Layout diagram

6   Comparison with Open-ZB

As a part-to-part equivalence cannot be checked in case of software and a piece of hardware, comparison is limited to the features implemented as well as the amount of power dissipation by both designs. The main features implemented are given in Table 3.

As we can see, all the main features except security is implemented in open-ZB [7]. Hence for comparison purpose, it has been disabled from the Hardware MAC also. The software stack has been implemented on the Micaz platform. As the stack is written in NesC language, it has been compiled to C code first and then made it an executable. This final executable is burned in the Micaz platform. A mesh network with a PAN coordinator and two other devices was formed with Beacon Order (BO) = 7 and Superframe Order (SO) = 6 and

Fig. 11. Experimental setup of Open-ZB stack on Micaz platform

transmission of data is done for a simulation time of 20 s. The experimental setup is shown in Fig. 11. For energy and packet simulation AvroraZ emulator is used which is an extension of Avrora.

Results of the software emulation are given in Table 4. For the 20 s simulation, energy consumed by the device is 0.454 J with a processor frequency of 7.37 MHz which is also less than what is used in hardware MAC. It is clear that approximately 95% of the total energy is spend in the MAC layer and it is very much larger than what we saw in the hardware MAC.

Table 3. List of main features present (Y) and not present (N) in Hardware and Software

Feature	Hardware MAC	Open-ZB
Transmit and receive data	Y	Y
Superframe format	Y	Y
CRC-16	Y	Y
CSMA-CA mechanism	Y	Y
Frame filtering	Y	Y
Frame formatting	Y	Y
Security	N	N
Beacon generation	Y	Y
Beacon reception	Y	Y

Table 4. Number of clock cycles and power consumed by the software stack

Clock cycles ($\times 10^3$)			Power (mW)	
Total	Active	MAC layer	Total	MAC layer
147456	97680.329	49775.671	22.7	21.565

7   Conclusion

A complete hardware approach on MAC Layer compliant to standard [1] is presented in this paper. A comparison with the software stack Open-ZB is also provided for the analysis of power efficiency in hardware as well as software. Even though there is an advantage of frequency for the Software stack, a great reduction of power is seen from the results obtained from RTL design synthesis and the software compilation and emulation. A comparison without the security feature is good enough because it will add up the power in both cases almost in the same manner for the reason that it is implemented as an entirely separate unit in most of the cases. This can be the basis of any hardware attempt on MAC Layer and if extended, for a complete sensor node. Also, comparison to other stacks mentioned in [7] can be done with the security feature enabled. In a different perspective, there is a good scope for performance analysis also.

References

1. IEEE 802 Working Group: IEEE Standard for Local and Metropolitan Area Networks—Part 15.4: Low-Rate Wireless Personal Area Networks (LR-WPANs). IEEE Std, vol. 802, 4-2011 (2011)
2. Zhang, M., et al.: MAC controller for Wireless Sensor Network on IEEE 802.15. 4 standard. In: 2012 6th International Conference on Signal Processing and Communication Systems (ICSPCS). IEEE (2012)
3. Chen, S., Yao, J., Yuhou, W.: Analysis of the power consumption for wireless sensor network node based on Zigbee. Proc. Eng. **29**, 1994–1998 (2012)
4. Di Francesco, M., et al.: Reliability and energy-efficiency in IEEE 802.15. 4/ZigBee sensor networks: an adaptive and cross-layer approach. IEEE J. Sel. Areas Commun. **29**(8), 1508–1524 (2011)
5. Chintalapudi, K.K., Venkatraman, L.: On the design of MAC protocols for low-latency hard real-time discrete control applications over 802.15. 4 hardware. In: Proceedings of the 7th International Conference on Information Processing in Sensor Networks. IEEE Computer Society (2008)
6. Sun, Y., Li, L., Luo, H.: Design of FPGA-based multimedia node for WSN. In: 2011 7th International Conference on Wireless Communications, Networking and Mobile Computing (WiCOM). IEEE (2011)
7. Basmer, T., Schomann, H., Peter, S.: Implementation analysis of the IEEE 802.15. 4 MAC for wireless sensor networks. In: 2011 International Conference on Selected Topics in Mobile and Wireless Networking (iCOST). IEEE (2011)
8. Kothari, N.B., Sudarshan, T.S.B., Gurunarayanan, S.: SOC design of a Low Power Wireless Sensor network node for Zigbee Systems. In: International Conference on Advanced Computing and Communications, ADCOM 2006. IEEE (2006)

9. Cunha, A., et al.: Open-ZB: an open-source implementation of the IEEE 802.15. 4/ZigBee protocol stack on TinyOS. In: IEEE International Conference on Mobile Adhoc and Sensor Systems, MASS 2007. IEEE (2007)

10. Open-ZB - Open-source Toolset for IEEE 802.15.4. Website. http://www.open-zb. net

11. Cunha, A., Alves, M., Koubaa, A.: Implementation of the ZigBee network layer with cluster-tree support. IPP-HURRAY Technical report, HURRAY-TR-070510 (2007)

12. Cunha, A., et al.: ZigBee over TinyOS: implementation and experimental challenges. In: 8th Portuguese Conference on Automatic Control (2008)

13. Levis, P., et al.: TinyOS: an operating system for sensor networks. In: Weber, W., Rabaey, J.M., Aarts, E. (eds.) Ambient Intelligence, pp. 115–148. Springer, Heidelberg (2005). https://doi.org/10.1007/3-540-27139-2_7

14. Gay, D., et al.: The nesC language: a holistic approach to networked embedded systems. ACM SIGPLAN Not. **49**(4), 41–51 (2014)

15. ATmega128L 8-bit AVRMicrocontroller Datasheet Atmel ref: 2467MAVR-11/04 Website. http://www.atmel.com

Design of CMOS Based Biosensor for Implantable Medical Devices

G. Gifta[⊠], D. Gracia Nirmala Rani, Nifasath Farhana,
and R. Archana

Thiagarajar College of Engineering, Madurai, India
giffy.zion@gmail.com, gracia@tce.edu,
nifasathfarhanatce@gmail.com, archanarajtce@gmail.com

Abstract. In the recent years medical potential of Implantable Medical Devices (IMD) has attracted increasing attention of surgical methods to improve the human health care. IMD is used as diagnostic or therapeutic devices. It is fabricated to replace the missing biological structure or improving the functioning of damaged biological structure. Bio sensor is a major block present in an implantable device it is an analytical device used for the detection of an analyze that combines a biological component with a physicochemical detector. To design an low power amplifier for biosensor is a challenging task, This paper present a low power CMOS based OTA with 1 V power supply produce an output current of 154 pA and power consumption of 19 µW. The proposed system has been developed by using 0.18 µm CMOS technology on CADENCE Design Environment with simulation results.

Keywords: Ultra low power · Electrochemical-biosensor · OTA · CMOS technology

1 Introduction

Recent advances in integrated biosensors resides within implantable medical device deals with the detection of many hazardous biological elements within our human body which includes cholera toxin, mycotoxins, rabies virus from biomolecules such as glucose, DNA, RNA, antibodies and proteins. The accuracy level in detection of disease by using biosensor is very high and the cost for designing of biosensor is very low. It is more comfortable and flexible for human body. Bio Senor is an analytical device which detects the biological components like tissue, antibodies, nucleic acids and cell receptors. There are many types of biosensors i.e.: Blood glucose biosensor, optical biosensor, Electrochemical biosensor, Potentiometric biosensor and Thermometric biosensor. This paper deals with design and development of electrochemical biosensors.

The above diagram describes the components of biosensors. Electrochemical Biosensor is a device which measures electronic current, ionic by conductance changes carried by bio-electrodes.

The biosensor which consists of five elements such as bio-element, transducer, amplifier, processor and display. The transducer is an element that convert the

© Springer Nature Singapore Pte Ltd. 2019
S. Rajaram et al. (Eds.): VDAT 2018, CCIS 892, pp. 695–704, 2019.
https://doi.org/10.1007/978-981-13-5950-7_57

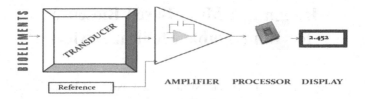

Fig. 1. Flow diagram of biosensor

bio-recognition element into a measurable signal. The transducer produces a electrical signal which is used for amplification. It converts the bio-element into voltage signal. Then the voltage signal is given as an input to an amplifier which is an Operational Tran conductance Amplifier (OTA) followed by pixel amplifier which is mostly used in biomedical application. So it has low voltage, low power consumption, has low noise and easy implementation. The processor which performs signal conditioning such as amplification and conversion of signals from analog into digital form. Input parameter of biosensors having weak signal in the range of PicoVolt to NanoVolt has to be amplified. The processed signals are then quantified by the display unit of biosensor. The output signal on the display can be numeric, graphic, or image which depends on the requirement of end user.

The transconductance operational amplifier design is done using 180 nm technology [8] which uses a low pass filter to eliminate noise at higher frequencies only. A single stage OTA design using 90 nm technology [7] possesses good frequency response, the topology carries the disadvantage of lack of tunability & limited linearity. Two stage OTA based on floating gate has compared with two stage CMOS OTA using 180 nm CMOS technology [5] the technique employed leads to a significant increase in DC gain and decrease in the settling time without extra power consumption. High CMRR OTA design using 180 nm technology with the power supply at 1.6 V and multifunction filter design implemented using 2.5 V [4] employs to lead more voltage sources growing aging population and aggravating environmental problems have led to increasing interests in wearable and implantable medical devices [3] but the wearable devices are affected by bad weather condition and human sweat etc. An active bandpass filter based on operational transconductance amplifiers (OTA) using simple CMOS current mirrors using 180 nm technology [2] with the frequency of 1.18 GHz and bandwidth of 15 MHz.

Our objective is to design a two stage OTA with pixel stage consumes minimum power and gives a high gain used in biosensor for biomedical application.

The paper is being organized as follows. Session II deals the problem formulation and Sect. 3 presents the proposed design of the CMOS OTA for the required specification Results and Discussions are considered in the Sect. 4. The conclusion is drawn in the last section demonstrates the various issue in different topologies of OTA. It identifies a very simple and different topology which gives electrical parameter like DC gain, linearity and Power supply rejection ratio (PSRR). Op-amp can also used to avoid closed loop instability, frequency compensation but OTA are widely used to meet the required performances. For two stage operational transconductance amplifier, the simplest compensation technique is to connect the capacitor between differential transconductance stage and common source amplifier stage. Depends upon the input and output characteristics OTA can classified into four types. There are (i) single-stage OTA (ii) Two-stage OTA. (iii) Telescopic OTA (iv) cascade OTA (v) Folded cascade OTA. Single stage OTA implementation is very easy but it gives very low gain when compared to two stage. Cascade OTA is a two transistor stack which is used to obtain high gain and output impedance, it reduces the output capacitance in compared to the normal configuration which is used for high frequency responses but for amplifier stability it requires compensation technique. To avoid low gain of a single stage OTA, telescopic OTA has been designed by adding some additional transistors. By adding more transistors the output voltage swing is reduced. For two stage we need less number of transistor enough to design. Folded cascade OTA was design to compensate telescopic OTA. It permits low supply voltage still having high output voltage swing but it consumes more power when compared to telescopic Two stage OTA has high output voltage, very high gain when compared to other topologies and at low frequency PSRR of the OTA is very high.

2 Proposed Design

Figure 2 shows the circuit diagram of the CMOS OTA followed by Pixel amplifier. The OTA topology plays a major role in the design of low power system. It is the basic building block of any signal processing system. These Amplifiers are mainly classified into Single ended output OTA and Differential ended output. In this design we proposed a Differential Two stage CMOS OTA. The first stage is differential pair input voltage with current mirror load and the second stage is gain stage or common source amplifier stage. Bulk driven technique is applied at the input of OTA, so it can operate at minimum supply voltage. The two stage differential OTA have several advantages over single-ended output OTA such as one frequency compensation capacitor, consume less power and reduce the distortion. The two stage OTA has differential input voltage which generates a output current. This can be called as a voltage controlled current source (VCCS). The OTA is mostly used in all biomedical application.

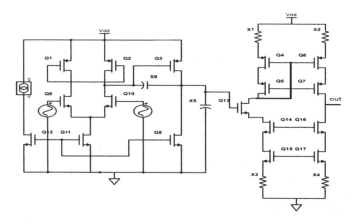

Fig. 2. Proposed circuit of transconductance amplifier

The threshold voltage remains almost constant for all OTA, so reduction in power consumption is an challenging task. The proposed OTA design aimed to reduce the power supply voltage. The proposed transconductance amplifier which has two stages known two stage CMOS OTA as shown in Fig. 2. The two stages are input differential transconductance stage followed by gain stage. The second stage which increases the gain and maximizes the output signal is an important factor in power consumption. The bias circuit is used here for fixing operating point for each transistor. The proposed OTA which has many advantage of high gain, one frequency compensation capacitor, and less number of transistor. The OTA finds its application in analog to digital convertors, bio-medical signals amplification, sensing signals and designing of filters. Then CMOS OTA configuration in which transistor Q12 provides biasing for entire operational amplifier. The transistor Q12 and Q11 form a differential pair and thus the input of the first stage of operational amplifier. The transistor Q9 and Q10 supplies differential pair with bias current IDC. The input of the operational transconductance amplifier depends on the basis of bias current. The input differential pair is actively loaded with current mirror formed by Q2 and Q1. Node 1 forms the output of the first stage of op-amp. The second stage consists of Q3 which is common source amplifier actively loaded with the transistor Q8. The transistor Q3 and Q8 which act as an output transistor. The transistor Q8 does not provide biasing for Q3 indeed Q3 is biased from gate side. The size of the transistors is discussed in Table 1. The capacitors are used in the design for frequency compensation between first and second stage. The proposed OTA have attains high performance in CMOS technology at low voltage application.

The main aim of our work is to reduce power consumption, noise and have high gain so we designed Pixel amplifier stage along with two stage OTA. Transistor Q13 acts as an input transistor of pixel amplifier.

Table 1. Specification table

Transistors	(W/L) ratio
Q1, Q2	8u/1u
Q3	87u/1u
Q4, Q5	3u/24u
Q6, Q7	10*3/24
Q8	38u/1u
Q9, Q10	3u/1u
Q11, Q12	6u/1u
Q14	2.1u/12u
Q15	1.5u/48u

Transistor Q13 acts as an input transistor of pixel amplifier. A current splitter array can generate femto ampere current but cannot generate bidirectional current pulses, to resolve this problem a capacitor X5 of 2 pF is added to the input of pixel amplifier. The output of OTA has been given as an input to pixel amplifier through capacitor, Pulse of voltage are applied on capacitance to generate current pulse. The capacitor X6 of

800 fF added between first stage and second stage of OTA, as it is used for frequency compensation. The pixel amplifier consists of three stage cascoded amplifier of nmos and pmos. The transistor which consist of flicker noise and thermal noise. To avoid these noise the transistor one cascaded pmos and nmos transistor has been replaced with resistors X1, X2, X3, X4. These transistors can act as a resistors in linear region. By these we can able to reduce thermal noise. Next comes to flicker noise, to reduce it the size of the transistors has to be increased. Therefore, to reduce input referred current noise contribution of Q4 and Q6, the transistor area was set at very large area to reduce flicker noise. Large transistor length of Q4 and Q6 also helps provide accurate current gain by reducing transistor mismatch effects. As a result, the source terminal voltage of transistors Q4 and Q6 are equal. The voltage terminal of transistors Q15 and Q17 also becomes equal. The resistor X1 and X3 has been given as 10 MΩ and the resistors X2 and X4 was given as 1 MΩ. The pixel amplifier stage is designed to obtain a high gain and to reduce the noise level.

3   Result and Discussion

The CMOS OTA has been designed, simulated and implemented by using 0.18 nm CMOS technology with the power supply of 1 V. The main parameter in the design is power consumption and it has been analyzed and plotted with respect to the schematic design entry of the block. The DC analysis with differential input produces an output current for the designed OTA and pixel stage has been plotted. The Transient analysis of the designed amplifier at different time periods has been plotted. The AC gain for two stages and pixel stage of the amplifier was plotted.

3.1   Transient Analysis

The Fig. 3 shows the amplified output of an operational transconductance amplifier (OTA). This can be obtained by keeping the differential input voltage at 500 nV at

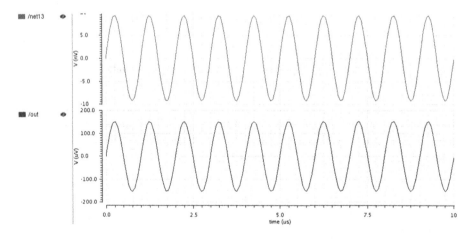

Fig. 3. Transient response of amplifier

inverting terminal and 800 nV at the non-inverting terminal, 20 nA of biasing current, 1 K frequency and 1 V of supply voltage with time period of 10 us.

3.2   AC Analysis

The OTA is an voltage to current converter circuit whose differential input voltage produces an output current circuit in which is obtained in Fig. 3. As

$$I_{out} = (V_{in+} - V_{in-})G_m$$

Where V_{in+} and V_{in-} represent the voltage at inverting and non-inverting terminals. The OTA output voltage can be obtained by

$$V_{out} = I_{out} R_{out}$$

The voltage gain is the ratio of output voltage to that of differential input voltage in which the transconductance amplifier gain is obtained by

$$G_{voltage} = R_{out} G_m$$

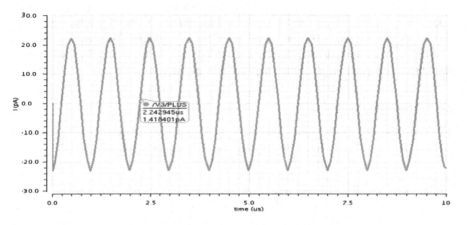

Fig. 4. Output current plot of transconductance amplifier

To characterize the pixel amplifier's DC response, a waveform generator was used to generate a sinusoid voltage signal that was applied across a resistor to generate an input sinusoid current with power. Transient current response of the pixel stage when *Iamp* = 154, *Iwidth* = 200 ns as shown in Fig. 5.

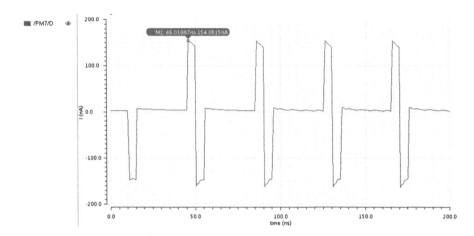

Fig. 5. Output current plot of pixel amplifier

3.3 DC Analysis

In proposed design of CMOS OTA gain can be calculated at two stages. In first stage gain of the amplifier is as 64 dB as shown in the Fig. 6. And in the second stage of the amplifier the gain obtained is 90 dB as shown in Fig. 7.

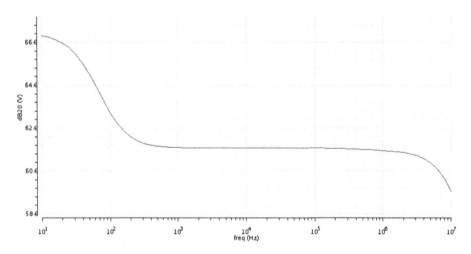

Fig. 6. Output gain of first stage in amplifier

In this paper, the pixel amplifier has been designed at cutoff frequency of 1 kHz. As the frequency of pixel amplifier ranges from 50 Hz to 19 kHz, has a low frequency gain of 31 dB as shown in Fig. 8.

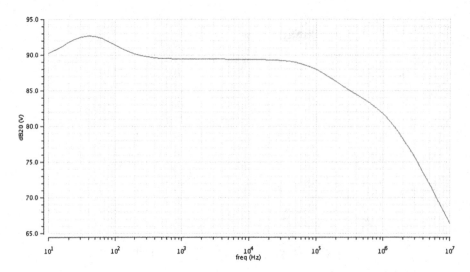

Fig. 7. Output gain of second stage in amplifier

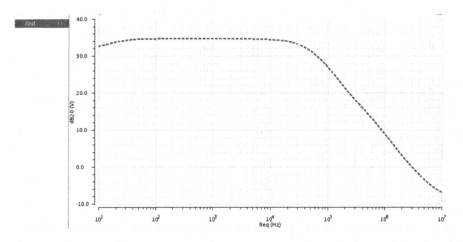

Fig. 8. Output gain of pixel amplifier

3.4 Power Plot

In any type of Integrated circuit (IC) power consumption is the most challenging parameter. The design of proposed system is aimed at reducing the power in the range of µW shown in Fig. 9, thereby improving the performance of the low power biomedical circuits.

Then the various values of power plot that is obtained by the previous results are compared with our design's power values at 180 nm CMOS technology in Table 1. Hence the comparison of other studies with our design has been analyzed at different values of power supply with 180 nm CMOS Technology. So an improved OTA is being proposed with more effective design in order to reduce the power consumption.

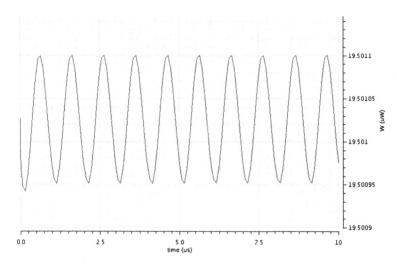

Fig. 9. Power plot of amplifier

From the above comparison table we can conclude that the power consumption for our design has been reduced of about 12.6 µW. Hence this low power CMOS OTA could be implemented at different implantable medical device (Table 2).

Table 2. Comparison table

Ref.	Process (CMOS Technology)	Power supply (V)	Bias current (I_{bias}, A)	Gain (dB)	Power consumption (W)
[1]	90 nm	1.3	20u	80.43	3.3 m
[2]	180 nm	1.5	57u	71.20	4.8 m
[3]	130 nm	1.5	2.85 m	58.7	15.85µ
[4]	32 nm	0.5	1n	13	18.85µ
[5]	130 nm	1.25	550 m	12	3.2 m
[6]	250 nm	2.5	20u	36	86µ
[7]	0.5 nm	1	10n	161	21µ
This Work	180 nm	**1**	**20p**	**90**	**12.6µ**

4   Conclusion

This paper demonstrates the design of biosensor with transconductance amplifier and pixel amplifier has a low power consumption of 19.5 µW which is implemented by 0.18 nm CMOS technology with less number of transistors. The OTA is used in sensing signals in which it attains a high gain of 90 dB analyzed from simulation results. The proposed biosensor has features of high speed, high gain and low frequency which have been used in much low power biomedical application in which the battery life of the implantable medical device can exists longer.

5 Future Work

Low power is becoming the key research area in today's electronics industry. The low power consumption is becoming an important parameter in battery operated devices as speed, area and gain. So we have to design such an efficient circuit which will provide us high Gain, high Unity Gain Bandwidth, with the minimum power consumption. We can even try different techniques from the literature to implement with our design to get the better performance.

References

1. Haitao, L., Manson, A.J.: Ultra compact microwatt CMOS current readout with pico ampere noise and kilohertz bandwidth for biosensor arrays. IEEE Trans. Biomed. Circuits Syst. **53** (11), 2371–2376 (2018)
2. Jarjar, M., El Ouazzani, O.: Design of an OTA-based microwave active bandpass filter. In: International Conference on Wireless Technologies Embedded and Intelligent Systems (WITS) (2017)
3. Zhang, Huang, S., Chen, M., Zeng, X.: An area-efficient error-resilient ultralow-power subthreshold ECG processor. IEEE Trans. Biomed. Circuits Syst. **18**, 273–288 (2016)
4. Gaonkar, S., Sushma, P.S.: Modeling, design and analysis of high CMRR two stage gate driven operational transconductance amplifier using 0.18 μm technology. In: International Conference on Computing for Sustainable Global Development (INDIACom) (2016)
5. Vijeta, Wairya, S.: A study of two stage operational transconductance amplifier using floating gate MOSFET. Int. J. Eng. Comput. Sci. **4**(10), 14643–14648 (2015). ISSN 2319-7242
6. Yong, G., Li, X., et al.: A health IOT platform based on integration of Intelligent Packing, cohersive Bio sensor and intelligent medicine box. IEEE Trans. Biomed. Device Circuits **20**, 636–646 (2014)
7. Khare, A.V., Dahigaonkar, D.: Effect of scaling on operation of low voltage OTA. Int. J. Eng. Sci. (IJES) **2**, 191–193 (2013)
8. Maiellaro, G., Ragonese, E., Jacob, S., Benwadih, M., Coppard, R., Cantatore, E.: High-gain operational transconductance amplifiers in a printed complementary organic TFT technology on flexible foil. IEEE-Trans. Circuits Syst. **60**, 3117–3125 (2013)

Design and Fabrication of Versatile Low Power Wireless Sensor Nodes for IoT Applications

Saket Thool[(✉)], Raghavendra Deshmukh, and Rajendra Patrikar

Centre for VLSI and Nanotechnology, Visvesvaraya National Institute of Technology, Nagpur 440010, MH, India
saketthool@gmail.com, rbdeshmukh@ece.vnit.ac.in, rajendra@computer.org

Abstract. Recent times world has witnessed a wireless sensing networks (WSN) technology attracting for a wide range of real-world applications, mostly due to its shrinking size and cost while demonstrating improved performances and functionalities. One of the crucial factors that affect the operation of WSN is its power consumption and battery life. This paper provides an overview for designing of a low power WSN for IoT applications. Through a combination of ZigBee wireless technology, with a strong networking function, it can realize the communication between a number of Wireless Sensor Nodes. Cost-effective and low power reliable system is implemented using this protocol. Core2530 is one of the Zigbee stack available for such network solution. While considering sensor platforms and its applications, power consumption is one of the important factors to take into consideration. This paper presents the development of low power wireless sensor node for condition monitoring of railway rolling stocks.

Keywords: Embedded · IOT · WSN · ZigBee · Vibrations

1 Introduction

The term Wireless Sensor Node was introduced in the field of wireless communications several years ago, when "Internet of thing" was trending as technology. Since then the academic community as well as industry has paid a great deal of attention to Wireless Sensor Networks (WSN). The continuous advancement in technology had made WSN cheaper, smaller and more efficient in terms of power and versatility for a wide range of applications. Despite it, the most common application of Wireless Sensor Nodes is data collection, retrieving the important data out of collected raw data through wireless sensor network. The sensors involved in WSN application are mostly micro-electro-mechanical systems (MEMS) technology based such as accelerometers, pressure sensor, gas sensors etc. Recent advances in wireless communication and digital electronics have enabled us to develop low power wireless sensors nodes [1]. WSN has been

© Springer Nature Singapore Pte Ltd. 2019
S. Rajaram et al. (Eds.): VDAT 2018, CCIS 892, pp. 705–719, 2019.
https://doi.org/10.1007/978-981-13-5950-7_58

found to be a critical tool for smart home application and environmental monitoring system. In this work, the development of low power wireless sensor node has been discussed (Fig. 1).

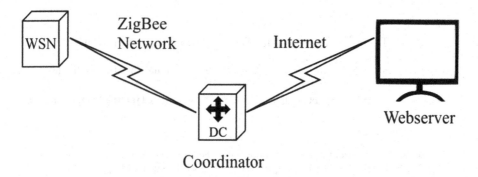

Fig. 1. Overall system description

In this work, we have fabricated WSN for vibration monitoring of railway rolling stock using IoT. It is capable of sensing vibrations in XYZ direction up to a range of ±12 g and temperature of the same. The work in this paper has been organized into following sections as Introduction, Designing of Wireless Sensor Node, the Hardware structure of WSN, Software for low-power design of WSN, Results and discussion obtained followed by a conclusion.

2   Designing of Wireless Sensor Nodes

One of the key requirement in the design of wireless sensor nodes is low power. Thus, In the process of selection of commercial off the shelf (COTS) components, low power consumption requirement was taken into consideration. The main components of Wireless sensor node are as shown in Fig. 2. Components which are proposed as follows.

Table 1. Absolute power ratings.

Block	Component proposed	Absolute power ratings
Transceiver	CC2530F256R	29 mA
Microcontroller	STM32F103C8T6	11 mA
Sensor - accelerometer	AIS3624DQ	10 uA
Sensor - temperature	TMP37	50 uA
Battery	Li-ion 18650	3800 mAH

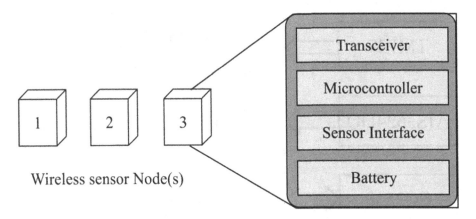

Fig. 2. Sensor node architecture

With help of above asserted COTS components, Wireless Sensor Nodes have been fabricated. It consists of Zigbee chip CC2530 from Texas Instruments which was flashed with custom ZigBee stack provided by WaveShare Electronics [2]. It is a true System-on-Chip solution for RF transceivers based on an enhanced 8051 core suiting for low power system perfectly [5]. STM32F103C8T6 ARM M4 controller from STMicroelectronics served as the main controller for data acquisition and TI's CC2530 as Transceiver Module. Two different sensors were used in this work one for vibration measurement, AIS3624DQ which is industrial grade accelerometer from STMicroelectronics and another one was TMP37 a temperature sensor from Analog Devices. The theoretically calculated power consumption for WSN is 41 mA. The power unit accommodates a Li-Ion 18650 battery with 3.3 V nominal voltage with a low-dropout (LDO) regulator. Standby time of fabricated WSN by theoretical computations is found to be 3800 mAh/41 mA, 92.68 h to be precise.

3   Hardware Structure

The complete system needs a single power supply to run stably. Figures 3 and 4 combinedly shows block diagram of WSN. The entire wireless sensor node mainly divided into two main parts, the Transceiver module, and data acquisition module.

3.1   Transceiver Module

This module applies CC2530 flashed with WaveShare stack to construct Zigbee communication Network as shown in Fig. 4. CC2530 that lives up to Zigbee protocols supports TTL level serial interface. Therefore, communication can be

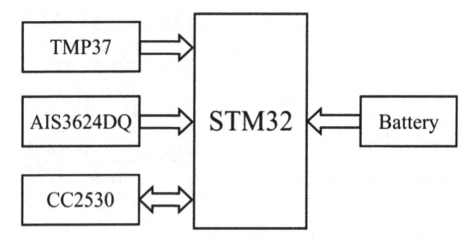

Fig. 3. Hardware structure wireless sensor node

conducted with the core processor and there is no need for interface conversion
[4]. It also supports 2.4 GHz, The ISM band is the RF band of choice for most
current and future wireless devices in the field of industrial, scientific and medical
field it offers larger bandwidth and follows IEEE 802.15.4/ZigBee standards,
which meets the design of low cost and low power consumption requirements
[3]. It has Active-Mode RX current consumption of 24 mA and Active Mode TX
current consumption of 29 mA [5]., which is quite good in number as compared
to popular ZigBee available in the market.

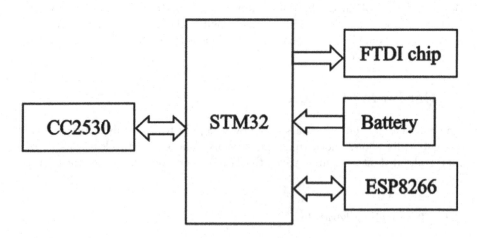

Fig. 4. Hardware structure data concentrator

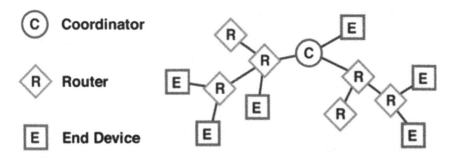

Fig. 5. Topology example of a ZigBee network [6]

Coordinator, Router and End devices are basic components of ZigBee network as shown in Fig. 5. In our fabricated system wireless sensor node (WSN) and data concentrator (DC) uses the same hardware design. WSN was configured as Router/End Device since router device can act as a router as well as End Device and data concentrator is configured as Coordinator. In system designed data concentrator creates a ZigBee network when it starts with configured Personal Area Network (PAN) ID, all other routers and end devices with same PAN ID will join this ZigBee network. In this module CC2530 and main controller communicates over the serial port with a data rate as low as 2400 bps.

3.2   Data Acquisition Module

This module consisted of accelerometer AIS3624DQ and Temperature sensor TMP37. AIS3624DQ is connected on SPI bus of STM32. It is ultra-low-power 3-axis accelerometer having a digital output of 16 bit with 12-bit resolution [7]. TMP37 is connected on ADC port of STM32. It is low voltage, precision centigrade temperature sensors, provide a voltage output that is linearly proportional to the Celsius (centigrade) temperature [8]. Averaging of data acquired is done before transmitting to reduce noise and error in data. Block diagram for Data concentrator is described in Fig. 4, transceiver module is common in both Sensor Nodes and Data Concentrator (DC). Besides that, two extra blocks are there ESP8266 and FTDI chip.

3.3   FTDI (Serial Port)

FTDI's FT230 is Single chip for USB to asynchronous serial data transfer interface. Here this chip is integrated on DC to communicate with laptop over serial com port. With help of this chip telemetry viewer is communicating with DC for observing Sensor Nodes Data.

3.4   ESP8266 (Wi-Fi Module)

In this proposed DC (Data Concentrator) it consists Wi-Fi module for Data Concentrator to server/base station communication. ESP8266 module collects the data from stores collected sensor nodes data to the MySQL database with Transmission Control Protocol (TCP) as shown in Fig. 13.

4   Software Technique Used in Designing of Low-Power Wireless Sensor Node

Endeavoring to reduce overall power consumption of Wireless Sensor Nodes the proposed software techniques are used. Unlike General sensor node in which Data concentrator (DC) has no control over WSN, WSN keeps broadcasting the data irrespective of whether the data is logged or not. This results in unnecessary power loss and hence the battery lifetime of Sensor node is decreases significantly [9].

4.1   General Idea of the System (WSN)

In proposed software technique the data is requested from Wireless sensor node by DC as shown in flowcharts Figs. 6 and 7. We have done successful communication without receiving unwanted signals using a fabricated wireless sensor node with proposed software techniques. When an acknowledgment is successfully received by WSN it will send the collected data for that instance and this cycle continuous unless the loop is broke. If an acknowledgment is not received within the interrupt timer it will reset the interrupt and will start over again. This technique can reduce the power consumption and hence battery life of WSN can be increased.

4.2   General Idea of the Data Concentrator (DC) System

As shown in Fig. 6 data acquisition is completely controlled by Data concentrator (DC). WSN will not send data without receiving an acknowledgment from DC as shown in the flowchart of Fig. 6.

4.3   General Idea of IoT/WoT

IoT can be referred as a use of standard internet protocols for thing-to-thing, human-to-thing or thing-to-human communication in the physical world. The data from the sensors need to be leveraged by analysing the data in real-time. Data concentrator uses ESP8266 WIFI module which acts as a gateway between data collected and webserver. Some of the famous websites providing cloud-based free IoT development platform are Thingspeak, adafruit, and postscapes.

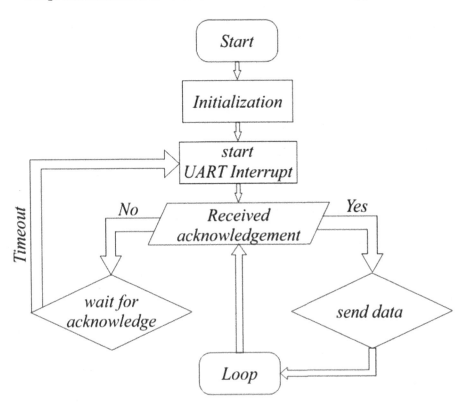

Fig. 6. Flowchart for wireless sensor node

While using these main drawbacks which user faces is latency between data posted. Thus, this makes it harder to realize in precise real-time applications. For this reason, WoT term is coming into reality which has very less latency and more capabilities over IoT. Generally, TCP protocol is used by WIFI/Ethernet modules to send data to websites with POST/GET requests. In this work, we have created the Web server with the help of PHP, Apache, and MySQL. In our system, a WIFI enabled PC acts as a Base-station. The webserver is created using XAMPP software. MySQL script for collecting data using POST request is written. The data collected through post request is stored in the database created with PHP. It has the key feature of timestamping of new data as soon as it inserted into a database. This collected WSN's data was plotted in the form data vs timestamp with help of chart.js java script. Thus, making it easier to log and observe the live data.

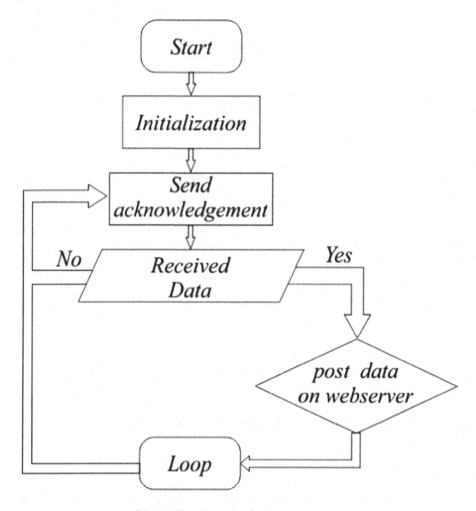

Fig. 7. Flowchart for data concentrator

4.4 General Idea of Observing Data on Serial Port

Data collected from WSN at data concentrator can also be observed on a serial monitor such as Telemetry viewer or Arduino IDE. After forming a ZigBee network, we just need to connect data concentrator to the serial port of the PC. The main advantage of using telemetry viewer is that we can export the observed sensors real-time data in csv format directly.

5   Result and Discussion

The system is fabricated using commercial off the shelf components with consideration of low power consumption as specified in Table 1. The hardware design for WSN and DC are same except WIFI module which is additional in data concentrator.

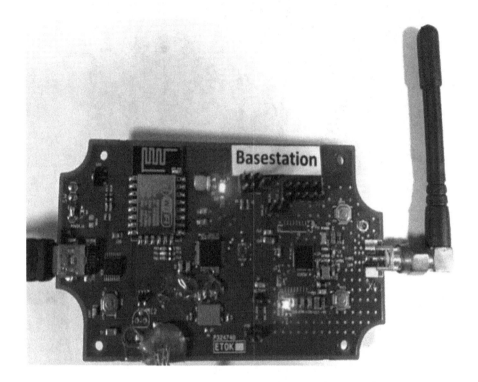

Fig. 8. Fabricated data concentrator

Figures 8 and 9 shows the fabricated DC and WSN respectively. Flowchart specified in Figs. 6 and 7 have efficiently conserved intermediate power losses during communication. The Fig. 12 shows the power consumption of WSN when data is transmitting, and in ideal state. For estimating power consumption we use the keithley current measurement unit. The final packaged WSN to be fixed on rolling stock is shown in Fig. 10. The package is of ip68 standard with industrial grade. Figure 11 shows the tentative location where the WSN will be mounted.

In the fabricated WSN ideal consumption is 34.5 mA and during communication it is 40.5 mA as specified in Sect. 2, the theoretical and observed value of power consumption is nearly same. In Sect. 2 we assume the current

Fig. 9. Fabricated wireless sensor node

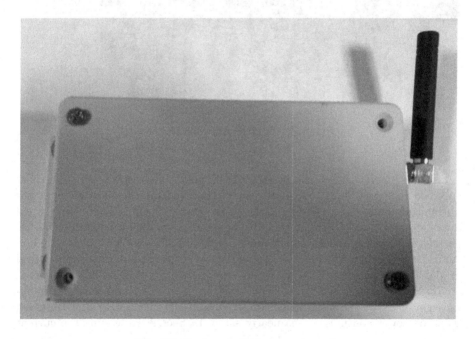

Fig. 10. Packaged wireless sensor node

consumption of 40.5 mA is constant and calculated standby of 92.68 h was found, whereas with software techniques proposed it is observed that current consumption is not constant for whole time. From Fig. 12 it was observed that out of total communication interval, 60% of it is pull downed to ideal state. Under these conditions, the lifespan of WSN will be more than stated in Sect. 2.

Fig. 11. Tentative location to mount sensor node

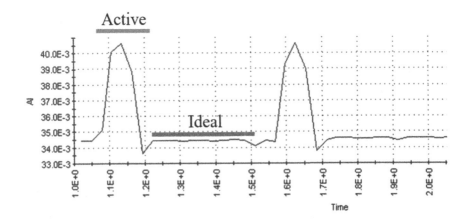

Fig. 12. Power consumption of WSN

716   S. Thool et al.

d1	d2	d3	d4	d5	d6	d7	d8	field9	ID	1
355	180	1195	28	-210	-200	1560	30	2018-04-05 15:56:38	7974	
330	135	1140	28	350	225	1275	28	2018-04-05 15:56:37	7973	
305	235	1270	28	-135	-210	1570	30	2018-04-05 15:56:35	7972	
325	145	1290	29	-120	-215	1585	30	2018-04-05 15:56:34	7971	
345	95	1285	29	-70	-270	1595	30	2018-04-05 15:56:33	7970	
440	185	1255	28	-125	-185	1590	30	2018-04-05 15:56:32	7969	
270	115	1205	29	-80	-195	1580	30	2018-04-05 15:56:31	7968	
355	190	1185	29	-145	-185	1605	30	2018-04-05 15:56:30	7967	
360	185	1170	29	-125	-210	1595	30	2018-04-05 15:56:29	7966	
345	205	1290	29	-45	-260	1530	30	2018-04-05 15:56:28	7965	
330	185	1280	28	-120	-190	1580	30	2018-04-05 15:56:27	7964	
325	95	1195	28	-120	-140	1520	30	2018-04-05 15:56:27	7963	
350	205	1350	28	-70	-160	1550	30	2018-04-05 15:56:25	7962	
350	180	1335	29	-75	-175	1505	30	2018-04-05 15:56:24	7961	
310	95	1325	28	-85	-205	1555	30	2018-04-05 15:56:23	7960	
390	140	1255	29	-165	-210	1435	30	2018-04-05 15:56:22	7959	
360	110	1165	28	-145	-165	1555	30	2018-04-05 15:56:22	7958	
300	190	1275	29	-95	-240	1585	30	2018-04-05 15:56:21	7957	
380	145	1215	28	-80	-110	1560	30	2018-04-05 15:56:20	7956	
455	185	1295	29	-90	-195	1590	30	2018-04-05 15:56:19	7955	
275	175	1280	29	-60	-215	1495	30	2018-04-05 15:56:18	7954	
320	150	1215	29	-95	-235	1525	30	2018-04-05 15:56:17	7953	

Fig. 13. PHP database of sensors data

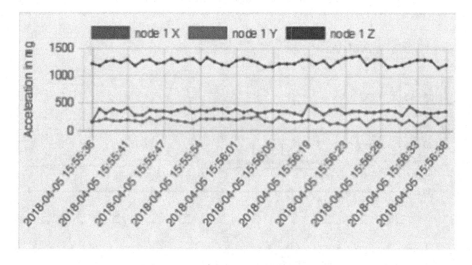

Fig. 14. Vibration data from node 1

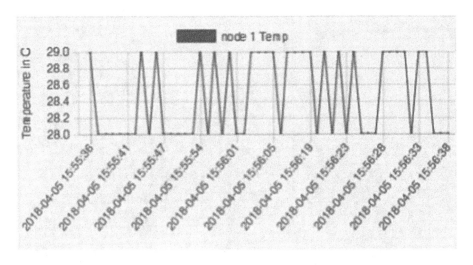

Fig. 15. Temperature data from node 1

In part C of Sect. 4, a key feature of IoT is briefed. Figure 14 shows a data received at base-station with timestamping feature. It also allow us to log the data from sensors.

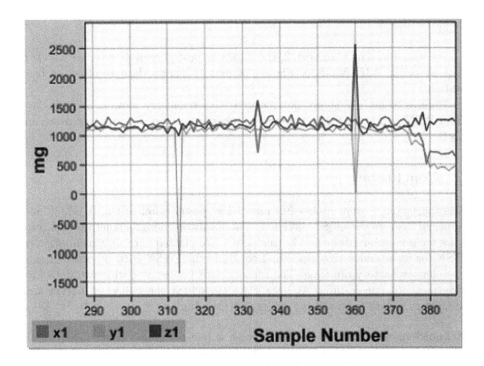

Fig. 16. Vibration data from node 1

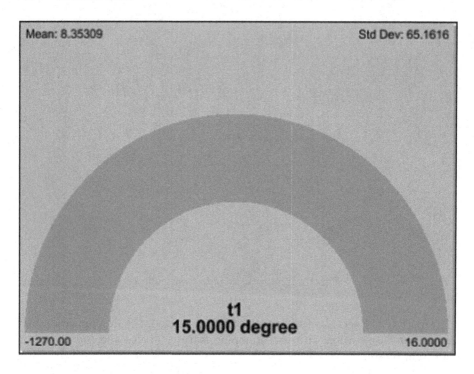

Fig. 17. Temperature data from node 1

As stated in part C of Sect. 2, the data was posted on webserver with POST request using WIFI module. Figures 14 and 15 shows data received at base station.

Figures 16 and 17 shows data logged with telemetry viewer. Sensors data from WSN is transferred to telemetry viewer from data concentrator over com port.

6   Conclusion

The fabricated system makes full use of low power wireless chip CC2530 and powerful arm processor STM32F103. The hardware design structure and software techniques are discussed in this paper. We plotted current consumption of WSN for ideal and active mode and conclude that WSN with proposed design have longer battery life time. The sensors data is observed with two data logging methods successfully. At last, a system which can collect vibration and temperature data from railway rolling stocks is built.

Acknowledgement. The work in this paper is research project under C2SD-SMDP sponsored by Ministry of Electronics and Information technology (MeitY), New Delhi at Centre for VLSI and Nanotechnology, VNIT, Nagpur.

References

1. Song, E.Y., Lee, K.B.: IEEE 1451.5 standard-based wireless sensor networks. In: Mukhopadhyay, S.C., Leung, H. (eds.) Advances in Wireless Sensors and Sensor Networks. LNEE, vol. 64, pp. 243–271. Springer, Heidelberg (2010). https://doi. org/10.1007/978-3-642-12707-6_11
2. Zigbee stack by WaveShare Electronics. https://www.waveshare.com/wiki/ Core2530
3. Li, Z., Bai, X., Chen, X., Fan, X.: The MSP430 Series of Ultra-low Power Microcontroller Principle and System Design. Xidian University Press, Xi'an (2008)
4. Zhao, J., Lian, X., Wu, Y., Zhang, X., Wang, S.: Design of wireless temperature and humidity data collection system based on MSP430 and CC2530. In: 3rd International Conference on System Science, Engineering Design and Manufacturing Informatization (2012)
5. Texas Instrument CC2530 datasheet. http://www.ti.com/lit/ds/symlink/cc2530. pdf
6. Homepage. http://thomarmax.github.io/QtXBee/doc/pre_alpha/xbee_zigbee_ basic_concepts.html
7. STMicroelectronics AIS3624DQ accelerometer datasheet. http://www.st.com/ resource/en/datasheet/ais3624dq.pdf
8. Analog Devices TMP37 datasheet. http://www.analog.com/media/en/technical-documentation/data-sheets/TMP35_36_37.pdf
9. Serizawa, K., Lu, J., Kuwabara, H., Zhang, L., Maeda, R., Hayase, M.: Development of low-power and ultra-small wireless sensor nodes for bio-logical information monitoring. In: Electronics Packaging (ICEP) (2016)

Author Index

Printed in the United States
By Bookmasters